Effective Business Communications

SIXTH EDITION

Effective Business Communications

Herta A. Murphy

Professor Emeritus of Business Administration
and of Business Communication
University of Washington

Herbert W. Hildebrandt

Professor of Business Administration
and of Business Communication
University of Michigan

McGRAW-HILL, INC.
New York   St. Louis   San Francisco   Auckland   Bogotá   Caracas   Hamburg
Lisbon   London   Madrid   Mexico   Milan   Montreal   New Delhi   Paris
San Juan   São Paulo   Singapore   Sydney   Tokyo   Toronto

To my husband, Gene
—H.M.

To my wife, Dee
—H.H.

EFFECTIVE BUSINESS COMMUNICATIONS

1 2 3 4 5 6 7 8 9 0   HAL HAL   9 5 4 3 2 1 0

ISBN 0-07-044157-X

This book was set in New Caledonia by Ruttle, Shaw & Wetherill, Inc.
The editors were Bonnie K. Binkert and Peggy Rehberger;
the designer was Leon Bolognese;
the production supervisor was Janelle S. Travers.
New drawings were done by Vantage Art, Inc.
Arcata Graphics/Halliday was printer and binder.

Picture credits:
Cover photographs, contents, and part openers:
(1) Andrzej Dudzinski/Science Photo Library/Photo Researchers
(2) Courtesy Motorola
(3) and (4) Courtesy Siemens Information Systems
(5) Courtesy Motorola
(6) Tony Craddock/Science Photo Library/Photo Researchers

Picture credits for the prologue and the graphics section appear below each picture. Copyrights
included on this page by reference. Photo trademarks: Freestyle™ is a trade mark of Wang
Laboratories, Inc.

Library of Congress Cataloging-in-Publication Data

Murphy, Herta A.
    Effective business communications / Herta A. Murphy, Herbert W. Hildebrandt.—6th ed.
        p.   cm.
        Includes index.
        ISBN 0-07-044157-X—ISBN 0-07-044159-6 (test bank).—
        ISBN 0-07-044158-8 (instructor's manual).—ISBN 0-07-044160-X (study guide).
        1. Commercial correspondence.   2. Business report writing.
I. Hildebrandt, Herbert William, (date).   II. Title.
HF5721.M85   1991
651.7—dc20   90-6239

Preface

Communication—written or oral—consistently receives one of the highest rankings for competencies that managers should possess to achieve excellence in business. That assertion has guided the contents of the previous five editions of this widely adopted text, *Effective Business Communications*. In this sixth edition we have maintained the strengths of former editions while also incorporating new material based on significant developments in business communication.

This book is designed to develop communication skills needed by those preparing for, or already in, a business or management position. Student-readers learn how to deal with problems common to businesspeople—how to organize effective letters, reports, and speeches in order to communicate successfully in the business and non-business environment.

Noted for its solid research base, the text includes a wealth of up-to-date material, abundant examples, and thought-stimulating exercises and problems, based on business practice. They provide students with meaningful learning experiences as communicators in a wide variety of real-life situations.

The text has proven its adaptability to almost any business communication course length and level. Its comprehensive coverage and flexible organization make it suitable to one- or two-semester or quarter-length courses at two- and four-year colleges and universities as well as in continuing education and management training seminars. Further, *Effective Business Communications* has proven its value as a handy reference guide after the course is completed.

NEW MATERIAL AND CHANGES

- **A new prologue** positions the reader in the high technology office of today and tomorrow. Colorful pictures enhance the prose and emphasize the benefits of modern technology for communicating in the 1990s. Students, as future businesspeople, need to understand how to use electronic methods to create, transmit, store, retrieve, reproduce, and disseminate messages for international as well as local communications. Other chapters in this edition also discuss uses of electronic business equipment wherever necessary.
- **Legal issues,** covered in an appendix in previous editions, are now moved forward to Chapter 5, because of the increasing importance of this topic for written and oral business communications. The chapter

cautions businesspeople about the legal implications of communicating in our litigious society.

New examples include actual incidents involving business communication issues and the resulting court decisions. The cases parallel the terms and ideas expressed in the chapter. New exercises and problems deal with ethical issues as well as the use of LEXIS, a legal database. This comprehensive discussion of the legal aspects of business communication is based on input from business law professors, and recent research by practicing legal scholars. Legal cautions are also covered, to a lesser extent, in Chapters 8, 9, 13, 14, 24, and 25.

- **The process of preparing effective business messages** is now presented in a revised Chapter 6. New checklists in frames have been included with guidelines for opening and closing paragraphs. After the planning and organizing steps, the composition process focuses on editing, revising, and proofreading, through the use of time-saving computers with helpful software.
- **Employment-related communication topics** are thoroughly presented in Chapters 12, 13, and 24, as well as in Chapter 5. Suggestions are provided for evaluating one's own achievements, obtaining employment help, and discovering international employment opportunities. New examples for resumes and application letters—including a list of 86 active verbs—have been added to others in Chapter 12. Also included are new discussions on interviews and suggestions for applicants and employers regarding how to handle negative or illegal questions. Fair and unfair preemployment inquiries are presented in a Chapter 5 checklist.
- **Goodwill messages,** Chapter 15, now includes 5 new letters. These are in addition to the 17 other friendly examples on various topics.
- **Business reports,** Chapters 16–19, offer new materials on using electronic databases to gather information, constructing professional quality graphs and charts with computer software, and preparing international reports. The report writing chapters emphasize the importance of applying logical reasoning in preparing reports. A major new section on parenthetical documentation—useful for writing messages to persons within or outside the organization—has also been included. In the proposals chapter, an enlarged section now includes coverage of proposals to foundations and the federal government. It also has a sample budget and outlines of parts that make up three types of formal proposals.
- **Oral communications,** Chapters 20–24, include significant new and revised materials. Among them are four new checklists, and expanded sections on stage-fright, nonverbal behavior, listening, audience analysis, business meetings, interviews, and common pitfalls in reasoning. New sections discuss process and policy as purposes of informative speaking, policy and procedure in persuasive speaking, and present new international examples. New numbered figures provide meaning-

ful illustrations of various audiences, leadership styles, and speaker-listener feedback.

■ **International and intercultural communications** now occupy an enlarged Chapter 25, emphasizing that international communications affect businesses more than ever. Today, businesspeople may communicate around the block or around the world. The chapter includes discussions on major cultural variances that affect communication, including an expanded section on verbal and nonverbal differences. Additionally, the chapter offers updated sources for those considering international work.

■ **Format, appearance, and uses of business messages** are updated in Appendix B. The Appendix provides effective models for letters, memorandums, and special time-saving messages. It stresses the importance of the computer and software as time-saving tools and offers guidance in preparing internationally acceptable documents. Additional consideration is given to the widespread use of the telex and facsimile as means of business communication.

SPECIAL LEARNING FEATURES AND BENEFITS

Examples

A consistent strength of previous editions—and this sixth—are the examples. They support the discussions on how to use you-attitude in good and bad news messages, in direct and persuasive requests, in conflicts, and in many other situations. Most of the over 400 examples are drawn from actual business and professional organizations. (To protect privacy, names and figures have been changed.) Classroom tested, the examples have benefited from our combined 65 years of teaching experience with thousands of students and consulting experience with business firms.

Some examples show *how* and how *not* to express ideas in various sentences, paragraphs, and complete messages. Poor and better examples are contrasted in parallel columns. The many framed examples highlight well-written letters, memos, resumes, reports, headings, outlines, graphs, and other helpful materials.

Checklists

Continuing the successful tradition of including useful checklists, this edition has 59, all in a new, easy to read, framed format. They provide concise and useful guidelines to students for writing business messages, preparing for other aspects of communication, and for review. They are not "recipe lists." These checklists *suggest* rather than prescribe. They are adaptable to various situations in and outside the workplace. Contents page xxiv lists all checklist titles.

Exercises and Problems

Over 300 end-of-chapter exercises and problems present a wide variety of assignments. Some ask only for word, sentence, or paragraph corrections. Many include messages for students to analyze, evaluate, and revise. Others provide detailed cases for which students can develop well-organized outlines and prepare written and oral messages. Still others require surveys, interviews, group planning or collection of data for written and oral reports.

Cases

Most chapters include mini cases and problems which lend themselves to in-class analysis—impromptu evaluations and writing and speaking assignments. Incidents as seen particularly in the legal chapter invite students to analyze situations that are later resolved in a summary of the actual court decisions.

Seven C Principles

Based on sound communication principles, the mnemonic seven C's provide important suggestions for all written and oral communications. They are basic guidelines for choosing content and style of presentation *adapted to the purpose and recipient of each message*. They help make messages complete, concise, considerate, concrete, clear, courteous, correct.

Visuals

The sixth edition provides more illustrations, graphs, charts, and tables than ever before to enhance the text and further clarify important points in communication. In addition to the attractively designed two-color format, *Effective Business Communications* offers two full-color inserts: the first, in the prologue, vividly portrays communication in the modern business office; the second, in Chapter 16, offers examples of effective computer-generated visual aids.

Marginal Notes

For the complete message examples in Chapters 7–25, marginal notes in color are added as brief, helpful guides and outlines to focus student attention. While headings set the direction of a discussion, marginal notes, or side notes, instantly clarify. They often parallel long illustrations and act as brief rolling summaries.

References and Explanatory Notes

Bibliographic references to scholarly studies support the textual discussion. Explanatory notes provide additional information for those who wish to further pursue particular topics or ideas mentioned in the text. In the sixth edition, every reference and note—indicated with a superscript—is listed in a new chapter-by-chapter References and Notes section placed before the Index, for easy access. Each citation lists the corresponding text page number for each superscript.

Outlines and Summaries

Every chapter opens with an outline of the main chapter topics followed by a brief overview of all sections. At its conclusion, each chapter offers a summary of the most important concepts discussed. The outlines and summaries assist instructors in quick class preparation and help students focus on important text concepts for examination review.

Databases

This sixth edition includes numerous references to large databases in law, the social sciences, and business that are available to students. This information encourages students to electronically research sources useful to written or oral forms of communication. Specific electronic database references are included in the text, where appropriate.

Appendixes

Three appendixes supplement the text:

- **Appendix A: Mechanics and Style** presents guidelines, examples, and 67 short exercises on common mechanical problems communicators face.
- **Appendix B: The Format and Uses of Business Messages** provides updated guidelines, new and revised discussion material, plus examples of proper format for letterhead, letters, memos, and special time-saving media. Exercises that require evaluations and revisions of messages are also provided.
- **Appendix C: Symbols for Marking Letters, Memos, and Reports** includes over 70 symbols for correcting and amending student papers and business documents. The appendix is featured on the inside back cover of the text for quick and easy reference to answers to common questions on business writing.

SUPPLEMENTS FOR INSTRUCTORS AND STUDENTS

Instructor's Manual

This manual of over 200 pages is based on our years of teaching experience and on suggestions from many users of the text's previous editions. It offers instructors the following materials to facilitate lecture preparation:

- Background information, including course content and organization; suggestions for conducting various courses using this textbook; grading; plus longer, unique cases with simulation exercises.

- Suggested answers to the exercises, problems, and cases in the text chapters and appendixes.
- Over 75 transparency masters for classroom use. Some illustrate significant text concepts; others extend the textual material; many display suggested answers for chapter exercises and problems.

Test Bank

A test bank with over 1000 examination questions by Anita Bednar of Central State University is available. Each chapter contains a variety of true-false, multiple-choice and essay questions with answers and text page references conveniently located for easy reference.

Computerized Test Bank

The test bank is also available as *RHTest,* a computerized test preparation system. It offers instructors the following options: to quickly create and print a test covering one or more chapters of the text; to choose test questions randomly or by number; to view each question on the screen during the selection; to add additional questions to the test; to edit or delete questions; to add a heading or instructions to a test; to print scrambled versions of the same test. It is available for Apple and IBM compatible computers.

Customized Testing Service

This service is available to instructors by mail, phone, or toll-free number from McGraw-Hill. Instructors can order custom prepared tests from items in the printed test bank. An original test and a separate answer key will be provided to the instructor.

Software Package

WordPerfect, The McGraw-Hill College Version is available for the instructor and student. This powerful and easy-to-use word processing program is for use with IBM PCs and compatible systems. The program comes with a color-coded template and illustrated user's manual with step-by-step lessons to enhance the learning process.

Film/Video Library

Free rentals of videotapes on issues pertinent to business communications are available from The University of Illinois Media Library. A complete listing of available tapes related to topics covered in the text, is included in the instructor's manual. Please contact your local sales representative for information and arrangements for ordering videotapes.

ACKNOWLEDGMENTS

No book is only the work of its authors. Such was and is true of the current edition. Immediately we must state that whereas we depended on many people and reviewers, the final product—and decisions relating thereto—is entirely our own.

We value our students and express our appreciation to them because it is as a result of their input that new topics and new samples have been included in the sixth edition.

Over 600 executives, from all over the world, have used the fifth edition. They have offered numerous suggestions on internationalizing the current edition and including more real-life examples; they deserve our applause.

Associations also deserve special recognition. The Association for Business Communication, the International Association of Business Communicators, the Speech Communication Association, the World Communication Association—each, and some of their members either reviewed or contributed to this new edition. Their academic influence—through research studies and suggestions—have improved the book's foundation.

Reviewers of draft manuscripts were exceptionally thorough, specific, and helpful. Their constructive comments, given in the spirit of improving the text, helped us greatly in our revision of the text. With admiration, we thank these dedicated reviewers:

Martha Blalock, University of Wisconsin, Madison
Andrea Corbett, University of Lowell
Thomas Dukes, University of Akron
Janet M. Howard, Brigham Young University
Robert O. Joy, Central Michigan University
Carol D. Lutz, University of Texas at Austin
Frances Land Ritter, Roosevelt University
Joan C. Roderick, Southwest Texas State University
Caroline Schoon, University of South Dakota
Marilyn Shanahan, University of Nebraska, Omaha
Paula Williams, Northern Illinois University

We also appreciate the published reviews by William Buchholz, Bentley College; Thomas Dukes, University of Akron, and Donald Skarzenski; each on one of our three previous editions. Their encouraging comments and suggestions truly contributed to this sixth edition.

A special recognition is given to our colleagues versed in law. They led us through the thickets of legal aspects for business communication. Especially, we thank Lorraine R. Goldberg, University of Washington; George Cameron and George Siedel of the University of Michigan, all legal scholars eminent in business law.

Other colleagues, professionals, and business managers who contributed examples, suggestions, or specific information for this text and supplements deserve our sincere gratitude. We thank:

Elsie Allbright, researcher and writer
Anita Bednar, Central State University
John Buller, Bon Marché
Robert Cooney, Press Associates
Jennie Hunter, Western Carolina University
Virginia Johnson, Minnesota Mining and Manufacturing Company
Robert O. Joy, Central Michigan University
Jeanette Murphy, U.S. West Communication Services
Barbie Nelson, Western Union
Jerry Pollock, U.S. Postal Services
Eugene Smith and Jeremiah Sullivan, University of Washington
Karen Wenzel, Bell and Howell

Also, to the authors and companies that have given permission to quote excerpts from their publications and conferences, and whose names are mentioned in the Reference Notes, we express sincere appreciation.

Librarians deserve a special bow. Not only did they search, but led us through many data base mazes. From a vague statement as "I think it's from around July 1988" they listened, searched, located, and gave a hard copy of the missing data. We appreciatively acknowledge Julie Wheaton, Jo Ann Sokkar, and Nancy Karp.

While many visuals appeared crudely on our screen, it took master hands to bring vividness and vitality to those initial drawings. Two people are acknowledged: Carol Mohr and Christi Bemister. Student assistants also helped: Jinyun Liu and Joseph Crepaldi. Keeping everyone sane, balancing floppies, redrafting manuscripts, finding the lost was Joanne Ripple, secretary extraordinare.

McGraw-Hill has been our publisher since 1972. That long, and warm, relationship continues. Unknown to us are the many artists, editors, designers, compositors, and typesetters behind the scenes. A sincere thank you to them all. More visible—via phone, fax, personal visits, or overnight mail—were Bonnie Binkert, Senior Editor, and Mimi Melek, Assistant Editor. Their expertise is appreciated by us, as is also the efficient work of Larry Goldberg, Peggy Rehberger, Leon Bolognese, Janelle Travers, Caroline Izzo, Daniel Loch, Mike Phillips, and the sales representatives.

Our personal dedication of the book is to the two persons who endured out of love our affairs with modern office technology and hundreds of messages. Our public dedication is to students: they are the future users of communication. They have our sincere good wishes for their future success in oral and written communications.

Herta A. Murphy
Herbert W. Hildebrandt

Contents

**PART THREE
Special
Messages**

**PART FOUR
Reports**

**PART SIX
Significant
Concerns for
Effective
Business
Communicators**

APPENDIXES

Courtesy Hewlett–Packard

THE ELECTRONIC OFFICE OF TODAY AND TOMORROW

Information is power. Speed and efficiency in business communications depend to a great extent on how an organization handles information. As an employee, manager, owner, or supervisor in a rapidly changing business environment, you will need to understand how to use the technology of today's information age to create, transmit, and store information.

Microcomputers

Courtesy Apple Computer

❏ A message originator completes a first draft on an office personal computer (PC) and then uses the electronic network to send the draft to a colleague's PC for review. Both individuals simultaneously review and finalize the draft. The originator now enters the electronic (E-mail) addresses of four regional offices and sends the message via a keystroke.

Courtesy GTE Airfone

❏ A marketing manager, on a flight from Tokyo to Chicago, picks up an Airfone, dials his central recording office, and dictates a summary of his meetings directly into a headquarters computer. Within a short time, a fax of that dictation is returned to his aircraft, still in flight.

❏ A sales manager carries five proposals with her, each over 20 pages long. Copies will be made on her arrival in Moscow—from the 3 1/2-inch disk in her briefcase.

❏ Managers from the New York and Tokyo offices of an international corporation meet to discuss new marketing strategies. They use a voice translation system that interprets spoken Japanese into English and vice versa.

❏ A secretary faxes a document prepared at a company's main office to 50 worldwide subsidiaries—where the document arrives in the native language of each subsidiary.

Most office employees already have or soon will have access to a microcomputer. This electronic instrument—often linked with a laser printer—is at once a typewriter, video unit, storage unit, and minicomputer. While many use this equipment primarily for word processing, others use it as a stand-alone computer, capable of a phenomenal range of

calculations and information processing once found only in large mainframe installations.

Laptop computers (portable microcomputers) are already in widespread use. Soon they will possess the same range of capabilities as the desktop microcomputer. Documents created on a laptop are displayed on a screen—a cathode ray tube or CRT—and can be revised and stored. The final document can later be printed and disseminated, next door or around the world.

Software

As the microcomputer is the hardware or the instrument itself, software is the electronic program or set of instructions that tells that instrument how to accomplish its tasks. Software gives the microcomputer the capability of accomplishing a wide variety of writing and graphic functions. Thus, users can create, edit, and revise prose, insert, highlight, or remove copy, format and paginate, merge documents, select and color graphics, and create visual aids that will enhance the appearance of a document or a presentation.

Desktop and Portable Recorders

Currently in development are recorders that translate speech into its written equivalents. Until that is perfected, your voice can be converted into digital impulses on hand-held or desk recorders and transmitted to a central office for transcription. From around the world, those messages can arrive in the United States either over telephone lines or via satellite. Foreign offices or offices around the country are instantly reachable. Time-lags are no longer a problem in information transmission.

Storage of Information

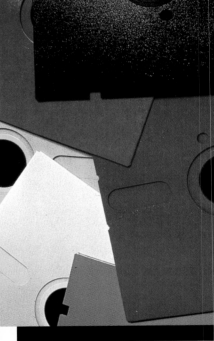

Thousands of pages of copy, or complete files and subfiles, can be stored at a microcomputer workstation on small 5 1/4- or 3 1/2-inch high-density disks—the software of most microcomputers. Sections of files or

entire documents are instantly accessible.

Micrographic instruments greatly reduce the amount of space required to store information. For instance, one 4- by 4- by 1-inch microfilm will hold 25,000 document pages—approximately the capacity of a six-drawer file cabinet. An optical disk can store from 40,000 to a million images.

Electronic Retrieval

A keystroke on a microcomputer instantly retrieves documents from an electronic file. In fact, you could work in Kuala Lumpur, Malaysia, and via a keyboard system link up with a satellite, connect with your home office in the United States, and access a company record. You would instantly have available the latest data for making a decision. At least five retrieval options are available:

❏ A microcomputer—wherein you input the needed cues—can locate a specific document in an electronic storage system in seconds.

❏ A monitor (usually a CRT screen) permits you to page through the stored document, ultimately selecting the precise section.

❏ A camera can photograph the screen image and store it for immediate or later reproduction.

❏ A printer can reproduce the screen image, specific pages, or the entire document, in seconds. It can also produce as many copies as you need.

❏ An optical disk—faster than digital retrievals—allows rapid access to files containing many thousands of stored images.

Reproduction

Reprographics is the process of reproducing printed and graphic material. Via photocopying machines or xerography machines, documents can be reproduced instantly; laser printers and digital machines can also

Desktop Publishing

This phrase is a recent buzzword in the vocabulary of the modern office. Desktop publishing is an integrated electronic system that uses a microcomputer, a software package, a laser printer, and, usually, an electronic network (a linkage with other microcomputers) to produce various documents to fill the needs of an organization. With such a system, several persons can collaborate on the same document from different workstations, electronically review and amend the produced internally. This system permits selecting a wide variety of visual elements including different styles and sizes of typography, color, high-lighting devices such as arrows and pointers, photographs, pictures, and charts. For instance, newsletters, monthly in-house magazines, advertisements, brochures, catalogues, posters, and news releases are among the end products often created through desktop systems. The sophistication of the end-product is limited only by the quality of the software and the skill of the user.

be used to print letter-quality copies of your immediate work or work in a file.

❑ Xerox, Kodak, Canon, Minolta, IBM, and many other companies manufacture machines to reproduce documents. Machines of this type are in widespread use and enable users to print one copy or hundreds, collated in the proper order. The need for carbon copies of letters and the retyping of complete reports are tasks of the past.

❑ Many of these copiers also have the capacity to enlarge or decrease the size of the original document. This feature permits users to highlight certain documents or sections of documents for visual emphasis and to reproduce large documents in a more manageable size.

common piece of work either concurrently or consecutively, and print the final document. Thus, material once requiring professional typographers in printing offices can instead be

Currently, desktop publishing is the latest stage on the continuum from the hieroglyphics of the ancient world to an integrated electronic system.

developments such as image phones that allow you to see the caller will add a dimension now lacking in voice-only telephones. Both the oral and nonverbal cues of communicators will add to the clarity of the communication situation.

The use of electronic mail (E-mail, or EM) will continue to grow. Local area networks (LANs), or distributed data processing networks (DDPs), which tie workstations together, will increasingly link word processors throughout office buildings or around the world. Messages can be sent anywhere, without regard to time differences, for current or later reading.

Voice mail or voice mailbox permits leaving a message on an answering system of another person unable to respond immediately. Telephone tag is eliminated; messages are stored on the receiving machine for later listening.

Dissemination

Telephones will continue to be a main means of communication. Telephone equipment has become increasingly sophisticated, with special features such as programmed dialing, built-in speakers that allow you to call or answer without picking up the handset, conference calling, connection capability to PCs, fax machines, and other office communications equipment. New

Facsimile (fax) machines are the fastest growing information-dissemination machines in business. After you dial your receiver's telephone number, a document is inserted in your machine and its image is instantly sent to the receiver across town or across continents. The benefits of using this equipment seem innumerable:

❏ Executives on a business trip can send their handwritten, confidential notes via fax to their office, where a secretary can type a final copy and send it back to the executive.

Pitney Bowes Fascimile Systems

❏ Sales representatives in a customer's office can send orders directly to the home sales office.

❏ Weekend writers can send a draft of a report, along with corresponding charts and graphs, to the home of another executive for review.

Satellite Communications

Over 150 satellites are in geosynchronous orbit 22,300 miles above the earth. These instruments both disseminate and receive communications. Services include telephone and mobile communication, data transfer,

Courtesy Federal Express Corp.

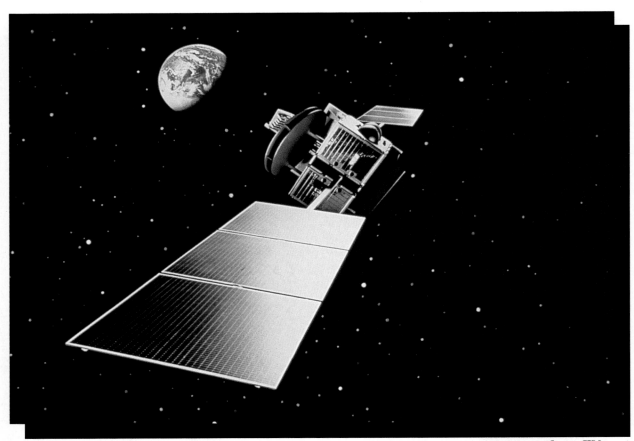

Courtesy GTE Spacenet

time-sharing telex, facsimile, mail-grams, electronic mail, broadcast video, tele-education, and video-conferencing. Instantaneous contact is maintained with any out-of-country location; videotapes or live broadcasts of company events electronically tie a company together; training films update an entire company at the same time.

Surface Carrier Services

Both government and private carriers of letters and packages continue to deliver overnight materials. Indeed, a Mailgram may be sent electronically through the Western Union net-work, often directly from one's word processor.

TELECONFERENCES, VIDEOCONFERENCES, AND VIDEOTAPES

Teleconferencing refers to the audio linkage, via telephone, of people who are in different locations. Videoconferencing refers to audio and video linkage, combining the use of special cameras, videotapes, telephones or computers, and devices such as electronic whiteboards and computer-assisted design (CAD) systems. Participants at a videoconference, for instance, can present a proposal to a geographically distant review committee, consult experts as questions arise or modifications are requested, use video and CAD devices to illustrate the proposal, resolve problems, record modifications, and come to a decision, thus saving travel time and expense.

ASSERTIONS FOR THE FUTURE

A maze of cables and instruments now fills the high-technology office—and this is only the beginning. You will

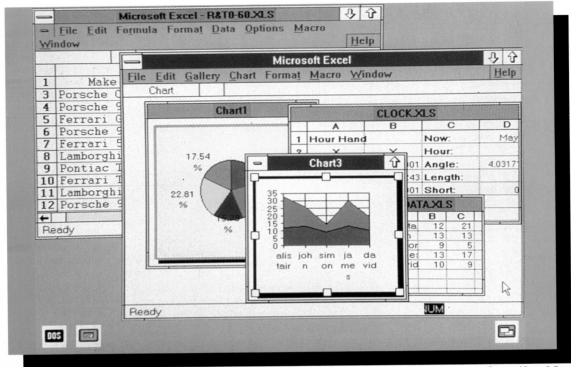

have to know not only how to operate the instruments, but also how to organize thoughts and ideas, how to merge content and style, how to keystroke and transmit, how to think and react, and how to write and edit more rapidly than ever before. Your work may be literally on global display. This text will help prepare you for the high-tech office.

Among communications developments, the following are imminent:

❏ International communications will increase; employees must and will broaden their global horizons. A greater awareness of foreign cultures will occur.

❏ Nonverbal communication on the electronically sent printed page and via the voice through an image phone will instantly communicate something about the sender. Communicators will focus on being effective in both written and oral communication.

❏ Almost anyone—with password limitations—will have easy access to common data files. Traditional communication meetings and phone calls will be supplemented by electronic data.

❏ Response time to messages will decrease. With instruments available 24 hours a day, a response may be sent at any time, and answered at the receiver's convenience, thus saving time, money, and the invariable telephone tag games.

❏ Graphics, in dazzling color and configurations, will increasingly join traditional written business communications. Business communicators will have to be aware of software packages and communication programs and know how to use and blend the available technology to produce effective messages.

A final conclusion is this: although technology may be the means, you are the one to input and receive information from that technology. This book intends to help you create effective business communication through understanding its process and structure.

PART ONE

Background for Communicating

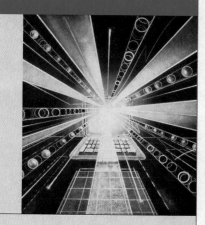

Chapter 1

Importance of Effective Communications in Business

f you can communicate effectively in speaking and writing, you have an important, highly valued skill. Managers and top-level executives of American business, industry, and government have repeatedly expressed their concern regarding the need for better communication. In numerous surveys (page 9), business executives have ranked ability to communicate in first place among the personal factors necessary for promotion within management. And they have selected business communication as one of the most useful college studies in their work.

This chapter includes answers to the following questions regarding the importance of effective communication in business:

> How new is concern for effective communication?
>
> Why is effective communication the "lifeblood" of every organization?
>
> How can it help you in your career and personal life?
>
> How can you meet the challenges of communicating for business?

ANCIENT HERITAGE FOR COMMUNICATION PRINCIPLES

Oral communication obviously preceded written communication. In fact, the ancient Greek and Roman world depended heavily on oral communication. It was necessary to communicate well on one's feet: in government assemblies and in the law courts.

A school of teachers called *sophists* taught ancients to speak well, for to defend oneself and to speak eloquently were marks of a learned person. More formal instructors called *teachers of rhetoric* taught ideas that in later years appeared in published works. Thus, today we recognize names such as Socrates, Plato, Aristotle, Cicero, and Quintilian—to mention a few—as contributors to the history of communication.

During the Medieval and Renaissance period the oral tradition continued. And as writing became more important as a permanent record of communication, authors and books on written communication principles appeared. Names such as Desiderius Erasmus, Richard Sherry, Angell Day, and many others were forerunners of those associated with our modern principles of written communication.

Hence, some of today's principles of writing are founded on a mixture of ancient oral and written traditions. Business communication is then one offshoot from an earlier world where communicating well was a foundation of learning.

"LIFEBLOOD" OF EVERY ORGANIZATION

So important is communication that without it an organization cannot function. An *organization* is a group of people associated for business, political, professional, religious, athletic, social, or other purposes. Its activities require human beings to interact, react—communicate. They exchange information, ideas, plans; order needed supplies; make decisions, rules, proposals, contracts, agreements.

Because this book is concerned primarily with effective *business* communication, the discussions and illustrations you will read focus mainly on business messages. However, you can apply them also to other organizations, to the professions, and to your personal communications.

Both within and outside the organization, effective business communication—oral and written—is its lifeblood. Founded on established principles, effective communication is essential, beneficial, and also costly.

Internal Communication

A vital means of attending successfully to matters of company concern is through effective internal communication—"downward," "upward," and "horizontal." It helps increase job satisfaction, safety, productivity, and profits as well as decrease absenteeism, grievances, and turnover.

When employees receive appropriate *downward* communication from management, they can be better motivated and more efficient. They need and want not only clear job directions and safety rules but also facts about organizational strategy, products, and viewpoints on important controversial issues. They are concerned about employees benefits—health care, insurance, promotions, pensions, training, work environment, retirement. In all, the many pressures from employees force employers to be accountable for their decisions through effective downward communication. Employers that communicate effectively have happier employees.

Likewise, *upward* internal communication has become increasingly more significant. Many executives sincerely seek frank comments from employees—in addition to the usual periodic reports. They listen more closely to opinions, complaints, problems, suggestions—especially when these are clearly and effectively stated.

Effective *horizontal* communication between peers is also essential in organizations ranging from two to thousands of employees. These peers must exchange ideas to help solve problems, perform job duties, prepare for meetings, and cooperate on important projects.

Among various ways of communicating within companies are memos, reports, meetings, face-to-face discussions, teleconferences, and video conferences. This book includes suggestions that may be applied to these communications.

External Communication

Messages to persons outside the company can have a far-reaching effect on its reputation and ultimate success. The right letter, proposal, report, telephone call, or personal conversation can win back a disgruntled customer, create a desire for a firm's product or service, help negotiate a profitable sale, encourage collections, motivate performance, and in general create goodwill.

Furthermore, communications to the *public* regarding social accountability have become significantly more important during the past two decades. Because of demands by many special interest groups (labor unions, environmentalists, government agencies, plus political action committees), the press, reputable American organizations, and even political offices are seriously concerned about enhancing their public image. Important are well-planned public speeches by their executives, tactful replies to comments and criticisms from consumer groups, free informative pamphlets, annual reports, 10-K reports, and interviews with news media. All these messages are transmitted with greater emphasis on honesty, openness, and concern for the public.[1]

Elements in Overall Communication Costs

In multinational corporations thousands of hours are devoted daily to interviews, conferences, memos, reports, employee manuals, letters, advertising, news articles, bulletins, newsletters, and other messages. Time is the chief element in the overall cost of written and oral communications. They require the time of executives and assistants for researching, thinking, planning, organizing, dictating, typing, editing, revising, proofreading, mailing (the written), presenting (the oral), and filing records. Among other costs are materials (stationery, office supplies, postage, computer disks, software), equipment, and fixed charges (heat, rent, light, depreciation, etc.). These elements likewise affect overall costs to the recipients who read or listen to and respond to the messages they receive. Important developments and adaptations of office technology such as computers, electronic mail, and videoconferences (see the prologue) can help in various ways to reduce the time and costs of communicating efficiently.

Still another significant fact to be considered is the wasteful cost of unclear, incomplete, inaccurate, inconsiderate, and unduly long or late communications. Poor messages are, indirectly, more expensive because they destroy goodwill, waste time, and alienate customers. Often they require several additional messages, when one message should have accomplished the desired result. Furthermore, in some fields—aviation, construction, medical, mining, oil drilling, others—inadequate instructions can result in loss of life and millions of dollars.

In summary, effective communication within and outside the organization can contribute in various ways to its lifeblood and overall costs. Successful messages help to enhance morale, efficiency, goodwill, safety, productivity, profits, and public credibility.

BENEFITS IN YOUR CAREER AND PERSONAL LIFE

Your jobs, promotions, and professional reputation often depend on the success or failure of your written and oral communication. Also you will find that ability to communicate effectively is a valuable asset during many activities in your personal life.

A Valuable Job Requirement

Especially if your career requires mainly mental rather than manual labor, your progress will be strongly influenced by how effectively you communicate your knowledge, proposals, and ideas to others who need or should receive them.

Preference for communication skills is found in the job descriptions listed by numerous companies wishing to employ college graduates. For example, Dr. Francis W. Weeks, emeritus executive director of the Association for Business Communication,[2] found in a six-year study of job listings at the University of Illinois Coordinating Placement Office that 340 jobs in 30 fields required communication ability. Among the job descriptions found in that study—and also priorities indicated in surveys done in the 1980s—were requirements like the following:[3]

> Must be able to communicate effectively with all levels of management
>
> Must have substantial experience or training in oral and written presentations and must demonstrate good writing skills
>
> Will prepare special analyses, research reports, and proposals
>
> Needs ability to compose effective correspondence
>
> Must have ability to communicate and "sell" ideas
>
> Must be able to cultivate and maintain good customer relationships
>
> Needs skills in gathering, analyzing, and interpreting data and in writing analytical reports

Job and career opportunities in which effective communication is the *main* responsibility are available in various areas, such as customer relations, labor relations, marketing, personnel, public relations, sales, teaching. Also, technical and scientific fields need editors, producers, researchers, and writers. Advancement can be made to management, research, training, and consulting positions.

Communication skills are important, too, in local, state, and federal governments. Congressional and senatorial offices, for instance, require large staffs to handle both outgoing and incoming mail, to and from constituents. Additionally, there are the many administrative departments of government, each seeking to communicate clearly internally and externally. Searching for people to eliminate foggy double-talk from government reports is ongoing.

Even if your work is mainly with figures, as in the accounting profession, the ability to communicate to those who read your financial reports is essential. The *Journal of Accountancy*, by an experiment cited in *Horizons for a Profession*, emphasized to the profession the importance of writing. A group of accountants who were considered the "most knowledgeable and forward looking segment of the accounting profession" ranked 53 subjects that a beginning C.P.A. should be familiar with. First place went undisputedly to written and oral English—even over accounting theory and practice.[4]

The federal government's Defense Contract Audit Agency (DCAA), for instance, has a two-volume manual which accountants must follow in auditing government contracts. While instructions are detailed as to which material should be audited, one chapter is devoted entirely to writing, "Preparation and Distribution of Audit Reports."[5]

An Essential for Promotion

The prime requisite of a promotable executive is "ability to communicate." Notice it is the top rung of the ladder in Figure 1-1.[6] Too often those who

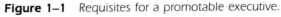

Figure 1–1   *Requisites for a promotable executive.*

cannot communicate effectively in either oral or written communcations remain "buried" in lower, dead-end jobs.[7] Members of management spend 60 to 90 percent of their working days communicating—speaking, writing, and listening.

Over the past 40 years, many surveys and articles have confirmed the statement that effective communication is essential for success and promotion in business. They have included, altogether, responses from thousands of top-level executives, middle managers, and university business graduates across the United States and in foreign countries. When the respondents were asked to answer the question "What has been the most valuable subject you studied in college?" such titles as Business Communications, Business Letter and Report Writing, and Written and Oral Expression were always listed among the top three. Respondents—including top, middle, and operations managers—have repeatedly asserted that business communication skills significantly influenced their advancement to executive positions.[8]

U.S. executives in the 1980s held views similar to those expressed earlier. In 1980–1987 surveys of 7,419 newly promoted vice presidents, presidents, and chief executive officers in the United States, respondents ranked business communication, both oral and written, as their *first* choice among 13 curricular options preparing one for business leadership. These executives came from 39 major industry groups, including businesses with under $10 million to over $10 billion in gross operating revenues.[9]

A survey of 6,223 U.S. middle managers[10] produced basically the same conclusions. Managers from the Far East also rated business communication as their first choice among 13 curricular options.[11]

As a trainee on a new job, you have opportunities to speak about problems with co-workers and to submit memos, reports, and letters that test your ability to communicate clearly and quickly. A frequent complaint of managers is the inability of college graduates to make themselves heard, read, or understood. Your messages can reveal how well you are doing a job, and they help management to evaluate your fitness for a substantial promotion. For example, imagine that you are one of several highly trained employees in an organization that requires everyone to submit frequent oral and written reports to clients or company personnel. If there is an opening for promotion and you each rate about the same except that you alone can write and speak effectively, then clearly you have the advantage over the others. One alumna who had five promotions in five years emphasized that her success was based on her ability to prepare concise reports for senior management.

A Help for Meeting Personal Responsibilities

Effective communication—written and spoken—also helps you to better accomplish various aims in your personal activities. You will sometimes need to write letters, proposals, or reports, or to present your views orally as committee chairperson, club officer, or private citizen. In these roles you might communicate with public officials; business, industrial, or professional people; or personal friends. Whatever your purposes, you will usually achieve them more effectively when you apply the same skills that help you communicate effectively in business.

Additional benefits that enthusiastic students of business communication have gained are better grades in some of their other college courses that require analytical problem solving and high-quality, well-organized reports.

THE CHALLENGE OF COMMUNICATING FOR BUSINESS

Because communication plays such a major role in the operation of a firm and in possible promotion for the individual, communicating for business should be a challenge meriting your best efforts. Like any other worthwhile activity, the quality of your individual attitude and preparation affects communication.

Developing the Right Attitude

The "personality," image, or culture of your company is an extension of many individual personalities and traditions. You are one of these important personalities, whether you are an executive or a new clerk responsible for routine messages. With the right attitude, you—as well as other communicators—have opportunities to build goodwill and get favorable responses.

Help Your Company Image

Ask yourself if your company's image is a little better because of you. Some company communications are so important that they can win thousands or even millions of dollars worth of business or goodwill. If you were working on such a message (for a letter, report, speech, or crucial interview), you would probably devote several hours—perhaps days or weeks—to your best thoughts, imagination, and planning. But what about the other messages—especially the minor, routine kind that you will handle daily? They may not be individually worth a million dollars, but each is part of the lifeblood of your organization. Each is an opportunity to build goodwill. Furthermore, such messages might lead to major business transactions. Collectively, the effect of thousands of routine messages is far-reaching.

"To the customer, you are the company" is good advice that public relations officials often give to their employees. AT&T's board chairman forcefully expressed this view when he urged all the firm's employees to be responsive to their customers' needs and concerns:

> If you were to sit at my desk and read and answer the mail I get about telephone service, you'd come to realize, if you don't already, how much "little things" mean; how sometimes lifelong impressions of the character of our business are formed on the basis of a single contact with just one employee. Rather significant, I'd say, when you consider that the Bell System employs more than a million men and women. . . .

The key element in all the letters . . . I get is how the customer was treated by an employee of the company. . . . Intermixed with complaints are a goodly number of commendation letters . . . about how an employee treated the customer in a manner so unusually satisfying that the customer felt compelled to write to me about it.[12]

Be Enthusiastic and Capable

Doing an honest job enthusiastically and competently helps both the doer and the receiver. Answering even routine inquiries should and can be an interesting challenge. For example, an insurance company correspondent may often receive similar questions from policyholders who have lost their insurance policies. Instead of responding with an abrupt, impersonal, boring, routine-sounding message, the correspondent needs a different outlook. Though lost-policy cases are familiar to him or her, they certainly are not routine to the reader. Thus the better approach is to send a personalized, helpful message, considerate of the reader's viewpoint.

If you catch yourself sending stale, repetitive messages, try a new—and in many cases a more personal—approach. Like any other job, written and oral communication can be more successful when the individual develops the right attitude.

Preparing Adequately

Most people can learn to communicate effectively for business if they desire to do so and are willing to devote whatever effort is necessary to prepare themselves adequately.

In addition to the right goodwill-building attitude, the following qualities are desirable:

Intelligent, sound judgment when choosing ideas and facts for each message

Patience and understanding—even with unjustly insulting persons

Integrity, backed up by a valid code of ethics

Reasonable facility with the English language

Applied knowledge of the communication process and principles and of successful methods for sending and receiving messages

SUMMARY

In a real sense communication is not a new subject. Thus business communication, written and oral, has its heritage as far back as the ancient Greeks and Romans. There, oral communication was foremost. In later periods, written communication grew in importance, as the need for more permanent forms of communication evolved.

Effective business communication is the lifeblood of every organization in its internal messages to and by employees as well as in its external contacts with customers, suppliers, and the public. It is also a key to success in your career and a help in your personal life. The volume and costs of business communications are great; so are challenges and opportunities for those with the right attitudes and preparation. When you diligently apply the basics of effective business communications with common sense, you can continue to improve your communication ability.

In the following chapters and appendixes, you will study various principles, techniques, examples, cautions, and typical business communication situations. Your communications will involve thinking, analyzing, solving problems, gathering facts, planning, and organizing messages according to acceptable contemporary procedures for effective business communication. Through these experiences you should gain a better understanding of people, learn how to win favorable responses from them, and learn how to make friends for your company. The background provided should give you the confidence to tackle almost any task you might face when writing letters, memos, proposals, or reports and when communicating orally.

EXERCISES

1. Pick up a copy of a recent *Wall Street Journal* and look at the section called "The Mart." Conduct a mini investigation as to how many job positions require communication capabilities.

2. Define or otherwise identify these terms or individuals related to early communication principles; all will require research beyond this chapter.

> Rhetoric
> Logos
> Sophists
> Seven liberal arts
> Aristotle
> Cicero
> Quintilian

Chapter 2

The Process of Communication and Miscommunication

C ommunication is a process of transmitting and receiving verbal and nonverbal messages that produce a response. The communication is considered effective when it achieves the desired reaction or response from the receiver. Simply stated, communication is a two-way process of exchanging ideas or information between human beings.

In actual practice, however, the communication process is not simple. It involves more than sender————message————receiver. Sometimes it is quite complex and imperfect, and malfunctions can occur easily and may result in miscommunication. This chapter includes a brief overview of communication elements, concepts, and problems regarding verbal and nonverbal communication. The information presented is adapted from various studies in such fields as psychology, sociology, semantics, speech communication, and human relations.

ELEMENTS OF COMMUNICATION

The process of communication involves five elements or factors:

- Sender-encoder
- Message
- Medium
- Receiver-decoder
- Feedback

The model in Figure 2-1 illustrates partly how these factors interact in the communication process, affected by various internal and external conditions and decisions.

Role of Sender-Encoder

When you send a message, you are the writer or speaker, depending on whether your communication is written or oral. You are likewise the "encoder." You try to choose symbols—usually words (and sometimes also graphics or pictures)—that will correctly, tactfully express your message so the receiver or receivers will understand it and react with the response you desire. Both external and internal stimuli affect message encoding and sending.

First, an external stimulus prompts you to send a message. This prompt may arrive in any number of ways: letter, memorandum, penciled note, electronic mail, fax (facsimile), telex, or modular telephone, or even via a casual conversation in the hallway. Regardless of the stimulus source, it could be a business transaction, a written question, a meeting, a past-due bill, an interview, or an unexpected request for a favor. As you think of ideas for the message, you react also to various conditions in your external environment—physical surroundings, weather, noise, discomforts, cultural customs, and others.

Next, internal stimuli have a complex influence on how you translate ideas into a message. When you encode, your own world of experience affects your choice of symbols—mental, physical, psychological, semantic. Attitudes, opinions, emotions, past experiences, likes and dislikes, education, job status, and communication skills may influence the way you communicate your ideas. Also especially important are your perception of and consideration for the receiver's viewpoint, needs, skills, status, mental ability, and experience. In all, you decide which symbols best convey your message and which sending mechanism to choose among the available written and oral media.

Message

The message or the core idea you wish to communicate consists of both *verbal* (written or spoken) symbols and *nonverbal* (unspoken) symbols. Examples are discussed later in this chapter and others.

Whenever you compose a message, you need to consider what content to include, how the receiver will interpret it, and how it may affect your relationship. A simple "thank-you" message will be relatively easy. In contrast, to inform 200 employees of bad news about salaries or to bid on engineering plans to construct a $100 million industrial building will require much more complicated, carefully planned messages.

Medium

How will you send your message? Should it be sent via an electronic word processing system to be read on the receiver's screen, through the printed word or through graphic symbols on paper, or via the medium of sound? Briefly, should one write or speak?

Like message content, the choice of medium (oral or written) is influenced by the interrelationships between the sender and the receiver. Some research suggests that the urgency of a message is a major determiner of which medium to use. Then one may consider factors such as importance, number of receivers, costs, and amount of information.

Figure 2–1   A communication model.

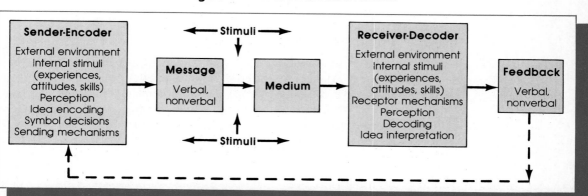

Based on research[1] the following describe some of the characteristics found in oral and written media:

Oral	**Written**
Immediate feedback	Delayed feedback
Shorter sentences	Less spontaneity
More conversational sentences	Less colloquial quality
Focus on interpersonal relations	Focus on content
Highly contextual nature	Greater linguistic emphasis
Prompter action	Later action
Less detailed, technical information	More detailed, technical information
More personal pronouns	More involved sentence structure
More slang and contractions	Useful for permanent record
More imperative, interrogative, exclamatory sentences	Possibility of detailed documentation
	Possibility of review

If your message requires an immediate answer, an oral channel may be the better choice. But if the message contains complicated details and figures or if its subject requires filing for future reference, a written communication is necessary. Furthermore, whether your message receiver is inside or outside your organization affects your choice of the medium.

Inside Your Organization

For internal communication, written media may be memos, reports, bulletins, job descriptions, posters, notes in pay envelopes, employee manuals, or even electronic bulletin boards. Oral communication may be by staff meeting reports, face-to-face discussions, speeches, audio tapes, telephone chats, teleconferences, or even videotapes. Another oral channel, though unplanned by the sender, is the "grapevine," through which news and rumors often travel quickly—oftentimes quite accurately, sometimes inaccurately.

Outside Your Organization

External written communication media may be letters, reports, proposals, telegrams, cablegrams, Mailgrams, faxes, telexes, postcards, contracts, ads, brochures, catalogs, news releases. You may also communicate orally—face to face, by telephone, or by speeches in solo or panel situations—personally before groups or via teleconferences, videoconferences, or TV.

Receiver-Decoder

The message receiver is your reader or listener—also known as the *decoder*. Some messages, of course, may be directed to many readers or listeners.

As Figure 2-1 indicates, the receivers as well as the sender are influenced by external environment and internal stimuli. They receive messages through the eyes and ears, but are also influenced by nonverbal factors such as touch, taste, and smell. All these factors demand interpretation according to individual experiences.

A problem is that all of us do not have identical experiences with the subject or symbols chosen by the sender. Even within the United States, attitudes, abilities, opinions, communication skills, and cultural customs vary. Add a foreign country into the communication process, and the problems increase. Hence, misinterpretations occur; personal biases intervene, as each receiver through his or her receptor mechanisms tries to perceive the intended meaning of the sender's idea.

Feedback

Ultimately the receiver reacts, with either a response based on clear interpretation of the symbols or an incorrect response because of miscommunication. What the sender receives may be oral or written feedback—a "yes" or "no," a request for further clarification, a desirable or an undesirable decision, or a detailed helpful report. If the receiver incorrectly perceived (decoded) our message, we have miscommunicated. The success or failure of the communication is indicated by the feedback we get.

GENERAL COMMUNICATION CONCEPTS AND PROBLEMS

No two people in the world are exactly alike mentally, physically, or emotionally. Thus the innumerable human differences plus cultural, social, and environmental differences may cause problems in conveying an intended message.

Each person's mind is a unique filter. Communication difficulties are more likely to occur when the communicators' filters are sharply different. The message sender's meanings and the receiver's response are affected by numerous factors. Among these are their:

- Presumptions of understanding
- Perceptions of reality
- Attitudes, opinions, and emotions

The consequences of miscommunication may range from mild or humorous to extremely serious and costly, as revealed in the following examples of suggestions for improvement.

Presumptions of Understanding

A fundamental communication principle is that the symbols the sender uses to communicate messages must have essentially the same meaning in both the sender's and the receiver's minds. One cannot presume that the identical message in the mind of the sender will be perfectly transmitted to the receiver. The business world and the world in general are littered with errors as a result of presuming that a message is perfectly understood.

A way to clarify semantic problems is to view the semantic triangle (Figure 2-2). This triangle suggests three things: (1) A symbol is simply a sign for something that exists in reality. Thus your name—really a symbol or word—is a representation of you. (2) Only through common experience is a connection made between the symbol or word attached to you and you as a person in reality. (3) The closer the common experiences surrounding symbols and the things (referents) to which they refer, the closer the level of understanding between sender and receiver.

For instance, the terms *debit* and *credit* are well known to accountants. To a person unfamiliar with these terms, they can be confusing, to the extent that the person may even mix up which term means "adding to" and which "subtracting from" an account.

Meanings to a great extent are therefore in people. The knowledge we each have about a subject or word affects the meanings we attach to it. Different word interpretations are especially noticeable in *"bypassed" instructions* and in reactions to *denotations, connotations,* and *euphemisms.*

Bypassed Instructions

When the message sender and receiver attribute different meanings to the same words or use different words though intending the same meanings, bypassing often occurs. Many words have several dictionary definitions; a few have over 100. In one abridged dictionary the little word *run* has 71 meanings as a verb, another 35 as a noun, and 4 more as an adjective. Moreover, for some words people have their own unique meanings, based on their experiences, and those meanings are not in a dictionary. Thus, confusion sometimes arises, as these "listening" incidents illustrate:

1. An office manager handed a new assistant a letter, with the instruction "Take it to our stockroom and burn it." In the office manager's mind (and in the firm's jargon) the word "burn" meant to make a copy on a company machine that operated by a heat process. As the letter was extremely important, she wanted an extra copy. However, the puzzled new employee, afraid to ask questions, burned the letter and thus destroyed the only existing copy!

2. An equipment supervisor told a new night-duty employee, "You'll have to crack all the valves before you clean the settling tank." The next morning the supervisor found a floor full of smashed castings. "Crack" to the supervisor meant opening each valve just enough to allow minimum flow. You may be surprised that the supervisor was discharged

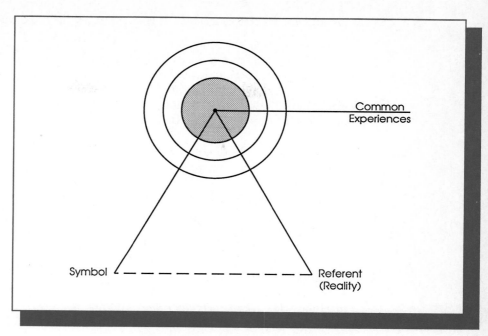

Common
Experiences

Symbol

Referent
(Reality)

Figure 2–2   *Communication triangle.*

because of the inadequate instructions that resulted in costly miscommunication.

3. A superintendent (John) said to Tim, a maintenance worker, "Plant 2 is having trouble with its automatic control. Whatever the trouble is, go out there and get rid of it." The next day, after receiving angry complaints from Plant 2, John berated Tim for yanking out completely and discarding the entire control unit and installing a new one, even though Plant 2 had purchased the original unit only five months before. The company had new, rigid cost-cutting rules to repair, rather than replace, all salvageable equipment whenever possible. But John had failed to inform Tim of those rules. Thus Tim thought that because the control unit was causing the trouble, that's what he should "get rid of." John had wrongly assumed his instructions were clear, but Tim's meaning was entirely different from John's.

Bypassing occurs not only in business and industrial offices but also among government officials, military leaders, professionals, and all of us in our everyday contacts. To avoid communication errors of bypassing when you give instructions or discuss issues, be sure your words and sentences will convey the intended meaning to the recipient. Also, when you are the recipient of unclear instructions, before acting on them, ask questions to determine the sender's intended meaning.

Reactions to Denotations, Connotations, and Euphemisms

Many of us have at some time been surprised that a remark intended as a compliment, matter-of-fact statement, or joke was interpreted by the receiver as an insult. A statement intended as a good deed can be distorted into something self-serving. Some of these communication problems may occur because words have both denotative and connotative meanings, and the sender has not considered the receiver's probable interpretations and reactions.

Denotations.   The denotative meaning is the meaning on which most people will probably agree. It often is the dictionary definition. The word informs the receiver, and it names objects, people, or events without indicating positive or negative qualities. Such words as *car, desk, book, house, water* convey denotative meanings, provided, of course, that the communicators understand the English language and provided that the receiver has a similar understanding of the context in which the word is used.

Connotations.   In addition to the more literal denotative meanings, some words have connotative meanings that arouse qualitative judgments and personal reactions. The term *meeting room* is denotative. *Director's lounge, executive suite, rickety firetrap, rat-filled joint*—though they each denote a meeting place—also have connotative meanings. The word *student* is denotative; *bookworm, scholar, dropout, school dummy, gunner* are connotative. They tell how the sender evaluates the subject. Some words—such as *efficient, gentle, prompt*—usually have only favorable connotations. Others—such as *lazy, cowardly, rotten, delinquent*—usually have unfavorable connotations. Some words have favorable connotations in some contexts but unfavorable meanings in other instances. Compare, for example, *fat check* and *fat girl; free enterprise* and *free* (rude, bold) *manners; sucker* (customer) and *sucker* (candy); *cheap product* and *cheap price*. In common usage, words that usually have opposite meanings can sometimes have the same meaning, as in the two expressions *slim chance* and *fat chance*.

The connotative meanings for words are also affected by the communicators' different backgrounds and interests. Words such as *amnesty, unions, speed, grass, crack, hippies, gay, fair wages, women's liberation* may arouse mixed feelings and arguments, depending on people's associations with them. For additional examples on connotations, see the discussion in "Slanted" Statements, page 23, and Choose Nondiscriminatory Expressions, pages 78–82.

Euphemisms.   Tactful writers and speakers use euphemisms whenever possible to replace words that might have blunt, painful, lowly, or distasteful connotations. Euphemisms are mild, innovative expressions with which most people do not have negative associations.

Expressions like the following have obvious connotative advantages: *maintenance worker* or *staff member* instead of *janitor; slender* instead of *skinny; Salisbury steak* or *hamburger* instead of *choice ground dead steer*. Instead of saying an employee was *fired*, a communicator may use such euphemisms as *laid off, terminated,* or *a victim of reorganization* or *staff cutbacks.*

Euphemisms and any expressions that have pleasant associations for the recipients are especially helpful in advertising and selling. Usually, mass-produced consumer items—like soap, lotions, toothpaste, soft drinks—have similar functions and ingredients though made by different manufacturers. Advertisers then market their products by associating them with pleasant experiences the users will gain—popularity at social functions, physical attractiveness, enjoyment at sports events, etc. Advertising slogans or labels can help make or break a product's effectiveness. For example:

> *One basically sound product—a vibrating mattress, which could have been a great help to sufferers of insomnia and industrial fatigue—failed mainly because the advertisements stressed, "Shake yourself to sleep." The connotation of the word "shake" was the deathblow to the marketing effort.*

To communicate effectively you need to be aware of the usual connotative meanings of various terms and also to realize that some people may have their own unique meanings because of their experiences and background. Thus, choose your words carefully, considering both their connotations and their denotations to convey the idea you want and to achieve the desired results.

Perceptions of Reality

The world of reality is complex, infinite, and continuously changing. Also, human beings' sensory perceptions—touch, sight, hearing, smell, taste—are limited, and each person's mental filter is unique. People perceive reality in different ways. We make various *abstractions, inferences,* and *evaluations* of the world around us.

Abstracting

The process of focusing on some details and omitting others is *abstracting.* In countless instances, abstracting is necessary and desirable—for both written and oral communication. However, the alert, honest communicator should be cautious about at least two semantic traps of abstracting—the "allness" fallacy and "slanted" statements.

Necessary, Desirable Abstracts. Whether you write a memo, letter, or report or converse by telephone, you will be limited somewhat by time, expense, space, and purpose. You will need to select—honestly—facts that are pertinent to accomplish your purpose and to omit the rest (as you do, for example, in a one-page application letter about yourself).

The chapter you are now reading is also necessarily an abstract; it condenses into these few pages some highlights of numerous studies relating to communication and miscommunication.[2]

You, as the communicator, must also anticipate the likelihood that others may not be abstracting as you are. Their points may be as important as yours though they select differently from the infinite details in reality. For example:

When reporting on an event—a firm's new-store dedication ceremony, a factory explosion and fire, a football game, a traffic accident—no two witnesses give exactly the same descriptions. The participants will perceive different details than the observers, but some parts of the whole may be mentioned by all or several observers. Juries often must determine which witness's details are the most credible.

Differences in abstracting occur not only when persons describe events but also when they describe people, equipment, projects, animals, objects.

"Allness" Fallacy.   We should not yield to the *allness fallacy*—the attitude that what we know or say about something or someone is all there is to know or say. The more we delve into some subjects, the more we realize there is so much more to learn and to consider. Semanticists suggest that we at least mentally add "etc." to remind us that statements are incomplete and to keep from making incorrect, unfounded judgments.

Even authorities on certain subjects humbly admit they don't know all the answers. Though they sometimes disagree among themselves on various topics, they continue to study all available facts. So do conscientious, open-minded business executives, government leaders, educators, scientists, and students.

Unfortunately, it is true of some people that the "less they know, the more sure they are that they know it all."

A conspicuous example is that of the high school sophomore chatting casually with a man who (unknown to the student) was a distinguished scientist devoting his lifetime to studying botany. The smug sophomore commented, "Oh botany? I finished studying all about that stuff last semester." As Bertrand Russell states, "One's certainty varies inversely with one's knowledge."

A characteristic of some children, and also adults, is to use a liberal application of words such as *every* and *always* in describing an event, thus reflecting their basic assumptions that what they are saying is true 100 percent of the time. Such assumptions are rarely correct. Use of words such as *never, all,* and *none* reflect similar misconceptions.

Thus, it is best for us to avoid assuming we know all about any subject or circumstance simply because we have a few facts. Otherwise we may have an inadequate, erroneous impression of the whole, as did the six blind men who each felt only one part of an elephant. The one who felt only the swinging tail thought an elephant was like a rope. The others' ideas of an elephant—based on the parts they felt (shown here in parentheses)—were a spear (its tusk), a wall (its broad side), a snake (its trunk), a tree (its knee), a fan (its ear).

"Slanted" Statements.   Conscientious communicators—as both senders and receivers of messages—should try to determine whether the facts they are acquainted with are truly representative of the whole. Are they slanted with intentional bias and opinion? Slanting is unfair in factual reporting. The reporter should be careful to include quoted statements in context and exclude connotative expressions of personal approval or disapproval of the persons, objects, or occurrences being described. For example, the reporter is not permitted to write, "A small crowd of suckers came to hear Tom Jones yesterday noon in that rundown hotel that disfigures the central area." Instead, the write-up may state, "Between 100 and 150 people heard an address yesterday noon by Tom Jones in the auditorium at the Edge Hotel on Center Street."

Likewise, the voting secretary who writes minutes of meetings must be careful to avoid slanted reporting. To omit some items merely because they may seem less important or are contrary to the secretary's personal biases is both unfair and inaccurate. He or she must not allow personal preferences to influence perception and reporting.

Inferring

Conclusions made by reasoning from evidence or premises are called *inferences.* Every day most of us find it necessary to act on some inferences. We make assumptions and draw conclusions even though we ourselves do not (or cannot) directly see, hear, feel, taste, smell, or otherwise immediately verify the evidence. Some inferences are both necessary and desirable; others are risky, even dangerous.

Necessary, Desirable Inferences.   For business and professional persons inferences are essential and desirable in analyzing materials, solving problems, and planning procedures. Systems analysts, marketing specialists, advertisers, architects, engineers, designers, and numerous others all must work on various premises and make inferences after they have gathered as much factual data as possible. Even our legal procedures allow inferences from experts as acceptable evidence. Also, as consumers in our daily activities, we may make inferences that are necessary and usually fairly reliable.

> *When we drop an airmail envelope into a mailbox, we infer that it will be picked up, flown by plane, and ultimately delivered to our intended readers. We infer that the gas station attendant pumps gasoline (not water) into our car's tank, that the elevator in our building is capable of taking us to the desired floor, and so on.*

When we base our inferences on direct observation or on reasonable evidence, they are likely to be quite dependable; but even so, there are disappointing exceptions. Conclusions we make about things we have not observed directly may be true or untrue.

Risks of Inferences.   As intelligent communicators we must avoid faulty inferences. We must realize that inferences may be incorrect and unreliable and may cause miscommunication. We need to anticipate risks before acting on the inferences.

> *Suppose that a personnel manager notices that Sue Jones, a new management trainee, has been staying at least an hour after closing time every evening for the past two weeks. He might infer that Ms. Jones is exceptionally conscientious, that she is incapable of doing the required work within the regular time, that she has been given more responsibility than should be expected of a new trainee, or even that she is snooping around for confidential materials after others have left the office. Before acting on any of these inferences, the manager should get more facts!*

In some industries executives may make a disastrous decision that ultimately causes loss of lives as well as money if they assume wrongly that an inference in a report is a verifiable fact.

On any job you do—for an employer or others—be sure to consider the bases of inferences. Inform those who may be acting on your inference what portions of your statements are mere assumptions. If you are presenting or receiving a report on which an important executive decision may rest, be especially careful to distinguish clearly among verifiable facts, inferences based on facts, and mere "guesstimates."

Making Frozen Evaluations

Another drawback to effective perception is the *frozen evaluation*—the stereotyped, static impression that ignores significant differences or changes. Stereotyping is often based on faulty inferences. To help assure that your comprehension of reality will be correct, you need to recognize that any person, product, or event:

May be quite different from others in the general group

May have significant differences today when compared with characteristics yesterday or some time ago

May deserve more than a two-valued description

Individual Differences within Groups.   In reality no two elements of a general group or classification are exactly alike. When people ignore significant individual differences and consider all parts of a group to be the same, they have formed a frozen—stereotyped and unfair—evaluation. Even manufactured assembly-line products differ under a microscope. Flashlight F320 number 1 is not exactly the same as number 2 or number 1,020. Though you may have trouble with one F-brand flashlight, that does not necessarily mean all flashlights of that brand are also defective.

The same caution applies emphatically to human beings. Some people adhere to their faulty stereotypes about all members of a group merely because of an experience with one member's promptness, honestly, or appearance. Such stereotyped generalizations—based merely on assumptions that all parts of a whole are alike—unjustly disregard important differences in individual characteristics.

Differences within Time Periods.   Frozen evaluations are also made when people disregard the possible changes that may have occurred over a period of time. Every thing and every person in the world changes. No one, no thing remains static; neither should our evaluations remain static.

> *Perhaps you've known a customer who asserts, "I'll never again buy any coat with the Realex label! The one I bought last year came apart at the seams." He or she should realize that (1) probably not all Realex coats last year ripped at the seams (Realex coat number 1 is not exactly the same as Realex coat number 10,500) and (2) Realex coats last year may not be the same as Realex coats this year or next year.*

A customer's payment record this year is not necessarily exactly the same as last year. Nor can you be sure that a successful sales campaign this month will again be successful next month. Furthermore, though a certain area may have been ideal (or disappointing) for skiing the past several weeks, its weather may be quite different next week.

In all, we should remember to avoid frozen evaluations made on the basis of what was true at one time. Changes occur in products, people, laws, business conditions, organizations, environment, and so on.

Differences in Degree.   The communication practice of making only a strict, two-valued, "either-or" evaluation may be a source of miscommunication. If communicators designate people, products, or statements as either good or bad, strong or weak, honest or dishonest, hard or soft, large or small, fast or slow, black or white, true or false, they may be *polarizing.* They are overlooking important areas in between the extremes. To be fair and accurate, communicators should be specific in each case, using details and figures whenever possible.

In short, to be discerning communicators, we must consider significant differences for a unit of any group—and changes in any one unit during a period of time. We must ask *which* person, *which* product, *which* event, exactly *when* and *to what extent* any particular statement is true. This caution is useful for all communicators. It is especially applicable for report writers, who must be able to identify their sources, dates, and specific details of important facts.

Attitudes and Opinions

Communication effectiveness is influenced also by the attitudes and opinions the communicators have in their mental filters. People tend to react favorably when the message they receive agrees with their views toward the information, the set of facts, and the sender. In addition, sometimes unrelated circumstances affect their attitudes, emotions, and responses.

Favorable or Unfavorable Information

The effective communicator should be considerate of the receivers and whenever possible emphasize—honestly—points the receivers will regard as favorable or beneficial. Rejecting, distorting, and avoiding are three common undesirable, negative ways receivers react to information they consider unfavorable. For example:

> *Suppose some employees perceive that a recently announced change in company policy is contrary to their beliefs or benefit. In reacting, they may reject or resent the company and their boss, perhaps falsely accusing them of being unfair. Or they may, instead, distort the meaning and misinterpret the true purpose of the policy change. Or they may avoid the message, situation, or people by putting off acceptance, hoping that the delay will somehow prevent the change and protect them.*

Incorrect Set of Facts

Occasionally people react according to their attitudes toward sets of facts, rather than to the facts themselves. For instance, a customer may be happy over an adjustment or a loan that a company extends, but angry when learning that a neighbor received a better deal for what the customer assumes (perhaps wrongly) to be the same circumstances. This person may have inadequate information.

Closed Minds

Some individuals have a closed mind toward receiving new information. The closed-minded person is one of the most difficult to communicate with. Typically, this person has only inadequate and mainly incorrect knowledge of the subject. Yet he or she refuses to consider any new facts, even from an expert who has made a long, careful study of the problem and the proposed change. The closed-minded person says in essence, "My mind is made up. Don't bother me with facts. I want what I want." Sometimes this type of person, even before reading or hearing the documented facts, unjustly labels them or the sender's views as distorted, or calls the sender a liar. In all, closed-minded people stubbornly reject, distort, or avoid a viewpoint before they know the facts. Sometimes better communication is possible if these adamant persons can be encouraged to state their reasons for rejecting a concept. They may reveal deep-rooted prejudices, opinions, or emotions. However, if they react only with anger and refuse to give reasons or to consider the other person's facts, effective communication will be impossible. To settle such a dispute, the intervention of a mediator or even a court of law may be necessary.

Sender's Credibility

Often, people react more according to their attitude toward the *source* of facts than to the facts themselves. A staunch Democrat will be more likely to accept an idea from another Democrat than the same idea from a Republican. A conservative executive may be less likely to accept statements from the office grapevine than from the department manager.

Stated positively, employees, customers, and people in general react more favorably when a communicator has credibility—when they respect, trust, and believe in the communicator. Also, when an adult must present a disagreeable message to another adult, the recipient will usually be more open to suggestions if the sender communicates on an adult-adult basis instead of like a critical parent to a child, for the latter communications arouse negative responses.

Other Circumstances Affecting Attitudes, Emotions, Responses

When personal or business or environmental upsets occur, emotions and attitudes toward various messages may be adversely affected. Worry, anger, fear, despondency, hatred—even when due to circumstances entirely unrelated to the particular message—can adversely affect it. On a day when everything at home is wrong and disturbing, a person's written and oral communications at the office might sound unusually gruff, gloomy, or uncooperative. When everything is rosy in someone's personal life, that person's business communications may also reflect this better emotional condition. In an emotionally charged situation, words must be chosen extremely carefully, for even one slip may trigger an emotional reaction and ruin the success of a message.

If you can predict the probable attitude, opinion, or prejudice the receiver already has about a certain matter or person, you can better focus your communication in ways to reduce tension and resistance. Also, if you are the receiver, try not to let your personal, biased viewpoints affect your perception of a message. Observe, read, and listen to various sources for useful information.

When both sender and recipient are open-minded, each may find areas in which the other person is right, so that a compromise can be reached. In the words of an old Indian prayer, "Let me not criticize my neighbor until I have walked a mile in his moccasins."

NONVERBAL COMMUNICATION

The preceding sections about the communication process and problems focused mainly on *verbal* communication—by written or spoken symbols, usually *words*. As Figure 2-1 indicates, we also communicate *nonverbally—without words*. Sometimes nonverbal messages contradict the verbal; often they express true feelings more accurately than the spoken or written language.

Numerous articles and books have been written on the importance of nonverbal messages. Some studies have found that from 60 to 90 percent of a message's overall effect comes from nonverbal cues.[3] This section presents a brief general overview of nonverbal communication in these broad categories:

- Appearance
- Body language
- Silence, time, and sounds

How Appearance Communicates

Appearance conveys nonverbal impressions that affect recipients' attitudes toward the verbal messages even before they read or hear them.

Effect on Written Messages

The envelope's overall appearance—size, color, weight, postage—may impress the receiver as "important," "routine," or "junk" mail. Telegrams, Mailgrams, Express Mail, and private courier mail also have distinctive envelopes that signal urgency and importance. Next, the letter report or title page communicates nonverbally even before its contents are read. Also important are the appearance of a message's stationery and its length, format, and typing. The enclosures—quantity and attractiveness (with or without charts, graphs, pictures)—also give significant nonverbal impressions.

> Some students after a job interview suggest that by simply looking at and feeling an envelope they can immediately determine whether it contains a "ding" letter—one which suggests the company is not interested in them. (Their inferences may be right or wrong.)

Effect on Oral Messages

Whether you are speaking to one person face to face or to a group in a meeting, personal appearance and the appearance of the surroundings convey nonverbal stimuli that affect attitudes—even emotions—toward the spoken words. Communication success can be profoundly influenced.

Personal Appearance. Clothing, jewelry, hairstyles, cosmetics, fingernails, neatness, stature are parts of personal appearance. They can convey impressions regarding occupation, age, sex, nationality, social and economic level, job status, and good or poor judgment, depending on circumstances.

> Stereotypes that depict accountants as wearing three-piece suits, organizational behavior and human-resource people as wearing sweaters, or people who wear caps as driving pickup trucks are unfair inferences based on personal appearance.

Appearance of Surroundings. Aspects of surroundings include room size, location, furnishings, machines, architecture, wall decorations, floor (carpeted or bare?), lighting, windows, view, and other related aspects wherever people communicate orally. How does the appearance of the surroundings affect attitudes toward and the interpretation of spoken words? Here are two examples, among hundreds:

> *Why will an executive or professional whose office is a luxurious top-floor suite with a panoramic view convey a different nonverbal message (about status, success, advice, size of bill) than he or she will if the office is in a dingy, poorly lighted basement room? Why do full professors seek corner offices with windows on two sides?*

In some factories and business firms, lower-status employees may work in small, crowded, unattractive areas. Thoughtful managers can help improve morale and efficiency when they perceive employee attitudes toward surroundings and follow suggestions for improving appearance.

How Body Language Communicates

Included under body language are facial expressions, gestures and posture, smell and touch; all are noticeable nonverbal communication symbols. Sometimes they are more meaningful than words, but we must be careful when interpreting them in our daily interpersonal communications. They are important also for special occasions, interviews, and speeches to groups, as suggested in later chapters.

Facial Expressions

The eyes and face are especially helpful means of communicating nonverbally. They can divulge hidden emotions—anger, annoyance, confusion, enthusiasm, fear, hatred, joy, love, interest, sorrow, surprise, uncertainty, and others. They can also contradict verbal statements.

> *A new employee may answer "yes" hesitatingly, ashamed or embarrassed to tell the truth when asked if she or he understands the supervisor's oral instructions. Yet that employee's frown or red face and bewildered expression in the eyes should prompt the observant supervisor to consider restating the instructions more clearly.*

Direct eye contact (but not staring) is usually desirable when two people converse face to face. The person whose eyes droop or shift away from the listener is thought to be shy or perhaps dishonest and untrustworthy. But we must be careful not to overgeneralize. Because people differ, there are exceptions on individual nonverbal cues, as shown in this example:

> *Some folks assume, wrongly, that they can tell what people have been doing just by looking into their eyes. However, a person's eyes may be misty and red because he or she has been ill, or crying, laughing, drinking heavily,*

smoking, sleeping, suffering from infection, walking in the wind, swimming, or working near harmful vapors.

Moral? Get more facts before judging anyone's facial expressions conclusively.

Gestures and Posture

Do actions speak louder than words? They do in some occupations, as well as in many interpersonal situations. Employees who direct traffic on crowded streets or in noisy stadiums, or guide huge trucks when backing up in narrow places, can effectively communicate by pointing arms or fingers in the desired directions—without uttering any words. And, of course, deaf people communicate silently by hand and finger movements.

Clenched fists pounding on a table or podium may indicate anger or emphasis. Continual gestures with arms while speaking may signal nervousness; they may also distract listeners' attention from the spoken words. Handshakes reveal attitudes (and sometimes handicaps) by their firmness or limpness, promptness, and movements.

Legs, too, communicate nonverbal messages. Consider, for instance, possible attitudes of these people: a sitting man with legs stretched on top of his office desk during an interview; a quiet person with head bowed and knees on the floor; a standing person shifting weight from one leg to another in rhythmic motion while humming—or pacing back and forth while speaking.

Posture nonverbally conveys impressions of self-confidence, status, and interest. Confident executives may have a relaxed posture and yet stand more erect than a timid subordinate. Interested persons occasionally lean forward toward the speaker, while those who are bored or annoyed may slump—as well as yawn and repeatedly glance at their watches.

Smell and Touch

Various odors and artificial fragrances on human beings can sometimes convey emotions and feelings better than spoken words. (Some odors on equipment can indicate smoke, fire, decay, or dangerous leaks in containers or pipes, thus helping to save lives if detected early.)

Touching people in different ways (and places) can silently communicate friendship, love, approval, hatred, anger, or other motives and feelings. A kiss on the cheek, pat on the shoulder, or slap on the back is prompted by various attitudes and emotions. Also, "touching" in a crowded bus in which passengers are squeezed together is offensive to many North Americans.

Voice

Perhaps you have heard people speak words that were pleasant but in a tone of voice that betrayed their true feelings? *Paralanguage* is a term denoting the subtle variations in meaning between *what* is said and *how* it is said.

The words "Wow! How prompt you are today!" could be a compliment. But if the tone of voice is sarcastic and said to someone who arrived an hour late, the true meaning is criticism, perhaps anger.

You can also convey different meanings by the rate, pitch, and volume of your voice. Speaking fast may indicate nervousness or haste. A soft voice soothes and calms; a loud, shouting voice may foretell danger, urgency, a serious problem, joy, or anger. Furthermore, by emphasizing different key words in a sentence you can purposely indicate your feelings about what is important.

Consider the sentence "Tom completed two reports." If you accent "Tom," you are stressing who deserves credit for the reports. If, instead, you emphasize the word "completed," or "two," or "reports," you can change the meaning of your message with each different vocal emphasis.

How Silence, Time, and Sounds Communicate

Silence

Though at first thought silence may seem unimportant, it can actually cause serious hard feelings, loss of business, and profits.

Suppose you wrote an urgent letter to the customer relations manager of a large company, stating why you need a reply by March 5. If you receive no answer by that date and none for two months after that, what is your reaction to the silence? Do you worry whether your letter was lost? Do you angrily assume the manager is rude and just considers your request unworthy of his or her time? Do you wonder if the manager is annoyed by something in your letter or if your envelope is perhaps at the bottom of a stack under other priority mail?

Time

Waiting when an important request is ignored causes problems and attitude changes. In the preceding example, after the long silence, should you write again, telephone, wire, or just drop the matter and buy from a competitor? You should also consider whether in your request for a "reply by March 5" you gave the manager enough time to reply. Time is important in many other ways too. Being on time for appointments, for work each day, and for deadlines communicates favorable nonverbal messages in our culture.

As will be noted in more detail in Chapter 25, concepts of time vary across cultures, and even in the United States. Americans and Germans, for instance, are quite punctual. Middle Eastern business people think little of arriving after an agreed-upon time not out of discourtesy, but rather a feeling that the task will be accomplished regardless of time.

Sounds

In addition to a speaking person's voice, other human sounds—clearing the throat, sighing, laughing—communicate nonverbally. Also, nonhuman sounds—of bells, whistles, steam shovels, cars, trains, airplanes—all can be significant nonverbal communicators. Many people set their watches by certain whistles or rush off to work or to catch their transportaton when they hear certain signals. Sounds can also indicate leaky pipes or defective machines that need immediate attention. And they can sometimes serve as convincing evidence—contrary to the written or spoken words of a mechanic—that the repair work just completed is unsatisfactory!

SUMMARY

Effective communication depends to a large extent on insights into human nature and on the ability to get desirable responses. It is a complex process that involves sender-encoder, message, medium, receiver-decoder, and feedback. This chapter has included merely an introduction to the process of communication. Its aim has been to give you helpful ideas of why communication problems may occur, particularly some characteristics of the oral and written medium.

To be an effective communicator, realize that human beings' mental filters and experiences differ. Each connects different attitudes, abilities, skills, and cultural customs to the words we use. To presume that our message will be always perfectly understood is unrealistic. Bypassing (assigning different meanings from the same symbols), denotations, connotations, euphemisms all intrude on perfect messages between senders and receivers.

Other hindrances to precise communication include the concepts of abstracting, of using two-valued words and "allness" terms, of slanted statements, and of drawing incorrect conclusions or inferences.

Try always to consider differences in word (and sentence) interpretations. Keep an open mind for getting as many accurate facts as possible about reality. Admit that there is more than can be said, and allow for the influences of attitudes, opinions, and emotions. Remember also the importance of nonverbal communication—by appearance, body language, silence, time, sounds. Above all, try to better understand the people with whom you communicate. This ability will be useful and will be developed further as you apply the principles in the remainder of this book.

EXERCISES AND PROBLEMS

1. Divide your paper into five columns with the following headings: Sender-Encoder, Message, Medium, Receiver-Decoder, and Feedback. Under each column list possible causes of miscommunication, problems that con-

tribute to the breakdown of communication; include examples from your own experiences, if possible.

2. Consider three of the following names: Mary, Mikhail, Barbara, Jimmy, Liz, George, Peter, Carol, Ronald, Abby. Prepare to share with the class your thoughts, opinions, experiences (and emotions, if any) about each. Using communication terms in this chapter, explain how and why details of your reactions are different from those of classmates.

3. The comment "Harold Joiner is a member of five business clubs and two athletic clubs" may be intended as a compliment. Why might some listeners interpret it as derogatory?

4. Give two examples of how the opinions and prejudices in your mind affect your communication.

5. Try and answer the question why there is a broken line on the semantic triangle between symbol and referent in Figure 2–2 on page 19.

6. Discuss whether each of the following statements is an inference or a verifiable fact based on observation:
   a. The boss is a "swinger."
   b. Employees under 20 and over 65 are inefficient.
   c. The union requested double pay for each hour of overtime.
   d. The union requested too much money.
   e. XYZ skis are no good.

7. What general communication principles do the following statements and incidents illustrate? Discuss each briefly.
   a. A friend of yours states: "I'll never buy our groceries from Tiptop Market. Haven't been there since the first week after they opened four years ago. Their produce department is a mess, and prices are too high."
   b. In a public utility, an order went out setting up a new procedure; on the basis of that order, five different powerhouses set up five different procedures.
   c. An article in tonight's newspaper states that a nationwide strike appears all but certain after union negotiators walked out of contract talks and accused management of forcing a strike. But the chief negotiator said he couldn't "conceive how anyone could say what we gave them was a provocation for a strike."

8. Suppose you see Helen (the tenant who lives alone in an apartment directly above you) leaving at 8 p.m. from the front of the building. You have observed that she leaves at the same time each weekday evening. Yesterday she told you she is a doctor in a downtown hospital and her shift starts at 8:30 p.m. Tonight at 8:55 you hear footsteps in the apartment above you.

    a. Name three spontaneous inferences you could make.

    b. Discuss possible reasons why those inferences may be right or wrong. What action, if any, should you take?

9. Discuss two examples of how your nonverbal communications contradicted your spoken words.

10. Bring to class an example of a written business message that conveys an unfavorable nonverbal message, and bring a second written message that conveys a favorable nonverbal message. State specific reasons for your evaluations.

11. A popular humorist and actor has stated that sometimes the same jokes that cause one audience to laugh spontaneously don't even get a chuckle another night in a different town. Discuss this comment in terms of a communication principle.

12. Can you share with the class an example of (a) bypassing instructions or (b) judging the whole by a part? Discuss the causes and consequences.

13. Figure 2–2 is a representation of what occurs between a symbol and the object in reality for which it stands. In a similar way symbols (flags, songs, religious artifacts, school insignia) stand for something else. With that as background, read the following incident and then be prepared to discuss the incident from a communication perspective.

> *Your firm employs 230 people, is located in a midwestern community, and produces medical products. Producing the product demands close attention to quality inspections, most often occurring in a "clean room" (a room with controlled air inflow wherein employees must dress in protective clothing).*
>
> *The foreman of the day shift of the clean room has been with the company for six years, is respected, and is well-liked by the company administration. But he is known to express opinions which are counter to those of his co-workers. One day he was particularly disturbed about an increase in his property taxes and took the American flag off the wall, threw it down on the floor, and stamped on it. His co-workers were incensed. They feared that next time he would burn the flag. Most members of the day quality-inspection team demanded his immediate dismissal.*

Chapter 3

Business Communication Principles I

I. **Completeness**
   A. Answer All Questions Asked
   B. Give Something Extra, When Desirable
   C. Check for the Five W's and Any Other Essentials

II. **Conciseness**
   A. Eliminate Wordy Expressions
   B. Include Only Relevant Statements
   C. Avoid Unnecessary Repetition

III. **Consideration**
   A. Focus on "You" instead of "I" and "We"
   B. Show Reader Benefit or Interest in Reader
   C. Emphasize the Positive, Pleasant Facts
   D. Apply Integrity and Ethics

IV. **Concreteness**
   A. Use Specific Facts and Figures
   B. Put Action in Your Verbs
   C. Choose Vivid, Image-Building Words

V. **Summary**

VI. **Exercises and Problems**

To compose effective messages you need to apply certain specific communications principles. They tie in closely with the basic concepts of the communication process and are important for *both written and oral communications*. They provide guidelines for choice of content and style of presentation—*adapted to the purpose and receiver of your message.* Called the "seven C's," they are completeness, conciseness, consideration, concreteness, clarity, courtesy, correctness. This chapter discusses the first four C's, and Chapter 4 the remaining C's. (You will find the C's in other chapters too.)

COMPLETENESS

Your business message is "complete" when it contains all facts the reader or listener needs for the reaction you desire. Remember that communicators differ in their mental filters; they are influenced by their backgrounds, viewpoints, needs, experiences, attitudes, status, and emotions.

Completeness is necessary for several reasons: First, complete messages are more likely to bring the desired results without the expense of additional messages. Second, they can do a better job of building goodwill. Third, they can help avert costly lawsuits that may result if important information is missing. Last, papers that seem inconsequential can be surprisingly important if the information they contain is complete and effective. In high-level conferences, in courtrooms, and in governmental hearings, the battle often centers on an ordinary-looking message that becomes important because of the complete information it contains.

As you strive for completeness, keep the following guidelines in mind:

■ Answer all questions asked.
■ Give something extra, when desirable.
■ Check for the five W's and any other essentials.

Answer All Questions Asked

Whenever you reply to an inquiry, try to answer all questions—stated and implied. A prospective customer's reaction to an incomplete reply is likely to be unfavorable. The customer may think the respondent is careless or is purposely trying to conceal a weak spot. In general, "omissions cast suspicions," whether you are answering an inquiry about your product or recommending a former employee for a new job. If you have no information on a particular question, say so clearly. If you have unfavorable information in answer to questions, handle your reply with both tact and honesty.

The replies in situations 1 and 2 were incomplete, because the respondents omitted the answers to one or more questions or omitted important information in an explanation that answered a question.

SITUATION 1   *A distributor of software, when replying to a dealer's letter, answered only four of seven questions. Because the original questions were unnumbered and somewhat buried in five long paragraphs, the respondent apparently overlooked or disregarded three of them. The reply, incomplete and unfriendly, caused the distributor to lose the business and goodwill of a potential customer.*

Sometimes before you can answer an inquiry, you need certain specific information from the inquirer. Then it is a good idea to list the needed details on a reply form that the inquirer can fill out and return to you. In this way both your answer and that of your respondent will be complete. In situation 2 the eight messages about one transaction resulted in delay and annoyed and disappointed customers. Had the bank supplied a reply form, the desired sale could have been completed promptly with four messages: the first inquiry, the bank's reply with an enclosed form asking specific questions, the owner's authorization (on the form), and the banks's final liquidation notice and check.

SITUATION 2   *On May 8 the owner of mutual fund stock wrote to a New York bank's investment department that he wanted to sell his shares. He asked, "Just how does your bank want me to authorize this sale?" He received the following reply May 19:*

```
If you wish to terminate account #99998 and liquidate the
shares held by this bank, we need a letter of instructions
signed by both you and your wife just as the account is reg-
istered. Please be sure to give us the name of your fund,
your account number, and the name of the person to whom pro-
ceeds are to be mailed.
```

The customer's reply, signed by both himself and his wife, included the fund name, account number, and this statement:

```
Please sell our 37 shares effective this date--May 23, 199-,
and send proceeds to us.
```

On May 28 they received the following telegram:

```
RE MLF FUND A/C 99998 UNABLE ACCEPT INSTRUCTIONS TO LIQUI-
DATE ON A SPECIFIC DATE FORWARD NEW SIGNED INSTRUCTIONS.
```

In their reply the customers wrote essentially the same letter as their second, but they omitted the words "effective this date. . . ." A week later they received from the bank another request—this time to include in their reply both the name and the address to which the proceeds were to be mailed! (The bank had not asked for the address, and the customers assumed the proceeds would be mailed to their home address.) The next day they wrote their fourth letter. Finally—July 8, two months after the original question— they received a formal notice of liquidation with a check for the proceeds. However, during the delay, the price of the stock had fallen considerably, and they lost money on their sale.

Give Something Extra, When Desirable

The words "when desirable," in the above heading, are essential. Sometimes you must do more than answer the customers' specific questions. They may not know what they need, or their questions may be inadequate. For example, suppose you are president of the Regional Business Executives' League for your industry and receive the following inquiry from an out-of-town member:

> I think I would like to attend my first meeting of the League, even though I'm not acquainted in your city. Will you please tell me where the next meeting will be held?

If you answered only this one question, your letter would be incomplete. Realizing that your reader is a newcomer to your city and to your league's meetings, you should include in your reply a welcome plus such needed details as directions for reaching the building; parking facilities; day, date, and time of meeting; and perhaps also the program for the next meeting. Your message will then have the "something extra" that a reader really needs and appreciates.

Sometimes the something extra is a detailed explanation instead of a mere brief statement. The last paragraph of letter 1 below contains an invitation that is meaningless for any new depositor who does not know what "facilities" are at his or her disposal. Letter 2 clearly explains the services offered and thereby makes the invitation meaningful. (If a writer can enclose a descriptive brochure, the letter can be shorter and still complete if it merely mentions the services and refers to the enclosure for details.) The following examples show only the message of each letter (without address and salutation).

LETTER 1   *Incomplete letter to a new savings depositor.*

> Thank you for the confidence you have shown us by the account you recently opened.
>
> All our facilities are at your disposal, and anytime we can be of service, please call on us. Our appreciation is best expressed by our being of service to you.

LETTER 2   *Revised, complete letter to the new savings depositor.*

> Thank you for the confidence you have shown in First Federal by the savings account you recently opened. Our goal is to make all our services to you both pleasant and helpful.
>
> Among the conveniences and services available to you at First Federal, you may be especially interested in these:
>
> > YOUR PASSBOOK DEPOSITS earn $6\frac{1}{2}$% interest compounded monthly.

> BETTER-THAN-CHECKING service helps you pay bills by
> phone, earns interest on your money, and permits using
> our 24-hour Cash Machines.
>
> MORTGAGE LOANS help you to buy, build, or refinance a
> home or to borrow for property repairs and improve-
> ments.
>
> With our MONEY MARKET CERTIFICATES you can earn inter-
> est at various current high rates, depending on time
> and amount of your investment. The enclosed leaflet
> gives you more details about these and other services
> available to you at First Federal.
>
> FREE CUSTOMER PARKING is provided in the lot north of
> our office. The teller stamps your parking slip, en-
> titling you to free parking while doing business here.
> Office hours are 9:30 a.m. to 4:30 p.m. weekdays except
> for Friday, when the doors remain open until 6:00 p.m.

You are most welcome to come in whenever we can assist you.
Please consider this association your financial headquarters
for your savings and borrowing needs.

Check for the Five W's and Any Other Essentials

Another way to help make your message complete is to answer, whenever desirable, the "five W" questions—*who, what, where, when, why*—and any other essentials, such as *how*. The five-question method is especially useful when you write requests, announcements, or other informative messages. For instance, to order (request) merchandise, make clear *what* you want, *when* you need it, to *whom* and *where* it is to be sent, and *how* payment will be made. To reserve a hotel banquet room, specify the accommodations needed (*what*), location (*where*), sponsoring organization (*who*), date and time (*when*), event (*why*), and other necessary details (*how*).

The following example shows how a sales message failed because it omitted one essential statement.

The fund-raising chairman for a local alumni chapter of a national fraternity wrote a persuasive but unsuccessful letter personally addressed to each of the chapter's 140 members. It explained convincingly why funds were urgently needed to help provide adequate care for the many severely abused and neglected children in the community. It named the local nonprofit child care agency that would receive 80 percent of the dollars raised, and a national committee that would receive the remaining 20 percent. The last paragraph asked each addressee:

> Please send your generous tax-deductible contribution in the
> enclosed envelope to Tom Smith.

Unfortunately, the letter omitted answering one important question: To whom should the check (or money order) be payable? The letter had no letterhead—only a round sticker at the top with the national fraternity's name and "Prevent Child Abuse." Recipients did not know if the contribution should be to Tom Smith, or the local child care agency, or the national committee, or the national fraternity, or the local chapter, or the fund-raising chairman (whose name was typed at the bottom, with no signature). As the letter included no address or phone number, members could not get needed information. Only five sent their check, and only one of them had the correct payee—the local chapter's name.

CONCISENESS

A concise message saves time and expense for both sender and receiver. Conciseness is saying what you have to say in the fewest possible words without sacrificing the other C qualities. Conciseness contributes to emphasis. By eliminating unnecessary words, you help make important ideas stand out.

To achieve conciseness try to observe the following suggestions:

- Eliminate wordy expressions.
- Include only relevant statements.
- Avoid unnecessary repetition.

Eliminate Wordy Expressions

1. Use single-word substitutes instead of phrases whenever possible without changing meanings.

Wordy	Concise
along the line of (salary)	about (salary)
at this time	now
consensus of opinion	consensus
date of the policy	policy date
due to the fact that	because
during the time that	while
during the year of	during
few and far between	seldom, scarce
for a price of	for
for the purpose of	for; to
for the reason that	since; because
from the point of view of	as
have need for	need
in accordance with your request	as you requested
in due course	soon
in many cases	often; frequently

Wordy	Concise
in most cases	usually
in order to	to
in some cases	sometimes
in spite of the fact that	although
in (for) the amount of	for
in the city of	in
in the event that	if
in the neighborhood of $60	about $60
in view of the fact that	because
please don't hesitate to write	please write
under date of	dated
under the circumstances	because

2. Omit trite, unnecessary expressions, such as "allow me to say," "in reply I wish to state," "please be advised." Also, instead of "please find attached" (or "enclosed"), use concise statements like "attached are," "enclosed is," or "the enclosed list includes."

3. Omit "which" and "that" clauses whenever possible.

Wordy: She bought desks that are of the executive type.

Concise: She bought executive-type desks.

4. Avoid overusing "It is," "It was," "There is," "There was," "There are," "There were" at sentence beginnings.

Wordy: It was known by Mr. Smith that we must reduce. . . .

Concise: Mr. Smith knew we must reduce. . . .

Wordy: There are four rules that should be observed.

Concise: Four rules should be observed.

5. Whenever possible, use a verb in the present tense and active voice.

Wordy: The total balance due will be found on page 2 of this report.

Concise: The balance due is on page 2 of this report.

Include Only Relevant Statements

The effective, concise message should omit not only unnecessarily wordy expressions but also irrelevant material. To be sure you include only relevant facts, observe the following suggestions:

1. Stick to the purpose of the message.

2. Prune irrelevant words and rambling sentences.

3. Omit information obvious to the receiver; do not repeat at length what that person has already told you.

4. Avoid long introductions, unnecessary explanations, excessive adjectives and prepositions, pompous words, gushy politeness.

5. Get to the important point tactfully and concisely.

Wordy: At this time I am writing to you to enclose the post-paid appointment card for the purpose of arranging a convenient time when we might get together for a personal interview. [*30 words; 5 prepositions.*]

Concise: Will you please return the enclosed card and name a convenient time for an interview? [*15 words; 1 preposition.*]

Wordy: We hereby wish to let you know that we fully appreciate the confidence you have reposed in us. [*18 words.*]

Concise: We appreciate your confidence in us. [*6 words.*]

The following overly wordy letter is to the business administration placement office by a person who graduated from a university the previous year. He had difficulty finding a satisfactory job. Notice his pompous words and irrelevant material. If he talked and wrote this way to employers or customers, would they probably react negatively toward him? Compare his letter with the revised example, which the placement officer prefers.

The university Placement Office has sent me at periodic intervals a form inquiring as to my current employment status. As you may recall from our discussion last spring, I was most desirous of making a favorable change in vocational locale. After following up several recommendations made by your office (Goodwin, etc.), I was unable to negotiate an immediate change, and upon receiving suave assurances of rapid promotion from my superiors, promptly regressed into the torpid complacency which characterized my thinking upon graduation. However my present intention to move is more than a harbinger of that most fragrant of seasons but rather stems from a feeling of disillusionment and inadequacy with my vocational environment.

May I once again prevail upon you to assist me in this undertaking by informing me at your convenience of any job opportunity for which you think I would be well-suited. As indicated in my last reply to your office, I no longer look

```
to accounting as my forte but instead am seeking a selling
situation which is both challenging and remunerative.

Thank you for your patience and understanding in this
matter. You may reach me at 555-1234 during the day or at
555-4321 in the evening. [200 words.]
```

Here is the concise revision, with only relevant statements.

```
Because my interests are now in sales, please tell me about
any sales opening that is challenging and also pays well.

You can reach me at 555-1234 during the day or at 555-4321
in the evening. [36 words]
```

Avoid Unnecessary Repetition

Sometimes repetition is necessary for emphasis. But when the same thing is said two or three times without reason, the message becomes wordy and boring. Here are three ways to eliminate unnecessary repetition:

1. Use a shorter name after you have mentioned the long one once: Instead of the "Thompson Product Manufacturing Company," "Thompson Company."

2. Use pronouns or initials rather than repeat long names: Instead of citing "North Central Auto Insurance Company, Inc." again and again, use "it" or "they" or "NCAI."

3. Cut out all needless repetition of phrases and sentences. For example, the following letter from a business executive to a firm the company had dealt with for five years shows unnecessary repetition at its worst:

```
Will you ship us sometime, anytime during the month of Octo-
ber, or even November if you are rushed, for November would
suit us just as well, in fact a little bit better, 300 of
the regular 3- by 15-inch blue felt armbands with white sewn
letters in the center.

Thanking you to send these along to us by parcel post, and
not express, as express is too stiff in price, when parcel
post will be much cheaper, we are. . . .
```

The writer took 80 words to say what is said in 25 below:

```
Please ship parcel post, before the end of November, 300
regular 3- by 15-inch blue felt armbands with white sewn
letters in the center.
```

CONSIDERATION

As discussed in Chapter 2, the interrelationship of the message sender and receiver profoundly affects communication effectiveness. Consideration means that you prepare every message with the recipient in mind and try to put yourself in his or her place. Try to visualize your readers (or listeners)—with their desires, problems, circumstances, emotions, and probable reactions to your request. Then handle the matter from *their* point of view. This thoughtful consideration is also called "you-attitude," empathy, the human touch, and understanding of human nature. (It does *not* mean, however, that you should overlook the needs of your organization.)

In a broad but true sense, consideration underlies the other six C's of good business communication. You adapt your language and message content to your receiver's needs when you make your message complete, concise, concrete, clear, courteous, and correct. However, in all four specific ways you can indicate you are considerate:

- Focus on "you" instead of "I" and "we."
- Show reader benefit or interest in reader.
- Emphasize positive, pleasant facts.
- Apply integrity and ethics.

Focus on "You" instead of "I" and "We"

Your receivers are usually more concerned about themselves than about you or the company you represent. They are more likely to read your message when they see *their name* and the pronoun *"you"* rather than "I," "we," or "us."

Usually it is desirable to get your reader into the first paragraph. (Exceptions are presented later in this section.) If psychologically desirable, begin with "you" or "your," and keep your reader in the message (tactfully) until you finish. The opposite of the you-attitude is the we-attitude, in which the writer views every matter from his or her own (or the organization's) standpoint rather than from the reader's:

We-Attitude	You-Attitude
I want to send my congratu-lations for. . . .	Congratulations to you on your. . . .
We will ship soon the goods in your May 4 order.	You should receive by May 8 the Apex screens you ordered May 4.
We pay 8% interest on. . . .	You earn 8% interest on. . . .

The we-attitude department store message, letter 1 below, contains 20 "we-our-us-I-my" pronouns (underlined) and only 3 "you's" (in italics).

LETTER 1   *We-attitude.*

May _I_ take this opportunity to express _my_ thanks for the account *you* recently opened with _our_ store. _We_ are pleased to
furnish a wide variety of products for the home or individual customers.

_We_ want *you* to take full advantage of _our_ store services,
for _we_ have the largest stock in the city. Also _we_ make deliveries of _our_ customers' purchases free of charge within
30 miles of _our_ store.

*The next two paragraphs—omitted here to save space and reading—have
four "we's," three "our customers," and no "you." The last paragraph is:*

_We_ welcome *you* to Bekinson's. If _we_ can be of additional
service in any manner, please call on _us_.

In contrast, letter 2—rewritten for more you-attitude—contains 20 "you's"
and "your's" (in italics) and only 2 "we-our-us" pronouns (underlined):

LETTER 2   *You-attitude.*

Thank *you* for the account *you* recently opened at Bekinson's.
Serving *you* with *your* needs for clothing and home furnishings is a pleasure.

You can satisfy all *your* shopping needs when *you* visit any
of Bekinson's 32 well-stocked departments. _Our_ courteous,
skilled salesclerks are ready to assist *you* in selecting the
merchandise that best meets *your* requirements.

If *you* prefer to shop within the comfort of *your* home,
instead of coming to the store, *you* need only telephone 555-
8823. A Personal Shopper will gladly take *your* order for
any number of items, answer *your* questions about brands and
sizes available, and see that the goods *you* order reach *you*
by store delivery within a few days.

When *you* shop at Bekinson's downtown store, *you* are invited
to use the free customer parking privilege provided just
across the street.

You are always welcome at Bekinson's. Please call on _us_
whenever *you* need additional services.

As the foregoing examples illustrate, a letter is likely to have better you-
attitude when it contains more "you's" than "I's." But there are notable excep-

tions! An extreme example is the collection letter with "you" or "your" in almost every sentence; if those sentences are insulting, sarcastic, tactless, or untrue accusations and threats against the debtor, the letter surely lacks you-attitude.

In two kinds of situations it is advisable *not* to use "you."

1. When the reader has made a mistake:

    Poor: You failed to enclose your check in the envelope.

    Better: The envelope we received did not have a check in it.

    Poor: Your contract tells you plainly that. . . .

    Better: I am glad to explain more fully the contract terms.

2. When the reader has expressed an opinion different from your own:

    Poor: You are entirely wrong in your attitude.

    Better: The proposed plan has three aspects which are extremely important and which we need to explain now.

Show Reader Benefit or Interest in Reader

Whenever possible and true, show how your readers will benefit from whatever the message asks or announces. They will be more likely to react favorably and do what you suggest if you show that benefits are worth the effort and cost. In situations where actual direct reader benefit is impossible or irrelevant to the subject matter, the message should at least show interest in and concern for the reader's needs or viewpoint.

Even a simple request gets better response when a reader-benefit plug accompanies it.

For example, an insurance company that wanted to update its address files sent to half its policyholders a double postcard with this message:

Because we have not written you in some time, please help us bring our records up to date by filling in and returning the other half of this card.

Only 3 percent of these cards came back. To the remaining half of its policyholders the firm sent the same request—reworded to show reader benefit:

So that dividend checks, premium notices, and other messages of importance may reach you promptly, please fill out and return the other half of this card.

This request brought 90 percent of the cards back in a few days!

Merely inserting the word *you* does not ensure you-attitude, as shown in this sentence:

```
You will be glad to know that we now have a Walk-Up Window
open 7-9 a.m. and 3-8 p.m. every weekday.
```

Some readers may wonder, "So what?" The revised sentence includes reader benefit:

```
You can now take care of your banking needs also at our new
Walk-Up Window. It is open with a capable teller to serve
you 7-9 a.m. and 3-8 p.m. Monday through Friday.
```

Reader-benefit appeals help collect payments on bills, soften the blow in a turndown, and sell products. Though your company is in business to make a profit, you omit that selfish-sounding idea; the reader assumes it anyway and is motivated only by what benefits he or she receives. Reader-benefit appeals are desirable also in job applications, favor requests, and announcements to your customers, prospective buyers, stockholders, and employees. Whether you are writing to one person or to large numbers, try to personalize the reader benefits (as in letter 2, page 45) instead of stating them in a general way ("our customers," as in letter 1, page 45).

If your organization provides employee benefits—such as health insurance and various retirement plans—management should make every effort to assure that all employees understand and appreciate those benefits. Many may be unaware that their employer spends more than one-third of the total payroll on employee benefits. To inform employees effectively, management can use such media as memos, employee manuals, bulletins, policy statements, company magazines, newssheets, reports, posters, films, and notes in pay envelopes.

Emphasize the Positive, Pleasant Facts

A third way to show consideration for your reader (or listener) is to accent the positive. This means (1) stressing what *can* be done instead of what cannot be done and (2) focusing on words your recipient can *consider favorably.*

Statement of What Can Be Done

The reader (or listener) wants to know what you *can* do for him or her. For most people negative words like *no, won't, cannot, never, impossible* trigger unpleasant emotional reactions. By making clear what you can or will do, you (by implication) often make clear what you *cannot* do, without using a single negative word. Furthermore, whenever possible and helpful, tell why or how.

Negative—Unpleasant	Positive—Pleasant
It is <u>impossible to open</u> an account for you today.	As soon as your signature card reaches us, we <u>will gladly open</u> an. . . .
We <u>don't refund</u> if the returned item is <u>soiled and unsalable</u>.	We <u>refund</u> when the returned item is <u>clean and resalable</u>.
When you travel on company expense, you will <u>not receive</u> approval for <u>first-class</u> fare.	When you travel on company expense, your <u>approved fare</u> is for <u>tourist</u> class.
To <u>avoid</u> further <u>delay</u> and <u>inconvenience</u>, we are sending this report by Express Mail.	So that you will <u>get</u> this report <u>as soon as possible</u>, we are sending it by Express Mail.

Words Your Recipient Can Consider Favorably

Among the *positive* words to which people react *favorably* are *benefit, cordial, happy, help, generous, loyal, pleasure, thanks, thoughtful*. Words with *negative* connotations that often arouse *unfavorable* reactions include *blame, complaint, failed, fault, negligence, regret, reject, trouble, unfair*, and many others. For example, in the following opening of a letter the negative words (underlined) focus on ideas you'd rather not have the reader think about.

> We <u>regret</u> that, since you <u>closed</u> your account, your name will be missing from our long list of satisfied customers. We sincerely <u>hope</u> that, despite the best efforts of our fine staff, there were <u>no occasions</u> on which you felt we <u>failed</u> to serve you properly.

A better opening expresses appreciation for the customer's patronage in the first paragraph, as shown below. Then the second paragraph welcomes him or her to other services.

> Having you as a member of Apex Savings Bank was a pleasure. thank you for giving us the opportunity to serve you.
>
> We noticed recently that you closed your account with us. Perhaps you reached that particular goal for which you were saving, or it may be that an emergency arose which called for a large outlay of cash. Whatever the reason, we were happy to have some small part in your financial program. You are cordially invited to use our other profitable, time-saving services that can provide benefits for you in various ways.

Apply Integrity and Ethics

To be truly considerate, you need also to apply integrity—high moral standards, personal honor, truthfulness, sincerity—to your written and oral messages. Integrity is indispensable in our jobs, in business transactions, in social and political activities, in everything we do. Without it, business communications would prove worthless, and our confidence in people would be shattered.

Ethics is concerned with what is right human conduct. Codes of ethics provide standards enabling us to determine the fundamental distinction between right and wrong human behavior. Often, gray areas involve fine decisions between complete truth and a partial falsehood. An honest businessperson needs a strong conscience as well as knowledge of communication principles and company policies.

The following statements, adapted from "Honest Communication," an essay by the Royal Bank of Canada, express well several important basic concepts:

> Honesty is not a simple subject, because it goes to the very heart of human nature. Honesty is born when one perceives what is right and wrong and chooses to do what is right. . . . Confidence in one's honesty cannot be established simply by avoiding only what is illegal. . . . The rules of ethics are far wider than mere legality. . . .

> Promises made in speeches, letters, and advertising should be fulfilled scrupulously. . . . Honesty in business communication reaches its most visible public testing point in advertising, labeling, and selling. . . . Half-truths, exaggerations, and misleading descriptions of products or services are not honest communications.[1]

Because you are an agent of your company, you help build your company's image. To make this image one of integrity and ethical conduct requires consistently fair standards and honesty in communications with persons outside and inside your organization.

Integrity with Persons outside the Organization

When you show consideration for your customers, you try to let them know you are aware of and are doing something about their interests and needs. This does *not* mean, however, that you yield to the temptation of showing favoritism, allowing deviations for one customer that you would not allow for all other customers in similar circumstances, or arranging money kickbacks and bribes to obtain government or commercial business. If customers insist that "everyone else does it," the temptation to comply with their wishes may be difficult. Nevertheless, widespread existence of evil does not make evil right. *High ethical standards may require "doing the harder right instead of the easier wrong."*

Studies have shown that the behavior of superiors and pressures from top management to meet competition and increase profits were the chief factors influencing executives to make unethical decisions. Typical examples include misrepresenting contents of products, substituting materials without customer knowledge after the job contract has been awarded, scheduling inaccurate delivery dates to get a contract, and so on. Therefore, an ethical boss can be an important influence for ethical employee communications.[2]

Among 10 examples of behavior that advertising and marketing executives considered most unethical (in a 1981 study by Lewis and Reinsch)[3] were these dishonest communications to persons outside the firm:

Making false product or service claims to a potential customer in order to obtain $1,000,000 (or $500,000 or $1,000)

Shading the truth in published financial statements

Divulging confidential data to persons outside the company

Needed Ethical Communication within the Organization

Employees must also be fair to their employer and to each other. Weak ethical standards, economic pressures, and competition for promotions or increased income have tempted many to unethical behavior.

Dishonesty toward Employers.   Employee internal thefts and dishonest practices like the following are estimated to cost businesses billions of dollars yearly:

Wasting time on the job—by taking excessive lunch and coffee breaks, "snoozing" in the stockroom, claiming sick leave when not ill, and so on. One survey of 325 employers revealed (according to a report in the *Star,* Dec. 21, 1982) that a worker steals an average of more than four hours a week from the boss.

Failing to report an employee error that will cost the company losses ranging from $10 to $100,000.[4]

Unfair padding expense accounts with dinner dates and travel items far above the actual costs to the reporting persons.

Purposely ordering larger quantities of supplies or equipment than needed so that employees who order can take valuables home for their own use.

Unfair Communications with or about Co-workers.   Examples of dishonest behavior by employees toward each other include these—and many others:

Issuing false instructions to a co-worker in order to make that person look bad or perform poorly

Giving false information to a superior in order to improve the giver's position in the department

Falsely reporting high work evaluations for personal favorites so they will get unjustified promotions

Spreading false rumors against a competitor for a promotion in the department or company[5]

How do unethical practices affect you and other business communicators? The following statements, though printed in 1977, are important anytime:

> Corrupt practices corrupt personnel, impair integrity of the corporation, challenge the corporate chain of command, and threaten the free-market system. . . . Corporations should establish internal codes of honest conduct for guidance of company personnel and procedures for their effective enforcement. It should be made plain by the board and management that economic results will not excuse violations of the code. . . . Honesty is not merely the best policy. It is the *only* policy.[6]

CONCRETENESS

Communicating concretely means being specific, definite, and vivid rather than vague and general. The following guidelines should help you compose concrete, convincing messages:

- Use specific facts and figures.
- Put action in your verbs.
- Choose vivid, image-building words.

Use Specific Facts and Figures

Whenever you can, substitute an exact statement or a figure for a general word to make your message more concrete and convincing.

Vague, General, Indefinite	Concrete and Convincing
This computer reproduces campaign letters fast.	This computer types 400 personalized 150-word campaign letters in one hour.
Our product has won several prizes.	[Name] product has won first prize in four national contests within the past three years.
These brakes stop a car within a short distance.	These Goodson power brakes stop a 2-ton car traveling 60 miles an hour, within 240 feet.

Often vague, general words are *opinion words*; they may have different meanings to the sender and the receiver. For instance, how fast is *fast*? A bicycle rider and a racing-car driver will have different meanings for this word. How large is *large*? A person reared in a village of 150 people may consider a population of 15,000 large; yet to a native of a city with 10 million inhabitants,

15,000 is very *small*. The following words can also lead to uncertainty, misunderstanding, or confusion:

a few	high	low	more	quick	soon
early	long	many	most	slow	tall

In some cases it is, of course, permissible—and even desirable—to use general expressions. Exceptions to the "facts and figures" rule occur:

1. When it is not possible to be specific, for you may not have nor be able to get definite facts or figures.

2. When you want to be diplomatic. Thus, instead of saying, "We have sent you four notices of your overdue payment," you may be more tactful (to a usually prompt paying customer) by saying, "We have sent you *several* reminders of this. . . ."

3. When you want to allow the person to form his or her own opinion, or when exact figures are unimportant, as in "A *few* (or *Many*) of our employees attended the parade."

Put Action in Your Verbs

Strong verbs can activate other words and help make your sentences definite. To compose strong sentences, you should (1) use active rather than passive verbs and (2) put action in your verbs instead of in nouns or infinitives.

Active versus Passive Voice

When the subject *performs* the action that the verb expresses, the verb is said to be in the *active* voice. In "Mr. Jones *repaired* the computer," the subject (Mr. Jones) did the repairing; the verb "repaired" is active.

When the subject benefits from or otherwise *receives* the action the verb expresses, the verb is said to be in the *passive* voice. In "The computer *was repaired* by Mr. Jones," the verb "was repaired" is passive. A passive verb has three characteristics: (1) The subject doesn't do the acting, (2) the verb consists of *two or more* words, one of which is some form of "to be" (*is, is being, am, are, was, were, will be, has* or *have been, had been,* or *will have been*), and (3) the word *by* is expressed or implied (*by whom* or *by what*).

Passive (Subject Receives the Action)	Active (Subject Performs the Action)
Tests <u>were made</u> by us.	We <u>made</u> tests [*or* Tests <u>showed</u> that . . .].
A full report <u>will be sent</u> to you by the supervisor.	The supervisor <u>will send</u> you a full report [*or* You <u>will</u> <u>receive</u> . . . from the supervisor].

Passive (Subject Receives the Action)	Active (Subject Performs the Action)
These figures <u>are checked</u> by the research department.	The research department <u>checks</u> these figures.

Active verbs help make your sentences more:

1. *Specific.* "The board of directors decided" is more explicit than "A decision has been made."

2. *Personal.* "You will note" is both personal and specific; "It will be noted" is impersonal.

3. *Concise.* The passive requires more words and thus slows both writing and reading. Compare "Figures show" with "It is shown by figures."

4. *Emphatic.* Passive verbs dull action. Compare "The child ran a mile" with "A mile was run by the child."

Sometimes, however, you may prefer the passive voice instead of the active, as in the following situations:

1. When you want to avoid personal, blunt accusations or commands. "The July check was not included" is more tactful than "You failed to include. . . ." "Attendance at the meeting is required" is less harsh than "You must attend. . . ."

2. When you want to stress the object of the action. In "Your savings account is insured up to $100,000," you have intentionally stressed "your account"—not the firm that does the insuring. Also, "You are invited" is better than "We invite you."

3. When the doer isn't important in the sentence. In "Three announcements were made before the meeting started," the emphasis is on the announcements, not on who gave them.

Action in Verbs, Not in Nouns

Seven verbs—*be, give, have, hold, make, put,* and *take* (in any tense) might be designated as "deadly" when the action they introduce is hidden in a "quiet noun." The examples below show how each deadly verb with the noun and preposition (all underlined) can be changed to an action verb that shortens the sentence.

Action Hiding in a "Quiet Noun"	Action in the Verb
The function of this office <u>is</u> the <u>collection of</u> payments and the <u>compilation of</u> statements.	This office <u>collects</u> payments and <u>compiles</u> statements.

Action Hiding in a "Quiet Noun"	Action in the Verb
Mr. Jones will <u>give consideration to</u> the report.	Mr. Jones will <u>consider</u> the report.
The contract <u>has a requirement for</u>. . . .	The contract <u>requires</u> that. . . .
They <u>held the meeting in</u> the office.	They <u>met</u> in the office.
He <u>made the payment for</u> his first installment.	He <u>paid</u> his first installment.
The chairperson <u>puts</u> her <u>trust in</u> each committee member.	The chairperson <u>trusts</u> each committee member.
We will <u>take a look at</u> your record.	We will <u>look</u> at your record.

Action in Verbs, Not in Infinitives

Action can also be concealed by infinitives. Notice, in the following example, that both main verbs in the left-hand sentence follow "is" (or some form of "to be") plus the preposition "to," and they don't convey much action.

Action Hiding in Infinitive	Action in the Verb
The duty of a stenographer is <u>to check</u> all incoming mail and <u>to record</u> it. In addition, it is his or her responsibility <u>to keep</u> the assignment book up to date.	A stenographer <u>checks</u> and <u>records</u> all incoming mail and <u>keeps</u> the assignment book up to date.

Choose Vivid, Image-Building Words

Among the devices you can use to make your messages forceful, vivid, and specific are comparisons, figurative language, concrete instead of abstract nouns, and well-chosen adjectives and adverbs.

Comparisons

Sometimes adding a comparison helps your recipient build a meaningful picture. Consider the vague images you get from the sentences in the left-hand column below as contrasted with the vivid impressions gained from those at the right.

Vague	Vivid
There are a great many solder joints in the spacecraft, and each must have just the right amount of solder.	The spacecraft has $2\frac{1}{2}$ million solder joints. If an extra drop of solder had been left on these joints, the excess weight would have been equivalent to the payload of the vehicle.
This is pure clover honey, made by honeybees.	Honeybees have gathered nectar from approximately $4\frac{1}{2}$ million clusters of clover and traveled about 150,000 miles--or equal to six times around the world--to deliver this package of Bradshaw honey to you.

Figurative Language

Figures of speech may express an idea more vividly than literal language.

Literal (and Dull)	Figurative
She is usually the one who gets things started in the organization.	<u>Jean Jones</u> is the <u>spark plug</u> of the organization.
X product helps you lose your double chin in four weeks, if you use X as directed.	If <u>two chins quarrel for a place on your collar</u>, X product <u>helps settle the argument. Only one chin remains</u> after you use X just four weeks as directed.

Concrete instead of Abstract Nouns

Still another way to enliven your message is to use concrete nouns instead of abstract nouns, especially as subjects of your sentences. Concrete nouns represent subjects your recipient can touch, see, smell, feel, hear, or taste. Abstract nouns as subjects designate intangible concepts. They bring only vague "pictures," if any, to a person's mind.

Abstract	Concrete
<u>Consideration</u> was given to the fact that. . . .	The <u>committee</u> considered . . . .
<u>Termination</u> of the insurance contract will be in June.	The insurance <u>contract</u> ends in June.

Abstract

```
Analysis of the situation
suggests that Mr. Smith is
right.
```

Concrete

```
I think Mr. Smith is right.
```

One more caution: If you are referring to an *inanimate object*, avoid using the neutral word *thing* whenever possible. Use a more specific word that is related to the "thing"—such as *event, element, fact, idea, condition, method, plan, purpose, principle*.

Adjectives and Adverbs

You can sometimes build a more realistic and interesting word picture by adding well-chosen adjectives and adverbs. In the examples below, adjectives are underlined; adverbs are in capitals.

Colorless

```
The camera has a system that
gives you good pictures.
```

Realistic, Vivid, Interesting

```
The Poney camera has a
UNIQUELY precise metering
system that assures you
PROPERLY exposed, true-color
pictures.
```

```
This cookware is guaranteed
to withstand changes in tem-
perature.
```

```
Creston cookware withstands
changes in heat and cold--
from zero to 450 degrees
Fahrenheit. The guarantee
assures you that you can
SAFELY move any piece from
your freezer to your micro-
wave oven.
```

SUMMARY

Effective written and oral business messages should be adapted to the purpose and receiver of each message. The basic business communication principles—also known as the *seven C qualities*—provide guidelines for choosing content and style of presentation. The four discussed in this chapter are completeness, conciseness, consideration, and concreteness.

The *complete* message should contain all facts the reader or listener needs for the reaction you desire. You can make your messages complete by answering all questions asked, giving something extra when desirable, and checking for the five W's and H (*who, what, when, where, why, how*) as well as any other essentials.

A *concise* message includes all necessary ideas and facts in the fewest possible words without sacrificing the other C qualities. You can shorten or omit wordy expressions by using single-word substitutes, eliminating "which" and "that" clauses whenever possible, and avoiding overuse of "it is" (or "was") and "there is" (or "are" or "were") for sentence beginnings.

The message should include only facts relevant to its purpose. Sentences should omit pompous words, irrelevant details, excessive adjectives, and statements the receiver already knows. You can avoid unnecessary repetition of long names by using pronouns, initials, or shorter names. The concise message helps emphasize important points and saves costly time for both sender and receiver.

Considerate means you are genuinely thoughtful of your message recipients and consider their probable reactions to your messages. You can indicate you-attitude by focusing on "you," the reader or listener; by showing benefit to or interest in the receiver; by emphasizing positive, pleasant facts; and by applying integrity and ethics—consistently fair treatment, honesty, and sincerity. Consideration involves the golden rule—showing to others the same fairness and honesty we expect for ourselves. Remember, both your own integrity and that of your company are revealed in your business messages.

Good *concrete* writing and speaking include specific facts and figures, with examples. Generally you should use active rather than passive verbs and place action in verbs, not in nouns or infinitives. To help make messages vivid and specific you can use comparisons, figurative language, and concrete instead of abstract nouns, plus well-chosen adjectives and adverbs.

EXERCISES AND PROBLEMS

1. Discuss orally how to make each of the following requests complete and concrete:

    a. `Harry, we need to get this out pretty soon. And, Sally, as soon as convenient, would you. . . .`

    b. `The coat you had in your window last Thursday is exactly the style I would like to have. Please send it to me on my charge account.`

    c. `I am interested in the portable TV you advertised in yesterday's newspaper. Will you please tell me more about it?` [*The firm advertised one TV set in the city's morning paper and a different set in the evening paper.*]

    d. `Please reserve three seats for the opera` <u>`Turandot`</u> `Saturday night.`

    e. `My daughter and I wish to repaint two bedrooms, each of which is 10 × 12 feet. Please send us the right amount of paint--in pink--to do this job, and charge my account.`

2. Choose an active verb to replace each "deadly" verb hiding in some of the following nouns.

    a. Be of assistance.
    b. Make substitution.
    c. Have intention.
    d. Make a decision.
    e. Put on a demonstration.
    f. It is my intention to.
    g. Held a meeting and had a discussion.
    h. Improvement in quality has been made.
    i. Evaporation of the liquid takes place.
    j. We will give thought to your proposal.

3. Which of the following verbs are passive and which are active voice? Revise the sentences that have passive verbs so they will have active verbs.

   a. Each member was given a copy of the annual report.
   b. The printer is planning to expand operations on Monday.
   c. Each courteous clerk wins goodwill for Mace Department Store.
   d. Final preparation will be made by the planning committee.
   e. The finance committee has been making a careful study.
   f. By January, the committee will have interviewed all applicants.
   g. Mr. Thom's secretary has completed the assignment.
   h. The contract will be signed next week.
   i. A farewell banquet has been planned in honor of Miss Bray.
   j. Many customers are reached by television advertisements.
   k. An account was opened by Mrs. Simms.
   l. It is suggested that you come early.

4. Revise the following sentences to eliminate the negative aspects.

   a. We regret that we cannot extend your payment date for more than two months.
   b. This policy will not pay except when the damages exceed $50.
   c. Your bicycle has been repaired, and we hope you will have no further trouble with it.
   d. To avoid the loss of your good credit rating, please send your $130 check this week.
   e. This information is being sent to you now so that we will avoid later misunderstandings about our credit terms.
   f. We know you will agree that our prices are not any higher than those of competitors.
   g. On c.o.d. orders we require a 20 percent deposit to safeguard ourselves against loss in case of refusal of merchandise.
   h. We will hold shipment of this hardware until we receive your confirmation.
   i. Unfortunately, I will not be able to give you any definite price until you let me know the size and quantity of cartons you need.
   j. There will be a delay of four days in filling your order, because the material for your coat has to be ordered from Boston. We are sorry about this delay, but there is nothing we can do about it.
   k. Because of shortages of material, we will not be able to ship before June 10.
   l. I am sorry I cannot send you the booklet you requested, as we have not yet received it from the publisher.
   m. I can't meet with you at 11 a.m. Monday May 8, but. . . .

5. Change the following sentences so that they emphasize you-attitude instead of we-attitude.

a. We allow 2 percent discount for cash payments.
b. This is just the kind of job I am looking for, since it offers me a chance to get practical experience in personnel work.
c. We value your patronage, for satisfied customers are the foundation of our success.
d. Since we have our own obligations to meet, we must ask your immediate attention to your past-due account.
e. We do not send receipts, because of the extra work involved for us; of course, you have your canceled checks anyway.
f. Our pamphlet is designed to help its readers get the most out of raising beautiful roses.
g. We hope to have the pleasure of showing you what we think is the finest assortment of Italian boots in the city.
h. To help us improve our production schedule, we would appreciate your ordering two weeks in advance.
i. I wish to tell you that we are sending your new coat tomorrow.

6. Revise the following sentences to eliminate wordiness and other errors.
   a. The picture that is enclosed will give you an idea of the appearance of this home.
   b. In the event you would wish to schedule playings of there anniversary records to certain or all of you're employees, arrangements for these programs may be made by getting in touch with Lon Jones. As you probably know, his phone extension is 562. [*Can you cut these 43 words to 22?*]
   c. Their would still be continuation of the controversy, I must say, after the new plan is instituted.
   d. You will note when you study the cost of stationery that the expenditure of stationery gradually and steadily increased for 1988, 1989, 1990, and 1991.
   e. I have your letter of October 14 and wish to say that we'll be glad to give you a refund for the blouse you bought here last week.
   f. Permit me to take this opportunity to call your attention to the fact that we have brought your account up to date.
   g. For your information we are attaching hereto a carbon copy of the letter sent to Mr. Ava Knocash under date of April 25.
   h. Please find enclosed herewith a copy of the report which is 15 pages in length.
   i. I wish to take this opportunity to sincerely acknowledge receipt of your order for 1 bushel of Washington red delicious apples and thank you for placing it with our company.
   j. Please be assured that we are now rechecking and reviewing all our specifications as it is our earnest and most sincere desire to be certain and for sure that this machine

```
   gives you satisfaction and good service in every possible
   way in the future.
k. In addition, will you please permit me to state in this
   letter that we will welcome any suggestions or comments
   that you may have any time if you think of any methods for
   the improvement of our service to our customers.
l. Proceed without undue delay to discharge your obligation.
```

7. Regarding ethics and integrity choose one or more of the following:

   a. Bring to your class for discussion a specific example of ethical conduct in a difficult predicament, and an example of behavior you consider shady or downright unethical. Your examples may be from business, industry, government, or other situations and may include ethical dilemmas on which your classmates can express conflicting opinions.

   b. Discuss an action or statement that is not illegal but is unethical.

   c. Evaluate the following actions that have occurred in business:

   (1) A manager wrote to a customer:

   > ```
   > Your request will be given our careful attention, and
   > we assure you our objective is to be fair.
   > ```
   > [*This writer merely threw the case into a file folder and told his secretary he had no intention of working on it or assigning anyone else to do so. He hoped that after a long wait the customer would forget.*]

   (2) An advertisement stated:

   > ```
   > Nationwide, three out of four people prefer this amaz-
   > ing new product.
   > ```
   > [*Actually, the product was not nationally known, and only four persons in each of five states were surveyed.*]

Business Communication Principles II

Threshold: the preceding chapter discussed four of the seven business communication principles: completeness, conciseness, consideration, concreteness. To make your messages easily understood, friendly, and accurate, you should also apply the remaining C principles: clarity, courtesy, and correctness.

CLARITY

Clarity means getting your message across so the receiver will understand what you are trying to convey. You want that person to interpret your words with the same meaning you have in mind. Accomplishing that goal is difficult because, as you know, individual experiences are never identical and words may have different meanings to different persons, as discussed in Chapter 2.

Here are some specific ways to help make your messages clear:

- Choose short, familiar, conversational words.
- Construct effective sentences and paragraphs.
- Achieve appropriate readability (and listenability).
- Include examples, illustrations, and other visual aids, when desirable.

Choose Short, Familiar, Conversational Words

When you have a choice between a long word and a short one, use the *short, familiar* word that your reader or listener will quickly understand. Also, use *synonyms* instead of Latin terms (L) if they, though short, may be unfamiliar to your message receivers.

Say:	Not:	Say:	Not:
about	circa (L)	home, house	domicile
after	subsequent	pay	remuneration
announce, de-clare	promulgate	show, uncover	disclose
error	inadvertency	that is	i.e. (L)
for example	e.g. (L)	use	utilization

Avoid technical and business jargon whenever possible when you talk or write to a person who is not acquainted with such words. If you must use those words, define them briefly and clearly. If you don't, you'll confuse, embarrass, or irritate the reader, and perhaps be forced to explain later, as in the following story:

A plumber wrote the National Bureau of Standards to tell them hydrochloric acid is good for cleaning out clogged drains. (Before you go any further into the story, visualize the plumber. Assume you don't know him and have never exchanged correspondence. It is a pretty good guess he isn't a college graduate—maybe he didn't finish high school. But he probably is a good plumber—at least conscientious—because he's writing to the bureau to tell them something he thinks will help other people.)

In reply to the plumber's message, a technical specialist of the bureau wrote:

```
The efficacy of hydrochloric acid is indisputable, but the
corrosive residue is incompatible with metallic permanence.
```

The plumber then wrote to thank the bureau for agreeing with him—when, of course, the bureau was actually disagreeing with him. Sensing the plumber didn't understand, another member tried to set the man straight by writing:

```
We cannot assume responsibility for the production of toxic
and noxious residue with hydrochloric acid, and suggest you
use an alternative procedure.
```

Again the plumber thanked the bureau. Then, in desperation, the department manager wrote:

```
Don't use hydrochloric acid. It eats hell out of the pipes.
```

The moral of this story is to write and speak on the *receiver's level of understanding*. Here are a few business words used by mortgage loan firms—and the synonyms a layperson will more likely understand:

Possibly Unfamiliar or Unclear	Expressions Familiar to the Layperson
assessed valuation	property value for tax purposes
charge to your principal	increase the balance of your loan
easement for ingress and egress	agreement allows passage in and out

Notice how the following sentence with *unfamiliar* words is expressed clearly in the revision using *familiar* words:

```
After our perusal of pertinent data the conclusion is that a
lucrative market exists for the subject property.
```

REVISION

```
The data we studied show that your property is profitable
and in high demand.
```

Construct Effective Sentences and Paragraphs

Arranging your words in well-constructed sentences and paragraphs is also an essential task that requires adaptation to your reader. Important characteristics to consider are length, unity, coherence, and emphasis.

Length As Short As Desirable

Generally, short sentences are preferred. The suggested average sentence length should be about 17 to 20 words. Because a pleasing variety of length is desirable, you can have a range of from 3 to 30 or more words. But when a sentence exceeds 40 words, try to rewrite it into more than one sentence. Also, if *all* sentences are short (under 10 words), the result is primerlike language—choppy and undesirable.

A general rule in most business writing is to keep paragraphs as short as possible. If well organized, they can help to emphasize facts, add to a message's physical attractiveness, and improve readability. The first and last paragraph of a letter or memo should preferably be kept to no more than four or five lines. Keep all other paragraphs as short as possible, but vary the length up to eight or nine lines.

Unity, to Express Main Ideas

In a sentence—whether simple, compound, or complex—unity means that you have one main idea, and any other ideas in the sentence must be closely related to it. "I like Jim, and the Eiffel Tower is in Paris" obviously is not a unified sentence.

In a paragraph, unity likewise means you have one main idea or topic. Usually a *topic sentence* is a good way to express the main idea. (Of course, a one- or two-sentence paragraph needs no topic sentence.) The preferred position for the topic sentence in most paragraphs is at the beginning, where it receives the best emphasis. The sentences that follow it contain details to help develop the main idea. However, if you think your reader will consider your main topic unfavorable or unclear, you may be wise to place the supporting details first and then lead up to the topic sentence at the end.

Coherence, for Clear Meanings

In a coherent sentence the words are correctly arranged so that the ideas clearly express the intended meaning. Place the correct modifier as close as possible to the word it is supposed to modify. In the following examples notice why each "unclear" sentence conveys a wrong meaning, and how it is corrected in the "clear" sentence.

Unclear: `Being an excellent lawyer, I am sure you can help us.`
Clear: `Being an excellent lawyer, you can surely help us.`

or

Clear:	As you are an excellent lawyer, I am sure you. . . .
Unclear:	His report was about managers, broken down by age and sex.
Clear:	His report focused on age and sex of managers.

or

Clear:	His report about managers focused on. . . .
Unclear:	After planting 10,000 berry plants, the deer came into our botanist's farm and crushed them.
Clear:	After our botanist had planted 10,000 berry plants, the deer came into his farm and crushed them.

For coherence in a paragraph, each sentence should be relevant to the main idea expressed in the topic sentence. Transitional words and phrases correctly placed within paragraphs help point the way from one sentence to another. Likewise, they can lead the reader from one paragraph to another. For examples of transitional words, listed under eight headings, and for examples (also exercises) of dangling participles, see Appendix A.

Emphasis, for Forceful, Clear Expression

The quality that gives force to important parts of sentences and paragraphs is *emphasis*. Writers must decide what needs emphasis, and then choose correct sentence structure. In a complex sentence the main idea should be placed in the main clause; the less important points are in subordinate (dependent) clauses or phrases. For instance, in the first sentence below, the two ideas appear to be of equal value. In contrast, if the important idea is that the "airplane was difficult to control," the second sentence would be more meaningful and emphatic; its main idea is in the main clause.

No emphasis:	The airplane finally approached the speed of sound and it became very difficult to control.
Emphasis:	As it finally approached the speed of sound, the airplane became very difficult to control.

To help compose a paragraph, this second sentence could become the topic sentence. It would be placed in the most important position—preferably at the beginning. Several supporting sentences within that paragraph would explain specifically about the difficulty in controlling the plane.

The following 69-word sentence to an insurance agent is confusing because it is too long and the main point is not emphasized clearly. Isn't the revised paragraph clearer—with topic sentence at the beginning and with shorter sentences?

We have been advised that the allotment for the above-numbered policy was filed effective April 1991, but inasmuch as the premium due March 1, 1991, of $85.30 has not been remitted and inasmuch as allotment payments are not applicable to premiums due and payable in advance of the effective date of

```
allotment, we hereby request that you contact the insured
directly and request payment of this premium due.
```

REVISION

```
Allotment payments can be applied only to premiums falling
due after the effective date of allotment. Since the allot-
ment did not become effective on this policy until April
1991, it cannot pay the March 1, 1991, premium of $85.30.
Therefore, we ask you to collect it.
```

Achieve Appropriate Readability—and "Listenability"

Besides aiming for qualities of unity, coherence, and emphasis, you should adapt your business messages so that their word-and-sentence level will be appropriate for your recipients' general education level.

Among the many guides that measure readability is Robert Gunning's popular Fog Index.[1] It is based on two factors: sentence length and percentage of hard words. This Index is designed to help you determine the educational level of your writing and speaking.

Fog Index Guide

1. *Find average sentence length.* Use a sample at least 100 words long (beginning preferably with the first word of a paragraph). Divide the total number of words in this passage by the number of complete thoughts. (A simple or complex sentence has one complete thought, with a subject and predicate. A compound sentence contains two complete thoughts.) Your quotient gives the average sentence length.

2. *Figure the percentage of "hard" words.* Count the number of words of three syllables or more. Include any unexplained abbreviations (CMO, BSD), but don't count words:
   a. That are (correctly) capitalized (*Washington, Smithsonian*)
   b. That are combinations of short, easy words (like *bookkeeping, salesperson*)
   c. That are verb forms made into three syllables by adding *ed* or *es* (like *created* or *trespasses*)

   Divide the number of hard words by the total number of words. Your quotient is the percentage of hard words.

3. *Add the average sentence length and the percentage of hard words and multiply by 0.4.* The product, the Fog Index, is the reading level (number of years of education) required.

For an example, if a paragraph has 110 words in 6 sentences, the average sentence length is 18.3 words. If 14 of the 110 words are considered hard words, the percentage is 12.7. From these figures you can compute the Gunning Fog Index—12.4—as shown below:

Words in example.	110
Sentences	6
Average sentence length (110 ÷ 6)	18.3
Percentage of hard words (14 ÷ 110)	12.7
Total.	31.0
Multiplier	0.4
Fog Index (grade level of high school senior)	12.40

After you have read the basic procedure for using the Gunning Fog Index, these additional guides from Robert Gunning may help you: (1) Count anything as a word that has space around it. Thus *March 1, 1992,* is 3 words; *one thousand dollars* is 3 words: *5 1/4* is 2 words, *five and one quarter* is 4 words, but *5¼* is 1 word; *twelve-month* is 1 word; *$5,000* and *$9,752,461* are each 1 word; if spelled out, the latter figure is 10 words. Exception: Do not count the numbers (I, II, 1, 2, 3) or letters (A, B, a, b, c) that precede items or paragraphs. (2) Count hyphenated words as polysyllables only if one part is a word of three syllables or more. For example, *seventy-two* is four syllables. (3) Do not regard numerals as polysyllables, regardless of pronunciation. For example: *$987,652,431.50* is one syllable.

Studies have shown that almost everyone appreciates easy reading and listening if the message has a Fog Index of between 8 and 12 (eighth- to twelfth-grade level). (*Reader's Digest* and *Time* have Indexes between 9 and 10; *Scientific American* averages 11 or 12.) If your writing level to the average person is on the thirteenth level or higher, your message runs the risk of being ignored or misunderstood.

Among the writings and documents that especially need simplifying to be understood by the average reader are those from legal, insurance, medical, and government offices. Their messages sometimes have a Fog Index of 26 or more—at least 14 school years beyond a high school graduate. Also, in many other large companies, the employee grapevine has indicated that management's messages are too often misinterpreted.

Limitations and Cautions

Readability formulas[2] are popular and helpful in improving clarity, but there are limitations and cautions. First, a person must be careful not to use too many simple words and short sentences, for the message would be monotonous, elementary, and choppy. Second, some "long" words really aren't so difficult as some two-syllable words (for example, *employee* versus *avid*). Also, you must count the same word as many times as it appears in the passage. Third, a message with crude, harsh, unethical, or insulting words—lacking courtesy or consideration for the receiver—may still get a desirable Fog Index. Fourth, though a message may be incomplete, vague, and incorrect in grammar or style, such errors are not shown in the Fog Index. Fifth, in long messages one should select random samples to see if readability is consistent.

Used with discretion, however, the formula will serve the purpose of a *guide* to the readability of letters, reports, books, magazine articles, or any other business writing—and speaking. Mr. Gunning considers his Fog Index a "simple warning system"—not a cure-all for writing problems. He suggests using this formula "to check if your writing is in step with that which has proved easy to read and understand."

Include Examples, Illustrations, and Other Visual Aids, When Desirable

In addition to focusing on clarity of words, sentences, and paragraphs, you can also sometimes use various visual aids effectively.

When you have a complicated or lengthy explanation in a letter, speech, or report, you'll often find you can improve the clarity by giving your recipients an example, analogy, or illustration. Furthermore, visual aids—such as headings, tabulations, itemizations, pictures, charts—are definite aids to clarity and easy understanding. Also, typographical aids can be useful. Some important statements may be underlined, numbered, colored, or typed in all CAPITALS or *italics* or on short lines with wider margins. Throughout this text—especially sections on reports—are examples of messages that use illustrations and visual aids to help clarify the material for readers.

COURTESY

Courteous messages help to strengthen present business friendships, as well as make new friends. Courtesy stems from sincere you-attitude. It is not merely politeness with mechanical insertions of "please's" and "thank-you's." To be courteous, considerate communicators should follow—in addition to the four guidelines discussed under Consideration (Chapter 3)—these suggestions regarding *tone* of the communications:

- Be sincerely tactful, thoughtful, and appreciative.
- Omit expressions that irritate, hurt, or belittle.
- Grant and apologize good-naturedly.

Be Sincerely Tactful, Thoughtful, and Appreciative

Tact instead of Bluntness

Though few people are intentionally abrupt or blunt, these traits are a common cause of discourtesy. Sometimes they stem from a mistaken idea of conciseness, sometimes from negative personal attitudes (discussed briefly in Chapter 2). A time to be especially wary of bluntness is on those days when everything seems to go wrong. Avoid expressions like those in the left-hand column below; rephrase them as shown in the right-hand column.

Tactless, Blunt	Tactful
Your letter is not clear at all; I can't understand it.	If I understand your letter correctly, . . .
Obviously, if you'd read your policy carefully, you'd be able to answer these questions yourself.	Sometimes policy wording is a little hard to understand. I'm glad to clear up these questions for you.
Apparently you have already forgotten what I wrote you two weeks ago.	As mentioned in my May 15 letter [or memo] to you, [continue with the facts]. . . .

Writing a letter to a customer generally requires more conscious "niceties" than writing a memo to someone within your organization. A one-sentence memo like the following is all right to an employee or colleague if it adequately covers your particular message:

Tom,
Please call me (ext. 312) to tell me the casting number on
the side of the trunk safety lock you need for the '88 Ford.

But in letters to customers, you usually avoid a one-sentence body, because it sounds blunt. Instead, you need to add a few tactful words, as in this example:

We will gladly replace the safety lock on the trunk of your
1988 Ford.

So that we can know the right lock to fit your trunk, please
send the casting number. It is imprinted on the side of the
lock. If you have a question, please call me (555-8899) any
weekday between 8 a.m. and 5 p.m.

Thoughtfulness and Appreciation

Writers who send cordial, courteous messages of deserved congratulations and appreciation (to persons both inside and outside the firm) help build goodwill. (For examples of goodwill messages see Chapter 15.) The value of goodwill or public esteem for the firm may be worth thousands (or millions) of dollars. Much money is spent on advertising to attract new customers and to keep desirable old customers. While advertising may bring buyers into the front door of your firm, discourteous letters can drive customers out the back door!

Sometimes silence can also be considered significantly discourteous. A thoughtful, courteous businessperson—no matter how busy—should not ignore answering customers' or colleagues' inquiries. Even a short, courteous note written on the bottom of the request and returned promptly, or a tactful phone call by the secretary, is usually better than no reply. Totally ignoring the inquiry or request communicates unfavorable nonverbal messages that may lead to loss of business or employee morale. Thoughtful communicators answer messages as soon as possible, preferably within a few days.

Omit Expressions That Irritate, Hurt, or Belittle

The thoughtful business communicator should avoid expressions that might offend the reader. Such expressions are discussed here in three groups: irritating, questionably humorous, and belittling statements.

Irritating Expressions

The following list contains irksome expressions to be avoided, particularly when used with "you" and "your."

contrary to your inference
delinquency (delinquent)
I do not agree with you
if you care
I'm sure you must realize
inexcusable
irresponsible
obnoxious
obviously you overlooked
owing to your questionable
   credit we are unable to
simply nonsense
surely you don't expect
we are amazed you can't
we don't believe
we expect you to
we find it difficult to believe
   that
we must insist
we take issue
why have you ignored

you are delinquent
you are probably ignorant of
   the fact that
you claim that
you did not tell us
you failed to
you forgot to
you have to
you leave us no choice
you neglected to (overlooked)
you say
you should know
you surely don't expect
your apparent disregard of our
   previous request leaves us
   no alternative
your complaint
your failure to
your insinuation
your neglect
your stubborn silence

Questionable Humor

Humor is often quite effective in business writing. However, before you try to be funny, be sure your humor is good-natured and appropriate for the situation. A flippant attitude can be in poor taste, as letter 1 indicates. Letter 2 conveys the same message informally but courteously.[3]

LETTER 1 *Offensive rather than humorous.*

```
Dear Mr. and Mrs. Smith:

We were mighty happy to learn about the package the stork
brought you. And what a distinguished tag you put on him. .
```

. . Joshua Gerald Smith II. You tell Josh that as soon as
he's ready, his Prudential agent will be around to help him
set up his insurance program.

In the meantime, I guess it's up to us to take care of the
little fellow's insurance needs for a while--you know, educational funds and a little nest egg to help him start his
journey through life.

I'll phone you in a couple of days to find out when it will
be convenient for you to talk about insurance for your new
bundle of joy. Till then, keep his powder dry!

LETTER 2   *Courteous.*

Congratulations on the birth of your son, Joshua.

Like other thoughtful parents, you no doubt want him to have
a happy, well-protected future. It may seem early to be concerned about financing his college eduation. But we at Prudential have seen too many youngsters miss out on college
because their parents put off the problem too long.

If convenient for you, I would like to call at seven
o'clock, Friday evening, June 20, to show you how Prudential
can help you solve this problem. I will phone Thursday to
confirm the appointment or to arrange a different time that
you prefer.

Belittling Statements

Talking down to or belittling a person is another form of discourtesy that can
have a profoundly unfavorable effect, as in the following case:

> *XYZ Chemical Company annually shipped to AMC Company thousands of
> dollars worth of chemicals in returnable drums. To substantiate a railroad
> claim, AMC's accountant needed the exact charges on certain drums. He
> checked with the local XYZ representative, who asked him to contact Mrs.
> Lancaster in Diamond, California. After writing to her, the accountant
> received the following reply, which he said caused a "much greater explosion
> within our department than all XYZ chemicals combined could have."*

In reply to your letter of October 10 addressed to Diamond,
California, attention Mrs. Lancaster, you made two mistakes.
In the first place, we have no Mrs. Lancaster, and in the
second place, Diamond is not a place to send mail. We charge
$8.50 on the Carbon Bisulphide-Carbon Tetrachloride Mixture
drum to AMC Company, in your city, for the drum only. We
trust this is what is meant.

Grant and Apologize Good-Naturedly

Whenever you grant a customer's request, begin your letter with the best news first and inject a courteous, ungrudging tone. Notice the difference in tone of the following two paragraphs:

Grudging:

```
Your request causes a great deal of extra paperwork to
change monthly payments. However, in compliance with your
request we hereby reduce your monthly interest and principal
payments called for in our note to $_____, plus $_____ for
taxes and insurance; effective [month, day, year], your total
monthly payment will be $_____.
```

Good-natured:

```
As you requested, we will reduce the monthly interest and
principal payments called for in your note to $_____, plus
$_____ for taxes and insurance. Thus, starting [month, day,
year], your total monthly payment will be $_____.
```

If a request has caused you extra work, you may tactfully tell the customer somewhere in the letter—but not the first paragraph—to notify you by a certain time if he or she again wishes to change something.

Occasionally you may get a "nasty" letter from a customer who is wrong in his or her accusations. A courteous reply can lead not only to an apology from the customer but also to future staunch loyalty as a booster for your firm.

When someone in your organization makes a mistake, you can apologize and correct the error perhaps even before the customer discovers it. Sometimes a small, courteous printed form is useful to admit an error promptly and to explain how (and when) you are correcting it. Of course, if the matter is serious or complicated, a special letter will be more appropriate, as shown in Chapter 8.

CORRECTNESS

The correctness principle comprises more than proper grammar, punctuation, and spelling. A message may be perfect grammatically and mechanically but still insult or lose a customer and fail to achieve its purpose. The term *correctness*, as applied to a business message, means the writer should:

- Use the right level of language
- Check accuracy of figures, facts, and words
- Maintain acceptable writing mechanics
- Choose nondiscriminatory expressions
- Apply all other pertinent C qualities

Use the Right Level of Language

The three levels of language—formal, informal, and substandard—overlap because of our ever-changing language. English, with almost a million words, has the richest, largest vocabulary on earth. Some words once considered substandard have moved into the informal level, and some once-informal words are now acceptable on a formal level. The first two—formal and informal language—are both correct, but they are quite different from one another, have different uses, and should not be interchanged.

The *formal level* of language is used for writing scholarly dissertations, master's and doctoral theses, legal documents, top-level government agreements, and other materials in which formality is expected. The expressions used are often long, unconversational, and impersonal—just what the term *formal* implies.

In contrast, the *informal level* refers to the language of business—for letters, reports, newspapers, and other business communications. Instead of formal words, you will use short, well-known, and conversational words, as the following list illustrates:

Formal	Informal	Formal	Informal
anticipate	expect	endeavor	try
ascertain	find out	interrogate	ask
conflagration	fire	procure	get
deem	think (believe)	terminate	end
edifice	building	utilize	use

The following poem by Enid C. Stickel provides a humorous example of how people try to formalize their language.

Readability Gap

Colleges aren't schools,
They are learning institutions;
Problems don't have answers,
They have viable solutions.
People don't spend money,
They re-allocate resources.
Newsmen don't use tipsters,
They rely on informed sources.

Speakers don't make speeches,
They give oral presentations.
Bosses don't set quotas,
They just indicate objectives.
Workers don't take orders,
Though they implement directives.

Machinery can't break down,
But components can malfunction.
A court does not command
It just issues an injunction.
Programs don't have failures,
They have qualified successes.
And jargon doesn't hurt you—
It just constantly distresses!

The third level of language—*substandard*—should be avoided. If you use words on this level in writing (or in speaking), your readers will begin to question your ability to use good English. Here are a few examples:

Substandard	**Acceptable**	**Substandard**	**Acceptable**
ain't	isn't, aren't	haven't got	don't have
between you and I	between you and me	in regards to	regarding
		irregardless	regardless
can't hardly	can hardly	nohow	anyway
hadn't ought	shouldn't	should of	should have

The following sentences illustrate the three levels of language:

Formal:

```
Although item 21 is enumerated in this report, the
writer has ascertained that it is currently not in
the organization's inventory nor in the writer's
possession.
```

Informal:

```
Although item 21 is listed in the report, it is not
in our stock now and I don't have it either.
```

Substandard:

```
Irregardless of the report that item ain't on our
shelves now, and I haven't got it either.
```

Check Accuracy of Figures, Facts, and Words

Absolute accuracy is essential for effective written and oral messages. When figures, facts, and some words are incorrectly used, they can cause serious problems, as shown in the following examples.

Risks from Incorrect Figures and Facts

One erroneous digit—creating, for instance, $35,000 instead of $85,000—makes a difference of $50,000 and may result in a lawsuit. Even small errors of a few cents can annoy customers and undermine goodwill. Furthermore, a wrong figure in an account number muddles up records and leads to untold problems.

To be sure of the accuracy of facts, communicators should verify all statements before writing, and again before signing or approving, messages. Of course, they also need to be up to date on laws that affect their organization. Guessing or assuming that facts are right can be costly. Just because a certain fact was true about a customer last year—or even last month—does not assure that it is true now, as the following case illustrates:

Mr. Henry Simson sent in a claim for medical benefits to his insurance company. In turn, the correspondent handling the case wrote back to Mr. Simson, saying, "We are pleased to enclose a check for $277.54 for benefits due you because of your confinement at the Mountain View Hospital." Unfortunately this correspondent shouldn't have sent the check, because *that hospital was not certified as a full "general" hospital, a requirement under the terms of Mr. Simson's policy. Innocently, Mr. Simson cashed the check.*

A month later the mistake was discovered and a notation made on Simson's file that no future payments were to be made for confinement at the Mountain View Hospital.

Two months afterward Mr. Simson again sent a claim for medical benefits because he once again had been a patient in that same hospital. The person who handled the claim this time consulted Simson's file, found the notation, and wrote a letter refusing the claim. However, this refusal was wrong because between Simson's two admissions the Mountain View Hospital had been certified as a full general hospital. If the correspondents at the insurance company had checked all the facts, such a mix-up would not have happened.

The good business writer must be continually alert to accuracy, because of changing rates, regulations, laws, and conditions locally and nationally, and within his or her organization. Chapter 5 presents legal aspects of business communications.

Words Often Confused

Like most things in life, English is ever-changing. Even the dictionaries can't keep up with its fast pace, but they can usually help you choose correct words to convey your intended meaning. The following are a few of the many words that are often confused in usage.

a, an	Use *a* before a word that begins with a consonant sound or a long "u" sound. Use *an* before a word that begins with a silent "h" or a vowel sound.
anxious, eager	*Anxious* implies worry, whereas *eager* conveys keen desire.
between, among	*Between* involves two people or two groups; *among*, three or more.
biannually, biennially	*Biannually* means "two times a year"; *biennially*, "every two years."
continual, continuous	*Continual* means "recurring regularly" (like lapping ocean waves). *Continuous* means "without stopping."
counsel, council	*Counsel* means (as a verb) "to advise" and (as a noun) "lawyer", "advice." *Council* (noun) is an advisory or governing group.

effect, affect	In business usage only *effect* is a noun; it means "result," "condition," or "influence." Both words are verbs—to *effect* is "to bring about"; to *affect* is "to influence."
eminent, imminent	*Eminent* means "high in station, merit, esteem," "prominent." *Imminent* is "about to happen," "threatening" (said especially of a danger or castastrophe).
imply, infer	*Imply* means "to insinuate" or "suggest"; *infer* means "to conclude." A writer *implies;* the reader *infers*.
lay, laid, laid lie, lay, lain	A person or a sheet *lies* (rests) on the bed, but a person *lays* the book on the table or *lays* himself or herself on the bed. If you can substitute *place(s)* and answer *what?* use the proper tense of *lay*.
principal, principle	*Principal* (as an adjective) means "chief," "main"; as a noun, it means "sum of money" or "head of a school." *Principle* means "rule" or "basic truth."
which, that, who	*That* refers to persons or things; *who*, to people; *which*, only to things.
who, whom	Use *who* as the subject of a verb—"*Who* will win?" Use *whom* as the object of a verb or a preposition—"*Whom* can you trust?" (You can trust *him* or *her,* not *he* or *she.*) "For *whom* will you vote?"

Maintain Acceptable Writing Mechanics

Acceptable writing mechanics include correct punctuation, capitalization, syllabication, and spelling—plus correct sentence and paragraph structure, already mentioned under Clarity. This area also includes using correct format for letters, memos, reports, and envelopes—as discussed in other chapters of this book.

If you need review on dangling participles, numbers as words or figures, abbreviations, punctuation, and other details that plague writers, study the helpful suggestions in Appendix A. And if you need help on parts of speech and sentence structure, be sure to consult an excellent, up-to-date grammar book.[4]

Two common weaknesses in writing mechanics deserve special, though brief, mention here: incorrect spelling and careless omissions.

Spelling Errors

Business executives and customers expect you to spell correctly and may begin to question your overall ability if you misspell—especially the customer's name and everyday words like *convenience, questionnaire, stationery, personnel,* and *accommodation.* Errors of transposition (*nad* instead of *and* or *recieve* instead of *receive*) are also spelling errors that show carelessness.

English spelling does have many inconsistencies. Among them are short words like these—with vowel sounds pronounced the same yet spelled differently: *made, paid; rule, school; say, weigh; dough, blow; sign, line; trend, friend; bear, bare.*

Inconsistencies in plurals are highlighted in this anonymous poem "Pluralistics."

> We'll begin with a box and the plural is boxes,
> But the plural of ox should be oxen not oxes.
> Then one fowl is a goose but two are called geese,
> Yet the plural of moose should never be meese.
> You may find a lone mouse or a whole set of mice,
> But the plural of house is houses not hice.
> If the plural of man is always called men,
> Shouldn't the plural of pan be called pen?
> If I speak of a foot and you show me your feet,
> And I give you a boot would a pair be called beet?
>
> If one is a tooth and whole set are teeth,
> Why should not the plural of booth be called beeth?
> Then one may be that and three would be those,
> Yet hat in the plural wouldn't be hose.
> And the plural of cat is cats and not cose.
> We speak of a brother and also of brethren.
> But though we say Mother we never say Methren.
> Then the masculine pronouns are he, his, and him,
> But imagine the feminine, she, shis, and shim.
> So English I fancy, you all will agree,
> Is the funniest language you ever did see.

If you are one of the many educated men and women who are better able to solve complicated business problems than spell correctly, you can take three precautions: refer to a dictionary often, hire a top-notch assistant who is a good speller, and use a computerized speller. The software programs that check spelling will help you find typographical spelling and transposition errors such as *recieve* and *nad.* However, they cannot detect a correctly spelled word in the wrong context. For instance, if you happen to type "State *Conversation* Commissioner" instead of "State *Conservation* Commissioner," the computerized speller does not recognize that error. Thus the safest procedure is to be sure a dependable person proofreads and corrects every message before it is mailed.

Careless Omissions

Another way to maintain correct writing mechanics is to double-check for any careless omissions of punctuation marks or words needed for grammatical accuracy. Sometimes even small omissions can lead to costly miscommunication, as this example illustrates:

A traveling client had instructed his stockbroker to buy for him as many shares of a certain company's stock as was possible and desirable. One day the broker found an opportunity to purchase 3,000 shares. Because the price had risen considerably, he asked the client to wire his decision— whether or not to buy. The client considered the price exorbitant. He wired:

`NO. PRICE TOO HIGH.`

Unfortunately, the period was omitted after the first word, and the broker bought the unwanted shares.

Choose Nondiscriminatory Expressions

Another important requirement for correctness is "equal treatment of the sexes" and nonbias toward people of different races, ethnic origins, and physical features. Conscientious business communicators (as well as authors) should be continually alert to use nondiscriminatory expressions whenever possible. The suggestions selected here are guidelines that can be particularly useful for your written and oral business communication. Try to choose nondiscriminatory language when you refer to occupational roles and achievements, personal characteristics, physical and mental attributes, humanity at large, names, and various title designations.[5]

Occupational Roles and Achievements

People should not be stereotyped or arbitrarily assigned to a leading or secondary role because of gender, race, ethnic group, or some physical "handicap." People can be in a variety of professions at all levels—doctors and nurses; principals, professors, and teachers; lawyers, judges, and social workers; bank presidents and tellers; accountants; pilots; plumbers; computer operators; and many others.

Personal Characteristics

Women and girls of any race or ethnic origin should be shown as having the same ambitions, abilities, mental strengths, and weaknesses as men and boys. Both sexes include some people who are industrious, active, strong, independent, courageous, competent, decisive, assertive, persistent, serious-minded, successful. Both include logical thinkers, problem solvers, and decision makers pursuing career goals.

Stereotypes of the logical, objective male and the emotional, subjective female should be avoided. Among them are the scatterbrained female, henpecking shrew, frustrated spinster, and nagging mother-in-law clichés. Also taboo are biased words used exclusively or more frequently against members of a particular race, age, disability, or ethnic background. Examples include such words as *aloof, pagan, untrustworthy, lazy, useless, stingy, hot-tempered, insane, handicapped.*

Physical and Mental Attributes

Men and women should be treated with the same respect, dignity, and seriousness. Neither should be trivialized or stereotyped. In descriptions of men in the home, references to general ineptness should be avoided. Men should not be characterized as dependent on women for meals or clumsy in household maintenance. Women should not be described by physical attributes when men are described by mental attributes.

Not this: Henry Harris is a prominent lawyer, and his wife Ann is a striking brunette.

But this: The Harrises are an attractive couple. Henry is a handsome blond, and Ann is a striking brunette.

Or: The Harrises are highly respected in their fields. Ann is an accomplished musician [or active in civic affairs], and Henry is a prominent lawyer.

Here are suggestions for changing some other undesirable expressions into acceptable ones:

No	Yes
girl (as in "I'll have my *girl* check that").	I'll have my *secretary* (my *assistant*) check that. (Or use the person's name.)
female-gender word forms, such as *authoress, poetess, Jewess.*	*author, poet, Jew.*
career girl or *career woman.*	name the woman's profession: *Attorney Ellen Smith; May Sanch, a journalist (editor, agent, doctor, business executive, lawyer).*
Housewives are feeling the pinch of higher prices.	*Consumers* (*customers* or *shoppers*) are feeling the pinch of higher prices.

Humanity at Large

In references to humanity at large, language should include women and girls. Common problems encountered when trying to meet this goal stem from "*man*-words" and singular pronouns.

Man-Words.   The word *man* has long been used to denote not only a male person but also, generically, humanity at large. However, to many people today the word *man* has become so closely associated with a "male human being" that they consider it no longer broad enough to be applied to any person or to human beings as a whole. In deference to this position, alternative expressions should be used whenever such substitutions do not produce an awkward or artificial construction. The following are some possible substitutions for man-words:

No	**Yes**
mankind	humanity; human beings; human race; people
the best man for the job	the best person (or candidate) for the job
man-made	synthetic; manufactured; artificial; constructed; of human origin
manpower	human power; human energy; workers; work force, personnel

In cases where man-words must be used, special efforts should be made to ensure that pictures, a footnote, or other devices make explicit that such references are meant in their generic sense—all human beings and both sexes.

This suggestion does not apply, of course, to words that begin with *man* but are not derived from the masculine. For instance, *manner, manager, mantle, manufacture,* and over a hundred others need no substitutions. Also, some words derived from masculine words can't be easily changed. Most people, for example, object to changing *freshman* to *freshperson* or *freshwoman.*

Singular Pronouns.   Because the English language lacks a generic singular pronoun signifying "he or she," it has been customary and grammatically sanctioned to use masculine pronouns in expressions such as "anyone . . . *he*" and "each customer . . . *his* bill." Nevertheless, we should avoid whenever possible the pronouns *he, him,* and *his* when referring to the hypothetical person or humanity in general.

Alternative	**No**	**Yes**
1. Reword to eliminate unnecessary gender pronouns.	The average American drinks *his* coffee black.	The average American drinks black coffee.
2. Recast into the plural.	The average *American* drinks *his.* . . . The shopper . . . *she*	Average *Americans* drink *their* coffee. . . . Shoppers . . . *they*
3. Alternate male and female expressions and examples.	Supervisors often say, "*He's* not the right man for the job," or "*He* lacks the qualifications for success."	Supervisors often say, "*She's* not the right person for the job," or "*He* lacks the qualifications for success."

Alternative	No	Yes
4. Replace the masculine pronoun with *one, you, he or she, her or his.* (Use *he or she* and its variations sparingly to avoid clumsy prose.)	This sale benefits every charge customer. *He* may purchase up to . . .	This sale benefits every charge customer. *One* (or *he or she*) may purchase up to. . . .
5. Repeat the noun (or a similar noun) if at least a few words intervene.	The executive benefits from this policy every month. *He* may choose from. . . .	The executive benefits from this policy every month. Each *executive* (or *manager*) may. . . .
6. Sometimes change to passive voice instead of active voice.	Every employee has an assigned parking place. *He should park his* car in. . . .	Every employee has an assigned parking place. Each car *should be parked* in. . . .

In long reports, to avoid severe problems of repetition or inept wording, it may sometimes be best to use the generic *he* freely. But you should add, in the preface and in the text, statements that the masculine pronouns are intended to refer to both men and women. *Each communicator must use good judgment regarding which alternatives to choose.*

Names, Occupational Titles, and Parallel Language

In referring to men and women, speakers and writers should, whenever possible, treat the sexes equally—by using the individuals' own names, nonsexist titles, and parallel language.

Own Names.   Women should be referred to by their own names in the same ways that men are. Both should be called by their full names, by first or last names only, or by titles. Unnecessary reference to a woman's marital status should be avoided. Whether married or not, a woman may be referred to by the name by which she chooses to be known, whether her name is her original or her married name, or a combination (Smith-Jones).

No	Yes
Ron Smith and Helen	Ron Smith and Helen Brown
Helen and Smith	Helen and Ron
Mrs. Brown and Smith	Ms. Brown (because she prefers *Ms.*) and Mr. Smith
Miss Kohn and David Green	Hilda Kohn and David Green, or Miss Kohn and Mr. Green, or Dr. Kohn and Dr. Green

Occupational Titles Ending in -Man.   Whenever possible, occupational titles should be nonsexist. Terms ending in *-man* may be replaced by terms that can include members of either sex, unless they refer to a particular person.

Yes, for Men	**Yes, for Men or Women**
businessman	business executive, businessperson, manager
cameraman	camera operator, photographer, technician
chairman[6]	chairperson, chairman and chairwoman, head, leader, coordinator, moderator, person presiding at (or chairing) a meeting, presiding office, or chair
congressman	member of Congress, representative (but Congress-*man* Koch and Congress*woman* Swanson)
mailman, postman	mail carrier, letter carrier
salesman	sales representative, salesperson, salesclerk, sales agent, sales associate

Parallel Language.   Words like the following should be in parallel terms:

No	**Yes**
men and ladies	men and women, gentlemen and ladies
man and wife	husband and wife

The foregoing discussion and examples have introduced you to ways you can reconstruct, substitute, or omit expressions in order to correct discriminatory communication. However, always remember that good judgment is necessary. Before you change any words, check their meanings and roots to be sure they need to be changed. For some expressions, changes could be unnecessary and ridiculously incorrect.

SUMMARY

So that your written and oral business communications will be easily understood, friendly, and accurate, you should also apply the C principles of clarity, courtesy, and correctness.

Make your message *clear* by using words that are familiar to your receiver. Aim for unity, coherence, and emphasis in your sentences and paragraphs. Have an *average* sentence length of around 17 to 20 words and an average paragraph length of 4 to 5 lines in letters, 8 to 9 lines in reports. The readability and listenability level should be appropriate for your recipient's general educational level—eighth to twelfth grade for the average person. To make figures stand out clearly, you may find tabulating to be useful. Also, give your reader helpful examples with appropriate, easy-to-read headings or other visual aids whenever you need to explain complicated material.

The *courteous* communicator is sincerely tactful, thoughtful, and appreciative. In both written and oral messages courtesy requires omitting expressions that irritate, belittle, or have questionable humor. The courteous person also grants and apologizes good-naturedly and answers mail as promptly as possible.

Overall *correctness* in business communication requires correct language level and accurate facts, figures, word choices, grammar, spelling, and punctuation. Necessary also is nondiscrimination toward people because of their gender, race, ethnic origin, or physical characteristics. When you sign your name or initials to the business message, you assume responsibility for everything in it. Included for correctness are all the pertinent C qualities and principles discussed in this book.

Suggestions for editing, revising, and proofreading are in Chapter 6.

■ Checklist of Business Communication Principles

Completeness:	■ Answer all questions asked. ■ Give something extra, when desirable. ■ Check for the five W's and any other essentials.
Conciseness:	■ Shorten or omit wordy expressions. ■ Include only relevant statements. ■ Avoid unnecessary repetition.
Consideration:	■ Focus on "you" instead of "I" and "we." ■ Show reader benefit or interest in reader. ■ Emphasize the positive, pleasant facts. ■ Apply integrity and ethics.
Concreteness:	■ Use specific facts and figures. ■ Put action in your verbs. ■ Choose vivid, image-building words.
Clarity:	■ Choose short, familiar, conversational words. ■ Construct effective sentences and paragraphs. ■ Achieve appropriate readability—and listenability. ■ Include examples, illustrations, and other visual aids when desirable.

(continued)

Courtesy:	■ Be sincerely tactful, thoughtful, and appreciative.
	■ Omit expressions that irritate, hurt, or belittle.
	■ Grant and apologize good-naturedly.
Correctness:	■ Use the right level of language.
	■ Check accuracy of figures, facts, and words.
	■ Maintain acceptable writing mechanics.
	■ Choose nondiscriminatory expressions.
	■ Apply all other pertinent C qualities.

EXERCISES AND PROBLEMS

1. Correct the following sentences so that the meanings are clear. If necessary, use more than one concise sentence.

    a. *From an employee news bulletin:*

    ```
    Remember next Friday's paper drive! Bring your papers
    (and your neighbors). Put them in paper bags and tie
    them.
    ```

    b. During a job interview the executive wants to hear what you can do in a few seconds.

    c. Enclosed are your contracts on Gary Green in triplicate.

    d. Mr. Jones visited factory employees May 9 and lectured on ''Destructive Pests.'' A large number were present.

    e. Your Memorial Day speech will be followed by a firing squad.

    f. *Advice in a newspaper's published recipe:*

    ```
    One should put a cup of liquid in the cavity of a turkey
    when roasting it.
    ```

    g. *From one insurance company to another insurance company:*

    ```
    Frankly, the information we have while it may disclose
    some contributory negligence on our assured's part which,
    of course, is questionable, we still feel that your as-
    sured had he not been driving at the high rate of speed
    that he was could have swerved to his right and avoided
    our assured's vehicle but due to the fact he was coming
    down a hill at such a tremendous rate of speed with no
    control over his car and struck our assured there was
    ```

```
    enough room to the right of your assured to have turned
    slightly and, therefore, avoided the accident.
```
h. Working in a grocery, several professors chat with him daily.

i. She wanted a policy for her house that cost $100 a year.

j. Although working full time on an outside job, Tim's grades remained good.

k. Thank you for your letter concerning the 10 pianos we received by airmail this morning.

l. When only 4 years old, this customer's mother died.

m. As an experienced certified public accountant, I would like to ask your help with a problem my high school bookkeeping instructor assigned to us today.

n. All the fauna exhibited a 100% mortality reaction.

o. We bought a ham at your store that contained glass chips.

2. Check the Fog Index of two pieces of business writing—one that you consider easy to read and one that is difficult. Then tell the class how the Fog Index of each agrees with your readability level. Use examples from this list:

a. Letter from a company to a customer.

b. Annual report.

c. Magazine read by members of the profession which is your major.

d. The *Wall Street Journal.*

e. Article on the front page of your daily newspaper.

f. Report or textbook. One sample selection from a 500-word report, article, or booklet is sufficient. In long reports (or books) five or six separated samples may be desirable.

3. Assume you are writing to the average citizen. What synonyms for the following words would be better understood?

accelerate   allegation   default   rescind
aggregating   contingent   discrepancy   validity

4. Translate the following gobbledygook into the original proverbs. Then compare sentence length (total words) in each concise proverb with the total words in the gobbledygook counterpart.[7]

a. All's well that is finalized effectively.

b. Be it a minimal dwelling in a depressed socioeconomic area, there is no place like home.

c. All programmed activity and nonutilization of recreational outlets make Jack a less than fully realized personality.

d. Do not attempt statistical estimates of your chickens before it is feasible to correlate volume variances with projected expectations.

e. The utilization of a superfluity of culinary personnel maximizes disorganization and has a deleterious effect on the broth.

5. Correct the errors in the following paragraph:

```
In rgard to your letter of the fifteenth, let me explain our
policy on our Certificates of deposit.  Your certificate
comes due on November 9, 199-.  At this time the intrest
check will be dispersed as you indicated at the time of your
initial deposit and the certificate will be automaticly re-
newed unless you contackt us prior to the experation date.
```

6. *Exercises on choice of words:* Choose the correct word or words that should be used in each sentence listed below.

  a. This act will not (effect, affect) my confidence in you.
  b. I am (anxious, eager) to (tell, advise) you that you are right.
  c. (Continuous, continual) rains are drenching the fields.
  d. We assure you (its, it's) a pleasure to do as you suggest.
  e. Enclosed (please find, is) my check for ($100.00, $100).
  f. RXZ College employs 10 (imminent, eminent) scholars.
  g. The dissension (between, among) the five departments has been settled by a (well known, well-known) authority.
  h. The man (who, which, that) was crossing the street was struck by a car (who, which, that) Mr. Smith was driving.
  i. (A, An) university regent held (a, an) one-hour meeting with (a, an) honor society (council, counsel).
  j. We sold (fewer, less) fans last month.
  k. We had (already, all ready) received the suit when your letter arrived. I am (already, all ready) to write this customer.
  l. Your rug should (lie, lay) (smooth, smoothly) on the floor.
  m. The (principal, principle) of honesty should be evident here.
  n. Be courteous to (whomever, whoever) comes to your desk.
  o. A large number of bills (is, are) outstanding.
  p. Do you know (who, whom) the manager promoted yesterday?
  q. The decision is a secret between Ron and (I, me).
  r. We have a large (quantity, amount, number) of suits here.
  s. Either Ellen or (myself, I, me) will call you Monday.

7. Assume that the following words appear in the letters and reports your secretary has typed for your signature. Without the help of any source, determine which words are misspelled and correct the errors. Then check all words (in a dictionary or a computerized spell-checker or in class) to see how many you had right. If you need a pocket-size dictionary to help you spell correctly, try *20,000 Words*, compiled by C. E. Zoubek and G. A. Condon, McGraw-Hill, New York, 1985.

1. accommodation	**6.** batchelor's degree	**11.** colledge
2. acquainted	**7.** benefited	**12.** compliment (meaning
3. attatched	**8.** brosure	supplement)
4. attendence	**9.** catalog	**13.** concensus
5. attornies	**10.** childrens'	**14.** congradulate

15. consede
16. convience
17. correspondant
18. defendent
19. descendant
20. develop
21. disatisfaction
22. dissadvantage
23. envelop (noun)
24. excellant
25. existance
26. Febuary
27. heighth

28. incessent
29. insistance
30. interupt
31. it's (possessive)
32. knowlege
33. labled
34. manageing
35. mispelled
36. occured
37. oppurtunity
38. paralel
39. preceed
40. prefered

41. proceed
42. proceedure
43. questionaire
44. reccomodation
45. recieve
46. recind
47. referance
48. referred
49. resistence
50. sargeant
51. seperate
52. servicable
53. stationary (paper)

8. Assume that you received from a leading corporation a complicated, unclear letter to stockholders. You wrote the chairperson suggesting the need for simpifying communications to the average stockholder, and for setting clearly the purpose of the meeting. The following is the chairperson's reply. Is it courteous and clear? Why or why not?

```
Yours is the first criticism we have had from the many thou-
sands of stockholders who have already sent in the proxies
saying that the purpose of the meeting was not understanda-
ble to them.  I do not see how I can state the facts any
more clearly and simply than was done in my letter of Janu-
ary 18.
```

9. Suggest acceptable nonsexist alternatives, if desirable, for the following words:

bellboy	delivery boy	lumberman	repairman
checkroom girl	foreman	maiden name	showmanship
committeeman	furnaceman	manhole	workman
craftsman	layman	man-hours	

10. For the following interdepartmental memo (a) number the paragraphs (1 to 4), (b) under every paragraph number, list all sexist statements—each on a separate line—and (c) opposite each statement write an appropriate nonsexist version.

```
TO:      Mrs. Erica Cosmos              DATE: May 10, 199-
FROM:    Tom Grant
SUBJECT: CPC Staffing Requirements

I would like your support along with that of Charles to
serve as cochairmen of our Staffing Requirements Committee
for the Communications Planning Centers.  As you know, the
CPCs are a most important sales tool, and we need highly
qualified manpower with top salesmen.
```

The other committeemen I have appointed to work with you are
Scott Durke, Fred Picker, Miss Helen Jaynes, and Mrs. Thoms.

One of the important jobs at the centers is that of professional sales demonstrator, which requires many man-hours of
work. This man will be an entry-level group manager, responsible for all equipment sales demonstrations. He must
of course be extremely knowledgeable about all our products
and services. Currently this assignment is being handled by
Miss Carolyn Mayer at our XY Center and by Kermit Smith at
ABC Center. Both are doing a superior job.

We would like this task to be a one-year rotational assignment and be filled with the best available candidate--man or
lady. This job experience can greatly benefit the assigned
individual and make him more valuable to our company on
future reassignments. Please get your committee together
this week to begin an extensive search for good people that
are available for these assignments. If you need help typing announcements or other materials, I've asked the gals in
the typing pool to be available.

11. Encircle the correct choice of "a" or "an" before each entry in this list:

a	an	hotel	a	an	heroic effort
a	an	honorary degree	a	an	hour
a	an	unit	a	an	heir
a	an	historical event	a	an	union
a	an	honest opinion	a	an	unanimous decision
a	an	unique method	a	an	humble opinion

Chapter 5

Legal Aspects of Business Communication

I. Incidents

II. Defamation
   A. Publication
   B. Privilege
   C. Defamatory Terms

III. Invasion of Privacy
   A. Use of a Person's Identity or Private Facts
   B. Physical Surveillance of Records, Reports, and Letters

IV. Misrepresentation and Fraud
   A. Innocent Misrepresentation
   B. Fraudulent Misrepresentation
   C. Sales Warranties
   D. Mail Frauds

V. Some Pertinent Laws Regarding Employment, Credit, and Collections
   A. Employment—and Preemployment Inquiries
   B. Credit and Collections

VI. Other Areas of Caution in Business Communication
   A. Unmailable Materials and Unordered Items
   B. Copied Documents
   C. Copyright Material

VII. Incident Decisions

VIII. Summary

IX. Exercises and Problems

When you apply integrity, honest consideration for your reader, and the golden rule in your business communications, you should be safe in the eyes of the law. Yet as a cautious, sensible businessperson—and as a consumer or member of a governmental organization—you need to realize that there are legal dangers even in some true statements. On the other hand, not all untrue words that appear to be libelous will lead to a lawsuit. Even while books about laws are being prepared for publication, many new laws—and interpretations of those laws at state and national levels and contracts between unions and management—may be enacted. No single chapter or book can begin to cover all specific legal interpretations applied to business communication.

Thousands of statutes have been passed, and thousands of court and arbitration decisions have been made, in the 50 states' courts and in the national court system. The laws of one state have no binding effect in other states, but federal laws apply throughout the country and have precedence over conflicting state laws.

The purpose of this chapter is to call to your attention some of the legal risks and complications that may occur in business communications. Remember, however, that statutes in various states differ, that numerous new laws and different interpretations are made from time to time, and that each legal case must be analyzed individually upon its facts. Ignorance of the law excuses no one. For advice on specific situations, you should consult an attorney. The discussion here is necessarily a brief introduction only; no guarantee is made for its completeness. Yet if you are aware of the risks discussed here, you can avoid harmful utterances and costly misunderstandings.

This chapter focuses on the following issues:

- Defamation
- Invasion of privacy
- Misrepresentation and fraud
- Some pertinent laws regarding employment, credit, and collections
- Other areas of caution

Before discussing these subjects, the chapter begins with true incidents that led to arbitration or court hearings. The decisions on them are at the end of the chapter.

INCIDENTS AND COURT STATEMENTS

The following 12 mini cases (incidents) are taken from trade publications and court cases relating to human relations problems in business. You may wish to read the incidents first, form an opinion, and then turn to the arbitrator and court decisions on pages 113–114. When reading the decisions, one realizes how careful everyone must be when communicating in and outside an organization.

Incident 1

A secretary wrote a letter to members of the board responsible for overseeing the secretary's supervisor.

—It included derogatory comments about her supervisor.
—It suggested that her supervisor managed badly, and even wore mannish clothing.

Two members of the board complained about the letter and requested a 10-day suspension for the secretary. The secretary requested an arbitration hearing.

Incident 2

Some bankers and their staff used confidential customer information to gain more insurance business for their bank. That information was part of the bank's files. They therefore turned to it and increased their business—until someone complained.

May a bank or any organization use confidential customer information to further additional business activity without the written consent of the customer?

Incident 3

A reporter filed and had printed a story about a local government agency which dispensed welfare benefits to applicants. Both he and a certain employee of the agency knew that disclosing confidential information—as stated in the agency's personnel manual—made the employee liable to dismissal.

Examination of the newspaper articles suggested that the writer was given access to certain internal documents. It was further discovered that he and the employee did make private information public. The employee was discharged. The union immediately filed a grievance and argued that discharge was improper.

Incident 4

An employee did good work for many years, but when a new supervisor was hired, it quickly became clear that relationships would deteriorate between the employee and new supervisor.

The supervisor knew that in the future some kind of action would have to be taken. She therefore began to keep a written record of all occasions when corrective action was required for the employee. Only after outside complaints about the employee were brought to the supervisor's attention did she send an official letter of warning to the employee.

(continued)

During the grievance procedure, the employee learned about the secret record of her alleged uncooperative behavior. "You have no right to keep a written record of alleged discretion without my knowledge," she said. "I wish the issue arbitrated."

Incident 5

An executive in a company was told that he would be replaced by a younger man. In consideration of his many years of work, he was permitted to use his office to find a new position within the company. Actually, the employee remained for more than a year, eventually reaching age 55, at which time he filed age discrimination charges with the Equal Employment Opportunity Commission.

The issue went to court, where the company argued that timeliness of a discrimination claim is measured from the day an employee receives reasonable notice of dismissal. The employee argued that what occurred a year or so earlier was not a clear and unequivocal discharge.

Incident 6

Nonverbal communication in the office was important to a company, particularly as expressed through the dress of its employees. The only criterion mentioned was "use common sense." Computer operators thus came to work in whatever clothing they chose.

A newly hired manager announced that in the future people should look "more professional." One young woman reported to work with culottes and was sent home by the manager, who even docked her for the time needed to change clothing. She demanded arbitration.

Incident 7

Disgruntled consumers are numerous. They communicate their discontent either orally or in written form. Courts seem to have been influenced by two criteria:

—Ignorant purchasers
—Sophisticated buyers

Does a customer claiming that a company did not reveal all of a product's deficiencies, even after signing of the contract, have a valid reason for legal action (even if the company was unaware of the deficiencies)?

Incident 8

Dear investment officer:

You requested that I submit the enclosed financial information in order to qualify for a loan from your Minnesota bank. That information is enclosed in the attached documents.

If you have any further questions, please get in contact with me.

Can one be taken to court for sending, from one state to another, a letter containing false information?

Incident 9

Here are the facts of the matter:

—An employee is suspected of wrongdoing.
—The employee has a box of private written materials in the workplace.
—The employee's box is opened and viewed by police, without a warrant.

To what extent are private notes or writings that are kept in one's place of work open for inspection?

Incident 10

RESUME FOR TOO SHEE LIU

Name: Too Shee Liu

Date of Birth: August 21, 1960

Family Members: S. Tanakaa, Father
                      G. Wong, Mother (Teacher)
                      S. Wong, Brother (Teacher)

Health Conditions: Good

May a U.S. employer request the above information in a resume? (All names have been changed.)

Incident 11

On March 14, Ms. S. visited a retail shoe store in [*city*], Idaho, to purchase softball shoes and a glove. While she was there, a salesman recommended the "Spot-Bilt Monsters," noting they were the best and most popular softball shoe on the market. Ms. S. indicated in her subsequent complaint that she relied on these representations. She paid $15 toward the purchase and placed the shoes on layaway.

On April 11, Ms. S. made a second payment on the shoes. She contended that on this occasion she was told by the owner of the store that the Spot-Bilt Monsters were highly recommended and were great softball shoes. These shoes, in addition to the usual cleats on the bottom of the shoe, also have "sidewall cleats," which protrude from the outside edge of the shoe.

On June 12, while wearing the shoes in a women's softball game in her state, Ms. S. attempted to slide into home plate when the outer cleat of her right shoe caught in the dirt and severely fractured her ankle. She filed a complaint in the county superior court on July 24, alleging several causes of action. The complaint named as defendants the retail store and the manufacturer of the shoe.

Ms. S.'s complaint alleged the following causes of action: (1) negligence, (2) strict liability, (3) breach of implied warranty, (4) breach of express warranty, (5) misrepresentation, (6) outrage, and (7) violation of the Consumer Products Act (CPA).

Incident 12

Dear Mr. Z.:

You passed the required examinations necessary for the position. Indeed, your qualifications are all appropriate, except for one that gives us difficulty.

We require that all candidates for deputy sheriff meet a minimum height requirement of 5 feet 9 inches. . . .

The candidate was unhappy with the decision and argued in a state superior court that three persons less than 5 feet 9 inches in height were employed as county sheriffs; he was being discriminated against. That court ruled that discrimination did occur, but the decision was appealed. Do you think the appeal was successful?

DEFAMATION

The unconsented and unprivileged "publication" of a false and malicious state-ment that tends to injure one's character, fame, or reputation is *defamation*. Oral defamation is *slander*. Written defamation is a *libel*. Truth is usually an acceptable defense to a defamation suit, but there are exceptions. Also, some false statements may be either *absolutely privileged* or *conditionally privileged*. Because the words *publication* and *privilege* have important legal significance, they are discussed first; then follows a sampling of defamatory terms[1] and court statements pertaining to defamation.

Publication

In the legal sense, the unconsented intentional or negligent communication of defamatory matter to a third party is *publication*. Any means of communication by which some third party (anyone other than the person attacked) actually receives the defamatory idea can effect a publication. The fact that the LEXIS database lists over 2,400 instances of defamatory statements in state courts alone suggests issues of publication are real.

If you tell Mr. X to his face privately that you consider him incompetent or a swindler, you are within your legal rights; only he has heard your statement. But if you intentionally communicate the defamatory statement to at least one other person who is not "privileged" (as defined later), you can be in serious trouble. The derogatory qualities that make a statement defamatory are the same for libel and slander. Because libelous statements are more permanent, different levels of proof are required by the aggrieved party for damages when libel is alleged than when slander is alleged. The writing (for libel) may be any permanent communication—such as a letter, postcard, telegram, circular, pic-ture, photograph, cartoon, newspaper, recorded tape, phonograph record, and radio or television broadcast.

Even a sealed letter addressed and mailed to the person you are accusing can result in actionable publication if you knew or should have known that it would be intercepted by or shown to a third person. For this reason, a letter containing unfavorable information about a person (or organization) and any collection message about past-due payments should be mailed only in a sealed envelope and addressed so that it will be read only by the addressee. Adding the words *Personal and Confidential* or *Personal* is a good precaution. However, remember that some secretaries open and read all their employers' mail; the reading would result in publication. Another precaution is to use an opaque envelope and to fold the message into the envelope in such a way that it cannot be easily read when held up to a light.

Accidental communications to third persons (for example, eavesdroppers or unauthorized letter readers) are not actionable unless you knew of or should have foreseen such possibilities. A mere possibility that someone may see or overhear the statement is not enough.

Dictation to a stenographer is considered by most authorities to be a publication that is conditionally privileged with respect to matters reasonably related to the ordinary conduct of the business.

Privilege

A legal right to communicate defamatory information in certain situations is *privilege*. The privilege may be *absolute* or *conditional*.

Absolute Privilege

In these three general areas absolute privilege applies: judicial proceedings, legislative proceedings, and the acts of important government officials, usually executives. The privilege is concerned with statements by and about various persons.

Judicial officers, attorneys, witnesses, parties, and all other participants in judicial and quasi-judicial proceedings are absolutely privileged to make defamatory statements and to file such papers during and as part of the trial, if they bear some relationship to the matter under consideration. Letters between parties or attorneys relating to a controversy are also privileged. However, defamatory statements about a case made outside the ordinary course of a judicial proceeding, such as comments to reporters in the hallway, are not entitled to the absolute privilege for judicial proceedings.

Similarly, legislators and government officials are absolutely privileged to make defamatory statements in the performance of their official functions, but not if the statements are irrelevant to the public matter then under consideration. For example:

> A member of the highway commission in New Mexico made a defamatory statement about a highway contractor at a commission meeting with reporters present. A superintendent of banks in California made libelous statements concerning his former attorney. In each case the Supreme Court of the respective state held that these public officials were protected by an absolute privilege in the exercise of their executive function. In contrast, a public official would not be absolutely privileged to defame his subordinates when publicly explaining why he dismissed them.[2]

The risk of liability for criticism of public persons decreased significantly in the United States after the Supreme Court decided the *New York Times* case in 1964. Under the *Times* rule, public officials cannot recover libel damages unless they prove actual malice. Criticism or comment about the public conduct or fitness for office of public officials and statements about the public conduct of other voluntary public figures are privileged even if they are based on or include erroneous material—unless there was actual knowledge of falsity or reckless disregard for whether the material was true or false.

Conditional (Qualified) Privilege

In several kinds of situations a conditional (qualified) privilege applies when the interest of either the participants or society dictates that communication in good faith should not be hampered by fear of lawsuits. Thus defamatory statements made in the ordinary commercial activity are qualifiedly privileged, whether they are interoffice messages or ones sent to persons outside the company, when the recipient has a lawful interest in the topic of discussion. This aspect of conditional (qualified) privilege is significant regarding recommendations of applicants.

Requests for Recommendations.   When you request someone to send you information about another person, show in your letter that you have an interest to protect the received information and promise to keep it confidential if this is permissible. Also, to receive all the important facts you need, it may be advisable to include a question like, "Do you have any other information (or . . . know of any personal habits) that might help or hinder this applicant's success in the position for which we are considering her (or him)?" Such statements help protect the informer against a libel suit.

Requested Recommendations.   The person who answers an inquiry about the performance of an employee or the credit record of a customer is obligated to take reasonable precautions that the information sent is accurate. He or she must *avoid intentional deceit or malice.* "In a personnel report it is generally believed that the writer owes a moral duty to state what is known about a former employee. What is stated honestly and in good faith is privileged communication even if it is subsequently shown to be untrue."[3]

Thus, whenever you send requested information to an inquirer (prospective employer or creditor, for instance, who might suffer a loss if he or she employs or lends to an unworthy applicant), make every effort to tell the truth and to reply in good faith without malice. If a respondent intentionally or carelessly misleads the inquirer who seeks information about another person (for instance, a job or credit applicant), he or she may be sued for damages. The reply should neither mislead the recipient into hiring or lending to an unworthy applicant nor maliciously prevent a worthy applicant from being considered fairly for employment or credit.

Writing letters of recommendation is a serious responsibility. A failure of true candor resulted in a highly publicized court trial after a hospital hired a physician who had been praised in four glowing recommendation letters by his senior colleagues. They neglected to mention job-related difficulties (concerning rape and assaults of patients). In the words of a respected pediatrician, "If the person you recommend doesn't measure up, your future credibility is zero."[4]

When the truth about an individual or an organization is unfavorable and directly related to a question you are asked to answer, *try as much as possible to protect the good name of the one involved.* Also indicate in your reply that the information was *requested,* and ask that it be kept *confidential,* if possible.

Remember, however, that under public disclosure laws some information cannot be kept confidential.

Some employers have been reluctant to state unfavorable but true and relevant information about an employee because they fear facing a lawsuit threatened (or implied) by the applicant. Nevertheless, the prevailing view is that the employer's right to freely express his or her opinion should not be restricted by another person's insinuations. If an employee threatens legal action in an attempt to restrain an employer from stating or committing to writing what is true, the threat is a baseless attempt to intimidate. An employer certainly can state "It is my opinion that the employee has failed to live up to the quality of work we require at this institution. We have certain standards, and we feel he (or she) did not meet those standards." It is necessary, of course, to specify what the expected standards are and to have records and documentation that will support the statements made.[5]

Unsolicited Information in Recommendations.   Is it illegal to provide unsolicited information in a personnel report (or recommendation letter)? No, but in this case the standard for truth is higher. Dr. Carson Varner has presented the following example:

> Suppose you are writing a recommendation for an employee who has worked as a janitor and is applying for a job as bank teller. The inquiry to which you are responding is: "How has the candidate been as an employee?" You know the janitor has been in jail, and it is generally believed the janitor was convicted twice for embezzlement, and you write this in your recommendation. Suppose it turns out the janitor has been in jail for involuntary manslaughter not embezzlement (the distinction might be critical for a bank job) and the janitor sued you for libel. Normally, the recommendation is privileged, but does it apply here? Here you were only asked to comment on the janitor's performance on the job and not about the background; therefore the information is not privileged, but subject to another standard.

> Were you careless or negligent in stating what you knew? If so, you could be held liable for damages caused. On the other hand, let us assume the janitor had started the rumor or everyone had believed it for years and the janitor had made no attempt to correct the rumor. In this case the jury could find you were not careless in your statement and therefore not liable.[6]

In summary, if one responds to an inquiry, one should basically have no fear of saying what one knows or adding relevant information in good faith. The response to such an inquiry is qualifiedly privileged, and truth is generally an adequate defense. But if one speaks or writes maliciously (for example, because of a desire to reap personal gain against a competitor or to hold an applicant up for ridicule), one may be held liable in any case. Privilege does not extend to defamatory statements unrelated to the purpose of the particular privilege (for instance, defamatory remarks not relevant to job qualifications). Also, the former employer may lose the privilege if the response uses such violent or abusive language that the real motive in the reply is clearly malice or some other improper purpose. Furthermore, if the former employer knows the statement is false, clearly the privilege is defeated. If he or she is negligent or unreasonable in believing it to be true, jurisdictions differ as to whether the privilege is lost.

Privilege does not apply to unreasonable disclosure and publication of particulars concerning a debtor to his or her employer or relatives, and to the public by such devices as "deadbeat lists" or obvious communications forms that may be read by others who have not requested the information and have no immediate need of it. These practices may also constitute invasion of privacy.

Defamatory Terms

Among the terms that have been judged libelous, the following is a representative (but incomplete) sampling of words to be avoided or used with caution when you refer to a person or an organization:

adultery	faker	Jekyll-Hyde	scandalmonger
alcoholic	falsified	personality	sharp dealing
altered records	forger	kept woman	shyster
bad moral char-	fraud (fraudu-	kickbacks	slacker
acter	lent)	mental illness	sneak
bankrupt	gay	misappropria-	swindler
blackmailer	gouged money	tion	thief
cheats	grafter	misconduct	unchaste
communist	hypocrite	misrepresen-	unethical
corrupt	illegitimate	tation	unmarried
crook	incompetent	perjurer	mother
deadbeat	inferior	plagiarist	unprofessional
dishonest	informer	price cutter	unworthy of
disreputable	insolvent	profiteer	credit
drug addict	intolerance	quack	villain
		racketeer	worthless
		rascal	

Also unacceptable are any words or expressions imputing:

■ A loathsome disease
■ A crime, or words falsely charging arrest, or indictment for or confession or conviction of a crime
■ Anti-Semitism or other religious, racial, or ethnic intolerance
■ Connivance or association with criminals
■ Financial embarrassment (or any implication of insolvency or want of credit)
■ Lying
■ Membership in an organization that may be in ill repute at a given period of time
■ Poverty or squalor
■ Unwillingness or refusal to pay a debt or evasion of payment of a debt

Some statements are defamatory because they malign a characteristic necessary in a person's work (provided the occupation is legal). Thus, in most jurisdictions, it is defamatory to impugn the financial responsibility of a merchant, but not of a teacher, because ability to obtain credit is essential only to the merchant. Also it has been held defamatory to attribute communist sympathies to a public official, but not to an engineer. And, as already discussed, it is defamatory to impugn the competence of an employee to perform duties required by his or her job. But such statements may be conditionally privileged if made in the ordinary course of business activity, as discussed above under Privilege.[7]

The truth is usually a defense in a libel suit in which there is no conditional privilege, especially if there is no evidence of malice. Traditionally, legal malice has meant spite, ill will, or a desire to do harm for harm's sake. However, some cases, including those that involve constitutional privilege, have extended the meaning of the word *malice*. These distinctions are too technical to warrant discussion here.

In the following court statements each underlined legal term suggests how it was used in the courts under the heading of "defamation."

"Plaintiff must prove to your satisfaction from the evidence the following things: . . . that the employee of the Defendant Reynolds Metals Company who made the defamatory statement knew at the time said statement was made that it was false and that it was defamatory. . . ."

Supreme Court of Alabama, 1989 Ala.; June 16, 1989, filed.

"Here, the specific meaning of the allegedly defamatory terms is far from clear. 'Sleazebag' apparently has yet to earn a mention in popular dictionaries. 'Sleazy' is defined as being "thin or poor in texture.""

United States District Court for the District of Colorado, 669 F. Supp. 356; 1987 U.S. Dist.; 14 Media L., Rep. 1659, September 16, 1987, Decided and Filed.

"When a supervisory employee comments on the job performance of a subordinate worker, the supervisor's comments are entitled to a qualified privilege under New York Law . . . The applicability of a qualified privilege to statements made by an employer/supervisor reviewing or evaluating the performance of an employee is well established."

United States District Court for the Northern District of New York, 1989 U.S. Dist.; December 21, 1989, Decided; December 22, 1989.

"There is nothing in the law contested which attempts to prevent a corporation from hiring whomsoever it pleases, or from discharging its employees when it sees fit. Neither is there anything in the law which requires a corporation to give a letter of recommendation to employees discharged or leaving its service. All that is required is a statement of the employer showing the character of services rendered by the employee and the reason for his leaving the service of his employer."

Supreme Court of the United States, 259 U.S. 548; 66 L. Ed. 1056; 42 S. Ct. 524, June 5, 1922, Decided.

". . . charge to jury in slander action by former employee whose discharge from employment of defendant corporation by defendant personnel manager was accompanied by a false accusation of theft, which set forth that a conditional privilege adhered between the personnel manager and other employees who had a mutual interest in the hiring and discharging of employees, gave defendants the basic protection to which they were entitled."

Supreme Court of Michigan, 360 Mich. 129; 103 N.W.2d 789; June 6, 1960, Decided.

"In this case, the defendants raise two specific arguments which would entitle them to judgment as a matter of law. First, the defendants claim that none of the alleged defamatory statements were published within the statute of limitations period. Second, the defendants argue that all of the statements, whether or not they were defamatory, were qualifiedly privileged and the defendants did not abuse their privilege."

United States District Court for the District of Massachusetts, 1989 U.S. Dist., December 19, 1989, Decided.

INVASION OF PRIVACY

The unconsented, unprivileged, and unreasonable intrusion into the private life of an individual is *invasion of privacy*. Unlike defamation, privacy can be violated although no publication to third persons takes place and even though the matters delved into are true or not particularly harmful to reputation. The concept of right of privacy is analogous to that of trespass, which gives one the right to keep unwarranted intruders off one's land, not because of any resulting emotional distress or loss of rents, but merely to ensure the solitude of landowners. Though the boundaries in this concept have not been definitely determined, its primary concern is the protection of a mental interest—such as freedom from mental anguish resulting from invasion of one's privacy.[8]

This section discusses two aspects of invasion of privacy: use of a person's identify without permission and physical surveillance of records, reports, and letters by persons not entitled to examine them.

Use of a Person's Identity or Private Facts

If a person's name, photograph, or other identity is used for commercial benefit without permission on a sales letter or advertisement (or other permanent publication), that person may have cause for legal action because his or her right of privacy has been violated.

Recovery and monetary awards have also been granted for publication of x-rays and other medical pictures, for pictures of a deformed infant, and for undue publicity of a delinquent debt.

Furthermore, the personal information customers are required to give when they apply for credit, insurance, medical care, or a job should be accurate and kept confidential. Unfortunately, in some cases the data collection methods result in incorrect, misleading, unfounded, or outdated information. (Some private investigating agencies gather information by questioning neighbors, landlords, and friends about lifestyles, health, and traits of applicants.) Some people who have been turned down on their application have found it necessary to sue when they discovered that incorrect personal information about them was filed (perhaps computerized) by a firm and then passed on to other firms without the customers' knowledge or permission. Customers should have the right to privacy.

Unreasonable publicity of someone's private life may also result in legal action and costly money awards to the offended person, as in the following case:

> In the "pink letter case" a suggestive letter bearing a woman's signature was mailed to 1,000 men. Handwritten in a feminine hand, the letter was mechanically reproduced on pink stationery and mailed by a mailing agency. The name signed to the letter was that of the principal character in a motion picture the letter was advertising. Unfortunately, it also turned out to be the name of a woman living in Los Angeles—the only person by that name listed in the City Directory or the telephone directory. When the letters began arriving (in hand-addressed, pink envelopes), many wives must have looked at their husbands with a quizzical eye. But it was worse for the plaintiff, who began getting telephone calls from the men. She also worried for fear that some irate wife might shoot her—for the letter invited the men to meet the signer in front of a certain theater on a certain day and to look for a girl "with a gleam in her eye, a smile on her lips and mischief on her mind." The court felt that the plaintiff should be compensated for invasion of right of privacy.[9]

If you wish to use the picture or identity of a person for your advertising or sales letters, for instance, be sure first to get previous consent and make clear just how the picture or identity is to be used. A person may have indicated consent by willingly posing for a photograph, but alteration of the photograph or use of it in a way to carry objectionable implications is an invasion of privacy. Photographers should carry releases (permission to use photos) in their camera case so that on-the-spot permission can be obtained.

Yet, not every use of another's likeness or identity is actionable. In some states it must be unreasonable under the circumstances, as well as unprivileged. Using pictures of an all-American football team on a beer company's calendar that also contained advertising was held (in one case) not to be an invasion of team members' privacy, because they were public figures and there was no false implication of endorsement.

Physical Surveillance of Records, Reports, and Letters

The right of privacy may also be violated if private records, reports, and letters are read by persons not entitled to examine them.

Powerful binoculars, long-range telephoto cameras, and "zoomer"-type television cameras have been used effectively (and illegally) in recent years to look through windows at important papers lying faceup on desks, at models of new products and designs, and at charts displayed at conferences. These techniques have become so common in certain areas of industrial espionage that elaborate security precautions are taken to keep designs and models in windowless rooms and to keep blinds drawn at all times in certain offices.

Modern technology has added to these existing situations the possibility of passing visible light or reflected infrared energy through an envelope and taking pictures of the contents. These pictures can then be read (deciphered) by persons skilled in reading handwriting or typing where lines are inverted or superimposed. You can help to greatly reduce or even prevent this type of surveillance by using—when desirable on certain very confidential material—envelopes with a random pattern inside them to make them opaque or by inserting more than one sheet of paper in them.

Quotations from two cases are included below to suggest how terms referring to invasion of privacy have been used in recent court cases.

"(The historical judgment, which the Fourth Amendment accepts, is that unreviewed executive discretion may yield too readily to pressures to obtain incriminating evidence and overlook potential <u>invasions of privacy</u> and protected speech.) Petitioners would have been forced to articulate their exact reasons for the search and to specify the items in Dr. Ortega's office they sought, which would have prevented the general rummaging through the doctor's office, desk, and file cabinets."

Supreme Court of the United States, 480 U.S. 709; 107 S. Ct. 1492; 1987 U.S.; 94 L. Ed. 2d. 714; 55 U.S.L.W. 4405; 42 Empl. Prac. Dec. (CCH), P36,891; 1 BNA IER CAS 1617, March 31, 1987.

> "However, the federal courts have not yet recognized such a 'principle,' and we fear the potential effect . . . on the long accepted, and vitally important, axiom that the sender of a letter retains an expectation of <u>privacy</u> protected by the fourth amendment in the contents of the letter after it is sent."
>
> United States Court of Appeals for the Eighth Circuit, 853 F. 2d 1479; 1988 U.S. App.; August 12, 1988, Filed.

MISREPRESENTATION AND FRAUD

Misrepresentations are of two kinds: innocent and fraudulent.

Innocent Misrepresentation

The fundamental legal meaning of *innocent representation* (or simply *misrepresentation*) is a "communication which is not in accordance with the facts, but which the communicator thought or merely assumed to be true." To be legally significant the misrepresentation must be relied on by the person to whom it is made, and it must be material. A misrepresentation is *material* if it would influence the judgment of a reasonable person.

Fraudulent Misrepresentation

When the communicator knows that the representation is not true and the person to whom it was made relies on it to his or her disadvantage, a *fraudulent misrepresentation* (or *fraud*—sometimes called *deceit* in tort actions) exists. Fraudulent misrepresentation may be the basis of an action for contract rescission or of an action for damages. If the remedy sought is rescission of a contract, the person who made the misrepresentation must have known it was not in accord with the facts and the victim must have relied on it.

Fraud will be the basis of an action for monetary damages if the person making a misrepresentation knows that what he or she is communicating is not true and, in addition, if the communication is material, resulting in injury to the person who relied on the untrue statement. A fraud, like an innocent misrepresentation, is material if it would influence the judgment of a reasonable person.

Section 5 of the Federal Trade Commission (FTC) Act, as amended, outlaws practices that are deceitful or are otherwise unfair to consumers. Included are (among others) false advertising regarding prices, performance capability, quality, and character of goods or services. Also included are endorsements by persons misrepresented as "experts" or "doctors," and many other misstatements intended to deceive.[10] A test for fraud is to ask, "Would the other party have entered into the contract had he or she known the truth?"

Sales Warranties

In most sales contracts, the seller undertakes certain obligations concerning the nature, title, and quality of the goods being sold. When these obligations are expressly stated or implied and when they actually induce the sale, the obligations are called *warranties*. They are guarantees by the seller with respect to the goods sold. Warranties may be "express" or "implied."

An *express warranty* affirms a fact or a promise the seller made to the buyer in bargaining concerning the nature of the goods. It may include a description, grade labeling, use of a sample or model, statements or pictures in an advertisement. Such a promise becomes a basis for the contract even though the term *warranty* or *guaranty* is not used.

Implied warranties are considered part of the bargain even though the parties themselves say nothing about them. For instance, the seller warrants that he or she is conveying a good title to the goods. Also, under the Uniform Commercial Code (adopted by all 50 states) if the seller is a merchant with respect to goods of that kind, he or she warrants that the goods are salable and are fit for the ordinary purposes for which such goods are used. Whether or not the seller is a merchant, if the seller knows or has reason to know that the buyer intends the goods for a particular purpose, and the buyer is relying on the seller to select a product suitable for that purpose, there is an implied warranty that the product is fit for that purpose. However, sellers have the ability under the UCC to disclaim or exclude warranties.

The Magnuson-Moss Warranty Act (a federal law enacted in 1975) states that if a seller chooses to give an express warranty for a consumer product to a consumer, the seller must disclose the warranty terms in simple and readily understood language. For products costing over $15, the warranty must be labeled "full" or "limited." Among other requirements, *full warranty products* must be repaired or replaced by the seller without charge within a reasonable time if there is a defect. If a warranty is limited, the limitation must be conspicuous so that buyers are not misled. Further, the act provided that if the sellers give a written warranty, they cannot disclaim or modify the implied warranties. If a warranty is limited in a reasonable manner, the duration of the implied warranties may be limited.[11]

Mail Frauds

According to the U.S. Postmaster General, in the Post Office Department's informative booklet *Mail Fraud Laws*, fraudulent schemes sent through the mail are costing American consumers an estimated $500 million a year. Among the many dishonest practices to trap the unsuspecting consumer are fake contests, home improvement offers, auto insurance frauds, charity appeals, missing-heir schemes, fake business opportunities, worthless medical cures, and fake correspondence-school programs promising "exciting, high-paying jobs."

The U.S. Chief Postal Inspector lists the following ways you can help enforce mail fraud laws:

To stop a dishonest scheme, inspectors must find that you and others buying a product or service were cheated as a result of claims the seller made in an intentional effort to defraud. Mail fraud violations occur when a general scheme or pattern of fraud exists.

When you believe mail fraud exists, hold all letters, including envelopes and other evidence related to the questionable scheme. See if your neighbors or business associates have also received similar material.

Bring such information to the attention of a postal inspector in your area by contacting him or her directly or through your postmaster.

Inspectors cannot investigate a case simply to force a supplier to speed up deliveries, to obtain funds, or to otherwise act as an intermediary in settling unsatisfactory transactions. In such instances the dissatisfied buyer should:

Seek an adjustment or settlement with the seller.

Bring the complaint to the attention of the Better Business Bureau, chamber of commerce, trade association, or publication that carried the ad.

Seek relief through civil suit if a breach of contract may be involved.[12]

Most states now have consumer protection divisions in the attorney general's office, and they can be very helpful too.

The following sample quotations from four court cases illustrate the use of terms relating to misrepresentation and fraud:

> ". . . the insured had a scar on his brain, of which he was not aware, and as a result thereof suffered from epilepsy. In a suit by judgment creditors, it was held that the insurer was not entitled to rescind the policy because of an innocent representation by the insured in the application that he had no physical defects."
>
> United States Court of Appeals Fifth Circuit, 343 F. 2d 55, March 16, 1965.

> "The investor/plaintiffs allege the FDIC acquired their notes with actual knowledge of the fraudulent misrepresentations and omissions and without good faith. Specifically, the investor/plaintiffs allege the FDIC had full knowledge of the financial condition of the bank and of the material misstatements made to the plaintiffs by FPB officers and employees."
>
> United States District Court for the Eastern District of Louisiana, 661 F. Supp. 163; 1987 U.S. Dist.; February 27, 1987, Decided and Filed.

"The sales contract, which was negotiated in the United States, England, and Germany, signed in Austria, and closed in Switzerland, contained *express warranties* by petitioner that the trademarks were unencumbered and a clause providing that 'any controversy or claim [that] shall arise out of this agreement or the breach thereof' would be referred to arbitration before the International Chamber of Commerce in Paris, France, . . ."

Supreme Court of the United States, 417 U.S. 506; 94 S. Ct. 2449; 1974 U.S.; 41 L. Ed. 2d. 270, June 17, 1974.

". . . complaint—mail and wire fraud, bribery and violations of the Foreign Corrupt Practices Act—were all committed in connection with the underlying scheme. Focusing on the complexity of the scheme, the court held that if the appellants' allegations proved to be true, the wire and mail fraud communications used to implement the scheme account for numerous violations of federal law. . . ."

United States District Court for the District of New Jersey, 713 F. Supp. 737; 1989 U.S. Dist.; May 11, 1989, Decided and Filed.

SOME PERTINENT LAWS REGARDING EMPLOYMENT CREDIT, AND COLLECTIONS

Employment—and Preemployment Inquiries

Title VII of the Civil Rights Act of 1964, with amendments in 1972 and 1978, prohibits discrimination in employment as to hiring, firing, compensation, termination, and conditions or privileges of employment on the basis of race, color, religion, sex, or national origin. (Exceptions are allowed in some businesses or enterprises—such as church organizations, modeling agencies, entertainment producers—when religion, sex, or national origin may be bona fide occupational qualifications necessary for normal operations.)

The law forbids discrimination, *not* the asking of certain questions. But some questions may be unfair or risky to ask because they appear to be for the purpose of discriminating, and in fact do discriminate. They might later be the basis for legal action. Even if an employer wins the court case, the damage in public relations may be extremely serious. Thus many firms have policy guidelines with narrow rules on what recruiters may or may not do when interviewing.[13]

The following checklist of fair and unfair preemployment inquiries[14] is in line with the federal *Uniform Guidelines on Employee Selection Procedures*. Some states, as well as cities and counties, may have stricter regulations regarding a few of the preemployment inquiries. Thus, because of variations, it is advisable to check your own local and state laws or consult a counselor when in doubt.

■ Checklist—Preemployment Inquiries

Subject	Fair Preemployment Inquiries	Unfair Preemployment Inquiries
a. Age	Inquiries as to birthdate are permitted in some states; in others, only whether applicant is of legal age.	Any inquiry that implies discrimination (without job-related justification).
b. Arrests (see also Convictions)	None. (Law enforcement agencies are exempt from this rule.)	All inquiries relating to arrests.
c. Citizenship	Whether applicant is prevented from lawfully becoming employed in this country because of visa or immigration status. Whether applicant can provide proof of citizenship, visa, or alien registration number after being hired.	Whether applicant is citizen. Requirement before hiring to present birth certificate, naturalization papers, or baptismal record. Any inquiry that would divulge lineage, ancestry, national origin, descent, or birthplace.
d. Convictions (see also Arrests)	Inquiries concerning specified convictions that relate reasonably to fitness to perform particular job being applied for, provided that such inquiries be limited to convictions for which date of conviction or of prison release is within seven years of job application date. All general conviction inquiries must be accompanied by a disclaimer informing the applicant that a conviction record will not necessarily bar him or her from employment.	Any inquiry which does not meet the requirements for fair preemployment inquiries.
e. Family	Whether applicant can meet specified work schedules or has activities, commitments, or responsibilities that may prevent meeting work attendance requirements.	Specific inquiries concerning spouse, spouse's employment or salary, children, child care arrangements, or dependents.
f. Handicap	Whether applicant has certain specified sensory, mental, or physical handicaps that relate reasonably to fitness to perform particular job. Whether applicant has any handicaps or health problems that may affect work performance or that employer should take into account in determining job placement.	Overly general inquiries (e.g., "Do you have any handicaps?") which would tend to divulge handicaps or health conditions which do not relate reasonably to fitness to perform the job.
g. Height and weight	Inquiries as to ability to perform actual job requirements. Being of a certain height or weight will not be considered to be a job requirement unless the employer can show that no employee with the ineligible height or weight could do the work.	Any inquiry that is not based on actual job requirements.

Subject	Fair Preemployment Inquiries	Unfair Preemployment Inquiries
h. Marital status (see also Name and Family)	None.	Whether applicant is married, single, divorced, separated, engaged, widowed, etc.; whether Mr., Mrs., Miss, Ms.
i. Military	Inquiries concerning education, training, or work experience in the armed forces of the United States.	Type or condition of military discharge. Experience in other than U.S. armed forces. Request for discharge papers.
j. Name	Whether applicant worked for this firm or a competitor under a different name; if so, what name. Name under which applicant is known to references if different from present name.	Inquiry into original name and whether it has been changed by court order or marriage. Inquiries about name that would divulge marital status, lineage, ancestry, national origin, or descent.
k. National origin	Inquiries into applicant's ability to read, write, and speak foreign languages, when such inquiries are based on job requirements.	Inquiries into applicant's lineage, ancestry, national origin, descent, birthplace, or mother tongue. National origin of parents or spouse.
l. Organizations	Inquiry into organization memberships, excluding any organization the name or character of which indicates race, color, creed, sex, marital status, religion, or national origin or ancestry of its members.	Requirement that applicant list all organizations, clubs, societies, and lodges to which he or she belongs.
m. Photographs	May be requested *after* hiring, for identification purposes.	Request that applicant submit photo, mandatorily or optionally, before hiring.
n. Pregnancy (see also Handicap)	Inquiries as to duration of stay on job or anticipated absences that are made to males and females alike.	All questions as to pregnancy, and medical history concerning pregnancy and related matters.
o. Race or color	None.	Any inquiry concerning race or color of skin, hair, eyes, etc.
p. Relatives	Names of relatives already employed by this company or by any competitor.	Names and addresses of any relative other than those listed as proper.
q. Religion or creed	None.	Inquiries about applicant's religious denomination or affiliations, church, pastor, parish, religious holidays.
r. Residence	Inquiries about address to the extent needed to facilitate contacting the applicant.	Names or relationship of persons with whom applicant resides. Whether applicant owns or rents home.
s. Sex	None.	Any inquiry.

Credit and Collections

Because of the widespread use of credit by consumers, the federal government and the states have enacted a series of laws to protect consumers and try to assure that they are treated fairly in credit transactions. Because state statutes vary, you will need to investigate those in your state. Space here allows only a brief introduction to some of the federal laws. They are detailed in the United States Statutes at Large. (Volume and page numbers are in parentheses after each act described below.)

Equal Credit Opportunity Act requires that financial institutions and other firms engaged in credit extension make that credit equally available to all creditworthy customers without regard to sex or marital status. Subsequent amendments have extended the act's protection to all persons, regardless of race, color, religion, national origin, or age. The credit extenders have certain rights to make necessary inquiries for determining creditworthiness. (**88**:1521–5) (1974)

Fair Credit Billing Act aims to protect the consumer against inaccurate and unfair credit card practices. The act specifies procedures for consumers to challenge any charge account statements they believe are incorrect. It states procedures for creditors regarding acknowledging, investigating, problem solving, account closing, collecting, and reporting of debtors to credit-rating offices. It includes penalties for creditors that don't conform to the rules. Creditors must send to customers printed instructions twice a year explaining the procedures. In certain situations, the act also protects consumers who use credit cards other than charge cards to make purchases. (**88**:1511–17) (1974)

Fair Credit Reporting Act requires that consumer reporting agencies (credit bureaus; investigative, detective, and collection agencies; computerized information-reporting firms; lenders' exchanges) adopt impartial, fair procedures for meeting the needs of consumers regarding consumer credit, personnel, insurance, and other information. It specifies guidelines with regard to confidentiality, accuracy, relevancy, and proper use of such information. It stipulates the circumstances under which consumer reporting agencies may furnish consumer reports, the type of information they may and may not furnish, and the requirements for disclosing to the consumers the substance and sources of information as well as for reinvestigating to correct disputed information or errors. (**84**:1114–16) (1970)

Fair Debt Collection Practices Act states what bill collectors (other than creditors and attorneys) can and cannot do. In the collection of debts or in attempts to collect any claim alleged to be due or owed, the collector should not unreasonably oppress, harass, abuse, or intentionally cause mental distress to any person. Harassment and abuse include abusive language, anonymous or repeated telephone calls at odd hours, anonymous c.o.d. communications, or any communications that look like messages from a credit bureau or government agency or like a court summons. (**91**:874) (1978)

Federal Truth in Lending Act aims to assure meaningful disclosure of credit terms so that consumers will be able to compare more readily the charges by different credit sources. It requires lenders and creditors to disclose the terms, conditions, finance charges, and service or carrying charges (including annual percentage rate) before a consumer signs a contract. It also gives a consumer the right to rescind within three business days after signing a contract that will result in a secondary security interest's being acquired in his or her residence. If the transaction is rescinded, the borrower (consumer) has no liability for any finance charge. (**82**:146–158) (1968)

OTHER AREAS OF CAUTION IN BUSINESS COMMUNICATION

Noteworthy also are a few highlights regarding some mailed items and cautions on copying of documents and copyrighted material.

Unmailable Materials and Unordered Items

Suggestions on how you can help enforce mail fraud laws are listed under Fraud, in this chapter. Among the many other *unmailable materials* that may violate United States postal laws are letters and printed matter concerning lotteries, obscene literature, extortion threats, and solicitation of illegal business. Space does not permit discussion of these items here. You can obtain booklets on most of these subjects through your local postmaster or the U.S. Government Printing Office, Washington, D.C. 20402. And if you are in doubt about the mailability of any particular material, you may submit a request to the Office of the General Counsel, Mailability Division, Post Office Department, Washington, D.C. 20260. A ruling will be furnished as promptly as circumstances permit.

The sending of *unordered merchandise* through the mail does not violate postal laws unless it is sent c.o.d. However, persons receiving such unordered items can:

If the package has not been opened, write "Return to Sender" and put it back into the mails.

Treat unordered merchandise as an unconditional gift if living in a state where the laws apply.

The sending of *unsolicited credit cards* is illegal, as specified in the Consumer Credit Cost Disclosure Act.

The following is a quotation from one court case on the topic of unsolicited material:

> "The Congressional findings which were part of the Goldwater amendment also specifically referred to the protection of persons from the receipt of <u>unsolicited material</u>. The statute need not be construed to cover broader ground than its sponsors intended."
>
> United States District Court, E.D. New York, 328 F. Supp. 297; 15 A.L.R. Fed. 464, June 10, 1971.

Copied Documents

Another caution pertains to the copying of certain documents. Congress, by statute, has forbidden the copying of the following documents and items under certain circumstances: United States government obligations or securities, such as Treasury and Federal Reserve notes, National Bank currency, certificates of indebtedness, silver and gold certificates, paper money, and others; also United States savings bonds (except for campaign publicity for their sale); Internal Revenue stamps (except in copying for lawful purposes a legal document on which there is a canceled revenue stamp); postage stamps canceled or uncanceled (except for philatelic purposes, provided the reproduction is in black and white and is less than ¾ or more than 1½ times the linear dimensions of the original); postal money orders; bills, checks, or drafts for money drawn by or upon authorized officers of the United States; and other representatives of value issued under any act of Congress.

Among other materials that may not be copied are certificates of citizenship or naturalization (except foreign naturalization certificates); passports (except foreign); immigration papers; obligations or securities of any foreign government, bank, or corporation; draft registration cards and selective service induction papers bearing certain information; badges, identification cards, passes, or insignia carried by military personnel or members of the various federal departments and bureaus such as the FBI and Treasury (except when ordered by the head of such departments or bureaus). In some states copying auto licenses, automobile certificates of title, and driver's licenses is also forbidden. For these items—and others not listed here—penalties of fine or imprisonment are imposed on those guilty of making illegal copies.

Copyright Material

The U.S. Copyright Law that went into effect January 1, 1978, forbids the copying of copyrighted material without permission of the copyright owner—except for certain limited "fair use" privileges and single copies made for noncommercial purposes, as specified in the bill. It includes details about permissible uses of single or multiple copies from books, articles, essays, poems, graphs, charts, cartoons, pictures, and so on, and states when written prior permission must be obtained.

Circular 1, "General Information on Copyright," contains in its 10 pages answers to some of the frequently asked questions about copyright. For a list of other material published by the copyright office, write to Register of Copy-rights, Library of Congress, Washington, D.C. 20559, and ask for "Publications of the Copyright Office."

INCIDENT DECISIONS

Here are the arbitrator and court decisions regarding the 12 incidents on pages 91–94. Were your opinions—or "guesstimates"—similar to these decisions?

Incident 1

The arbitrator argued that little in the letter was considered constitutionally pro-tected free speech. However, he did shorten suspension to five days.

Incident 2

Holding companies and their subsidiaries cannot either directly or indirectly use confidential information to further any activity without the express written con-sent of the customer involved.

Incident 3

The discharge of the employee held. Employees cannot make private informa-tion public about a client or another employee.

Incident 4

The arbitrator held that supervisors cannot keep secret files on employees with-out inspection of those files by employees.

Incident 5

The court held that the employee's first notice for dismissal was clearly commu-nicated; the employee also lost on the issue of timeliness.

Incident 6

The arbitrator suggested that precedents as to interpreting "common sense" had different interpretations; the company had acted unreasonably.

Incident 7

Courts have split on the question of whether to allow recovery for innocent misrepresentation when a contract has been signed. It is difficult for a company to know all deficiencies in a product. Thus innocent misrepresentation is a difficult criterion for measurement.

Incident 8

The federal mail fraud statute has stood for more than a century as a means of preventing various forms of fraud via the mails. The courts ruled that mail fraud prosecution was proper in Minnesota and the home state of the sender.

Incident 9

The Supreme Court asserted that the scope of the private-party search did not diminish the employee's actual or subjective expectations of privacy. In other words, one's written material—of a private nature—is not open to inspection without a warrant.

Incident 10

Some states do permit inquiries regarding birthdate; the other information violates employee selection procedures. See pages 108–109.

Incident 11

Ms. S. appealed the trial court's summary judgment dismissal of her claim against the retail store for violation of the Consumer Protection Act (CPA), negligence, and breach of express warranty. She contended material issues of fact existed that made the summary judgment inappropriate. The retail store cross-appealed, contending that the court erred in denying its motion for attorney fees. (The Court of Appeals affirmed the dismissal of the case by a lower court and denied attorney fees to the retail store.)

Incident 12

The state supreme court reversed the original decision. It indicated that the state human rights commission had the authority to make a preemployment inquiry regarding height as an unfair employment practice.

SUMMARY

As you can quickly see, there are numerous communication traps into which you may fall. The court decisions are not consistent between states, nor are the decisions awarded in cases taken to arbitration. Your task is to be cautious. Remember to:

Be honest and fair in all your business transactions and correspondence.

Avoid any statements and acts that may be considered defamation, invasion of privacy, or fraud. When answering requests for recommendations of former employees, customers, or others, include relevant facts truthfully without malice. As a seller or buyer of merchandise, be aware of federal and state laws regarding warranties; also be aware of how to help curb fraudulent schemes sent through the mail. Do not make assertions if you are not sure of their truth or accuracy.

Keep yourself well informed on legal responsibilities regarding employment, credit, collections, and other areas of concern—based on both federal laws and those in your state. Recognize the importance of honest, prudent actions by yourself and your subordinates.

Consult an attorney when in doubt about the handling of any complicated situation that might involve legal risks. Each case must be analyzed individually.

EXERCISES AND PROBLEMS

1. *Short written or oral report:* Choose one of the following acts (or perhaps any other related to your major field of interest). Then consult the U.S. Statutes at Large for details about that act.

   - Equal Credit Opportunity Act
   - Fair Credit Billing Act
   - Fair Credit Reporting Act
   - Fair Debt Collection Practices Act
   - Federal Truth in Lending Act
   - The new Copyright Law
   - The new Bankruptcy Act

   Prepare a short report or oral presentation with information that will be useful to your class members—and yourself.

2. *Memo report on guidelines for ethical practices:* The purpose of this assignment is to broaden your knowledge of guidelines for ethical practices among advertisers. You can obtain information from the Fair Practice Code of the Council of Better Business Bureaus, from the Direct Mail/Marketing Association, and from some pamphlets by the U.S. Postal Service regarding

laws, regulations, and mail fraud. Write a short (two- to four-page) memo report to your instructor, stating highlights of your findings.

3. **Evaluations:** On a scale of 1 (very ethical) to 5 (highly unethical) rate each of the following behaviors. Be prepared to discuss the issues in class.
   a. Rewriting an unfavorable report in order to show favorable (but false) results.
   b. Divulging confidential data to persons outside the company.
   c. Giving a superior false information in order to improve your own position in the office.
   d. Writing office evaluations in order to gain raises and promotions for personal favorites.
   e. Rewriting personnel reports to justify hiring a friend rather than a minority candidate.

4. **Definitions of ethical terms:** Basic to understanding ethics and its derivatives are some terms which have variant meanings. Each of the following terms relate to ethical behavior and communication. Define each as the basis for a class discussion or a short paper.

   Ethics   Dilemma
   Right   Standard of behavior
   Justice   Laws
   Values

5. **Report on a case involving legal problems of business communication:** Law journals and other publications are mainly of interest to attorneys and students interested in law. However, they contain many cases involving business communication that could be brought to the attention of others. If a student is interested in law he or she may wish to become familiar with the LEXIS system. Report to the class what the system is and summarize one case which involved problems of communication.

Chapter 6

The Process of Preparing Effective Business Messages

Whether you are preparing a written or an oral business message, you need to plan, organize, compose drafts, edit, revise. The written message must also be proofread and corrected before it is mailed. These steps are essential in the process of preparing successful communications.

Also essential is thoughtful adherence to communication principles—the seven C qualities—and awareness of legal aspects, as discussed in preceding chapters. Even if your organization has the best modern office technology for inputting ideas, processing messages, and storing, retrieving, reproducing, and disseminating them, the need for careful preparation of communications is the same.

This chapter presents planning steps, basic organizational patterns, suggestions for openings and closings, and composing procedures—writing, editing, revising, proofreading. Here the discussion and exercises focus on written messages—mainly letters and memos. Other chapters include further details about them and also additional suggestions for preparing reports and oral presentations.

FIVE PLANNING STEPS

To communicate effectively, first go through the following steps before you write your message:

- Know the purpose of the message.
- Analyze your audience—readers or listeners.
- Choose the ideas to include.
- Collect all the facts to back up these ideas.
- Outline—organize—your message.

Know Your Purpose

Your first step when planning your communication is to determine your specific purpose. For instance, is it to get an immediate replacement for defective articles? Or is your main purpose to announce your firm's new location? Or to apologize for a serious error? Or to persuade prospects to buy your product? Or to explain why you are not granting a customer's requested refund?

In addition to the specific purpose of each message, all communications have, of course, an underlying general purpose—to build goodwill. For example, in a refusal or a collection letter, the purpose should be twofold—not only to refuse a request or to ask for money, but also to maintain the customer's goodwill.

Analyze Your Audience

After reading about the communication process, principles, and legal aspects (Chapters 2 through 5), you realize how important it is to adapt your messages as much as possible *to the recipients' views, mental filters, and needs.* If you are

well acquainted with your recipients—or even if you have met them only once—
you can actually visualize individuals. Most of your writing, however, will probably be directed to people you have never met.

If you are sending a message to one person, try to picture that person the
best ways you can—business or professional person or laborer; superior (boss),
colleague, or subordinate; man or woman; new or longtime customer; young,
middle-aged, or elderly client. Consider the person's educational level, attitudes,
and so on. If you are addressing a form message to many people, remember
the caution that every person within any group has a unique filter and special
interests! Try to discover some characteristics common to all of them, and then
imagine you're talking to one individual within that group.

In all communications consider the areas on which your recipients are likely
to be well informed or uninformed; pleased or displeased; positive, negative, or
neutral; interested and enthusiastic or uninterested and unreceptive.

Choose the Ideas

With your purpose and recipient in mind, your next step is to choose the ideas
for your message. If you are answering a letter, you can underline the main
points to discuss and jot your ideas briefly in the margin or on a memo pad. If
you are writing an unsolicited or a complex message, you can begin by listing
ideas as they come to you. Then consider what facts will be most useful for that
person.

The ideas you will include depend on the type of message you're considering. For example, in a welcome letter from a savings and loan association to
new customers, is your purpose only to welcome them? If so, then one or two
sentences should suffice. They might merely thank new customers for selecting
your association and welcome them. But should the purpose of this message be
only to welcome? Shouldn't you also make them aware of your policy concerning
savings accounts, the overall services available to them, and your association's
eagerness to be their financial headquarters? Thus, the five ideas listed below
should be included in the welcome letter. (After you have gathered all the facts
and outlined your message, you might write a letter like letter 2, pages 38 and
39.

- Welcome the customers and thank them for opening an account.
- State some of your services—free parking, save-by-mail, mortgage
  loans, special accounts.
- Tell them the hours you're open to serve them.
- Mention the percentage of interest they earn.
- Assure them you're ready to help with their problems or wishes.

Collect All the Facts

Having determined what ideas to include, ask yourself if you need any specific
facts, updated figures, or quotations. Be sure you know your company policies,
procedures, and product details if this message requires them. Perhaps you

should check with your boss, colleague, subordinates, or the files for an exact percentage, the name of an individual, a date, an address, or a statement. Sometimes you need also to enclose a useful brochure, table, picture, or product sample.

Outline—Organize—Your Message

Before you write the message, outline it (in your mind or on paper). The order in which you present your ideas is often as important as the ideas themselves. Disorganized writing reflects disorganized, illogical thought processes or careless preparation.

Choose the organizational plan after you have determined your purpose, collected all needed facts, and asked yourself "How will the reader or listener react to these ideas?" The basic plans are discussed briefly in the next section, and more specifically in other chapters.

BASIC ORGANIZATIONAL PLANS

Your choice of organizational plan depends on how you expect your reader (or listener) to react to your message. And that reaction, of course, depends to some extent on what is already in that person's mental filter, as well as on the content of your message.

For letters and memos you can choose one of four basic organizational plans: the *direct-request*, *good-news*, *bad-news*, or *persuasive-request plan*. The first two use the direct (deductive) approach, which begins with the main idea; the last two, the indirect (inductive) approach, which states the main idea later.

Direct (deductive) approach
for
direct-request
and good-news plans

Indirect (inductive) approach
for
bad-news and persuasive-request plans

Main idea

Main idea

All these plans are to be considered as flexible guides only, not as rigid patterns. Your own judgment must help you decide the best organization and content of each message. Other chapters discuss and illustrate various ways you can use these plans.

Direct (Deductive) Approach

When you think your reader (or listener) will consider your message favorable or neutral and the information understandable (without any obstacle), you can use the direct approach. You *begin with the main idea or best news*. After the opening, you include all necessary explanatory details—in one or several paragraphs—and end with an appropriate, friendly paragraph.

The direct-request and good-news plans have three basic parts. Notice their similarities as you compare the brief outlines side by side in the checklist below.

Use the direct-request plan when the main purpose of your message is to make a request that requires no persuasion, because the reader will say "yes" readily.

Use the good-news plan to grant requests, announce favorable or neutral information, and exchange routine information within or between companies.

■ Checklist for Organizational Plans Using the Direct (Deductive) Approach

Direct-Request Plan	**Good-News Plan**
1. Main idea	**1.** Best news or main idea
a. Request, main statement, or question	
b. Reasons, if desirable	
2. Explanation	**2.** Explanation
a. All necessary and desirable details	**a.** All necessary and desirable details
b. Numbered questions, if helpful	**b.** Resale material°
c. Easy-reading devices	**c.** Educational material
	d. Sales promotion material°
3. Courteous close, with motivation to action	**3.** Positive, friendly close, including, if appropriate:
a. Clear statement of action desired	**a.** Appreciation
b. Easy action Dated action, when desirable	**b.** Clear statement of action desired, if any
d. Appreciation and goodwill	**c.** Easy action
	d. Dated action, when desirable
	e. Willingness to help further
	f. Reader benefit

° *Resale material* is usually favorable information about a product or service that the reader (customer) has already bought or is planning to buy. The customer made the selection. *Sales promotion material* usually includes the vendor's suggestions for additional products or services the customer may find useful. The vendor originates the suggestion about selection.

Indirect (Inductive) Approach

When you think your reader (or listener) will probably react unfavorably (negatively) to your request or information, you should usually not present the main idea in the first paragraph. Instead you will need to begin, preferably, with some relevant pleasant, neutral, or receiver-benefit statements; then give adequate explanation *before* you introduce the unpleasant idea.

Thus the bad-news and persuasive-request plans both use the indirect approach. Notice—in the side-by-side checklist outlines below—that each has *four* instead of three parts. You need to take a little longer to present bad news and to persuade.

■ Checklist for Organizational Plans Using the Indirect (Inductive) Approach

Bad-News Plan

1. Buffer (pleasant or neutral statements with consideration for reader)

2. Explanation
   a. Necessary details, tactfully stated
   b. Pertinent favorable, then unfavorable, facts
   c. Reader-benefit reasons

3. Decision (implied or expressed), along with offer of additional help or suggestions

4. Positive, friendly close
   a. Appreciation
   b. Invitation to future action
   c. Clear statement of action desired
   d. Easy action
   e. Dated action, when desirable
   f. Willingness to help further
   g. Reader benefit and goodwill

Persuasive-Request Plan

1. Attention
   a. Reader benefit
   b. Reader-interest theme

2. Interest
   a. Descriptive details
   b. Psychological appeals
   c. Reader benefits

3. Desire
   a. Statement of request
   b. Conviction material to help create reader's desire to grant request

4. Action
   a. Clear statement of action desired
   b. Easy action
   c. Dated action, when desirable
   d. Special inducement
   e. Reader-benefit plug

The bad-news message is one of the most difficult to prepare, because your receiver will consider it unfavorable. Likewise, in the persuasive request you expect resistance. Your receivers will probably find obstacles and react negatively unless they are persuaded. So you try to show them how they or someone in whom they are interested will benefit from granting your request.

BEGINNINGS AND ENDINGS

Two of the most important positions in any business message are the opening and closing paragraphs. You have probably heard the old sayings "First impressions are lasting" and "We remember best what we read last." Whenever possible, place the main favorable ideas at the beginning and ending of a message. (This advice applies also to business sentences and paragraphs.)

Because openings and closings are so significant, this section includes brief suggestions to help you concentrate on common essentials before studying various message types in later chapters.

Opening Paragraphs

Often the opening of a written message determines whether the reader continues reading, puts the message aside for later study, or discards it. The following checklist and examples are suggestions for good openings that help make favorable impressions:

■ Checklist for Opening Paragraphs

1. Choose an opening appropriate for the message purpose and for the reader.
   a. Main idea or good-news subject first—for direct-request, neutral, and good-news messages
   b. Buffer first—for bad-news messages
   c. Attention-getting statements first—for persuasive requests
2. Make the opening considerate, courteous, concise, and clear.
   a. Get reader into opening.
   b. Keep first paragraph relatively short.
   c. Focus on the positive.
   d. Use courteous, conversational words.
   e. Avoid unnecessary repetition.
3. Check for completeness regarding:
   a. Sentence structure
   b. Date of letter you are answering.

1. Choose Openings Appropriate for Message Purpose and Reader

Main Idea or Good-News Subject First.   Begin with the main idea or good-news subject when you are sure the reader will consider the information favorable or neutral. It is, of course, also important that the reader can understand the main idea if it is in the first paragraph. These openings are desirable in direct-request, neutral, and good-news messages.

Request:	So that the account of Mr. R. B. Jones, deceased, can be transferred to your name as Executor, will you please return to us the following:
Good news:	Three copies of <u>Brown's Garden Book</u> were sent to you today by parcel post as you requested.
Announcement (five W's):	You and your family [*who*] are invited to a machinery demonstration [*what*] next Saturday from 10 a.m. until noon [*when*] in the ballroom of the Statler Hotel [*where*]. The purpose of this demonstration is to show and explain to management the operation of the latest data processing equipment [*why*].

Buffer First.   When you have bad news for the reader, begin with a buffer—some statement on which you can agree. Don't spread gloom with your first words; try to get in step first.

Poor:	We regret your loan application did not meet our regulations and board policies for approving a loan.
Good:	Your application for a loan has received our careful attention. It is evident you are doing your best to provide a comfortable home for your family.

Attention-Getting Statements First.   When you have a persuasive request (sales letter), begin with relevant statements that will induce the recipient to read further, as in this opening to a licensed pet owner:

> Like most conscientious cat or dog owners, you know that proper food is just as important to a pet as it is to a human being. And you know, too, that if you try to make up a scientifically balanced diet for your pet, it involves more time and effort than you can spare. That's where Muskies can help!

2. Make the Opening Considerate, Courteous, Concise, Clear

Get your reader into the opening whether your message is good or bad news, a direct or persuasive request. Don't emphasize the writer. Focus on the positive, what *can* be done. Use courteous expressions, avoiding anything that might anger the reader.

Keep the first paragraph relatively short—five typewritten lines or less. As in all paragraphs, use conversational words—in clear, concise sentences. Avoid unnecessary repetition of what the reader told you.

3. Check for Completeness

Avoid opening with an incomplete sentence like:

```
Reference your letter [or Received your letter] of March 26,
concerning Ms. Helen M. Smith's application.
```

Usually, subordinate the date of the letter you are answering, but include it if doing so is beneficial to either the reader or you—generally, for record keeping.

Poor:
```
As per your recent letter, we have shipped your order
today by Railway Express.
```

Good:
```
The five dozen Conform hats you ordered October 10 were
shipped to you today by Railway Express.
```

Closing Paragraphs

The closing is more likely to motivate the reader to act as requested if it is appropriately impressive. Here you have the opportunity to bring final focus on the desired action and leave a sense of your courtesy with the reader. What you say in the closing depends on the purpose of the letter and the ideas in previous paragraphs.

The checklist and examples below again focus on ways to apply the C qualities in closings for various letter and memo situations.

■ Checklist for Closing Paragraphs

1. Make your action request clear and complete with the five W's and the H (how) if you want your reader (or someone else) to do something.
  a. *What and who:* Clearly state what action you desire and who should do it.
  b. *How* and *where:* Make action easy.
  c. *When:* Date the action, if desirable.
  d. *Why:* Show reader benefit, if possible.
2. End on a positive, courteous thought.
  a. Include any apologies and negatives before the last paragraph.
  b. Be friendly.

     c. Show appreciation.

     d. Occasionally add a personal note.

  3. Keep the last paragraph concise and correct.

     a. Avoid trite expressions.

     b. Omit discussion and worthless details.

     c. Use relatively short and complete sentences.

1. Make Action Request Clear and Complete with Five W's and H

Whenever you are requesting action by your reader or someone else, your closing paragraph will usually be more effective if you make clear *what, who, how, where, when,* and (if appropriate) *why.*

What and Who?   *Clear statement of the action you desire your reader (or someone else—perhaps even you yourself) to take.* Should the reader phone your office for an appointment? Sign a card or a document? Return it, and to whom? Come to your office in person? Send you certain details, merchandise, forms, payments, or opinions? Ask another person to do something? Give you permission to do something?

How and Where?   *Easy action.*

> Include your phone number (with area code) and extension if you want the reader to phone you.
>
> Enclose a form (card, order blank, questionnaire, document) and an addressed reply envelope (perhaps with postage paid) if you want the reader to furnish information or sign and mail something.
>
> Give complete instructions regarding *how* and *where* if you don't include a form and envelope.
>
> State your office hours and location if you want the reader to come to you in person. Do you have a free parking lot? Where?

When and Why?   *Dated action; special inducement to act by a specified time.* Name the date (and the time, if pertinent) whenever you need the reply by a certain time. Tactfully state the reason you need it then—perhaps to meet a report or printer's deadline or to use in a speech you are giving at a certain meeting.

When appropriate, mention some benefits the reader will gain by prompt action. A reader-benefit plug in the ending paragraph or paragraphs is a stimulus to action.

In the following example, notice how the vague action request is improved by inserting some of or all the W's and the H:

Vague: Please take care of this matter at your earliest
          convenience.

Better: So that we can discuss suitable arrangements for your
          meeting, please call me at 555-9900, ext. 25, before
          Thursday, June 2, any weekday between 1 and 5 p.m.

2. End on a Positive, Courteous Thought

Include Any Apologies and Negatives before Last Paragraph.   Finish with
positive statements.

Negative: I regret we cannot be more helpful in the study you
            are making.

Positive: The best of success with your term paper. You have
            an interesting topic to research.

Be Friendly.   Offer to help the reader further or again if that is appropriate.
Words like *please* or *will you* help soften commands.

Good: If you have further questions about this method, please
          write. Or call me (555-4422) any Monday or Friday
          morning.

Poor: Send us your check today.

Good: To keep your credit in good standing, please send us
          your check for $123.94 today.

Show Appreciation.   Everyone likes sincere praise when earned. But don't
thank people for doing something before they have agreed to do so.

Avoid: I thank you in advance for your cooperation in informing
          your employees of these tours.

Say: I will appreciate your cooperation in informing your
          employees of these tours.

Occasionally Add a Personal Note.   When unrelated to the subject discussed
in the message, a personal note is appropriate sometimes as an added last
paragraph or preferably as a postscript.

    You're fortunate to be in Alaska this month. Our thermometer
    registered 108°F at 3 p.m. here yesterday.

3. Keep Last Paragraph Concise and Correct

Trim your last paragraph to five or fewer lines of complete sentences. Avoid trite expressions and worthless repetition.

Poor:
```
Again, we thank you for your inquiry. Enclosed you will
find a self-addressed stamped envelope.  Hoping to hear
from you soon about your preference, I remain [or I am]
```

Good:
```
Please fill out this form and return it in the enclosed
stamped envelope by [date].  Then you can soon begin to
enjoy the comfort of. . . .
```

COMPOSITION OF THE MESSAGE

Write or Dictate Your Drafts

When you have completed the five planning steps and considered your openings and closings, you are ready for the first draft of your message.

For routine, short communications, you will usually be able to dictate or write quite easily with little or no revising. Try to compose from your outline. Choose appropriate words; construct sentences and paragraphs the reader will easily understand. Temporarily forget about mechanics of spelling, punctuation, sentence structure; you can check on them after the first draft is finished.

For other writing—especially complex, longer messages and reports, new form letters, and any communication that is to be published—you should expect to edit and revise, sometimes substantially.

Edit and Revise

After you have finished the first draft of a complex message, you will need to evaluate its content, organization, and style. The following are suggestions for editing and revising to make sure the message meets all principles of good business communication.

1. *Edit your draft objectively, with concern for your message recipient and your purpose.*
   a. Check the "C" qualities in *what* you say and *how* you say it. Is the message complete, concise, considerate, concrete, clear, courteous, and correct? (A brief summary of these principles, discussed in Chapters 3 and 4, is on the inside front cover of this book. Consider also pertinent legal aspects, Chapter 5.) Are all facts and data included accurately?
   b. Are your main ideas emphasized adequately?
   c. Are opening and closing paragraphs appropriate?
   d. Check all paragraphs for sentence structure, topic sentences, logical

presentation of facts. (For various checklists pertinent to your message see index.)

e. Does the message accomplish its purpose?

2. *Revise—several times if necessary.*

a. Delete unnecessary material.

b. Add new material where desirable.

c. If a paragraph should be moved to a different location or omitted, this can be done easily and quickly with a few keystrokes on the computer or word processor. When using a typewriter, changes can be made with scissors and tape or paste. Either way, such revisions are achieved without time-wasting retyping of the entire draft.

d. On complicated, long reports and proposals (also, important letters or memos addressed to many readers) you may need to talk over some aspects with colleagues. Whenever desirable, consider suggestions from knowledgeable associates. Be willing to revise drafts several times. Occasionally you may feel like the doubtful report writer who remarked to his supervising editor: "You mean you want the revised revision of the fifth revised revision revised?"

Top correspondents and authors have confirmed again and again that the best writers rewrite and rewrite and rewrite. Tolstoy revised *War and Peace* 5 times; James Thurber rewrote his stories as many as 15 times; Franklin D. Roosevelt's speeches often went to 18 drafts.

Proofread

Careful proofreading is also essential after your best revised business message is typewritten, and before it is mailed. Any errors in typing, spelling, punctuation, figures, names, and grammar should be corrected so that your paper will reflect favorably on you and your company. Computer software programs check many of these errors, but not all. For example, some spelling checkers search only for spelling, not for context. If a sentence is about a *house* and the word is spelled *mouse,* a human brain with good sense must find that error.

Remember, some uncorrected errors in mailed messages can be not only embarrassing but also extremely costly—in loss of goodwill, sales, income, and sometimes even lives. Advice from careful communicators is to proofread at least two or three times before signing a message.

SUMMARY

Before composing any message, consider carefully the five planning steps regarding purpose, audience, ideas, facts, organization. They furnish the basis for an effective message. Also, when you express your ideas, follow guidelines for the seven "C" principles, and consider pertinent legal aspects.

Choose a direct or indirect organizational plan, depending on your reader's (or listener's) probable reaction to the message. Pay particular attention to the opening and closing paragraphs, because of their strategic importance. After preparing your message, edit it for content, organization, and style, according to the various pertinent checklists (offered as suggestions, not rigid patterns) in this book. Wherever desirable, revise your drafts. Then see that the finished typewritten message is proofread and all errors are corrected before you sign it for mailing.

*Chapters 1 through 6 have focused on your responsibilities for composition and accurate **content** of your business messages. Another important matter is their **appearance**. Though typing each message is usually your secretary's job, you assume responsibility for everything when you sign your name on the message. Its stationery, standard and optional parts, plus format and layout all contribute to favorable or unfavorable impressions. **Appendix B** includes framed examples, guidelines, and other useful information regarding these additional features for various business messages.*

EXERCISES AND PROBLEMS

1. *Evaluations of openings:* What is your reaction to each of the openings below: Is it good, fair, or poor? Why? If two openings are given (indicated by "versus"), which do you prefer? Why?

   a. You made several errors on the reply form you submitted, and you neglected to answer three questions.

   b. Jean Doe, about whom you inquired in your July 6 letter, has kept an account with us since August 18, 1978.

   c. You have failed to correct the existing delinquency on the above-captioned loan, and furthermore, you have made no arrangements for repayment.

   d. We are in receipt of your note regarding the two toaster ovens that you say are defective.

   e. Good news! After reviewing the facts again, we are issuing the desired policy.

      versus

      This is in reply to your letter of March 19, requesting us to review the application which was previously declined.

   f. We will be pleased to consider issuing the desired policy, provided you submit a new application by November 15.

      versus

      A new application must be submitted by November 15; otherwise, we cannot consider issuing the desired policy.

   g. Congratulations on making the final payment on your home improvement loan #4-5555. We are sure you had a happy feeling of satisfaction when you could finally say to yourself, "Well, that debt is paid in full."

      versus

      Our records show that the balance on the loan account above has been paid off.

2. *Evaluations of closings:* What is your reaction to each of the closings below? Is the closing good, average, or poor? Why?

   a. `We hope our error has not inconvenienced you too much.`
   b. `When it is convenient, please let me know your decision.`

   versus

   `I trust you will avail yourself of the opportunity of mak-`
   `ing either of these changes and, when your decision is`
   `reached, notify me at your earliest convenience.  I await`
   `the pleasure of your reply.`

   c. `Please let us know when we can help you again.`
   d. `We appreciate your interest and will keep you informed of`
   `all developments.`
   e. `Hoping to hear from you, I remain. . . .`
   f. `Fill out this form and return it to me.`
   g. `As soon as you return the four completed forms, I'll air-`
   `mail one to Chicago for prompt rating.  In this way, you`
   `will receive the renewal as quickly as possible.`
   h. `Again, let me repeat how sorry I am to have not answered`
   `sooner.`

3. *Evaluations and suggested improvements for two letters:* The following two letters consist of an inquiry from a church to a bank and a reply to the inquiry.

   a. Which organizational plan does the inquiry follow?
   b. Evaluate the opening and closing paragraphs of the inquiry.
   c. What is the purpose of the reply? What organizational plan should be used?
   d. Evaluate the opening and closing paragraphs of the reply.
   e. Does the reply include the ideas necessary to fulfill the purpose? Are the ideas organized effectively? What improvements can you suggest?

INQUIRY

`Gentlemen`

`We would like to request your permission to post a church`
`directional sign "First Christian Church" with directional`
`arrow at the edge of your property parking lot on First`
`Avenue, near Central.`

`This is an attractive, small sign on a neatly painted post.`
`It is very important to our church because of the fact that`
`Central Street is probably the shortest street in [city].`
`The size of the sign is about 15 × 15 inches.`

`The exact location of the sign will be specified to us as`
`soon as we bring written permission from you and from our`
`office to Mr. Smith at City Hall.  He will then advise us as`
`to how and where to place the sign so that it will give a`

good appearance and not interfere with either traffic or
your business operations.

Please indicate your permission hereon and return your reply
to this office as soon as possible.

We appreciate your cooperation.

REPLY

Dear Reverend Glouster

Thank you for your recent letter requesting permission to
post a church directional sign in the corner of our parking
lot on First Avenue near Central.

Unauthorized parking in the lot during our business hours
has been a continuous problem for our bank. The parking lot
already has several signs posted for different purposes. An
additional sign in this corner of the parking lot could
cause the public confusion regarding the use of the parking
area. We, therefore, find it necessary to decline your
request.

Your parishioners are welcome to continue to use this parking lot on Sundays and at other times that you have church
services that do not conflict with the business hours of the
bank. We appreciate and wish to continue the cordial relationship with you and members of your church.

4. *Evaluations of reply to a displeased customer:* The following reply is
   from the Blank Fish Company, Anytown, to an out-of-state customer who
   complained that she found two "ugly specimens" in her favorite brand of
   canned shrimps.
   a. What is (should be) the purpose of this message?
   b. What organizational plan should be used?
   c. Evaluate the opening and closing paragraphs and the explanation.
   d. Point out the portions that are "resale" material and "apology." Are they
      well placed? Discuss.
   e. Do you think the letter helps restore the customer's confidence? Why?

Thank you for giving us the opportunity to reply to your
experience with Blank Brand shrimp. We appreciate your
thoughtfulness in writing.

Your enclosure turned out to be small pieces of the root
section of a common seaweed that grows on the shrimp beds in
great abundance. We are stumped how this substance could
stick to a shrimp through three successive washings and inspections in the canning process and still escape detection

by our packers. But it did, and we are sorry that it happened.

It is of little help to explain that this harmless vegetable
substance became totally sterile when the shrimp were cooked
in the can. You did exactly the right thing when you wrote
about the incident.

Today we are sending you by parcel post two cans of Blank
Brand shrimp with out compliments. You are the discriminating consumer we want to please.

5. *Revision of a wordy memo:* Assume that the following wordy memo from
   an auditor of disbursements in a head office was sent to the auditor of
   disbursements in a branch. Both work for the same organization. Your job
   is to revise this monstrosity. Can you make the revision no longer than four
   or five sentences? (A "rear support" is a metal holder for a large ledger or
   dictionary you usually find only in libraries.)

   a. What is the purpose of this memo?
   b. In seven words or less write an informational subject line.
   c. Should (or does) the writer remain neutral regarding the decision to be
      made by the reader?
   d. Is it desirable to convey that his company asked Hunter Company to
      make the shorter supports available?
   e. Make clear to whom the reader should send the unwanted supports.

We previously sent you copies of our correspondence with the
Albert M. Hunter, Inc., relative to the Hunter Wage Charts.
Particular attention is directed to our comments relative to
the rear supports $4\frac{1}{2}$ inches in length, which in our opinion
were too long, in our letter dated April 8. As a result of
our comments, Albert M. Hunter, Inc., developed rear supports $2\frac{1}{2}$ inches in length which they furnished us to replace supports $4\frac{1}{2}$ inches in length.

On July 19 we sent you by express 26 sets of the rear supports $2\frac{1}{2}$ inches in length. We are of the opinion that the
rear supports $2\frac{1}{2}$ inches in length are a considerable
improvement over the rear supports $4\frac{1}{2}$ inches in length and
have accordingly replaced the rear supports $4\frac{1}{2}$ inches in
length on the Hunter Wage Charts in use by us with rear supports $2\frac{1}{2}$ inches in length.

We assume that you will also wish to replace the rear supports $4\frac{1}{2}$ inches in length on the Hunter Wage Charts in use
by you with the rear supports $2\frac{1}{2}$ inches in length. If you
make the replacement, please return the rear supports $4\frac{1}{2}$ in
length to us in order that we can return them to Albert M.
Hunter, Inc., in accordance with their request.

```
For your information, the rear supports 2¹/₂ inches in length
to replace the rear supports 4¹/₂ inches in length were fur-
nished by Albert M. Hunter, Inc., free of charge with the
understanding that the rear supports 4¹/₂ inches in length
would be returned to them.

If you prefer to continue using the rear supports 4¹/₂ inches
in length, please return the rear supports 2¹/₂ inches in
length to us in order that we can return them to Albert M.
Hunter, Inc.
```

6. ***Revision of a wordy letter:*** Revise the following three-sentence letter—from a college bookstore to a small manufacturer. Though the purpose is stated at the beginning, the letter rambles and seems artificially friendly. Improve it wherever desirable.

```
Once again with your kind permission, will you please make
for us four armbands, blue felt, white sewn letters, and
white chain stitching as per the attached layout, and if you
please Mr. Cowell, we have marked on the layout and for the
operator to kindly make these up just as we show them, and
not change them.  What we mean by that, in a most friendly
way, this is a little order which you made up for us a few
days ago, and the operator, thinking it would be perfectly
all right, transposed the position of some of the lettering,
so that they were not uniform all the way, and too, inadver-
tently on one or two of them left one or two of the letters
out, and we are not complaining about that at all, all we
want to say sincerely is that we are grateful for your tak-
ing care of these little things for us, and we are not reg-
istering any complaint at all, for we are using them for
samples and do not expect you for one moment to do this
again without your regular charge, for you making nothing on
it, and you are just like us, we know, doing this to satisfy
a customer, we being a customer, for other things, and if we
weren't we would not have the nerve to ask you to make
these, so therefore, if you please, this is for a bunch of
women and they are a little bit more particular than men,
and if the operator will just follow what we have laid out
everything will be fine.

Thanking you so much, and with best wishes and kindest
regards, we are. . . .
```

7. ***Evaluations of three replies:*** The sales manager of Right Fit Hanger, Inc., recently wrote to three television stations asking if they would like to handle her product on a commission basis. She had heard that some stations occasionally used their open time in this manner. Which of the three replies below do you think adheres best to the writing principles for business? Why? Compare your choice with the other two replies.

REPLY A

I don't know where you got your information as stated in the opening sentence of your letter. "I have been informed that your station promotes items on a commission basis," and we don't appreciate it. If you want to do business with us, buy; if you don't, don't write us.

REPLY B

This will acknowledge your recent letter of offering your all-plastic clothes hanger on a commission basis.

I am quite sure that you did not run your advertisement in the Sunday newspaper supplement on a commission basis. By the same token, we will not accept business on a percentage or per inquiry basis.

For your information, I am attaching our rate card.

REPLY C

Your information must have been somewhat misleading inasmuch as NUTZ has never promoted items on a commission basis.

We would be delighted to handle the Right Fit hanger, and I personally think it is an item of great demand.

Enclosed is our rate card so that you can choose the time, frequency, and length of message that will promote your product as you wish it. As soon as your reply to these points reaches us, we will be glad to put all our resources at your disposal.

8. *Revision of a memo:* Revise the following memo announcement so it has better you-attitude and more active than passive verbs. Correct any other errors. This company employs both men and women to sell its products.

```
TO:        Customer Service Personnel     DATE: March 1, 199-
FROM:      Tom S. Powers
SUBJECT:   Deposit and Cash Receipt Books
```

Effective March 1, 199-, the following changes will be made in the use and care of deposit and cash receipt books by our salesmen:

1. The deposit and/or cash receipt book(s) issued to a salesman will be used only by the client to whom the book is issued.
2. Whenever a deposit or other monies are collected, the salesman will remove from the receipt book(s) the custom-

er's copy(s) and give this to the customer as is now
done. In addition, at the end of his shift, each salesman will no longer turn in the receipt book(s) with the
money and tickets for those transactions.
3. Deposit and receipt books are not to be left laying
around in a vehicle or other places. They are to be
under the strict control of the individual the book(s) is
issued to.

Normally a salesman will have one deposit book and one cash
receipt book. Additional books may be issued by a service
supervisor. All used up books are to be returned to the
supervisor for forwarding to the accounting department.

PART TWO

Major Plans for Letters and Memos

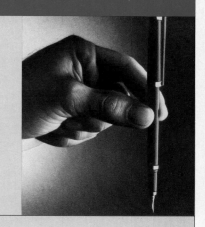

Chapter 7

Direct Requests

After you have completed the planning steps—regarding your purpose, audience, pertinent ideas, and needed facts—you can concentrate on organizing and composing your message.

When the main purpose of your written message is to ask the reader to answer questions or do something, you are writing a *request* letter or memo. Whether you organize it according to the *direct-* or the *persuasive*-request plan depends on the nature of the request and, most of all, on how you think the reader will react to that request. You can usually handle the following messages with the direct (deductive) approach:

> Inquiries
>
> Claims (routine complaints) and requests for adjustments
>
> Requests regarding routine business or public causes
>
> Invitations, orders, reservations
>
> Early-stage collection messages

This chapter outlines briefly the direct-request organizational plan, discusses the first four types of direct requests, then compares them briefly in capsule checklists. Chapter 14 discusses early-stage collection messages.

ORGANIZATIONAL PLAN

For a routine inquiry or request you assume that the reader will—without persuasion—do as you request, when he or she understands what you want and why you want it. Thus you use the direct-request plan, discussed in Chapter 6. Though direct requests vary in content, they have three basic parts:

> 1. Main idea—your request or question, statement, and reason
> 2. Explanation—details needed to help the reader respond correctly
> 3. Courteous close—with motivation to whatever action is desired

INQUIRIES

To get facts you need and cannot conveniently or economically obtain yourself, you write inquiries requesting information. The questions asked are important in all inquiries, whether they are in a letter, memo, or long survey questionnaire. Thus, this section begins with suggestions about phrasing and arranging questions. Then follows a discussion of direct requests that seek information about persons and messages inquiring about products, services, and other matters requiring no persuasion.

Wording and Arrangement of Questions

So that you can get exactly the information wanted, you must be especially careful when planning the questions to be included in your inquiries.[1] The following suggestions apply to all kinds of direct-request inquiries:

1. Make your questions specific. If the product about which you inquire is technical, include specific physical dimensions, technical specifications, exact intended use of the item, architectural drawings, or whatever else will help the respondent. A single general question such as "Will you give us any information you can on this applicant [*or product*]?" will probably bring a reply so general that it will be almost useless.

2. Use a separate paragraph for each main question if it requires explanations.

3. If you have more than one question, consider numbering them. If you have only a few short questions, you may place them in the body of your letter. If you ask more questions and they require explanations, it is generally better to list them on a separate sheet or sheets. Allow enough space for adequate answers.

4. Word your questions to get more than "yes" or "no" answers if you need a detailed opinion or description. For example a yes or no answer to "Did the applicant have duties that required responsibility?" would probably be inadequate. To obtain a more helpful answer, you might ask: "What kinds of duties requiring responsibility did the applicant perform especially well?" In contrast, a yes or no answer would be adequate for such a question as "Does the applicant have an account with you?"

5. Word some questions for simple checking of "Yes," "No," or "Don't know" if you send a questionnaire to a list of persons and you plan to tabulate numerous answers.

6. Cover only one topic in each question. "How long is your product guaranteed, and do you accept c.o.d. orders?" should be in two separate questions.

7. If you wish the respondent to rate a person, product, or service, it may be better to define each category on your rating scale. For instance, the following example shows one of eight questions on an employer's questionnaire about an applicant for employment. Notice how both the squares and the definitions make responses easy. The best choices may be placed at the right (as in the example) or at the left, but consistent placement of best choices is more convenient for both the reference and you—especially if you must compare many replies.

```
ABILITY TO GET ALONG WITH OTHERS
  Is the applicant a likable, friendly, and tactful per-
  son, or an egotistical, unpleasant, or thoughtless per-
```

son? Will this person attract the people with whom he
or she deals or keep them at a distance? Is he or she
poised in normal social situations? (Check one.)

☐	☐	☐	☐	☐
Egotis- tical, un- friendly, or tact- less	Somewhat neutral, does not easily attract friends	Approach- able	Likable, friendly, and tactful	Excep- tionally pleasant and agreea- ble; will attract others

8. Carefully arrange your questions—generally starting with the ones that are easiest to answer.

9. Word your questions in a neutral way so you will not influence the answers.

Inquiries about Persons

When you need information about a person, you usually direct your request to a reference—a responsible source of information. You ask the reference—by phone or letter—to give information about an applicant for a job, a loan, credit, membership in an organization, an award, or some special training or insurance protection.

Inquiries to a reference may be made by the applicant or, more frequently, by the person who seeks information about the applicant.

Applicant's Request to a Reference

Sometimes an applicant asks references if they will send a recommendation directly to someone who needs confidential information about that applicant. For instance, suppose you are seeking admission into a graduate school that requires at least four confidential recommendations. Perhaps you can approach some of your selected references in person or by telephone. To others, however (if they are out of town or if you have a questionnaire they need to fill out), you will have to write a letter.

In the first paragraph it is courteous to state why you are writing to this person and what the recommendation is for. If you haven't been in touch with the references for some time, you may need to refresh their memory about who you are.

The explanation should include a brief summary of pertinent facts about yourself. If, for example, the reference is a former professor, you might choose, from the following, a few facts that would be appropriate.

1. The course you studied under the reference—when, where, and your grade.

2. Your major and your grade-point average (GPA) in the major.

3. Your overall GPA in college.

4. Positions you held and dates employed.

5. Honors, honor societies (Phi Beta Kappa, Beta Gamma Sigma, etc.), studies in any special honors programs, scholarships awarded.

6. Leadership qualities; for example, offices held in living group, on campus, or in political groups.

7. Activities—tutoring, United Nations Model Congress, etc.

8. Guidelines, if possible, for the recommendation. Enclose, if you can, a form or letter from the graduate school, stating what information it seeks from the reference about you—distinguishing intellectual traits or abilities, leadership capacity, quality of work done, character, integrity, or other traits.

9. Statement of your goals and objectives.

Your closing should state to whom the letter or form is to be sent. State the full name and address, unless this information is printed on the form. And, of course, include a statement of appreciation. (Many colleges now supply preprinted forms for the applicant and the recommender to complete. The recommender's statement is sent to the college placement office, then duplicated for prospective employers or graduate schools.)

If it is necessary for you to obtain recommendations about your work in specific courses or jobs in which your work was just mediocre, be sure to provide an explanation regarding the quality of your work, if possible. In Figure 7-1 (Inquiry 1) the applicant shows consideration for the reader by courteous tone, by the facts included about courses she studied, by mention of factors that influenced the quality of her chemistry studies, and by the reasonable time allowed for response.

Inquirer's Request to a Reference

The most frequent requests to references are those telephoned or written by persons who need confidential information about an applicant. Suppose, for example, that you are the employer, lender, creditor, insurance underwriter, or officer of any organization that is considering an applicant for a special reason. The inquiry, whether by phone or letter, to each reference the applicant has listed can be organized according to the direct-request pattern.

Your opening statements (oral or written) usually include the applicant's full name, and why you are calling or writing to the reference.

The explanatory section should include:

1. Sufficient details about the requirements of the job, loan, credit, scholarship, or membership for which the applicant is being considered.

4963 Cloverdale Avenue
[City, State, ZIP]
February 10, 199-

Professor James R. Hartstrom
320 Mason Chemistry Building
State University
[City, State, ZIP]

Dear Professor Hartstrom:

Introduction of request and reason

This letter is to reintroduce myself and to ask a favor of you. The University of *[name]* Dental School has requested a recommendation from my organic chemistry professor.

Explanation: details about past relationship

Almost three years ago--in winter and spring quarters *[year]*-- you were my chemistry professor at State University. The courses I took from you were Chemistry 241 and 242; both met at 3 p.m. Monday through Friday. The grades I received were C's, but I believe I would have done better if circumstances had been different that year. Besides the lapse of two years between my inorganic and organic studies, my part-time job in the Applied Physics laboratory was until 3 p.m. four days a week. Because this work caused me to come to your class about 15 minutes late, I sometimes missed important laboratory work, a fact that necessarily affected my grade. In our several conferences, however, you often commented very favorably on my work.

More details, leading to reason for this request

Currently I am a senior, graduating this quarter with a grade point average of 3.03 (out of 4.0) in Business Administration. I am applying for admission to the Dental School at the University of *[name]*. To this date I have completed successfully all the predental requirements, and want to begin dental studies next fall.

Easy and dated action

The enclosed Reference Form is one the Dental School requires regarding my studies in organic chemistry. Professor Hartstrom, will you please fill out and return this form in the enclosed stamped envelope to the admissions officer? I will appreciate your mailing this information within the next two weeks--before the admissions deadline March 1.

Sincerely,

Elizabeth A. Franklin

Elizabeth A. Franklin

Enclosure

Figure 7-1   Inquiry 1   *An applicant's well-written request to a former professor.*

2. If appropriate, a few pertinent facts the applicant has already told you—such as length of time worked for the reference, job title, achievements. This way you can check on the applicant's accuracy and honesty.

3. Clearly stated questions (preferably numbered, if the request is in writing) courteously asking exactly what you want to know about the applicant. They may include relevant information about unique capabilities, character, special qualities. Be sure preemployment questions meet legal requirements. For suggestions, see Chapter 5.

Comments in the last or next-to-last paragraph usually include, if possible, a promise of confidential treatment of the reply, and (if appropriate) provisions for easy action. When you write to a business executive at a business address, you can usually omit the enclosed easy-action reply envelope because many business executives prefer to use their own firm's stationery. However, when you write to a reference at home (for instance, to a personal reference whose business address is unknown to you) or to someone who may be in a one-person office or in a nonprofit organization, it is appropriate to enclose a stamped reply envelope.

To save space, most examples in this and following chapters include only the body of each message, without the letterhead and other parts. You can assume the salutation is the usual "Dear Mr. [Mrs., Miss, Ms.]" plus the reader's surname unless otherwise indicated. Please refer to Appendix B for framed examples of letters, memos, envelopes, and some special time-saving messages. It includes also format and layout guidelines for various standard and optional parts of these messages.

The letter below (inquiry 2) is from a hardware store manager to a reference who is a department store manager in another city.

INQUIRY 2   *Personal request listing numbered questions in letter.*

Name; why being considered; reason for request

Mr. Victor Dryer, one of your former employees, has applied here for a position as assistant manager of our electrical supplies department. He gave your name as a reference.

A few facts; appreciation; request

We need a qualified person who can, in about two years, become department manager. Mr. Dryer states that he was in charge of your electrical appliances section for about a year. I will appreciate your frank answers to the following questions and any other pertinent facts you can include:

1. When was he in your employ and why did he leave?

Questions

2. How satisfactory were his services as a section head in your store?
3. Do you know of any personal habits or characteristics that might hinder or help his success in a position of responsibility?

A promise

Your statements will, of course, be kept confidential. I look forward to your helpful reply.

Inquiry 3 is an exceptionally thorough inquiry that interweaves explanation and unnumbered questions for each qualification. It is an example of the care that a reputable firm takes in placing an outstanding candidate. (Also, some questions might occur over the telephone.)

INQUIRY 3   *Personalized request interweaving explanations with questions.*

Full name;
reason for request

We are seriously considering Ms. Barbara Rankin for a position in our research department. As she gave your name for a reference, I will appreciate your comments.

Details—
applicant's work

Ms. Rankin has been working in a part time clerical position for about a year in our branch office. Now she has expressed interest in getting into more professional work and pursuing her career in writing for our head office.

Details; specific
request and
explanation

Because of Ms. Rankin's outstanding record in college, and the fine work she has done for us, we are making every effort to find, or create, a position for her here. For that reason I am asking for help in finding out as much as possible about her relative strengths and weaknesses. We can then do a better job of fitting her talents to our needs and in assigning her work that is neither beyond her present capacity nor out of line with her interests and skills.

Two implied
questions

Ms. Rankin, I understand, worked about two years part time in your advertising office. I will welcome information about how effectively and concisely she writes, particularly how readily she can compose business letters to advertisers.

In addition, may I have your impressions of her in the following areas:

Question with details	`--Ability to organize her work`
	`--Originality, initiative, reliability`
	`--Ability to work smoothly with others while under pressure`
	`--Degree of supervision and guidance under which she is likely to do her best work.`

A promise	`Any and all comments you may care to make will be a great help and, of course, will be viewed as confidential.`
Easy action (phone)	`I will appreciate either a letter or a collect phone call from you, whichever you prefer. You can reach me at [area code and phone number], usually between 9:00 and 11:30 Monday through Friday.`

For a personnel department that needs references on hundreds of new applicants, sheer volume will require a duplicated form that can be used again and again. Some paragraphs may then have spaces for typewritten fill-ins:

`____[name]____ of ____[city]____ states that he or she was em-`
`ployed by you as ____[type of work]____ from ____[date]____ to`
`____[date]____ . Your name is listed as a reference.`

After the explanation of what is needed and a courteous request, the questions are stated. These may be open-ended with space for detailed comments, or similar to the illustration in suggestion 7, pages 141 and 142, or to this example:

Your Estimate of:	Superior	Good	Average	Below Average	Unsatis-factory	Comments
Potential ability to sell a quality product						
Personality						

At the end of the questionnaire form, lines are provided for the reference's signature, title, and date of reply.

Inquiries about Products or Services

Both as a consumer and as a business- or professional person, you will have many occasions to seek information from the seller of products and services or from customers, employees, and others.

Direct Request to the Seller

When your inquiry goes to a seller—whether a manufacturer, retailer, investment broker, or hotel clerk—the addressee's self-interest should make him or her glad to comply with your wishes. Perhaps you want a free catalog, price list, or booklet about products, deliveries, or payment plans. At such times your complete direct request need be only one sentence, such as:

> Please send me your latest sporting equipment catalog and the descriptive folder you advertised in the April issue of <u>Sportsman Illustrated</u>.

If, however, you have a unique problem, you may need to ask questions for which the recipient does not have prepared answers. Following the direct-request plan, present your main idea (request, reason, or both) in the first paragraph. For most inquiries to a seller concerning a product or service, it is entirely optional whether to present the request or reason first. But if you think your request is somewhat unusual or will be time-consuming for the reader to answer, state the reason first. After the opening paragraph, include all needed explanations and questions. The final paragraph contains the action request.

Inquiry 4 is written by a purchasing manager requesting information from a distributor about a product she is considering buying. Notice that the letter begins with the major request, but if you prefer to begin with the reason, you might interchange paragraphs 1 (request) and 3 (reason).

INQUIRY 4 *About a product praised in a newspaper article; numbered questions in letter to writer/distributor, dated March 17.*

Major request

Your article in the March 15 [*name*] newspaper attracted our attention regarding serious risks of contracting cancer from chemically contaminated drinking water in this area. We will appreciate answers to the following questions about the Solid Carbon Block filters you highly recommend:

Specific numbered questions

1. In what sizes are these filters available?
2. Of what materials are they constructed?
3. What is the price of each filter size?
4. How many filters should an office like ours install? The two drinking fountains we have are for our customers and 20 employees. Also, in the small employee lounge is a water faucet they use for the water they drink, or add to coffee and tea if they prefer.
5. What guarantee do you offer?

Reason for request

Before deciding whether our firm should invest in one or several water purification products, we need as much information as possible about leading brands.

| **Suggested action** | ```
If you have a factory agent in this region, we
will welcome a demonstration before April 25,
preferably after receiving your written reply
to these five questions.
``` |

Direct Requests to Customers, Employees, and Others

As the seller of products or services, you can often use direct-request inquiries to win back "missed" customers who have not bought from your firm for some time. You can also obtain information and opinions from customers and others about your firm's products or services.

"Miss-You" Messages.   Many firms have revived hundreds of unused accounts by mailing a series of direct requests—ranging from colorful postcards to form letters on specially designed stationery. Such messages concentrate on telling readers they are missed, appreciated, and important and on asking them to come back. Some may also ask what is wrong, as in inquiry 5. Then if the former customers have a complaint, they can express it; if they have none, they will probably say so and perhaps place another order. Either way, the silence has been broken, and a dead account may be revived. Also, the firm may have gained useful comments about its products or services.

INQUIRY 5   *Miss-you letter aiming for an answer to "What is wrong?"*

| **Main idea** | ```
Perhaps you have the answer to a question that has
worried us.  For a long time no order or mail has
arrived here from you.
``` |
| **Explanation** | ```
We have missed the privilege of serving you--a good
business friend.  Often we have asked ourselves:
"What did we do or say to offend this good customer?  What causes this absence?"  We've checked
all the orders and correspondence from you, plus
our shipment schedules and prices to you--and
everything looks OK.  But something must be wrong,
to keep you from us so long.
``` |
| **Request and easy action** | ```
Please tell us about it frankly.  Let us help if
possible.  Just write your note on the margin or
back of this letter and mail it in the enclosed
postpaid envelope addressed to me.  We will very
much appreciate your reply.
``` |

Other Inquiries about Your Firm's Products or Services.   Often you will need information from employees, colleagues, or other persons. Whenever questions are easy to answer and no persuasion is necessary, messages similar to inquiry 6, a *memo* launching an employee survey, can be adapted to other readers—inside or outside your organization

INQUIRY 6   *Memo seeking employee needs and preferences about parking on company premises; questionnaire attached.*

```
TO:       All employees        DATE: May 1, 199-
FROM:     Parking Division, Personnel Department
SUBJECT:  Your preferences about parking permits
```

Reader benefit

In an effort to improve the parking situation for all employees, the parking division is conducting a survey of your needs and preferences.

Request and dated action

Will you please fill out the attached questionnaire and return it, unsigned, to your supervisor by Friday, May 8, at 5 p.m. Then you will be sure that your feelings are included in the survey. The results of employee opinions and suggestions will be tabulated and announced at the next employee meeting, May 15.

CLAIMS (COMPLAINTS) AND REQUESTS FOR ADJUSTMENTS

Whenever you are dissatisfied with a product, service, or policy, it is to your advantage—and the company's—to communicate with the right person promptly about the desired correction. Oral complaints to sales representatives or clerks often do not bring desired results. A better procedure is to write an effective letter to the proper company official who does care when a problem exists and who will do something to correct it. Most business managers want to please customers.

When you state your complaint, you usually make a claim or request for some kind of adjustment. All such requests are grouped together in this section and labeled *claim letters*. Claim letters should be organized by the direct-request pattern whenever they involve a routine matter that is covered by a guarantee or by established procedures for customer relations.

Typical situations for direct-request claims about merchandise involve defective materials or workmanship, malfunctioning parts, soiled or shopworn items, or products that are not what customers ordered. Claims about services include delivery mix-ups, broken promises, discourtesy, carelessness, clerical or bookkeeping errors, and minor inconveniences relating to violation of published company policies. (For those claims that involve controversial issues, substantially large sums of money, repeated errors, and other serious matters, you will need to write a persuasive request, as discussed in Chapter 10.)

Characteristics of Well-Written Claims

To be fair to the seller, product or service, and yourself—write promptly. Also, be sure your letter has all the C qualities. Show by your attitude and wording that *you have confidence in the readers' fairness*—confidence that they will make the adjustment after they get the facts.

When you complain about the poor condition of a product, for instance, state all the pertinent facts logically, courteously, and impersonally, without exaggeration or irrelevant material. Guesses and opinions about who may be to blame are unwise and unhelpful. Let the reader determine causes; you present specific facts as you see them. And when your purpose is to call attention to employees' poor service, make clear you are doing so because you think the behavior is not representative of the firm's usually good customer relations policies. Cite phone call records of the date and time each call was made as well as the name of the person spoken to.

Anger and name-calling are, of course, taboo. Antagonizing the recipient merely lowers the chances of satisfactory adjustment—or at least of being considered a reasonable person. One extra caution: When you write as an agent for your employer or business, you must be even more careful to avoid tactless, intemperate accusations. Such outbursts not only reflect unfavorably on you and your company, but also may place you in danger of a libel suit.

Also, a good letter may state both sides of the case. For example, you might comment (in the explanation) on something you *like* about the firm's products or service. Even humor (not sarcasm) is appropriate when the matter is relatively small.

Organization and Content of the Simple Direct Claim

Begin your direct claim with the main idea—the need for an adjustment or correction of an error. State your account number, the date, or both, and the number of the invoice, sales slip, or work order. Such facts can be on a subject line or within the first or second paragraph.

In the explanatory paragraph or paragraphs include all facts the reader will need to understand your claim clearly. For instance, if you wish free repairs on an item that is malfunctioning within the guarantee period, present evidence of the date of your purchase, model number, price; make it clear that you followed carefully the operating instructions (if you did); and state clearly what is wrong.

In your action paragraph, ask for what you want, or leave the decision to your reader. Depending on the circumstances, you will usually request one or more of the following:

1. Refund—for all or part of purchase price (as in claim 1).

2. A new shipment with the correct item ordered (claim 1).

3. Free replacement of defective parts, the whole item, whole shipment, or service (claim 2). Often it is better not to return goods until you have the seller's instructions (and suggestions for a satisfactory adjustment).

4. Free repairs.

5. Reduction in the price (because of a product or service defect).

6. Free inspection, leading to redecorating, complete overhaul, etc.

7. Explanation of or change in policy or procedure (claim 2).

8. Credit to your account (or a credit slip).

9. Cancellation of an order or part of an order.

10. Correction (and perhaps explanation) of a billing error.

CLAIM 1   *(Dated June 9) to a sportswear department manager, from an out-of-town cash customer who needs an exchange or a refund.*

Main idea: request and reason	Enclosed is the sweater that Nelson's delivery truck left here yesterday and which I wish to exchange for the correct size or a refund.
Explanatory details	When I selected and purchased this Hudson sweater in your department last week, on June 4 (for $40.50 cash), I asked that a size L be sent to my home. The size I received is an S, and of course I can't wear it. My sales check is #7902, dated June 4, written by salesclerk #801.
Specific request Dated action	Please send me the correct size L in exactly this same style and color or, if this is not available now, a cash refund of $40.50. As I am leaving on a trip June 18, it is necessary that I receive the sweater or the check before that date.

Claim 2 concerns faulty products sent to a business firm. Notice that the writer presents facts without anger and with a good you-attitude.

CLAIM 2   *A gift store owner's considerate complaint to a wholesaler.*

Main idea: request and need for adjustment	Your shipment of Excel tumblers—invoice no. 48165—was checked in yesterday and put on sale, then hurriedly withdrawn when the stockroom reported it contains completely defective products. We are asking you for an adjustment on these tumblers.
	The news about this shipment was especially disappointing to us because we had already advertised that the sale was to begin today. I personally washed and examined a dozen glasses of each size, four each of which (not neces-

Details

> sarily the worst) we are sending you by express for your examination and comment.
>
> The mars, scratches, and abrasions, or whatever the defects should be termed, do not indicate faulty moulds. In fact, I've never seen anything in domestic or imported glass to equal the variety of imperfections apparently present to some degree in every glass of this shipment.

You-attitude

> I realize fully that you had no opportunity to check this merchandise and that only through your customers can you learn of its condition and in turn seek an adjustment from the factory.

Action

> We are withholding sale of the glasses and payment of the bill until we hear from you regarding a satisfactory adjustment with a shipment of desirable products.

REQUESTS REGARDING ROUTINE BUSINESS OR PUBLIC CAUSES

The messages in this section include business or professional people's requests that are directly related to routine business or to public issues that affect their firm or industry. The discussions and examples are grouped in two categories—whether the requests go to persons outside or within the organization.

Requests to Persons Outside Your Organization

As a business or professional person you may need to ask your customer, supplier, transportation company, or others to sign an enclosed signature card or document. Or you may need missing answers on a customer's credit application, or a correction of an irregularity in a check sent to your firm. Also, you may have requests for public officials about concerns that are in the best interests of your community, business, or industry. These and numerous other matters may be handled by the direct-request plan.

Notice that the following letters are concise, clear, courteous. And they begin with the reason or the request (or a statement that leads to the request) either in the first paragraph or at the beginning of the second.

When a similar request goes to several or many customers, you can use processed form letters. Each may be personalized with the reader's name, address, salutation, and pertinent specific insertions in certain places, as was done, for instance, in request 2.

REQUEST 1   *A bank's trust department asks an estate executor to return an affidavit, signature card, and passbook (individually typed message).*

Reason; request	So that we can transfer the account of Mr. R. S. Roe, deceased, to your name as Executor, will you please do the following:
Specific requests; on separate lines for emphasis	--Sign the enclosed affidavit. --Fill out the enclosed card and sign it. --Return to us the signed affidavit, card, and your passbook #222-222.
Reader benefit; easy action	The same day these important materials reach us, we will transfer the funds to a new account, with no loss of earnings. Please use the enclosed airmail envelope to speed your reply.

REQUEST 2   *From the customer services manager of a mortgage loan firm to a recent borrower, regarding insurance premium payments (personalized form letter).*

Reader benefit and main idea	Your Homeowner's Mortgage Protector insurance that you purchased recently provides valuable benefits for you and your family. As the policy certificate states, the insurance premium must be paid each month along with the mortgage installment.
Thanks and specific request	Thank you for your check in payment of your April 1 mortgage installment that arrived on time. Please send the [amount] insurance premium to reach us before April 8.
Request, with future specific payment amount, due date, and reader benefit	Next month and for all future months just combine your mortgage and insurance payments into one check for [amount]. Please mail it on or before the first day of each month. Then you'll be sure your property is protected.

In request letters to public officials the opening paragraph may preferably begin with the main idea, then mention a reason, and end with a frank request, as in the following example:

From a business executive to a senator in Washington, D.C.:

The proposal to increase the truck weight and sizes on the interstate highway system deserves your serious consideration. I believe such an increase would be extremely unwise and wish to join the many others who ask that you oppose such a measure.

For a direct request pertaining to a civic cause or public officials, see the checklists on whatever type of situation best applies. If you prefer, merely follow the Direct-Request General Plan in the first column and, as always, use your good judgment about what details to include.

Requests to Persons within Your Organization

The memos included here are straightforward requests exchanged between employees, colleagues, supervisors and subordinates, who are part of an organization. (Most memos of authorization for special studies and reports also fall in this direct-request group, as shown on page 536.)

The next example illustrates a manager's request to six persons within his organization. Notice its good features—the five numbered details for easy reading and the definite, courteous instructions about the desired action.

REQUEST 3   *Memo from a sales manager asking field representatives to send monthly reports.*

TO:	Ron Lenheart	Dick Robinson
	Mary Mason	Emma Simpson
	Tom Nedlock	Harold Tompkins

FROM: James Pearson   DATE: May 10, 199–
SUBJECT: Monthly Reports

Request

Starting June 9, will each of you please submit to this office a monthly report including the following information:

Numbered details

1. Major orders received during the previous month
2. Lost orders the previous month
3. Anticipated major orders for the current month
4. Industrial trends in your area
5. General comments or suggestions about problems

Helpful sample

A sample report form you will use is attached. In your June 9 report, items 1 and 2 will focus on the month of May, and item 3 will mention major orders for June 199–.

Clear statement of when and where report should be sent

On or before the 9th of every month, please mail your monthly report to me, and a copy to Gail Rankin, our controller. Our addresses are at the bottom of the report form.

Courtesy

```
I will appreciate your cooperation. The in-
formation is essential for our company rec-
ords and overall plans.  We look forward to
receiving your first report by June 9.
```

INVITATIONS, ORDERS, RESERVATIONS

Though quite different from each other, invitations, orders, and reservations are similar in that the reader is asked for participation, merchandise, or facilities. They use the direct approach.

Invitations

Invitations that require no persuasion can be classified as both good-news announcements (Chapter 8) and simple requests. Regardless of how you classify them, they are organized according to the same three-part plan: main idea, explanation, action.

The main idea in the first paragraph is the invitation request. Try to include in it as many of the five W's as you can. In the explanation paragraph of your direct-request invitation, include all details that your reader will appreciate and need. The ending paragraph clearly states the desired reader action and makes the action easy. If you need a reply by a certain date, be sure to say so, as in the following letter to business executives. The salutation is "Dear Alpha member."

Request

```
The next meeting of Alpha is one you are espe-
cially invited to attend.  As your yearbook
shows, this is
```

What
Who

```
     The FORUM RECEPTION, sponsored jointly by
        the Chamber of Commerce and our Club

                  to be held
```

**Where

```
        at Lake City Community Hall, [address]
```

When

```
   on Thursday, April 21, 199-, 3:30-5:30 p.m.
```

A detail about the program

```
A highlight of the program is the panel dis-
cussion on the topic "Problems of the Small-
Business Executive in King County."  You will
find the discussion timely, challenging, and
thought-provoking.
```

Easy action; dated

```
To make your reservation, please call either
Trish Norden (555-7777) or Mike Browne (555-
9999) before Tuesday, April 19, 5 p.m. How
about phoning right now while you think of it?
```

Reader benefit

> For your convenience, free parking is avail-
> able on the north side of the hall. We look
> forward to receiving your reservation and to
> seeing you April 21 at the reception and
> program.

Orders and Reservations

When you are ordering supplies or equipment and do not have an order blank or a purchase form of the company with which you are placing the order, you can accomplish your purpose by writing a letter according to the direct-request plan. The same is true when you wish to reserve hotel accommodations, a meeting room, parking facilities for a conference, or any other premises. In both order and reservation messages, the main idea in the first paragraph is that you are ordering or reserving something. Your explanatory paragraphs give whatever details the order or reservation requires. The last paragraph focuses on desired action.

Order letters include three kinds of facts: details about *what you are ordering, directions for shipment,* and *manner of payment.* State clearly the quantity, color, style, size, price, payment, location, shipment date, place—plus any special instructions your reader might need. The following letter illustrates the organization and content of an order letter with items tabulated for easy reading.

Request

> Please ship via United Parcel Service (UPS)
> the following supplies to reach our main of-
> fice at 9251 Grand Avenue [*city, state, ZIP*] by
> Wednesday, June 3.

Quantity	Description (and/or Unit catalog number)	Price	Total

Details

		Total	$_____

Payment

> These items are to be charged to our account
> on the usual 2/10, net 30 terms.

Shipment;
courtesy

> As we plan to distribute the ballpoint pens
> for customer gifts on the opening day of our
> new branch, June 5, this shipment must arrive
> on time. We count on your company's usual
> promptness in filling orders.

To reserve hotel accommodations and other premises, the content of your explanatory paragraphs will depend somewhat on the event and number of persons needing rooms.

- If you are reserving for one or two people, you may need to state only dates, preferred room size, location, any special facilities required, and inquire about rental fees.
- If, however, you are chairperson of a conference for 200 expected attendants, your letter will require many other details. These may include inquiries about available meeting rooms, sizes, seating arrangements, lecterns, visual equipment, exhibit tables; facilities for meals; parking; and rates. (Hotels usually provide reservation forms for the meeting attendants to mail regarding their preferred rooms, arrival times, and payments.)

SUMMARY

The eight Capsule Checklists on pages 168 and 169 provide a quick summary of each type of direct request discussed in this chapter—inquiries; complaints; requests about routine business or public concerns; and invitations, orders, and reservations that all require no persuasion. In direct-request messages, introduce your main idea at or near the beginning, include whatever details your reader needs, and end courteously with easy and dated action, if appropriate.

Caution: Remember that *these Capsule Checklists—and all others in this text—are to be used only as guidelines and reminders, NOT as "recipe lists."* In every message, use your best judgment for planning and wording of content after you have considered your purpose, reader, facts, and pertinent circumstances.

EXERCISES AND PROBLEMS

Inquiries about Persons, Products, Services

1. *Evaluations:* Comment orally on the good and poor qualities of the following inquiries about persons (sent to references). Which ones do you think will best accomplish their purpose? Why?

   a. *From a national oil company:*

   > We are considering Mr. Lawrence Jones for a position with this company, and he has given your name as a personal reference.
   >
   > May we have your frank comment as to his ability and personal qualities? Do you know of any reason for our not giving him full confidence? We shall appreciate any additional comments that will help us in reaching a correct decision, and also in adapting him to our organization if we employ him.

Since this matter is very active at present, we shall appreciate a prompt reply and are enclosing a stamped and self-addressed envelope for this purpose.

b. *From the Big Brother volunteer service organization to "Dear Mr. Wills" (subject line is "About: Robert Zurbach"):*

The above-named gentleman has applied to us to serve as a Big Brother. He has given your name as a reference.

We feel you, in your contacts with him, would be able to advise us as to his stability and moral character. As a Big Brother, he will be working with a young, fatherless boy, establishing a friendship and offering moral and character guidance to the boy.

We would like your frank appraisal, which will be held in strict confidence. Since your evaluation is necessary to complete the application, we will appreciate hearing from you soon.

c. *Night letter telegram from a regional utility company:*

ROBERTA R ADSEN BEING CONSIDERED FOR POSITION AS MANAGE-MENT TRAINEE, ULTIMATE ASSIGNMENT TO KEY STAFF IN PUBLIC RELATIONS, HAS GIVEN YOUR NAME AS REFERENCE. WE WOULD APPRECIATE IMMEDIATE NIGHT LETTER COLLECT STATING TO WHICH DEGREES (A. OUTSTANDING, B. VERY GOOD, C. ADEQUATE, D. UN-SATISFACTORY) APPLICANT POSSESSES THE FOLLOWING QUALITIES: (1) MENTAL ABILITY--ALERTNESS, OPEN-MINDEDNESS, FLEXIBIL-ITY, (2) SOCIAL ADJUSTMENT--COURTESY, TACT, COOPERATIVE-NESS, (3) SELF-EXPRESSION--CLARITY, COHERENCE, SENTENCE CONSTRUCTION, SPEECH DIRECTNESS, (4) APPEARANCE, BEARING, MANNER. PLEASE ADD ANY OTHER PERTINENT INFORMATION IN-CLUDING MATURE JUDGMENT, STRENGTHS, OR WEAKNESSES BASED ON HER ACADEMIC STANDING OR YOUR PERSONAL KNOWLEDGE.

d. *Letter used by a law school to get information about the many applicants who seek admisstion (subject line has applicant's name):*

The above-named person has applied for admission into [*school*] Law School. Because your name was listed as a reference, we will appreciate a letter of recommendation from you.

No special form is required. Letters should be detailed, with frank appraisals of the applicant as to (1) qualities of intellect, (2) communication skills, (3) character, (4) maturity, (5) personality. Comparisons of

the applicant with other students known by you to have
been admitted to law school are helpful.

2. ***Evaluations:*** Prepare to discuss orally the strengths and weaknesses of the
following letters designed to get information. Comment particularly on organization clarity, completeness of explanations, and motivation for action.

   a. *To subscribers of a magazine (salutation is "Dear Journal Reader"):*

> You're right. Another questionnaire. But we feel it's
> an important one, and the short time required to complete
> it should be well spent, for it will help shape the course
> YOUR magazine, the <u>Journal</u>, will take in important years
> ahead.
>
> We say YOUR magazine because it's written and edited
> with readers like you in mind. That's why the editors
> would like to take stock of what you like and dislike
> about the <u>Journal</u>. What parts are good? What needs im-
> provement? What might be cut down or eliminated? What
> might be added?
>
> Your answers will help the <u>Journal</u> keep in step with
> the rapidly changing field of [*name of field*].
>
> You will note that we have not provided a space for
> your signature. This is by design. We believe that ano-
> nymity will produce more straight-from-the-shoulder opin-
> ion and constructive criticism. Thank you for your help.

   b. *From a firm of research counselors in New York to an addressee in a
state 2,500 miles away. The addressee is an employee of a city light
company (letter is an obvious form with a "Dear Sir" salutation):*

> May we ask a favor that takes only a minute of your time?
> We are conducting a special study to help determine how
> familiar people in industry are with one of our clients.
>
> We would appreciate it very much if you would answer the
> questions on the attached sheet and return the question-
> naire to us in the enclosed stamped, addressed envelope.
> Your reply will be confidential, of course, and the re-
> sults of the study will be shown in statistical form only.

3. ***Inquiry to suppliers of word processing equipment:*** Assume you are
purchasing manager for Ajax Company, an industrial firm with 1,100 employees. You desire to install a word processing center in your company to
cut down on the cost of processing your daily paper load. You will need
equipment to take care of (1) original input (machine, handwritten, or central

dictation), (2) reproduction (composer systems such as magnetic tape type-writers, paper tape typewriters, or copying machines), (3) the delivery system (PBX, private wire, telephone, or various other options), (4) the storage file (magnetic tape or cards, paper tapes, computer storage, microfiche, micro-film, or office storage file cabinet).

From several suppliers that handle word processing equipment you will request the following information: what different models are available, spe-cial features of each model, estimated price of equipment, service policy cost, in-service training availability, portability, facility needed to house equipment, and noise level when in operation. (You intend to compare the information you receive from the various suppliers, make a decision in two months on purchase for your firm, and present this to your board of direc-tors.)

Write a letter that can be sent to several companies, requesting the information you will need.

4. ***Memo—customer's damaged calculator, watch, etc.:*** You are the owner of a seafood restaurant in the downtown area of your city. On January 8, Alfred Carlyle was in the lounge area waiting to be seated for dinner when a cocktail waitress accidentally spilled beer over the contents of his open briefcase. To make matters worse, the waitress proceeded to drop two heavy mugs, causing damage to the customer's calculator and smashing his watch crystal. In the uproar that followed, the patron demanded to see the manager, a rather haughty man whom you hired three months ago because of his success in managing two other seafood restaurants in the area. On the night in question, the manager was miffed by the patron's belligerent, threatening attitude and refused to compensate the patron for the damages just incurred. Incensed, Mr. Carlyle stormed out of the restaurant, threatening to file a legal suit. The event was witnessed by many other diners.

Today—four days later—you have just received a letter from the patron condemning the manager's handling of the situation and demanding com-plete reparation for his damaged possessions. He has included a list of the articles in question, along with their current or appraised value. The total comes to $250. He states that if his claims are not answered to his satisfaction immediately, he will turn the matter over to his lawyer. In the meantime, he is advising his many friends and acquaintances not to frequent your restaurant. You are eager to resolve this problem as soon as possible, since you fear that any negative publicity could seriously hurt your business. Write a memo to the new manager, Dan Chen, requesting that he accommodate the patron, send him a $250 check, and attempt to reestablish Mr. Carlyle's goodwill toward your restaurant. (Consider whether you should ask Mr. Chen to see you before he writes to Mr. Carlyle, and whether he should send you a copy of his letter before it is mailed.)

5. ***Letter—Inquiry to a reference about Elma Renton:*** As executive admin-istrator of staff personnel at City Hospital, you are currently searching for

the right person to be chief pharmacist. One of the applicants you interviewed yesterday is Elma Renton (age 35), who worked at the Excello Pharmacy in Omaha from January 1984 until June 1990. For a reference she has given the name of James Bonson, chief pharmacist at Excello, 952 Fourth Avenue, Omaha, NE 68100-9999.

Your hospital, one of the leaders in the country, established a new 300-bed teaching and research wing two months ago and now plans to open a new pharmacy five months from today. Both personal qualifications and technical skill are important for the responsible job of chief pharmacist. You need to know whether Ms. Renton has the ability or potential to organize the new pharmacy in your modern, well-equipped hospital. You need a frank evaluation of her as a worker, because this job will demand a tremendous amount of initiative, drive, and sustained working capacity. Also, because she will have people working under her direction, she must be able to organize them into a tightly knit and happy working group. You'd like to know if she was liked and respected by subordinates, associates, and supervisors. Also, it would be helpful to know what duties she performed at Excello Pharmacy. Write a tactful, well-organized inquiry to Mr. Bonson for the information you need. Keep your questions within the laws regarding fair preemployment inquiries.

Claims (Complaints) and Requests for Adjustment

1. *Evaluations:* Which of the opening paragraphs in the following claim letters do you consider effective? Why? Tell how to improve the poor ones.

    a. In line with your policy on consumer satisfaction published in your recent catalog, I am requesting a cash refund of $45.38 for a toaster I purchased two weeks ago for cash. The reason I have directed this request to your office is that your department manager said such a refund would not be possible. [*Written to the adjustment department manager.*]

    b. In the past year I have ordered nearly $200 in goods from your store, by mail. Two weeks ago I came there in person and bought a gray overcoat. As I was heavily loaded with packages, I asked the clerk to send the garment to me by store delivery. When the overcoat arrived, I was busy and so I didn't open the package until two days ago.

    c. Never in my life have I been treated so rudely as I was the other day in your store, by two jerks you call employees. I tell you, the way I was insulted gave me a good indication of what kind of people you're hiring these days. I'm so mad I will never go back to your store again.

2. *Evaluations:* Comment on the following claim letters. Consider tone, organization, clarity, accuracy, and probable effectiveness in getting the desired

result. What changes, if any, do you recommend? Please be specific. Try to determine first what each writer really wants.

a. *From a business firm in Detroit to an airfreight corporation in Pittsburgh:*

> Re your airbill #54663, we originally shipped this same
> amount of mdse. to Cincinnati UPS (United Parcel Service),
> got overnight delivery, and it cost only $15. Now, your
> shipment from Cincinnati to us took over 15 days to get to
> us, and you want $48.36. Now, if you want to rebill and
> charge ICC surface rates, we will pay you, but if you
> think 15-day delivery is air express . . . better check
> the rubber bands on your airplanes or start feeding those
> pigeons better.

b. *From a charge customer to a department store with five branches. [This handwritten letter had merely the date at the top and the writer's signature ("Mrs. Joan M. Smith") at the end. Her envelope had no return address. The store has 250 Smiths and no Joan M. Smith.]*

> I cannot understand your statement each month showing that
> our account has a past-due payment. This is very irritat-
> ing since our payments have been:
>
>   1/10/ [year] -- $25.00
>   2/3/ [year] -- $30.00
>   3/4/ [year] -- $25.00
>   4/3/ 5/6 [year] -- each $50.00
>
> It is my understanding that our payments each month are to
> be only $20.00 per month. As you can see ours have been
> much more than that--so where do you get this "overdue"
> bit?
>
> I am at this time sending another $50.00 check, which I'm
> sure you will agree does not make my account past-due.
> Please get my records straight as I don't believe this
> makes my credit rating look too good.

c. *From a landlord to apartment tenants:*

> It seems some of your typing late at night disturbs some
> tenants. Perhaps when all is quiet it is easier to hear.
>
> I was wondering if you type on the nook table--as that is
> bad because the table is fastened to the building. A felt
> pad will help if you do not already have one. The univer-
> sity bookstore has them just for that purpose.
>
> I know your typing is important to your schoolwork; how-
> ever, I would like to keep everyone happy.

3. ***Letter—the "runaway" bus:*** Last Saturday you took a 7:40 a.m. Transcontinental bus to St. Louis, a city 200 miles from where you live. The bus was scheduled to make five stops along the way and to arrive in St. Louis at 11:40 a.m. This would be just in time for you to attend an important regional luncheon at the Marlborough Hotel, starting at 12 noon. (You were to be a panel speaker at this function and had accepted the appointment two months ago. You planned to return the same afternoon on the 5 p.m. bus.)

At about 10 a.m. the driver of your 7:40 a.m. bus, after making four scheduled stops to pick up passengers, turned off the freeway for an *unscheduled* stop at a roadside snack bar—a 6-foot open-air counter with no chairs and no roof. He told passengers they would be there a "few minutes to stretch and have a snack" if they wished. As your hands were sticky after eating a candy bar, you stopped in the rest room to wash them. Only three minutes later when you came outside, the bus was gone! The driver had apparently left without a warning toot or a count of noses! Thus you were stranded off the freeway, 15 miles from any scheduled bus stop; and no other bus was to pass on the freeway ½ mile from the snack bar for three hours. You would surely miss the entire function. What could you do? (You're not a hitchhiker.) The snack bar operators stated this was the second time in a week that the same bus driver had left a passenger stranded at the same place. Rather than have you miss your luncheon, one of the two operators generously offered to drive you in her car until she caught up with the bus. You both hoped it would be just a few miles, because she had to get back to her job. However, after 25 miles you reached the next town—at the fifth scheduled stop—just as the bus driver was starting the motor, ready to leave for the last lap of his trip. You hurriedly pressed $15 cash into the hand of your Good Samaritan and hopped on the bus. Not one word of apology came from the bus driver! At the luncheon all your friends agreed with you that the driver should be reported.

Write an effective letter to the customer service manager in St. Louis (ZIP code 63100) requesting whatever adjustment (and explanation) you think is fair. Send a copy to the bus company's head office in Chicago. Make your message as concise as possible; assume whatever is necessary for completeness.

4. ***Letter—incorrect billing by Airway Freight Corp.:*** You are accounting department manager of Flowers by Welcome, a reputable florist. Today (April 5) you received a $106.50 bill from Airway Freight Corporation, 947 Columbus Building, Indianapolis, IN 46288-3344. The bill shows two deliveries—airbills #18694 and #25479—unpaid since January 20 and February 9, respectively. You have canceled checks and invoices showing that both these shipments were paid when delivery was made. In fact, your firm always pays freight when it arrives. You resent the computerized statement across the bottom of today's bill: "THIS IS OUR FINAL REQUEST BEFORE REFERRING THIS TO A COLLECTION AGENCY. REMIT NOW." This is the first billing you have received. Your firm's general manager has decided

that as of today he is switching to another airfreight company that takes better care in bookkeeping. He says that any company this careless in keeping records probably is no less careless in handling freight. Write to the general manager of Airway Freight Corporation after you have determined your purpose and what evidence you need to enclose with your message. Use good judgment in the tone and content of your letter.

5. ***Letter—tar on suit:*** With a group of 15 other business people you took an interesting tour last Tuesday through the Bay Lumber Mills. All of you had attended a conference, and the tour was scheduled as part of the conference. After walking from one building to another, you happened to be the target for a glob of tar that dripped from a roof of one of the mills as you entered. It fell on your left shoulder, on your new suit. One of the employees suggested that after the suit was cleaned, you should send the bill to that lumber mill. Now you have had the suit cleaned, and you want reimbursement. To get the desired refund ($9.85), write a courteous letter to Mr. Daniel Jenks, Public Relations Manager, Bay Lumber Mills, Racine, WI 53499-8888.

Miscellaneous Requests, Orders, Invitations

1. ***Evaluations and Improvements:*** The following messages deal with routine business situations. Analyze each and then decide whether the message is adequate. Suggest improvements.

   a. *A printed form letter from the manager of a savings association to customers; customer's name and address are inserted at the top; it has no salutation:*

   _____Please sign the enclosed withdrawal slip and return it to us.
   _____Would you please send us your signature card. _____
   _____Would you please send us your social security (reporting) number.
   _____We need your *original* hazard (fire) insurance policy (with extended coverage) in at least the amount of $_____.
   _____An error was made on your last transaction, which has already been corrected on our records (we'll correct your passbook the next time we have it).
   _____We are returning your check because _____
   _____Your construction interest payment starts _____
   199_, in the amount of $_____; thereafter, interest payments will be $_____ until regular payments ($_____) start _____, 199_. YOU MAY MAKE FULL PAYMENTS AT ANY TIME AND RECEIVE CREDITS TOWARD FUTURE PAYMENTS.
   Thank you.

b. *Memo from a company's social director to all supervisors:*

SUBJECT: <u>Christmas gifts for our departmental secretaries</u>

With Christmas just around the corner, it's time for me
to raise my ugly head above ground once again to remind
you it's time to consider our departmental secretaries.

If you wish to contribute toward a gift for each gal,
please leave your donation in my box by December 10. A
buck or two from each of you will be adequate.

2. *Memo—tuition for management course:* Your employer encourages young executives to enroll for additional university training whenever possible, and the firm pays tuition for desirable programs. You (assistant personnel manager) would like to attend the Graduate School of Business Administration Management Program at the [*name*] University in your city. Because most classes meet Monday evenings and a few on Saturdays, they will not interfere with your job. You believe the course will definitely make a graduate more knowledgeable in the management field, thereby increasing his or her worth to the company. Some of the topics you foresee as particularly valuable to your present job are management communication, performance appraisals, and basic human motivation. The program, over one academic year, costs $1,500; $300 is required to be submitted with your application, and the remaining $1,200 by October 8. Today is August 15. Enclose your application with your memo to Mr. D. J. Helwick, executive vice president, for his approval.

3. *Memo—company blood bank:* You are area coordinator for your company's blood bank. Last year, through the cooperation of various departments, your blood bank had ample credits to provide the 289 withdrawal units requested by employees. Now the annual drive is approaching again. On March 5 and 6 your company's employees are to participate in this worthwhile cause, from 10 a.m. to 5 p.m. (You decide on the place and on other necessary details.) You want donors to sign up for the time most convenient for them. Provide sign-up sheets in convenient places, and write a memo to all 200 employees, attaching a folder about the blood bank and donor qualifications.

4. *Memo—fuel conservation by employees:* To conserve fuel, because of the current fuel shortage, you—as operations manager of a large company—want to request all employees to observe certain simple fuel-saving steps. Without fuel your plant cannot operate; so it is to everyone's interest that as much gas and diesel fuel be saved as possible.

   You ask that all vehicles be shut off when idle. Examples include when drivers are on lunch breaks or other breaks; when chip trucks are under bunker for any time (diesel manufacturers recommend engines should not idle for more than five-minute periods); when trucks are being loaded with lumber, logs, or other materials; when trucks are standing idle at any other times not in use. Also, you want all employees having company cars to obtain fuel at outside sources. And you request that operators run machines in such a manner as to conserve fuel without loss of efficiency. Excessive speed where not necessary consumes more fuel. You believe that cooperation of all employees could result in a 5 to 10 percent savings. Ask the superintendent and shop stewards to make sure proper steps are being carried out. Mention in your memo that you will make personal inspections periodically. Plan an attractive, easy-to-read format for your requests.

5. ***Invitation letter to a Business Show:*** You are sales manager of an office equipment company that specializes in a large selection of computer systems for business. You have decided to display your equipment and supplies at a business show sponsored in your city by the Business Management Association. An admissions fee is charged to defray the expense of the show, but you have purchased a block of tickets to distribute to your regular customers and to other good prospects for your products. The three-day event starts one month from today. At the show, you will display: Apple Macintosh, IBM compatibles, microcomputer systems, Postscript Laser printers, modems, and Aldus Pagemaker software programs for desktop publishing. Books, accessories, and factory authorized technicians will also be available.

Write a letter, which will be personalized and typed on a computer, to invite your customers to see your display and converse with a technician at the show. It will be in your city's convention center. The letter will go to purchasing agents, office managers, and computer services supervisors. Enclose a ticket to the show, and give them the exact dates with exhibit times. You will be happy to furnish more tickets if others from a company wish to attend. All they need to do is call your office (give your number). You will send the extra tickets immediately.

6. ***Evaluation:*** The following is the first draft of a form letter request from a mortgage loan company to borrowers. The revision that was mailed is illustrated in request 2, page 154. Which do you think should be more effective and why? Compare the two letters' organization, openings and closings, paragraphs, action requests, clarity, completeness, and consideration. Be specific.

```
Dear Homeowner:

We wish to inform you that the Homeowner's Mortgage Protec-
tor Plan Certificate that you recently received is to be
read carefully and then filed with your other valuable pa-
pers. The benefits provided by the plan are very valuable.
```

```
The protection will become effective on the date indicated
on the certificate after the premium has been paid.  The
premium that is shown on the enclosed certificate should be
added to your future monthly payments.

If your mortgage payment has already been made for the month
the protection is to become effective, the premium should be
sent now so that you will be fully protected for the month.
Next month, combine the payments.

We are pleased you have secured this protection for yourself
and family.  The acceptance of this plan by so many of our
customers indicates to me that it is certainly a valuable
and worthwhile project.
```

7. ***Invitation letter—grand opening of new quarters:*** As administrative assistant to the president of Benson Savings Association, write a letter inviting customers and their families to be your special guests at a grand opening of your new quarters on Thursday, Friday, and Saturday, the last three days of this month. There will be handsome gifts for both ladies and gentlemen, special door prizes with drawings every two hours, and refreshments. Children will receive balloons. Also, each current passbook holder will receive a special present. Your new building is graciously furnished, with a number of authentic period antiques. A "SPECIAL GUEST" name tag, which you will enclose with your invitation letter, entitles customers to their gifts.

8. ***Memo—request for annual report by managers:*** You are assistant director of your company's regional office. You need to write a memo to all 15 plant managers asking them for a report by June 30 of this year. In this report—for the past fiscal year, June 1 through May 31—you want them to be sure to cover the following points: the major accomplishments of their plant during the past year, major problems facing them for next year, objectives for their plant for next year, plans for accomplishing them, and anticipated difficulties. Also, you want a brief summary—one paragraph on each subject—covering their plant's operations last year in the areas of organization planning, quality performance, production and scheduling performance, community relations, personnel management, costs of operation, health and safety, product development, and any other matters they think significant. If they will please organize their reports in this manner, the reports will be especially useful to you in preparing your Annual Division Report and in making plans for next year. You feel the company has had a good year, and you look forward to an even better one next year.

   Arrange your request in an easy-to-read format (perhaps consider some tabulating?) and achieve a pleasant tone.

9. ***Letter—insurance company interviews for college seniors:*** Assume you are the new assistant manager of the Topco Insurance Company's office in your city. Your company will hold interviews on a nearby college campus February 20 for business students graduating in June this year. You want to send a concise, personalized form letter to graduating seniors inviting them to sign up for an interview (whenever you specify) or to call you for further information. You will also grant off-campus interviews. You believe your company has jobs that graduates might be interested in. They can be in the fields of accounting, marketing, computer programming, personnel, and administration. Graduates can build a business career with no capital investment, get comprehensive training to develop their talents, and earn a monthly life income after 40 years of qualified service. Should you include anything else?

10. ***Letter—management seminar for local and regional directors:*** As customer relations director of Executive Services, Inc., you now have the pleasure of announcing your firm's three-day management seminar. Your letter is to be a form, individually addressed to local and regional directors of large firms that have supervisors and assistant managers in various departments. Make clear that from each firm one or more of these managers may attend. Enclose with your announcement a formal seminar folder, giving the cost and a detailed program. Make clear in your letter the place, dates, and highlights of the training sessions, and create a pleasant, goodwill-building tone.

■ CAPSULE CHECKLISTS FOR DIRECT REQUESTS*

A	Inquiries about Persons		D
	B	**C**	
Direct-Request General Plan	**To Reference by Applicant**	**To Reference by Person Interested in Applicant**	**Inquiries about Products or Services**

1. MAIN IDEA
  a. Request, main statement, or question
  b. Reason(s), if desirable
	1. Main idea
	  a. Reason for writing to this person
	  b. Introduction of request
	  c. Memory refresher
		1. Main idea
		  a. Applicant's full name
		  b. Why you are considering this applicant
		  c. Why you are writing to this reader
			1. Main idea
			  a. Major request
			  b. Reason(s) for interest in product or service

2. EXPLANATION
  a. All necessary and desirable details
  b. Numbered questions, if helpful
  c. Easy-reading devices
	2. Explanation
	  a. Summary of pertinent facts about yourself: courses, major, GPA, outside work, tests, scores, honors, scholarships, leadership
	  b. Guidelines for the recommendation; kinds of information the inquirer needs
	  c. Enclosure of form(s) and resume, if helpful
		2. Explanation
		  a. Requirements for job, loan, credit, scholarship, membership (legal?)
		  b. A few pertinent facts applicant told you about him- or herself
		  c. Specific questions for:
		    (1) More than "yes-no" answers
		    (2) Explanations if necessary
		    (3) Itemization—in body or on separate questionnaire
			2. Explanation
			  a. Specific questions
			    (1) Preferably for more than "yes-no" answers
			    (2) Explanation, whenever necessary
			    (3) Itemization if more than one and desirable for clarity and/or ease of response
			  b. Promise of anonymity, if desirable

3. COURTEOUS, CLOSE, WITH MOTIVATION TO ACTION
  a. CSAD[†]
  b. EA[‡]
  c. DA[§]
  d. Appreciation and goodwill
	3. Courteous close
	  a. CSAD,[†] to whom recommendation should be sent
	  b. EA[‡]
	  c. DA[§]
	  d. Appreciation
		3. Courteous close
		  a. Appreciation
		  b. Promise of confidential treatment
		  c. EA[‡]
		  d. DA[§]
		  e. Offer to reciprocate, if appropriate
			3. Courteous close
			  a. Suggested or specific action desired
			  b. DA[§]
			  c. EA, when appropriate[‡]
			  d. Appreciation and courtesy

* All lists include possible content. For any one message, choose only the pertinent, appropriate items.
† CSAD = clear statement of action desired.
‡ EA = easy action.
§ DA = dated action, if desirable.

■ CAPSULE CHECKLISTS FOR DIRECT REQUESTS* (Continued)

E **Complaints,** **Claims, Requests** **for Adjustment**	**F** **Requests regarding** **Routine Business** **or Public Causes**	**G** **Invitations**	**H** **Orders and** **Reservations**
1. Main Idea a. Purpose(s) (need for adjustment or correction of error or procedure)	1. Main idea a. Reason b. Request (inter-changeable)	1. Main idea a. Invitation request with all pertinent W's: who, what, when (day, date), where, why	1. Main idea a. Statement of order or reservation
2. Explanation a. Something good about reader, product, or service, if true b. All facts pertinent to claim, stated with no anger, threats, sarcasm, exaggeration, or persuasion c. Desirable qualities: promptness, faith in reader's fairness, good humor, when appropriate	2. Explanation a. Desired details and, if helpful, instructions b. Itemization, preferably when more than two items are requested c. Reader benefit, if any	2. Explanation a. All necessary details—if to a function: program, time, apparel, costs, refreshments, location, directions, parking; if to submit material: length, method, format, etc. b. Setup and enclosures as needed for easy reading	2. Explanation a. Details about: (1) Needed items or facilities—quantity, size, color, style, catalog number, price (or rate) (2) Payment—method, time deposit (if any) (3) Shipment—date and place (4) Special instructions, if any b. If reservation: function, number in expected attendance, requirements
3. Courteous close a. CSAD:[†] Free replacement, free repairs, refund, credit, price reduction, inspection, explanation, apology or change, new shipment, or adjustment left up to reader b. EA[‡] c. DA[§] d. Appreciation and courtesy	3. Courteous close a. CSAD[†] b. EA[‡] c. DA[§] d. Courtesy	3. Courteous close a. CSAD[†] b. EA[‡] c. DA[§] d. Courtesy	3. Courteous close a. CSAD[†] b. EA[‡] c. DA[§] d. Courtesy

* All list include possible content. For any one message, choose only the pertinent, appropriate items.
[†] CSAD = clear statement of action desired.
[‡] EA = easy action.
[§] DA = dated action, if desirable.

Chapter 8

Good-News and Neutral Messages

A message that conveys good news is usually easy to write (or state orally) because you are telling your reader something pleasant. A neutral-reaction message is also relatively easy to compose, because it is about something the reader considers neither good nor bad news—just information that may be useful. Such messages should be organized by the direct approach—the good-news plan. This chapter discusses the following kinds of letters and memoranda you can organize with this plan:

Favorable Replies

   Answering inquiries about individuals

   Granting adjustments on claims and complaints

   Approving credit

   Acknowledging orders you can fill

   Granting favors and other requests—pertaining to business, government, and organizational procedures or individual needs

Unsolicited Favorable Messages

   Announcements about:

      Sales and events

      Procedures, policies, and responsibilities

      Honor and activities of people

   Transmittals

Other messages adaptable to the good-news plan are included in later chapters. (Replies to sales-related inquiries about products are in Chapter 11.)

ORGANIZATIONAL PLAN

You can use this direct-approach, good-news plan whenever you answer a request or initiate an unsolicited message yourself, if the news will be favorable or neutral—at least not unfavorable—to your reader. As with direct requests, the plan has three parts:

---

1. Best news or the main idea
2. Explanation, with one or more of the following, when desirable: all necessary details, educational information, resale, sales promotion
3. Positive, friendly ending—clear statement of action desired, if any; motivation to action; willingness to help further; appreciation

---

If your message is mainly good news or favorable information but also has some unpleasant fact, you can still use this plan tactfully and honestly.

Because the items in the explanation section form the basic core of your message, good judgment is necessary in deciding which items to include. The following suggestions highlight the content and uses of four items:

1. *All necessary details.* Include whatever facts, terms, reasons, and other explanations pertain directly to the best news or the main idea. Consider, for instance, whether the reader needs specific details on the why, what, when, who, where, and how of the news or main idea.

2. *Educational information.* Include instructions for use and other educational facts about a product or service the customer has bought if such information is necessary to help the customer get the utmost benefit from the purchase or from the relationship with your firm. If you enclose an instruction booklet, a short paragraph within the letter may call special attention to certain pages in that booklet.

3. *Resale material.* Include appropriate favorable information about a product or service the reader has already bought or is planning to buy, or about your organization. Such material usually answers the question "What will this do for me?" and strengthens the reader's confidence.

4. *Sales promotion.* Include suggestions about other products or services related to those the customer has bought or is considering buying. Whenever you do so, you indicate your desire to be of further service to the customer. This material should be presented without sales pressure; the emphasis should be on what the customer may need or appreciate and not on a desire to get more business.

FAVORABLE REPLIES

To help build goodwill, any progressive organization replies to all reasonable requests courteously, helpfully, promptly (within a few days, if possible). If you know there will be a delay, a brief acknowledgment should state why and then tell the inquirer approximately when to expect a complete answer. In such a message you can still begin with the best news first—information that is useful to the reader or shows you are doing something. Don't start with such negative statements as "We are sorry we cannot answer your request here. . . ." Emphasize the positive, for example:

```
Your request for information about solenoids has been for-
warded to our chief systems analyst, Mr. Richard Hacket, in
our Chicago offices.  You can expect to receive his helpful
comments regarding your special needs soon after he returns
from Alaska next week, September 10.
```

In every good-news reply your compliance with the reader's request is more important than any expression of gratitude or pleasure. Depending on circumstances, you can begin by saying that you have done it (the preferred beginning), that you are doing it, or that you will do it. Thereafter the material you select for the explanation and ending varies significantly with the circumstances.

The discussion in this section includes guidelines for and examples of favorable replies to requests for information about individuals and products, and to requests for adjustment, credit, orders, and favors. It also provides a basis for deciding how to answer other types of good-news replies.

Answering Inquiries about Individuals

Among the most frequent non-sales-related inquiries you might need to answer are requests for information about personnel and credit applicants. The following section focuses on recommendation letters about personnel for jobs, but also briefly discusses replies to inquiries about applicants who are considered for reasons other than jobs.

When you furnish pertinent information about an applicant's qualifications, character, and general conduct, the message should preferably be addressed to the specific person interested, instead of "To whom it may concern."[1]

You have a fourfold responsibility when you write recommendations. You must be fair (1) to the applicants, so they can get what they are best qualified for, (2) to the inquirers (prospective employer, creditor, landlord, or whomever), for they are depending on your frank comments, and (3) to your own conscience and reputation for integrity. Also, (4) you must abide by civil rights laws and be aware of possible legal problems. Discussed below are the expanded good-news outline, recommendations on outstanding candidates, and appraisals on candidates with shortcomings.

Expanded Good-News Plan for Recommendations

The following suggestions serve as a basis for confidential recommendation letters (or even phone conversations) when facts are mainly favorable or neutral.

1. Main idea
    a. State the applicant's full name and what his or her relationship was to you—employee, customer, friend, tenant, club member. Mention dates, length of time, and type of job, credit, tenancy, or whatever is pertinent. Use facts; don't guess.
    b. Include an expression of pleasure, if sincere, in your statement of purpose for the letter, *replying confidentially to a request.* A subject line can cover part of item b with such words as "Confidential report by request, on Thomas W. Jones as a prospective field representative."

2. Explanation
    a. Answer all questions—direct or implied—unless doing so would be legally risky. (See Defamation, Chapter 5.)

b. Arrange answers in the best psychological order, depending on facts.

c. Back up your statements of evaluation (excellent, outstanding, and so on) with specific facts about performance record. For a job applicant:

    (1) Tell specific job duties that applicant performed.

    (2) If the inquiry states requirements of the job for which the applicant is being considered, talk about those duties that will be significant.

    (3) When desirable, mention work habits that show personality characteristics.

d. Be honest and fair with negative material. (If the candidate has unfavorable habits or characteristics, please consider the six suggestions on page 177 in the section Recommendations for Candidates with Shortcomings.)

3. Ending

a. Include if possible a candid statement of your personal opinion about the applicant's probable fitness for the position (or whatever the applicant is being considered for—a lease, credit, membership).

Recommendation Letters for Outstanding Candidates

When everything you want to say is favorable, the requested recommendation is easy to write, as in letter 1 below:

LETTER 1   *A Marine Corps commanding officer's sincere solicited recommendation to the regional manager of a nationally known business firm about a corporal seeking a management trainee position.*

Pleasure; purpose; name; job length of time	I am glad to answer your inquiry about Wayne S. Prochas. Because Wayne has worked with me nearly two years as a correspondence clerk, I know him well.
Answers to questions Duties performed	During this time he has demonstrated outstanding abilities in both general office and management work. In 20 years of military service I have only once before made such a high recommendation, and currently I have over 800 officers and men in my command. With speed and efficiency Corporal Prochas has attended to the administrative correspondence of more than 800 men attached to this command, and he has never once complained of the workload or poor conditions under which he has had to work.
Personality and character	I recognize in this man a great potential, because he is intelligent, industrious, and so well liked by all who come in contact with him. Wayne does his work with no supervision and can be relied on to deliver a finished product at all times. Also I get the very

```
                           definite impression that he could, if placed
                           in a position to do so, generate ideas as well
                           as process those of others.

                           As to conduct, personal habits, and ability to
                           handle himself properly, this man has no
        Personality        faults, to my knowledge.  He doesn't appear to
                           have to work at being a gentleman.  It seems
        and                to come naturally to him.  His loyalty is un-
        character          questionable, and by his practices he has in-
                           fluenced others to a great extent.


                           I have two regrets: firstly, I cannot take
                           this man to my next command and, secondly, I
                           do not possess the word power necessary to de-
        Unqualified        scribe this man.  But I do say this; my infor-
        recommendation     mation is accurate, and I am sincere.  He will
                           make a real contribution to any organization
                           he may choose to join.  I recommend him very
                           highly without any reservation.
```

Though the statement following "secondly" in the last paragraph above seems overdone (and could be revised), this commanding officer is to be commended for his sincerity and for including more than mere glowing adjectives to describe a man he considers outstanding.

Recommendations for Candidates with Shortcomings

If the candidate has the needed good qualities, you must decide whether to include or omit negative material. You may be able to give a qualified or even an unqualified recommendation without stating the shortcoming. In any case, mention a weakness only if it meets these conditions:

1. It is pertinent to the job (or credit, etc.) for which the candidate has applied.

2. It is *sufficiently serious* to affect the applicant's probable fitness for that responsibility.

3. It is a fact (not hearsay or a statement made because of your personal prejudice, jealousy, malice, or discrimination).

4. It occurred often enough (and recently enough) to be worth mentioning.

5. It answers a specific question asked or implied, and you mention it in a spirit of goodwill based on the preceding four items.

6. You state it *discreetly within legal limits.*

Recommendations are incomplete and misleading as personnel reports if they omit truthful, pertinent, helpful information. Nevertheless, many employers have been reluctant to make any negative—though truthful—statement (in writing or orally) for fear of a costly lawsuit or unfavorable publicity if the applicant should sue. Others, however, feel they have a moral duty, when responding to a legitimate inquiry, to state what they honestly and in good faith believe to be true and pertinent to the questions asked about a former employee. Basically, one should have no fear of stating the pertinent facts *prudently*.

An applicant who was discharged, after warnings, because he was caught three times stealing from the cash drawer should probably not be employed in a job handling company funds. But he may be a fine employee in other work. Likewise, such serious shortcomings as the following, unless corrected, will probably affect an employee on the next job, too: excessive drinking or drug use, poor health causing frequent absences, unwillingness to cooperate, dishonesty, extreme emotional instability. (If an applicant discloses a job-affecting problem that is a disease, the employer should persuade that person to get treatment. But if the problem continues, the employer may need to terminate employment.) Whenever you must make negative statements, know the legal aspects.

If you are writing a recommendation letter about a candidate who, apart from one serious shortcoming, is satisfactory (or excellent), organize your letter so that you establish the applicant's more favorable characteristics before you mention the defect. In letter 2, for example, the negative facts answering two questions are embedded; the message ends with candid, positive statements. In the subject line this writer chose the word "Appraisal" instead of "Recommendation." (Four lawyers and an assistant attorney general have declared this letter legally appropriate.)

LETTER 2   *A department manager comments on a former employee who had a serious alcohol problem. (This letter, dated July 28, answers inquiry 2, page 145.*

Confidential Appraisal by Request on Victor L. Dryer

Full name and brief summary

Mr. Dryer worked hard for us as a salesperson in the electrical appliances section for about a year. He was such a dependable salesperson that when the section manager resigned to go to the east, we placed Vic in charge and found him well-qualified for the job. He

Answer to part of question 1

was with us 22 months--until June 30 this year.

As section manager, Vic had much responsibility. Besides ordering all merchandise for the section, he was also in charge of the five salespeople working under him. He was well

Answer to question 2	liked by subordinates and customers. He had a knack of being tactful and thoughtful with every customer. Because of his personality and his knowledge of the stock, he pleased a good many steady patrons and helped increase total sales within his section.
Favorable comment before and after the negative answer to part of questions 3 and 1	Vic's work at the store was entirely commendable for about 16 months. Then he developed what he described as an alcohol problem, which noticeably affected his disposition and his attendance. When I talked with him about the change and I suggested a treatment program, he mentioned serious worries. He tried to lick the problem alone and did so for three weeks. But after he had missed at least a day's work every week for six months, I regretfully had to let him go.
More about question 3	Vic's other personal habits are good. His personality, honesty, and physical appearance are an asset to any company. He takes an active part in outdoor sports and is in fine health, except for the problem I mentioned. He will quite probably successfully recover from it during a helpful professional program.
Favorable, job-related appraisal	Vic is intelligent and well educated (a marketing graduate of Broadway College). Because he knows the electrical appliance business well and has so many other fine qualities, he can be a top-notch department or section manager especially in the electrical field.

Besides recommendations of job applicants, you may sometimes be asked to recommend people for other reasons. Whether the inquirer is considering a person as a tenant on leased property, or for membership in a distinguished organization, or for credit or an honorary award, you can adapt the Expanded Good-News Plan for Recommendations to help you write honest favorable recommendations.

Granting Requests for Adjustment

An *adjustment letter* is the reply to a complaint (called a *claim letter*). In general, the best attitude is to give the customer the benefit of any doubt. Most persons are honest in their claims, and it is usually better to make the desired adjustment than to risk losing a customer.

Even though your firm's adjustment policy may be generous, the ultimate success of your good-news adjustment letter depends on not only *what* you say but also *how* you say it. Never refer to a complaint as such. Call it "your experience," or just refer to the reader's "letter."

The discussion in this section concerns (1) tone of adjustment-granting messages, (2) organization and content when the seller is at fault, (3) variations when the buyer or a third party is at fault, and (4) organization when the fault is not yet determined and will be investigated.

Tone of Adjustment-Granting Messages

Consideration and courtesy are exceptionally important when you grant an adjustment. Because your reader has been inconvenienced, irritated, and perhaps angered, he or she is especially sensitive to the tone of your message. Even when the letter grants a request, it can destroy goodwill if its tone is poor. Compare, for example, the following "poor" sentence (in which the antagonizing expressions are underscored) with the suggested "better" version:

Poor: `Nevertheless, `so that we can keep you as a satisfied` customer, we are `willing` to `allow you` to exchange these toys.` *[The motive sounds selfish; "willing" and "allow you" sound condescending and grudging; the sentence lacks you-attitude.]*

Better: `Because we want you to be completely pleased, we will gladly exchange the toys for you.`

When you (or anyone else in your firm) are definitely at fault, saying "I'm sorry," "We apologize," or even "Please forgive us" is quite disarming. You are more likely to lose face by *not* apologizing than by doing so. One apology (preferably in the *explanation* section) is enough, for most situations.

Organization and Content When Seller Is at Fault

The discussion in this section aims to help you plan carefully when granting an adjustment if your company is at fault.

Opening Paragraph.   Try to begin with whatever you think the reader will consider the best news. If the customer asked for something specific—like a refund, exchange, credit memo, or speedier service—grant or promise immediately. However, if the request or attitude makes a "granting" opening inadvisable, try to get in step with the customer in some other appropriate way. For example, if a customer has found a bug in a jar of prunes and vows never to buy your products again, you can't very well *begin* by saying you're sending another jar of prunes to replace the faulty one! Instead, you might express appreciation for the thoughtfulness in writing and might agree with a comment made in the complaint. In the following examples the first two grant immediately, and the last three open with various statements to get in step with the reader.

**Customer's Request
or Complaint**

Suggested Opening

1. That you "eliminate the delays" in your merchandise shipments or risk losing business.

You will be glad to hear that we have found a new way to speed deliveries of fresh vegetables to you. From now on your produce can reach you within two hours after we receive your order.

2. That you replace immediately five defective copies of a book needed by May 15.

Today five copies of book title] were sent to you by air express, shipping charges prepaid. You should receive them three days before May 15.

3. That you refund to a friend the $30.50 purchase price because of your firm's error. (Your customer bought a birthday gift for a friend. Instead of charging it to your customer's account, your store incorrectly sent the "gift" to the friend c.o.d. That was two months ago; the friend does not yet know about the mix-up.)

[*To the customer's friend.*] You have had the unusual experience of paying for your own birthday gift which your friend James L. Tomson had purchased for you from our store. The mix-up is due entirely to our error, for which we extend to you our sincere apologies. [*Note: In this case the refund check is mentioned only after the explanation.*]

4. That two special toys ordered four weeks ago did not arrive in time for Christmas.

Please give us the opportunity to restore the Christmas spirit for your children. We surely want to do the best we can to make them happy with new toys.

5. That the service of a certain waiter in your restaurant was disappointing, and the customer's guests were embarrassed.

You are perfectly right to expect prompt and courteous service from our waiters. That service is exactly our goal for every guest, and we thank you for taking time to write us.

Explaining What Caused the Mistake.   When your firm is at fault, admit it frankly. Don't say, "mistakes are bound to happen," or that because of the size of your firm there will naturally be frequent errors. Don't promise the error will never happen again. If it *does,* the situation will be doubly embarrassing. Generally it is desirable to include at least *some* explanation. Paragraphs like the following—from two adjustment grants—help the reader understand how the error occurred:

1. You guessed correctly. Apparently all the order and shipping papers, including the ones that should have been kept for our use, were sent to you. As a result, we have no record of the ordered paint. We are certainly sorry that you were inconvenienced by our slipup. Always we aim to be careful in processing every customer request accurately and promptly.

2. Sometimes we find that a package miscarries in the mails. This occasionally happens because of an error in addressing the label, or damage to the label in the mail, obliterating the address. Apparently, the latter happened with your parcel.

Resale.   If the person complaining seems to be losing faith in your firm, resale is desirable. If possible, include concrete evidence of your efficient service, safe and correct shipments, or care in producing or selecting high-quality products. If certain steps have been or will be taken to prevent recurrence of whatever the customer is complaining about, mention them. Sometimes you can honestly state that a new procedure is developed "on the basis of helpful comments like yours."

Sometimes, it is desirable to resell the customer on keeping both the replacement you are sending *and* the original slightly defective shipment. (You save return-shipping charges and the bother of processing the damaged merchandise.) A consumer may be glad to keep slightly damaged articles if you substantially reduce their price. Likewise, a dealer customer may be willing to accept a below-average shipment that can be used for a special sale and quick profits if you give sufficient inducement—price reduction, consignment terms, or perhaps longer payment time.

Sales Promotion Material.   If a retailer sells only one type of costly product (like furnaces, home insulation, or roofing), which the average consumer buys only once in a great while, sales promotion material would be out of place. However, if the seller carries a variety of often-replaced items, sales promotion may be desirable. Without sounding greedy, you want to encourage the customer to continue to buy other goods from you. Also, if the customer returned the original shipment and is receiving credit or a refund, she or he really needs a different replacement. Sales promotion material is then appropriate.

Ending Paragraph.   For a pleasant close you may (1) tie suggested action in with sales promotional material, (2) comment on the pleasure the reader will gain from the high-quality new article you have sent, (3) express appreciation that the reader took time to write, or (4) issue a cordial invitation that the customer continue to come to your firm for top service. Omit negative thoughts, such as an apology or a reminder of the inconvenience the mistake caused.

Don't suggest future trouble or imply that the customer may stop buying from your firm.

Letter 3 concerns a situation in which the seller is at fault. The disappointed customer stated the intention of never buying this canned food product again. Notice that the writer does not begin by "granting" or even giving the free assortment; the main idea is appreciation and resale. The assumption is that only after reading the explanation—and more resale—will the customer be in a mood to accept the replacement. The last paragraph effectively ties in a gift with a hint of sales promotion.

LETTER 3   *A good adjustment-granting letter from the assistant manager of a national packing firm's quality control department to an out-of-state customer who found a fly in a can.*

Main idea: thanks; resale

Thank you for writing us of your experience upon opening a can of DeMona spinach. We are very concerned about this because of the particular care taken in the preparation of all DeMona products to assure you of receiving wholesome and high-quality food items.

Explanation, with resale

Upon arrival at the packing plant, the spinach is run through a large perforated cylinder, where it is tumbled and shaken apart to eliminate particles of soil, etc. From there, it is transferred to wide traveling belts where inspectors remove all imperfect leaves and any other defects present. The spinach then goes into the washers in which a series of paddle wheels keeps it in constant agitation while high-pressure jets of water wash, rewash, and rewash. After that, it is subjected to a further careful inspection as it is placed in the cans; therefore, you can see we do everything possible to produce a clean, wholesome product.

Easy action; apology

To further investigate this incident, we will appreciate your sending us the code mark that was embossed on the lid of the can in question. This will enable us to refer the matter directly to the plant where the spinach was packed. If you made a note of it, please send it to us on the enclosed reply card. We appreciate your bringing this situation to our attention and offer you our sincere apology.

Gift to retain goodwill and promote sales

Within a few days you will receive an assortment of DeMona fruits and vegetables. We want you to enjoy them so thoroughly that you will continue to be a regular DeMona satisfied customer.

Variations When the Buyer or a Third Party Is at Fault

When someone other than the seller is at fault, you may be justified in refusing—instead of granting—the request. Nevertheless, firms will occasionally grant a buyer's claim even though the buyer or a third party is at fault.

Buyer at Fault.   If you decide to grant the adjustment claim though the buyer is at fault, you have two choices for letter organization.

1. Using the preferred direct approach, you begin with the best news—granting the request. Then in a tactful explanation you should help the customer to realize that mistreatment of the product caused the damage. Your goal is to maintain goodwill so that the customer will continue to make future purchases from your firm. This method is used in letter 4.

2. The alternative choice, the indirect approach, is to begin with a statement that gets in step with the reader (perhaps something on which you both agree, or your appreciation of the customer's promptness or whatever is appropriate). Then explain the mistake, and after that grant the claim. The reason for this alternative is that sometimes the psychological effect on the reader is better if you allow the claim *after* you have shown tactfully that the buyer, not your firm, is at fault.

LETTER 4   *A sales manager grants a refund on a blouse that faded because someone washed it incorrectly; best news first.*

Best news: refund	Because we want you to be completely pleased with your purchases at Lon's, you are receiving the enclosed refund. It covers the original price of your Barlow blouse, plus sales tax, for a total of $49.50.
Resale, with tactful (impersonal) explanation of necessary washing care	The Barlow is one of the finest lines of blouses made. The synthetic fibers and special dyes that make possible the beautiful colors in these blouses do, however, require special care. When these blouses are laundered, washing by hand in a solution of mild detergent and lukewarm water gives the best results. As the instruction tag on every blouse states, these garments are very sensitive to heat and should always be dried at room temperature, never in an automatic dryer. Also, any staining substance that contacts the material must be loosened in cold water, because hot water often causes a chemical change that affects the dye and results in fading.

Resale; additional emphasis on care; educational enclosure

Although the Barlow line does require special care, its beauty and elegant fashion lines outweigh the special care required by the fine fabric. Because of the many new materials on the market, I think you will find that the enclosed booklet on laundering all types of synthetics is helpful for continuing their attractive appearance.

Sales promotion, with implied action and courtesy

As you are one of our regular customers, we invite you to our special upcoming June sale. A complete line of summer fashions, including new pastel and print blouses, will be waiting for your inspection. The sale begins June 12, at 9 a.m., but the general public will receive an announcement on June 14. Come as early as you can--to select your favorite styles. It is a pleasure to help you.

Third Party at Fault.   Sometimes merchandise is damaged or lost while it is in the warehouse or truck of a third party—distributor, broker, shipper, or someone else. Then the third party has the legal responsibility to adjust the claim, and many sellers prefer not to get involved.

However, some wholesalers that sell to small retailers assist them in the claim-filing procedures, or they even file the claim directly on behalf of the dealer. Letter 5, from a retailer to an individual customer, is unusually generous and considerate.

L**ETTER** 5   *A gift shop owner replaces a lamp damaged in shipment.*

Best news: replacement

A new Brighton lamp should reach you in two days to replace the one you received in damaged condition. We sent it today by prepaid express.

Explanation showing seller not at fault

As the Ace Truckline gave us a receipt acknowledging that they received the original lamp in perfect condition, the porcelain base must have been cracked in transit. We are sorry this happened, for we know how much you want this beautiful gift for your cousin's wedding anniversary. Although our responsibility ended when the truckline accepted the package, we are glad to make this replacement for you.

Suggested action to help claim with carrier

Will you please give the original lamp to the express driver when the second lamp is delivered? We will then enter a claim with the truckline.

Courtesy; resale

> Thank you for writing promptly. Our concern now is that you receive the lamp in time for the anniversary, and in perfect condition.

Organization When the Fault Is Not Yet Determined

Sometimes the final adjustment decision cannot be made until the seller determines who is responsible for the mistake. In such cases, letting the buyer know promptly that you want to investigate the claim should have a neutral effect on the reader, for you are neither granting nor refusing the request. The best organization is (1) express interest in the problem, (2) assure the customer you are looking into the matter, (3) include brief resale if desirable, and (4) courteously state that you will give the facts as soon as they are available.

LETTER 6   *A hatchery manager promises to investigate.*

Interest in problem

> Thanks very much for your report on the N&H "Nick Chick" Leghorn pullets delivered to you on March 2. I sympathize with you, for pullets you buy from Nerving should meet the high standards of previous lots. We want to do everything possible to cooperate with you.

Possible causes of problem; promise of investigation

> Tints, egg size, broodiness are characteristics both genetic and environmental. That fancy phrase simply means pullets can be influenced by both breeding and raising, management, etc. Because so many factors are involved in the conditions you describe, we are asking our Oregon representative, Mr. Vern Jacks, to call you within the next few days. He can run tests on the pullets. You will find him cooperative and helpful.

Resale

> Most hatcheries would be satisfied if 90% of their stock were good 90% of the time. Not Nerving's. We are aiming for 100% on both counts and won't rest until we reach that goal. Of course, when you are dealing with "life," numerous variables make this difficult. But, we keep trying. That's why letters such as yours help in pointing out where improvements can be made.

Courtesy

> We want you to be a satisfied customer, Mrs. King. If we are at fault in any way, you are assured we'll do our level best to make amends. Thanks again for writing; you help us take steps to make things right.

Approving Credit

The message telling the customer of your granting credit[2] often includes all parts of the basic good-news plan—best news first, then terms, resale, sales promotion, and appreciation. Many firms have preset form letters acknowledging credit approval and containing all needed information.

Decision or Shipment in First Paragraph

If the customer has not yet ordered any merchandise on credit, begin with the credit-granting decision and a cordial welcome. If an order was sent with the request for credit, begin with the date and method by which the goods are being shipped (thereby implying the credit approval). Make clear the purchase details (name and quantity of goods sent, item prices, freight, and total charge); for more than two or three items, attach an invoice copy. Mention cordially that the shipment has been added to the customer's new account.

Explanation of Credit Terms

In your explanation section, mention briefly the basis on which credit was earned, and clarify the terms. If, for instance, an applicant's references all speak highly of prompt payment habits, it is psychologically a good idea to mention those habits. The applicant is then encouraged to continue this good reputation in dealing with you.

Clear explanation of the credit terms helps reduce collection problems later. Suppose, for example, your wholesale firm's terms are 2/10, net 30. You must be sure that every new credit customer (dealer) knows whether your terms are based on invoice date, delivery date, or the end of the month (e.o.m.). Misunderstanding on this important detail can cause a customer's payments to be as much as a month off. Compare these vague and clear statements regarding credit terms.

Vague: Our credit terms are the usual 2/10, net 30.

Vague: Under our credit terms of 2/10, net 30, you earn a
               2 percent discount if your payment is made in 10 days.
               [*Ten days after what?*]

Clear: Our credit terms are the usual 2/10 net 30, based on
               invoice date.

You can place the terms either before or after the resale and sales promotion. If before, you are more certain the reader will notice them, because you're emphasizing the terms; if after, you seem to be stressing the other person and not "what's in it for me." Another noteworthy fact is that using the word "grant" reflects we-attitude, while stating that the customer has "earned" good credit uses you-attitude.

In a retail firm, you will make clear what kind of account you are opening for the consumer—monthly, flexible, major-purchase (furniture, appliances, etc.) with fixed payments, or other. Explain the billing procedures,[3] the consumer's payment obligations, and the finance charges.

Be tactful in telling the customer when payments are due. Compare, for example, the poor tone in "we expect you to pay" or "you are expected to pay" with the improved tone in "Payments are due within 10 days after the billing date." In this sentence the indirect approach is desirable. Good tone is also possible with courtesy, as in "Please send your payment within 10 days after. . . ."

Resale and Sales Promotion

The credit-granting message should preferably include customer-benefit resale information on the firm's services. Also, it is sometimes desirable to include sales promotion material (in the next-to-last or last paragraph) about such news as a forthcoming sale, new seasonal merchandise, or products allied to those ordered (if any). Such news encourages the customer to use credit. To keep your letter short, you can enclose a leaflet describing departments and services such as the following:

For the consumer: Free parking, mail and telephone shopping, personalized services for men, home-planning bureau, bridal consultants, tearoom, other restaurants, child care, gift wrapping, free and frequent deliveries, special discount or purchase privileges.

For the intermediary (retailer or wholesaler): Nearby warehouses, factory representatives, quantity discounts, free window or counter displays, national advertising, cuts and mats for newspaper and other advertising, repair services, manuals, factory guarantees, prompt and speedy deliveries, research department.

Future-Service Ending

Close your credit approval with statements which indicate your desire to serve the customer well in the future or which specify particular services. Inviting readers to a special sale, for example, helps to get them to use their accounts. The tone must in no way sound greedy for orders, but courteous suggestions for easy action are appropriate.

LETTER 7   *A retailer's processed form letter granting credit to a consumer; applicant's name is in the inside address and salutation.*

Best news: **welcome;** **new account**	Welcome to you as a Nelson credit account customer. Your new charge plate is enclosed, and we invite you to use it often. This plate will identify you at all Nelson stores, so please sign it in ink before putting it into your wallet or purse.

Credit terms	You will receive your statement soon after the first of each month, showing purchases up to the 23rd of the preceding month. Bills on this monthly account are payable by the 10th of each month. (Unpaid bills are subject to a 1½ percent finance charge monthly.)
Resale on store services	As one of our regular charge customers, you will receive announcements of all our sales before they are advertised for the public. If you should wish sometimes to shop in the comfort of your own home without a trip to town, you can do so conveniently by phone. Just ask for "personal shopping services," tell your needs to the shopping assistant, and then just say "Charge it to my account."
Invitation to future use of account	The enclosed leaflet explains the numerous Nelson services available for your convenience. Do use them often to save yourself both time and money. We look forward to giving you friendly, courteous service in any of our colorful stores . . . for many years to come.

Acknowledging Orders You Can Fill

An order acknowledgment performs several important functions. It lets the buyer know that his or her order has been received, is appreciated, and is given attention. It helps to build goodwill. Furthermore—and very important—by identifying and accepting the order, the acknowledgment completes a valid contract between buyer and seller. For these reasons the acknowledgment must be definite and complete, in keeping with the situation.

Orders your firm can fill immediately fall into two types—first orders and repeat orders. Though acknowledgment for both types should identify the shipment and show appreciation, the message content will be quite different.

Acknowledgment of First Order

The new customer needs to know that his or her order is being filled promptly and correctly, that it is appreciated, and that—because of your products and services—dealings with your firm will be pleasant and profitable.

Sending the Ordered Items.   Usually the best beginning for your first-order acknowledgment is to state what, when, and how you shipped. If possible, state approximately when the shipment should reach its destination. Express appreciation for both the order and the remittance (if you received the latter). If you can fill most of an order promptly and the rest soon thereafter, usually it is best to begin with what you can ship now (or what is already on its way to the customer). Later in the letter explain why and when the remainder of the order will be sent separately.

Then take care of any needed details about shipping charges and payments. If you opened a new credit account for this customer, you will of course explain the credit terms.

Here are a few overworked expressions to avoid in first-order acknowledgments; they are followed by comments, suggested revisions, or both:

Vague, trite, and a little inaccurate: "We have shipped your order. . . ." (The order is really *the piece of paper* on which the customer authorizes you to send requested items; your firm fills the order and ships merchandise, groceries, livestock, or whatever was ordered.)

Better: "The bedspread (#204) and the electric blanket (#B43) you ordered September 4 were sent to you today by parcel post. You can expect them in a few days. Thank you for your order and your enclosed $95.20 check in full payment."

Trite: "Welcome to our long list (or family) of satisfied customers." (Omit such trite statements and show elsewhere in your letter by actions—prompt service, reader-centered resale, sincere thoughtfulness—that you appreciate the order and want to please the customer.)

Specific Resale Material.   For the first-order acknowledgment, resale on company *services* is appropriate to both the consumer and the retailer. Resale on *products* ordered is usually more desirable for the consumer than for the retailer. Before ordering, the retail manager who will resell your products has usually studied their merits carefully—through sales literature, catalogs, and perhaps your sales representative—and you generally need not repeat what has already been read. However, the manager may appreciate any special product features he or she can emphasize to customers.

To a consumer, resale material from the "home office" is sometimes extremely helpful. After placing a large first order with a firm (either by mail or through a sales representative), the consumer may regret having signed the contract—especially when the item purchased is a luxury. But the order acknowledgment from headquarters with detailed reader benefits about the product and warranty helps reinforce the buyer's confidence in the purchase.

Looking Forward to Future Orders and Reader Satisfaction.   To end the first-order acknowledgment, you can tie suggested action in with resale or sales promotion; enclose order blanks or whatever else is needed for easy action. If you wish, invite the cash customer to fill out and return a credit application form (as in letter 8). Avoid suggesting that credit be automatic.

LETTER 8   *A wholesaler's acknowledgment of a dealer's first cash order.*

Best news: **shipment**	You can expect to receive the two dozen Top-skill lawn edgers, #L592, and the five power mowers, P952, in time for your garden sale

Monday, May 15. They were shipped by prepaid
express this afternoon.

**Appreciation; check
acknowledgment**

Thank you for your order and your $2,325.60
check, which exactly covered the items as
priced in your new dealer catalog. As you
know, the suggested markup on these items is
30 percent.

**Resale on services
for dealer; cus-
tomer benefit**

Your customers will be pleased with these
highly popular Topskill tools. Currently
they are advertised in special 1/2-page, two-
color ads in <u>House and Home</u> and <u>Western Gar-
den</u> magazines, April through July. You can
assure your customers that every Topskill is
factory-guaranteed according to the contract
that accompanies each tool. A special feature of the Topskill edger is its ability to
trim neatly within 1 inch of flower beds and
rockeries. On the mower, a simple twist of
the dial knob adjusts both wheels and roller
for precise cutting height and ease of operation.

Services to dealer

Illustrations of counter and window displays
and other free sales helps are sent with this
letter. Just let us know your needs on the
enclosed checklist.

**Suggestion for
credit**

You may be interested in our regular credit
terms of 2/10, net 30--based on invoice dates
of your future orders. If so, just fill in
and return the enclosed form; we will gladly
consider your credit application. Also, if
you have any questions with which we might be
able to help, just write us. We'll do our
best to serve you promptly.

Acknowledgment of Repeat Orders

Most orders come from repeat customers who know and like a firm's products
and services, and who don't expect a typewritten letter of acknowledgment.
Usually the goods can be sent as quickly as an acknowledgment can be mailed.
In some cases standard purchase order forms give complete instructions about
terms and delivery date, and they stipulate that the buyer will be notified only
if the order cannot be filled as requested. In others, an adequate good-news
order acknowledgment is an inexpensive (perhaps printed) form, a carbon copy
of the shipping invoice, or a postcard.

Though most repeat orders are filled without letter acknowledgments, an unusually large order may occasionally warrant a personalized letter. This may include appreciation, a statement of how the order is being handled, and perhaps a few cordial comments about your past relationship and future plans to supply the customer's needs.

Granting Favors and Other Requests

Whenever you decide to grant a favor, you have a comparatively easy letter to write. Whether the favor is serving on a committee, speaking without pay at a convention, donating money, or lending your firm's equipment without charge, the good-news plan is best to use. Usually all you need is the acceptance first, pertinent comments or explanation, and a cordial ending.

By following the good-news plan plus the suggestions and cautions discussed in this section, you can also write effective favorable replies to other kinds of requests—from customers, employers, employees, friends, government officials, or anyone else. Good judgment is necessary, of course, to adapt your messages to the circumstances and your readers.

UNSOLICITED FAVORABLE MESSAGES

The previous section considered messages that are written because someone inquired. This section discusses *unsolicited* favorable and neutral-reaction messages—specifically, announcements and transmittals.

Announcements

Favorable and neutral-reaction announcements should follow the good-news plan—best news or main idea first; then adequate explanation, resale, or educational material; and, finally, the appropriate ending. Some messages combine an announcement with an invitation. How should you classify them? Either way. Whether you call them announcements (discussed in this section) or invitations (Chapter 7), you use the same three-part organizational structure.

Included in this section are group and personal announcements about sales and events; procedures, policies, responsibilities; and honors and activities of people.

Announcing Sales and Events

Whenever you wish to announce a sale or an event (luncheon, conference, celebration, meeting, or other function) about which you need merely to inform your readers, you can use the good-news plan. The opening paragraph usually includes as many of the five W's as possible—who, what, where, when, why.

An excellent way to build and strengthen goodwill with regular customers is to let them know you appreciate them. For example, message 1 announces a sale before newspaper publication.

MESSAGE 1   ***Letter:*** *a store's preannouncement to charge customers about a forthcoming sale (processed form without an inside address; salutation is "Dear Customer"; complimentary close is "Sincerely"; signature is by the manager.*

Reason: best news; five W's

Because you are a regular [*store name*] charge customer, you are invited to a special sale of unusual spring coat values. It is one of the
Designer Room's greatest coat events. This
announcement comes to you now so that you can
make your selection during a three-day period
before newspaper ads appear.

Displayed items for emphasis

PREANNOUNCEMENT SELLING
Wednesday, Thursday, and Friday
February 6, 7, and 8
NEW SPRING COATS BY OUR FOREMOST MAKERS
all priced far below regular

THESE ARE FINE COATS such as you will see at
much higher prices after this great sale. Every
one is a new, just-arrived 199- fashion!

Details

ATTRACTIVE COLORS include whites, pastels, neu-
trals, and bright shades. You will also find a
wide selection of styles--casual and dressy, or
town tweeds--in various lengths; coats that wrap
or button.

Easy action and motivation

TAKE ADVANTAGE OF THIS OPPORTUNITY FOR FIRST
CHOICE AND SUPER SAVINGS! Come in early . . .
February 6, 7, 8 to choose your coat. Prices
will return to regular immediately after this
outstanding coat event.

Announcing Procedures, Policies, and Responsibilities

Some business firms commonly use "directives" to announce to employees official statements of company policy, procedures, and employee responsibilities. They provide loose-leaf policy manuals in which employees can file current directives (usually typed in memo form) and from which they can remove those that are outdated. The manual may cover a wide variety of topics ranging from assigned parking facilities and office hours for employees to policies about salary increases, retirement benefits, overtime, handling of inflammable goods, and treatment of customers.

Two cautions to remember when you write directives are (1) make your statements absolutely clear to all levels of your employees, from top executive to the part-time janitor, and (2) avoid a bossy or threatening tone. Show confidence that all will cooperate if they understand what they are to do.

Of course, many messages about procedures, policies, and responsibilities are not directives. They can be processed announcement letters to customers (and others) or memos, like message 2, to employees.

MESSAGE 2   *Memo: announcement to all employees about enrollment for company insurance plans.*

```
                                       DATE: Sept. 22, 199-
        TO:       All Kenmore employees
        FROM:     John K. Wood, Retirement and Insurance
                  Officer
        SUBJECT:  Open Enrollment Period for Company
                  Insurance Plans
```

Why; when; for whom; where; what (itemized)

```
The annual enrollment period for employee insur-
ance plans will be between October 4 and 27 at the
retirement and insurance office.  During that
time, you may

1. Enroll in medical, life, salary-continuation,
   or accident insurance plans for the first time
2. Transfer from one basic medical plan to another
3. Add previously uninsured dependents to medical
   insurance plans
```

Effective date

```
Changes and additions made during the open enroll-
ment period will take effect November 1, 199-.
```

Enclosure: instructions

```
Please refer to the attached individual Insurance
Program Summary, which shows the premiums, company
contributions, and payroll deductions for plans in
which you are currently enrolled.  Then read the
rest of the attached material, which explains just
what to do if you wish to make changes in your
coverage.
```

Offer of more help

```
Brochures describing the plans and individual
counseling services are available at the retire-
ment and insurance office, 4th floor; or phone ex-
tension 987 if you wish one mailed to you.
```

Announcing Honors and Activities of People

To inform employees and customers about promotions, awards, honors, new appointments, retirements, and other recognition-deserving activities of various persons, it is thoughtful to send announcements.

The first paragraph—which states the good news—often begins with words like "We are pleased to announce that. . . ." or "With great pleasure we inform you. . . ." The second paragraph gives details about the new officer, award, or whatever pertains to the announced honor or activity. Suggested action may be that all join in congratulating the person or wishing the person success and happiness.

Transmittals

As the name implies, the main purpose of transmittals is to transmit something, which is usually mentioned in the first paragraph. Transmittals, also called "covering letters," have many uses. They range from short (5- to 10-line) notes to official letters that accompany, explain, or justify documents. In general, they follow the good-news plan.

For routine business to consumers, employees, or other persons a cordial, short note is sufficient to transmit one or more items—such as a check, policy, passbook, warranty deed, or map. Often processed fill-in forms are used, with various listed items and spaces for checking those that are enclosed.

Transmittals that accompany official documents, bids, applications, proposals, or formal reports should be carefully worded letters. (Two are illustrated in Chapter 18.)

SUMMARY

Whenever you answer a request favorably or announce news that will be pleasant or neutral to your reader, keep in mind the three-part organizational good-news plan. The nine Capsule Checklists on pages 168 to 169 give you a brief summary review of the basic plan and various adaptations when you answer requests for information, adjustment, credit, order filling, and favors and when you announce or transmit something.

EXERCISES AND PROBLEMS

Favorable Replies to Inquiries about Individuals

1. *Telegram—recommendations about Roberta R. Adsen:* You—personnel manager for Trustline Insurance Company—have just received the night letter telegram in Exercise 1.c., page 159, about Roberta R. Adsen. She worked in your claims department 20 hours a week for two years while attending [*name*] University, in the school of business administration. She was meticulously accurate with figures, conscientious, courteous, friendly. Although only a part-time employee, she earned two promotions during the two years. She thrived on responsibility. She was intelligent, thorough, honest, resourceful, receptive to suggestions, always eager to correct any shortcoming. Her letters and oral explanations to customers were clear, tactful, effective. You recall she took two university courses in business communication and she happily showed you her grades—A and B. She was poised, self-confident, neat in her work. You know of almost no adverse information except that while working in the claims department filing section she usually

dressed quite shabbily. Also her spelling was sometimes inaccurate. Write your night letter telegram, choosing ony pertinent facts.

2. ***Memo—recommendation about James R. Bockman:*** As staff supervisor in the test support division of KLM factory, you have been asked by the personnel department to write your recommendation on James R. Bockman, Clock #5-409. Today is August 31. Your statement about Jim's summer employment will become part of the permanent personnel records. A carbon copy of your memo is to be sent to Jane Kaber and Mark Saylor, both department heads in your firm. Jim arrived in your department on June 2 this year and was assigned to your most tedious job—#9477 (you can decide what this job is)—which lasted three months. Jim is returning to college next month, as agreed when he was hired in June. Jim reasons well and has the ability to organize his workload. Should he apply for reemployment next summer, you would gladly welcome him into your group. Jim learns quickly and has adapted himself to your methods with minimum difficulty. His attitude, attendance, and cooperation are excellent. He is highly thought of by his lead personnel and supervisors. Write a recommendation, using correct memo format.

3. ***Letter—recommendation about Emmet Gart:*** You are assistant manager of the loan department of the Central Bank, your city, and you have received a letter of inquiry from Ms. Janet Tock, public relations director of the National Environmental Council. She is considering Emmet Gart for a field representative job and asks your recommendation of Gart, who worked for your bank as a field collector of unpaid loan installments. Gart's job was to call at debtor's homes and collect their payments, which were past due. In the new job, he would work with business executives to upgrade environmental conditions.

   Emmet worked for your bank from April to November last year and quit on impulse with one week's notice after a disagreement with an immediate supervisor. This supervisor happens to be the strictest of all your supervisors in his collection policies. He insists that every item of property be promptly repossessed when a debtor is delinquent in his or her payments. Emmet Gart, on the contrary, believed in the gentle "soft sell" method. He was pleasant, honest, and extremely patient with customers, often much more so than the supervisor wanted. With one customer in particular, Emmet and the supervisor clashed; it was finally the cause of Emmet's leaving. The customer had borrowed $8,000 to lease a fleet of trucks for an out-of-state construction job. Although he was financially able to pay the monthly installments, he was habitually late; furthermore, he threatened to transfer all his business—including his checking and savings accounts—to a competing bank unless the collection department stopped harping about his late payments. Gart sided with the customer, arguing that so long as the customer cheerfully paid extra interest on all his late payments and because he always did pay (though late), the bank should "go easy" in its dealings with him, to save his goodwill. One day the supervisor angrily told Gart to repossess his customer's trucks or quit; Gart chose the latter, for he refused to compromise what he thought was the right course of action.

When you heard about the incident, you called Emmet back to your office and tactfully told him that his record had been very satisfactory with the bank and you hoped he would reconsider and stay. Emmet's collection record for the six months he was with your bank was second to the top of your 10 collectors in the field. He was exceptionally well liked by customers and fellow employees. Gart thanked you for your invitation to return and said he would like to, but because he would have to remain under the same stern supervisor, he thought it best to return full time to his university studies and give up the job until another opening might occur the following summer.

Emmet is a sociology and English major at the university, and an ardent supporter of social justice. He spoke occasionally about his desire to do something worthwhile in the community to help improve the environment and help the underprivileged. You honestly believe he will be happier in the type of work for which Ms. Tock is considering him. Write a tactful, frank recommendation, after you have sorted out the important and the irrelevant facts.

Granting Adjustments

1. Evaluate the following adjustment letter from a manufacturer to a retailer. What do you like and dislike about it? Suggest specific improvements where needed—in the tone, organization, accuracy, and adequacy of explanation and resale.

   ```
   Thank you for telling us of the problem you have had with the
   suits you purchased.

   Some time ago, a batch of material having bad formulation es-
   caped detection by our quality control people.  The line in-
   spectors caught most of the finished suits before they were
   invoiced.  However, some were shipped.  Apparently your order
   was among them.

   The situation has since been corrected, and we don't believe
   you will have this problem with a replacement.  Accordingly,
   a special shipping label is enclosed for returning your de-
   fective merchandise to us.  It will be promptly exchanged
   upon receipt.  Please let us know if we may be of further
   service.
   ```

2. ***Letter—Garson Hotel's errors on bill for NMS meeting:*** You are service manager of Garson Hotel in which the Miami chapter of the National Management Society (NMS) was host to the annual spring district meeting.

Approximately 90 officers and spouses were present. The meeting started on Thursday night for the early arrivals, but the main meetings began on Friday and lasted until Saturday noon.

In making preliminary arrangements the Garson general manager and you agreed to provide a large additional meeting room as a private lounge for any social gatherings before and between the scheduled sessions from Thursday evening to Saturday noon. It was complete with tables, chairs, a beautiful view, and a beverage bar. The special fee was $390.

The meeting was a success, and everything was fine until the final accounting from the Garson credit office was presented to the Miami chapter. The charge on the lounge was $450, and there was also one long-distance telephone charge of $4.75 billed to NMS. The call was made at 5 p.m. Saturday, but all NMS members had checked out before 1 p.m. The treasurer of the Miami chapter, of course, appealed the two charges. When checking, you found that the phone caller had rented a room near the lounge; he was a resident of the city to which the call was made. You've written to him and asked him to send his check to you for the cost of the call.

As service manager of Garson, write a letter to Mr. James Manual, treasurer of the Miami chapter of NMS, Box 890, Miami, FL 33199. Admit the error and tell him to disregard the two charges ($60 for the lounge and $4.75 for the phone call). Remind him of the excellent facilities, good meals, extra service, and other good reasons for the Miami chapter to use Garson Hotel for another NMS meeting sometime in the future.

3. ***Letters to Mrs. Ray and the Landons regarding "mystery toaster":*** Assume that two months ago Mrs. Joseph Ray, one of your longtime good customers, bought a dual-control, four-slice, chrome-plated electric toaster from your store and asked that it be sent as a wedding anniversary gift to her out-of-state friends Mr. and Mrs. Thomas Landon. Since then she has found no charge for the $70.50 on her monthly statements from your store; neither has she received a thank-you from the Landons. Last weekend, as a guest at the Landon home, she noticed they were using the exact toaster she had sent them. To her chagrin they called it their "mystery toaster" because it had reached them c.o.d., although neither of them had ordered it. Because they needed one, they kept it. Mrs. Ray then told them of her gift. She is furious with your store and wants you to make a proper adjustment immediately. This situation requires two letters—one to the Landons and one to Mrs. Ray. Will you send her a copy of your message to the Landons? Also, should your letter to the Landons mention the refund in the opening paragraph? Why or why not? The salesclerk forgetfully omitted Mrs. Ray's name on the sales slip. Finding only the name and address of the Landons (who have no account at your store), the shipping department sent the toaster to the Landons c.o.d.

4. ***Letter—lost Beta Gamma Sigma pins:*** As assistant manager in the customer service department of Finecraft Company, "jewelry's finest crafters,"

in Hartford, Connecticut, you need to answer today (January 4) a special delivery complaint from Ben Brown, vice president of the Beta Gamma Sigma business honorary, at the University of Missouri chapter. He asks what happened to the order he mailed to you almost three months ago (October 5). The chapter needs 38 crested pins for an initiation to be held three weeks from today. Your records show you received his official order and that the pins were shipped to him November 8 by first-class mail. Since the package has not been returned to you unclaimed, you can only assume it was lost in the mail. Company procedure requires that the customer complete the enclosed insurance affidavit so that you can file a claim and tracer with your insurance company. Upon receipt of the affidavit, properly executed, you will immediately enter a replacement order. Write a goodwill-building adjustment. (This chapter has bought jewelry from you for many years.) You'll rush the pins to reach Ben before initiation.

5. ***Letter—Ms. Donn's too small boots:*** As customer service manager, you received a complaint letter today from Ms. Sue Donn stating that the boots your store sent by mail last week are too small. These boots were on special sale for $48.50. The usual store policy is to accept no returns on special-sale merchandise. (This rule is one reason that you can offer goods at such low prices.) However, in this case you will make an exception to the rule because she did not know (and the store did not inform customers) that this style of boot must be larger than for dress shoes. You'll be glad to take the boots back, and you will credit her account for $48.50. Ask her to pack them in the same box in which they came and to mail them with your name on the address label. If she wants a larger size, you will send it· to her for the sale price. In case no larger size is available, suggest how she might indicate a second choice of boot she'd like you to send. Make action easy for Ms. Donn so the package will come to your attention with all the information you need to benefit both Ms. Donn and your store.

Other Favorable Replies about Credit, First Orders, Favors

1. ***Letter granting credit to Ms. Jane Vaso:*** You are a correspondent in the credit department of the leading department store in a city of 150,000 population. Several weeks ago Ms. Jane Vaso wrote you, saying she just moved to town from a distant city and wants a credit account with your store. In turn, you sent her an application form to fill out because the local credit bureau had no information available on her. She filled out the form and returned it to you promptly. You checked her facts—including the references—and found she has an excellent credit reputation. The references complimented her for prompt payment throughout the years she traded with them. Your assignment is to notify her that you have granted her credit with your store. Her present address is 1924 Fourth Street, Sacramento, CA 95807-6222. Assume your department store has the services you'd expect in a city of 150,000. In preparation for this assignment, you (or a representative from your class) might want to find out what services are available at a

comparable department store and also the type of message the store sends to a customer like Ms. Vaso.

2. ***Letter from wholesaler granting credit to Thomas Bruce:***
You are credit manager of Recreational Supply, Inc., a wholesale firm in Rochester, New York. Today (January 20) you approved a credit request from Mr. Thomas Bruce, owner-manager of Tom's Sporting Goods in Toledo, Ohio. He has ordered:

20 little league baseball bats, catalog #BB897	$3.60	$ 72.00
30 baseballs with cork centers, BC2125	2.90	87.00
10 Deluxe table tennis sets, #TT8126	10.00	100.00
Total		$259.00
Shipping charges		12.50
		$271.50

This is his first order to your firm. It came to you through your field representative, Betty Giori, who reports an exceptionally favorable location of Tom's Sporting Goods—within two blocks of both junior and senior high schools and in the heart of a residential shopping area catering to young families with children. Mr. Bruce (a college graduate seven years ago, majoring in recreation) bought the store three years ago with savings and a small inheritance. Although his capital investment is limited, he is a well-liked manager with progressive ideas. As a former captain of his college football team and as a little league coach for four years, he is widely known and respected in the community. His character and ethical standards are above reproach. His references report that he has always paid his bills, although often payments have run past the 30-day periods. You decide to grant him credit on your usual 2/10, net 30 terms based on invoice date, and to give him a little "education" (tactfully) on what he gains from paying within the discount period. (The discount will be figured on $259.) You are setting a credit limit of $300 until you see how well he keeps his account up to date. The items he ordered were sent by Railway Express today; delivery will be within two days. The little league bats (of white ash) are approved by the American Baseball Association; the Deluxe table tennis sets (with five-ply basswood paddles and sure-grip vinyl handle bindings), as well as the bats, are nationally advertised in *Sport Parade* and *Parents* magazines. You're enclosing with the shipment some counter and window displays, plus the needed order lists and blanks and your new spring catalog.

3. ***Memo to Sam Edwards regarding compensation:*** As J. T. Wall, president of a steel manufacturing company, you recently received a memo from Sam Edwards requesting a review of his compensation. Sam, who has been your salaried vice president of sales for over 15 years, would like to be on commission pay similar to the other sales reps in his department. He understands that such a change in pay will require him to pay for many of the expenses that are currently charged to the company, such as a lease car and membership in a nearby golf club.

Sam spends about 70 percent of his time each week working on client accounts and 30 percent attending to managerial tasks. He has been a consistently good performer in the field, but somewhat lackluster performing his designated administrative duties. Lately, Sam has become restless because the reps working for him have salaries much larger than his. They are paid a 2 percent commission on all sales they make, whereas Sam currently receives $65,000 annual base pay plus $13,000 worth of fringe benefits. You have a sincere respect for Sam, now nearly 57 years old, and believe he is a valuable asset to the company. His hard work and personable nature have allowed him to establish a long list of faithful customers during 15 years. He is also a good manager and team leader, and all the reps in the department admire him. You have decided that Sam will retain his title and duties as vice president of sales, but, to allow him more time to work on his accounts, you will redistribute some of his more routine paperwork to Kathy North, your new administrative assistant. Sam's commission will be based on 2 percent of recorded sales.

Today is August 27, 199-. Write a memo informing Sam of your decision to comply with his compensation request. Though Sam will now have to pay for his lease car and auto insurance, you will continue paying his membership to the country club as a bonus for his 15 years of service. Decide whether to make the new payment plan retroactive to August 1, 199-, so that it would include the $1 million deal he signed with a new client two weeks ago.

4. *Letter accepting invitation to be dinner guest and speaker:* In the five years since you graduated from college you have become active in the local chapter of a national business organization relating to your major work. (Make up a pertinent name.) Last month you were presented with the "Executive of the Month" award, and a short article appeared about you in this organization's national magazine. Today you receive a complimentary letter and invitation from the president of the organization's chapter in another city (100 miles away) to be dinner guest (6 p.m.) and banquet speaker (20 minutes) on Thursday evening, one month from today. Your spouse or a friend will also be a welcome guest, and the organization will provide for your car expenses and hotel overnight costs. There is no fee for speaking. After thinking the matter over, you decide to accept, even though you must be back at your office at 8 a.m. the next (Friday) morning. The topic suggested for your talk is one that's dear to your heart. Write your pleasant acceptance and make clear any details the president will need to know. Assume any additional necessary facts. The chapter's publicity will go to press 10 days from today, so of course you need to respond fairly soon. The earliest you can get to the banquet is 6:30 p.m. (Make up the name and address of the chapter president.)

Good-News and Neutral Announcements

1. *Letter and check for overdue freight bill:* You are an accountant for D&M Company. Today (January 13) you discovered an error you made

regarding freight bill #720015, dated October 3 last year, from Mason Carloading Company, 708 Central Avenue, Oakland, CA 94600-6655. Through your oversight you have not yet paid this bill, though payment was due last October 13! Your firm tries always to pay its bills on time. It was an honest mistake, and you want to apologize for it. You received freight bills #720015 and #71129 from Mason on the same day. Since these two freight bills were identical except for the bill number, you had put them together assuming that one was a copy of the other. You hope this incident will not hinder any future good relations your firm may have with Mason Carloading. Write an appropriate letter with which you transmit your check for the $90.98 that was due three months ago.

2. **Memo—Ken Maxwell's retirement:** You have recently been appointed chairperson of your company's employee finance committee. One of your longtime employees—Ken Maxwell—will retire June 30 this year after serving the company in various capacities for one-third of a century. For the past two years he has been editor of the employee newsletter, which goes to 100 employees. Known for his witty columns and good-natured humor, Ken is generally well liked. Last month, when he returned from a trip to France, he wrote (and related) humorous stories to the delight of the office grapevine. His enthusiasm for improving the employee newsletter caused him to spend the whole biennial operations budget in the first year, but by special know-how he has done well this second year. During the previous 31 years, after starting as bookkeeper, he progressed to two management positions.

   To honor his years of dedicated service there will be a reception from 3 to 4:30 p.m. in a company meeting room you select. Your committee plans goodies, punch, and a minimum of maudlin speeches. To help "punch up" the punch, pay the caterer, and, if possible, present a little token to Ken, you must now write a memo to all "friends of Ken Maxwell." Let them decide how much to give, but tactfully set a suggested minimum. Some past and present department chairpersons will perhaps recall how Ken extricated them from problems from time to time. Spouses are welcome, too, at the reception. If you can, add a little light humor to your memo.

3. **Letter—club's annual spring luncheon:** You are chairperson of the City Business Club's annual spring luncheon, and you've been working hard on plans for the past two months. A senator of your state, the Honorable Nancy T. Bon, has accepted your invitation to be principal speaker. Because you anticipate that recent events in the state capital will generate a high level of interest, you have moved the luncheon to a larger room at the local athletic club. You have decided to permit each member to bring one nonmember guest. The purpose of these luncheons is to provide an opportunity to get reacquainted with other business executives in your community and to hear a challenging and provocative message from a prominent public figure. The program this year should provide both. The date is Thursday, July 10, 199-. The total number you can accommodate is 180. Your cutoff date for reser-

vations is July 6. Luncheon will begin at 12 noon. Write the letter announcing this event and make action easy for reservations. Be specific.

4. **Letter—bank's new "Prime Service":** You are customer services manager of Ace Security Bank that serves 54 percent of the households in your city and suburbs. For many months you've heard customers complain that the 9:30 to 4:30 banking hours should be longer and that waiting times to teller windows should be shorter. All banks in your state have the same hours. People who work Monday through Friday until 5 p.m. are unable to get to a bank during their working hours. When they go on a lunch hour, they dislike waiting in long teller lines.

   After several conferences with your board of directors and department managers, you all have today (March 1) made a bold decision for changes. You'll give new "Prime Service" for all your customers in your 26 branches throughout the city and the adjacent surburbs. Beginning May 1 this year, all your banks' branches will be open 9 to 6 p.m. Mondays through Fridays and 9 to 1 p.m. Saturdays. After six months, branches not generating enough business will close on Saturdays. In all your branches 24-hour Person-to-Person assistance will be available by telephone seven days every week. Any personal questions about loans, investments, account balances, lost checks, interest rates, and other financial matters can be discussed with a personal banker anytime day or night. You have also provided Express-Teller windows, added cash machines, and offered $5 to any customer waiting longer than five minutes in any teller line.

   Write your good-news one-page announcement letter that will be sent to all your customers across the entire area. Can you make your message visually easy to read?

■ CAPSULE CHECKLISTS FOR GOOD-NEWS MESSAGES*

A Good-News (and Neutral): General Plan	B Answering Inquiries for Information about Individuals —Letters of Recommendation

1. BEST NEWS OR MAIN IDEA	1. Best news or main idea
	  a. Applicant's full name and relation-
	    ship to you, or how you know appli-
	    cant—job(s) held, tenant, customer,
	    club member, etc.
	  b. Reason for writing (by request)

2. EXPLANATION
  a. All necessary details
  b. Resale material
  c. Educational material
  d. Sales promotion
	2. Explanation
	  a. Answers to questions—direct or
	    implied
	  b. Best psychological order for four-
	    fold responsibility to:
	    (1) Applicant
	    (2) Person considering applicant
	    (3) Your conscience
	    (4) Civil rights laws
	  c. Specific facts about
	    (1) Applicant's job, duties, conduct
	    (2) Applicant's work or other habits
	    (3) Applicant's personality, etc.
	  d. Honesty and judgment about
	    negatives
	  e. Caution on legal aspects
	  f. Confidentiality
	  g. Offer, phone call

3. POSITIVE, FRIENDLY ENDING
  a. Appreciation
  b. CSAD†
  c. EA‡ and motivation
  d. Willingness to help further
  e. DA§
  f. RB¶
	3. Courteous close
	  a. Candid statement of your personal
	    opinion about applicant's probable
	    fitness for whatever he or she is
	    being considered
	  b. Positive (not negative) attributes at
	    end

° All lists include possible content. For any one message, choose only the pertinent and appropriate
  items.
† CSAD = clear statement of action desired.
‡ EA = easy action.
§ DA = dated action, if desirable.
¶ RB = reader benefit.

■ CAPSULE CHECKLISTS FOR GOOD-NEWS MESSAGES (Continued)*

Granting Requests for Adjustment

C Seller at Fault (A)	D Buyer or Another at Fault (B)	E Approving Credit

1. Best news
   a. Whatever will please buyer most
   b. Courtesy
	1. Best news
	   a. Same as C.1.a
	   b. Get-in-step-with-reader, courteous comment and concern
		1. Best news
		   a. Credit approval (if no purchase)
		   b. Shipment (if goods ordered)
		      (1) Description
		      (2) Quantity
		      (3) Prices, costs
		      (4) Method, charges
		   c. Courtesy

2. Explanation
   a. Brief resale with tactful explanation of error (if desirable)
   b. Instructions for buyer action, if needed
   c. Concrete resale on firm, services, or goods, if desirable
   d. Cautions
   e. Sales promotion on replacement of returned items(s) or on allied goods
	2. Explanation
	   a. Brief resale with tactful explanation of error, showing seller not at fault
	   b. If use of 1.b above, best news after explanation
	   c. Concrete resale on firm, services, or goods, if desirable
	   d. Cautions
	   e. Sales promotion on replacement of returned item(s) or on allied goods
		2. Explanation
		   a. Basis for credit; compliment
		   b. Credit terms; payments, discounts, limits
		   c. Resale on services
		      (1) *Consumer:* parking, shopping services, departments, conveniences, deliveries, price benefits
		      (2) *Intermediary:* warehouses, discounts, selling aids, advertising, guarantees, repairs, deliveries
		   d. Resale on product choices
		   e. Sales promotion?

3. Courteous close
   a. Suggested action and expectation of future pleasant use of goods and services.
   b. EA‡
   c. Positive idea; help
   d. RB¶
	3. Courteous close
	   a. Suggested action and expectation of future pleasant use of goods and services
	   b. EA‡
	   c. Positive idea; help
	   d. RB¶
		3. Courteous close
		   a. Expectation of pleasant service and orders (not greedy)
		   b. Suggested action
		   c. EA‡
		   d. RB¶
		   e. Courtesy; suggestion of further help, if pertinent

° All lists include possible content. For any one message, choose only the pertinent and appropriate items.
† CSAD = clear statement of action desired.
‡ EA = easy action.
§ DA = dated action, if desirable.
¶ RB = reader benefit.

■ CAPSULE CHECKLISTS FOR GOOD-NEWS MESSAGES (Continued)*

F Acknowledging First Orders	G Granting Favors	H Announcements	I Transmittals

1. Best news
  a. Shipment details
    (1) Description
    (2) Quantity
    (3) Prices, costs
    (4) Method, charges
  b. Thanks for remittance and/or order
	1. Best news
	  a. Acceptance of favor, request
	  b. Courtesy
		1. Best news; main idea. When appropriate:
		  a. Five W's (all or most); reader in first and all other paragraphs
		  b. Statement of pleasure, compliment, congratulations
		  c. Admission of errors, with good news
			1. Best news; main idea
			  a. Transmittal of specific item(s)
			  b. A concise reason
			  c. Courtesy

2. Explanation
  a. *For credit customer:*
    (1) Basis for credit—compliment
    (2) Credit terms; payments, discounts, limits
  b. *For cash or credit:* Resale on services same as E.2.c. (1) and (2) Resale on products ordered; highlights on special features—adapted to buyer
  c. *For cash customer:* Perhaps credit application form enclosed, with invitation to return it for consideration.
	2. Explanation
	  a. Pertinent comments, and details regarding favor—what is being or will be done, etc.
	  b. Questions, if necessary, pertaining to favor
		2. Explanation
		  a. Details to emphasize, reader benefits, if possible
		In admission of error:
		  b. Explanation, apology; emphasis on sincere desire to serve well
		  c. Resale on firm, products, or services, as appropriate
			2. Explanation, if needed:
			  a. Comments
			  b. Instructions

3. Courteous close
  a. Expectation of pleasant service and orders (not greedy)
  b. Suggested action
  c. EA‡
  d. RB¶
  e. Courtesy, suggestion of further help, if pertinent
	3. Courteous close
	  a. Cordial, pertinent comment; perhaps a forward look, good wish, compliment, or request
		3. Courteous close
		  a. CSAD†
		  b. EA‡
		  c. DA§
		  d. RB¶ and/or offer of further help
		  e. Courtesy
			3. Courteous close
			  a. CSAD†
			  b. EA‡
			  c. DA§
			  d. Offer of further help or other items or RB¶ about items transmitted

* All lists include possible content. For any one message, choose only the pertinent and appropriate items.
† CSAD = clear statement of action desired.
‡ EA = easy action.
§ DA = dated action, if desirable.
¶ RB = reader benefit.

Chapter 9

Bad-News Messages

Whenever you must send a message that your reader will consider disappointing or unfavorable in some way, the situation requires special planning and careful choice of words. Your goal is to create and maintain goodwill toward your organization.

This chapter discusses the right attitude for transmitting bad news, suggests plans for bad-news messages, and presents various examples of the unfavorable replies and unsolicited messages.

THE RIGHT ATTITUDE

Everything you learned in preceding chapters about the communication process, consideration, and courtesy toward our reader or listener applies to bad-news messages. In such messages it is especially important that the *tone* is appropriate. Because the right attitude toward your recipient will improve the tone and thus the effectiveness of your message, keep the following additional suggestions in mind when you write bad-news letters and memos:

1. Try honestly to see things from the other person's point of view. Your goal is to convince your reader tactfully that your decision, though contrary to his or her request or action, is fair, necessary, and reasonable—and possibly even to his or her advantage in the long run.

2. Avoid leaning on company rules or policy with selfish statements such as "It would be inconvenient for us [*or* against our policy] to do as you ask." Include, if possible, the *customer-benefit reasons* that are behind your rules.

3. Look for the best in the other person. Although a customer may be mistaken, try to have confidence that she or he honestly wants to do the right thing. The following expressions show faith in the reader:

   ```
   We are confident that you. . . .
   You are probably wondering how you can. . . .
   You will agree, I believe, that. . . .
   ```

4. When praising a person, single him or her out; when criticizing, put the person in a group. Mention mistakes impersonally.

Single out:	`You certainly made the right decision, Mr. Brown.`
As a group:	`Sometimes people, unknowingly, make a wrong decision.`
Impersonal:	`Some figures here need to be rechecked for errors.`

5. Shield the reader's pride. (See also Courtesy, pages 68–72).

Tactless:	`If you had read the instructions I gave you, you`
	`would have noticed that they specifically state`
	`you had to sign the acceptance form within 30`
	`days.`

Tactful:	`Our commitment was good for 30 days. In the in-`
	`structions you received with the . . . you will`
	`find. . . .`

6. Talk with, not down to, the reader.

Condescending:	`We are willing to look into this matter` `for you.`
Agreeable:	`Thank you for taking the time to tell us` `about. . . . We always appreciate. . . .`

PLANS FOR BAD-NEWS MESSAGES

The underlying purpose of every bad-news message is to present the unpleasant facts with you-attitude—in such a way that the reader will consider you fair and reasonable and, preferably, remain a friend of the organization you represent. Your choice of message plan is influenced by the circumstances—your purpose, the reader's probable reaction, your relationship to the reader, and the facts in each case. You have two choices of plans: the indirect or the direct.

Indirect Plan

Before you read the suggested indirect pattern for stating bad news, try an experiment on yourself. Suppose you, as a customer, have been waiting for a reply to your request for something you want very much from a business firm—a refund or perhaps a loan important to you. How would you react if the reply began with a negative statement similar to these:

`We regret [we are sorry, wish to state] that we are unable to`
`refund the $300 down payment you made on the car.`

or

`Your application for a loan [refund] has been denied [re-`
`fused, rejected].`

Wouldn't you feel more receptive toward the firm and its bad news if the reply had opened with at least a brief agreeable statement—like the following—and then presented an explanation *before* the bad news?

```
We appreciate your letter telling us how you feel about the
199- hard-top Mercury you purchased from us three months
ago.
```

or

```
Thank you for giving us the opportunity to consider your
loan application for financing your proposed home purchase.
```

Most people appreciate hearing at least some explanation before the bad-news decision, especially if it seriously affects them. Usually a good rule to consider is "Be quick to give good news, but take longer to tell the bad news." Thus, whereas the good-news message uses a direct approch, the bad-news message usually follows the indirect approach. Using this approach, the bad-news plan has the following four-part suggested organizational structure:

---

1. Buffer
2. Explanation and analysis of circumstances
3. Decision, implied or expressed, with resale and/or helpful suggestions
4. Friendly, positive close

---

1. Buffer

If possible, fill your first paragraph mainly with reader-interest information—to get in step with your reader. Your buffer should be pleasant, relevant, honest, and neutral. It should begin close to the general subject of your letter. Avoid statements that might mislead the reader into thinking you are granting the request; they merely build the reader up for a sad letdown. Apologies are unwarranted if your firm is not at fault.

The following are ways to begin a bad-news letter tactfully:

a. *Agreement.* Agree with your reader on something, if possible (perhaps business conditions, costs, or any other pertinent item).

b. *Appreciation.* Thank the reader (for a check, information, application, request, inquiry, cooperation, or whatever applies).

c. *Assurance.* Assure the reader of careful consideration and honest explanation of all available facts about the problem.

d. *Compliment.* Try to compliment the reader on something good about his or her past record or request (sincerity, careful listing of facts, etc.).

e. *Cooperation.* Show a sincere desire to be as helpful as possible.

f. *Good news.* If you can grant any part of a request and you think your reader will be pleased, begin with that good news.

g. *Neutral courtesy.* Keep your opening paragraph noncommittal. For instance, if you must announce an unfavorable price increase or service decrease, use neutral words such as "needed change."

h. *Understanding.* Show you understand or sympathize with the reader's problem (desire to have a dependable product, to pay at least a partial amount due, etc.).

2. Explanation and Analysis

Include honest, convincing reasons why under the circumstances the matter must be handled differently from the way the reader wants it. However, stating a reason is unnecessary when the matter is routine and obvious (for example, a clerical error) and when you'd get mired in negative or confidential material if you tried to explain. When you decide to include explanation, place it *before* the decision and remember these suggestions:

a. Try to convince the reader you are acting in his or her best interests in the long run, or at least according to a law that is enforced equally for all. Avoid the insincere: "Much as I would like to . . .; however, . . ." Also avoid reasons that suggest benefit only to your firm.

b. Explain courteously all pertinent facts behind your decision. Mention first the favorable factors, then the less favorable ones.

c. If the reason is confidential or too complicated to explain, then show—as a substitute—that the request has been carefully and sincerely considered (for the reader's benefit as well as your company's).

3. Decision, Implied or Expressed, with Resale and/or Helpful Suggestions

To make the decision clear, positive, concise, you have these alternatives:

a. If the reasons are so sound that your reader will conclude you *must* refuse the request, payment, or such, you can omit negatives entirely and make the bad-news decision clear by implication. For example, if you are already scheduled as luncheon speaker in Chicago, May 6, omit saying, "Thus, I cannot attend your luncheon in Miami that day."

b. If an implied decision might be misunderstood, express your decision briefly and clearly, near the end of the explanation. Be careful never to mislead or cause your reader to be uncertain about your decision. The best place for a negative decision is in the middle—not the beginning—of a paragraph, and never in a paragraph by itself. Avoid "must refuse," "cannot grant," and similar negatives.

    c. If you can, offer a constructive suggestion, counterproposal, compromise, alternative course of action, or ray of hope for the future. By emphasizing what *can* be done, you may clearly imply what *cannot* be done, without actually using the negatives.

    d. If desirable, resell the reader on your company's services or practices and policies.

4. Friendly, Positive Close

End on a positive note, with one or more of these ideas:

    a. Offer assurances that the reader is appreciated as a customer (or as an interested inquirer and possible future customer).

    b. Invite future patronage, cooperation, suggestions, or compliance with the decision. Include mild, no-pressure sales promotional material if you think your reader is in the right mood for it.

    c. If you are awaiting the reader's approval or if the reader must take some action, make clear what the action is, when to do it, and how to do it easily.

    d. Express continued interest, service, and reader benefit, or sincere wishes for the reader's success with a suggested alternative. (Don't refer to or repeat the bad news. Also, omit such statements as "I trust our decision is satisfactory" and "Let us know if you have any further problems.")

Direct Plan

Though you can use the indirect bad-news plan for most unfavorable messages, there are situations that may warrant the direct approach. Again, the choice depends on the particular circumstances. You may decide to begin directly with the bad news if you have one of the following:

A routine or small matter on which the reader is likely not to be seriously disappointed or personally emotionally involved—especially a message between employees of two business firms or within the same firm (and perhaps also to a person who is known to prefer reading and bad news in the first paragraph).

An urgent message that should be called to the reader's attention forcefully—as in the late stages of a collection procedure.

If you use the direct approach, the pattern is essentially the same as the direct good-news plan, except that the opening contains bad instead of good news.

> **1.** Bad-news decision (with or without a brief buffer)
> **2.** Explanation
> **3.** Appropriate, courteous ending

Most examples of bad-news replies and unsolicited messages in this chapter are organized by the *indirect* approach (hereafter referred to as the bad-news plan). For examples of the messages organized according to the direct approach, you will find the words *direct plan* in the title.

UNFAVORABLE REPLIES TO REQUESTS

This section focuses on unfavorable replies to requests for information about non-sales-related subjects, adjustment, credit, orders, and favors.

Answering Non-Sales-Related Inquiries When the Information Is Undesirable

Occasionally you may have to write bad-news answers to inquiries about matters not relating to sales. In most cases your reply may follow the bad-news approach. In some, the direct plan or perhaps a different alternative may be desirable, as shown in the following example regarding an unfavorable recommendation.

When you receive a request for a recommendation on a person about whom you have only unfavorable information, and whom you honestly cannot recommend, you have these alternatives:

1. Call the inquirer on the telephone and discuss the matter (with prudence).

2. Write a brief refusal note similar to the following:

```
On the basis of my experience with Tom Dawson, I am sorry
that I do not have sufficient information to recommend him
for the position [credit] for which you are considering
him.
```

3. Write an honest, frank, confidential, legally appropriate letter using the bad-news plan. Because of libel laws, it is imperative to be cautious and scrupulously accurate. (See also the comments on pages 177–179 and the discussion of legal aspects, pages 95–101, Chapter 5.)

The *best overall policy* is be honest, tactful, and aware of your fourfold responsibility—to the applicant, to the addressee, to yourself, and to civil rights laws. Omit any statements you cannot verify in a court of law!

When you're writing to someone in your own organization about a relatively small matter with which the reader is not emotionally involved, you probably should use the *direct* refusal plan, as in the following memo.

MESSAGE 1   *Memo in direct-plan format for bad news about company equipment.*

TO: Ann Brown, Purchasing
FROM: Harry Mills, Plant 2
SUBJECT: New ventilating fans needed

Bad news

Today Fred Jones, representative of Ace Electric, told me that the noisy fans you asked about can't be repaired or adjusted again. He says they're a total loss. The only thing possible for ventilation is to buy new fans.

Details

Three fans, model XA22, should do the job well. They'll cost us $90 apiece, installed. Jake says he can install these fans this coming Saturday.

Action request

If you approve, I'll go ahead and make arrangement. Fred needs two days' notice, because he'll order what we need from the factory. Will you give me a jingle by Wednesday afternoon?

If you write for a nonprofit organization that gets many requests for free information—and if you often need to send bad-news replies—you may, to cut correspondence costs, even devise a form letter listing the most recurring negative facts. The following letter has a "Dear reader" salutation.

MESSAGE 2   *Form letter to handle a nonprofit organization's multiple inquiries for which many answers may have to be bad news.*

Buffer: thanks and reader benefit

Thank you for your recent inquiry. In the interest of replying promptly to the hundreds of requests we receive--and for economy--your request and all others are answered by this form letter.

Facts: implied decisions

1. The item or information you requested is
   (a) Enclosed _____.
   (b) Out of print. Copies are in many libraries _____.
   (c) Not yet available _____; will be sent later _____.
2. Your request will be filled as soon as our supply is replenished _____.
3. The free supply of this report is exhausted _____. Copies may be purchased from [*name and address*] for _____ cents a copy.

Suggestions for future action

```
If the check mark for your request is no. 1.c or
2, you can depend on us to send the promised ma-
terial as soon as possible.  If your request has
other check marks, we wish you success in finding
the desired items elsewhere.
```

[Signature]
[Name and title of writer]

Refusing Adjustments on Claims and Complaints

When you refuse a request for adjustment, helpful material to include—besides your buffer and explanation—is resale, constructive suggestions, and even sales promotion where appropriate.

This section discusses two kinds of unwarranted customer claims on which you may have to write a refusal: (1) when the customer is at fault regarding a product and (2) when the customer is mistaken in a complaint about an account or a service.

When the Customer Is at Fault regarding a Product

Often, customers who claim free replacement or repair of a "malfunctioning" product are at fault because they violated instructions for using it. Or a customer might return as "new" an article that cannot be resold because of something the customer did wrong. Also, many customers seek a refund or credit on items simply because they have changed their mind. The next three examples illustrate satisfactory adjustment refusals in such cases.

Misuse of a Product.   Notice that in message 3 the writer calls attention to the user's mistake indirectly and shields the reader's pride. She doesn't say, "You violated the instructions," or, "You obviously failed to read the directions." Instead, the message includes a tactful, logical explanation, an implied but clear refusal, a constructive suggestion, and an easy-action, reader-benefit ending.

MESSAGE 3   *Letter from the customer-service manager of a mail-order house refusing to replace free a broken, misused garden hose.*

Buffer: agreement, appreciation

```
When you buy a Widgeon product, you are right
to expect high quality.  We appreciate your
returning the hose for our inspection so that
we can meet our goal--satisfying your needs
with quality products.
```

Resale; assurance about honoring guarantee

```
To provide each of our thousands of Widgeon
customers with the specific hose he or she
needs, we carry a wide selection.  Each type
of garden hose described in the Widgeon cata-
log is guaranteed to give you the service for
which it was designed.
```

Reason for hose breakdown

As stated in the catalog, the Opaque Plastic Hose you bought is recommended only for use in mild climates, and also it is not to be shut off at the nozzle. Since Mount Vernon's weather ranges in temperature annually from -15 to +105°F, you can see how these extremes may have affected the splitting of the hose. Laboratory analysis indicates that the damage was caused by excessive water pressure re- sulting from either shutting the hose off at the nozzle or from water pressure greater

Implied refusal

than that normally found in most cities. Be- cause Mt. Vernon has the normal water pres- sure of 60 pounds per square inch, the split occurred because someone shut the hose off at the nozzle.

Constructive suggestion

Two Widgeon hoses--the Gold-Line Plastic and the Neoprene Rubber--are especially recom- mended for shutting off at the nozzle. In addition, you can use the Neoprene Rubber hose even in harsh weather. Both are de- scribed on the enclosed copy of catalog page 977.

Easy action; reader benefit

After you have decided which hose best meets your needs, fill out the enclosed order form and mail it in the envelope with your check or money order for $28.97 or $33.97, which includes shipping costs; or indicate that you wish c.o.d. shipment. Either way you can be watering your garden again just three days after we receive your order. And you can be sure of many years' dependable service from your hose.

Unsalability of Return Product.   Some products (for instance, prescription drugs and undergarments) cannot—because of state or national statutes—be accepted for return after they have left the store. In such cases the explanation is easy. However, sometimes a customer may try to return a product he or she has damaged or owned for so long that the store can no longer resell it. Then a tactful, detailed letter like message 4 may be necessary.

MESSAGE 4   *Letter from a retail clothing store's adjustment manager refusing to accept a returned evening gown.*

Buffer: assurance; thanks

To please our customers is the foremost aim of Bon-James. Thank you for writing us ex- plaining your wishes about the evening gown you purchased here last month.

Reader benefit; facts about exchange policy in general

We want you and all our customers to enjoy the confidence of knowing that any purchase from us is for merchandise of outstanding quality and style and that it is absolutely clean, fresh, and new. Wearing apparel may be returned for full credit anytime within 30 days provided the garment is in clean, resalable condition.

Findings in this case

Implied decision

To maintain the high standard on the goods we sell, we carefully check returned merchandise before it is again placed for sale. This examination of the gown you mailed to us disclosed facial makeup at the neckline and several brown spots near the hemline. Because cleaning would render the garment "used" to anyone wishing to repurchase it, the gown is unacceptable for resale.

Helpful suggestions

You can be sure that the skillful touch of our fitter will make the sleeves of your Dior evening gown just the length you like best. For this reason, we suggest that you stop in to see Mr. Davis, who served you when you purchased the gown. He will hold it for you until you can come in for a fitting, or if you want us to send it to you without any changes, he will arrange its prompt return.

Easy action

Resale

Please check and mail your preference on the enclosed card. You can depend on us to do everything possible to help you feel pleased with the gown. You can wear it for several years with confidence that it is a highly fashionable evening garment. As you may recall, it was an outstanding success in the designer show held in New York on June 2.

When the Customer Is Mistaken about an Account or a Service

In addition to refusing adjustments on returned merchandise, you may also have bad news for customers who make erroneous claims resulting from a variety of intangible grievances. Among them are unwarranted claims about their account balances and unjustified gripes about various aspects of your firm's service. Many firms now handle most of these complaints by telephone whenever possible.

Unwarranted Claims about Account Balances.   When customers think you have made an error and you find your records are correct, you must give the customers the bad news that they owe more than they claim. You need to assure them that you have carefully rechecked their records and want to cooperate fully. Be sure to explain each additional charge clearly, for your readers may have forgotten that a purchase or late charges were added or that some past checks were returned by the bank for various reasons. If the matter is too complicated for a phone explanation, a letter will be more helpful—with a tabulation of figures or a photostatic copy of the record.

Unjustified Gripes about Company Services.   Careful and tactful explanation is desirable to establish your company's accuracy and resell the reader on its usual high-quality service. For instance, the printer who is wrongly accused of misspelling a name on the customer's stationery may have to send a copy of the customer's original handwritten order showing the identical spelling. Professional cleaners may reduce customer gripes by sending a printed note like the following, with a cleaned garment or rug that has unremovable stains:

> We've tried and tried, but find that the stains on this [*item name*] cannot be removed without possible injury to the color or fabric. This has been called to your attention so that you will know it has not been overlooked.

If a customer does complain, a detailed oral or written explanation may have to include specific facts about the extra care and time devoted by the experienced workers skilled in modern spot-removing processes. Likewise, similar procedures are desirable in other types of business to help answer complaints about their services. The message should tactfully convince the customer that the firm has well earned the fee and in fairness must charge for an honest job.

Refusing Credit

Even when refusing a credit application, you want to try to keep the reader's goodwill, and perhaps continued business on a cash basis. A person's credit reputation is important. Thus, a credit manager has responsibilities to make sound, informed decisions concerning credit.

To avoid risk of a lawsuit and unfavorable publicity, a credit manager must be careful about what he or she writes and how reasons are expressed. Refusals of both retail and mercantile credit are organized by the bad-news plan, though their contents differ. Some credit departments use the telephone for all refusals. Even if you work in such a department, you will find you can apply many writing principles in this chapter to your oral refusals.

Retail Credit Refusals

For various reasons, approving credit purchases of some customers may be undesirable or impossible. Also, sometimes a customer who has credit established must be told that further credit purchases will be stopped until a current balance is reduced or even paid in full. Other decisions may involve those people who move into a city and want credit immediately, unsettled divorce actions that bring different problems, young people who are just getting started in married life and who may be good risks but yet have no established credit record, and others.

Opening Paragraph.   The refusal usually begins with a buffer that refers to the firm's appreciation or careful consideration of the reader's request for credit or to his or her interest in the store, or to both.

Explanation.   Explanations in retail credit refusals vary considerably; four ways of handling the reasons for refusal are used:

1. Reason is omitted entirely (see letter 1).
2. "Insufficient information" is the only reason given (see letter 2).
3. Factors generally considered in evaluating credit applications are stated without indicating specifically which apply to the reader (see letter 3).
4. Specific reasons are stated (see letter 4).

The first three of these methods can be easily adapted by credit departments that find it necessary to use form letters because of a large number of applications (often over a wide geographic area). Because of similar names among the thousands of individual requests, mix-ups and errors do occur. Thus credit managers for firms that handle numerous requests find it safer to omit specific reasons, especially those that pertain to undesirable character and poor pay habits. From the customer's standpoint the refusal that omits the reason entirely is the least helpful (although it may save some embarrassment). The "insufficient information" reason and the list of general reasons are considered by some customers to be unclear or insincere. Nevertheless, methods 2 and 3 are usually acceptable under certain circumstances, provided the constructive suggestion is tactful and helpful.

The fourth method of refusing credit—stating specific reasons—is desirable when the following conditions exist:

- The situation requires a personalized, typed reply (as in an application for a large loan).
- The reason is not poor (dishonest, unreliable) personal character.
- The desired relationship between the credit department and the applicant is somewhat personal.
- The applicant cannot come for a personal interview and is likely to be offended with anything but an individual, helpful letter.

Such letters are usually longer—and harder to write—than the first three types, but when tactful and accurate, they are highly appreciated by the recipient, because they indicate what must be done to earn (or restore) a good credit standing.

Some large firms use printed forms with courteous opening paragraphs and then a list of perhaps 20 reasons for credit refusals. In front of each is a small square. The sender checks only the reasons applicable to the reader. These forms may also state (at the bottom or on the reverse side) the applicant's rights according to law.

Decision, Resale, Suggestions.   In stating your decision, avoid such negatives as "did not approve," "unfavorable," "does not meet," "must decline." Instead of stressing what is wrong, suggest (whenever possible) how the situation can be improved. Often you can combine resale and constructive alternatives with either the decision or the ending paragraph. In line with circumstances, the applicant may be invited to take one or more of these steps:

1. Come to an office to discuss the case if he or she has questions or thinks an error has been made (letters 2 and 4).

2. Apply again later when conditions have improved (letter 3).

3. Contact another lender or credit agency that you name.

4. Examine the record at the credit bureau and write any needed corrections.[1]

5. Use the layaway plan or another suitable credit plan (letter 3).

6. Continue buying from the company on cash or c.o.d. basis (letters 1, 2, and 3).

Ending Paragraph.   The suggested action ties in with one of the above suggestions and, if possible, includes a reader benefit. Compare form letters 1, 2, 3, and the personal letter 4. (The last paragraph of letter 2 refers to buying on a cash basis. Because some customers consider this suggestion obvious—maybe even offensive—you can avoid reference to cash by wording the last paragraph in a way similar to that in letter 3.)

LETTER 1   *No stated reason. An unhelpful retail credit refusal.*

Buffer: **appreciation**	Thank you for your confidence in us as expressed by your recent credit application.
Decision	After careful consideration, we find that at this time it would be better for you to continue your purchases from us on a cash basis.
Forward look **(weak)**	We hope you will give us frequent opportunities to serve you from our wide selection in all our stores.

LETTER 2   *Insufficient information. A popular retail credit refusal inviting a conference as well as cash purchases.*

Buffer: thanks	We sincerely appreciate the preference you have shown Mack's by your application for a charge account.
Explanation: insufficient information **Decision** **Suggestions: conference**	As you know, the usual custom before opening a new account is to get information that will serve as a basis for credit. Such information as we have thus far obtained is insufficient for us to pass favorably upon your request at this time. If you feel there are other details that would favorably affect your credit, you are welcome to call on us so that we can consider all the facts.
Cash buying; resale	In the meantime, please let us supply your needs on a cash basis. We will make every effort to serve you well with high-quality merchandise and friendly service.

LETTER 3   *List of factors (general reasons) usually considered. A retail credit refusal inviting reapplication and a layaway plan.*

Buffer: thanks	Thank you, [*reader's name*], for your recent inquiry regarding the status of your credit applicaton.
Explanation: list of factors considered	A number of factors are taken into considera-tion when reviewing an application. Length of time at one residence and employment are of vital importance--as well as income, assets, and the paying record of current and past obligations.
Implied decision; assurance; invitation	You are assured that all the above available information has been carefully analyzed in your case. Your circumstances may improve in the future, at which time we would be pleased to reconsider your new request for credit.
Reader-benefit invitation to purchase; no mention of cash	In the meantime, we invite you to save on your household and clothing purchases at Ranney's regular everyday low prices and frequent sales. Also, of course, you're welcome to use our easy layaway plan for bigger purchases.

LETTER 4   *Specific reasons: inadequate income. Personal typed loan refusal.*

Buffer: compliment; favorable aspects	You are to be complimented on your desire to provide the best possible housing for your family. Also, both your loan application and your credit report indicate that you

have maintained a steady employment record. This too is commendable.

Explanation: reasoning from general to specific

In mortgage lending, however, extensive studies have revealed that a certain relationship between a person's income, fixed monthly expense, and loan amount should exist to make a loan advisable. Our maximum loan is 2½ times the annual income, or payments may not exceed 20 percent of the monthly income. Since your income at present meets neither of these requirements, you

Reader-benefit decision

can understand why we feel that an additional financial burden will not serve your best interests.

Suggestion

If you would like to stop in my office, I will be glad to go over with you the minimum requirements for a smaller loan. This discussion might help you in setting and planning your desired goal for home ownership. As time goes on and your income increases, you will be able to improve your financial position to the point where we can help you buy a newer and larger home.

Future help

Feel welcome to come in any day between 9 and 5. We sincerely want to help you reach your desired goal.

Mercantile Credit Refusals

Wholesale or mercantile credit is that which is extended by one business firm to another. The preferred organizational pattern for these credit refusals is the bad-news plan.

For the buffer, you have choices similar to those used in retail refusals—appreciation and assurance of careful consideration.

The most noticeable difference between retail and mercantile credit refusals is that the latter are generally more forthright in the reasons for refusal and are individually typewritten. The decision is based on the firm's financial statement plus other credit ratings (by Dun and Bradstreet, special rating agencies, creditors, and sales agencies of the wholesaler or manufacturer considering the applicant). As with retail credit, the emphasis should be on the positive—the desirable goal—rather than on what is wrong now.

A mercantile credit refusal may include one or more tactful reader-benefit suggestions (especially for someone inexperienced in business):

1. Reduction of apparently excessively high inventory by special means

2. Ways to build up customer's volume of sales (and working capital, if pertinent); perhaps offering assistance of your firm's sales representative

3. Advantages of modest buying, local financing, and cash discounts

4. Cash purchases—smaller, more frequent orders

5. Cash on delivery or cash with orders earning discount privilege

6. Review of the applicant's credit situation at a future time

One good test for any letter is what your reaction to it would have been if you had received it. Would you feel offended if you were the retailer? Would you buy from the wholesaler? True, you're not getting credit, but does the writer seem sincere and interested in helping you?

Acknowledging Orders You Can't Fill Now or at All

Whenever you get an order that you cannot fill immediately, your acknowledgment will be at least temporarily bad news to your customer. The customer is expecting the goods ordered, and any intervening message from you signals possible delay and inconvenience. This section discusses bad-news acknowledgments regarding incomplete or vague orders, back orders, and substitution orders.

Incomplete or Vague Orders

If an order that omits necessary information comes from a customer who has never before ordered the items in question, you probably cannot guess what is wanted. Telephoning or writing to the customer is always better than risking errors and annoyance.

If the order lists some items that you *are* sending now, mention them first, of course. If not, begin with a buffer—usually short resale on the product for which the order is incomplete, appreciation for the order, and, if a first order from a customer, welcome. Then, before you request the missing information or payment, state a reader-benefit reason—that you want to be sure to send exactly what will be liked best. Shield the reader's pride by omitting such words as "you forgot" or "you failed to." Include explanatory facts that the customer needs to complete the order, such as sizes or color choice available. If a letter (instead of a phone call) is necessary, include pictures, catalog numbers, sketches, swatches, and other helpful items when appropriate. Make customer action easy, and assure prompt shipment, if true.

Orders for Out-of-Stock Items to Be Back-Ordered

If your stock of an ordered item is temporarily depleted and you expect a new shipment within a reasonable time (one or two weeks), you can usually back-order and assume the customer would rather wait than cancel the order.

As with the incomplete-order acknowledgment, your main goal in the back-order letter is to keep the customer sold on your goods and to serve him or her well. Because of the necessary delay while waiting for the return of the out-of-stock item, your message should again be organized by the bad-news plan.

Your buffer can be resale on the ordered item (to reinforce the customer's confidence in her or his choice), appreciation, and (if appropriate) a welcome.

Your explanation should focus on the positive aspects—the date the goods will or can reach the customer. Omit such negatives as "cannot send," "out of stock," "exhausted," "won't have any . . . until." Preferably include a reason for your being out of the item, so the customer won't think your firm is inefficient. If such reasons pertain to high popularity or exceptional demand, this even strengthens your resale and the customer's desire for the item. In your action-getting close, positive suggestion is again useful. The easiest way for the customer to "show" approval of the back order is to take no action. Thus back-order acknowledgments often include the positive:

```
Shipment will be made as soon as we receive the new sup-
plies, unless you instruct us to the contrary.
```

If the wait might be unreasonably long, ask the customer to let you know (perhaps by an easy-action reply card) whether he or she approves of your shipping on the later date. Your emphasis whenever possible should be on acceptance, not cancellation. Sometimes a bit of sales promotion material on seasonal or related goods is appropriate, if it is included clearly for the customer's benefit—as a service to the customer rather than just another sale for your firm.

A short message like letter 5 is sufficient for one temporarily out-of-stock item.

LETTER 5   *Acknowledging a charge customer's order on an item to be back-ordered.*

Buffer: thanks, acknowledgment	```Your order for one dozen of the popular Perkup 26-inch window fans, at $42 each, is sincerely appreciated.```
Resale; explanation	```The demand for this newest three-speed, reversible fan has far exceeded our most optimistic expectations at this time of year, with the result that we have twice reordered from the factory. The manufacturer has assured us that our new supply will be delivered within 10 days.```
Decision: expected delivery date; reader benefit	```You may plan on receiving a rush shipment of your fans before March 20. Your customers will like the way these automatic, thermostatically controlled Perkups enable them to enjoy cool breezes indoors regardless of the heat outdoors.```

Orders for Out-of-Stock Items on Which You Suggest a Substitute

When you get an order for a certain model or brand which you cannot supply soon enough by back order or which has been discontinued, you can often suggest a substitute by telephone—provided you honestly think it will meet the customer's needs.

Usually it is safer to ask permission to substitute before you ship, as in letter 6, especially if the customer must pay a higher price for the newer line and if the items are breakable or otherwise costly to ship. (Unfortunate shippers who have sent large substitute shipments without permission have sometimes had to pay many dollars in express charges both ways for rejected merchandise returned by a displeased customer.)

LETTER 6   *Suggesting a substitute in place of an ordered, discontinued item.*

Buffer: brand resale, thanks	You can be sure that your decision to buy a Semco was a decision to buy the finest. Many thanks for your order on June 27 for a Semco office storage cabinet.
Explanation for new model (substitute)	Early this year, in line with business executives' increasing need for better internal security, the Semco factory came out with a new model storage cabinet, the C-402. Because it has all the features our customers have been asking for, we now stock this model exclusively. Though it's possible that George's Supply in North Center may still have the model C-302 you ordered, we are sure you will want our newest model after you check these improved features of the C-402:
Reader-benefit features of substitute	... HEAVIER-GAUGE STEEL than any other cabinet on the market assures extra heavy duty for extra safety. ... REINFORCED DOORS and BASE provide added sturdiness. ... DEPENDABLE YALE LOCK makes cabinet tamper-proof for stored articles. ... ADJUSTABLE SHELVES--six of them--allow easy storage for almost any size supplies. ... NEW COLORS blend with your office decor: mint green, fog gray, or walnut brown.
Easy action	For all these advantages, the C-402 is inexpensively priced at only $94.95, delivered to your office. To give me your "OK" for shipment, just call me at (212) 555-9999 any weekday be-

```
                        tween 8 and 5.  I'll have your new Semco cabinet
                        on its way to you the same day.
```

Reader-benefit
resale
```
We'll be happy to deliver it on open account,
giving you a full 30 days for payment.  You'll
be glad you bought the newest Semco: C-402.
```

Notice that the buffer begins with appreciation and general resale—emphasizing the strongest point of reader appeal that the two articles have in common—the Semco brand. It omits any point of difference (model number, in this case) between ordered and substitute items.

The explanation and bad-news decision stress what the firm *does* have instead of what it does not carry. The new substitute—model C-402—is introduced with one of its merits *before* the bad news that the ordered item—model C-302—is unavailable. One good way to do this is to state that you now stock the substitute *exclusively* (if true), but don't use the word *substitute,* because of its negative connotation. If the substitute is a different brand instead of merely another model of the same brand, do not mention the ordered item by brand name more than once (or at all), because you want the reader to focus attention on your product. However, don't knock your competitor's product; sell your product on its own merits. If you can mention where the ordered product may be obtained, subordinate that statement in a dependent clause, as in letter 6. If the price of the substitute is higher, be sure to state adequate selling points to justify the difference. Instead of "is inexpensively priced at," you might write, "is well worth the small additional $5," or "is an excellent value even at $5 more than the older model," if you think your reader would appreciate knowing the price difference. If your substitute is lower in quality but an excellent value because of price or other reasons, stress these benefits.

The ending asks for authorization to send the substitute—or tells why you have already sent it. Then make clear that the item comes to the customer on trial or subject to approval. Sometimes substitution is also made in rush orders for very similar, same-price, inexpensive items or when the company absorbs the price difference.

Declining Invitations and Requests for Favors

Customers, noncustomers, and employees may extend invitations or request various privileges or favors, other than information, which you may have to refuse. Some are business-related; others, nonbusiness and personal.

Among the numerous business-related favors that customers ask and that you may have to refuse are changing requirements or payment due dates, borrowing your company's equipment or premises, seeing your firm's confidential material, getting special reduced rates, or skipping several payments on a contract. Requests concerning nonbusiness activities may involve donations of your time, money, property, or other assistance.

The bad-news plan is usually the safest to use in most of these refusals. As always, good judgment is necessary for appropriate choices of buffer, tactful explanation with acceptable reasons before the decision, a helpful suggestion, and friendly close. Message 5 is an example of such a letter refusing a request that would require the writer to donate his time.

MESSAGE 5   *Letter: a refusal to accept the office of regional director.*

Buffer: agreement; compliment; appreciation

NRX Association has a great deal to offer business people. I've always found it worthwhile. And so I appreciate even more the compliment you expressed in nominating me for the office of regional director.

Reasons

Implied refusal; emphasis on positive

To perform this job adequately, I realize I should travel to the three State Days this coming year and correspond regularly each month with the 12 branches in this region, before sending monthly reports to our national office. I've given your invitation a good deal of thought, in the light of my present responsibilities as executive trainee at the ABC Company here. My job requires that I devote long hours to the program daily. Often I work Saturdays, too. In addition, Sally and I must spend a great deal of time with our 2-month-old son. Considering everything, I'm convinced the job would be better filled by someone else for the coming year.

Suggestion

If you'd like a suggestion, you might find Albert Solen would be interested in this type of office. He's been active in NRX for 10 years, 2 of them as our excellent branch president. He's an established accountant at the National Gadget Company and is single. Al enjoys being helpfully involved and in my opinion would be a perfect regional director. I'm enclosing a card with Al's address in case you would like to contact him.

Cordial wishes

You have my best wishes, Jim, for getting the right person. You're doing a terrific job for the organization.

On somewhat routine matters between departments of the same firm it is quite permissible to begin directly with the bad-news decision, as in this memo:

MESSAGE 6   *Memo—Direct Plan: refusal of a requested specification change in an airplane factory.*

```
TO:          J. R. Lander        DATE: June 16, 199-
FROM:        T. M. Jepson
SUBJECT:     Food and Beverage Elevator
REFERENCE:   RPD-5244-12 dated 6-15-[year]
```

Refusal

As shown on page 5 of the specifications, paneling for elevator walls remains a valid requirement. Thus the referenced request to use paint instead of vinyl paneling is unacceptable.

Explanation

Because of the particular uses for this elevator and the expected altitudes for flights, it is necessary that all walls have the extra protection of the exact vinyl as in the specifications, instead of mere coats of paint.

Request

Will you please, therefore, see that the paneling requirement is met, according to specifications.

UNFAVORABLE UNSOLICITED MESSAGES

You may sometimes have to send unpleasant messages that are not in response to inquiries. This section illustrates unfavorable announcements about prices and services, rules and procedures, plus miscellaneous bad news. You are generally wise to use the bad-news plan whenever you think your readers will be seriously disappointed or even angered by your bad news. However, when you write to employees or other business associations on routine matters, you may use the direct plan.

Announcing Bad News about Prices or Services

When your firm finds it necessary to increase prices or curtail services to customers, a buffer opening followed by reasons before the unhappy decision will help break the news gently, as in message 1.

MESSAGE 1   *Letter from a wholesaler announcing limitations in services.*

Buffer:
neutral courtesy

In reviewing 199- business and trying to plan for a future in which Gray's can continue to give you good service, it has become evident that some modifications must be made.

Reasons

Our problems are not unlike yours or anyone else's in business today. All expenses in business have been constantly increasing without corresponding increase in profit margin on goods and services. Rather than increase prices in general, the following

Decision

changes as an alternative plan will become
effective July 1 this year:

(1) Free local delivery will be continued
only on orders of at least $15. Orders for a
lesser amount, if received by 1 p.m., can be
delivered the next business day by United
Parcel Service or sent by our regular delivery service if the customer wishes, but the
actual cost of this service will be added to
the invoice.

Details on
the decision

(2) Out-of-town shipments will continue to be
shipped as instructed by the customer or, in
the absence of instructions, will be routed
by the least expensive of parcel post, United
Parcel Service, or Auto Freight. Actual
shipping costs will be added to the invoice.

(3) Collect telephone calls will be accepted
only in cases where we have been in error.

Fairness to
customers;
courteous invitation

A decision on these three changes was made
after a very careful analysis of our costs in
relation to service. We are sure you will
agree that these changes are minimal and fair
to our customers. If you have any suggestions on how we may improve our service to
you, we will greatly appreciate your writing
or calling us right now.

In contrast to the *buffer opening* of message 1 to customers, you can use *bad-news direct-approach openings* similar to the following when you announce the same decisions in *memos* to your employees:

So that Gray's can continue to give good service without a
general increase in prices to our customers, the following
restrictions in delivery and telephone services will become
effective July 1 this year.

Even for employees, however, you should follow the bad-news plan and begin with a buffer when they are likely to be personally affected or seriously disappointed by your bad-news decision. Suppose, for instance, that your company management has decided to close the employee cafeteria food service mornings and evenings and keep it open only during noon hours. To partially offset this decrease and to provide for changing employee food preferences, the snack bar service will be increased. Message 2 illustrates a poor way to announce these changes to employees; message 3, a good way. Notice the difference even in subject lines.

MESSAGE 2   *Memo—Direct Plan: a poor, negative, incomplete bad-news announcement to employees about decreased cafeteria service.*

Janury 25, 199-

TO: All employees of ABC
FROM: Karen Whitson, Food Services Director
SUBJECT: <u>Closing of Cafeteria for Breakfasts and Suppers</u>

Starting next Monday, February 1, there will be no more breakfasts or suppers served in the cafeteria.

This facility will hereafter be closed every morning and afternoon. Lunches will be served in the cafeteria only between 11 a.m. and 2 p.m.

However, to provide continuing service to our employees, the snack bar will be open from 8 a.m. to 5:45 p.m. and will offer a wider selection of food.

MESSAGE 3   *Memo—Indirect Plan: an improved version of the preceding bad-news announcement to employees.*

January 25, 199-

TO: All employees of ABC
FROM: Karen Whitson, Food Services
         Director
SUBJECT: <u>Changes in Company Snack Bar and
         Cafeteria Service</u>

Buffer: reader benefit; noncommittal statement

To keep food prices at their present level, in spite of rising costs, and to meet your changing needs--the snack bar and cafeteria services will be modified <u>starting Monday, February 1.</u>

Reasons

Employee benefits

Changes are necessary because during the past three years fewer employees have been eating breakfasts and suppers in the cafeteria and costs of operating it have steadily increased. So that you can continue to benefit from both low prices and good-quality food, we are altering the services and believe you'll like them.

Decision: favorable changes first

<u>Snack Bar Services</u>--The snack bar will be expanded to offer a wider selection of food than ever before. From the semi-self-service counter and the vending machines you can choose:

```
Packaged Cereals  Fruits and     Sandwiches
Doughnuts            Juices       Hamburgers
Rolls             Soft Drinks     Salads
Coffee, Tea,      Ice Cream       Potato Chips
  Milk            Pies and Cakes  Soup
Hot Chocolate     Candy Bars
```

Decision: emphasis on the positive

Cafeteria Service--Each day a lunch special consisting of a hot main course, salad, dessert, and drink will be served, as before, for less than $5. The cafeteria will serve only lunches.

New Hours--The new hours effective February 1 are:
Snack Bar---8 a.m.--5:45 p.m.
Cafeteria---11 a.m.--2:00 p.m.

Employee benefits

In addition, the cafeteria doors will remain open between 8 a.m. and 6 p.m. for those of you wishing a meeting place during work breaks or a place to enjoy food brought from home or the snack bar.

Forward look; employee benefits; invited action

You are invited to use these facilities whenever you can. They are available to you at no extra price on snacks or lunches. If you have any suggestions on the new cafeteria or snack bar services, please jot them on a slip of paper and drop them into the suggestion box, at the cafeteria door.

Penalizing for Nonconformity to Rules or Procedures

Announcements about penalties for deviating from required procedures or disregarding previous notices quite often begin with the bad news. The direct plan should be used especially when the situation is urgent or when the writer wants the reader to be sure to read the main idea, as in message 4 signed by a bank's branch manager.

MESSAGE 4   *Letter—Direct Plan: processed announcement about dormant savings accounts; typewritten inside address and salutation.*

Main idea

A new [name] state law will definitely affect the status of your inactive account #111-2222.

Explanation

Effective March 1, 199-, accounts will be considered dormant after two years of inactivity. The dormant fee will be $15 a year, and dormant accounts earn no interest unless they are activated.

Our records indicate that there has been no activity on your account for several years.

Suggestion: easy action
Having your passbook updated to reflect the 5½% interest earned from past quarters will prevent your account from becoming dormant. At your earliest convenience before March 1 please complete and return this form in the enclosed postage-paid envelope.

Pleasant close
If you have any questions concerning your account, please come in or call me at 555-6625. We are here to serve you.

The form below this letter asks the saver to check an answer to one of two questions: (1) whether he or she is enclosing the passbook for updating or (2) whether it is lost and thus a Lost Passbook Affidavit should be sent by the bank. Lines are provided for the saver's signature and address change, if any.

Conveying Other Bad News

You may have to write other bad-news, unsolicited (and solicited) messages. As a rule, you can handle most of them well by the bad-news plan.

However, an exception to the usual rule for customer bad-news letters is when you must announce that you made a mistake that is not in the customer's favor. In such cases it is often better to admit your error in the opening, as in the next example.

MESSAGE 5   *Letter—Direct Plan: announcement of an error that unfavorably affects the reader.*

Tactful lead to bad news
Giving accurate service to you and all our customers is always our goal. Today, however, we apologize for a slipup made on a premium statement sent to you last week.

Details
The correct amount of your February 199- premium was $128.61, and we billed you for only $120.55, a difference of $8.06. We overlooked the difference in insurance premiums between your former policy and the new policy, which has given you additional coverage since January 1.

Request; easy action; goodwill
May we ask you to sign the attached form and send it to us with your check for $8.06? Just slip it into the enclosed stamped envelope and mail it. You can be sure we'll do our best to see that you get accurate service in the future.

The letter of resignation is another bad-news announcement you may have to write. It should include your reason for resigning (ill health, better position, or whatever), appreciation and pleasant comments about people you are leaving, perhaps a statement of regret, definite effective date for the resignation, and a sincere, cordial ending.   Whether you resign from a job for which you have been paid or from an elective office, you consider your readers and your relationship to them before you decide to organize by the indirect or direct plan.

MESSAGE 6   *Letter—Indirect Plan: resignation sent to a board of directors.*

Buffer: agreeable statements	During the past four years I've greatly enjoyed working with the many fine people of our organization. Civil defense is an important and challenging cause.
Reason	Recently I received unexpected news that seriously affects my activities. Because I have developed a heart condition, my doctors have instructed me to slow down and particularly emphasized my giving up civil defense. While the condition is not dangerous at present, it is a "warning" type.
Decision and date of resignation	As you may guess, this is pretty much of a blow to me, but it isn't smart to ignore the advice of our doctors. Thus with much reluctance and regret I must ask to be released from my position as state director of civil defense. It is difficult for me to request that you accept my resignation to become effective immediately after your next month's board meeting.
Good wishes	I assure you that my good wishes will continue to be with you and the great work you are doing.

If this writer had felt that the busy board of directors would prefer reading the main idea in the first paragraph (though it is bad news), he could have chosen the direct plan. The letter might then begin with a sentence like the following and continue with reason, pleasant comments, resignation date, good wishes.

> With reluctance and regret I must ask to be released from my position as state director of civil defense.

SUMMARY

Whenever you write unfavorable news—whether you are replying to a request or initiating an unsolicited message—you are usually safe to follow the indirect, four-part bad-news plan. If you use the direct plan, be sure that the type of message, the situation, and the relationship between you and your reader warrant that approach. The 13 Capsule Checklists on pages 244 to 247 review both plans (columns A and B), adapt the indirect plan to 8 kinds of bad-news messages, and suggest choices of either direct or indirect plan on three kinds of announcements.

EXERCISES AND PROBLEMS

Refusing Adjustments on Claims and Complaints

1. *Larry Pider's sweater:* You are manager of the adjustment and claims department in Apex, a small apparel store with a relatively low volume of business. Because of its low volume, it is the store's unwritten policy to grant few refunds and replacements on items returned 30 days after purchase.

    A customer, Mr. Larry Pider, recently returned a cardigan sweater with which he was dissatisfied. The sweater was blue knit, size 42, and contained a label that indicated that the sweater was "wash and wear but must be washed by hand using a mild detergent." Mr. Pider decided to return the sweater, because after he had washed it in his washing machine, using the wash-and-wear cycle, the sweater would no longer fit. He had no record of when it was purchased because he had misplaced his sales slip. However, when he came to the store, he stated that he bought the sweater over two months ago. He also indicated that he had washed it on several occasions, using the wash-and-wear cycle on his washing machine. The sweater, as returned, now appeared to be a size 40 instead of a size 42.

    The customer argued that the label on the sweater said wash and wear and that the store should be accountable. The settlement was not made when the customer came into the store, but you promised to respond to him in writing in a few days.

    Write a letter to Mr. Pider, 4301 Hill Lane, Duluth, MN 55862, refusing the request for a refund or a free replacement on the knit sweater, because the instructions said specifically to wash the sweater by hand and with a mild detergent. You believe the garment was not properly laundered. However, provide some other alternatives in your reply so that Mr. Pider will be inclined to forget about the requested adjustment. You might offer an inducement such as an invitation to a special customer sale or a discount on another purchase.

2. *Bill for long-distance calls:* You are customer service director for the telephone company in your region. One of the letters you must write today is a refusal to Lars Blint, a student at Central Community College (about 50 miles from your office). Here is his letter:

    ```
    The enclosed bill from you for $81.90 contains long-distance
    calls that I won't pay for.  Apparently someone in your
    ```

```
office got numbers screwed up and charged my account instead
of someone's else's.  I know I made eight of the calls on
this bill, but the other two I didn't make.  I don't know
anyone in those towns, and therefore I refuse to pay the
$20.75 charges on them.

Your bill says I supposedly made those calls on June 18.
Well, that day I'm sure I didn't make any long-distance
calls, because I was busy planning for the little celebration
party I had that same night.  It was a special event.  I
didn't see anyone using my phone that night, either.  Anyway,
whoever made the calls should have to pay for them, not me.

Enclosed is my check for $61.15, which I think is in full
payment of what I owe you.
```

Your operations staff members have thoroughly investigated this claim. Your highly accurate equipment registers every call—whether it is directly dialed or placed through an operator as a collect call. If it is the latter, the operator makes a definite, written report on each call. The two calls Mr. Blint questions were placed at 9:35 p.m. and 10:03 p.m., June 18; each was directly dialed; one was 20 minutes long, $9.60, and the other 25 minutes, $11.15. The number from which these calls originated is definitely that of Lars Blint. As every phone book states near the front under "long-distance information and rates," any calls dialed must be billed to the number from which the call is made. Thus Lars must pay for the entire bill, including the $20.75 unpaid balance. Can you include one or two helpful suggestions for him? (Perhaps, because he knows the date, time, town, length of each call, and the cost of each, he could check among his June 18 guests to see who placed the calls.) Your staff even checked all equipment and operations records and found no equipment problems recorded for June 18.

Write Lars Blint, 1852 Seventh Avenue (make up his town and ZIP), a tactful refusal that will keep his goodwill and, you hope, get his full payment before your company has to disconnect his telephone! Remember to emphasize positive aspects.

3. *Graphlix camera repairs:* Your firm sells and repairs cameras and electronic equipment. One of your out-of-town customers sent to you for repair a Graphlix camera, Model 619, bearing the serial number 71961. She claims the camera is defective and asks for free repairs, because she has had it only six months on a one-year guarantee. Examination shows that the camera is not defective, but it has been dropped and badly misused. These repairs are needed: replace broken lens, $48; repair range finder, $9.50; repair and readjust electronic eye, $9. These repairs will put the camera in first-class shape; it cost originally $285. Write to the customer, Ms. Jean A. Norton, 4220 Brooklyn Avenue, Camden, NJ 08166-3200, letting her know why and what she will have to pay for these repairs. You are the customer service manager. Your guarantee accompanying all cameras states they are guaran-

teed for workmanship and materials under normal operating (use) conditions, but *not* when immersed in water, dropped, or given other unusual "shock" treatment. Make action easy for Ms. Norton.

4. ***Bleachez liquid's nonremoval of a seat belt stain:*** As consumer service assistant manager of the Bleachez Company you have today received a complaint from Mrs. F. A. Torno, 8912 Ashworth Street, Gary, IN 46460-3875. She writes that after using your Bleachez liquid to remove a stain from her new, white seat belt, she found that the belt turned an "ugly yellow." She wants you to pay the $18 for a new belt. However, from her description of the yellow discoloration, it appears that the belt had been treated with a resin (for soil resistance and "body") that is not compatible with any dry or liquid chlorine bleach. Your label states that Bleachez removes fruit, vegetable, etc., stains from washable cotton, linen, nylon, and other synthetic materials. But you advocate that Bleachez not be used for stain removal unless the entire item can be immersed in the properly mixed solution and then rinsed well, which is important to stop the bleach action. Thus, Bleachez should not be used on a car seat belt, because of the inconvenience of removing the belt and all metal trimmings before immersing the material in the right solution. Though you can't guarantee 100 percent results, she may wish to immerse the belt for a few minutes in a solution of 1 gallon of water, 2 tablespoonfuls of sodium sulfite (from a drugstore or photo supply shop), and ½ cup of white vinegar, and then rinse throughly. Although you must refuse her claim, make your reply tactful, helpful, and positive.

Refusing Credit

1. ***Mrs. Dell's charge account problem:*** Mr. and Mrs. John R. Dell, 4908 Zain Street, Peoria, IL 61608-3211, have been your credit customers at Best-Ever department store for the five years they have lived in your city. Their account shows that average monthly purchases are about $50 and until two years ago their account was almost always paid on time. During the past two years, however, the payments have not been made when due. The account balance is now more than $500, and no payments have been received for four months.

In today's mail was a letter from Mrs. Dell, which said that she had tried to purchase some furniture last week and the salesclerk told her that the items could not be charged. She left the store in an angry mood, and this letter from her is the result. Among all the things mentioned in the letter are two that are of importance: (1) she threatened to take the matter up with the local better business bureau and the local credit bureau, and (2) she said that she would never again purchase anything at your store.

Write to Mrs. Dell and explain, in a tactful manner, why her recent credit purchase was turned down. Remind her, for example, of the current balance in the account and of the credit terms that she agreed to when the account was first opened, and point out that neither the better business bureau nor the credit bureau will take any action, because your store has broken no laws. Mention anything else that will support your position. You will not, of course, resort to threats but will encourage immediate payment of the account so it can be reopened for her future convenience.

You will also want to include, as best you can, some statement of goodwill or a statement concerning her future as a customer of your store. This is not, of course, the time to try to sell her anything, but you can remind her of the quality products you sell, the several convenient locations in the area shopping center, the customer announcements that go out several days before sales are announced to the general public, and similar points. Tact and firmness are both important, but so is your effort to regain the Dell family's goodwill. Can you show your concern by willingness to help her work out an agreeable, beneficial solution?

2. ***Mr. Tiller's Midway Plumbing and Heating:*** You are the assistant credit manager of Commercial Plumbing Supply Company, wholesalers of bathroom fixtures and plumbing hardware. Compose a credit refusal to Mr. Dick Tiller, owner of Midway Plumbing and Heating, 3950 Empire Boulevard, Columbus, OH 43265-7110.

After examining the business's financial statements, credit ratings from Dun and Bradstreet and the credit bureau of Columbus, and reports from two of Midway's creditors, you must tactfully deny the credit application because of a slow open-account payment record and the firm's low working capital ratio. Midway has been making an average of $260 cash purchases monthly, and you want to keep the firm as a cash customer. You also feel that in a year or two the company may have improved its creditworthiness to meet your credit standards. The company has grown steadily since it was organized four years ago.

Carefully consider these factors and use the most appropriate organizational pattern—direct or indirect. Provide several reader-benefit suggestions for strengthening Midway's credit eligibility. Assume, as needed, other pertinent realistic facts and suggestions regarding Midway's financial position.

3. ***Credit record on Mr. Mesher's account:*** You are the manager of a wholesale fabric business. You distribute fabrics to many stores in your state. You allow them 30 to 90 days to pay for goods, and sometimes longer if necessary. Just recently you have run into a very difficult situation. You extended credit to one small fabric shop that was run by a very personable fellow, Mr. John Mesher. He has come in several times to your warehouse and ordered and picked up fabric. He seems quite at home with all the personnel in your company, and everybody likes him. For these reasons, when he was unable to pay his bill in 90 days, you gave him an indefinite extension. He continued to place eight more orders this year, and his bill is now $795. It has now been a year since he has paid for anything. Of course part of the blame is yours for letting it go on as it did, but you have decided that you can no longer extend credit to this man until he starts paying his past bill. You had

explained that you had to stop credit, and he said he understood, but when he called up on what he termed "emergency" situations, you always said, "Well, only this time." The situation is now out of hand, and you want your money. Decide on a course of action, and write Mr. Mesher an effective letter (Hilltop Fabrics, 895 Fourth Avenue, York, PA 17492-6655).

4. *Mrs. Cobb's application for credit:* As credit manager of Fair Department Store, you have received a credit application from Mrs. Ross Cobb, who seems to be doing a noble job of making the family ends meet on her $1,200 monthly wages. She and her husband and four children rent a $410-a-month cottage, at 21 Tree Lane, Mobile, AL 36666. Her husband has been unable to work for three months because of illness, but he hopes to get a job within two or three more months. You honestly feel that a charge account is not what this family should have now. Cash purchasing from your complete catalog, where they pay as they go, lets them know where they stand at any time. Also, you have end-of-month sales regularly, with savings up to 50 percent. Send Mrs. Cobb a catalog supplement with all the news about your sales. Perhaps when Mr. Cobb is working, you will reconsider her application for your monthly payment plan. Make your letter specific and genuinely helpful.

Acknowledging Orders You Can't Fill Now or at All

Incomplete Orders

1. *Suit for Ms. Welt:* As customer service representative for Evans Clothing Store, Glendale, California, you have today (Tuesday, May 6) received an order from Ms. Loraine Welt, 846 Fifth Avenue, Burbank, CA 91547. She writes that last Saturday evening on her way to a theater in Los Angeles, she happened to pass your store windows on the west side. In the center window she saw a suit that she would like you to send her in size 12, in "white and blue. I think the price was $92.50; just charge it to my account. It's just the thing I'd like to take with me on a trip; we'll be leaving Tuesday, May 13. Will you please send it to reach me no later than Monday?" In checking with your window decorator, you learn that six suits were displayed in the center-west window last Saturday. Worse yet, three of them were in blue and white: (1) horizontal stripes in the jacket top, with navy blue skirt, (2) vertical stripes for both the jacket and slacks, and (3) light-blue jacket with navy trim on the collar, and white skirt. Which does she want? Your secretary tried today to reach her by phone, but discovered that Ms. Welt has either an unlisted number or no phone. You must now write her a letter that goes in the 5 p.m. mail pickup and should reach her tomorrow or Thursday morning. If she will get her answer to you by no later than Friday noon, you can be sure to send the right suit to her on the store delivery truck Monday morning. Devise easy action for Ms. Welt; also make sure you will get all the information you need to fill her order immediately.

2. ***Marine supplies for Mr. Kamp:*** From Mr. Jonathan Kamp, assistant manager, Silver Marine and Pool Supply, 825 Arnold Avenue, Detroit, MI 48294-2244, you receive an order for:

```
10 boarding ladders, 3 steps              @ $30.50 each
50 ft #6424 Marine Mat and Dock Runner, red  @    8.20 per ft
3 doz. deluxe #78145 chair pads, floral   @    6.00 each
```

These items are to be shipped freight charges collect and billed on the firm's usual credit terms of 2/10, net 30. You can't ship two of these items, however, until you get more information. The boarding ladders come with 7- and 11-inch hooks—so they can seat securely on boats, rafts, pools, or docks. Which size does he want? It is even possible that he might want five of each, but you think it is risky to guess. The ladder prices are the same for both sizes of hook. These white, vinyl-covered hooks turn a full 360 degrees for fast and easy fitting, and they fold so that the ladder is flat for convenient storage. The steps are varnished oak hardwood, 16 inches wide.

The Mat and Dock Runner, #6424, is in aqua color, not red. The red is listed in your catalog (which Silver Marine has) as #6425. Though he probably wants the red and just wrote the wrong catalog number, you want to be sure before you ship this heavy roll. (Shipping weight is 3 pounds per foot!) This is an excellent runner for deck or dock. It is made of all-weather, nonslip, brush-action polyester pile with heavy rubber backing and is 36 inches wide.

You do have the chair pads and can ship them today. They are a durable, waterproof vinyl floral pattern, ideal for outdoor patio use. Today is June 12. Decide whether you should ship the pads today or wait until you can send the other items too. Write for the needed information, make action easy, and cover all pertinent details. You are assistant sales manager for Pool and Patio Wholesale Company, Oakland, CA 94621-3456.

Back Order

3. ***Mr. Roldo's wallpaper order:*** A charge customer, Mr. Thurston Roldo, at 945 Sound Drive, Portland, OR 97216-8200, orders five more rolls of the #WP4662 gold color, flocked, raised damask wallpaper ($17.95 a roll). He writes that he just finished papering the dining room with this pattern and his family likes it so much that they now want the hall to match. Your store (Milli's Interior Design Shop, Tacoma, WA 98411) is completely out of this pattern; you sold your last roll three days ago. You are the exclusive dealer for these distinctive wallpapers in the Northwest and get them direct from the Dayberry Mills in Massachusetts. A wire from the mills today promised that your special order of #WP4662 would reach your shop in 10 days. Write Mr. Roldo the appropriate letter to keep him convinced that this choice wallpaper is well worth waiting for. It is one of the most elegant you carry. Its beautiful flocked damask pattern has the lovely look and feel of velvet. Textured to simulate fine silk, all on tough vinyl, it is strong and

won't tear even when wet. Also, it's prepasted and pretrimmed and can be cleaned with soap and water. Shipping time between Portland and Tacoma is one day.

Substitution Order

4. ***Golden Agers' hotel reservation:*** You are the hotel reservation clerk for an ultramodern, very popular hotel in New York City. Every Thanksgiving holiday, various tourist groups of holiday shoppers make plans to come into the city and want to stay specifically at your hotel. Your facility offers the finest restaurants, great entertainment, attractive meeting rooms, indoor shopping facilities including the leading department store outlets, health spa, swimming pool, ice skating rink, etc. This is a facility for any season in the year. Therefore, the name is the All Seasons Hotel.

A request has been received from a group of "Golden Agers" (J. R. Brown, President, P.O. Box 921, Omaha, NE 68122-3444) who would like to stay at your hotel. They have done so in the past, but are late in sending their reservations for this year. Although your records show that this particular group has been your guest for the past five years, you must write them that your hotel cannot provide them with all the reservations they have requested. Offer them 35 of the 60 rooms requested and confirmation on the other 25 rooms in another hotel close by. Give a deadline date for their response.

Declining Favors, Invitations, and Miscellaneous Requests

1. ***Captain for United Way fund drive:*** Assume you receive the following letter from Mr. Eugene Hewsen, chairman of the local United Way campaign for this year:

Dear [**Mr.** *or* **Ms.**] [*your name*]

As you know, our city conducts a United Way fund drive annually. Many people volunteer their help to coordinate the
campaign. Will you be willing to serve as a captain this
year?

Captains are responsible for a particular geographical area.
Yours would be a 10-block area bounded by [*name*] Street on the
west, [*name*] Street on the east, [*name*] Street on the north,
and [*name*] Street on the south. You would be responsible for
selecting workers in each block, who in turn will canvass
each house in their particular block.

Needless to say, your effort will be for a most worthy cause.
Will you drop me a line . . . soon, saying you'll accept?

Unfortunately you must decline the request. Since the campaign is kicked off in September and you will be out of the state on vacation (or company business) that month, you won't be around to do your duty. Write a considerate reply. (Assume a local address for Mr. Hewsen.)

2. ***Rewrite of letter from a research firm's assistant manager:*** The following statements were in a letter the assistant manager of a research firm mailed to an inquiring college student. What is your reaction to this message?

```
I have your request for advice and booklets regarding prac-
tices and experiences of this company in consumer research
and market testing.  You list seven questions. Each is so
broad in scope that an adequate answer would require at least
a written chapter.  A comprehensive answer to all seven ques-
tions would comprise a thesis on marketing research.  I would
like to ask you a few questions:

1. Do students think a company has any responsibility to con-
   tribute to their education?  Do they think the company
   should help students prepare their thesis for the sake of
   building goodwill?  Or for the sake of securing a possible
   future customer?
2. If an affirmative answer is given to no. 1, what do stu-
   dents regard as a reasonable amount of cooperation?
   a. To check a few "Yes" or "No" questions?
   b. To furnish available and pertinent literature if avail-
      able?
   c. To write a dissertation for them on one subject? On
      seven subjects?
   d. To write a thesis for them?
3. How do university students think commercial companies
   would justify the time and expense involved in writing ed-
   ucational material for students in answer to broad-scope
   questions?

You need not answer the above questions nor reply to this
letter.  My questions are rhetorical, and I have no intention
of writing a reply to your questions.  My contribution to
your education is this letter, and in my opinion it should be
more valuable to you than an answer to your questions would
be.
```

Write a courteous refusal letter that you—this firm's manager—would have mailed. Assume you must, for an acceptable reason, refuse to answer the student's seven broad-scope questions. However, you'd be willing to give some helpful requested information—*if* the student would prepare a list of specific questions that can be answered easily in a few minutes. You'd accept a one-page (maybe two-page?) questionnaire. Try to include tactful suggestions and show consideration for the student's problem or needs. (Make up a name and address.)

Bad-News Announcements

1. ***Increased monthly garage parking rates:*** You are president of the Central Building Garage, Inc. Your company manages a 400-car garage used by business executives who occupy the Central Building. Because of steadily increasing operating costs (mainly wages), you have found it necessary to increase the monthly parking rates to $106 a month (instead of the former $96), plus the state sales tax. This increase will become effective February 1, 199-.

   For the past two years you have been absorbing the increased operating expenses, but cannot continue to do so any longer. After several conversations with Mr. P. L. Brown, vice president of Commercial Properties, Inc., the Central Building's owners, who lease to the business firms in the building and from whom you lease your garage facilities, you received permission for the rate increase. Now you will write two letters:

   a. To Mr. Brown, telling him your decision about the monthly rate and effective date. Inform him that you will notify all parking customers before a certain date. You might restate briefly the reason for this increase, refer to previous conversations, and show appreciation. Will you organize by the direct or indirect plan? Why?
   b. To all customers who have been renting monthly parking space from your garage. This increase comes to them as a bad-news surprise. Give them whatever details you think they will appreciate having. Will you organize the same way as for letter *a*? Why or why not?

2. ***Memo to boss regarding job offers:*** You have been an assistant account executive at a large advertising agency for eight years but recently received an offer from another well-respected agency for the post of account executive. The new job would entail a 20 percent salary increase and much more responsibility. Although excited by the offer, you are reluctant to leave your current position, where you enjoy your job and associates. Two weeks ago you wrote a note to your boss stating the terms of the offer, but emphasizing your desire to stay with your present agency if a competitive counteroffer were made. That offer, which you received three days ago, was disappointing to you. Your title would remain the same, your responsibilities would increase in only superficial ways, and your salary increase (9 percent) would be less than half what the competitor offered. After much deliberation, you and your spouse have agreed that the new position, offering better financial and career opportunities, should be accepted. Write a memo to your boss, Carl Logess, notifying him of your decision.

3. ***Memo to all employees regarding janitorial services:*** Today, March 25, you have just been informed that the only janitorial service in your small town is quitting business at the end of this month. Your general manager has negotiated a contract with janitorial services in a nearby town, but they will not begin work until April 10. Now you (personnel manager) need to

inform all employees that the entire office will have no outside cleaning help for seven workdays. All employees must keep their own work areas clean, and they must also keep restrooms and floors free from clutter. Perhaps you can suggest a rule regarding cigarette butts, bottles, cans? Each of your 14 employees—and managers too—must empty his or her own wastebasket into one of the large cans in the restrooms. (As these rooms have automatic hot-air dryers, those who wash their hands will not be bothered with any mess of paper towel disposal.) A vacuum cleaner and two brooms are available for use before 8:30 a.m. and after 5:30 p.m. Write a memo that creates a feeling of camaraderie and cooperation.

4. ***Letter to decrease mailing list of free magazine:*** For many years your company has been sending free copies of a glossy magazine, *Improving Your Outlook*, to anyone who requested to be on your mailing list. (If you prefer, assume a different title for this magazine.) Seldom do you hear from your readers. The cost of this little publication is about $3.10 each. In an effort to try to pare unnecessary expenses, your firm's directors have suggested that the mailing list be revised to include only those persons and firms that still read and appreciate the publication. They realize that after a passage of years those who originally requested to be on the mailing list may no longer be reading the magazine. Write a pleasant to-be-processed letter with positive tone that will offend no one, even though it basically conveys bad news. Your goal is to find out which readers wish to keep the magazine coming. They'll help you keep your mailing list up to date by taking a certain action that you request. Can you word your announcement in such a way that the readers will be dropped from your mailing list if you don't hear from them?

■ CAPSULE CHECKLISTS FOR BAD-NEWS MESSAGES*

Bad News		**C** **Answering Non-Sales-Related Inquiries When the Information Is Unfavorable**
A General Plan (Indirect)	**B** Exception (Direct)	

1. BUFFER
  a. Agreement
  b. Appreciation
  c. Assurance
  d. Compliment
  e. Cooperation
  f. Good news
  g. Neutral courtesy
  h. Understanding
	1. Main idea
	  a. Bad-news decision, sometimes with a brief buffer and/or reason
		1. Buffer
		  For unfavorable recommendations:
		  a. Applicant's name; relationship
		  b. Reason for writing; reply by request
		  For other inquiries:
		  c. Appreciation
		  d. Assurance
		  e. Understanding

2. EXPLANATION
  a. Necessary details—general to specific
  b. Favorable, then unfavorable facts
  c. RB‡ reasons
  d. Emphasis on desired goal
	2. Explanation
	  a. Necessary details—general to specific
	  b. Emphasis on desired goal
		2. Explanation
		  a. Answers to all questions
		  b. Pertinent facts (favorable and unfavorable)
		  c. Caution on legalities
		  d. Confidentiality
		  e. Offer, phone call

3. DECISION—implied or expressed—with resale and/or constructive suggestions
  a. Embedded statement of bad news—with suggestion of what *can* be done
  b. Helpful counterproposal, plans, alternatives
  c. Resale
  d. Sales promotion
	3. Decision omitted (already in B.1.a). Resale and suggestions often unnecessary and omitted; sometimes:
	  a. Helpful counterproposal, plans, alternatives
		3. Decision—with constructive suggestions
		  About applicant:
		  a. Honest nonendorsement
		  b. Possibility of changes since you last saw applicant
		  About other non-sales-related inquiries:
		  c. Same as A.3.a and b

4. POSITIVE, FRIENDLY, APPROPRIATE CLOSE
  a. Application
  b. Invitation to future action
  c. CSAD‡
  d. EA§ and motivation
  e. DA¶
  f. Willingness to help further
  g. RB†
  h. Good wishes
  i. Courtesy
	4. Positive, friendly, appropriate close. Sometimes:
	  a. Appreciation
	  b. Invitation to future action
	  c. CSAD‡
	  d. EA§ and motivation
	  e. DA¶
	  f. Willingness to help further
	  g. RB†
	  h. Good wishes
	  i. Courtesy
		4. Positive, friendly, appropriate close
		  a. Ray of hope for improvement
		  b. Willingness to help further
		  c. Good wishes

° All lists include possible content. For any one message, choose only the pertinent appropriate items.
† RB = reader benefit.
‡ CSAD = clear statement of action desired.
§ EA = easy action.
¶ DA = dated action, if desirable.

■ CAPSULE CHECKLISTS FOR BAD-NEWS MESSAGES (Continued)*

	Refusing Credit	
D **Refusing Adjustments on Claims and Complaints**	**E** Retail Credit	**F** Mercantile Credit

1. Buffer
  a. Agreement
  b. Appreciation
  c. Assurance
  d. Cooperation
  e. Neutral courtesy
  f. Understanding
  g. If granting a part is good news, opening is on that part
	1. Buffer
	  a. Agreeable comment
	  b. Appreciation
	  c. Assurance
	  d. Brief resale on product and/or firm
	  e. Incidental reference to the order, if any
		1. Buffer
		  a. Agreeable comment
		  b. Appreciation
		  c. Assurance
		  d. Brief resale on produce and/or firm
		  e. Incidental reference to the order, if any

2. Explanation
  a. Logical statement of reasons
  b. General RB† procedure, policy, instructions, guarantee
  c. Resale interwoven
  d. Education on use
  e. Impersonal facts on buyer's mistake
	2. Explanation
	  Choice of:
	  a. No reason
	  b. "Insufficient information" reason
	  c. List of all usual reasons
	  d. Specific reason(s): with RB† and emphasis on desired goal
		2. Explanation
		  a. Specific reasons
		  b. Favorable, then unfavorable, facts
		  c. Emphasis on desired goal

3. Decision—with resale and/or suggestions
  a. Impersonal, expressed or implied, but clear refusal; positive language, perhaps RB†
  b. Clear indication if you are returning product
  c. RB† suggestion(s) for using rejected product and/or another
  d. Resale on product, service, and/or firm
	3. Decision—with RB† counterproposal and suggestion(s)
	  a. Embedded statement of bad news—with suggestion of what *can* be done
	  b. Suggestions
	    Conference
	    Other lenders
	    Future review
	    Other credit plans available
	    Layaway
	    Cash or c.o.d. buying
		3. Decision—with RB† counterproposal and suggestion(s)
		  a. Embedded statement of bad news—with suggestion of what *can* be done
		  b. Suggestions
		    Inventory reduction
		    Sales or capital increase
		    Local financing
		    Cash or c.o.d. buying; smaller, frequent orders
		    Help of sales representative
		    Future review

4. Positive, friendly, appropriate close
  a. CSAD (tactful suggestion without urging)‡
  b. EA§ and DA¶
  c. Positive forward look
  d. RB† and satisfaction
  e. Courtesy
	4. Positive, friendly, appropriate close
	  a. Invitation regarding a suggestion; CSAD‡
	  b. Forward look
	  c. Resale
	  d. RB† and EA§
	  e. Courtesy
		4. Positive, friendly, appropriate close
		  a. Invitation regarding a suggestion; CSAD‡
		  b. Forward look
		  c. Resale
		  d. RB† and EA§
		  e. Courtesy

* All lists include possible content. For any one message, choose only the pertinent appropriate items.
† RB = reader benefit.
‡ CSAD = clear statement of action desired.
§ EA = easy action.
¶ DA = dated action, if desirable.

Acknowledging Orders You Can't Fill Now or at All

G	H	I	J
Incomplete or Vague	**Back Orders**	**Substitutions**	**Declining Invitations and Requests for Favors**
1. Good news, if any, and buffer a. Shipment details, if sending anything b. Buffer: short resale on vaguely described item(s) c. Brief order acknowledgment (date, item) d. Appreciation e. Welcome, if new customer	1. Good news, if any, and buffer a. Same as G.1.a b. Buffer: specific resale or ordered depleted item; no mention of depletion c. Brief order acknowledgment (date, item) d. Appreciation e. Welcome, if new customer	1. Good news, if any, and buffer a. Same as G.1.a b. Buffer: broad resale embodies both substitute and ordered item; omits differences c. Brief order acknowledgment (date, item) d. Appreciation e. Welcome, if new customer	1. Buffer a. Appreciation b. Compliment (to reader) c. Assurance d. Agreeable comment
2. Explanation a. RB† reason for requesting missing information b. Facts about choices available (sizes, colors, models) c. Descriptive enclosures	2. Explanation a. Approximate date goods expected to reach buyer b. Reasons unavailable now (RB?)† c. Resale	2. Explanation a. One or two merits of substitute (S) before revealing unavailability of ordered item (O) b. Sales point on why we carry S exclusively	2. Explanation a. Facts and (sometimes personal) reasons leading to refusal
3. Decision—with resale and/or suggestions a. See 2.a, above—implied decision b. Perhaps brief resale on the item(s) in general	3. Decision—with resale and/or constructive suggestions a. See 2.a above—implied decision b. Possibly mild sales promotion on allied item(s) to be shipped with back-ordered item c. Perhaps brief resale on back-ordered item	3. Decision—with resale and suggestions a. Unavailability of O—in positive terms (exclusively stock S—if true) b. Passive statement on where O may be bought c. Price and quality justification of substitute; RB† d. Sales promotion	3. Decision—with resale and/or suggestions a. Clear, tactful decision, implied or stated; emphasis on the positive aspects (desire to help, etc.) b. RB† suggestions—when, how you *can* help c. Alternative sources of help to reader
4. Positive, friendly, appropriate close a. CSAD‡ b. EA§ c. DA¶ d. RB (prompt delivery?)† e. Courtesy	4. Positive, friendly, appropriate close a. If shipment in reasonable time: no action; assumption that back order is OK b. If longer: CSAD‡; EA§; DA¶ c. RB†	4. Positive, friendly, appropriate close a. If S is already shipped: assurance of money-back "shipment on approval"; RB† b. If S is not yet shipped: CSAD‡; EA§; DA¶; RB†	4. Positive, friendly, appropriate close a. CSAD‡ b. EA§ c. DA¶ d. Good wishes e. RB† f. Courtesy

° All lists include possible content. For any one message, choose only the pertinent appropriate items.
† RB = reader benefit.
‡ CSAD = clear statement of action desired.
§ EA = easy action.
¶ DA = dated action, if desirable.

■ CAPSULE CHECKLISTS FOR BAD-NEWS MESSAGES (Continued)*

K **Announcing Bad News about Prices and Services**	**L** **Penalizing for Nonconformity to Rules or Procedures**	**M** **Conveying Other Bad News**

1. Main idea or buffer
  a. If routine (or reader not emotionally involved), B.1—(direct plan)
  b. Otherwise, A.1 buffer:
    (1) Agreeable comment
    (2) Neutral courtesy
    (3) Brief resale
	1. Main idea or buffer
	  a. If routine, urgent, or reader not emotionally involved: bad-news decision, sometimes with reason (direct plan, B.1)
	  b. Otherwise, A.1 buffer:
	    (1) Agreeable comment
	    (2) Neutral courtesy
	    (3) Compliment on past
	    (4) Hint of urgency or need for change
		1. Main idea or buffer
		  a. Same as L.1.a
		  b. Same as L.1.b

2. Explanation
  a. RB† reasons and analysis of increasing costs, etc.
	2. Explanation
	  a. Details about the requirements
	  b. Reasons leading to the penalty
		2. Explanation
		  a. Details on what is wrong

3. Decision—with resale and suggestions
  a. Effective date of new plan
  b. Clear statement and itemizing, if needed
  c. Enclosures or examples, if helpful
  d. Resale on your firm's products, services, prices
	3. Decision—with resale and suggestions
	  a. Clear, tactful statement of what will happen unless reader meets requirements
	  b. Suggestions for eliminating penalty in future
	  c. Forms and deadlines
		3. Decision—with suggestions
		  a. What needs to be done
		  b. How to do it

4. Positive, friendly, appropriate close
  a. Forward look
  b. Resale
  c. Invitation to action
  d. CSAD‡
  e. EA§
  f. RB†
  g. Courtesy
	4. Positive, friendly, appropriate close
	  a. CSAD‡
	  b. EA§
	  c. DA¶
	  d. RB†
	  e. Assurance
	  f. Good wishes
	  g. Courtesy
		4. Positive, friendly, appropriate close
		  a. CSAD‡
		  b. EA§
		  c. Goodwill
		  d. Courtesy

° All lists include possible content. For any one message, choose only the pertinent appropriate items.
† RB = reader benefit.
‡ CSAD = clear statement of action desired.
§ EA = easy action.
¶ DA = dated action, if desirable.

Chapter 10

Persuasive Requests

Besides situations in which mere *asking* is sufficient (routine direct requests), you will face situations in which you need to *persuade*. The favor or action you ask is such that you anticipate some objection. This chapter discusses the persuasive-request plan and how you can adapt it for the following messages:

> Persuasive requests for favors that:
> > Require time, knowledge, and/or effort
> > Ask donations of money or other valuables
> > Urge cooperation on goals and projects
>
> Other persuasive, nonroutine requests for:
> > Adjustment
> > Credit
> > Changes in policy or performance

The persuasive-request plan is also used for unsolicited sales, job application, and some collection letters, as discussed in Chapters 11 to 14.

ORGANIZATIONAL PLAN—AIDA

The persuasive request, like the bad-news letter, uses the indirect approach. You assume that if your request were stated directly at the beginning, it would be unwanted or bad news to your reader, who would then react unfavorably. Thus, before you mention the specific request, you will have to prepare the reader for it and, when possible, present facts to indicate that your proposal is beneficial or useful. Remember, your reader is not expecting your message, and you should attract his or her attention and arouse interest *before* revealing what you'd like done.

The basic structure for persuasive letters usually has four parts, commonly known as the AIDA formula for sales presentation:

> **A**—Attract the reader's favorable *attention*.
> **I**—Arouse the reader's *interest*.
> **D**—Create *desire* and convince the reader.
> **A**—Make clear the *action* the reader needs to take.

Although attention, interest, and desire are listed here as distinct steps, they are usually combined or blended so smoothly in the well-written persuasive message that it is difficult—and unnecessary—to separate them. Also, the parts do not always occur in the sequence given here; for example, it is possible to omit or deemphasize those points that have been covered in earlier letters, advertising, or personal contacts with the prospect. *You-attitude content and reader benefits are most important.* What you call the parts and whether you have three or four is unimportant. In fact, the persuasive-request plan is some-times called the four P's—promise, picture, prove, and push—or discussed under *three* parts—star, chain, and hook. In the AIDA persuasive-request ex-panded outline below, other names for the parts are indicated in parentheses.

1. *Attention.*   *(promise; star)*—*First Paragraph*

Attract favorable attention with a reader-interest or a reader-benefit theme. Begin with a relevant statement or a challenging question that entices the recipients to read on because they want to know "What's in this letter for me?" Highlight a point that is close to the reader's interests or needs, instead of talking about yourself or your organization.

Because many people throw away envelopes that look like part of bulk mailings, even the envelope plays an important part in getting favorable atten-tion. Among the devices used with varying degrees of success on envelopes are color, handwritten addresses, contest announcements, questions, and a few enticing words from the message printed on the envelope.

2. *Interest.*   *(picture; chain)*—*Middle Paragraphs*

Build upon the theme started in the attention-getting opening. Begin to tell what your project, product, or service is and what it will do for the reader (and/ or for others—if your goal is charity and altruism). Describe it clearly and specifically in two ways (not necessarily in this order):

a. *Its physical description*—important features, construction, appearance, performance, beauty, functions (any or all of which may be omitted for a long-established subject well known to the reader).

b. *Its value or benefits to the reader or others in whom the reader is interested.* Of the various features and uses that the project, product, or service has, emphasize the central selling point—that point you think is most likely to make the strongest appeal to the prospect. For instance, will your proposal bring comfort? Entertainment? Health? Recognition? Safety? Show the reader how your proposal gives one or more benefits like the following:

Appreciation (by others)	Entertainment
Approval (by others)	Extra earnings
Beauty or attractiveness	Fair treatment
Cleanliness	Friendships
Comfort	Good reputation
Convenience	Health
Cooperation	Improvement
Customer satisfaction	Love of home, family, others
Distinctiveness	Money and other valuables
Durability	Peace of mind
Efficiency	Pleasure
Enjoyment	Popularity

Position of authority

Prestige

Pride

Profits

Protection for family, business, self, or others

Provision for the future

Recognition

Reduced work

Relief from fear

Respect

Safety and security

Satisfaction of helping others (altruism)

Savings

Self-preservation

Solution to a problem

Success

Thrift habit

Usefulness

3. *Desire and Conviction.*   *(prove; chain)*—**Middle Paragraphs**

So that your readers will desire to do as you request and be convinced that they (or others in whom they are interested) will benefit from your proposal, you usually present proof. Give evidence that your statements are true. Include needed facts, pictures, figures, testimonials, tests, samples, guarantees, or any other proof your proposal may call for. Be aware of your legal responsibilities for truth.

A descriptive folder permits you to avoid cluttering your letter with many details. However, if you have an enclosure, mention it only after stating most of your selling points and then motivate your reader to read further details in the folder. Link your reference to the enclosure with a sales point. Don't depend on the enclosure to do your selling.

4. *Action.*   *(push; hook)*—**Last Paragraph**

Clearly state what the reader should do to comply with your request and thus to gain the benefits. Make action easy—by including a reply form, envelope, phone number, office hours, location, and so forth. Induce the reader to act now or within a certain time, and end on a reader-benefit plug, which may tie in with your opening statement.

PERSUASIVE REQUESTS FOR FAVORS

As a conscientious business or professional person you probably participate actively in various committees and organizations. And you have numerous opportunities to write (as well as to answer) favor requests that seek the recipient's donation of something—time, knowledge, effort, money, or cooperation. The AIDA plan helps you to ask a favor effectively, as described in the following section.

Getting Attention for Favor Requests

To begin your favor request with something close to your reader's interest or benefit, consider what appeals are likely to be most meaningful to her or him. Try to introduce a direct or indirect benefit that you can develop as a central selling point more fully later in the letter. You want to get the reader's attention *before* stating your request, but you need to use good judgment in introducing benefits. Be careful that your statements don't sound like high-pressure appeals or bribes, as in this poor opening for a letter inviting a political candidate to speak: "How much would it be worth to you to influence the views of 2,000 voters?"

Effective openings you can use—with discretion—for various favor requests are these:

1. Comments or assertions with which the reader will agree
2. Compliments—if sincere
3. Frank admission that your message is a request for a favor
4. Problem(s) that are the basis of your favor request
5. Question(s)—one or two rhetorical questions
6. Statement(s) of what is or has been done to solve or lessen a problem

Opening with Agreeable Comment or Assertion

To speak to students majoring in advertising:

```
Advertising is the spark plug of any business and a chal-
lenge to the creative thinker.  Yet what advice can you give
to the many students who cannot decide what area of adver-
tising to enter?
```

To help in getting community support:

```
One topic in which you and I share a special interest is the
education of our children.  The success of our school levy
will determine the quality of education received by Bellevue
students.
```

Opening with Sincere Compliment

To speak, without fee, to a local chapter:

```
Ever since your stimulating speech last year to delegates at
the KSA national convention in Atlanta, our TriCity chapter
members here have wanted to meet you personally.  We believe
you could be a profound influence on our future program and
growth.
```

To accept an important chairperson position:

```
Your exceptionally fine work in [name] projects emphasizes
that you deserve a place on the executive board of. . . .
```

Opening with Frank Admission of Favor

To be moderator at a national convention:

```
To get and keep our 199- NRMA Conference program on the
beam, we will need three top-grade people to serve as moder-
ators.  You can no doubt guess why I am making this appeal
to you.
```

To fill out and return a questionnaire:

```
WILL YOU HELP DMAA?
--AND HELP YOURSELF, TOO?

     I'd like to ask a favor of you. It concerns the gather-
ing of important facts and information regarding postal
rates.  Here, in a nutshell, is the story:
```

Opening with Basic Problem

To contribute to a lab fund:

```
DIAGNOSTIC LABORATORY IN DANGER!
INDUSTRY STANDS TO LOSE $60,000!
Contributions for the new diagnostic lab in [town name] have
stopped coming in.  Unless we can immediately raise $11,000,
we will lose the $60,000 appropriated by the last legis-
lature, on the condition we in the industry match it with
$35,000.  Only $24,000 of the necessary $35,000 has, so far,
been pledged.
```

Opening with a Question

To participate in a six-month research project:

```
Have you ever had the fun of participating in a market re-
search study?  As you know, market research is the study of
consumer reactions and attitudes to products.  This research
is extremely useful to manufacturers in helping them to give
you and your family products to better suit your needs.
```

To become a member of a university YWCA:

```
WHAT'S THE USE?
"What's the use of getting an education?"
  "What's the use of planning ahead?"
    "What's the use of living thoughtfully?"
      "WHAT'S THE USE OF ANYTHING?"
```

Opening That States What Has Been Done about a Problem

To send a gift to the Fund for the Blind:

```
Thousands of blind Americans wait eagerly each month for
their copies of the braille or talking book edition of
[name].  It is the only magazine of its kind available in
braille or talking book form (long-playing records) that is
exactly like the print edition read by their sighted
friends.  This means something very special to them.
    With the help of friends like you, we can supply these.
. . .
```

Arousing Interest and Creating Desire to Do the Favor

When you have decided on an opening that sets the theme and encourages the recipient to read on, you can continue to build on your idea. To get the reader's interest and desire, you need to (1) include all necessary description—physical characteristics and value of the project, (2) present facts and figures about direct or indirect reader benefits, and (3) handle negatives positively. This material consitutes the greater part of your persuasive request.

Physical Characteristics and Value of Project

If your reader is not a member of your organization or someone familiar with it, you need to give brief, but adequate, information about its purpose, scope, and members. But be sure not to *begin* your letter by talking about yourself and your organization, especially if the reader is an outsider. Place this material after a you-attitude opening.

In addition, you need to describe to all readers the problem or project to which the favor relates and to establish its values. For instance, if you are asking for funds to send underprivileged children to summer camp, you might describe (perhaps with the use of a folder) the physical camp facilities, size and number of buildings, surroundings, recreation areas, and number of children and counselors. Then you show the value of these facilities to the children—character building, friendships, appreciation of nature, fun, and so forth. Sometimes readers can visualize themselves in the shoes of those their funds can help, and in this way their interest is aroused in your project.

Direct and Indirect Reader Benefits

Usually near the middle of your letter you explain how the reader is to take part in the project. So that readers will desire to do as you ask, be sure to include all necessary facts and figures to convince them that their contribution will be enjoyable, easy, important, and of benefit to them (as much as is true and possible). Try to show direct or indirect benefits or both.

Direct Benefits.   To a person who does a favor, direct benefits vary with the type of favor. For example, if a person is to speak (without a fee and perhaps even without a traveling expense allowance) at a widely publicized convention, he or she may gain direct benefit from the favorable publicity as well as from personal contacts with the audience. If other prominent speakers are on the same program, say so, for this fact is an additional compliment to your reader. Be sure to tell the reader when he or she is to speak, where (date, day, hour), on what topic (or whether the speaker is to choose it), for how long, to whom, and to how many people.

Direct benefit may also come to the company that donates merchandise to, for instance, a charity or well-attended event. The people who see the company's name on the donated product will feel goodwill toward the donor and tend to buy its products when they need them. It is better, however, *not* to state such benefits specifically, but to let your readers determine them themselves.

In some favor requests the direct benefit offered may be a premium or gift or other small reward or token of appreciation. Those who participate in a questionnaire survey may gain, because the results will ultimately lead to improvements that make their work easier or help them to save money.

Indirect Benefits.   The participant who helps the members of a group he or she is interested in or a member of may receive indirect benefits. For instance, you can use indirect-benefit appeals to get a sales manager to speak (without a fee) to your school's marketing club or an auditor to talk to an accounting club. In each case, your reader's contribution may benefit him or her or the profession at least indirectly, because the reader helps a group of listeners whose interests are in a field of work he or she is interested in. Similarly, when you want to urge a busy person to accept a time-consuming office without pay, you can appeal to a sense of loyalty to the organization and the benefit his or her leadership can provide. Such indirect reader benefits are often persuaders.

In still other cases you can get a reader's cooperation by appealing on the basis of altruism—selfless devotion to the welfare of other human beings (or even animals). When persons contribute to a charity drive, for instance, they benefit by knowing they have helped bring happiness and hope to less fortunate people.

Positive Handling of Negatives

With the persuasive-request plan you must not only use appeals and stress reader benefits, but you also need to ask yourself, "To what will my reader probably object?" Then stress the positive aspects—what *can* be done—to minimize the negatives, as in the following examples:

1. Allowance for traveling expenses and/or speaker's fee is inadequate.

   a. Will you gladly meet her at the airport or any other location?

   b. Will she be guest of honor at a banquet? Maybe her spouse too?

   c. Will a car and/or parking be available for her use in your city?

          d. Is her part on the program so important that her employer will want to take care of her expenses?

          e. Can you arrange overnight accommodation?

2. Expected pledge or contribution is too large.

          a. Will you accept contributions in small installments?

          b. May he pledge now and pay after a future date?

          c. Can you show the great relief his gift will bring to those who need it?

3. Requested questionnaire looks long.

          a. Are the questions easy to answer? Why?

          b. Is taking part in the survey fun and important because . . . ?

          c. Can the entire questionnaire be finished in x minutes?

          d. Will the ultimate gain or reward be an incentive?

Asking for Action

Having included necessary facts, benefits, and positive aspects, you can confidently ask for the reader's acceptance. Make action clear, easy, and dated if necessary. If you need the reply by a certain date, tie this request in with reader benefit whenever possible—prominent billing on the program, adequate time for publicity, and so forth. Omit such negative statements as "*If* you can donate anything, please. . . ." It is better to say, "To make your contribution, just return. . . ." Your last sentence often can tie in with a statement featured in the opening paragraph, as a last reader-benefit plug.

Asking Favors That Require Time, Knowledge, or Effort

By using the persuasive-request AIDA plan, you can urge a busy person to be speaker at an important banquet or conference for little or no pay—and even partly or entirely at his or her own (or employer's) expense. You can encourage people to accept time-consuming terms as chairs of committees or to serve without pay on long-term committees and boards. You can obtain answers to research questionnaires that require more than routine effort by the recipient. You can give employees or club members a pep talk about attending certain functions, and you can increase membership in a business, professional, social, or religious organization. All these favors require time, knowledge, effort, or all three.

Request for a Speaker

In message 1, the president of an aircraft owners and pilots association invites an author (who is a member of the same nonprofit association in another city

500 miles away) to be principal speaker. The letter includes all needed details about date, time, place, audience, length and topic of talk. The underlying appeal or central selling point is the reader's ability to help in a serious crisis those of similar interests.

MESSAGE 1   *Letter inviting speaker to address banquet, without honorarium.*

Attention: reader-centered compliment

The article you wrote in the March issue of Flying has been of great interest to us in the Viewmont chapter of AOPA. We are currently in- volved in a battle to acquire a surplus Naval air station for general aviation use and find your ideas on airport facilities just the ap- proach we need to convince those not familiar with general aviation problems.

Interest: the problem

The request

Three months ago we learned that the Highpoint Naval Air Station would be surplus in August of this year. It seemed at first that general aviation would easily acquire this badly needed airport. But recently much opposition has de- veloped. The area residents simply do not un- derstand why another airport for "small planes" is needed. We have planned a banquet for the leaders of the community, to convince them of the genuine need for this facility and would very much like you as our dinner guest and speaker. Your views on the general crisis of airport congestion would be extremely help- ful in presenting our case. Will you tell us how you put the new program into effect last year in your city?

Reader benefit

Desire: conviction details

You will enjoy, I'm sure, the dinner and enter- tainment we have planned. The banquet will be held at the new Century Hotel, Monday, June 20, at 7 p.m., but the time can be changed if an- other hour is more convenient for you. You will, of course, be reimbursed for your travel- ing and overnight hotel expenses, and I person- ally will see that you are picked up and re- turned to the airport at your convenience. We expect about 100 persons to attend. After two local speakers present their opposing views, we would like you to speak for 20 to 30 minutes to conclude the arguments with an expert's opinion that will add much strength to our cause.

A brief letter from you indicating acceptance will assure the success of this function.

Dated action and value of reader's talk	Also, please include your preference as to dinner hour. Because the program goes to press in three weeks, will you send your decision by May 20? The members in this area will sincerely appreciate the contribution you can make to our obtaining another urgently needed general aviation airport in this area.

Request for Help in a Survey

Whether you are a student gathering firsthand information for a report, a business executive surveying your employees, or a research consultant working for numerous clients, you will get better cooperation from your readers when you write persuasively.

Message 2, for example, stresses reader benefit throughout. This letter also illustrates one way you can save money if you have a slim budget and a long mailing list: in place of the personalized inside addresses and salutation, you can use a reader-centered, attention-getting statement or question. A letter similar to the one below gained a 79 percent response.

MESSAGE 2   *Letter asking college teachers to return a questionnaire.*

Attention: reader benefit	Would knowing what other college teachers are doing in their business [name] courses help you?
Reader benefit or interest	Perhaps you, like many others, have wondered how the content, emphasis, and assignments of your basic course compare with those in other colleges that offer courses similar to yours in credit hours, size of sections, and prerequisites. Or you may have considered changing your courses, and you could use tips on what others are including.
Interest; description of project	To gather this information about this rapidly expanding field of study, we are making a nationwide survey of business [name] courses taught in schools holding membership in the American Association of Collegiate Schools of Business (AACSB). This study is planned to get specific details on the subject matter and written assignments in 199- and 199- courses.
Desire; facts; reader benefit	You are the only teacher in your institution receiving this letter and the enclosed form. All names of participants will remain confidential in the report of this study. By completing the questionnaire and returning it, you will be helping expand knowledge about the teaching of this vital subject matter. Also,

after all respondents' questionnaire replies
are summarized, you will know how your courses
compare with others. You will find the questions easy to answer, we believe, because most
of them require only your check mark.

*Dated, easy action;
reader benefit*

To make sure your college is included in this
study, please mail the form by May 1, in the
stamped envelope provided. In appreciation of
your cooperation in this study, you will receive a summary of the findings, if you wish,
before they are published. To protect anonymity, just insert your name and address on the
enclosed card and mail it separately from your
questionnaire.

The benefits offered to the college teachers for mailing the questionnaire
enclosed with message 2 are mainly intangible, yet they are adequate because
the readers are expected to have a keen interest in helping to improve their
profession. On the other hand, when you ask information from persons who
have no built-in interest in your questionnaire, you may—if your budget allows—
also have to offer a tangible inducement. For instance, the director of consumer
panels for a national market research firm, in a request to "Dear Homemaker,"
included a tangible gift (tableware), as well as intangible benefits (enjoyment,
usefulness, safety, and anonymity).

Asking Donations of Money or Other Tangible Valuables

Many people are even more reluctant to part with material goods than they are
to donate their time. Thus, all that you have learned about persuasiveness,
appeals, factual presentation, and reader benefits is even more important for
requests to donate valuables.

If you want your reader to donate money, describe the problem and tell
what is being or has been done, what needs to be done, and what your organization is doing about the problem. After stating meaningful facts, tell what it
will cost to do what your organization wants to do—and how the reader can
help.

If the donation is for a cause from which the reader benefits directly—as
in improved recreation facilities for a club of which he or she is a member—
you can choose from appeals such as comfort, enjoyment, friendships, health,
love of family. However, if the donation goes to charity, your main appeal is
usually altruism—the satisfaction of helping others. Statements like the following
help the conscientious reader who wonders how much he or she should give:

1. A gift of $20 will buy vitamins for 10 children . . . ,
   $45 will provide a cup of milk to 120 children . . . ,
   $100 may keep a father and mother alive to care for their
   own children . . . , $250 sends 200 pounds of medicines to
   our hospitals.

2. "What is a thoughtful contribution?" You can best answer this question. BUT we suggest that an amount approximating two hours' pay would be justified in light of. . . .

MESSAGE 3   *Memo from an executive persuading employees to contribute generously to an annual fund drive.*

TO: All Members of the Wigget staff
FROM: Alberta Jones, President
SUBJECT: An appeal for the UGN Fund
DATE: October 15, 199-

Attention: problem

All of you are aware that this year our community has a larger number of needy, desperate, afflicted people of all ages, creeds, and races.

What is being done

You know also of the fine work that the United Good Neighbors Fund does to provide community services through 82 Good Neighbor agencies. Hundreds of persons volunteer freely of their time and money to make this drive successful each year, with no thought of tangible rewards.

Reader benefit

Request

Your one contribution helps in many ways, and you are spared from being dunned by separate agencies. I am making a personal appeal this year that all of us reassess our values of this program and make an honest effort to give just a little bit more. Each of us sets the figure our conscience dictates, but I sincerely hope you can find it in your hearts to join me in increasing our donation this year. Our company's goal is $72,900.

Appeal to altruism

We are all most fortunate in not being on the receiving end of this program, and one way to count our blessings is by helping those less fortunate, as described in the enclosed leaflet.

Small installments

Appeal to pride, altruism

Remember, UGN pledge cards make it possible to contribute in small monthly or quarterly installments. Or, if you choose, you may pay by payroll deductions. Let's give serious consideration to the amount we contribute this year and try to make it one of which to be proud and which is helpful to those in need.

Easy action; date; appreciation

Please state on the enclosed pledge sheet the total you will contribute to UGN this year, and also mark which method of payment you choose. Then return the form in the enclosed envelope to

```
my office by November 1.  Your support will be re-
ceived with appreciation by the many agencies
within UGN.
```

Urging Cooperation on Goals and Projects

As a committee chairperson or officer you may sometimes need your readers' support for various goals and projects your organization considers important. Messages 4 and 5, sent to members and voters respectively, illustrate how persuasive requests can help move readers to action toward which they would otherwise be indifferent.

MESSAGE 4   *Letter from a chairman appealing for help to boost membership.*

Attention: agreeable comment and question

```
NPRA MEMBERSHIP
JUMPS 100%

Wouldn't you be delighted to see that headline in
the NPRA Journal?  And you can . . . for it can
be done easily without gimmicks or strings or
expense to you.
```

Reader-benefit goal

```
Increased membership will strengthen our effec-
tiveness and benefit each of us as well as the
entire field of public relations.  If you--each
member--will find us one new NPRA member, our
size can double.
```

Easy-action request

```
The method is simple and effective.  Go over your
firm's executive roster, your list of business
associates.  Think of everyone you know who might
be interested in public and customer relations.
Write the names and addresses on the enclosed
card, and mail the card in the accompanying enve-
lope.  That's all you need to do!  Our secretary,
Jim Harton, will take it from there.
```

Tie-in with opening

```
Isn't that easy?  Find one new member for NPRA
. . . and look for that headline soon . . . NPRA
MEMBERSHIP JUMPS 100%.
```

MESSAGE 5   *Letter signed by three citizens (one expert each in engineering, medicine, and law) persuading citizens to vote for a bond issue.*

Attention: reader-benefit comment

```
Dear Southside resident:

Each of us has the opportunity on May 19 to leave
a legacy for the future when we vote on the For-
ward Move bond issue--rapid transit.  This pro-
```

gram will substantially improve the quality of
your environment for many years to come.

Interest:
reader benefits

Rapid transit will reduce traffic congestion and
air pollution, both of which are becoming increasingly difficult problems in the Southside
area. In addition, it will be of enormous benefit to you as a resident of Southside. To you
and the employees in this area rapid transit
brings easy access to plants and businesses plus
increased mobility from the south side to all
parts of the greater *[city]* community.

*[Two paragraphs for "interest and desire" follow here and
include reader-benefit facts about two new underground bus
transfer stations and low taxpayer costs.]*

Reader-benefit
request

On the basis of the compelling need and an opportunity to preserve and strengthen your area, we
now ask you to vote "yes" with us May 19 on the
Forward Move bond issue.

OTHER PERSUASIVE REQUESTS

Adapting the AIDA Plan

You can also use the AIDA plan effectively when you must persuade your reader
to grant your request for adjustment, credit, or change in policy or performance.
For your attention-getting opening you can use any of the six suggestions
discussed for favor requests (pages 251 to 254). However, to present a concise,
logical argument, it is usually best to begin with an assertion. This statement
often is a principle—a major premise on which both you and the reader agree
or about which you wish to persuade the reader—for example, these two (which
can also be considered agreeable-comment openings):

1. No doubt you expect your authorized dealers to uphold the
   good name of your products.

2. Surely you want your company to have a reputation for
   fairness and honesty.

You will get the reader's interest and desire when you state all necessary
facts and details—interwoven with reader benefits. Include whatever description
the reader needs to see that his or her firm is responsible (if this applies) and
that your request is factual, logical, and reasonable. Your action request should
be a logical conclusion based on the major premise and the clearly stated facts.

Persuasively Requesting an Adjustment

When a product or service from a reputable firm is unsatisfactory but you know that your claim for an adjustment is outside the warranty or is otherwise unusual, your message should follow the persuasive-request instead of the direct-request plan. You also need to be persuasive when your request is *not* unusual but the seller disregarded your first direct request.

In letter 1, because of unusual circumstances, the customer persuasively asks for a new camera and certain other expenses—even though the printed guarantee includes a statement that the firm will service the camera but "cannot assume responsibility for loss of film, for other expenses or inconveniences, or for consequential damages occasioned by the equipment." This is an unusually long letter, but the details included are necessary to achieve the goal. The writer did get essentially what she wanted, though in slightly different form—six free rolls of film with processing mailers and an exchange of her camera with one owned by the manager of the local Picturetronics, Inc.

LETTER 1   *A consumer writes persuasively to a manufacturer's adjustment manager, requesting an unusual adjustment.*

Attention: assertion of major premise

"Let your Wessman camera preserve those precious moments for you." This appealing advertising slogan, plus your company's good reputation, helped me to choose a Wessman camera for my once-in-a-lifetime trip to South America. Because of unusual circumstances I now find it necessary to appeal to you.

Interest; facts about purchase

Six months ago I purchased my Wessman Instanshot camera from a reputable store here. That was two months before my trip, so I would have time to become thoroughly familiar with the camera before traveling in a foreign country. (I was a member of a group representing the Foundation for International Understanding, and our long-planned trip was a goodwill tour that I wanted to preserve in good pictures.)

[*For conviction, a paragraph here states facts on malfunctioning and repairs of the electronic eye, bar indicator, and flash attachment by an authorized dealer twice before the trip.*]

Conviction: more on the problem

Two days before my departure, they [*the repair shop*] called to report my camera was "now in excellent working order." Little did any of us guess the picture problems ahead. Nevertheless, the camera was again a disappointment only two days later-- on my first attempt to take a picture of friends before we left the airport. Twice the flash did not go off. Because it was Sunday morning and

**Reader in
writer's shoes;
writer's care
and trust**

only a few minutes before plane departure, there
was of course no way to have further repairs
then. Perhaps you can imagine how you would feel
at this moment. I had depended on your authorized dealer's word that my camera was in excellent condition! Always I handle a camera with
care according to instructions, for I know it is
a delicate precision instrument.

**Tie-in with
major premise**

Writer's losses

Throughout my trip there were numerous "precious
moments" I wanted to preserve with my new Wessman
camera. Most of these were on indoor occasions--
receptions, dinners, and other functions with
people. I can buy postcards of buildings and nature. But no one sells pictures of the precious
moments with other human beings who assembled
just for our group! Yet these moments are lost
forever because the flash attachment failed numerous times. These failures also resulted in my
ample supply of Wessman films being exhausted much
too soon. I thus had to purchase additional film
plus flashbulbs in foreign stores, at much higher
prices.

When my developed film was returned, I found that
72 negatives were total blanks. In other words,
72 times that flash attachment failed; 72 precious moments are lost instead of preserved, as
your slogan advertises.

**Appeal to
fairness
and pride**

Request

The people at Picturetronics, Inc., have said
they can't understand what is the matter with
this camera and they've done all they can. Even
they suggest that my camera must be one of the
very rare defective products from your usually
dependable, high-quality stock. Thus I am returning this camera to you for your inspection.
But after all the heartaches it has given me--in
losing instead of preserving precious moments--I
ask that you please keep this camera and send me
instead a new, dependable Instanshot camera.
Also, will you please reimburse me for the $51.20
I paid for wasted film, processing, and flashbulbs. Copies of sales slips are enclosed.

**Tie-in with
major premise**

By making these fair replacements, you will help
restore my faith in Wessman. Also, not only I,
but my friends who share my disappointment, will
again believe that Wessman does "preserve those
precious moments."

Retailers also sometimes encounter serious situations that require persuasive requests to their wholesalers or manufacturers after previous direct requests have failed. In such cases the attention-getting assertion in the first paragraph may even be a negative appeal: loss of reader benefits. For example, a retailer who sold a certain manufacturer's tools exclusively threatened to go to competitors' products if the manufacturer would not immediately improve both the quantity of tools and the promptness of deliveries sent to this distributor. The opening of his letter introduces the fear appeal:

```
Repetition is an accepted mechanism for achieving emphasis.
Although we have stated to you before our situation with re-
spect to Crown tools, we are writing again now to emphasize
to you the probable sad consequences of your current perfor-
mance and allocations.
```

[*In seven additional paragraphs the letter reviews specific facts regarding order backlogs, manufacturer's broken promises, disappointed construction contractors, cancellations by 69 customers lost to competitors, and further risks of lost reader benefits. After appeals to fairness, the letter closes with this reader-benefit request.*]

```
Therefore, please do everything you can this month to step
up your shipments to fill the backlog of orders while you
can still save this excellent market!
```

Persuasively Requesting Credit

Most credit applications are direct requests, made in the routine course of business. However, sometimes you may seek a special credit privilege that on the surface you appear to be unqualified for. In such cases a persuasive request is more effective. For instance, if you are just starting your first store and your capital, inventory, and current income are barely adequate, you will need to convince prospective creditors that they can depend on you to pay regularly. Or you may wish to ask for 120-day credit terms instead of the usual 30-day period. Whatever your unusual request may be, be sure to include sufficient facts and figures to show how you have planned carefully and perhaps how the reader will benefit—for example, from your expected expanding market.

Sometimes credit applicants' first direct requests are turned down, and they cannot understand why. If they still want credit with the firm, a persuasive request such as letter 2 may help accomplish that purpose. This letter brought a prompt, pleasant phone call, an apology, and the granting of a revolving credit account "gladly."

LETTER 2   *A persuasive request for credit after a turndown.*

Attention:
assertion
```
Your form letter of January 31 refusing my
request for the Blanks' Revolving Credit (BRC)
account and suggesting that I consider an Easy
Payment Account came as a mild shock.
```

Interest: applicant's work and knowledge

```
Without a doubt, Blanks maintains certain poli-
cies regarding credit applications from individ-
uals.  In my occupation as a bookkeeper and as
an assistant manager of City Paint and Hardware
Company, I process many applications for credit.
Therefore, I feel that when you considered my
application, either sufficient information was
not given or the fact that I am renting a house,
rather than buying, was regarded as grounds for
listing me as a person of "questionable"
credit standing.  In either assumption, I be-
lieve the following information will give you a
clear picture of my "present circumstances."
```

```
Employment and Income
     [7 lines]
```

Conviction facts

```
Assets and liabilities
     [8 lines]
```

```
References
  [11 lines]
```

Reader-benefit request

```
The Easy Payment Plan you suggest is an expen-
sive way to buy merchandise.  To buy on this
plan partially defeats the purpose of "SHOP AT
BLANKS AND SAVE!"  Small, easy payments do not
appeal to me.  Nor does dragging out payments
over a long period.  Your BRC account is one I
would use frequently.  And you can be sure that
you will receive prompt payments.  BRC fits my
present needs and my ability to pay.  Your
extending this privilege to me will be greatly
appreciated.
```

Persuasively Requesting Changes in Policy or Performance

Besides requesting nonroutine adjustment or credit, you may at times need to persuade a company to make other exceptions to its usual policy. Or you may wish to persuade individuals to change their actions, or to give employees a written pep talk, hoping to improve their future performance. The basic persuasive-request pattern is again applicable here.

Changes in Policy

In letter 3, an advertising consultant tries to persuade the public relations officer of RZC Company to depart from its usual policy of not giving away or lending products. An outstanding magazine feature writer (renamed "Jake Edlis" in this example) had written for permission to borrow, free, RZC Company's new XX boating equipment—to use, photograph, and mention in his new series of feature stories on outdoor life. Should the public relations officer consider the consultant's advice both ethical and desirable? The decision may be difficult.

LETTER 3   *An advertising consultant's persuasive request to change from the usual no-loan policy regarding company equipment.*

Attention: assertion	Though I know it is RZC's policy not to lend or give away its products, I think sticking to it in the case of Jake Edlis would be a mistake.
Interest; conviction	There are very few writers in the recreation field for whom I'd take a stand on this issue. Among them are _____, _____, _____, and Jake Edlis.
Company benefit	First, lending your boating equipment is a relatively small expense for the publicity RZC is bound to receive in return. The space value could, conceivably, amount to tens of thousands of dollars. As you know, Jake's write-ups reach about 16 million readers each month.
More company benefit	Second, RZC is in a big league now. Big leaguers play the game by getting respected writers like Edlis to use their products (many of them carrying big price tags) and write about them.
More company benefit **Risk of harmful results if change is not made**	Third, as a member of the Outdoor Writers Association of America and a well-known feature writer, Edlis is bound to talk to a lot of other "influentials" in the field. He could, intentionally or not, start word that RZC is willing to take lots of free space, but unwilling to extend the accepted courtesy of letting legitimate feature writers try its products without charge. Ultimately, this could lead to poor press relations and a resulting drop in our publicity lineage.
Company-benefit request	In the interest of maintaining exceptionally good press relations, please reconsider your company's "no giveaway" policy when someone with the stature of a Jake Edlis offers his services. I'm sure you'll be glad you did.

Changes in Performance

Persuasion is necessary whenever you need to convince individuals to change their performance and if direct requests have been or would be unheeded. Changing performance may include personal appearance and habits as well as business practices.

The next two examples[1] illustrate how important right tone and appeals are for getting reader cooperation. As you read letter 4, note these faults:

1. Overemphasis on negatives—"disturbed," "horrified," "will have to be removed," "senseless," "punishing," "destroying"

2. Overuse of "we"—meaning "Landlord, Inc.," rather than "all the people (us) in the neighborhood"

3. Manager's domineering, threatening, discourteous attitude, which places all parents on the defensive and seems to blame their children, although the vandals may have been outsiders

4. Total lack of reader appeals

LETTER 4   *A poor, negative, unpersuasive request from a building manager to tenants.*

```
TO ALL PARENTS LIVING IN 100 OAK AVENUE AND 50 ELM AVENUE

We have become seriously disturbed because of the recent
vandalism in your neighborhood.  Every day now, storage room
doors are being broken, tires removed from bicycles, parts
of baby carriages taken off, etc. etc., but today we were
horrified to see a beautiful living tree (in front of 50 Elm
Avenue) completely cut in half.  Now the tree will have to
be removed.

We would like all the parents to have a good talk with their
children in order to stop this senseless destruction.

We will start patrolling this section very closely from now
on, and if necessary, we will call in the municipal and
school authorities of Metropolis, in order to start punish-
ing children who are found destroying property.
```

In contrast, letter 5 eliminates the main faults of letter 4. Its tone is friendly, courteous, and positive. Equally important, this letter emphasizes community spirit, mutual concern, and cooperation. Letter 5 appeals to the parents' pride, love of family, health, and desire for security, and it includes the young people as citizens instead of accusing them indirectly of being vandals.

LETTER 5   *An appealing, improved version of letter 4.*

TO ALL FAMILIES IN THE ELM AVENUE SCHOOL
DISTRICT

**Attention:
a mutual problem**

I know you will be as sorry as I was to
learn that the lovely old elm tree that gave
our school its name was destroyed today.
Its beauty and grace are now lost to us forever, and all of us regret this tragedy.

**Interest; need for
mutual effort**

The destruction of our landmark appears to
be another in a recent series of acts of
vandalism in our neighborhood--a problem
that can affect all of us unless we make a
mutual effort to rid ourselves of it.

**Conviction: appeals
to safety, health,
security, and civic
pride**

A number of residents of our community have
volunteered to do patrol duty in their off-
hours, protecting the safety of our families
and our property. Though we appreciate
their desire to help, we need to ask ourselves if a patrol is what we really want.
Do we want our neighborhood to be a prison
for our children or a place of freedom and
healthful growth?

Shall we instead face this problem frankly
and constructively? Let us consider a few
facts. Does our community have adequate
provisions for recreational activities, or
should we be contributing more to the creativity, growth, and culture of Metropolis?
Have we done everything possible to make
this a city in which our young people will
be proud to grow up?

Request

It has been suggested that we discuss these
things both in our own homes and then together as a community. Will you meet with
us next Monday evening, January 18, at 7:30
in the auditorium of Elm Avenue School so
that we can plan a constructive program of
progress? Perhaps we can form a Civic Pride
Committee comprising both young people and
adults--a committee that can investigate our

**Appeals to pride
and cooperation**

needs and help us plan a calendar of events
to appeal to everyone. Our mayor and council members share our enthusiasm and have
agreed to be present.

Reader benefits

```
Let's make Monday evening "Family Night."
Fill the auditorium with families, ideas,
and appetites for cake, coffee, and sodas.
See you at 7:30!
```

SUMMARY

The persuasive-request plan has a four-part AIDA structure—consisting of attention, interest, desire and conviction, and action paragraphs. You can adapt this plan whenever you need to request favors that require the readers to donate time, knowledge, effort, cooperation, other intangibles, or money. You can also adapt this plan when you need to persuasively request an adjustment, credit, or changes in policy or performance.

The Capsule Checklists on pages 276–277 give a brief summary of the general plan and two main kinds of persuasive requests. (Chapters 11 through 14 and 22 include other messages using this AIDA plan.)

EXERCISES AND PROBLEMS

Requests for Favors

1. ***Rewrite of letter to Mr. Green, public relations director:*** What are the good points, weaknesses, and errors in the following letter? As program chairperson, rewrite it, applying the principles you have learned, to make your request so appealing that the reader will want to accept. Address it to Mr. Loren Greene, Director of Public Relations, KNRO Television, in a city about 80 miles from you. If your instructor approves, you may choose another topic instead of air pollution.

   ```
   What are your plans for Saturday evening, March 8?  The mem-
   bers of our [city] Business Leaders' Club feel it would be a
   pleasure to us to have you as the principal speaker for our
   annual banquet that night.

   Ways to fight air pollution is a topic that our members are
   concerned and realize the need of practical advice from expe-
   rienced executives.  Your many editorial comments on Channel
   15 KNRO have shown us your sincere interest and extensive
   study on this subject.  Our members and their spouses want to
   hear you in person.  This banquet is our biggest function of
   the year, and we would be honored to have you and your spouse
   as our guests.

   The banquet will be held in the Marlbron Room of the Plaza
   Hotel at 7 and will be informal.  A varied entertainment pro-
   gram and an excellent dinner at $18.50 per person have been
   arranged.
   ```

Your traveling expenses would be provided, and I hope that
you can take advantage of a visit to our city to settle any
personal affairs you may have here. The Plaza Hotel is
equipped with excellent facilities in the event you decide to
extend your visit.

I shall appreciate your assent to this request so that I can
welcome you on your arrival if feasible.

2. ***$6,000 cash needed for building extension:*** Assume you graduated from
college five years ago and you have become an active member of a certain
professional (or business, social, or religious) group that owns the building
in which its meetings and activities take place.

   You have just been elected treasurer of your organization for a two-year
term. For about 15 years this organization has been saving money to build
a much needed extension to its building. (Make up specific reasons why the
addition is necessary and beneficial to members.) It has been planned that
construction will begin next July 1—three months from today—and be
completed by October 1. (Assume today is April 1.) The addition, as sketched
by architects and approved by your executive board, will cost about $105,000.
Your books show $49,000 cash in the building fund; your organization can
get a $50,000 mortgage. You need to raise $6,000 cash between now and
about May 5, or construction cannot begin. Your task is to try to raise this
money. After several meetings with the executive board, it is decided that,
rather than asking your members to put on several fund-raising events (which
are time-consuming), or assessing them a definite amount, you will urge
them to make a donation. The board members want you to head this fund-
raising campaign.

   Write a letter, remembering that it is a form letter, to be sent to all
members. Assume a mailing list of 650. Try to keep your letter to one
typewritten page. Select the appeals (loyalty, pride, self-interest, and so forth)
that you think will be most effective in moving your readers to take the
requested action. Set May 1 as the deadline for donations, because adequate
time must be allowed for making financial arrangements before construction
begins. Make action easy and include any reasonable inducements for your
readers to act now. Naturally, you'd rather have checks returned with each
reply; however, for those members who would rather sign a pledge now and
pay later—before completion of construction—plan an easy-action reply
form you can use in your financial calculations.

3. ***Memo to obtain volunteers for Tomorrow's Managers:*** Assume International Valve Corporation is the largest industrial employer in your city.
Over the last five years, IVC has been the object of much unfavorable
publicity, stemming from violation of water and air pollution regulations and
controversy over discriminatory hiring practices. Its corporate image has
suffered.

   To increase its contributions as a responsible corporate citizen in the
city's economic and social life, IVC has launched a drive to increase the
participation of its employees in social service, civic, and cultural organiza-

tions. As a participant in one phase of this new direction, you (as public relations liaison) have been delegated the responsibility of writing a form memo to all IVC executives. You are to secure volunteers to serve as business advisers for Tomorrow's Managers. This organization sends business people into area high schools to assist students in forming and managing business enterprises to manufacture and market goods or services. The students thus obtain firsthand experience in how the free enterprise system functions.

IVC is sponsoring three advisers for Tomorrow's Managers. Each will devote two evenings a month to working with one of these groups at a city high school during the school year. There is no pay; the only benefits each volunteer receives come from working with young people, helping them to develop their business skills and understanding of business enterprises. And, of course, International Valve will benefit from improved visibility in the community as an involved, public-spirited business organization.

Write a memo that will get at least four volunteers for this project. Select and develop appeals focusing on benefits to IVC, the executives, and the high school students they will be advising. Anticipate and overcome objections that your readers might have. Date the memo August 8—schools open in one month.

4. **Letter to Dr. Johnson, an organization's national vice president:** Assume that you are program chairperson for your college chapter of a national organization composed of students whose major is the same as yours. For the past two years the members have repeatedly mentioned their desire to hear this organization's national vice president, Dr. L. F. Johnson. He is known to be an outstanding, dynamic speaker. Two of your members who heard him at the organization's national convention last June also have been enthusiastic about him. Because he lives 2,000 miles from your school and your chapter's treasury is small, everyone has just assumed that getting Dr. Johnson would be almost impossible. Fortunately, in yesterday's newspaper you happened to read that Dr. Johnson will be attending a one-day business conference in Somecity (you insert a city name), which is only 210 miles from you—just the day before your chapter's annual Founders' Day Banquet.

Now you want to persuade Dr. Johnson to accept your invitation to be principal banquet speaker. You cannot pay him any speaker's fee, but your budget enables you to pay traveling expenses equal to round-trip plane fare from (Somecity) to yours. Six planes daily fly between these cities; if he prefers a bus, buses run on an hourly schedule. A scenic ride by freeway takes about four hours, in case he prefers to drive a private car. Dr. Johnson will, of course, be your chapter's dinner guest. Maybe you can think of an inexpensive, courteous way to take care of him if he wishes to stay overnight after his talk? Assume any other necessary details that will make your letter complete—with you-attitude. Consider carefully the best appeals to use.

5. **Memo—rats in our building:** As building manager of your company's three-story structure, you have just received an unusual report from your sanitation engineer. He has found that at least two rats have been attracted into the

building recently. The employee practice of leaving food on bookshelves, desks, and other open locations will have to be discontinued or watched very carefully. Each office occupant must be made aware of the problem and the possibility that he or she is part of the cause. As rats will not bother to infest an area unless there is good reason to do so (food), the best way to maintain rat-free premises consists of denying them food, water, and safety. It would be economically unfeasible to make the needed structural changes for rat-proofing the entire building. (The cafeteria is, however, ratproofed.) About four months ago you wrote a simple announcement (without appeals—merely a direct request) to all employees. But apparently some (or most?) have forgotten about it. Now again two rats were seen, but many more, still unseen, could come into the building.

Thus you must write a persuasive request in a memorandum to all employees, urging them to cooperate on preventive action. Instruct them to exercise utmost care with lunches or other food brought into the building. Instruct them not to leave any food in their offices overnight. Also request them to be alert for signs indicating rodent or insect activity: droppings; gnawed food; odor; and dark rub marks along walls, ceilings, and ventilators and under doors, indicating a runway. Request that employees inform a certain office as soon as such evidence appears. Watch the tone of your memo, and be sure to consider the attitudes of your readers.

6. ***Letter—Group's visit to the White House:*** Assume that you are the state president of a group of professional people who will attend a meeting in Washington, D.C., May 23, and who would like to go through the White House together. There will be about 45 in your group, and you expect to have all the names and an exact number of attendees by May 1.

You are aware that any member of the United States Congress—senator or representative—can assist you in visiting the White House when in Washington. This assistance is commonly referred to as a congressional White House tour because you are given a special pass and a specific time to be at the entrance gate. Others, who are not aware of this, often stand in line for hours to make the visit, whereas those with the congressional tour tickets can walk in at the proper time.

Write to a a member of Congress (preferably the one who represents you) and ask if an afternoon tour at about 3:30 can be arranged. Explain the name and purpose of the association, at what hotel the group will be meeting, and any other pertinent information. Make up a reason why this request for May 23 requires persuasion, and include appropriate appeals. Ask for specific instructions about picking up the tour tickets before the date you will be using them.

Requests for Adjustments, Credit, or Changes

1. ***Barry's unfilled June 2 order:*** You are manager of Barry's Men's Wear in Sometown, Nebraska. You have two stores—one situated in the downtown area and one two blocks from a college campus. For years you have carried

exclusively Van Doner shirts, which you buy directly from the manufacturer. On June 2, only four days after this firm's fall catalog came out, you again ordered a complete Van Doner line for your two stores. You asked for delivery by September 2. But today (September 9) you have noted with alarm the many changes the manufacturer made in your fall order. Back-to-school goods scheduled by your sales staff for early delivery have been pushed to October and November. You haven't a plaid in stock and college opens next week. You've had to switch to other brands because you can't get all the Van Doner merchandise you'd like. You have faith in Van Doner merchandise; it's your preference of all brand shirts on the market. But this is the third time in four years that they have changed delivery time on your orders.

While you were in Springfield, Missouri, just a few days ago, you noted that the Lester Men's Store (a retail store for this shirt manufacturer) was stocked with everything in the Van Doner book, and Lester could not have ordered any sooner than you did. Just how does this manufacturer expect to keep good customers like you with that kind of treatment? Unless it can find some way to supply your stores adequately and promptly—by no later than September 21—you may have to find a replacement for Van Doner shirts. You feel you have helped considerably to build this manufacturer's business the past five years. (Your store's total Van Doner purchases were $220,000.) Right now you feel like giving your business to a competitor. Address your message to Mr. Harry Nomad, sales manager of Van Doner Manufacturing Company, 2200 Federal Avenue, Buffalo, NY 14266-5585. Be tactful, firm, appropriately persuasive, and clear in your request.

2. *Charge account turndown from a store:* Assume you have just received a credit turndown for a charge account with a local store. The reason stated for the refusal is correct. (Assume a legitimate reason such as being under age 18 or currently unemployed.) However, for various other reasons—perhaps a steady trust fund income you receive from a regular source, a verifiable record of integrity, or any other good reason that might outweigh the shortcoming—you know that you will be a prompt-paying customer. You always take care of all obligations you have. Write to the store's credit manager an honest, persuasive request for credit. Make your reasoning logical and appealing, so that your reader will be convinced that she or he should make an exception for you and grant you a charge account.

3. *Error in invoices for magazine subscription:* About three months ago you received a letter from a magazine publisher offering a special subscription rate to members of the National Business Association. (You are a member.) Because you think the magazine is an excellent source of current information in your major field, you decided to take advantage of the special offer—$8.50 for a one-year subscription, $16 for two years (24 monthly issues). Using the convenient order form provided, you indicated that you wanted the two-year subscription and that you enclosed your payment. You

attached your personal check, no. 552, to the order form and mailed it in the envelope provided.

The order was mailed exactly three months ago today, and your check cleared the bank the following month. You received your first issue of the magazine four weeks ago, along with an invoice for $16 for the subscription. The notice indicated that no further issues would be sent until payment was received. As you have your canceled check clearly showing that it was deposited by the National Publishing Company (the magazine's publisher), you realize that the company was in error. The same day you wrote a letter to Ms. Anne Plumb (Circulation Manager, National Publishing Company, 902 Broad Street, Philadelphia, PA 19108-4004), explaining the facts and asking her to see that your account (no. 0147392) was credited for the $16 and that the remaining 23 issues of the magazine were sent promptly.

Today you received a second invoice, stating that you still owe $16. The computer-printed bill had the following message: "We have not heard from you." Obviously, they should have heard from you: not once, but twice. Because your letter to Ms. Plumb seems not to have led to any action, you have decided to write a persuasive request for an adjustment directly to the party in power—the computer. Explain the situation again and ask for the appropriate action. A little humor may be acceptable, but remember the main purpose of your letter.

■ CAPSULE CHECKLISTS FOR PERSUASIVE REQUESTS*

A Persuasive Requests— General Plan	B Persuasive Requests for Favors	C Other Persuasive Requests for Adjustment, Credit, or Changes

1. ATTENTION (*promise; star*)
  a. Introduction of relevant reader-benefit or reader-interest theme—centered on reader, not on writer's organization
  b. Envelopes and letterheads sometimes specially designed for the message
	1. Attention
	  a. Sincere compliment
	  b. Questions
	  c. Agreeable comment or assertion
	  d. Basic problem
	  e. What has been done about a problem
	  f. Frank admission of a favor
		1. Attention
		  a. Preferably an agreeable assertion or a principle used as major premise
		  b. Sincere compliment
		  c. Question
		  d. Basic problem
		  e. Frank admission of a favor

2. INTEREST (*picture; chain*)
  a. Introduction of project, product, service, or problem; description; central selling point
  b. Appeals—direct or indirect reader benefits: appreciation, approval, beauty, cleanliness, comfort, convenience, cooperation, customer satisfaction, distinctiveness, durability, efficiency, enjoyment, entertainment, extra earnings, fair treatment, friendships, good reputation, health, improvement, love of home and others, money and other valuables, peace of mind, pleasure, popularity, position, profits, recognition, relief from fear, safety, satisfaction of helping others, savings, self-preservation, and others
 	
3. DESIRE (*prove; chain*)
  a. Development of description, benefits, central selling point, request, appeals; perhaps with an enclosure
  b. Appropriate handling of possible objections
  c. Conviction
    (1) "Outside" proof; perhaps with enclosures
    (2) Price and terms when needed and appropriate; perhaps in enclosure
	2. Interest
	3. Desire
	  a. Necessary physical description of project
	  b. Facts, figures, and reader benefits to convince reader that his or her contribution will be enjoyable, easy, important, beneficial—directly or indirectly
	    (1) In request for speaker: date, day, hour; place; function; topic; talk length; audience size, interests; honorarium; expenses; special attractions; appeals
	    (2) In requests for donation: problem; needs; past, present methods of meeting needs; costs; reader contribution; benefits; appeals
	    (3) In request for cooperation: problem; facts, suggestions, committee, etc., to help meet goal; reader's part; benefits; appeals
	  c. Positive handling of negatives and probable objections for favors that:
	    (1) Require time, knowledge, or effort
	    (2) Ask donations of money or other valuables
	    (3) Urge cooperation on goals and projects
	  d. Enclosures (brochures)
		2. Interest
		3. Desire
		  a. All necessary facts and details pertaining to request for adjustment, credit, or changes in policy or performance—interwoven with reader benefits and appeals (as in A.2.b)
		  b. Description as needed by the reader to see that his or her firm is responsible (if applicable) and that the request is factual, logical, and reasonable

■ CAPSULE CHECKLISTS FOR PERSUASIVE REQUESTS* (Continued)

A	B	C
Persuasive Requests— General Plan	**Persuasive Requests for Favors**	**Other Persuasive Requests for Adjustment, Credit, or Changes**

4. ACTION (*push; hook*)
  a. CSAD[†]
  b. EA[‡]
  c. DA when desirable[§]
  d. Special inducement when desirable
  e. RB[¶] (often tied in with opening statement)
	4. Action
	  a. CSAD[†]
	  b. EA[‡]
	  c. DA when desirable[§]
	  d. Special inducement when desirable
	  e. RB[¶] (often tied in with opening statement)
		4. Action
		  a. Logical conclusion based on the major premise and the clearly stated facts; then same as B.4

* Lists include possible content. For any one message, choose only pertinent and appropriate items.
[†] CSAD = clear statement of action desired.   [§] DA = dated action, if desirable.
[‡] EA = easy action.   [¶] RB = reader benefit.

Special
Messages

Sales Letters

very year millions of dollars' worth of goods and services are sold to consumers, businesses, and industries—by means of sales letters, both solicited and unsolicited. These kinds of messages are grouped in this chapter according to the organizational plans used.

Solicited sales letters include good-news and bad-news replies to sales-related inquiries. *Unsolicited* sales letters usually follow the persuasive plan. They may aim to make direct sales, serve as stimuli to future sales, or bring back lost customers.

SOLICITED SALES LETTERS

Requests for information about services or products you sell are inquiries related to sales. Included are questions about catalogs, prices, terms, discounts, deliveries, products, manufacturing methods, types of accounts available, sources of supply, and similar information.

Replies to many of these inquiries are actually sales letters and are called *solicited*, or *invited*, sales messages. The inquirer is often already your customer, or a potential buyer, who may become a steady, satisfied customer *if* you send a reply that impresses favorably.

Good-News Replies to Sales-Related Inquiries

When the information you can send in answer to an inquiry brings favorable or neutral information, you will *use the good-news plan*. This section discusses content of the three parts and suggestions for handling inquiries prompted by advertising.

Positive Opening Paragraphs

The best way to begin these letters is by courteously doing one of the following:

1. Answering favorably one of the inquirer's questions

   a. Yes, Ms. Jones,
      You can use Latex Enamel paint in your bathroom with complete assurance that it is washable.
   b. You're right! Model XL2, about which you inquired, can easily become an exceptionally good profit maker for you. Our dealers have reported it to be their most popular do-it-yourself maintenance kit.

2. Sending the requested material

   Enclosed are three samples of the nylon materials you asked about. We are glad to send these to you with our compliments.

Helpful Explanation Answering All Questions

In your explanation section, you should answer all questions—direct or implied. In many cases, you will also provide educational, resale, or sales promotion information. Arrange your answers so that the favorable responses are at the beginning and end of your explanation section, to accent the positive and "embed" the negative aspects. Maintain a you-attitude; keep the reader in every paragraph if possible.

Embedding the negative does *not* mean that you should omit or twist the truth. It means that you can emphasize what something *is* rather than what it is *not*. Like a good salesperson, you try to determine what the customer really needs. Contrast, for instance, the negative and the positive answers to the following questions:

1. **Question:**   Is the raincoat sprayed with ABC liquid so it is waterproof?

   Negative reply: No, I'm sorry to say the raincoat is not sprayed with ABC liquid. However, the material itself is made of durable vinyl, which is completely waterproof.

   Positive reply: The material in this raincoat is made of a durable vinyl that is permanently and completely waterproof. Thus you need never bother with any spray even after the garment has been cleaned many times.

2. **Question:**   Do you carry Bronson tape recorders? If so, how long would it take for you to send one to my office if I should decide to order it? [*The inquirer lives 500 miles from the seller, and only 100 miles from the factory. The seller is out of the item today, but notice that the inquirer has not yet ordered it.*]

   Negative reply: We are temporarily out of stock of the Bronson, and so we couldn't send you one right away. If we reorder especially for you, it will take 10 days after we receive your request.

   Positive reply: Yes, we do carry the Bronson tape recorder, and we can usually send it to you within one day after we receive your order. As it is an extremely popular model, we sometimes run out of it temporarily. In such a case, we will gladly reorder immediately so you can expect delivery within 10 days. Occasionally, for a rush order, we could have the item sent to you direct from the factory within two days after your request reaches us.

When quoting prices, be sure to use the same positive psychology by considering your reader's needs and circumstances. Unless the price of a particular product is a bargain, mention it only *after* you have stated most selling points and reader benefits. (Additional suggestions for quoting prices honestly and effectively are on pages 298 and 299.

Effective Action-Getting Paragraphs Leading to Sales

To get the desired action from your invited-sales reply, remember to make action clear, easy, dated if necessary, and beneficial to the reader when possible. Sometimes, numbering the steps the reader should take is effective.

Letter 1, from a manufacturer's consumer services manager, is a helpful reply to an inquiry related to sales. Notice that it includes specific suggestions for finding helpful retail merchants, and focuses on positive aspects instead of on negative regrets that the manufacturer can't quote retail prices.

LETTER 1 *A well-written reply that answers questions tactfully, encloses booklets, and suggests where to go for additional help.*[1]

Best news first; reader benefit	Thank you for your recent request for information about Armstrong products. We appreciate your interest and are enclosing for you various pamphlets showing how these products can help make a home easier to care for as well as more attractive.
Further help available	For retail information and addresses of nearby Armstrong merchants, we suggest that you refer to the Yellow Pages of your telephone directory. You will find Armstrong products listed under "Floor Materials," "Carpet," and "Ceilings." For additional information on our Thomasville and Founders furniture, please write to Thomasville Furniture Industries, Inc., P.O. Box 339, Thomasville, NC 27360-0339. Retail sources for Armstrong Cork Wallcovering can be obtained by writing to Katzenback and Warren, 950 Third Avenue, New York, NY 10022-1001.
Educational information	Your local retail firms selling our products will gladly supply retail cost information. We do not establish retail prices. Because of shipping and other considerations, prices necessarily vary in different zones of the country. In addition, when floors, carpet, or ceilings are professionally installed, your real cost is the "installed" cost, which, again, we cannot anticipate. We suggest that you obtain such information from local retail firms selling our

```
                    products. Most of them will gladly give you es-
                    timates without obligation to you.

                    So that you can see the newest in products, de-
                    signs, and colors, visit Armstrong retail mer-
Suggested action    chants near you.  From them you can get complete
                    and up-to-date information on current offerings.
                    We wish you every success with your selections.
```

Suggestions for Handling Inquiries Prompted by Advertising

Whenever a firm advertises, it should be prepared in advance for various kinds of inquiries. To save time and expense, you (or the marketing department) can compose pertinent form paragraphs, and entire messages, to answer the most-asked questions. Some messages should look personalized and individually type-written, even though the body may be essentially the same for other inquirers who asked the same questions. Costs of personalized messages can be decreased considerably by using word processing equipment.

On the other hand, many favorable replies do not need to be personalized—especially in routine situations when your reader will not object to a processed form. Most readers would rather receive promptly a high-quality, courteous, complete form letter than a poor personalized letter that is late, incomplete, or perhaps even inaccurately—and hurriedly—typewritten. Letter 2 is typical of the well-written, processed, sales-oriented replies that accompany booklets, samples, or other free information sent in response to a coupon or inquiry.

LETTER 2   *Processed sales promotion reply with easy-action order form.*

```
Good news with      Here is your . . .
courtesy; no        Foremost Radio catalog to aid you in your selec-
obligation          tions.  Thank you for requesting information on
                    Foremost communication receivers.

                    You will find much useful data in the section on
                    "precision construction and advanced design."
Resale              Other sections show you why Foremost sets are
                    the world's finest receivers.  They are the
Reader benefit      choice of radio amateurs, shortwave listeners,
                    industrial and scientific users.  A Foremost set
                    places the whole world at your fingertips.

                    All communication receivers listed in your cata-
                    log are in stock now for prompt shipment at the
                    prices shown.  You can get liberal trade-in al-
Reader benefits     lowances on standard communications receivers
                    (Hallicrafters, National, Apex, and Howell).  If
                    you prefer a time-payment plan, the attached
                    sheet gives you details.
```

Easy action

To assure delivery within 10 days, just enter your order on the enclosed order form and mail it now in the postage-free envelope. Your order may be accompanied by a deposit as low as 10 percent, with shipment to be made c.o.d. for the balance due, or you may include full remittance if you prefer.

Reader benefit

You can begin to enjoy the unusual reception of a famous Foremost set by placing your order now.

Bad-News Replies to Sales-Related Inquiries

If you have no honest favorable answer to your reader's direct questions regarding catalogs, prices, terms, products, and similar sales-related information, your reply should be organized by the bad-news plan. In some situations all four parts of such a message may be expressed adequately in four or five sentences.

When the inquiry is about a complex or more serious matter, however, much more detail may be necessary—especially in the explanation and resale portions. Letter 3—from the president of a wholesale cement firm to a contractor who had asked why the firm's prices were so high—illustrates how tact and specific details can help to retain a reader's goodwill despite bad news. Notice how it adapts to the four parts of the bad-news plan: buffer; explanation; decision, with reader benefit and resale; positive, friendly close, with offer of further service.

LETTER 3   *Goodwill-retaining bad-news reply to an inquiry about high prices.*

Buffer: thanks for inquiry and business

Thank you for your inquiry regarding the amount we charged you for your concrete. Because your business is very much appreciated and we understand your concern, it is important to me as well as to you that you understand why we billed you $528.08 instead of $465.13.

Explanation

Decision

Fairness to all; reader benefit

Because of a $1.65 hourly employee wage increase, an increase in the price of cement, and overall increases in direct and indirect operating expenses, it was necessary to increase the price of our concrete. For the past 11 months our prices for five sacks of our concrete have been $22.90 to individuals and $22.40 to all contractors. If we lower the price to one contractor, all others would rightly expect equal treatment. By maintaining our price, we treat everyone equally and can assure you that you are getting the quality of material you order and expect.

<table>
<tr><td>Resale</td><td>I realize you were able to buy concrete at a lower price in the past, but the company you bought the concrete from is no longer in business, specifically because their price was not sufficient to cover their direct costs and expenses. Neither you nor we would want this condition to happen to us. We are proud of our reputation for quality products and service and want to continue to serve you in the future.</td></tr>
<tr><td>Pleasant close: thanks; further service</td><td>Your letters are always welcome. Also, if you have questions or need supplies, please call me between 7:30 a.m. and 5:30 p.m. at 555-3333, or call evenings at 555-6666.</td></tr>
</table>

UNSOLICITED SALES LETTERS

Also known as "prospecting" and "cold turkey" letters, unsolicited sales letters are initiated by the seller for various reasons and are not direct answers to inquiries. Direct mail[2] successfully urges people to buy products ranging from mail-order catalog items to real estate. Not only large retail chains such as Montgomery Ward and Sears, but also thousands of lesser-known big-city and small-town merchants, wholesalers, and manufacturers sell effectively by mail. Many firms sell exclusively by mail. Even managers of shops selling services (for home and auto repair, health, beauty, protection, and others) stimulate their businesses by sales messages.

Although enormous potential income is possible using well-written sales letters, you need to be aware of the strong resistance many people have toward such messages. Common criticisms from readers who look unfavorably on sales letters are these: insincerity, appeals to the wrong group, hidden gimmicks, lack of personalization, excessive length, exaggeration.

In general, your success in sales letters will depend on three factors: the mailing list, the right appeals, and the presentation. The first two of these factors are *prewriting* steps. The remainder of this chapter discusses the steps to take before writing unsolicited sales letters, gives suggestions for writing them, and includes examples of four unsolicited sales letters. Chapter 5 includes various cautions regarding the seller's legal responsibilities in written and oral statements about the product or service.

Steps Before Writing the Unsolicited Sales Letter

Because your sales letter may go to hundreds—even thousands—of people, you need to do exceptionally careful planning before starting to write it. The five planning steps—about purpose, reader, ideas to include, fact gathering, and organization—are especially important. Usually you first gather facts on your product and your prospective buyer. Then give extra thought to the purpose, appeals, and presentation of your entire sales message.

1. Gather Facts about Your Product

Before you write a sales letter, you first analyze thoroughly the product you want to sell. (The word *product* as used here includes both tangible products and intangible services.) You gather information through reading, observing, testing, using, comparing, questioning, researching.

If yours is a tangible product, what are its physical characteristics—size, color, shape, content, composition? How is it made and from where did the raw materials come? How does it operate? What is its performance record? How does it compare with and differ from competitors' products in durability, efficiency, appearance, price, terms? What are its weaknesses? Strengths?

For your future buyers, benefits (psychological description) are usually much more significant than physical description. What will the product do for each user? What human needs or desires does it fulfill? For instance, a magazine may be a certain size, with *x* number of pages, on glossy paper, with hundreds of half-page pictures. But what information and enjoyment—even profits—does it bring to the user? What good does it do the buyer in business, home, family, and community contacts?

Whatever your product, you must know all its physical features and its reader benefits before you can confidently and effectively sell it.

2. Consider Your Reader and Mailing Lists

To sell your product effectively by letter requires also some knowledge of your readers and a selective, up-to-date, accurate mailing list. You'll use the mailing list both for a test mailing and for the entire mailing of one or several sales letters. *Testing* means mailing the letter to a small percentage (perhaps 5 to 10 percent) of the names on your list to see whether the letter brings the percentage of response necessary for you to make a profit.

When your product has almost universal use, you may have several different, reasonably homogeneous groups of prospects. Thus if you want to sell lighting fixtures by mail, you need to know the tastes, problems, preferences, and conditions of your various prospective users—homeowners; architects; store or office managers; plant, hospital, or school superintendents; and so forth—and you'll write a different letter to each group.

Selectivity.   Even an excellent sales letter about the best product in the world will not sell if the message goes to the wrong readers. You would not sell office filing cabinets to outdoor laborers, fishing boats to low-income people in a desert area, or Cadillacs to pensioners.

You can buy, rent, or make up a mailing list that includes the best potential buyers for your product. The more similar their characteristics and circumstances, the better. You can buy names and addresses of various specialized groups of people—classified by income level, age, marital status, sex, number of children, occupation, geographic location, education.

If you wish to make your own list, you will find one or more of these sources useful: telephone books, directories, membership lists, vital statistics, newspaper articles, and replies to your advertising. Furthermore, many firms have found that sometimes best of all are the prospect names from their own company records (on customers, stockholders, suppliers).

Currentness and Accuracy.   Postal authorities tell us that over one-fourth of all addresses change within one year. Names and titles may change too. The mailing list must be correct in addresses, spelling of names, use of prefixes (such as Mr., Miss, Mrs., Ms., Dr.), and titles (such as vice president or executive vice president). No matter how selective the list may be, it is good only when it is updated and correct.

3. Decide on Purpose

The purpose of an unsolicited sales letter may be to make a direct sale, to serve as stimulus for future sales, or to win back lost customers.

To Make a Direct Sale.   For relatively inexpensive convenience items or services, the purpose of the sales letter is usually to make a direct sale. Sometimes even for more expensive or complex items your purpose may be to sell with only one letter, as you will see later in this chapter. More often, however, for such products the direct-sale letter follows previous groundwork laid by former letters (in a campaign series), by demonstrations, by advertising, or by sales representatives.

To Serve as Stimulus for a Future Sale.   The long-range purpose of sales promotion messages may be to help build goodwill, supplement advertising, or give pep talks to distributors. Or they may serve as part of a campaign series involving complicated, costly products (like factory machinery) or services (like mortgage lending) that require planning or individual consultation with a company representative before purchase. In these letters the purpose may be to introduce the product and then follow up with a salesperson. The requested action may be that the customer ask for a booklet, catalog, or other information; invite a representative to call; or come to the salesroom.

To Win Back Lost Customers.   In other sales letters the purpose is to let customers who haven't bought anything for some time know you miss them, to find out why they haven't been buying from you, and to sell them on coming back. The requested action is usually that the customer return a questionnaire; often an enclosed order blank brings a direct sale. And good follow-up can help bring in future purchases by currently dissatisfied customers.

4. Choose Ideas and the Central Selling Point (CSP)

After you have collected facts on your product, obtained a mailing list of likely prospects, and determined your purpose, you are ready to decide on ideas to include in your sales letter. Instead of cluttering your letter with a long list of facts about your product, you should select for emphasis a central selling point and translate it into user benefits. You stress whatever appeal is most likely to convince the prospect that he or she should buy your product. Often this is the feature or benefit that differentiates your product from those of competitors. After you have stressed the central selling point, you can introduce other appeals about your product. (For a list of reader-benefit appeals, see pages 250 and 251.)

Your central selling point is always based on what you estimate are the prospects' needs. Will the product cut their costs? Protect them? Make them more attractive? If your product will appeal to different groups of prospects for different reasons, you will write a different sales letter to each group. In each letter you will *feature the central selling point and appeals that you estimate are most pleasing to the readers for whom you write it*. For example, to dealers who expect to resell your product, you will emphasize quick turnover and profits. To consumers you may feature comfort, pride in personal appearance, safety, or any other appropriate appeals. Remember also that individuals within any group have different mental filters and situations and may thus be motivated for different reasons (perhaps another central selling point that you stress in a later letter).

Suppose, for instance, you want to sell by mail vinyl jackets that are water-repellent, fully lined—with removable, warm inner lining—fashionable, and easily cleaned with a damp cloth. To readers living in rainy areas you might feature year-round comfort (dry in any downpour). To readers in arid regions your major appeal may be convenience (easily cleaned and wearable the year around). For students you might focus on both attractiveness (in style) and economy (infrequent replacements, factory prices, no dry-cleaning bills).

5. Organize and Plan the Sales Presentation

The fifth planning step—outlining and organizing—involves much more than deciding on the organizational plan and letter content. Your letter is part of an entire sales presentation, whether it is to be a single sales effort or part of a campaign series. Thus you will *consider*—perhaps with other executives and a consultant—*its length, appearance, timing, and enclosures, along with your budget and expected returns.*

Your presentation must move readers to take the desired action—and yield a satisfactory profit. The percentage of response needed for profitable returns may range from less than 1 percent to a much higher figure, depending on various factors. The returns the mailing brings must be sufficiently greater than its total cost—for the list, plus planning, consulting (with direct-mail specialists) about,[3] writing, revising, reproducing, testing, and mailing the letter with all its enclosures.

Number and Kinds of Enclosures.   Before writing your sales letter, plan the enclosures. Will the envelope contain any descriptive pamphlet, separate testimonials, pictures, samples, gimmicks, gadgets, order blank, reply envelope? Gadgets and gimmicks should be used only if they help to dramatize a point, not if they merely attract attention. (Some readers dislike them; others become absorbed in them and fail to read the letter.) The usual enclosures are leaflet, order blank, and reply envelope.

Length of Sales Letter.   If the enclosures adequately take care of all needed details, the letter should preferably be only one page. If a catalog or booklet is to be sent later upon request, or if a demonstration or sales representative is to follow, these methods will help make the sale. But if you do not have an enclosure—and especially if you want to make a direct sale—your letter may have to be longer than one page. Just be sure it is as concise as possible!

Many conflicting ideas exist about the desirable length of sales letters. However, direct-mail experts have proved again and again that long copy works—if it catches and holds the reader's interest and is sufficiently convincing.

Appearance of Sales Letter.   To a prospect a company is what it appears to be in its printed mailing. You need to decide (usually with the help of experts in direct mail, advertising, and processing) on the quality and color of paper to be used and also whether the printing will be in one or more colors. Among other factors to be considered in your planning are these:

Should special pictures, designs, handwritten "teaser" statements, offers of a gift, or other attention-getting devices or gimmicks be used on the outside envelope and the letterhead?

What about the sizes of the letterhead, envelopes, and other enclosures? Should any be oversize? Transparent? With what size, color, and kind of type?

Should the letter be personalized with the reader's name and address?

Should the letter have occasional underscoring, capitalizing, "inked" lines, arrows, or other marks to emphasize important ideas?

Timing of Sales Message.   Consider what is likely to be the best time of the week, month, season, and year to launch a certain sales campaign. The time of your mailing will naturally affect the wording of your sales letter and sometimes your choice of appeals (as for certain seasons, holidays).

Figures released by the National Association of Manufacturers show that 80 percent of orders are placed after the sales representative's fifth call. Remember, a sales letter is a "sales representative" too. Some firms effectively send the same letter (perhaps on paper of a different color) to the same prospects two or three times and receive orders only after the last mailing.

Suggestions for Writing the Unsolicited Sales Letter

After you have completed the prewriting steps about your product, mailing list of prospects, choice of ideas and main appeals, and the planned presentation, you are ready to develop the sales letter. This writing and revising will probably take hours, even days. You'll try to make your message complete, concise, considerate of the reader, clear, courteous, correct, and concrete—with specific facts, active verbs, and meaningful adjectives. If time and budget permit, you may decide—with the help of a consultant—to prepare several versions of your letter to test their pulling power before mailing one to the entire mailing list.

Your basic guide is the AIDA organizational plan—attention, interest, desire, action. Although the following discussion focuses separately on each part of the AIDA plan, the parts need not always be in this sequence, nor need all parts be in every letter. Some sales letters begin with desire-creating material such as testimonials or guarantees. Some start with action-inducing statements such as special offers or free trials. Some may skip product description and uses (the interest section) and devote most of the letter to proof—if, for example, the reader already knows the description and uses but needs conviction material to reinforce interest and create desire to buy the product. Circumstances vary—and so do sales letter content and organization.

Attract Your Prospect's Attention

The best way to catch the attention of a busy reader is by promising—or implying a forthcoming promise—*to benefit him or her by satisfying a psychological or a physical need*. Mention what the reader gains from the product before you name it. Even before the opening paragraph you can attract the reader's attention by inserting a benefit in place of an inside address.

Though the letter may go to thousands of people, each copy must "talk" in a natural, sincere, friendly way to an individual human being. The opening should be appropriate, fresh, honest, interesting, specific, and relevant to the central selling point. Avoid tricky, exaggerated openings, which have been so overused that the American public is unmoved or annoyed by them. Of course, if you can think of a novel, catchy opening that honestly relates closely to your central theme, go ahead and use it.

Also be careful to avoid openings that may outdate your letter soon. For instance, one letter addressed to "Dear Graduate" began "Now that you are out of school for three months . . ." Readers who had been out of school longer than that were of course annoyed by the inaccuracy.

Keep the first paragraph short, preferably two to five lines, sometimes only one. Short paragraphs look easy to read and thus are more likely to get the reader started. If unusual circumstances require you to have a long opening paragraph, it should be set up in an easy-to-read way—sometimes with double spaces between sentences or with some lines indented from both margins.

For your opening, you can choose reader-benefit attention getters like these:

1. A Comparison or a (Short!) Story.   *Selling a secretary's handbook along with a free kit (pictures of a cluttered and a tidy desk are at top of letter):*

It's really amazing! Betty and Sue work side by side in the same office. They have the same secretarial training and skills . . . both have identical workloads--yet Betty has usually completed her typewriting by 4:45 every day, while Sue usually can't even find her newspaper under the clutter of unfinished work still on her desk.
        And not only the janitor notices! Their boss has noticed the difference too. So besides the sheer delight of an easier day with much less pressure, let's face it, Betty will be in line for promotions, pay raises, and all the fringe benefits that go with them!

2. An Event or Fact in the Reader's Life.   *Selling car insurance:*

The fact that you are a college senior specializing in medicine and attending a well-respected university like [name] tells people about your character.
        For instance, it may qualify you for a special low-cost auto insurance program that might not otherwise be available to you.

3. A Problem the Reader May Face.   *Urging use of a catalog to shop by mail:*

During the next few weeks you and people all over the country will be doing Christmas shopping. Some will be early birds. Others will wait until the last minute, and if they are shopping in the stores, they will be pushed around and have to take what is left instead of being able to purchase the items they had in mind.

4. A Significant Fact about the Product.   *Selling TV cable service:*

More than 4,000,000 viewers in the UNITED STATES . . .
                        . . . and . . .
over 10,000 people in the [city] area alone enjoy sharp, clear, multichannel television reception by means of C.A.T.V. (Community Antenna Television).

5. A Solution to a Problem.   *Selling hospital insurance (picture of a check is at top of letter):*

You can receive a check like this, or even up to $5,000, when you or a member of your family goes to the hospital . . . IF you are protected by ABC Hospital Plan.

6. *A Surprising Question or Challenging Statement.* *Offering a special paint sprayer on 15-day free trial for homeowners, do-it-yourselfers, and professional painters:*

```
How would you like to beautifully paint a 9 × 12 room--walls
and ceiling--in less than one hour including cleanup time?
To paint 400 percent faster than with a 4-inch brush and 222
percent faster than with a 9-inch roller?
```

For some sales letters the attention-getting opening might be a testimonial, guarantee, special offer, or free trial—parts that are usually in later sections.

Arouse the Reader's Interest

Having attracted the reader's attention, you now arouse interest by beginning to "picture" your product and telling what it will do for the reader. You begin to develop the central selling point.

You can picture your product in two ways—physical description and reader benefits (listed on pages 250–251). You can place the benefits first, as in example 1, but usually they are interwoven with physical description, as in example 2.

EXAMPLE 1 *Stating benefits (money, extra earnings, usefulness) before physical description.*

```
When you use Family Investments, you find hundreds of ways
to make your money earn more and go further--for your home,
clothing, food, travel, taxes, and pleasure.  You get a rich
source of advice from accountants, automotive specialists,
real estate agents, tax consultants, life insurance experts,
bankers, stockbrokers, lawyers.

This leather-bound book contains 467 pages, divided by sub-
ject into 15 chapters, 165,000 words.  Sturdily built for
continual use, the book has 310 drawings, graphs, and tables
to illustrate points and clarify meanings.  In essence, us-
ing the book will be like taking a fascinating course in
managing your family's money--from highly paid profession-
als.
```

EXAMPLE 2 *Interweaving benefits and physical description.*[4]

```
The Apple IIc Plus personal computer gives you all the most
important benefits of the Apple II family--versatility, ex-
pandability, ease of use, and software compatibility--in one
compact, lightweight, elegantly designed package.  In addi-
tion, it has over five times the disk storage capacity of
```

```
previous Apple IIc models, and up to four times the process-
ing speed.

The Apple IIc Plus offers high-quality color graphics,
built-in connectors for easy accessory expansion, a full-
size keyboard, and a 3.5-inch high-capacity (800-kilobyte)
disk drive.  A completely self-contained power supply makes
the computer highly transportable, and the handle locks
downward to provide a stable, inclined keyboard for typing
convenience.  Naturally, the IIc Plus also offers the ease
of use that has characterized the Apple II family since its
inception.

If you're the first-time computer buyer who wants a system
that will just "plug in and go," the Apple IIc Plus is a
smart choice.
```

Create Desire and Convince the Reader

After getting your readers interested in one or several of your product's benefits, you need to create in them a desire to own your product, and to convince them that they should buy (if your purpose is to make a direct sale). Desirable statements about prices also help to convince.

The reader's progression from interest to desire to conviction is usually gradual. It is not necessary to worry about exactly where one step begins or ends; these steps are parts of an integrated whole. Together they develop your central selling point and help urge the reader to take the requested action.

Desire for Your Product.   Desire-creating material within the letter ranges from one paragraph—in a one-page letter with descriptive brochure—to several paragraphs if the letter itself is two or more pages long, with or without an enclosed brochure. The following example illustrates desire-creating paragraphs regarding an award-winning Image Search Plus system for business firms.

EXAMPLE 3   *Developing the central selling point and benefits.*[5]

```
Integrated Office Automation Made Simple
   Image Search Plus is a user-friendly system consisting of
the industry's top-rated software, PC-AT's, and digital
scanners that let you store and retrieve an actual image of
a document.  When you need to see it, simply punch it up and
read it on your monitor.  No walking.  No stopping.  No
waiting.  Imagine being able to update or refer to a file
while you have your customer on the phone.  It's the key to
office productivity.

Total Flexibility
   Whether you're starting with a single or multiuser system,
Image Search Plus gives you total flexibility.  As documents
```

arrive, you'll be able to scan, digitize, distribute, and
store them via hard copy, floppy disk, streaming tape, optical disk or by cable to remote displays. Entire files, single documents, or high-quality data can then be easily located with multiple cross-references, retrieved in seconds
and displayed on your system's monitor in the highest resolution available.

The Competitive Edge

   You'll have all your files updated and together, instantly
accessible by local and remote users and impossible to lose.
Employees will spend less time processing documents and more
time producing results. Almost immediately your Image
Search Plus system will make customer service a strong
point, improving production and giving you the competitive
edge.

Evidence to Convince.   The main proof about your product's features and
benefits comes preferably from evidence that persons outside your company
determine. These outside sources include *satisfied users; recognized testing
laboratories, agencies, and disinterested persons;* and *the prospect himself or
herself.* Seven popular kinds of proof are illustrated below.

1. Facts about Satisfied Users' Experience with the Product.   *These include
verifiable reports and statistics from users.*

   The green page in the enclosed brochure itemizes savings
   that 203 contractors have realized from EASI-POUR concrete
   mix. Notice that their actual savings range from 45 to 85
   percent. As you study the table, note its specific facts
   about the size of each job. Then compare the figures with
   your own average costs for similar projects.

2. Names of Other Buyers and Users.   *State how many persons or firms
already are using the product. Better yet, when appropriate, give the names
of well-known, satisfied users, or offer to send names and addresses upon
request.*

   Among the hundreds of business firms that are pleased with
   their use of ABC equipment are Marshall Field and Company,
   Alcoa Aluminum, Ford Motor Company, United Airlines, and
   Chase Manhattan Bank.

3. Testimonials.   *Because testimonials have been abused (with phony quotations by nonusers who are paid to make them), many people distrust them.
To establish the credibility of the testimonials you use, select persons or
firms that are bona fide users of your product and whose judgment the
reader respects. Be specific. Get their permission. Avoid exaggerations.*

> "Since we've been using EASI-POUR concrete mix, six of our
> workers can place and finish a section of concrete street
> with curb--12 feet wide and a football field long--in only
> <u>one hour</u>. Its paving ability and its quality surpass any
> concrete mix we've used during our 20 years of operation."
> Gene Aimes, project superintendent, East Contractors, Inc.

4. *Performance Tests.* *Whenever recognized experts, testing laboratories, or authoritative agencies in a field relative to your product have made satisfactory performance tests on it, their evidence offers convincing proof. Also effective are statements, reports, and statistics compiled by impartial, reliable witnesses.*

> **a.** Learnfun electric toys have earned the endorsement and
> seals of approval from Underwriters Laboratories, the
> Good Housekeeping Institute, the American Medical Association, and the National Safety Council.
>
> **b.** In every performance test by the United Automotive Association, ALERT batteries ranked at the top of the list.
> Read in the enclosed brochure the details of qualities
> tested, and decide for yourself why ALERT is the battery
> for you.

5. *Free Trial.* *If you have so much confidence in your product that you're willing to let the prospect try it on a free trial basis, your offer provides a very effective form of proof. The mail-order customer thus has the same opportunity to examine the product carefully as he or she would have before buying in a store. In fact, the customer gets the added privilege of using it before buying it.*

> You'll have a full 10 days to use your new glasses . . . to
> wear them walking, driving, working--without actually spending a single cent. . . . If for some reason, any reason at
> all, you don't like them, just send them back to me within
> 10 days and we'll forget the whole thing. What could be
> fairer?

6. *Guarantee.* *With the guarantee, the customer pays for the product before using it, but gets a written promise that if not satisfied, he or she will get a refund (or credit), free repairs, or free replacement of the entire article.*

> With every ARTEX product you buy you get this firm, money-
> back guarantee: "ALL ARTEX products are Unconditionally
> Guaranteed to please. If you are not completely satisfied
> with any ARTEX, return it within 30 days for full refund."

7. *Samples.* *Let the prospect examine, try on, or use the samples that you send (for instance, swatches of clothing or drapery materials; pieces of wire,* *rubber, or fireproof insulation) or that he or she calls for personally (such as gasoline for the car, or a food and beverage made fresh daily). The prospect is asked to perform some suggested action to convince him- or herself that the product meets the writer's claims.*

```
Just pick up the enclosed STICK-UP page, pull back the hardy
Celanar protective sheet.  Then place an assortment of odd-
sized clippings, ads, photos on the STICK-UP sheet in any
arrangement you choose.  Finally, return the protective cov-
ering and press down gently.

    Note how sharply and clearly you see every word through
    the transparent sheet, every shading of the material
    you've mounted on the STICK-UP page.

    But note this, too:  If the arrangement you've set up
    doesn't please you, all you have to do is pull back the
    Celanar cover, pick up the clippings or photos, and rear-
    range them any way you desire . . . as often as you wish,
    and there's no mess, no fuss, no sloppy paste pot! You
    save time and. . . .
```

Price of Your Product.   Your presentation on the selling features, benefits, and proof may have convinced the prospect that your product meets the need and he or she should buy it. But is the product worth the price, and can he or she pay for it? How does it compare with prices of similar available products?

If your price is a bargain, you might feature it as an attention-getting opening. If the price doesn't justify this emphasis, state it only *after* you have presented most of the selling features, benefits, and proof. Of course, if your letter is part of a campaign series to sell a costly item, the price might not be mentioned until near the end of the series. Sometimes price is not mentioned in the letter at all. If the product or service varies with the customer's needs (as for insurance or a complex heating installation in an industrial plant), the exact price quotation is given only after consultations with sales representatives.

If your prospect is likely to consider your price a drawback, try to bring the price within reach. For example, in addition to stating the full price, you can use the following methods to help convince the prospect that he or she can pay it:

1. Break it down into "easy" weekly or monthly payments.

2. State it in terms of unit price ($9 a book) instead of case lots, dozens, or sets ($210 for the encyclopedia set).

3. Interpret it on the basis of the benefits to be gained.

4. Emphasize its cost on a daily, monthly, or yearly basis—depending on the product's estimated life and service (only 3 cents a day).

5. Compare it with the amount the average reader spends daily (monthly) for nonessentials or luxuries.

The discussion of price is usually presented just before the action paragraphs—if price and action are clear-cut and distinct. Sometimes, however, they blend, as do interest and desire. In some letters, you will include price inducements with conviction details; in others, with action. Because offers of easy payment (as well as "no money down now" and credit card use) more often serve as special inducements to action, they are discussed in the next section.

Induce Reader Action

Having convinced your reader that your product is valuable, needed, and worthy of purchase, you now must encourage the most important step—performing the action you request.

All previous discussions in this book about handling negatives, overcoming price resistance, and inducing action are applicable to sales letters and are not repeated here. You also already know that a complete action section should:

State clearly the action you desire

Make action easy

Date the action (when desirable)

Offer special inducement to act by a specified time (when desirable)

End with a last reader-benefit plug (when appropriate)

To induce the reader to act within a certain time, you can use one or more of the following methods:

1. Credit Cards.   *The convenience of merely charging a purchase to a nationally accepted credit card—bank, national oil company, travel agency, diners' club, or other cards—is an effective inducement to action. The holder of such credit cards need not write a check or send a money order now, but merely return an order blank listing a credit card number.*

```
Send no money now.  To order, just check on the enclosed
form that you wish this purchase charged to your account
with one of the national credit firms listed.  Then be sure
to fill in your account number as shown on your credit card.
```

2. Easy Payments or "No Money Now."   *A budget plan or a future-payment plan by which the prospect pays nothing down now may serve two purposes—to convince the reader that he or she can afford to buy your product and to induce the reader to take the requested action. Thus, though the prospect may not have the entire price of the product, he or she will be able to order right away if the entire amount (or anything) is not required at once.*

```
For as little as $10 down you can begin to reap the benefits
of this useful encyclopedia before school starts.  Easy
```

```
monthly payments as low as $8 a month can be arranged at
your convenience.
```

3. Gift.   *If the prospect buys one item, two may be received for the price of one; or he or she may receive a gift that is different from the item you are selling.*[6]

```
Agree to try it for 10 days on our No-Money-Down offer, and
I'll send you a matching leather-look vinyl Tote Bag FREE.
This gift is yours to keep, even if you return the jacket.
```

4. Free Trial.   *The free trial serves two purposes—to convince the reader of your sincerity about the product's merits and to induce action now. The reader has nothing to lose; no money is spent now, and he or she need pay later only if the article is found satisfactory.*

5. No Obligation to Buy.   *When the purpose of your letter is to get the prospect to ask for more information, to come for a demonstration, or perhaps to ask a sales representative to call, the person is more likely to act if you promise there is no obligation to buy.*

```
Mailing the enclosed card does not in any way obligate you
to buy insurance, and no salesperson will call on you unless
you invite him or her.  To receive full details about this
plan, with specific figures at your present age--and your
free portfolio--just return the postpaid card above.
```

6. Higher Earnings.   *A promise of higher earnings if the reader acts before a certain date is also a good incentive.*

```
By sending your deposits in the enclosed envelope, so they
reach us by the 10th of May, you earn 6% interest from the
1st of the month.
```

7. Special Price for a Limited Time.   *Setting a time limit for bargain prices (perhaps on out-of-season items or items in limited supply), or for introductory prices on new items or to new buyers, effectively induces action. Offer a discount on the purchase price if the reader buys before a certain date or if cash in full is sent with the order.*

```
This special introductory rate (for new subscribers only)
brings you 40 news-packed issues of World Reports for only
$_____.
```

```
That is down to half-price for 40 issues if you bought one
copy at a time.  You get this special rate if your order is
postmarked before May 1.
```

Writing an effective sales letter is a lot of work, but it can be greatly rewarding. Many a sales letter mailed to thousands of prospects has brought thousands—even millions—of dollars in returns. Even the expert writers "agonize" over their copy. Good selling presents the benefits and the proposition in such a way that the readers become convinced and "sell themselves." On the other hand, if the letter sounds like a high-pressure sales pitch, the readers may become defensive. To achieve your goal may require meticulous editing and rewriting, but the results will be worth the effort.

Examples of Unsolicited Sales Letters

This section illustrates letters that aim to (1) make direct sales, (2) serve as stimulus to future sales, and (3) bring back lost customers. As you read them, notice how description is mixed with and reinforces reader benefits, how the central selling point (labeled CSP) is developed, and how reader-benefit appeals are emphasized.

Making Direct Sales

The letter below, sent to business owners, illustrates one way to sell relatively high-priced items successfully by one letter and detailed enclosures. The two items sold were priced at $170 and $295 (prices, though omitted in the letter, were in the enclosures). On a mailing of 4,500, this one-page letter brought in $45 in direct sales for every single dollar of costs.[7]

LETTER 1   *Selling radiator cleaning tanks to service-shop owners. CSP: less time to clean tanks. Appeals: reduced work; higher profits.*

IF THREE RADIATOR REPAIR EXPERTS WALKED INTO
YOUR SHOP THIS AFTERNOON . . .

Attention

And the first one, the owner of Midtown Auto
Radiator Service of New York City, said: "We
are cleaning 10 to 12 radiators in our tank and
find that it requires only 20 minutes to get
them thoroughly clean."

Interest

And the second person, proprietor of the Bronx
Radiator Service, said: "We clean nine radiators in one tank in half the time it used to
take to clean two."

And the third person, owner of Goldberg's Auto
Service of St. Johnsbury, Vt., said: "We have
found this the most satisfactory way to clean
radiators that we have ever used."

Desire

    . . . you'd certainly feel that you owed it to
    yourself to find out just what they used to
    bring those people such new speed and profits,
    wouldn't you? Well, here is how they--and
    YOU--are in a position to make such claims!

    You will find their explanations of exactly how
    they do it (along with reports of other leading
    radiator specialists from coast to coast) in
    the enclosed Bulletin #308. In addition, you

Conviction

    will find complete specifications on two sizes
    of radiator cleaning tanks that will enable you
    to clean up from 4 to 12 radiators at a time--
    probably in LESS time than it now takes you to
    clean ONE!

    Don't just take our word for it--read the genu-
    ine letters and see the actual, unretouched

Conviction; action

    photographs in the enclosed bulletin. Then
    prove these new speeds and savings in your own
    shop by mailing the Guarantee Order Form TODAY!

Another example of a successful sales message is Letter 2 with a one-sheet enclosure [see Figure 11-1(*a*) and (*b*)].[8] Some noteworthy qualities found in this message are the folowing:

Letter

- Short paragraphs, two to four lines, begin with words printed in ALL CAPITALS.
- CSP emphasis is on savings and guarantee, with you-attitude.
- Color for all words, figures, and signature improves visual appearance. (On this original letter the color was bright purple.)
- Ten words in letterhead are repeated across bottom of letter.

Enclosure

- For a wide variety of items, savings are stated attractively in percentages; some also in dollars.
- Specific groups of items are listed on both sides of sheet.
- On page 1 shown here, items in three columns range from adult clothing to home furnishings; all words and figures are purple.
- On reverse side (not shown here) under a title "BACK TO SCHOOL SAVINGS" are two columns with student clothing items, typewriters, word processors, luggage. Printing is also purple.
- On page 1 the word "save" appears 27 times; on page 2, 20 times.

Envelope

- All words and figures in return address and postage area are purple.
- A ½-inch purple and white border across the bottom states "OPEN ME BEFORE FRIDAY, AUGUST 25."

THE BON MARCHÉ
AUGUST SAVINGS SENSATION

FRIDAY, AUGUST 25, CHARGE CUSTOMERS' COURTESY DAY
SATURDAY & SUNDAY, AUGUST 26 & 27, CHARGE CUSTOMERS & THE GENERAL PUBLIC

Dear Customer,

Attention — YOU'RE INVITED to a very special sale. Special because you, our charge customer, have an opportunity to take advantage of savings before they are advertised to the general public. You get first choice and the best selection of the many, many excellent values during this event.

Interest — FRIDAY, AUGUST 25, is your day. The Bon Marche's August Savings Sensation merchandise will be signed and ready for you.

Desire — LOOK FOR THE SAVINGS SENSATION SIGNS throughout the store. You'll find hundreds of values. Top quality, famous brands, all guaranteed by The Bon Marche, including fashions and casual wear for the entire family, furniture and accessories for the home.

Actions — CHECK THE ENCLOSED SAMPLES OF TERRIFIC VALUES. They'll give you an idea of the great savings available for you. Then plan on shopping on Charge Customers' Courtesy Day at The Bon Marche.

Sincerely,

Robert B. Mang

Robert B. Mang
President

AUGUST SAVINGS SENSATION CHARGE CUSTOMERS' COURTESY DAY
FRIDAY, AUGUST 25

Figure 11-1(a)   Letter 2   *Inviting department store charge customers to a special one-day sale. CSP: savings on hundreds of top-quality items, all guaranteed.*

THE BON MARCHÉ
AUGUST SAVINGS SENSATION

SAVE 30%
MISSES SEPARATES
Pants, skirts and tops, were 9.99-32.00, now
6.99-19.60. Misses Sportswear.

SAVE 30%
MISSES 2-PC. DRESSING
Sizes s-m-l. Not in Bellevue Square.
Were 19.99. Misses Sportswear.

SAVE 30%
MISSES COORDINATES
Famous brands. Not in Bellevue Square.
Reg. 18.00-99.00. Misses Coordinates.

SAVE 50%
ENTIRE STOCK DRESSES
BUY 1 AND GET THE 2ND
AT 50% SAVINGS
Misses, petites and women's sizes. Second
must be of equal or lesser value. Dresses.

SAVE 33%
WOMEN'S WORLD
SPORTSWEAR
18W-24W. Reg. 28.00-40.00. Women's World.

2 FOR $40
SLEEPWEAR
Buy two and save 23-40%. Purchased
individually, price is as marked.
Reg. 26.00-34.00. Ladies Sleepwear.

SAVE 20%, 25% & 30%
BRA & PANTY STOCK-UP SALE
Buy one reg. price bra, **save 20%**.
Buy two reg. price bras, **save 25%**.
Buy three reg. price bras, **save 30%**.
Buy three reg. price panties, **save 20%**.
Buy six reg. price panties, **save 25%**.
Buy twelve reg. price panties, **save 30%**.
Sale does not include Wacoal, Christian
Dior, Oscar de la Renta or Natori.
Intimate Apparel and Budget Intimate Apparel.

SAVE 30%
FASHION ACCESSORIES
Includes jewelry, handbags, scarves, belts,
hosiery and exercisewear. Accessories.

SAVE 20%
WOMEN'S & MEN'S REG.
PRICE DRESS SHOES
Women's Liz Claiborne not included.

SAVE 25%
ENTIRE STOCK SPORTS
ILLUSTRATED™ SHORTS &
T-SHIRTS
Choose Supplex ™ running shorts and
T-shirts. Men's Activewear.

SAVE 25%
REG. PRICE VAN HEUSEN
WOVEN SPORT SHIRTS
Long sleeve "Design Elements". Sizes m-l-xl.
Reg. 22.00, **16.50**. Men's Sport Shirts.

SAVE 40%
MEN'S FURNISHINGS
SALE ITEMS
Basics and accessories. Men's Furnishings.

SAVE 10%
ANY REG. PRICE PURCHASE
IN MEN'S FURNISHINGS,
SPORTSWEAR PANTS OR
SPORT COATS
Men's Furnishings, Pants and Sport Coats.

SAVE ADDITIONAL
50%
BUDGET CLEARANCE ITEMS
Available where normally sold.

SAVE 20%
ANY BUDGET STORE
REG. PRICE PURCHASE

SAVE 50%
HOMEWORLD CLEARANCE
Decorative accessories, stationery,
housewares and linens. Homeworld.

SAVE 10%
REG. PRICE COLLECTIBLES*
& DECORATIVE ACCESSORIES
Royal Doulton collectibles, Hummels, Austin
statues, David Winter cottages and more.
*Does not include Lladro and Nao figurines.
Homeworld.

SAVE 20%
HOME DECOR
Includes china, crystal, silver, lamps,
stationery and silk plants. Special orders
cannot be accepted at this sale price.
Homeworld.

SAVE 10%
ENTIRE STOCK FURNITURE,
MATTRESSES & RUGS
Includes all regular or sale priced in-stock
items. Available where normally sold.
Homeworld.

SAVE 25-33%
REG. PRICE LINENS
Linens for your bedroom, bathroom, and
table top. Homeworld.

SAVE 10-20%
HOUSEWARES AND HOME
ELECTRONICS
Housewares and Electronics.

AUGUST SAVINGS SENSATION CHARGE CUSTOMERS' DAY
FRIDAY, AUGUST 25

Figure 11-1(b)   Letter 2 enclosure, presenting convincing specifics about valuable savings.

Serving as Stimulus to Future Sales

Many sales letters urge action other than an immediate order for a direct purchase. Some of these sell products or services which are complicated or expensive, or which must be specially tailored to fit the buyer's particular needs. Others sell continual use of the customer's credit card, which enables her or him to buy not only the firm's products but also other conveniences.

To Sell Complicated, Expensive, or Specially Designed Items.   For some products the buyer will need more time and information, as well as personal observation. In this category are real estate, industrial equipment, insurance, costly installations, pleasure boats, cars, and products or services the reader may have considered unnecessary.

A campaign series of letters is a popular means of stimulating ultimate sales of such products and services. You decide in advance how many letters you should send, the time intervals, and the content of each. Some might ask the customer merely to request further information. In other letters you might request that the reader call your office or store for a demonstration, or ask for a sales representative to visit, as in letter 3.

Depending on the kinds of products you sell, you can sometimes get a highly satisfactory return by mailing only a relatively few letters. For instance, a manufacturer of bulldozing equipment mailed one sales let   to only 58 business executives. To the requested action "Write, wire, or phone for further details" 30 readers replied; they bought $250,000 worth of equipment. Letter 3 was also an effective single letter. Though mailed to only 100 sales managers, it sold 1 million caps! Each letter was typewritten on one page and addressed personally to each manager.

LETTER 3   *Urging sales managers to request a sales representative to give more information about a distinctive advertising gadget. CSP: adjustable, lightweight, low-cost service caps. Appeals: appearance, savings, comfort, distinctiveness.*[9]

Dear Mr. Gates:

Attention
Literally and figuratively you can <u>hit the top</u> with your advertising.

How? With Paperlynen Adjustable Service Caps.

Interest
Paperlynen Caps offer the ideal medium for placing your name constantly before the public eye. Worn by storekeepers and your own employees, these caps not only will help sell your products but also are a constant goodwill reminder. And, as a means of cooperative advertising, they're excellent. In addition, Paperlynen Adjustable Service Caps are preferred because of these advantages:

Appearance

Adjustable to any and every head size; always fit;
look like linen; sanitary-clean

Low Cost

Cost less than expense of having ill-fitting cloth
caps laundered; this saving in addition to saving of
initial cost of cloth caps

Desire   Comfort

Light in weight; porous nature of crown permits free,
filtered ventilation

Distinction

Offer the opportunity of distinction through imprint-
ing your firm's name or trademark in a manner not
possible on ordinary caps. With cooperative advertising or as a dealer help, the storekeeper's name
may also be added.

Conviction   Several samples of Paperlynen caps are enclosed.
                Look at 'em, try 'em, test 'em. We're sure you'll
                like 'em.

Action   When you are ready for more information, call (333)
                555-1030 and one of our salespeople will be up to see
                you promptly.

To Sell Continual Use of the Customer's Credit Card.   From time to time
you may need to show the benefits that can be gained from a credit card. By
encouraging regular use of the card, you also help increase your future sales.
Besides the convenience of buying on a pay-later basis, your credit customers
receive additional benefits. Among them may be coupon discounts, special sales
not announced to the general public, low-cost insurance policies, gifts on various
occasions, and other appreciated advantages.

Benefits differ, of course, depending on the nature and scope of a business.
For example, a national company's travel club included these extra credit card
benefits in a sales letter:

You can charge a stay at any one of some 2,000 really good
    hotels all over America.
If you ever run into trouble on the road, you can use your
    card to charge car repairs up to $100 . . . and
You can reduce the amount of money you must carry, reducing
    the risk of loss or theft.

Bringing Back Lost Customers

Many businesses spend thousands of dollars on advertising to attract new customers and yet neglect regular customers. Studies have indicated that *indifference* on the part of the seller is the main reason customers leave one company for another. At least two-thirds of such customers drift away because they feel their business isn't appreciated, because they are treated discourteously, or because some grievances were unadjusted.

The best way to find out why customers haven't bought from you for, say, six months or more is to ask them—either in person or by mail. Warm, sincere, friendly letters can help you to learn why you lost customers and can also help you win them back. (Of course, it is important that after you know customers' reasons, you take steps to correct any weaknesses.)

The secret for winning back lost customers is to tell them that you miss them—and to keep telling them. Patience and persistence do pay off. For instance, one department store in Chicago reopened 2,724 accounts with sales totaling $73,001.34; a retail store in Long Beach, California, brought in $30,000 from lost customers; and a Buffalo merchant regained 47 percent of his lost accounts with 30 mailings over a period of five years.[10] Numerous other items have also had rewarding results (sometimes even with one letter).

Your first miss-you letters may be simple, direct-request inquiries without appeals. (See inquiry 5, page 149.) However, when direct inquiries bring no response, you need to mail persuasive requests that say, in essence:

We miss you.

Here are the benefits you get by coming back to us.

Please come again.

Sincerity, imagination, appropriate appeals, and sometimes good-natured humor characterize these messages, as illustrated in letter 4.

LETTER 4   *A unique message to win back "lost" hotel guests. CSP: high standard of personal service to "special guests." Appeals: enjoyment, comfort, convenience, prestige.*[11]

Dear Mr. Morgan:

Attention   Today we registered an ex-president; two senators, a congressman; several assorted corporation presidents; a foreign personage with party; generals by the one, two, and three star; plus a group of tourists. But not you.

Interest   I suppose you thought we'd be too busy to notice that you were among the missing. But that's not true. We haven't made The Mayflower the standard of personal

service by forgetting our special guests the moment
they leave the checkout desk.

What happened?

Desire

Have you sworn off roast beef when it's as succulent
as our Rib Room specialty? Are you punishing yourself
by giving up really comfortable, handsome, air-condi-
tioned guest rooms for lesser accommodations?

Do you feel guilty about staying at a hotel so perfectly located and so completely dedicated to your
convenience? Or have you just not been in Washington
lately?

We hope it's this last possibility.

Action

Please write and end our suspense as soon as possible.
Or, better yet, come back for a visit. Old friends
are best friends. And busy as we are, we miss one of
our very best friends: you!

With good judgment, sincerity, and imagination, you can develop a variety of appealing miss-you letters. If you prefer, you can buy special-theme messages from advertising specialists, with or without gadgets symbolic of various holidays, seasons, products, and services. Be sure, however, that they relate closely to your company's business.

SUMMARY

Sales letters may be either solicited (invited) or unsolicited. When you answer inquiries that are related in some way to your sales—regarding prices, terms, discounts, deliveries, products, manufacturing, types of accounts available, and so on—you have opportunities to write solicited sales letters. Follow the good-news plan if your information is favorable for the inquirer, and bad-news plan if it is unfavorable.

Use the persuasive-request plan for unsolicited sales letters—those you initiate yourself to make direct sales, encourage future sales, or win back lost customers. Begin with an attention-getting, appropriate opening; arouse interest through physical description or reader benefits; create desire and conviction by developing your central selling point and benefits, by offering proof, and by handling price in a positive way; then ask for action. If appropriate, offer special inducements so that the reader will act within a certain time.

The Capsule Checklists on pages 315–316 give a brief summary of how to adapt the good-news and the bad-news plans for replies to sales-related inquiries, and how to use the persuasive-request plan for unsolicited sales letters.

EXERCISES AND PROBLEMS

Good-News Replies to Sales-Related Inquiries

1. *Evaluations:* Letters **a** and **b** below are replies to routine, direct requests. Suggest improvements where needed in opening and closing paragraphs, you-attitude, and adequacy of resale material.

   a. *Individually typed reply from a steam specialty company:*

   Gentlemen:

   Replying to your letter of 30 Sept. 199-, please be advised that we are mailing to your attention, under separate cover, four copies of our current #57 General Catalog describing products of our manufacture, at no charge to your company.

   Appreciating your inquiry and hoping to be favored with your orders, we remain. . . .

   b. *Processed form reply from a clock manufacturer; personalized address and salutation:*[12]

   Here is the Seth Thomas booklet that you recently requested.

   As you look over the wide variety of styles offered for your choice, we are sure you will find the Seth Thomas clock you have always desired--either for your own home or for that certain someone who appreciates an outstanding gift. There are distinguished period designs, charming colonial reproductions, and smart moderns for those who appreciate this mode of furnishing.

   All clocks illustrated represent the finest in designing achievement and are truly the creations of experts in the craft of fine clockmaking. Their friendly presence in your home is a tribute to your appreciation of fine living.

   May we suggest that you visit your local Seth Thomas dealer. Many appliance stores handle Seth Thomas self-starting electrics--while keywound and electrics are offered by jewelry and department stores.

   For gifts that will surely become treasured possessions, select Seth Thomas clocks--they are always appropriate. And, for finer, friendlier living in your own home, be

```
          sure to choose an authentic Seth Thomas--"The Finest Name
          in Clocks."
```

2. *Evaluation and rewrite:* A motel manager in a resort town sent the following reply to a young man who inquired about rates and accommodations. He wrote that his wife and he were planning a three-week automobile trip and they expected to stay four nights in the town (Lagina) "sometime in July."

Comment orally on the good and poor qualities of this reply. How many errors can you find? Rewrite it so that it is accurate and contains appropriate you-attitude and resale material. Make any necessary assumptions.

```
          Thank you for your postal card regarding rates for Sum-
     mer.
          Our rates for two are $280.00 per week for most apart-
     ments & Oceanview are $310.00 per week.
          These Apartments consist of Bed Sittling room, fully
     equipped kitchen, bathroom and Shower and Garage.
          We are located in the North section of Lagina about a
     mile from the main business District.  The market is a block
     away and we are about two hundred yards from Crescent Bathing
     Beach.
          We do not allow Pets.
          On receipt of $20.00 deposit we will be pleased to
     reserve the accommodation you require.
          Thanking you for your courtesy, I am,
```

3. *Letter—custom stationery for Tomson Machinery Company:* As customer-service manager of Topco Business Forms, Inc., you just received an inquiry from Ann C. Batt, Purchasing Agent, Tomson Machinery Company, 2110 Lakeshore Blvd., Erie, PA 16593-4851. Ms. Batts wants to know if your company prints custom stationery—letterhead and envelopes. If so, she would like to know how a customer submits the design, what types of paper are available, what your prices are, and how long it will take for delivery.

Topco Business Forms does sell custom stationery, and the customer may be its "image maker." Tomson Machinery may choose a logo from your stock selection, or may submit its own design. (You will accept a sketch or a printed sample.) The customer has a wide range of choices in paper and ink color.

The best idea is for the customer to send a sketch or sample of the exact letterhead and envelope format desired and let you do the rest. Your answer to Ms. Batt will include a catalog that shows all the choices and the exact prices. Information about custom stationery is on page 24. Remind the customer that you have a minimum order quantity of 1,000, but prices for larger quantities are discounted.

Make sure that Ms. Batt knows about the order form and postpaid envelope in the catalog. Also, let her know that orders may be called in on your toll-free number (1-800-555-2871). Finally, your company has a 30-day free trial policy. If, for any reason, a customer is not completely satisfied, she or he need only return the merchandise within 30 days and the payment will be refunded or the invoices canceled.

4. ***Letter—advertising materials for Varto Electric Company:*** As correspondent for the Safety Electric Products Company, manufacturers of electric mixers, toasters, and other kitchen appliances, you need to answer an inquiry from Varto Electric Company, one of your new distributors (2970 South 11th Street, Tucson, AZ 85704-2277). They carry your complete line of seven products in their two stores, and they need the free newspaper mats to use in their local advertising campaign and also window display materials. Also, they would like to see a sample of the envelope stuffers (illustrative sales leaflets) that they might enclose with their customers' monthly statements. These leaflets are not free, although of course the one sample you're sending today is free. These colorful leaflets, which are revised periodically, cost $18.90 per thousand, but customers get good ideas from them. This is the first inquiry you have had from this new distributor since the welcome letter you sent 10 days ago. Your company advertises on TV in four states and in two national magazines.

Bad-News Replies to Sales-Related Inquiries

1. ***Letter—souvenir place cards for a football banquet:*** The following letter from a national manufacturer of party favors has several weaknesses. Rewrite it (to Jim Shore, chairperson of a college football banquet) to improve it in every way you can. Make up additional pertinent facts, if necessary, and try to be more helpful to this banquet chairperson. He wants individual souvenirs ("about 3 or 4 inches wide") to use as favors or place cards for the 250 persons expected to attend the banquet, six weeks from today. Although your factory does not have any such souvenirs in stock, you do manufacture special items to order. All you need is a design and three to four weeks' time; your skilled workers turn out really attractive novelties. Assume that your reader (the chairperson) lives 2,000 miles from your factory. Time is short. It is possible that the L. G. Baltwin Company (a retail supplier about 300 miles from Jim Shore's city) may have football souvenirs in stock. What can you say to be helpful?

```
Dear Sir:

We have pleasure in acknowledging your letter of 20 September
concerning your inquiry about small individual football sou-
venirs for your banquet.  Though we note that you had been
advised by Marcus Company to approach us in this connection,
we are sorry to inform you that we do not have football nov-
elties and thus cannot supply the material which you need.

We regret we cannot be of service to you for this occasion.
```

2. ***Letter—Atop Hot Chocolate Mix for Ms. Howton:*** You are consumer relations manager of a manufacturing firm whose popular varieties of processed convenience and diet foods are sold all across the United States. Today your incoming mail includes a letter from Ms. Jean Howton, 2194 12th Avenue, Berkeley, CA 94700-5555. She states two requests, and unfortunately, you cannot grant either of them. But you do want to help her and continue her interest in your products. She asks where in her city she can buy your Atop Hot Chocolate Mix; she hasn't found it anywhere nearby. She also asks that you please send to her two packages of that chocolate mix, for which she has enclosed her check. It's the amount she paid for two packages when she lived in Philadelphia until recently, and she hopes the price is still the same. She also added postage.

Her message is of sincere concern to you. Your firm aims to place the full line of the high-quality Atop products in every grocery store and supermarket. You cannot make direct sales to individual consumers, because you sell only to food wholesalers and distributors. So you're returning her check. Also you cannot insist that a given store or chain carry all or any of your products. Actually, some 60,000 items constantly compete for shelf space in supermarkets, though the average store can accommodate only about one-fourth of them. Thus, you can understand that managers prefer to handle the faster-moving items so they can turn inventories often and realize better profits. You don't know which stores carry your products in Ms. Howton's area. Inform her that you are notifying your southwest district sales office of her report and requesting that they advise her where in her city (or nearby) her desired product is currently sold. Suggest that in the meantime she might ask the manager of the store where she regularly shops to order this product for her. Though your message brings bad news now, it can—with adequate explanation, resale, and a friendly close—show your sincere effort to help this customer soon to have a convenient, regular source of supply. (You know that ideally Atop Hot Chocolate Mix should be located in the cocoa, diet, or instant milk sections of supermarkets.)

Unsolicited Sales Letters

1. ***All-purpose Weller folding card tables with matching chairs:*** As sales manager for Weller Manufacturing Company, Milwaukee, Wis., you want to send—to retail store managers who have been your regular customers—a letter that ties in with your national advertising campaign. During November and December your company's all-purpose folding card tables with four matching folding chairs will be featured in two consumer magazines in full-page, three-color ads. These ads will be read by 24 million people. You consider this the most powerful selling story you have ever put across. Now (October 1) you want to be sure that the 510 retail stores that carry your products are sufficiently stocked with a variety of these table-chair sets to meet the expected consumer demand. The wholesale price of each five-piece set is $91. The retail price is $130. (The $39 markup is 30 percent of the retail price.) Separate folding tables retail for $32 each, and each chair

is $27. Thus, by buying the combination set, consumers save $10. Each table is 36 inches square, with a vinyl-covered top and a bronze-tone-finish steel frame 28 inches high; shipping weight, 21 pounds. The matching folding chairs have 1-inch-thick padded vinyl seats, steel legs, and steel backs; shipping weight, 12 pounds each. Colors for both tables and chairs are green or mushroom beige in plain or floral patterns. These beautiful, practical, and low-priced items are just what consumers will need for Christmas and will find useful throughout the year for many years. In your sales letter, provide easy-action order blanks and promise prompt shipment; be as specific as possible. Orders you receive by October 18 can be filled and the sets shipped in time to be in stock by November 1.

2. ***Mod Man formal wear rentals:*** You are a part-time employee for Mod Man, Inc., a men's clothing shop "For men who think young." Your employer, knowing you are a college senior and that you're studying business communications, has just offered you a challenging opportunity to try your skill on a sales letter. After you write it, he will pay all expenses for reproducing and mailing it—plus a 10 percent commission to you on the direct sales your letter brings in.

   Here is his proposition: The store's men's formal wear rental department is sponsoring a special Senior Ball promotion. Your letter is to be mailed to all men in your college class. (If your college does not have a senior ball, assume you are writing to any other group of young people that do have an annual ball.) Assume at least 1,000 on your mailing list. Your employer has made arrangements with a local automobile dealer to have a brand new 199- convertible on display right in the store starting this weekend until two days before the ball. Someone who registers will win the free use of this car for the night of the ball, courtesy of Ron Kane Auto Sales, Inc. In addition, there will be four other big winners, each of whom will get Senior Ball tickets for two, a corsage of their choice, a $[*amount*] gift certificate for dinner for two at [*name*] restaurant (the best in your city), and their formal wear rental at no charge. All the readers have to do to get a chance to win is to register, and rent their formal wear from your store. You have the largest and most fashionable collection in the city: everything from white dinner jackets to full-dress tails, with 22 styles in between including double-breasted coats, turtlenecks, and ruffled shirts, and all at Mod Man's low rental rates.

   Your one-page letter will be processed in any way you choose—photocopy machine, computer, or printer—and will be on the store's letterhead. There is to be no enclosure. You may send the letter over your own signature, if you prefer. Design its layout in any way you choose. If you wish, you can give this promotion a special name (such as, "Your Prom Night on Us").

3. ***BBS Insurance Company policy special:*** As sales manager of the BBS Insurance Company of Illinois, which is licensed to do business in your state and in 44 of 50 states, you have a special offer that you believe is attractive. No salesperson will call on prospective customers; no one who applies will

be turned down if the application form is completely, accurately, and honestly filled out; the policy cannot be canceled for any reason if the premiums are paid on time; and the applicant can examine the policy at home for a full 30 days and then cancel it if not satisfied. Other features are noteworthy too. They will be included in a brochure from BBS if the prospective customer will just fill out the initial application-for-information blank.

Best of all, the policy will pay, in cash to the family, $100 per day for a period of hospitalization, plus certain other fees that are listed in the policy. No matter what other coverage one might have, the $100 per day will still be paid for as long as one full year.

The cost of hospital room occupancy and care is extremely high, and many families do not have adequate insurance coverage. If illness should strike such a family, the results could be disastrous—debt, loss of savings, emergency bank loans, mortgages, possible bankruptcy, and similar financial problems would have to be faced.

Write a letter that will be sent to the employees of the Acme Iron and Steel Company, in your city. You know that these employees have some health and hospitalization coverage, but the amount is insufficient for most serious illnesses. (Although you will not mention this, you will also send a second letter four weeks later if the first one is not answered. After that—no more letters.)

4. **A book for joggers and marathon runners:** Your company publishes sports books and how-to manuals for sales directly to consumers. Just off the presses is your newest book, *Everything You Always Wanted to Know about Running, but Couldn't Slow Down to Ask.* Because of the popularity of jogging and marathon running you feel that this book will be highly successful.

The book was coauthored by Mr. Jeff Long (an Olympic gold medal winner in the 10,000-meter run) and Dr. Gary C. Lane (an expert in the physiology of running and a consultant to the United States Olympic Team). Contained in the book are chapters on The Beginning Runner, The Physiology of Running, Developing the Running Attitude, Dietary Rules for Runners, and Selecting Jogging and Running Shoes and Accessories. Other chapters cover the history of marathons and Olympic track events, plans for developing speed and stamina, and information on avoiding injuries while running.

Because you think this book will be widely accepted, you have, for the first time, arranged for its sale through selected bookstores in several large cities. And to promote the book, the authors will travel to each city to conduct running seminars and autograph copies of the book. You, as regional sales manager, have been asked to write a letter to a prospect list that your company has purchased for this purpose. Describe the book in detail, and invite the prospects to attend the free seminars. Mention the time and location of the seminar and the name of the local stores where the books will be sold. If prospects take a copy of the book to the seminar, the authors will autograph it. The book will also be sold at the seminar. A runner's refreshment buffet (Perrier water, granola snacks) will be served.

■ CAPSULE CHECKLISTS FOR SALES LETTERS*

Solicited Sales Letters		Unsolicited Sales Letters
A Good-News Replies to Sales-Related Inquiries	**B** Bad-News Replies to Sales-Related Inquiries	**C** Persuasive Requests

1. Best news or main idea
  a. Positive opening with one of these:
    (1) Requested material
    (2) Favorable answer to a question
    (3) Introduction of main ideas
  b. Courtesy; appreciation
	1. Buffer
	  a. Appreciation
	  b. Assurance
	  c. Resale
	  d. Understanding
		1. Attention (*promise; star*)
		  a. Introduction of relevant reader-benefit theme by:
		    Comparison or short story
		    Event or fact in reader's life
		    Problem reader may face
		    Significant fact about product
		    Solution to a problem
		    Special offer or gift
		    Surprising question or challenging statement
		    Testimonials (here or in 3b)
		  b. Envelopes, letterhead, maybe special designs

2. Explanation
  a. Answers to all questions—direct or implied
    (1) Positive, helpful tone
    (2) Embedded negatives
    (3) Emphasis on what something is, what you can do or have
    (4) Reader benefits
    (5) Prices after most selling points (unless price is a bargain)
  b. Resale (with reader benefits), when appropriate
  c. Educational material on product use, if pertinent
	2. Explanations
	  a. Answers to all questions
	  b. Pertinent facts and details
	  c. RB¶ reasons for company policy
		2. Interest (*picture; chain*)
		  a. Beginning development of physical description, benefits, central selling point
		  b. Appeals: approval, beauty, cleanliness, comfort, convenience, customer satisfaction, distinctiveness, efficiency, enjoyment, entertainment, friendships, health, improvement, love of home and people, money and other valuables, peace of mind, pleasure, popularity, profits, safety, savings, self-preservation, and others (pp. 250 and 251)

3. Courteous close
  a. CSAD† (sometimes); itemized steps, if desirable
  b. EA‡
  c. DA§
  d. RB¶ and courtesy; offer of further help, if appropriate
	3. Decision—with resale and/or suggestions
	  a. Embedded statement of bad news with suggestion of what *can* be done
	  b. Ideas for help
	  c. Possible future changes
	  d. Resale on firm, products, services, if appropriate
		3. Desire, conviction (*prove; chain*)
		  a. Full development of needed description, reader benefits, central selling point
		  b. Proof by users, laboratories and agencies, prospect:
		    (1) Users' experiences with product
		    (2) Names of users
		    (3) Testimonials
		    (4) Performance tests
		    (5-7) Free trial; Guarantee; Samples
		  c. Price presented psychologically
		  d. Enclosures to strengthen desire, conviction

(Continued)

■ CAPSULE CHECKLISTS FOR SALES LETTERS (Continued)

Solicited Sales Letters		Unsolicited Sales Letters
A **Good-News Replies to Sales-Related Inquiries**	**B** **Bad-News Replies to Sales-Related Inquiries**	**C** **Persuasive Requests**

	4. Positive, friendly, appropriate close
	  a. Good wishes
	  b. Appreciation
	  c. CSAD†
	  d. Willingness to help further
		4. Action (*push; hook*)
		  a-d. CSAD;† EA;‡ DA;§ RB¶
		  e. Inducements
		    (1) Credit cards
		    (2) Easy payments or no money now.
		    (3) Gift
		    (4) Free trial
		    (5) No obligation to pay
		    (6) Premium
		    (7) Special price for limited time

° Lists include possible content. For any one message, choose only pertinent items.
† CSAD = clear statement of action desired.
‡ EA = easy action.
§ DA = dated action.
¶ RB = reader benefit.

Chapter 12

The Written Job Presentation

I. **Self-Assessment: Evaluating Your Achievements**

II. **Market Research: Making Preliminary Career Decisions**
   A. Written Sources of Career and Job Information
   B. Helpful People regarding Employers and Jobs
   C. Desirable General Qualifications of the Applicant
   D. Desirable General Qualities for the Written Job Presentation

III. **Resume (Vita, Qualifications Brief)**
   A. Opening Section
   B. Education
   C. Work Experience
   D. Achievements, Awards, Service Activities
   E. Personal Data
   F. References
   G. Sample Resumes

IV. **Job Application Letter**
   A. Opening for Favorable Attention
   B. Middle Paragraphs for Interest, Desire, Conviction
   C. Last Paragraph
   D. Sample Letters of Application

V. **Summary**

VI. **Exercises and Problems**

During your life it is highly likely that you will change jobs and positions, perhaps several times. Responding to advertisements, to posted job openings in your current organization, or to recruiters on campus demands some form of written presentation.

Actually, when you seek a first position or you desire a new position, you must sell a "product"—yourself. Therefore, research is needed before you write, as well as planning and "sales promotion" of those attributes that will attract the reader. This chapter discusses product analysis—your "self-assessment"—market research concerning job and career opportunities, and preparation of the resume and application letters.

SELF-ASSESSMENT: EVALUATING YOUR ACHIEVEMENTS

Whenever you sell something, you want to be sure you represent the product fairly. You need to analyze it to know *what* you are selling before you can start investigating *where* and *how* to sell it. The same is true when you are selling your services. For an adequate *self-appraisal,* take an inventory of your employment qualifications. Begin by listing your specific achievements, capabilities, interests, attitudes, and characteristics. You might write them under various general headings and subheadings like the following:

1. *Work Experience, Skills, Achievements.*

   Your part-time and full-time jobs (paid and volunteer) since high school—dates, employer and supervisor names and addresses, titles, duties, responsibilities, successes, promotions

   Your specific skills and aptitudes—speaking ability, report-writing ability, computers and other machines (office, industrial, craft) you can operate well

   Military service—dates, responsibilities, achievements

2. *Education—Evidence of Intelligence and Achievements.*

   Schools you attended (junior colleges, colleges, universities, technical schools, military academies, other)—dates, names, locations, degrees, major(s), scholastic standing in each, accomplishments

   Courses—in major, core, useful electives; grades; significant writings

3. *Extracurricular and/or Professional Organization Achievements.*

   Memberships, offices held, and noteworthy work in clubs related to your major, or in sports, church, social, community projects; coaching, student teaching, tutoring

   Achievements, honors, awards—scholarships, honor rolls, recognitions

   Travel, foreign language facilities, hobbies, personal business ventures, publications, attendance and responsibilities at conventions, and so forth

4. *Interests, Preferences, and Attitudes.*

Analyzing your interests, preferences, and attitudes can help you determine in what type of job you can use your skills comfortably and successfully.

Do I prefer to work with people, figures, machines, or ideas?

Which courses did I enjoy most? In which did I earn high grades?

Would I rather sell, create, or design? Lead or follow?

What are my strongest skills? How well do I work under pressure?

Which hobbies do I enjoy most? Do they relate to the job I'd like?

In which locality do I prefer to live? Have I strong preferences?

What have I done to correct my shortcomings?

What are my goals and priorities?

5. *Personal Characteristics.*

Rate yourself on the following characteristics considered important by employers who seek college graduates.

■ Checklist for Self-Appraisal

	Excellent	Good	Fair	Poor
■ Integrity, sincerity				
■ Ability to think logically.				
■ Enthusiasm, initiative, drive				
■ Dependability				
■ Ability to communicate orally . . .				
■ Ability to communicate in writing				
■ Intelligence				
■ Ability to listen well				
■ Maturity				
■ Analytical ability				
■ Ability to get along and cooperate with others				
■ Emotional stability				
■ Evidence of good judgment				
■ Ability to make decisions				
■ Health and energy				
■ Physical appearance				
■ Capacity for leadership				
■ Self-confidence				
■ Courtesy, tact, diplomacy.				
■ Adaptability				
■ Sense of humor.				
■ Neatness of work.				
■ Determination.				

An objective self-assessment like the foregoing inventory is strictly for your own use. It will not be mailed to anyone, but it helps you see patterns regarding your capabilities, desires, interests, and achievements.

MARKET RESEARCH: MAKING PRELIMINARY CAREER DECISIONS

The next phase of your job-getting campaign is to determine which jobs and employers require what you have to offer. This section includes suggestions to help you in these phases of your job-market research, whether you are a recent or upcoming graduate or a person who has worked a number of years and now wants to change jobs or careers.

Written Sources of Career and Job Information

Published sources and various people can help to inform you about careers and types of jobs available in your chosen field. Some also provide information about openings, products, services, geographical locations, sizes, problems, and facts about the employers. You will find useful printed materials such as the following in libraries and perhaps your campus career placement office:

Career Planning

- Bolles, R. N., *What Color Is Your Parachute? A Practical Manual for Job-Hunters and Career Changers,* Ten Speed, 1987.
- Felix, James V., *Accounting Career Strategies,* Career Plan Publications, 1982.
- Nivens, Beatryce, *The Black Woman's Career Guide,* Doubleday, 1987.
- Sekaran, Uma, *Dual-Career Families,* Jossey-Bass, 1986.

Resume Preparation

- Brennan, Lawrence, et al., *Resumes for Better Jobs,* Monarch, 1987.
- *Marketing Yourself: The Catalyst Women's Guide to Successful Resumes and Interviews,* Bantam, 1980.
- Turbak, Gary, *Action-Getting Resumes for Today's Job,* Arco, 1983.
- Washington, Tom, *Resume Power,* Mount Vernon Press, 1985.

General Directories

- *The Career Guide: Dun's Employment Opportunities Directory.*
- *College Placement Annual;* directory of employment opportunities for college graduates.
- *Dictionary of Occupational Titles,* U.S. Department of Labor.
- *Dun and Bradstreet, Million Dollar Directory;* firms with net worth over $1 million.
- *Fortune Directory;* the 500 largest industrials and 500 largest service firms in the United States.
- *Moody's Industrial Manual.*
- *Standard & Poor's Register of Corporations, Directors, & Executives.*

Overseas Employment Opportunities

- Kocher, Eric, *International Jobs: Where They Are, How to Get Them,* Addison-Wesley, 1988.
- Powell, James N., *The Prentice-Hall Global Employment Guide,* Prentice-Hall, 1983.

Other Written Sources of Job Information

Reading *annual reports, company 10-K reports,* and the many *recruiting booklets published by companies* will also give you useful information. You may gain better ideas of the kind of persons now working in a career field and the kind of people the company may be looking for in the future.

Also, occasional articles in *business and professional journals* discuss companies' new ventures, expansions, additional products, and so forth. Such leads may suggest employment possibilities for you. Furthermore, these publications, as well as newspapers, often have *advertisements for both help wanted and positions wanted,* often in *classified-ad sections.*

Helpful People regarding Employers and Jobs

Besides the printed materials, you can get helpful advice and sometimes tips about good openings from persons familiar with work or companies in your chosen career. The following may be useful sources of information:

- Alumni.[1] Some college placement offices maintain a current file of alumni willing to give career advice. Suggestions from those who graduated in your major field and are currently employed in it can be especially helpful.
- Business people and personnel departments in your chosen field or firm(s).
- Company representatives—traveling for various employers.
- Counselors—in your school placement office, among the faculty, and in activity programs.
- Employment agencies—including national, state, city, and private bureaus.
- Former employers and co-workers.
- Friends, relatives, acquaintances.
- Labor unions.

Desirable General Qualifications of the Applicant

Determining what the prospective employers' needs and requirements are is an important part of your research about the job market. You will then be better able to focus on jobs that are in harmony with what you can contribute as an employee. Desirable general qualifications all employers look for usually include (in varying degrees, depending on the job) *the five broad areas listed in the self-assessment,* pages 318–320. You will find detailed discussions on them later in this chapter. In addition, employers also look for proper attitude toward employment.

Willingness to Learn and Work

Especially if you are a recent college graduate, you should be willing to accept beginning or routine work within your chosen field, and to be a contributing team member.

You will more likely make a favorable impression when your attitude shows a *willingness to work diligently and learn,* building on your schooling and previous achievements. On the job you will need to learn the specific duties, procedures, and practices of the company that hires you. A college degree does open doors to employment, but you still have to prove your worth in your written application, interview, and actual performance on the job.

Sincere Interest in the Field and the Company

Show that you have a *genuine interest in your chosen field or job.* Your *interest in the company* should also be sincere. After you have studied the company, you can state why you feel it is the type of organization in which you can do your most productive work. Employers appreciate the applicant with *you-attitude and integrity.* Be sincere. In your resume and letter try to *show how you can be helpful to the employer.*

Reasonable Attitude toward Salary

Do not emphasize your own self-interest, such as what fringe benefits and salary the employer will offer *you.* Generally it is better to consider a challenging opportunity more important than a large beginning salary. Emphasis on salary—in the first written job presentation—creates an unfavorable impression. In general, especially if you are just beginning your career, it is best not to mention desired salary in the letter or resume. (This matter can be discussed during the interview.)

Desirable General Qualities for the Written Job Presentation

After you have evaluated your assets and researched job opportunities and employers' requirements, you are ready to prepare your written "sales promotion." The main goal is to get an interview and to persuade the reader—your potential employer—that you are the right candidate for the job.

Your written job presentation—the letter and resume—will make a more favorable impression on the prospective buyers if it has the seven C qualities. The following desirable *general* suggestions apply to both the resume and the letter. Later in this chapter the separate sections on Resume and Application Letter illustrate *specific* ways to include qualifications effectively.

1. *Present your message concisely, clearly, honestly, with consideration for the reader.* Desirable length is usually a one-page letter and a one- or two-page resume—unless you have many years of valuable experience pertinent to the job. Focus on your credentials that show how you can help the employer in the job you seek. Avoid overuse of the word *I*.

2. *Be yourself and don't use "canned" messages.* Your resume and letter should reveal your individuality and ability to communicate in writing. Avoid copying wording out of a text or words prepared by an employment agency.

3. *Be businesslike in your approach.* Avoid sounding cute or smart-alecky. Avoid slang or terms suggesting "hip" communication. Speaking about "cool" data, "on-target" goals, or a "gunner" attitude may sound all right to your friends but can produce a negative response in corporate offices.

4. *Check for accuracy of facts and mechanics.* Be especially careful to spell correctly names of persons, firms, and job areas. If necessary, have someone else, in addition to your word processor spell-checker, review for grammar, sentence and paragraph structure, organization, headings, punctuation, and parallelism of items. All errors must be eliminated.

5. *Make the appearance attractive and professional-looking.*
   a. Paper for the letter and resume should usually be 8½- by 11-inch high-quality white bond.
   b. Typing of both letter and resume should be error-free, with neat, black type; margins, ample for easy reading; erasures or corrections, unnoticeable. In the resume, to emphasize key words and headings, you can use underscoring, capital letters, italics, or boldface type.
   c. Duplicating—by offset (such as multilith), print, photocopy machines, or other neat professional methods (costing only a few cents per page)—is permissible for resumes, but *not for letters*. Each application letter must be individually typewritten.

6. *Personalize your presentation as much as possible.* Tailoring a resume for a specific job or company is desirable. However, even if you are sending out numerous resumes (neatly reproduced), you should preferably address each accompanying *letter* to a specific person *by name* with the correct title and should use that name in your salutation.

7. *Use good judgment in mailing your message.* Generally, be prompt. Sometimes it may be advisable to use special delivery to reach an executive at the best time, usually in the middle of a week. (However, some surveys show that letters answering a popular ad get better results if they arrive on about the eighth day rather than among the hundreds mailed the first seven days after the ad appears.)

RESUME (VITA, QUALIFICATIONS BRIEF)

This book uses the term *resume*—also spelled "résumé"—to describe the document listing your qualifications and career path. Some other terms for the same or similar material include *vita, qualifications document* or *qualifications brief.* Regardless of what you call the information, it should be prepared first, for it includes facts on which the letter will be based.

Your resume gives a concise picture of *you*—what you have accomplished in your education, your experience, and your activities that will benefit prospective employers. Content and layout vary widely; there is no one best type. However, an important rule is to place your most impressive qualifications first whenever possible and desirable. Present your information under headings in phrases instead of full sentences. Avoid using personal pronouns. Focus on your job-related achievements. *"Accentuate the positive" honestly.*

This section discusses the possible contents and ways of presenting a resume. From the following checklist you can select the parts that best fit your background and the job you seek, and then arrange them in any desirable order. Some schools have a common set of format requirements which all graduates must meet in order to be included in the school's resume booklet.

■ Checklist for a Resume

1. **Opening section**
   a. Your name, address (school and/or home), telephone number
   b. Job or career objective
   c. Summary of basic qualifications

2. **Education**
   a. Advanced schooling beyond high school—school names and locations, dates attended, degrees and certificates (include military)
   b. Major, significant, pertinent courses; academic honors; grade-point average, if high; special skills; significant speeches, research, reports
   c. Positions, such as assistant in classes, grader or research assistant to instructor (these could be under "work experience")

3. **Work experience**
   a. Employer names and locations, dates (beginning and ending month and year), titles and positions held, supervisory positions and number supervised, specific accomplishments
   b. Volunteer work, research, tutoring, publications, etc.

4. **Achievements, awards, service activities**
   a. School and community memberships, offices held, honors, publications
   b. Travel, languages, self-support, other facts

> **5. Personal data**—optional (unless job requires or state law forbids)
>   **a.** Age, health, military service, hobbies
>   **b.** Date of availability
>
> **6. References**—usually provided "upon request"

Opening Section

Information in the resume's opening section gives the reader a general picture of the applicant—who you are, what you want, what you have to offer, and where you can be contacted. (To protect privacy, examples in this chapter have fictitious names, addresses, and figures.)

Heading

The resume heading can contain your name alone; your name and the title of the job you are applying for; your name and address, plus your telephone number, or the name of the firm receiving the job presentation, or both. Also, you can choose other words besides *resume*, as in these examples:

1. `Resume of Robert A. Fletcher for Retail Management`

2. `John O. Bowman`
   `1504 Lamb Avenue`
   `Peoria, IL 61610-0010`
   `Phone: (309) 555-1072`

3. `Vita of Betty Jo Anderson for a position as Business`
   `Teacher in the North Shore School District`

4. `Qualifications Brief for Joan Otto`

Whatever title you choose, *include your address and telephone number* on your resume where your prospective employer can see and use them easily, preferably in the opening section. If you prefer to omit the address and phone number in the opening, you can include them in the Personal Data section.

Job or Career Objective

Based on your self-assessment and a market analysis, you narrow your options into a single sentence. It can be in the heading (see examples 1 and 3 above) or under a separate title.

You must decide whether to state a job objective. If yes, decide if it should be stated in terms of a functional area, or stated with a specific industry in mind.

If you have not narrowed your focus to a specific industry, it is better to state your objective in functional terms:

1. An entry-level sales position

2. A position as a staff accountant, moving from there into a supervisory position

3. A position involving institutional lending

4. A receptionist

If your plans are more precise, you may wish to include the type of industry, adding it to the functional statements:

1. An entry-level sales position to further the aims of a retail marketing organization

2. A position as a staff accountant in a public accounting firm, moving from there into a supervisory position

3. A position as an institutional lender with an east coast financial institution

4. A receptionist in a local high-tech computer firm

Summary of Basic Qualifications

Immediately after—or before—stating your objectives (what you *want*), you can sometimes include a heading suggesting what you can *offer* for the job. The heading can be "Significant Professional Achievements," "Summary of Basic Qualifications," "Capsule View of Public Relations Background," or others. Such a concise summary of major selling points is effective if you have two or more *outstanding* qualifications and achievements especially important for the job.

1. Six years of progressively greater responsibility in office management and business administration, with a master's degree in policy and organization. Record of accuracy, integrity, and ability to work with people.

2. Associate of arts degree in business--major in transportation; 4½ years of full-time experience, specializing in
in-bound cargo movement with steamship agency plus shipping department, order desk, and inside sales with manufacturing firm. [*By a community college graduate*]

3. Bachelor of arts degree with a major in personnel management, with emphasis in psychology, sociology, and busi-

```
        ness.  Four years of part-time experience working with
        people. Student counselor in Alaska, summer of 199-.
```

4. **Twelve years of experience in defense contract audits. Advanced from GS 7 (beginning auditor) to regional director. Ultimately responsible for entire Midwest region for Defense Contract Audit Agency (DCAA).**

Education

The most important qualification you can offer for the job (or the job area) should be in the first major section following the resume opening. If you are a recent graduate and education is your strongest selling point, cover this area first—in detail. The more years you are away from school, the less educational detail is required. But even applicants who have been away from school for years should include (usually later in the resume) names and locations of schools as well as dates attended and degrees earned.

If education is your main qualification, you may want to include all the items shown on the resume checklist (pages 324 and 325), provided this material strengthens your presentation. Additional recommendations are:

1. Include the school names, locations, dates attended, and degrees or certificates earned for all postsecondary schools you attended. (Even high school may be mentioned if its reputation or location and your achievements there somehow tie in with the job qualifications. If you earned special honors in high school, but haven't done anything really outstanding in college, high school data show prospective employers that you *do* have potential.)

2. Use the singular words "certificate," "bachelor," or "master" for your degree. Include the date.

3. Decide whether to include class rank and/or GPA. If your GPA is high, it should be included. If it is low, it may be omitted or included with supporting evidence that you used your time and skills well. For example, you financed 100 percent of your college expenses through part-time jobs.

4. The number and kinds of courses to list vary with the type of work requested. Show that you have an acceptable background in the area of the requested work. Also list useful elective courses related to your interest and the job. Good examples are courses in written communication, speech, and human relations; also, courses that will help you reach conclusions objectively or that developed skills needed for the job.

5. Note unique honors and scholarships. Tell prospective employers if you were awarded a tuition grant or scholarships, or if you earned a percentage of your expenses.

Illustrated below are various ways to show pertinent facts about academic background. List your education in reverse chronological order—most recent education first, and choose meaningful titles.

1. *Concise Listing of Schools, with Dates; Then Degrees, Standing, Majors.*   *Abbreviations, if clear, are permissible on resumes.*

```
             PROFESSIONAL TRAINING AND EDUCATION

University of Kansas         Lawrence, KS
   Business Administration                    1989-91
Everett Junior College       Everett, WA
   Liberal Arts                               1987-89
U.S. Air Force School        Denver, CO
   Electronics                                1984-86
Martin High School           Martin, WV
   College Preparatory                        1980-84



Degrees:   Bachelor of Arts in Business Administration,
           U.K., 1991
           Associate of Arts and Sciences, E.J.C., 1989
Standing:  Top 5 percent of class at both E.J.C. and U.K.
           Valedictorian, high school
Majors:    Operations Management and Finance
```

2. *Listing of Courses Functionally.*   *Twenty-year-old community college graduate with no paid experience.*

```
     Associate of Arts Degree--Technology/Accounting Major,
            Metropolitan Community College, Syracuse, NY



Accounting    Accounting Principles 1-2-3, Advanced Ac-
Techniques    counting, Federal Income Tax Accounting, Cost
              Accounting, Auditing, Governmental Accounting

Business      Business Organization and Management, Busi-
              ness Math, Business Law, Applied Economics,
              Business Statistics

Communication Written Communication, Speech
Skills

Machine       Data Processing, Office Computers, Rotary and
Operations    Electronic Calculators, Dictation Equipment,
              Facsimile
```

```
Working with    Introduction to Psychology, Office/Personnel
People          Management, Public Relations, Psychology of
                Human Relations
```

3. Inclusion of Schools and Grades with Coursework Pertinent to Job the Applicant Seeks.

```
Education

University of Missouri, Columbia--Sept. '87-June '91
Major:   Accounting
Grades:  Overall--3.7 (possible 4.0)
         Accounting--3.9

Other relevant courses in addition to accounting:

Strategic Planning        Principles of Economics
Human Resource Management Marketing Research
Business Report Writing   Banking and Finance

Broadway High School, Waco, TX: Sept. '83-June '87
Major:   General business and college preparatory
Grades:  3.8 (possible 4.0); top 5 percent of class
```

4. Inclusion of School, Degree, and Achievements.

```
The University of Michigan, School of Business Administra-
tion
--Bachelor of Business Administration, May 1991
--Concentrations in International Business and Marketing
--GPA 7.6/8.0
--Coauthor of class study on Avis Rent-a-Car
--Increase of membership by 12% as vice president of Inter-
  national Business Club
```

Work Experience

Any kind of work experience—related or unrelated—reveals information that helps the employer to evaluate you. Work experience similar to that for which you are applying indicates you like the type of work in question, and it may shorten the training period. If you are an older applicant with extensive experience, you will probably place Work Experience *before* Education. Also, you may prefer to include only the more recent jobs or those that best relate to the position you seek; employers appreciate conciseness, instead of a long list of irrelevant material.

Usually, list your jobs in reverse chronological order, with the present or most recent one first. Keep in mind the following points:

1. Include name[2] and location of each company, dates of employment, your position, and title, if any.

2. Support your career goal. Include skills and achievements which relate to your stated objective. Marketing, for instance, demands creativity; show how you were creative and innovative.

3. Include volunteer work if relevant. If you lack significant work experience, include useful pertinent organizational achievements under Service Activities.

4. State whether job was part-time (otherwise employer will interpret statement as full-time employment).

5. Use *action verbs* such as the following in stating achievements:

accomplished	defined	instructed	published
achieved	demonstrated	integrated	realized
administered	designed	introduced	recommended
advanced	developed	invented	reduced
advised	directed	investigated	researched
allocated	edited	led	revised
analyzed	employed	maintained	saved
approved	established	managed	scheduled
assisted	executed	marketed	secured
broadened	expanded	negotiated	sponsored
brought	formed	obtained	suggested
calculated	formulated	operated	supervised
clarified	generated	organized	taught
completed	guided	originated	trained
conceived	handled	performed	transformed
conducted	headed	planned	undertook
constructed	implemented	prepared	used
contracted	improved	presented	verified
controlled	increased	produced	widened
coordinated	influenced	promoted	won
created	initiated	proposed	worked
decreased			wrote

Arrange the facts for each job in the best "selling" order. *You can begin with your job title, your employer's name, the dates you held each job, or the functions you performed on each job.*

Be sure to follow rules of parallelism—making two or more elements in a series similar in grammatical word structure. *Manager, representative,* and *ac-*

countant are all parallel to each other because each is a job title. *Managing*—which is a kind of work, not a title—would not be parallel to the two titles. For duties: *keeping, drilling, filing, typing* are parallel; so are *kept, drilled, filed, typed.*

Be honest. Don't try to put on airs by camouflaging the title. For example, don't say "sanitary engineer" if you were a garbage collector; say "garbage collector."

1. Job Title First.

Service Representative, Upland Telephone Co., Norfolk, VA.:
          February 1989 to September 1991. Duties: assisted
          telephone customers regarding telephone installations,
          questions on bills, complaints, selection of additional
          telephones.

Accountant, Associated Hardware, Boston, MA: June 1985 to
          February 1989. Duties: figured discounts on state-
          ments, filed, typed, posted accounts, wrote checks.

2. Employer First.

California State Highway Department, 931 Ridgeway, Sacramento
          Drafter, March 1989 to December 1990*
                    Duties: drawing roadway profiles and burrow sites
          Personnel Assistant, May 1988 to March 1989*
                    Duties: keeping time and employee records for di-
                              vision and preparing vouchers
          Driller's Helper, January 1986 to May 1988**
                    Duties: drilling test holes for proposed highway
                              routes

Illinois State Highway Department, 210 Main, Springfield
          Engineering Technician, November 1983 to December 1985
                    Duties: Processing traffic data and interviewing
                              on truck surveys

* Part-time during school, full-time summers.
** Full-time.

3. Dates First.

June 1990 to   Legal Secretary--Took dictation, tran-
October 1991   scribed, typed, filed, received clients--for
                   McGee, Strom, Burner, Attorneys

```
                    9988 Hightower Building
                    Dearborn, Michigan 48121-0010

School Year         Receptionist--Weekday mornings used PC,
September 1989       transcribed, filed, operated switchboard--
to June 1990        for Barnes, Jayne, Jackson, Associates
                    Ridley Tower
                    Cincinnati, Ohio 45221-5555

Other jobs³         Worked in fast-food restaurant Fridays and
before              Saturdays two months, typed business letters
1989                for high school principal, picked strawber-
                    ries
```

4. Functions First.   *Though similar to category 1, this arrangement focuses on skills or duties (functions) instead of job titles. The executive chose to omit employer names in this section.*

```
              FUNCTIONAL REVIEW OF WORK EXPERIENCE

General         Vice President and General Manager of a highly
Management:     diversified million-dollar company.
1980-1991       --Directed five operating divisions
                --Reduced personnel turnover by 8%
                --Increased profits by 21%
                --Instituted techniques of modern creative man-
                  agement

Interna-        Manager of International Operations for company
tional          whose yearly sales exceeded $6 million.
Management:     --Enlarged overseas sales and operations by 8%
1972-1980       --Helped market new line of plastic products

Consulting:     Conducted seminars on a worldwide basis for . . .
```

Achievements, Awards, Service Activities

Though some resumes may include achievements in sections on education and work experience, you can also list them separately. Important here are the offices you held, as well as projects you directed and completed. Include athletics, published materials, foreign language fluency, speaking (such as debate), professional fraternities, student organizations, and community services that involve working with people. This is not the time to be humble. If you have earned an award, mention it in your resume.

Identify (in parentheses) any activity the employer might not know the significance of. However, if you are or were active in a church or political party, you need not identify them (because of civil rights), but do mention your responsibilities if pertinent, as in the following examples.

- Beta Gamma Sigma (national scholastic business honorary)
- Beta Alpha Psi (accounting honorary)
- Alpha Sigma Phi (social fraternity)
- ZIPS (leader of young people's church group)

Statements like the following may be noteworthy:

1. Recognition, achievement, awards
   a. President of school's March of Dimes program
   b. Rotary Club's "Student of the Year" award
   c. Dean's list, three semesters
   d. Chairman of school's German Club
   e. Vice President of senior class, [name] College

2. Service
   a. Assistant coach for Little League Football [city, state]
   b. Member of [year] World Service Team from my church, teaching and counseling junior high children
   c. Candy striper (student assistant at local hospital)
   d. Cofounder of "Garden Patches" for disadvantaged families
   e. Volunteer in local United Fund office

Personal Data

The category of personal information is now entirely optional. Civil rights laws prohibit discrimination in hiring on the basis of race, age, religion, sex, marital status, national origin. Exceptions include occupational restrictions that are reasonably necessary to the normal operation of particular businesses, enterprises, or occupations. For example, some jobs in modeling, sports, teaching, and professional entertainment (TV, movies, etc.) may reasonably require certain personal attributes.

Though no law forbids applicants from volunteering personal information, they must be careful not to include items that could possibly be used for discrimination and harm their chances for getting an interview and a job. *Omit any information that might be considered negatively,* and include only job-related information.

Some applicants include under Personal Data a few significant facts pertinent to the qualities needed for the job they seek. Among them might be health (nonsmoker), hobbies, and skills (to indicate endurance, strength, stamina, physical and mental performance); expenses paid for by working while attending college (to indicate determination, drive); travel (indicating knowledge of customs elsewhere).

Military experience, if significant for the job, may be in a separate section or listed under Education, or Employment, or Personal Data.

References

In general, if you are mailing your resume to a list of employers, or it is to be included in your school's resume file,[4] you'll be safer to omit references and state, "References will be sent upon request." (Then you won't risk having your references bothered by too many inquiries or becoming tired of recommending you over and over again. However, if you are writing to one employer (or a few) for a position you know is available, you can include references.

The least desirable reference is the "to whom it may concern" message you carry with you, and next are the references of friends. You (and the employers) know that friends you choose as references will say only nice things about you; otherwise you wouldn't give their names. The subjectivity of such references limits their value.

Sometimes it will be to your advantage to list references if the names you list are well known and respected by the employers. They may be more interested in you even before the interview when they see the name of a person they know and have confidence in or who is considered an expert in a particular field.

When you give references, list about three. The most appropriate names include present or former employers and professors. Also acceptable is a character reference whose name or occupation is respected. State each individual's full name, title, organization (if any), complete business address and telephone number. Since you obviously should get permission to use the names you're listing, you need not say "with permission." Relatives should not be used as references.

Sample Resumes

The foregoing discussions have included examples of various resume sections. Figures 12-1 through 12-4 illustrate a variety of resume contents and layouts. In all these resumes, dates are arranged in reverse chronological order, as is preferred.

In Figure 12-1 the main headings are in the left margin.

In Figure 12-2 the main headings and dates are in the left margin.

In Figure 12-3 main headings are centered; subheads begin at the left margin; dates are usually near the end of the same line. (If work experience is limited, as for recent graduates, the applicants can detail their job-related activities, skills, and hobbies, as Ms. Martin did on page 2 of Figure 12-3 when applying for a teaching position.) If it is desirable to have only one page, this resume could be condensed by rearranging headings and facts and omitting some details.

Figure 12-4—a functional resume—focuses on employment and job-related functions. It is especially appropriate for a person (like Mr. Felder) with impressive work responsibilities related to the job sought, with long job stability, and with few employers. It is also useful for applicants with little paid work experience but with considerable activities and job-usable skills (managing, selling, organizing, communicating, researching, helping people).

HOWARD SHUBBS

Campus Address   **Permanent Address**
[*Street*]   [*Street*]
[*City, State, ZIP*]   [*City, State, ZIP*]
[*Telephone*]   [*Telephone*]

Objective   A position in marketing or advertising--offering business
                     administration knowledge with analytical writing and commu-
                     nication skills.

Education   **School of Business Administration**
                     University [*name, city, state*]

                     B.B.A. degree candidate. May 1991. Concentration in marketing
                     with interest in advertising. Member of Marketing Club. Active
                     on advertising and product management committees. GPA = 3.16.

                     Business and Commerce
                     Community College [*name, city, state*]

                     A.A.—Associate in Arts degree, June 1989. Member of Phi Theta
                     Kappa, honorary fraternity. Received [*name*] Scholarship for
                     Outstanding Community College Student. GPA = 3.6.

Experience   **May Department Stores: Famous-Barr**   [*City, State*]

                     Intern. Summer 1990. Worked directly with buyers, assistant
                     buyers, store management, sales associates, and senior
                     merchandise management. In buying office, gained experience
                     in distribution, store communication, advertising, and
                     financial analysis. As assistant department manager, respon-
                     sibilities included trend analysis, implementation of mer-
                     chandise concepts, communication with buyers, promotion
                     preparation, and motivation of sales force.

                     Skirboll and Garber Advertising   [*City, State*]

                     Intern. Summer 1989. Gained experience in sales promotion,
                     public relations, media placement, agency presentations,
                     client relations, copy writing, and commercial production.

                     Commerce Weekly   [*City, State*]

                     Advertising display staff. January–April 1988. Responsible
                     for creation and layout of ads, and guidance of ads through
                     the areas of artwork, typesetting, and billing.

                     B & S Lawn Maintenance   [*City, State*]

                     Owner and partner. Summers 1984–1987. Marketed our services
                     to new and already established areas of our working community.
                     Increased customers from 15 in 1984 to 45 in 1987.

Activities   Research assistant for professor of marketing. Leader of
                     "Gerlex Products" marketing term project; organized advertis-
                     ing agency presentation of new marketing strategy for Gerlex
                     baby food. Member Zeta Beta Tau fraternity. Active on
                     fundraising committees. Team member in intramural softball and
                     football. Participant in Dean's Seminar Program.

Available   June 1, 1991. References furnished upon request.

Figure 12-1   *One-page resume with main headings in left margin; right-hand
margin justified (vertically straight).*

DAVID TUCKO
941 Masson Avenue
[*City, State, ZIP*]
[*Telephone*]

OBJECTIVE: A management position in accounting

EDUCATION: **The University of** [*name, city, state*]
School of Business Administration
M.B.A. candidate for June 199-. Concentration in accounting.
GPA 7.8 (8 = A, 7 = A-, 6 = B+).

The University of [*name, city, state*]
B.B.A. accounting, December 199-. GPA 3.9 (4 = A, 3 = B).
Member of Beta Alpha Psi; elected vice president 199-.
Recipient of various academic honors and awards.

EMPLOYMENT: **Guardian Industries,** [*City, State*]
April 199-   Manager of financial reporting. Major responsibilities:
to present   -- Prepared internal and external financial reports
-- Complied with SEC reporting requirements
-- Translated German financial statements and converted to
   U.S. generally accepted accounting principles
-- Maintained liaison with independent auditors; coordinated
   and reviewed major audit issues in Germany and Belgium.

Former positions were supervisor of financial reporting and
supervisor of corporate accounting. Major responsibilities:
-- Headed data processing division and the corporate
   engineering division, at corporate headquarters
-- Supervised corporate payables and payroll departments
-- Maintained liaison with plant and division controllers
-- Prepared long-range financial forecasts

Plante & Moran, C.P.A.s, [*City, State*]
January 199-   Audit supervisor for a major regional public accounting firm.
to April 199-   Responsibilities: planning, coordinating, and supervising
(plus summer   diverse audit and accounting engagements. Experience included
internships)   manufacturing, equipment rental, construction, auto dealer-
ships, and governmental entities.

W.S. Gorski & Co., C.P.A.s, [*City, State*]
December 199-   Part-time college employment as staff accountant, with
responsibilities for bookkeeping and tax return preparation.

ADDITIONAL   Passed the May 199- certified public accountant examination on
INFORMATION: the first sitting. Member of the American Institute of C.P.A.s
and the Association of C.P.A.s. Active in various sports.
Previously active in our church as a choir member, lector, and
representative on various committees.

REFERENCES: References will be furnished upon request.

Figure 12-2   *One-page resume with main headings and dates in left margin.*

RESUME OF LOUANNE A. MARTIN
1684 Mercer Avenue, [City, State, ZIP]
[Telephone]

Professional Objective: Business education teaching position in a
[state] Class A secondary school.

EDUCATION FOR BUSINESS AND TEACHING

[name] **University**, [city, state], September 1989 to June 1991

Major: Business Education, secondary school emphasis
Courses in accounting; business communication; business law;
computer programming; data processing; graphic arts; marketing;
office practice; secretarial procedures; teaching accounting,
shorthand; machine operations

Minor: Economics Courses in European and American economic history,
international economics, macroeconomics, microeconomics

Grade Point Average: 3.9 (out of possible 4.0)
Degree: M.B.A. (master of business administration)

University of [name], [city, state], September 1985 to June 1989

Grade Point Average: 3.8 (out of possible 4.0)
Degree: B.A. (bachelor of arts), with emphasis on business courses.

EMPLOYMENT EXPERIENCE

Student Teacher: Broadway High, [city, state], September to December 1990
  Supervisor: Ms. Jayne Hamilton
  Courses taught: Shorthand 2, Word processor Typesetting, Secretarial
                         Procedures, Computer Operations
  Responsibilities: Planned and supervised three complete units for
                         each class, ranging from 20-30 students, with
                         approval of Ms. Hamilton and Mr. Thomas Jones.

Bookkeeper and   Baron Ford Motor, 850 Fifth Avenue, [city, state],
Secretary: January 1988 to December 1990 (part time during
                         school; full time, summers): Mr. David Lowns,
                         office manager

  Responsibilities: Varied over the two years. Operated switchboard,
                         recorded accounts payable ledger, prepared reports,
                         typed letters, assisted office manager as secretary
                         and file clerk.

Figure 12-3 Resume (on two pages), with centered and side headings.

RESUME OF LOUANNE A. MARTIN
Page 2

EMPLOYMENT EXPERIENCE (continued)

Assistant Claims   Central Administrators, 360 Main Street,
Adjuster: [*city, state*] summer 1987

    Supervisor: Mr. Walter Arnold
    Responsibilities: Processed claims for health insurance, maintained all
                 billing files on customer accounts, and sent reminders
                 for premium payments

Part-time jobs before 1987:
                  Waitress in Jolly Home Restaurant, grocery
                  store sales clerk, library assistant

HONORARIES, CLUBS, ACTIVITIES

College
    Phi Beta Kappa, academic national scholarship honorary
    Beta Gamma Sigma, national scholastic honorary in business administration
    Recording secretary, Business Student's Association
    Vice president, Beta Beta sorority
    Recipient of two academic scholarships: from Lions Club and XYZ Business
    Association

High School
    National Honor Society and Torch Club--three years; secretary one year
    President, Business Education Club
    Editor, Annual
    Outstanding Graduate 1985, chosen by Alumni Association.

SKILLS AND HOBBIES

Write and speak the French language.
Office skills include operating computers (IBM, Apple, Zenith), copying
machines, electronic calculators; writing shorthand 125 wpm and typing 60 wpm.

Hobbies include hiking, working with people, swimming, professional
enrichment.

REFERENCES

Available with credentials at Placement Center,
[*name, address*] University

Figure 12-3   *(Continued)* Second page of resume.

Richard T. Felder
333 Olive Street
[*City, State, ZIP*]
[*Telephone*]

**Major
Qualifications:**

****** OBJECTIVE ******

A line management position with responsibility
for corporate or divisional profits. Alterna-
tively, responsibility for top-level contract
negotiations of client development.

Fifteen years of progressively greater management responsibilities, plus a master of business
administration degree with a major and continuing interest in management.

EMPLOYMENT

Dates:
Oct. 199- to present   Lanchet Industrial Supplies, Inc. [*city, state*]
July 199- to Oct. 199- ABN Products, International [*city, state*]

Functional Review of Work Experience:

General
Management

Directed development of a successful analysis and
profit planning system to help with management decisions
on profit lines and areas.

As vice president and general manager, am responsible
for five operating divisions. Reduced personnel
turnover and increased profits by over 20%.

Profit
Planning

Directed development of a successful analysis and
profit planning system to help with management decisions
on profit lines and areas.

International
Management

As manager of international operations, directed and
supervised overseas sales and distribution on four
producing divisions. Products ranged from intermediate
chemicals and pipeline coatings to treated wood.

Financial
Communications

Maintained financial relations with investment bankers,
security analysts, and clients through face-to-face and
written communications.

Report Editing
and Writing

Edited monthly Management Reports (printed for distribution to 950 company managers). Wrote and compiled award-
winning annual reports.

Staff
Management

As assistant manager of personnel, supervised a staff of
eight interviewers and testers for hiring both office and
warehouse personnel. Devised policies for training,
rating, and disciplining staff employees.

EDUCATION

M.B.A. in management, University of [*state*], 199-
B.A. in business administration (management and organization), University of
  [*state*], 199-, cum laude

PERSONAL DATA

Health: Excellent.   Languages: Fluent Spanish; some German and French.

FURTHER DETAILS AND REFERENCES UPON REQUEST

Figure 12-4   *Functional resume (one-page).*

JOB APPLICATION LETTER

The application letter is just as much a sales letter as any message selling a product or service—and the resume is an enclosure. In your letter you tell the prospective employer what you can do for her or him and why you feel you are qualified. You interpret only the important points in your resume as they *relate to the specific job requirements*.

The checklist below may be a guide when you plan the content of your persuasive "sales" application letter—organized by the AIDA plan. Subsequent pages discuss ways to develop each item.

■ Checklist for Job Application Letter

A. Attention (1 paragraph)
1. Businesslike beginning. Usually choose one or two:
    a. Summary—perhaps two or three outstanding qualifications
    b. Name—an individual or office the reader is familiar with or the publication in which the reader's ad appeared
    c. Question—for reader benefit
    d. News item—related to employer
    e. Other relevant reader-oriented statement
2. Mention of specific job or field of interest

B. Interest, Desire, Conviction (2 or 3 paragraphs)
1. Discussion of your qualifications from a reader-benefit or reader-interest viewpoint. Include:
    a. Education and training—related to job requirements
    b. Work experience—related to job requirements
    c. Significant personal attitudes, interests, activities, and qualities—related to job requirements
2. Reference to resume (once)

C. Action (1 paragraph)
1. Request for interview at reader's convenience, with suggestions when you will be available
2. Easy action
    a. Phone number
    b. Hours you can be reached
    c. Reply envelope or card enclosed only rarely. Consider reader!

Opening for Favorable Attention

The application letter should begin with a businesslike paragraph that attracts the reader's attention. It should make clear that you are applying for a job—not inquiring about one or studying this phase for a school report. Also, identify the job (or job area) you're interested in, as shown in the following examples.

Summary Opening

One of the most effective openings is a summary of your two or three outstanding qualifications related to the job you seek. (If you chose to insert these in your resume—as illustrated on pages 326–327—your opening paragraph in the letter can refer to them, but should not repeat the same words.)

1. Retailing experience in a department store similar to yours, business knowledge gained academically, plus a sincere interest in these areas have helped me learn the basic requirements for running a department efficiently. I would like to contribute the practical skills I have acquired by becoming a part of your management training program.

2. My understanding is that a continuity writer for your station must have an interest in the knowledge of classical music. She or he must have ambition and a desire to achieve. Above all, this person must be able to write. I have these qualifications and am asking to be considered for the job. [*Applicant had no work experience.*]

3. Your growth in the fast-food industry is the envy of many people. Such a phenomenal growth requires people who have already worked in the industry, made it a focus of attention in college, and then decided to make it their career. My preparation has followed these lines.

Name Opening

"Networking," speaking with different people concerning issues or job openings, is commonly used to find out about jobs. If a networking reference, or anyone well known to the reader has suggested you apply for a position, you can use that person's name in the opening—unless he or she has asked to you keep it confidential.

If you are answering a job ad, refer to it precisely.

1. Dr. Olga Schmit, professor of accounting and chairperson of the accounting department at [*university*], has informed me that your firm is looking for an accounting major who is interested in managerial accounting. Please consider me for the opening in your training program.

2. Your ad in the Sunday, October 6, 199-, <u>Times</u> for an aggressive person to sell your graphic communication products and services calls for qualifications that match mine very closely. With three years' successful selling as well as servicing of duplicators and electronic systems, plus genuine enthusiasm for selling and ability to solve complex graphic communications problems, I would like to join your staff as a sales trainee.

3. `Your name comes to me via a mutual friend, Mr. David`
   `Sarns.  He recommended that I contact you about your`
   `opening for an account executive.`

Question Opening

Another way to catch the employer's attention at the beginning is with a properly phrased question that shows understanding of a company problem or significant need and the applicant's desire to help.

`For your tourist store in [city] do you need a reliable assis-`
`tant store manager who speaks French and German fluently and`
`who has successful sales experience and a broad background`
`of business training?  I have these qualifications and would`
`like to put them to work for you.`

News Item Opening

Sometimes you can mention a news event about a significant achievement of the employer or his or her company, or a contemplated change or new procedure—if it ties in with your desire to work for a certain firm.

1. `In a recent [name of journal] article I read with interest`
   `that your firm is planning to open a branch office in`
   `Mexico.  Because my college background and work experi-`
   `ence, plus facility with Spanish, fit your basic require-`
   `ments for a research assistant, I would like to apply for`
   `that job in your branch office.`

2. `Your firm's consulting activities, and especially its work`
   `in "information systems," may make an individual with my`
   `qualifications and aspirations of interest to you.  My`
   `academic concentration on "open systems theory," coupled`
   `with practical experience, would enable me to perform well`
   `as a member of your management consulting staff.`

Middle Paragraphs for Interest, Desire, Conviction

After your attention-getting opening, you present your qualifications for the job you're applying for. In the short space you have (perhaps no more than three paragraphs) you can't repeat *unnecessarily* what is on the resume. You need to select and emphasize key points, considering carefully every word in every idea you include. *The emphasis is on how you can be helpful to the employer.*

As with most sales letters, facts and figures are more convincing than the writer's opinions. But these facts must relate to the buyer's needs. When you write each paragraph, ask yourself, "So what?" For example:

So what?	`I am a recent graduate of City Community College.`

Show how the facts relate to the job	`The specialized textile training I received at`
	`City Community College will enable me to provide`
	`the expertise in fabrics your clients want.`

So what?	`I traveled extensively in Europe.`
Show how the facts relate to the job	`My exposure to many different cultures has helped me understand some problems facing a multinational company.`

In a solicited letter answering an ad, be sure to cover in a positive way every qualification the ad specifies. If you have a shortcoming (maybe you're too young or have no work experience), emphasize other positive qualifications to strengthen the reader's confidence in your capabilities.

The order in which you present these paragraphs is also important. If you use a summary opening, you'll organize the paragraphs in the same order as the qualifications are listed in the opening—with the most important qualification first. If you don't have a summary opening, you'll still organize by discussing the most important qualification first. So that the reader doesn't divert attention to the resume before finishing the letter, don't refer to the enclosure until the next-to-last or last paragraph.

Education

Most recent college graduates consider education their most important qualification; if so, they should discuss it first—in the letter as well as in the resume. However, an applicant must be careful not to imply that a college degree—even a master's degree—is the only qualification for the job. Employers who hire college graduates look beyond the degree, to determine what the applicant can do or what the degree indicates about personality. They appreciate such signs of intelligence as ability to think logically, sound judgment, mental alertness, and good grades. In the paragraph on education you can:

- Show that you have both a broad background in business (or arts and sciences) and depth in a major or a certain area
- Highlight your overall education by showing how your college studies prepared you for the work (or area) you seek
- Explain how and why you supplemented your major with important electives outside your major

EXAMPLES

1. `Training I received in production control and planning at` [*name*] `College enables me to analyze, study, and recommend methods of work simplification in factory projects.  Additional studies on person and machine output rates, personnel relations, and business communications provided knowledge to make job analyses and to write clear, concise reports.`

2. `The accounting courses I studied at the University of` [*state*] `emphasized up-to-date procedures, principles, and theory--that provide a firm basis with which to grow in the auditing profession.  Courses in data processing, in addition to my work experience at a computer installation,`

```
have led me to be especially interested in the auditing of
such systems.
```

Work Experience

The jobs you've held—full- or part-time, related or unrelated to the position you're applying for—help strengthen your qualifications. Try to tell concisely how you performed some functions and what you accomplished. By discussing responsibilities you had in previous jobs, you can show:

- You gained experience that will help you understand (or learn faster) the special techniques required for the new job
- You can adapt to people and like to work with them
- You can handle responsibilities
- You're a hard worker

```
1. For the past four summers while working in your office as
   a shipping clerk and assisting in the accounting depart-
   ment, I have gained considerable knowledge of the tech-
   niques and terminology unique to the accountant in this
   industry.  This previous work experience with your company
   will enable me to adjust to your program with only minimal
   training.

2. During my employment at [name] Food Centers, I have or-
   dered merchandise for a store operating at a volume of
   $60,000 a week, formulated pricing policies, supervised
   merchandise allocation of the shelves as well as the ac-
   tivities of about 25 employees.  This background has
   helped me develop a working knowledge of the food industry
   and also the capacity to help make policy decisions on
   retail food store operations.
```

Personal Attitudes, Interests, Activities, Qualities

In another paragraph or two you can highlight a few personal attitudes, interests, activities, or qualities that relate specifically to the job requirements. You might discuss (1) your ability to work with people, (2) your attitude toward employment—your interest in the field, company, or geographic area, or (3) your personal qualities. If you have little or no job experience (or irrelevant education), these qualifications may be your main selling points.

Ability to Work with People.   If you genuinely like people and want to help them, you have a priceless quality to sell. You can convey to your prospective employer that you have this ability, as shown in the following examples:

```
1. As assistant manager of a Household Finance Corporation
   office and as a collection department supervisor for the
   National Bank of Commerce, I developed the ability to get
   along well with people.  For both customer service and
```

employee relationships it was necessary to exercise good judgment based on sometimes incomplete information, in varying situations or difficult circumstances. I enjoy opportunities to work constructively with people.

2. In several capacities I have been able to further develop my interest in communicating and working with people. Being the daughter of an Air Force officer, I have lived throughout the United States and in foreign countries and have spent most of my summers traveling. Furthermore, as hospitality chairperson of my sorority, I organized all events held at the house and acted as hostess for guests. As a result, I have learned to make friends quickly and to feel at ease with many types of people--attributes that will help me be beneficial in a retailing position.

Attitude toward Employment.   Interest in the field, company, or area should be substantiated by proof.

1. My interest in construction developed in high school, working summers and part time in residential home building. Upon graduation, I decided on a career in construction management, and consequently realized that a college background in business, combined with on-the-job experience, was essential preparation. As my interest and work experience indicate, I am very enthusiastic about a career in this field. Employment in construction completely financed my college education. Even in my spare time I am building a chalet, as the enclosed data sheet shows.

2. To supplement my marketing major, I sold men's clothing for three years part time or full time during school. This sales experience should give me a head start in your training program. I can sell, enjoy selling, and want to continue to sell. What's more, I proved my sales potential by winning the Arrow Shirt contest, which I have mentioned on the enclosed data sheet. Selling stocks appears to be a challenge, and I welcome that challenge.

Desirable Personal Qualities.   By citing various parts of my background—schooling, jobs, extracurricular activities—you can show you have personal qualities that are desirable for the job you seek.

1. As the enclosed resume shows, I found it necessary to work while completing my college education. In fulfilling the responsibilities for the jobs and the courses, I learned to be punctual and to apportion my time--requirements also confronted by an "audit team" in completing an audit within a time and fee limitation.

2. While attending the university, I worked part time or full time during the school year and up to 80 hours a week (on

```
two or more jobs) each summer.  I was entirely self-sup-
porting throughout my college career and feel I can offer
your company qualities of adaptability, perseverance, and
patience developed from working hard on many jobs with
many kinds of people.
```

Usually in the next-to-the-last paragraph, but sometimes in the last paragraph, direct the reader's attention to some data on the resume (see the preceding example 1 and the sample letters on the following pages).

Last Paragraph

The last paragraph of your letter usually asks for action—just as a sales letter does. Without begging or commanding, you ask for an interview and (if appropriate) say you will come to the employer's office when he or she suggests. Make action easy by giving your telephone number and hours to call if someone can't answer the phone throughout the day or evening.

If during normal business hours you are in classes or you work away from any office, but you have an answering machine, mention that. You could explain why you will call the employer to discuss arranging a convenient time for an interview.

1. ```
   As I will be in [city] from April 20 to April 25, I will ap-
   preciate the opportunity to see you during that time to
   discuss further my desire to serve as one of your inves-
   tigators.  After you have reviewed my qualifications and
   examined the enclosed resume, will you please name a con-
   venient time in a letter to me at my [city] address?
   ```

2. ```
   My class schedule allows me to come to your office any
   afternoon except Tuesdays.  May I have an interview to
   answer any questions about myself that you might have?
   You can reach me by telephoning 555-1234 before 10 a.m. or
   after 4 p.m.
   ```

Even if you're sending your job application hundreds of miles away, you might still ask for an interview if you think the company has a local representative who can screen you in person. You can ask the employer to send you the local representative's name or to arrange the interview for you with the local representative.

```
Although the resume and this letter give you some idea of my
qualifications, I am eager to have a personal interview with
you.  Or perhaps I could discuss my qualifications in
greater detail with your regional personnel representative.
Please let me know how I can get in touch with her or him.
```

Sample Letters of Application

The application letters illustrated in Figures 12-5 and 12-6 apply suggestions discussed in this chapter. Letter 1 illustrates content and layout of an effective application letter that can accompany the resume shown in Figure 12-2. Notice

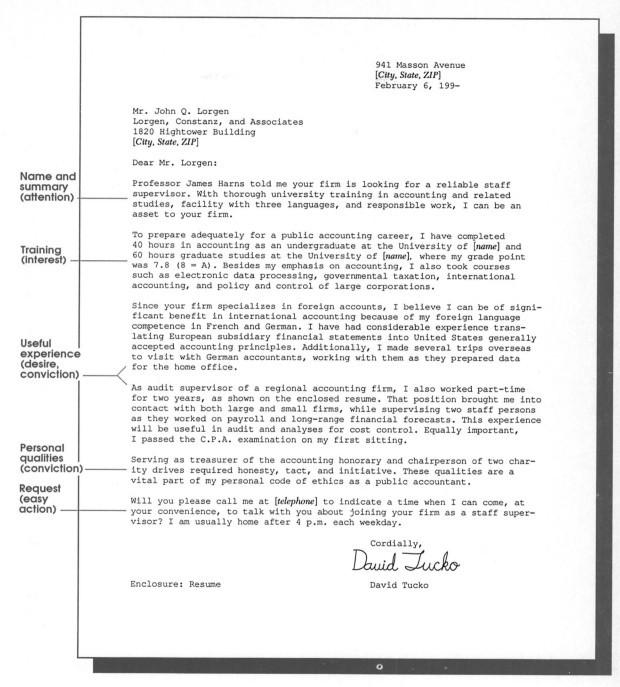

941 Masson Avenue
[*City, State, ZIP*]
February 6, 199–

Mr. John Q. Lorgen
Lorgen, Constanz, and Associates
1820 Hightower Building
[*City, State, ZIP*]

Dear Mr. Lorgen:

Name and summary (attention)

Professor James Harns told me your firm is looking for a reliable staff supervisor. With thorough university training in accounting and related studies, facility with three languages, and responsible work, I can be an asset to your firm.

Training (interest)

To prepare adequately for a public accounting career, I have completed 40 hours in accounting as an undergraduate at the University of [*name*] and 60 hours graduate studies at the University of [*name*], where my grade point was 7.8 (8 = A). Besides my emphasis on accounting, I also took courses such as electronic data processing, governmental taxation, international accounting, and policy and control of large corporations.

Useful experience (desire, conviction)

Since your firm specializes in foreign accounts, I believe I can be of significant benefit in international accounting because of my foreign language competence in French and German. I have had considerable experience translating European subsidiary financial statements into United States generally accepted accounting principles. Additionally, I made several trips overseas to visit with German accountants, working with them as they prepared data for the home office.

As audit supervisor of a regional accounting firm, I also worked part-time for two years, as shown on the enclosed resume. That position brought me into contact with both large and small firms, while supervising two staff persons as they worked on payroll and long-range financial forecasts. This experience will be useful in audit and analyses for cost control. Equally important, I passed the C.P.A. examination on my first sitting.

Personal qualities (conviction)

Serving as treasurer of the accounting honorary and chairperson of two charity drives required honesty, tact, and initiative. These qualities are a vital part of my personal code of ethics as a public accountant.

Request (easy action)

Will you please call me at [*telephone*] to indicate a time when I can come, at your convenience, to talk with you about joining your firm as a staff supervisor? I am usually home after 4 p.m. each weekday.

Cordially,

David Tucko

David Tucko

Enclosure: Resume

Figure 12-5   Letter 1   *Solicited application for a staff supervisor position. This letter accompanies Figure 12-2, page 336, the one-page resume.*

1684 Mercer Avenue
[*City, State, ZIP*]
January 10, 199–

Dr. Ralph E. Nelson, Director
[*City*] High School Employment Services
820 Fourth Avenue East
[*City, State, ZIP*]

Dear Dr. Nelson:

Question and summary opening (attention)

Next September, will one of your high schools need a business teacher who can make learning realistic and interesting for the students? If so, please consider me for the position. My qualifications include a liberal business background, work experience, and enthusiasm for teaching.

Liberal business background; specific courses (interest)

On June 10 this year I will graduate from [*name*] University, where I have emphasized business education and economics in my program. I am now prepared to teach any of these business courses that you offer: bookkeeping or accounting, business law, secretarial training, shorthand, and operations of various office machines--including data processors, computers, and typewriters. If you are considering adding a course in economics to your curriculum, I will gladly present to you my ideas about the advantages of teaching economics in high school.

Work experience (desire, conviction)

Three years of steady office employment and previous summer work have given me valuable insight into the growing need by business firms for vocationally trained high school graduates. This practical experience expanded my knowledge of business education. I am better equipped to communicate effectively with my students and to train them for high quality work and useful skills in business. The different positions I have held developed qualities of tact and adaptability, which I consider important when working with young people.

Personal attitudes and qualities (desire)

The semester of student teaching--mentioned on the enclosed resume--has convinced me that high school teaching will be my chosen career. I will work with the same zeal that helped me earn an A minus overall grade average with honors throughout my university and high school education.

Easy-action request

To discuss further your requirements and my qualifications, will you please grant me an interview? You can reach me by calling [*telephone*] any weekday before 9 a.m. or after 4:30 p.m. I could come to your office any time that is convenient for you.

Sincerely,

Louanne A. Martin

Enclosure: Resume

Louanne A. Martin

Figure 12-6   Letter 2   *Prospecting application to a school superintendent for a high school teaching position; accompanies resume Figure 12-3, pages 337 and 338.*

how well this applicant relates highlights of each paragraph to the job he seeks—staff supervisor in a C.P.A. firm that, the applicant knows, has an opening.

Letter 2 shows the content and layout of an application from a 23-year-old college graduate seeking a teaching position in a high school business department. It is a prospecting letter, because the applicant does not know whether an opening exists. Her letter accompanies the resume shown in Figure 12-3.

SUMMARY

Before you write a resume and job application letter, make an inventory of your employment qualifications. Analyze what you have to offer an employer and consider the kind of work you prefer for a job or career. Then research to determine which jobs and employers require what you can offer.

After you have evaluated your assets and noted requirements for desirable job opportunities, you are ready to prepare your written "sales promotion." The main purpose is to get an interview. First prepare a resume that has all the qualities for a well-written presentation. Organize pertinent facts under appropriate headings, use action phrases, and emphasize your strong points honestly. Education, work experience, and achievements should preferably be stated in reverse chronological order—with the present or most recent first.

The application letter is your sales message that accompanies the resume. It tells the prospective employer why you feel you are qualified for a certain job or area. Using the AIDA plan, you interpret important points in the resume as they relate to the specfic job requirements.

EXERCISES AND PROBLEMS

1. *Self-appraisal:* This assignment helps you to know yourself better before you launch a job-getting selling campaign. Make a thorough self-appraisal by taking an inventory of all your employment qualifications. After rereading especially the suggestions on pages 318 and 319, list your accomplishments under these five main headings: (1) work experience, skills, aptitudes, (2) education, (3) activities, achievements, social development, (4) interests, preferences, attitudes, (5) personal characteristics. Add whatever subheadings are desirable. You might place check marks or asterisks by the qualifications you think are your strongest for the work you'd like to do. Support your personal qualifications with specific facts about your achievements.

   Type all your qualifications under appropriate headings and subheadings; then insert them into a notebook. This "personal inventory," or "self-analysis," will help you to know what you have to sell.

2. *Market survey:* Make a market survey to find what career opportunities and jobs are suitable for your qualifications. See the suggestions on pages 320 and 321 regarding publications and people that can give you useful information.

3. ***Letter asking questions regarding a job or job area:*** The purpose of this assignment is to find out what qualifications the prospective employer looks for when screening you for your career job. Assume that in your market survey (Exercise 2) you discovered that sufficient existing publications are not available locally. So you will write to an organization of your choice (but not the firm to which you plan to send your application letter and resume), asking for answers to your questions or arranging for an interview with the appropriate officer. Although you're not getting answers from the prospective employer, you *will* from a source that should reveal comparable information on the qualifications considered most important.

   Prepare a list of 10 (or more) questions to which you must know the answers before you can write your application. All your questions must relate to a particular job or job area. (You may use the answers later for a report-writing assignment.)

   Listed below are several questions to consider. They're possible spring-boards for the questions to which you must find answers.

   a. What are the basic qualifications that you look for when you screen a recent college graduate for a job in [*your career area*]?
   b. For this type of work what major do you think is best?
   c. Outside the major, what courses (business or nonbusiness) do you think will be helpful on the job?
   d. What kind of previous experience do you look for in the applicant?
   e. How do you evaluate personality from a written job presentation?
   f. How important are grades?
   g. To get into this type of work, what initial job should I apply for?
   h. Do you prefer references in the initial written job presentation?

4. ***Resume and letter of application:*** Prepare a letter of application with an accompanying resume for the career job you plan to get into after completion of your college education. Address it to the firm of your choice and to the particular individual who should receive it.

   To make this material as useful to you as possible, date the letter the month and year you actually plan to send it. For example, if you're graduating this year, the date of the letter should precede that of graduation by enough time (four to nine months) so you'll have the job when you're ready to go to work. If you're a sophomore and have at least two more years of college and then two years of graduate school, again, use the date you'll actually be sending the letter.

   Use only facts, so far as possible, in both your letter and resume. If you are dating the letter in the future, assume the activities (especially schooling, work experience, government service) that will most likely take place between now and then. This timing permits you to update the written job presentation when you're ready to revise, type, and actually send it.

Try to make your message and resume so convincing and selling that they will stand out from many others that may be received the same day. Both should be neatly and accurately typed—100 percent correct in spelling and accurate in facts and figures.

5. *Evaluation of a classmate's job presentation:* On the day your application letter and resume (Exercise 4) are due to be handed in, bring them to class and exchange them (or copies) with a classmate—preferably one you do not know very well. Each of you will then evaluate the other's written job presentation. Assume you are the addressee of the letter, a stranger to the applicant. Would the letter and resume convince you to invite the writer to your office for an interview? Why or why not? On a separate sheet write your answers to these questions. Also list (a) specific good qualities of the letter and resume and (b) specific suggestions for improvements. Sign the sheet and return it to the writer, together with the letter and resume. If your instructor wishes, each student will hand in these comments along with the letter and resume. (No changes should, however, be made on these messages before the instructor reads them.)

6. *Evaluations:* Below are four application letters. Explain orally in class which ones will most likely result in an interview. Which are totally unacceptable? Why?

LETTER A *Application to a grocery chain for accounting position.*

With my vast and diversified working experience in a [*town name*] Safeway store and my 5 years' college training in accounting and economics, I am well-qualified to apply for an accounting position with Safeway Stores, Inc.

Having successfully completed studies in managerial and financial accounting while earning my degree at the University of [*state*], you will find that I can handle any accounting situation with ease and confidence.

While working in the many departments in Safeway in order to finance my college education, I became thoroughly familiar with every phase of operation of one of your stores. Because of my pleasing personality, my ability to get along well with others, and my excellent work record, I was chosen to supervise the night stock crew during the summers of [*year*] and [*year*].

My work experience with Safeway has been both valuable and enjoyable for me; therefore, I wish to continue working for your firm in my chosen field.

After you've had a chance to verify some of the things I've said about myself in this letter and on the enclosed data sheet, will you write me about the possibilities of working in one of your west coast offices?

LETTER B   *Application to a firm for sales position.*

Please consider my application for a position in your sales department. My qualifications are a bachelor of arts in general business, a thorough and working knowledge of accounting and finance, and a sincere interest in selling.

I am seeking a position in your company in selling because I feel that I have the necessary qualifications to do a good job for the company, while learning the basic components of your needs. I selected your firm because it is the most rapidly expanding company in this industry and a leader in research and development, which I recognize as essential to maintain your present status. I feel that I can contribute toward these goals. I have studied the basic background of the transportation industry and am deeply interested in furthering my knowledge, to the benefit of the company. I have enclosed a resume of my personal background, complete with a transcript of my grades.

After you've had time to review my application and data sheet, will you please call me or write. My address and telephone numbers are on the enclosed data sheet. Thank you for your consideration.

LETTER C   *Application to home appliance firm as sales representative.*

If hundreds of effective retail calls, thorough knowledge of point-of-sale, and imaginative merchandising help make a home appliance representative, then I've begun to learn the business. I would like to put this practical field experience to work for Sack's Home Appliance Company.

Fieldwork as an assistant district sales manager for the ABC Cleaning Products Company gave me an opportunity to plan and execute sales promotions that sold cleaners. I have proven ability to open nonbuying accounts, secure floor displays, sell additional packages, and achieve point-of-sale dominance.

In addition, I have conducted route analyses, set up key account systems, and conducted sales training meetings for wholesaler personnel.

Frequent contact with retailers and consumers enabled me to handle consumer complaints and utilize a good layman's knowledge of various home appliances.

After you've had an opportunity to review some of the things I've said in this letter and on the enclosed data sheet, will you write me frankly about the possibility of beginning a career with Sack's Home Appliance Company? I would appreciate an opportunity to discuss my qualifications.

LETTER D   *Application to a newspaper as assistant music and drama editor.*

In reference to your advertisement in Editor & Publisher (3/14) for an assistant music and drama editor, the offer is worth an inquiry because of my deep interest in theater. But, very frankly, I'm afraid it would have to be an exceptional salary offer to lure me so far from the east coast and what I'm convinced are its greater professional opportunities.

However, you will find samples of my reviews and a brief resume attached. Should you desire to continue this correspondence further, I will send you references and other material customary to a job application.

My experience in motion picture-theater reviewing with the Sun has been limited to "filling in" for the regular critic during his vacations or illnesses. Before that, I wrote a theater column in a weekly nespaper in Bath, Pa., a sideline to my daily reporting. I have engaged in all phases of amateur theater as an outside interest. I am not well versed in music--though I am confident in my critical capacities. Again, I have filled in at times for the Sun's music critic and, if need be, can also submit samples. I have handled general assignments and beats.

Your advertisement mentions "opportunity for advancement," without further elaboration. Your offer of the position of assistant music-drama editor would be considerably more attractive if coupled with a commitment to go to your Washington, D.C., bureau in two, or three, years or to whatever overseas bureaus the Daily Blat may sponsor, subject only to your complete dissatisfaction with the work produced for you.

The tendency, of course, of most newspapers is to fill the opening with the run-of-the-mill newsperson who is panting at the door and willing to accept chicken feed. Consequently, I have little reason to expect a favorable reaction to this letter. If I am mistaken, I hope you will advise me

of the maximum salary you can pay for this position, the
setup at the <u>Blat</u>, and any arrangements that you would consider feasible. I hope we can discuss this matter further,
but only with your understanding that I expect to drive a
hard bargain. My home address appears below and on the
resume. Please address your reply accordingly.

LETTER **E**   *Application to a company for a position in financial analysis.*

Able and motivated personnel are vital to any organization.
Specifically I believe my skills in financial management,
developed at [school], could benefit [company]. This belief and
eagerness to work in the [city] area prompt me to apply for
employment with [company].

For your review, my resume is enclosed. I will receive my
BBA in May 199-, and now seek a position in financial analysis for commercial or consumer lending. You may notice from
my resume that I am motivated to scholarship and involvement. Further, past job experiences have trained me in effective business communication and computer applications.

I wish to discuss my qualifications further in an interview.
I am frequently in the [city] area, and could be available any
weekday afternoon for a meeting. If it is agreeable with
you, I will contact you to arrange a mutually convenient
date.

Your consideration is sincerely appreciated.

7. **Letter of application and an annual report.** You on occasion may wish
   to write a blind request, that is, a letter to an organization or company in
   which you have no contacts. You simply know about the organization through
   its annual report, wherein is mentioned the name of the employment manager. Write a letter to that manager requesting a job interview.

Other Job Application Messages

The number of messages you'll send in getting your career job (or changing to another job) depends on economic conditions, need for graduates in your area, and your own qualifications and standards. If you're sending your job presentation when it's a seller's market and you have unusually good qualifications, you might get the job you want right away. But if the conditions are reversed, you can spend many weeks—even months—finding the right niche for yourself.

Many schools permit on-campus interviews with their students a year before graduation. That allows an early contact. If you wish to send a cover letter and resume to organizations not interviewing on your campus, you could begin from a year to three months before receiving your degree.

This chapter discusses the job interview, follow-up messages from you the applicant to the employer, and follow-up messages from the employer to you the applicant.

THE JOB INTERVIEW

Assume that your "sales" letter has achieved its purpose of getting you an interview, or assume that you have a time slot to interview with an on-campus interviewer. That interview may be the most important step toward getting the desired job. This section offers suggestions regarding preparation for the interview, conduct during the interview, answers to the interviewer's questions, and questions you might ask.

Preparing for the Interview

Always prepare for an interview. Your primary purpose is to get the best job suitable to your capabilities. The employer's goal is to get the best person available for the job.

New York Life Insurance Company's booklet *Making the Most of Your Job Interview* provides a good statement on the expectations of an interview:

> The employment interview is one of the most important events in the average person's experience, for the obvious reason that the 20 or 30 minutes spent with the interviewer may determine the entire future course of one's life. Yet interviewers are constantly amazed at the number of applicants who drift into job interviews without any apparent preparation and only the vaguest idea of what they are going to say. Their manner says, "Well, here I am." And that's often the end of it, in more ways than one.
>
> Others, although they undoubtedly do not intend to do so, create an impression of indifference by acting too casual. At the other extreme, a few applicants work themselves into such a state of mind that when they arrive they seem to be in the last states of nervous fright and are only able to answer in monosyllables.
>
> These marks of inexperience can be avoided by knowing a little of what actually is expected of you and by making a few simple preparations before the interview.

The following checklist offers helpful suggestions for preparing for the interview:

■ Checklist in Preparing for an Employment Interview

1. ***Know yourself.*** Know how your qualifications—both your strengths and weaknesses—compare with the job requirements. Review your achievements and how they relate to the position. Take with you two copies of your resume, a list of references, and—if appropriate—a few examples of your work.

2. ***Know the company.*** Read its latest annual report and an in-house newspaper for data on earnings, products, expansions, plant locations, events, and personnel. Review its recruitment brochure, if available. For any recent statements about the company, check the index to the *Wall Street Journal, Business Periodicals, New York Times,* or on-line databases and, if possible, talk to friends who work for that company.

3. ***Prepare questions and answers.*** Use your information about the company as a basis for your planned questions. You might ask if promotions come from within, why the job is open, where the job will lead. Also anticipate the questions the interviewer might ask and consider how to answer them. See Typical Questions in an Interview, pages 359 and 361; also Fair . . . and Unfair Preemployment Inquiries in Chapter 5, pages 107–109.

4. ***Have some idea about salary.*** Know the current beginning salary range for your type of job and experience. Don't raise the issue of salary until the interviewer does so. That may be near the end of the first or second interview—after you and the interviewer have discussed the job responsibilities and your credentials that affect your bargaining power.

5. ***Give careful attention to your appearance.*** Appearance conveys significant nonverbal impressions. Wear conservative, neatly pressed, appropriate clothing of good quality. Avoid gaudy colors and styles and anything low-cut. Women should keep jewelry and perfumes to a minimum. Suits in gray, brown, or dark blue are usually appropriate for any applicant. Men should choose conservatively cut suits and ties; women, tailored skirted suits. Be well-groomed, with a neat hair style, clean fingernails, and shined, unscuffed shoes. A pleasant smile is desirable too.

6. ***Check meeting place, time, and other details.*** Know precisely when and where the interview will be held; plan to arrive at least 1–15 minutes early; know a telephone number to contact. Know

the interviewer's name and how to pronounce it. Put a pen or pencil along with a small notebook in your pocket or purse.

7. **Rehearse.** Speak your opening statement out loud, perhaps in front of a mirror. Some applicants even hold a mock interview with a friend or a person in the school's placement office. If possible, videotape a session for assessing both your oral and your nonverbal presentation. Rehearse a good handshake too; it can make a positive impression during the first minutes of an interview.

Acting Professionally during the Interview

After you have followed the suggestions above, you can confidently proceed to the interview. Mentally prepare yourself for success. Give your appearance one final check.

When you meet the interviewer, smile and greet him or her by name, pronouncing it correctly. If he or she offers to shake hands, do so—with a firm grip, but not a bone crusher. Remain standing until invited to sit down, unless you're in a small room and the interviewer remains seated or sits down immediately.

These first few moments are critical. Your initial impression may color the remainder of the interview. Make eye contact and begin courteously, "Hello, I'm [*state your first and last name*]. I've looked forward to our meeting."

The overall impression will be influenced by your personality, oral communication ability, and appearance. To make the best impression—verbal and nonverbal—you need to be aware of some positive and negative behavior.

Positive, Desirable Behavior

1. *Show enthusiasm, vitality, interest.* You can do so by the alert way you sit and look, by facial expressions, by questions you ask, and by the answers you give. Speak with vitality and variety, not in a monotone.

2. *Be honest and sincere.* Stick to the facts; state achievements without exaggeration. Have high personal standards.

3. *Accent the positive aspects.* Use expressions that indicate you are competent and dependable, with a positive attitude.

4. *Listen attentively and concentrate.* Let the interviewer finish each question. Then reply precisely to the question. If possible, link your achievements with your answer.

5. *Use correct grammar and pronunciation.* Communicate accurately and clearly.

6. *Maintain appropriate posture and appearance.*

7. *Keep answers brief.* The more answers you can provide—during a half-hour interview—the more varied the information you can provide about yourself.

8. *Show interest in the company and/or industry.* Then tactfully relate your achievements to employer needs wherever possible.

9. *Show analytical skills.* Take time to weigh pros and cons of an idea. Note the short- and long-term benefits and consequences of a decision.

Negative Factors to Avoid

1. *Discourtesy.* Avoid smoking, using first names (unless invited to do so), showing disinterest, chewing gum, doodling.

2. *Interruptions.* Let the interviewer finish a question even though you presume to know where the question is headed.

3. *Jargon and slang.* Omit using such expressions as *yeah, y'know, cool, stuff like that.*

4. *Unfavorable comments.* Avoid slighting references about a former professor or employer. Focus on the positive, avoiding words such as *can't, won't, unable, hate, failure, incompetent.*

5. *Overaggressive or cynical attitude.* Avoid indicating a superiority complex and "know-it-all" feelings.

6. *Lack of poise and confidence.* If you have followed all suggestions in the checklist, you can be confident and less nervous.

7. *Disregard for the positive factors.* If you place the words "failure to" before each of the 9 suggestions for positive behavior, you'll have a total of 16 in this list of negatives to avoid.

Answering Interviewer's Questions

After the warm-up period (exchange of pleasantries to develop rapport) be ready for the interviewer's first questions about your qualifications or interest. Your answer may include excerpts from your education, work, or activities showing competence, dependability, ambition, creativity.

For some years Dr. Frank S. Endicott, former director of placement at Northwestern University, compiled a list of likely employment questions. In the following, his original list of 59 has been shortened to 25.

Typical Questions in an Interview

1. What jobs have you held? How were they obtained and why did you leave?

2. What are your future vocational plans?

3. In what type of position are you most interested?

4. What courses did you like best? Least? Why?

5. What do you know about our company?

6. What extracurricular offices have you held?

7. If you were starting college all over again, what courses would you take?

8. Do you think that your extracurricular activities were worth the time you devoted to them? Why?

9. What personal characteristics are necessary for success in your chosen field?

10. Do you prefer working with others or by yourself?

11. What kind of boss do you prefer?

12. Can you take instructions without feeling upset?

13. Can you get recommendations from previous employers?

14. Have you ever changed your major field of interest while in college? Why?

15. What interests you about our product or service?

16. Which of your college years was the most difficult?

17. Do you like routine work?

18. What size city do you prefer?

19. What is your major weakness?

20. Define cooperation!

21. Do you have an analytical mind?

22. What types of books have you read?

23. Have you plans for graduate work?

24. What are your own special abilities?

25. What are the disadvantages of your chosen field?

Additionally—drawn from the comments of students—the following also represent kinds of questions asked. While the list is brief, rehearsing potential answers will help you during the interview.

1. One of the things we're interested in is how you spend your time. Please describe a typical day.

2. List the qualities you feel are needed in this position.

3. Your last job seemed interesting: tell me about your likes and dislikes of that position.

4. Give both your short-term (5-year) and your long-term (15-year) goals.

5. Can you describe how you handled a difficult problem on your last job?

Of course the list of questions interviewers ask varies. No matter what the question, pause, try to organize your answer, and then offer it with a high degree of confidence. You may also refer to your resume, using it as support for an oral statement you are making.

"Bridging" Confrontational and Unfair Preemployment Questions

Most interviews—both the initial screening interview and a later follow-up with more people—will be direct. The questions will sincerely seek information related to the job. Occasionally, to test your poise under pressure, you may receive a confrontational question; you also may be asked an unfair preemployment inquiry that may be illegal if used for discrimination.

Confrontational Questions

Some interviewees have returned from interviews wilted. They allege that the interviews were confrontational, that the interviewers were abusive, abrupt, and discourteous. However, the interviewers may have been testing the applicants' confidence under pressure, how they handled a tense situation. Tough questions should not necessarily be considered a personal attack.

Preparing for some tough interview questions is similar to preparing for a TV interview. Leading executives spend considerable time and effort preparing for potentially hostile questions, using some of the same techniques you can use in your interview. Try to rehearse or hold a short mock interview for potentially negative questions. Try to bridge to a response which keeps you in control. The key word here is "bridge," using terms such as the following to move from a confrontational question to a more positive response:

- "There may be some truth in that statement [*bridge*], but my data and information lead to a different conclusion."
- "Certainly others have the right to their opinion [*bridge*]. My opinion is this. . . ."
- "That's an interesting comment [*bridge*]. A more complete analysis would include information discovered in my investigations."

In each case, you bridge to information you wish to speak about, avoiding a direct confrontation with a potentially negative and hostile question. Here are a few other questions that require tactful, honest answers:

Question	Answer
"How come your grades are lower than average?"	"What the grades do not reflect are the nonclassroom leadership positions I held on several committees. Also, to help pay college expenses I worked on part-time jobs—as shown in my resume."
"Some people feel M.B.A.s are arrogant and only concerned with the buck. . . ."	"That attitude, I know, is held by some people, including the press. In my opinion we cannot put all M.B.A. degree candidates into the same mold. . . ."
"What's your greatest weakness?"	"All things are interesting to me. But out of that love for work comes a bit of impatience. May I give you a complete incident . . . ?"

Even with the negative, risky question about your weakness, you can focus on the positive—determination to improve your strong qualities further—or perhaps mention a non-job-related trait that needs improvement. It is desirable for you to try to turn a potentially negative situation into a positive one.

Unfair Preemployment Questions

Federal laws prohibit employment discrimination on the basis of race, color, religion, sex, handicaps, and national origin. In Chapter 5, pages 107 to 109 include discussions on what are fair and unfair preemployment inquiries regarding 19 subjects.

If an interviewer asks you an "unfair preemployment" question, you may answer if doing so can't be a disadvantage to you. However, if your reply could hurt your chances of getting the job, tactfully decline answering. Whatever your decision is—to answer or to decline—tactfully let the interviewer know you're aware of the law.

Questioning the Interviewer

One of the signs that the interview is coming to a close is when you are asked for your questions. You may prepare these in advance, and they may preferably be about the company and the position. Some questions you might ask could include the following:

- What sort of person fits in best with the company?
- What is the scenario of the last person who was in the position?
- Is it possible to see a complete job description?
- For a person who works effectively in this job, what chances exist for advancement?

And so on and on.

One final comment. If you don't have a job offer, don't discuss salary or fringes which come with the job. You have just gone through the initial interview. However, if you are offered a position on the spot, that's the time to discuss salary and fringes, for then you are in a position to negotiate.

Leave the interview with the same confidence you had going in. Look directly at the interviewer, shake hands, suggest the meeting was worthwhile, and state that you hope to hear from the person again.

APPLICANT-TO-EMPLOYER FOLLOW-UP MESSAGES

Immediately following the interview, record important or especially interesting comments of the interviewer and perhaps significant facts you learned about the company or the job. Also evaluate your success during the interview. On which of your answers did you feel the interviewer seemed disappointed or annoyed? Did you forget to mention any persuasive points that could strengthen his or her good opinion of you?

To strengthen your chances for the job you have applied for, follow up your application letter and resume. Of the ways to follow up—in person, by letter, or by phone—the written message is one of the most effective, because employers can analyze applicants' qualifications at their convenience. They can also more easily compare a large number of applicants—either on the job or at home in the evening.

This section first covers the two all-important and most frequently used types of initial follow-up messages and then presents other types involved in getting a job.

The Initial Follow-Up

The first follow-up you'll write is either (1) a follow-up after the interview or (2) an inquiry about the application letter and resume when the employer hasn't replied.

Follow-Up after the Interview

To be courteous, and to make sure that you are not "out of sight, out of mind," write a follow-up message; this indicates your sincere determination in getting the job. Send to the interviewer (or appropriate company official) a written thank-you within two to five days after you have had your interview.[1] Remember, the interviewer spent valuable time to talk with you, and you need to acknowledge this time, attention, and consideration. Only when you are told during the interview not to write should you refrain from sending this message.

Usually this message is short—less than one page—and its organizational pattern is that of a good-news or neutral letter:

1. In the opening paragraph, state the main idea—express appreciation for the interview or say you're returning a completed (requested) form.

2. In the middle paragraph(s), discuss one or more of the following ideas:
   a. Mention how you *now* feel about the firm or a job with the firm—now that you have visited the plant, listened to the interviewer talk, and toured the facility.
   b. Add new material that might be helpful in determining your qualifications. For instance, if noteworthy, report that you have completed an assignment the interviewer gave you during the interview (such as to read a brochure, see someone, or take a test).
   c. If you think the interviewer questioned one of your qualifications or you think you might have made a negative impression concerning one statement during the interview, include honest, positive facts to rebuild confidence.
   d. Occasionally you can strengthen your presentation by stating (1) your favorable reaction to points covered by the interviewer and (2) highlights of qualifications discussed during the interview.

3. In the last paragraph you can use one or more of the following:
   a. Offer to send additional information upon request.
   b. Thank the interviewer for the interview (if this was not done in the first paragraph).
   c. Say you can come in for another interview.
   d. Indicate hope (or confidence) that your qualifications fit the firm's requirements.
   e. Mention you're looking forward to a favorable decision.
   f. Ask for an opportunity to prove you can help the firm's sales, growth, and so on.

With this organizational plan in mind, study the following two examples of effective follow-up messages. Both applicants were successful in getting the job they sought, though during the interview each appeared to have a shortcoming. In each case the employer stated that the follow-up letter helped greatly.

Message 1 is from a 22-year-old applicant seeking his first career job as a sales representative after college graduation. Notice how convincingly he surmounts what appeared to be a shortcoming by showing that his responsibilities *during* college were equivalent to two years' business experience *after* college.

MESSAGE 1   *A successful after-interview follow-up, to a national industrial firm.*

Dear Mr. Lawrence:

Attention, courtesy

Your interview with me yesterday was both enjoyable and informative. Thank you for your courtesies and the interest you took in my qualifications as a sales representative for your firm.

Interest, useful qualities

During the conversation you mentioned that you were particularly looking for a person who had at least two years' business experience since finishing college. I agree with you that the knack of working with people and the mature outlook gained from practical experience are valuable for a prospective sales representative. These qualities were firmly developed in me during my college years.

Desire, convincing evidence

As my resume shows, to obtain an industrial engineering degree I added an extra year of engineering and business courses to my studies. In various college activities my responsibilities were mainly with people. As publicity manager for College Engineer magazine—after careful planning plus enthusiasm and drive—I increased sales 25% over the previous year. As president of our fraternity, I worked harmoniously with our 80 members and sold the alumni on the support we needed. My part-time and summer jobs during college ranged from clerking in a grocery store to tutoring first-year students. I believe these activities, jobs, and additional studies have given me experience and judgment equivalent to the two years' business experience your firm would like its sales representatives to have.

Action, reader-benefit request

You will find, I believe, that I can develop into one of your top industrial sales representatives, Mr. Lawrence. Will you give me the opportunity to prove this statement?

Message 2 is from a 27-year-old recent accounting graduate applying for an accounting job in a community college. During the interview the college official was concerned whether the applicant—a quiet, soft-spoken person—had adequate qualifications for leadership; she would have to supervise the work of six bookkeepers in the college office. This letter helped her get the job:

MESSAGE 2   *A successful after-interview follow-up, to a college vice president.*

Dear Mr. Willard:

Courtesy, answered request

Your interview with me on April 4 regarding the accounting position in your office was sincerely appreciated. As you requested, I am enclosing the transcript of my grades from the University of [name].

Interest, leadership responsibilities

During my five years at the [name] Company I worked in a lead capacity with many people. The experience I gained would be useful for the job you outlined. For the first two of the five years, I was responsible for quality control in the Pensar division. As one of my duties I supervised 10 employees and trained new people to visually and dimensionally inspect vendor-made parts purchased for use on the program. When I requested night-shift duty so I could carry 10 to 15 credit hours at Mason Junior College, I was given full responsibilities for the inspection duties on that shift, a position I held three years.

Conviction, dependability

Four years of college studies (with no financial help) while holding full- and part-time jobs and raising a family indicate my perseverance. My school and work record of continuous four-year attendance (except for a three-day virus illness last summer) will assure you of my regularity and dependability on the job. We are buying a home in Blanktown and will enter our son in the school system here next fall; so my family is well established here.

Persuasive reader-benefit action request

I believe my education and 10 years of work experience will qualify me to assume the accounting and office responsibilities you pointed out to me. Please let me know your decision. You can depend on me to be a hard-working, mature staff member.

Inquiry about Application Letter and Resume

If you haven't received a response to your written job application within three weeks, you are justified in sending an inquiry. Although it is unlikely your material was lost in the mail, it is possible the receiver misplaced or forgot about it, or did not intend to respond. A well-run organization should acknowledge your material—and if it does not, you have the right to inquire.

This type of follow-up is usually shorter than the one written after the interview. Since many firms keep the written job presentation for six months or longer, all you really need do is give enough identification so that the employer can locate your material. The inquiry should include identification of the job sought, the date of the application letter previously sent, your continuing interest in the job, highlights of the previous application letter, and your telephone number. Avoid repeating information, but enclose an additional copy of your resume in case the previous material was lost. The following are two examples of acceptable inquiries, organized by the direct-request plan:

MESSAGE 3   *Emphasizes identification of applicant's file.*

Dear Ms. Bond:

Inquiry and explanation

On February 10, 199-, I sent you my application letter and resume for an opening in your management training program. Because I'm interested in your firm and its future, I'm inquiring whether you received this material.

Courtesy, action

Please let me know what information you wish about my background. And, of course, I can come for an interview whenever you suggest.

MESSAGE 4   *Includes highlights of the applicant.*

Dear Mr. Norden:

Main idea, reason

Perhaps you will remember I sent you my application for a position in your grain department on March 22. I am primarily interested in cash grain pur-chasing and the use of the futures market to assist in the operations of your company.

The principal points in my letter were that:

Explanation

1. A research project I conducted on the use of the commodity exchanges by members of the state grain industry developed insights that I can use effectively for your company. I am now finish-ing the writing of the results for my master's thesis, also on aspects of the grain industry.
2. My college degree is in business administration, and I plan to receive a master of arts degree in June 199- in marketing.
3. During 18 years on an Oklahoma farm, I became familiar with most of the grains in the grain industry.

Action,
courtesy

> I hope that you can use a person with my back-
> ground. If you wish any further information, I
> will be glad to send it to you.

Other Follow-Up Messages from Applicant to Employer

A job-hunting campaign can include quite a few other types of follow-up messages in addition to those just discussed. The following pages discuss and illustrate some of them.

Answer to a Noncommittal Letter

Assume that you have sent your application letter with resume—maybe even had the interview. Then you receive the following:

> We were pleased to receive your excellent application for
> employment.
>
> We are interested in your capabilities but regret that at
> the present time, we cannot make use of them; with your per-
> mission, however, we will keep your name on file and if any-
> thing should develop in the future, get in touch with you.
>
> Thank you for your interest in our organization.

What should you do? At first you might interpret this message as a routine refusal. However, the employer has said, "with your permission . . . keep on file," and you should assume that the message is sincere and you will definitely be considered when an opening occurs. A short message like the following is a quite satisfactory reply:

MESSAGE 5   *Answers employer's "keep-on-file" letter.*

Dear Mr. Lyons:

Courtesy

> Thank you for reviewing my qualifications for [*type of job*].

Interest
and brief
resale

> Will you please keep my name in your files so that
> you can consider me when a future opening in that
> field takes place? You can count on me to do a thor-
> ough, accurate job if I may join your staff.

Courteous
close

> I like what I read and hear about your organization--
> and hope some day to be part of such a company.

If you receive a message that says essentially what Mr. Lyons wrote but does not ask your permission, a reply is optional.

Reply to Request for Additional Information

Occasionally an employer, interviewer, or school will request additional information about your background. If such a situation arises, analyze your background thoroughly, so that you will include all the important details to back up and strengthen your presentation, with your reader's needs in mind. Then organize and write. You'll probably use an outline like the following:

First paragraph: Attention and courtesy	Thank person for interview and express eagerness to tell about whatever is asked for. Also identify the topic(s) you are discussing.
Middle paragraphs: Interest, desire, conviction	If asked about two qualifications (say, interest in field and interest in company), write separate paragraphs for each. The discussion will be persuasive—quite similar to the middle paragraphs that create desire in the application letter.

Last paragraph:
Courtesy, action
	You might express:
	    Availability for another interview.
	    Any other idea that rounds out and strengthens the message.

The following successful letter was addressed to the director of a law school's admissions office. The applicant was asked to fill out the necessary form and, separately, to tell about her interests in law and give highlights of her background.

MESSAGE 6   *Convincingly answers employer's request regarding law interests and background.*

**Attention,
courtesy**

As you requested, I am returning the completed Form
A and a brief discussion of two areas about which
you queried me: my interest in law and highlights
of my background.

Interest in Law

Before going into my background, I want to explain
why I want a degree in law. The need has been there
since childhood. Unlike most childhood fixations--
teacher, doctor, or dancer--the desire to be a lawyer has stuck with me since the age of 12. More
than a childhood dream is involved though. I feel
that a law degree and the ability to use it embodies
one of the most valuable assets a person can own.

**Interest,
answers to
questions**

To me, law pervades every aspect of our society.
Law is where the action is. It is one of the few
professions that enable a person to be actively involved in forming her culture while at the same time

enabling her to find a highly satisfactory role in
life.

Specifically I plan to concentrate on corporate law
with a later concentration on international legal
business relationships. This area needs good lawyers, and I want to prepare myself to fill that
need.

Background

Following is a brief sketch of my background that
will help you in assessing my ability to study law.
As the enclosed form shows, I was born in Germany
and was reared in South Africa from the age of 3.
In [year] I became a naturalized citizen of the United
States. I am bilingual, speaking and writing both
German and English without accent or faults in com-
position.

Desire

I used my undergraduate years to gain as wide a
knowledge of as many disciplines as I could. My
program emphasized political science, social
sciences, and some humanities, with a later concentration on general business courses. This was, in
my mind, the most useful road toward my eventual
goal.

Conviction

My transcript, which you should have received by
now, shows I spent five years on my bachelor's degree. The extra year was necessitated by a scarcity
of funds in my family. Part- and full-time jobs
have put me through school and have allowed me to
save enough money to attend law school. Although
outside work has detracted from study time, I feel
that the work discipline and the ability to communicate and work with all types of people more than
offset any loss in academic learning.

Action,
courteous
close

Should you need any additional information to aid
you in your decision, please let us know.

Acceptance of Invitation for Interview

Usually this message is conveyed by telephone; interviewers do not expect a
letter. Whether you write or phone, your good-news reply will begin with thanks
and acceptance. For an interview in a distant city, you might mention several
possible times within a certain week when you could make the trip. Then the
employer can choose the most convenient date and hour. In a letter, the last

paragraph should express sincere interest in the forthcoming interview. The following letter is a good example. It answers message 1, page 376, from a personnel services supervisor in a city 1,100 miles from the applicant's campus.

MESSAGE 7   *Accepts interview invitation and suggests dates.*

October 1, 199-

Dear Mr. Taggat:

Courtesy, good news	Thank you for inviting me to visit your office and plant. I very much want to study your organization and operation.
Explanation	Because of class schedules and previous commitments, the best dates are October 12-16, inclusive. Any one or more of these days permit ideal timing for the trip.
Action, courtesy	I'm looking forward to visiting your headquarters and talking with both management members and workers in production.

Follow-Up if No Reply after Interview

If you receive no reply by the promised date, remember it takes time for the employer to interview all applicants, route the qualifications to interested officers in the organization, and make a final choice. However, if you have waited what you consider ample time and also *beyond* the promised date of notification—especially if another firm is waiting for your reply—you might want to write a nonpersuasive inquiry similar to the one that follows.

MESSAGE 8   *Asks preferred firm for reply after interview.*

Courtesy, main idea	Three weeks have passed since I had the opportunity to talk with you about an opening in [*field*]. At that time you said you'd notify me of your decision by [*date*].
Explanation and question	Meanwhile, another firm has offered me a position and has requested a reply within the next 10 days. Before answering them, I would like to know whether you have reached a favorable decision as to my working for your company.
Interest, action	I sincerely prefer your firm, and will very much appreciate your reply before [*date*]. You can reach me by phone weekdays between 9 and 11 a.m. at [*number*] or by letter at the above address.

Request to Delay Decision

Sometimes you may need more time to decide whether to accept a job offer. The following letter (dated October 31) is an applicant's reply to a management trainee job offer (message 5 on page 379) that he received after a plant interview:

MESSAGE 9   *Requests extended time for decision on job offer.*

Dear Ms. Jones:

Reason, questions

Mr. Sawyer sent me a job offer as a management trainee in the industrial engineering department and suggested that if I had any questions I should get in touch with you.

Explanation

Before making a final decision concerning this offer, I will appreciate your allowing me until December 5 for my reply. My reason for requesting this extra time is to permit me to complete my interviews with several other companies that have already invited me to visit their plants.

Interest

Even with these other opportunities, I am at present more interested in [reader's firm] than all the others because many aspects of your company appeal to me. I was particularly impressed by the speed, efficiency, and precision of the manufacturing plant.

Action, courtesy

If you need my decision before the end of November, please let me know as soon as possible so that I will have the opportunity to make my final decision. Also, if you are giving me this extended time, I will be grateful for your message.

Acceptance of Job Offer

When you receive an offer you want to accept, reply soon—perhaps within a week. Begin with the good news—that you accept with pleasure. In this first paragraph identify the job you're accepting; the next paragraph might give details about moving (if distance is involved) and reporting for work. Naturally, what you say in this explanation depends on what the employer has already told you during the interview or in the job-offer letter. End with a rounding-out paragraph indicating you're looking forward to working for the firm. The following are acceptance letters by two applicants. The first example is dated December 1.

MESSAGE 10   *Accepts offer as management trainee and states time schedule.*

Dear Mr. Sawyer:

Good news

I am glad to accept your offer of $[*amount*] a month as a management trainee in your industrial engineering department.

Explanation

Since graduation is Saturday, March 10, 199-, my wife and I plan to leave [*city*] the following Monday, March 12. We should arrive in the [*city*] area the following day--Tuesday, March 13. Allowing a few days to locate living accommodations and to get settled, I should be ready to start work on Monday, March 19. Please let me know if this schedule is satisfactory with you.

Appreciation, courtesy

I am very pleased at becoming a member of your organization. It is with great appreciation that I look forward to what I am sure will be a challenging future with [*name of organization*].

MESSAGE 11   *Accepts employment offer and encloses signed copy.*

Dear Ms. Canavalla:

Good news decision

With pleasure I accept your employment offer. [*Name of firm*] has proved to me how exciting and dynamic the position will be. I look forward to a challenging career.

Compliment, interest

Very significant in making my final decision were the people I met. They were enthusiastic not only for their work, but for the company. That support tells me a great deal.

Action, courtesy

Enclosed is the signed copy of your employment offer. I look forward to further information from you or the Human Resources office.

Resignation from Present Job

Ideally you will have conferred with your present employer some time before accepting the new position. Though you may have orally conveyed the news that you are resigning, the employer may request a letter for company records. It should be dated at least two weeks or more before the effective resignation date, and may be organized by the direct plan, as in the following example dated May 1. (For an indirect-plan resignation, see page 233.)

MESSAGE 12   *Resigns from present position, stating main idea first.*

Main idea

As stated during our recent conference, I have accepted a position in the finance department of International Products in [*city*]. My reporting date will be June 11. Thus, please consider this resignation to be effective June 5.

Helpful promise

In the meantime you can depend on me to give my successor the help needed to ensure an effective transition here. I hope that you and my co-workers will continue to be my personal friends.

Courtesy

Again, thank you for your many kindnesses during the years I have worked in your firm. I wish you the best of good fortune in the years ahead.

Messages to Others Concerned

After you have accepted a new position, inform other employers whom you have interviewed recently. Also notify your campus placement office (or any other agency that helped you) so they will know your decision and suspend their activities regarding your job application. They deserve your thanks and courtesy. Someday you may need them again, so maintain good relations.

Rejection of Job Offer

When you refuse an offer, you're writing a bad-news message. The organizational plan is buffer, explanation, refusal (implied or expressed), and a friendly, positive closing. Even more important than the outline is your attitude toward the company. Remember, this firm seriously considered your qualifications and spent its time and money to bring you to the plant for an interview. If your refusal is discourteous, you leave an unfavorable impression.

In the following examples notice their outline, tactful tone, sincerity, positive approach, and genuine compliment to the firm.

MESSAGE 13   *Declines offer of position in management training program.*

Dear Ms. Olson:

Buffer

Thank you for offering me a position in your management training program.

Explanation, implied refusal

During my job hunting these last few months, I've sent applications to several firms I regard highly--only those I could be happy working for. Fortunately for me, both you and another firm offered me a job. Because my qualifications, interest, and

background fit in more closely with the other job,
I have already mailed my acceptance.

Courtesy

I do appreciate your consideration of my qualifications, the thorough one-day interview at the plant,
and the opportunity to meet all department heads in
production. I'll always think of your organization
as one in which management treats the employees as
a highly prized commodity. Again, thank you for
your consideration. I will always remember it.

MESSAGE 14   *Declines offer of position with promotional opportunities.*

Dear Mr. Rupp:

Buffer

With pleasure I received your offer of a position
with [company]. The future career and promotional
opportunities were well explained by you and others
with whom I interviewed.

**Explanation,
implied
refusal**

Because my work experience in your area of special-
ization was weak, I elected to join another company
where the training program fitted the early stages
of my career.

Courtesy

I personally thank you for your consideration, and
the opportunity to talk with people in other areas.
Your company will be remembered as one of courtesy,
integrity, and an honest desire to communicate with
young people beginning their careers.

EMPLOYER-TO-APPLICANT FOLLOW-UP MESSAGES

You should be able not only to write messages the applicant must send, but
also—since you will be in business someday—to dictate effective messages that
will go to the applicants.[2]

Invitations to Inverviews

Depending on circumstances, there are times when the employer writes directly
to applicants to arrange interviews either at the company offices or plant or on
a college campus near the applicants.

Applicant Invited to the Company for Interview

This message from you the employer is second in importance only to the job
offer itself. Thus you must make the reader feel that you genuinely want a

personal interview. Also clearly get across that you'll help in every way possible. For example, as in message 1, you'll send a round-trip ticket (or a check), reserve a hotel room during the stay if necessary, and reimburse all incidental expenses. In addition ask which dates will be convenient for a visit. Maybe you will make responding easier by enclosing a card.

MESSAGE 1   *Supervisor of personnel services invites applicant to interviews at plant and head office about 1,100 miles from the campus.*

September 25, 199-

Dear Mr. Brown:

Invitation, and expenses to be paid

Following our recent interview on your campus, we invite you to visit [*name of firm*] for interviews at our plant and head office. You will receive the necessary expenses for air travel to [*city*], and return, as well as incidental expenses.

Suggestions for easy action

If you would like to make this visit, please let us know when you can come and we will confirm a mutually agreeable date. A card is enclosed so that you can notify us of your decision. If possible, plan to spend one full day at the plant and office.

Courtesy, further plans

Thank you for the interest you have expressed in [*name of firm*]. Upon confirming an interview date, we will forward both a check covering your travel expenses and details for getting to the plant, and we will also reserve hotel accommodations in [*city*] if you so desire.

After you receive the applicant's acceptance of the invitation, you'll send a reply similar to message 2. You not only enclose a check for travel expenses, but also give all necessary details and indicate interest in the forthcoming visit.

MESSAGE 2   *Reply by certified mail gives details for visit and encloses check.*

October 4, 199-

Dear Mr. Brown:

Best news, date, request

Thank you for informing us of your intended visit to [*firm*] for interviews. The date we have set is October 15. The enclosed check is to cover your plane fare, meals, and miscellaneous expenses. Please retain any receipts for air travel and lodging for our expense account purposes.

We have arranged prepaid hotel accommodations for you for Tuesday, October 14, at the Hilton Plaza

Details

Hotel, [*city*]. You can come to the plant Wednesday morning in a company car which leaves our [*city*] office every morning at 7:10 a.m.

Details

To get this car you should report by 6:50 a.m. to the lounge, Room 1420, Industrial Building, [*address, city*]. Because of the early hour, you can plan on having breakfast when you reach the plant. You will be able to return to headquarters from the plant in the same manner, leaving there at 2:30 p.m. and arriving in [*city*] at about 3:10 p.m. for interviews here.

Application, action

The interest you have expressed in [*name of firm*] is appreciated, and we look forward to your visit on the 15th.

Employer Announces Impending Visit on Campus

Because some schools send resume booklets of all their graduates in advance to prospective interviewing companies, you may wish to invite certain students to an interview when you arrive on campus. Or, you may ask certain applicants to interview a second time when you are on campus or off campus. The following letter tells of an impending visit:

MESSAGE 3   *Invites applicant to a second interview on campus.*

Dear Ms. Webster:

Courtesy

Thank you for coming to the placement office at the University of [*state*] for an interview with [*name of firm*]. Since you and I had our visit, I have interviewed on approximately 20 other college campuses and talked to approximately 200 students.

Encouraging news

This has been my first opportunity to review the resumes of these students, from which I have selected approximately 15% suggesting further interviews. Mary, you are included in this group of students whose scholastic ability, personality, grooming, motivation, and overall personality place them in the upper 15% of those to whom I have talked.

Details, spring interview

Our spring interview date at the university has not been definitely established at this time, but as soon as it has been, I will drop you a note; if you are interested, arrange to be placed on our spring interview schedule in the placement office. You may recall that we select somewhere between 10 and 15 young men and women each year to go through our

Management and Underwriter Training Program, which runs from the third week in June until the middle or end of September.

Compliment, courtesy, action

Again we commend you for the fine scholastic record you have been able to maintain while being responsible for 100% of your college expenses. We look forward to visiting with you again in the spring, for I feel certain we both have much to offer each other by way of ability and opportunity for growth.

Follow-Up Messages from Employer after Interview

As a personnel representative or officer concerned with employing applicants, you will have a variety of other letters to write after interviews with applicants. The following pages include suggestions for such messages.

Request for Further Information

During the interview, you may have questions about the applicant's enthusiasm or sincerity toward the company or toward his or her chosen field. Or you might simply need additional information, as the letter below illustrates:

MESSAGE 4   *Requests a letter and return of enclosed application form.*

Dear Mr. Lund:

Comment, courtesy

Recently we had the pleasure of talking with you in connection with our college recruiting activity. Thank you for the time you gave us.

Interest, request

Our staff has had the opportunity to review your qualifications, and we are interested in learning more about you. Accordingly, will you please complete the enclosed application and return it to me by [*date*]. Also explain in an attached letter your interest in [*name of field*]. After this information reaches us, we will get in touch with you on a more specific basis.

Courtesy, action

Thank you for your interest in [*name of firm*]; we look forward to hearing from you in the near future.

Offer of a Job

When you send a job offer, begin by telling the good news in a friendly manner. In the first paragraph also identify the job and state the salary (usually on a monthly basis). In the following paragraphs, try to anticipate any questions the applicant might have—such as what moving expenses the firm will pay—and answer them. (Naturally you won't go into detail about expenses until she or he accepts.) Also, leave the door open for the applicant to ask questions before making a decision. Be sure your tone is appropriate—convey that you're interested in the applicant and sincerely want him or her to join your organization. The following message is from a general superintendent after a plant interview:

MESSAGE 5   *Offers employment as management trainee, and provision for moving costs.*

Dear Mr. Brown:

Good news

We are pleased to offer you employment as a management trainee, assigned to our industrial engineering department. Your starting salary for this position would be $[amount] a month.

Details

Should you decide to join our organization, we will provide the cost of travel for you and your wife and move your household effects.

Courtesy, invited easy action

Thank you for the interest you expressed when you visited the plant. We hope you will decide to make your career with us. If you have any questions concerning our offer or employment in general, please call Ms. M. A. Jones in the personnel office. Her telephone number is (123) 555-4889. We look forward to your reply.

Grant of a Time Extension

If you believe an applicant has a sound reason for requesting more time to consider an offer (as in the message on page 372), you may decide to grant the extension. Usually this matter is discussed conveniently by telephone. If you write a letter, grant the request in the first paragraph, explain (and in general terms set) the cutoff date, express interest in the applicant, and end on a friendly, positive note.

MESSAGE 6   *Grants one-month time extension for job-offer decision.*

November 7, 199-

Dear Mr. Brown:

Good news

As you requested, we will be glad to allow you additional time to decide whether you want to accept our previous offer to work for [firm].

We realize that you have many things to consider in reaching a final decision regarding employment.

Details

Therefore, we want to allow you as much time as possible for your evaluation of all opportunities.

I will appreciate knowing your decision as soon as possible. However, inasmuch as you will not be available until March 199-, your advising us a month from now will be quite acceptable.

Interest

We feel that you are well-qualified for the career employment opportunities available within [firm] and hope you will decide to make your career with us.

Action

If I can be of any further assistance to you, please write or telephone me. My number is (123) 555-4889.

Reply to Applicant's Acceptance

When the applicant has accepted your job offer, you will need to remember the value of public relations. The applicant doesn't expect a long letter, but a helpful you-attitude is always appreciated (see the following message). Sometimes an encouraging sentence can be included—*if true*—regarding the applicant's potential for broader responsibilities in line with the company's expected future growth.

MESSAGE 7   *Acknowledges applicant's acceptance of job offer.*

December 8, 199-

Dear Mr. Brown:

Pleasant comment

We are very pleased that you are coming with us, and we look forward to seeing you on March 19.

Plans for February

You will receive travel expenses in February, and we will contact you at that time regarding moving arrangements.

Action, courtesy

Please call on us if we can be of any assistance before that time.

Message Conveying Decision Not to Hire

The tone of your refusal is very important, for you want to avoid leaving the applicant with a lasting negative reaction to your firm. The people being turned down don't want weak excuses or outright false statements. They want honesty—but not discourteous, blunt, or crude expressions. They will appreciate sincere, complimentary remarks about qualifications, consideration of background, and proper attitude.

In the first paragraph state a buffer—show appreciation of their interest in the firm or the opportunity to talk with them, or thank them for coming in for interviews. In the second paragraph, explain. First say something neutral (for example, that you have reviewed the qualifications), and then refuse in as positive a way as possible. One of the best explanations seems to be that several other candidates have overall qualifications more similar to your requirements. Avoid negatives (*unable, regret, cannot, not suited, do not feel, do not have*). In the last paragraph, wish the applicants success, tell them you enjoyed talking with them, and thank them for their interest in the firm. Obviously you won't repeat in this paragraph what you said in the first.

Below is an effective refusal that follows the outline just discussed:

MESSAGE 8   *Informs applicant why other candidates are more qualified for the position.*

Dear Ms. Cotter:

Buffer, courtesy
Thank you very much for taking your time to be interviewed and tested for the position of systems engineering representative with [*firm*].

Details, polite rejection
We have reviewed your educational background, work experience, and aptitude tests, along with those of others we are considering for employment. Our analysis indicates that there are several other candidates whose overall qualifications are more in line with our requirements.

Courtesy
We enjoyed having the opportunity to interview you and sincerely appreciate your interest in [*firm*]. Please accept our best wishes for success in your chosen career.

SUMMARY

After you have mailed your job application letter and resume, you and the employer will usually communicate in other messages—oral and written. The interview is your most important oral message for getting the desired job. Thoughtful preparation is essential. Analyze the company, the job requirements, and your qualifications. Also plan answers to various questions the interviewer may ask you, and consider questions you might ask the interviewer. Check meeting place, time, and other details.

How you handle the interviewer's questions is important. Before the interview try to rehearse commonly asked questions in a mock interview. "Bridge" tactfully to your information on confrontational questions.

During the interview, your appearance, enthusiasm, sincerity, replies, and general conduct are important.

Your first written message after the interview is the thank-you letter, with perhaps some additional information and your feeling toward the company. In other follow-up employment messages you may need to request a time extension, ask that your name be kept on an active list, answer the employer's questions about specific details, decline or accept an offer, and also resign your present job.

As a personnel manager or interviewer, your message to applicants will include invitations to interviews, comments afterwards, requests for further information, grants or refusals for time extensions, offers of jobs, and tactful rejections.

EXERCISES AND PROBLEMS

1. *Evaluations:* Each of the following rejection statements was taken from actual rejection letters. Which is the most satisfactory? Keep in mind criteria such as adequate explanation of the reasons for the rejection, tone or warmth of the response, and wishes of future success for the applicant in his or her career.

   a. After reviewing your resume, we have found that while your credentials are impressive, we do not believe it would be mutually beneficial to pursue further discussions.

   b. We regret that it would not be mutually beneficial for us to continue the interviewing process any further. Please be assured that our decision in no way questions your ability to succeed in sales or sales management.

   c. I am sorry to say that we do not have any appropriate openings this summer, but appreciate your expression of interest in the firm.

   d. We have made our decisions on summer interns and, unfortunately, are unable to offer you a position. However, your credentials are excellent for future consideration. I also have two leads with clients for summer internship opportunities. If you are interested, please contact me as soon as possible.

   e. We take this opportunity to say thank you for your application. At the moment we are not hiring new personnel.

2. *Rejection letter from employer to applicant:* Although you have been with the Capital R. Corporation for two years, they have asked you to return to your alma mater to recruit persons for a position in accounting. You talked to 13 students, all of whom were qualified.

   While 12 of the students were marginally acceptable, they have already received their rejection letters. The thirteenth candidate's resume lies before you (the resume is that of David Tucko, Figure 12-2, page 336) along with your notes based on the interview. These notes include the following:

```
--Friendly and personable
--Dark hair, maroon jacket
--Excellent communication skills
--Does he really want accounting?
--May not wish to move to [city]
--Ambivalent regarding future
--A maybe; overqualified?
```

Your task is to write a rejection letter to David Tucko based on his resume and your notes.

3. ***Research about one large firm before interview:*** Assume you have written to a large corporation the application letter assigned in Exercise 4, page 350. Today you received an invitation for an interview next Friday (in your city). To prepare well for this interview, study a copy of the firm's recent annual report. List information about its products, personnel, and other items of interest to help you answer pertinent questions. (See the questions on pages 359–362.)

4. ***Follow-up letter(s) after your interview:*** Assume you sent your application letter and resume to the personnel manager of a particular firm; shortly afterward you received an invitation to come to her office for an interview. She is located in your city. During the 30-minute interview, she asked you questions about your qualifications and explained company policy, beginning salary, and other pertinent information. Write a follow-up for one (or each) of these possible outcomes:

   a. At the end of the interview she told you she'd notify you of her decision.
   b. At the end of the interview she asked you to write her about why you want to get into the type of work you're applying for.
   c. At the end of the interview she asked you to visit the manager in one of the organization's several local retail stores. While there, you should interview the manager and other employees to find out whether you want to make a career in this type of work. Then you're to write the personnel manager if you're still interested. Assume you are favorably impressed.

5. ***Inquiry about application letter and resume:*** Assume you mailed your application three weeks ago but have received no reply. Send an inquiry to the firm.

6. ***Your acceptance and refusal letters:*** Assume you received two offers for career jobs.

   a. Write the acceptance message.
   b. Write the refusal message.

7. *Employer's refusal letter to a job applicant:* As the employer, you must refuse a graduating senior the job she applied for, because her qualifications aren't as good as those of the others you interviewed. Furthermore, one reference indicated this person is a troublemaker. Write the refusal message.

8. *Letter requesting different date for interview:* As a graduating senior, you received the following letter from Mr. Alexander, recruiting coordinator. Unfortunately you can't see the representative on January 30. However, you're very much interested in working for this company. Write the appropriate message to the coordinator, making up any facts you wish, so long as you don't alter the assignment.

> Dear [*your name*]:
>
> Please forgive my resorting to a form letter to reach you--but time is getting short and I want to let you know that one of our executives plans to visit your campus soon.
>
> His primary purpose will be to interview [*year*] graduates for career employment with our newly merged organization. As you might imagine, we have an even greater horizon now to present to promising young people like yourself. Moreover, we have a number of good summer job opportunities for undergraduates this year.
>
> In any case, I have been alerted to your fine summer employment record with us and assure you our interest in you continues strong. Accordingly, if you want to explore a position with us, I urge that you sign up to see our corporate recruiting representative when he visits your placement office on January 30.
>
> If you cannot make that date, please drop me a line and let's try to arrange for you to visit some nearby branch office. I am enclosing a return envelope for that purpose, together with a copy of our annual report and some other literature for your reference.
>
> Meanwhile, accept our sincere best wishes on your forthcoming graduation.

9. *Reply to invitation for interview in head office:* Assume that three weeks ago you had an interview on campus with a representative of a national company whose head offices are 1,000 miles from you. Before parting, the interviewer asked if you would be willing to come to the head offices someday for further interviews, and you had replied that you would

be glad to. Today you receive the following letter, dated February 2, from the personnel manager:

Dear [*your name*]:

It is with a great deal of pleasure that I confirm our invitation to visit us in [*city*] in order to pursue further the possibility of your joining [*firm name*]. We have arranged a schedule for which we would like to have you arrive at our executive offices at [*address*] at 1:30 p.m. on Monday, April 10; be prepared to stay with us through the following day.

As I pointed out during our brief meeting, at [*firm name*] we feel strongly that the matter of selection is a "two-way street," and we look forward to this chance of making you better acquainted with us and the opportunity we offer. Also, of course, we would like to review your qualifications more fully.

I know you have already accepted our invitation for further interviews, but we would appreciate a letter indicating that you still plan to come. It might be a good idea if you were to make airline reservations right away and let me know the flight numbers. I will then reciprocate by sending you an open ticket drawn on the airline you designate.

We will make a hotel reservation for you for the night of April 10, and for the night of the 9th too if schedules require you to come the night before. As a last point, please keep track of the incidental expenses incurred by your trip so that we may reimburse you for them.

That would seem to cover it, [*your name*], but please let me know if you have any questions. I'll be looking forward to seeing you again.

Write the complete, thoughtful, friendly letter this invitation calls for. Before you do so, however, consider the kind of airline passage you should reserve. Should it be first-class? Coach? Economy? Why? Why do you think the employer leaves the choice up to you? You might also discuss in class the kinds of incidental expenses that will be appropriate for you to include in your later request for reimbursement—after this second interview.

10. ***Practice interviews with classmates:*** If you and your classmates would like practice interviews, try this assignment. For one interview half the class members will volunteer to be job applicants and the other half will

be employers' personnel representatives. For a second interview all students will switch roles.

Each interview will be based on an application letter and resume the applicant has written (as, for example, Exercise 4, page 350) and, presumably, mailed. In class, students will merely exchange these papers.

Each interview should preferably be about 20 to 30 minutes in length between students who do not know each other well. Both the applicant and the assumed personnel representative (or higher executive, if appropriate) should make all necessary preparations before the interviews. The applicant (interviewee) should review pages 358–362. The employer's representative (interviewer) will find helpful suggestions in Chapter 24, regarding how to conduct an interview. He or she will, of course, also study the applicant's resume before conducting the interview and know something about the company the interviewer represents.

Collection Messages— Written and Oral

C ollecting past-due accounts is an important part of any business. After a borrower gets a loan or a customer purchases something on credit, payment should be made within a specified period—according to the terms of the agreement. When obligations are not paid on time, collection messages become necessary. Reasons customers are not paying are usually one or more of the following: they've overlooked the invoice or statement; they're dissatisfied with the merchandise, delivery, billing, or handling of a complaint; they're temporarily short of funds; they're chronic debtors.

Collection messages have an important, twofold purpose: to *get the money* and to *keep customer goodwill*. These messages may be delivered by mail, phone, personal visit, telegram, or Mailgram. To carry out the twofold function requires an understanding attitude and effective messages appropriately planned and timed throughout the collection stages. Most collection procedures have similar basic characteristics whether the messages concern retail credit (to customers) or mercantile credit (to business firms), and whether they are for open account or installment credit. For various reasons, they also have differences. This chapter discusses the right attitude for effective collections, collection stages, telephone collection procedures, and some prohibited collection practices.

RIGHT ATTITUDE FOR EFFECTIVE COLLECTIONS

A debtor may be touchy about how and when the creditor asks for payment even though it is for a legitimate debt. The longer past due the payment is, the more difficult the situation becomes. The right collection attitude for a creditor requires an understanding of human nature, careful choice of collection appeals, and knowledge of both the debtor's past credit record and regulations affecting collection policies.

Understanding of Human Nature

When you send a collection message, remember you are communicating with a person, not with an account number. Each person has a different mental filter, with attitudes, prejudices, perceptions, and problems. All human beings have feelings and react negatively to offensive expressions, sarcasm, anger, and insults just as quickly as you do.

The fairest assumption to make is that your customers honestly want to pay as agreed. The majority of customers will pay when reminded. However, conditions change, and with them the customers' ability and willingness to pay may also change. Some debtors conscientiously promptly write or telephone their reasons for lateness and explain when they will make their next payments. Some remain silent, and a few are repeatedly uncooperative.

A tactful, courteous attitude coupled with firmness and patience always collects more money in the long run than impolitely worded demands. As a collection manager you need to decide carefully *how* and *when* to contact customers about past-due accounts. If you're too lenient, some individuals may pay other bills that seem more pressing and you won't get the money coming to you. However, if you threaten or harass customers, they may not pay either.

Tactless expressions like *you are delinquent* should not be used. Instead, phrases such as *two payments are past due* or *the delinquency of this account* are less offensive because they are impersonal. All the C qualities (Chapters 3 and 4)—especially consideration, concreteness, and courtesy—are important for effective collection messages. Also, the suggestions for proper attitude in bad-news letters (pages 208 and 209) apply to collections.

Choice of Collection Appeals

As you will read later in the discussion on Collection Stages, those collection messages that must be *persuasive* should include well-chosen appeals. These choices relate closely to the debtor's payment record. Both positive and negative appeals are effective in persuasive collection messages.

Positive Appeals—Cooperation, Fair Play, Pride

Cooperation, the mildest appeal, caters to one's desire to be considerate of others—in this case, loyal to the creditor who has been courteous and friendly in asking for what is rightly due. (This should not, however, be a whining "poor me" appeal.)

The *fair-play* appeal is usually developed by reviewing the facts—how long a payment has been past due—and showing that since the creditor has carried out his or her part of an agreement, the debtor (customer)—to be fair and honest—should keep his or her promise and pay. Resale on items bought is also effective.

The *pride appeal* should be subtle, not a high-pressure tactic. You can develop this appeal in various ways by referring to what you know the customer is proud of—a good credit rating, (sometimes) the items bought, or the respect and good reputation enjoyed in the community.

Negative Appeals—Self-Interest and Fear

Individuals who care little about cooperation or fair play may be motivated to pay when you show what they will gain by doing so and will lose by further delay.

The *self-interest* appeal usually has two objectives—to show the value of the present advantages the customers have and to convince them that further delay may cause them to lose the advantages.

Fear appeal, instead of stressing the value of keeping various benefits, stresses the loss of such benefits (good credit standing or possessions). The past-due account will be reported to the credit bureau and turned over to an attorney or collection agency, or be taken to court as a lawsuit, which will be extra expense for the debtor.

You can use effectively one or a combination of these appeals in a persuasive message. Your choice of appeals is influenced by the debtor's payment record, your knowledge of collection policies, and the message's place in the collection stage.

Knowledge of Collection Policies and Laws

Besides understanding human nature and choosing collection appeals carefully after considering the debtor's past credit record, you and your assistants need also to know your firm's collection policies and government regulations. They may relate to various time limits on installment or mortgage late payments, foreclosures, and procedures regarding consumer credit and collections.

An effective collection policy necessitates bringing the debt to the debtor's attention *promptly* and *regularly*, with *increasing firmness* as the past-due period lengthens. Just how soon after payment due date the messages should be sent, and what you say in these messages, varies also according to the type of credit account, the particular debtor's situation, your firm's collection policies, and various legal aspects (see Chapter 5, pages 110 to 111). These factors also influence the time interval between collection messages and overall length of the collection process, as is discussed later in this chapter.

To summarize, the right attitude for collection messages requires tact, courtesy, consideration, fairness, firmness, and a positive viewpoint. It requires understanding of human nature, knowledge of collection appeals and the customer's past payment record, plus adherence to your firm's collection policies and government regulations.

COLLECTION STAGES

The first notification the customer receives after purchasing on credit or borrowing money on a loan is a statement (bill) or invoice showing the amount owed. This notification usually lists the transactions for the time period involved and states the terms and date of payment.

If the customer does not pay by the due date, you begin to send a series of messages called a *collection series*. Though the length, content, and collection methods of a collection series may vary according to circumstances, a well-planned series usually has three stages. The messages in each stage vary in number but usually follow a somewhat typical organizational plan and general assumption.

1. *Reminder* stage	Plan:	Routine direct request
	Assumption:	Oversight or minor problem
	Number:	Varies from 1 to 5 or 6
	Appeals:	None, usually
2. *Discussion* stage	Plan:	Persuasive request (modified)
	Assumption:	Something unusual happened
	Number:	Varies from 2 to 5 or more
	Appeals:	Positive
3. *Urgency* stage	Plan:	Persuasive request (modified)
	Assumption:	Debtor may need to be scared into paying
	Number:	Usually 1 or 2
	Appeals:	Negative; sometimes also positive

Regardless of stage in the collection procedure or other differences, *all collection messages should make clear two facts—the amount due and the account number*. These two facts are of course always on the printed statement. In the letter they may be in a subject line, or between the date and inside address, or under the reference initials, or within the body of the letter. (To save space in this chapter, only the body of each letter is shown. Assume that the amount due and the account number are definitely in one of the other named parts if not in the letter example.)

Also, an easy-action postpaid envelope is appreciated and often speeds the reply.

Reminder Stage

Messages in the reminder stage aim to jog the customer's memory. They are direct requests, ranging in number from one to five or six. You first present the *main question or subject*, then *explain* (when necessary), and end the message *by requesting action*. You don't attempt to persuade or to use any appeals. Although some reminders—especially those sent to installment credit and the routinely slow-paying customers—might have a personalized inside address, generally they are obvious processed forms to avoid any suggestion that you are questioning the customer's integrity or ability to pay. They may be one or more standard statements (usually not itemized), computerized card-size messages, or an obvious form letter on company letterhead stationery.

Some companies use the telephone first, calling if a monthly payment is even one week late. After the first mailed statement or call, statements might include messages on colorful stickers like the following three. They can be purchased in quantities from a printer.

Below are examples of a computerized message and a short letter reminder that is an obviously processed form on the firm's letterhead.

REMINDER 1   *A computerized form 3¾ by 6½ inches in size on green pastel paper. A large department store sends it to a customer along with a second statement (and sometimes a leaflet advertising new merchandise items—for sales promotion).*

```
Customers say they appreciate being reminded when their ac-
counts are a little overdue.

So, we trust you will accept this reminder in the friendly
spirit with which it is intended.

If our letters happen to cross and your check arrives in the
next mail, please disregard this notice and accept our
thanks for your payment.
```

REMINDER 2   *A short form letter request from an oil company to a credit card customer who had previously received a statement and a form-notice reminder.*

```
                    Dear Customer:
```

Main idea and amount due	```It's easy to misplace statements and overlook form notices. That's why we're sending this let-ter to remind you of your balance amounting to $[amount].```
Action	```Your account [number] is somewhat past due, and we would appreciate your sending us a check in the next few days.```

Humor, witty short poems, anecdotes, and pictures that relate to the creditor's business or products can be quite effective—if they are used in the reminder stage—for small debts. Various humorous reminders can be purchased or specially designed. Good judgment and originality are necessary, of course, for appropriate humorous reminders. Consider seriously how the customer who owes money might react to the humor.

Discussion Stage

If you receive no response after the routine-request reminders you sent to the customer, you progress into discussion-stage messages that are *persuasive* requests. In this stage you usually personalize your messages by using an inside address and a salutation with the customer's name. You assume that something unusual has happened. For some reason unknown to you the customer cannot or does not want to pay. (Do *not* revert again to the "oversight" assumption used in the reminder stage.) *Your purpose now is to get the debtor to send the payment or at least an explanation*—if there is a reason for not paying.[1] Then you may be able to make mutually satisfactory alternative payment arrangements.

Depending on the type of debtor and account, discussion messages range in number from two to five or more. To get the customer to read your message, you will need to attract attention in the first paragraph. You try now to begin with a reader-interest theme—something beneficial, pleasant, interesting, or important to the reader.

Your paragraphs showing desire and conviction may include facts, figures, and reasons why the debtor will benefit by doing as requested. Well-chosen *appeals* (see pages 389 and 390) will help convince the customer and stimulate a desire to do what is right. Usually your first message is an inquiry, asking if something is wrong and inviting the customer to send either an explanation or a check; the positive "cooperation" appeal may be effective. Successive messages become progressively stronger, ending with a hint of negative appeal in the last discussion message. You may also include more than one appeal in any message.

Some small business and professional firms that have no collection department may depend heavily on using the telephone. Or they may continue their collection efforts by merely attaching colorful discussion-stage stickers on their monthly statements that show the amount due and the account number. Stickers like those shown below can be useful in the early part of the discussion stage.

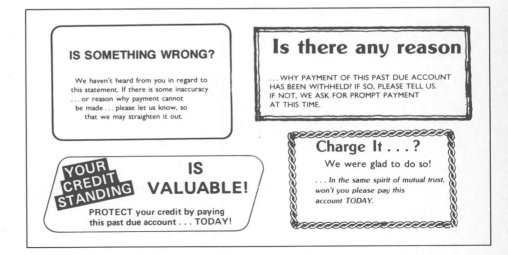

For more persuasive requests it is better to write personalized letters. If necessary, they can be essentially form messages—individually typed by computer or electronic typewriters—identical for many customers but personalized by insertions of the amount due and other pertinent information, as in letter 1. Notice how skillfully this letter avoids suggesting a negative idea about the reason for nonpayment. It does *not* ask if something is wrong with the store's merchandise or service or billing; yet if any of these should happen to be problems, the customer is free to mention them and thus help to "expedite any possible adjustment." Easy action is provided by lines at the bottom for the customer's reply and by an enclosed envelope.

LETTER 1   *A tactful, persuasive, personalized form letter from a department store to a usually promptly paying customer.*

> `Dear` [*Mr., Mrs., Ms., name*]

Attention: **compliment**	`The privilege of serving you is certainly our pleasure. For this, we extend our sincere thanks.`
Appeal: **cooperation**	`You have always been cooperative in the past by keeping your account paid on time according to your credit agreement. As we have received no remittance from you for over three months, we wonder if you have a question concerning the balance.`
Request for reason or check **Easy action**	`Whatever information you request will receive our prompt attention, as we want to expedite any possible adjustment. A note at the bottom of this letter will do. Then just mail it--or your check for $`[*amount*]`--in the enclosed envelope.`
Goodwill	`Your cooperation will be greatly appreciated.`

In letter 2 a wholesaler includes several appeals to the mercantile customer. By reviewing the facts about the overdue account and mentioning the high-quality merchandise plus a willingness to help, the writer makes a fair-play appeal. In addition, the compliments on the dealer's good payment record and the reiteration of the value of a favorable credit rating develop both pride and self-interest appeals.

LETTER 2   *Wholesaler's effective personalized letter to a mercantile customer.*

Attention: **agreeable** **comment**	`It would be nice if we could get together in person to talk over your overdue account, but the demands of our business and the distance make this impossible.`

Facts; compliment	Your account is 80 days past the final due date on our terms of 2/10, net 30. This is exceptional, considering your past prompt payment record with us, and we would like to know what is wrong.
Pride, self-interest appeals	You have worked many years to establish your favorable credit rating, Mr. Jones. It allows you to stock high-quality furniture such as the Allwood chairs when you need them and even take advantage of a discount if payment is made within 10 days. You can have an adequate supply of merchandise on hand at all times, without maintaining a large amount of cash for working capital. Your credit rating not only makes conducting your business easier but also allows you to establish yourself with new suppliers quickly and easily.
Fairness appeal	Is there anything we can do to help you overcome a difficulty? We want to be fair with you. I'm sure we can work out some kind of a plan for payment that will be compatible with your situation. Of course, the most satisfactory solution would be a full payment of the $629.57 in the return mail. If you cannot manage this, then send us a frank explanation of the problem you are facing and we will see what plan we can come up with to clear your account.
Easy action, with suggested time	The enclosed envelope is addressed to come directly to my desk unopened, Mr. Jones. I look forward to seeing it again next week with your check for the full $629.57 inside. If this is not possible, then use the envelope to send me a full explanation of your situation so that we can help you find a solution.

The writer of the next letter uses the positive pride and self-interest appeals plus the negative appeal of loss of comforts and advantages. Even though this borrower owes three payments, the letter (from a bank's lending officer) avoids a scolding tone and tries to keep the customer sold on the values of home ownership.

LETTER 3 *Bank officer's helpful, persuasive request to a home-loan borrower.*

Attention: pride appeal	You have probably often heard the statement "There's no place like home."

Appeals to self- and family interests	You and your spouse made a wise decision when you invested in your present four-bedroom home. Close to schools, your church, and stores, it has the ideal location for your growing family. Your loan department person- nel here at [*name of bank*] were glad to help you with financing by extending you the loan you needed seven years ago.
Comfort, security	So that you can continue to enjoy the comfort and security of owning this home, it is impor- tant that you keep up your payments on your loan. Four messages have been mailed to you about the three payments that are now past due:

May 10	$275.00
June 10	275.00
July 10	275.00
Late charges	35.24
Total	$860.24

Easy-to-read facts

Economic self- interest and risk-of-loss appeals	It is easy to become so accustomed to a privi- lege that we take it for granted. You were fortunate to buy when you did, for today the same kind of home--even without the playroom and patio you have--would cost you at least $9,000 more, at a higher interest rate. You'll agree you can't afford to risk losing the comforts and advantages you now enjoy.
Action	So please send your check for $860.24 today, or call me at [*number*] so we can discuss a sat- isfactory solution.

In any business you may find some customers who are repeatedly late in paying their bills. To such persons, who have in previous delinquencies received a variety of detailed letters from you (with inquiries and positive appeals), you may wish to concentrate on a negative appeal. The following letter emphasizes what the customer with a poor credit rating will experience.

LETTER 4   *Persuasive request with strong fear appeal to repeatedly late payer.*

Attention	How valuable is your credit rating to you?
Positive self-interest appeal	If you possess a good rating, you are able to buy on a charge basis whenever necessary. You can buy quality, expensive items without paying the entire cost in cash at time of

purchase. Also, if an emergency arises,
your credit will be helpful.

Negative self-interest appeal

However, if your record in various places
shows you are a poor credit risk, this valuable possession of credit will be lost. You
are likely to be subjected to the unpleas-
antness of drastic collection measures. In
addition, your credit reputation will follow
you wherever you go. It will take years to
restore a good rating. You may be deprived
of items you would like to purchase, because
of the necessity of paying cash.

These are facts. We mention them only so
that you will not take lightly the possible
loss of your credit that may follow unless
your account with us is paid.

Action

It is still possible to salvage your credit
reputation. Please use the enclosed envelope to mail your check for $[*amount*] today
in payment of this account, which has been
overdue since [*date*]. If you cannot pay it all
immediately, you will find us willing to
discuss a definite arrangement to take care
of it. Please call me at [*number*].

For chronic "delinquents" you might omit the offer (in the last paragraph) to discuss a payment arrangement and simply ask for full payment.

Urgency Stage

During the reminder and discussion stages most messages may have been signed by someone in the credit or collection department. In the urgency stage—for greater impact on the past-due customer—messages may be signed by a higher executive, such as a vice president or even the president, in some firms.

These messages follow the persuasive-request plan and use the strongest negative appeal—fear. In addition, it is often desirable to include at least one positive appeal—giving the debtor a chance to avoid the drastic action and extra costs—before the account is turned over to a collection agency or lawyer or the merchandise is repossessed. The action request is firm and definite about the amount the debtor must send and the office to which it should be sent.

As the following examples illustrate, you can use one or two messages in the urgency stage. If two, the first one doesn't set a date for the drastic action, but the final message *always* sets the date.

EXAMPLE 1   *First of two messages in the urgency state.*

Fairness; review
of facts

The time has come when we must write the kind
of letter we dislike very much. In previous
letters we urged you to pay your long-overdue
bill, which is now $365.70. But we have re-
ceived no replies to any of our requests.

Fear; self-interest;
fairness

Must we now turn your account over to our
attorney for collection? A lawsuit would require you to pay not only the bill but also
the court costs. We don't want to do this
without giving you one last chance to write
and let us know your side of the story.

Self-interest;
reader benefit

We have been good business friends for many
years, [name]. Please don't make it necessary
for us to end our friendship in such an unpleasant way. Write us immediately--or better
still, send us your check to pay this debt,
now 115 days past due. But do it today,
please!

If you are using only one letter in this collection stage, you can use example 1, adding the following paragraph before the final one:

For that reason we will delay action for six days--until
July 22--before turning your account over to Smith, Smythe,
and Smothers.

If you feel that in the discussion-stage messages you have given the debtor sufficient time to "discuss or pay" (especially when dealing with chronic late-payers), you might use a telegram or Mailgram as the first message in the urgency stage. According to Western Union, companies using Mailgrams report collection efficiency improvement of up to 70 percent.[2] You can, of course, send any length of message you wish. (For methods of sending mailgrams see page 810.) Here are two short messages that have shock value:

EXAMPLE 2   *Mailgrams as the first of two messages in the urgency stage—especially for chronic late-payers.*

a. YOUR ACCOUNT #[number] WILL BE REFERRED TO AN OUTSIDE COL-
    LECTION AGENCY. ONLY YOUR REMITTANCE FOR $[amount] WILL
    STOP FORMAL CREDIT ACTION. SEND IT TODAY. TO: [address].

b. IMPORTANT YOU CALL COLLECT IMMEDIATELY [phone number] BE-
    TWEEN 8AM AND 4PM CENTRAL STANDARD TIME CONCERNING YOUR

```
CREDIT CARD ACCOUNT [number].  PLEASE TELL THE OPERATOR YOU
RECEIVED THIS MESSAGE.
```

EXAMPLE 3   *Final letter that sets a date. (Letter is signed by the collection manager or a vice president.)*

```
Your account has just been referred to me, marked for
"final action."

Because it is the policy of this company that every contact
with our customers shall be one of courteous interest in
their behalf, I am writing you this letter as a last appeal
that you mail us your check for $623.02, or call personally
to see us.  I have withheld any action on your account and
feel sure we can work out some mutually satisfactory ar-
rangement for settlement.

The record of your account will be held on my desk for 10
days.  Please send the entire balance due.  Unless I hear
from you by June 25, I shall have no alternative but to as-
sign your account for collection.  I anticipate you will not
force me to take a step that would have such a serious ef-
fect on your credit reputation.
```

Some firms collect almost entirely by Mailgrams, using discussion-stage as well as urgency-stage messages. If you wish, you can store your collection-letter formats on a Western Union computer, and file with that company the names and addresses of customers. Then you simply direct Western Union to send, for example, "format 31" to customers 10 through 50 and indicate amounts due. Each debtor gets a personally addressed Mailgram. A lending officer, for instance, might send a message similar to Example 4, which includes her or his name and "Assistant Cashier" at the end.[3]

EXAMPLE 4   *Mailgram that sets a final date for payment of overdue installments.*

```
REPEATED REQUESTS HAVE BEEN MADE FOR PAST-DUE PAYMENTS ON
YOUR LOAN AT OUR OFFICE.  YOUR MANNER OF REPAYMENT IS UN-
SATISFACTORY AND WILL NO LONGER BE TOLERATED.

WE MUST RECEIVE YOUR OCTOBER AND NOVEMBER INSTALLMENTS IN-
CLUDING LATE CHARGES AND SERVICE FEES NO LATER THAN NOVEMBER
25.  FAILURE TO MEET THIS REQUEST WILL FORCE US TO TAKE
WHATEVER STEPS ARE NECESSARY TO PROTECT THE BANK'S INTEREST.
```

PLEASE MAIL YOUR REMITTANCE FOR $[*amount*] **TO** [*bank name, P.O. box number, city, state, ZIP*].

EXAMPLE 5 *Final message that sets a date. This form goes to customers who live within the specific credit bureau's jurisdiction.*

No. 1982915

Please Read This Carefully

_____ 199 _____

To: _____

_____
Address   City   State

It is the purpose of this notice to inform you, as a matter of courtesy, of our

intention to assign your account to the **COLLECTION DEPT.,**   **(NAME) CREDIT SERVICES, INC.**

for collection unless your remittance is in our hands on or before _____ 199 _____

This can be avoided if **PAYMENT IN FULL** is made on or before the above date, but you must **ACT WITHOUT DELAY.**

The amount is $_____

Mail to: _____ (CREDITOR)

_____ (ADDRESS)

By _____

_____

Pay your bills in full TODAY So that your Credit will be good TOMORROW

(Emblem: GUARD YOUR CREDIT AS A SACRED TRUST)

TELEPHONE COLLECTION PROCEDURE

Both written and oral messages can be effective for collecting past-due payments. Basically, the goals, attitudes, and procedures are similar whether you collect by written communication or through oral contacts—face to face or by telephone. You need also to be aware of prohibited collection practices.

The following quotation expresses some advantages of using the telephone in collecting:

> One of the chief advantages of this method is that it is somewhat surprising to the debtor and may, therefore, catch him unguarded with small alibis and grievances with which to excuse his delinquency. It furnishes the collector a good opportunity to impress him emphatically with the urgency of payment, varying the appeals as the need arises. Frequently, when the reason for nonpayment is understandable, although the failure of the debtor to communicate it is not, a plan of payment may be worked out, usually with a partial payment to be made immediately. Thus, by telephoning nearly all can be accomplished that could be gained by a personal solicitation. Telephoning, however, is often the speedier method, the more flexible, particularly in tracing skips, the less costly, even in the use of long-distance service, as long as it is used with efficiency and discretion.[4]

Because of the growing importance of the telephone in all three collection stages, this section focuses briefly on two special phases of telephone collection techniques: precall planning and the actual collection conversation.

Precall Planning

The steps a collector and every businessperson should take before any important telephone call—or a personal conversation—are similar to the first five planning steps before writing.

1. Determine Your Purpose

Besides the general goal of collecting the money and keeping goodwill, you probably have a specific purpose too. Be sure to check all previous letters and calls, and any response to them. Is your purpose now to work out a special payment arrangement? Or to remind the debtor of a promise made recently but not kept? Or to urge the debtor to pay by a certain date? Or to present an important decision?

2. Visualize Your Customer

First determine the right person to talk to. He or she should be the *only* one who is responsible for paying the bills. Try to judge whether the customer would respond better to a hard or a soft line. If the customer has just received the first overdue notice, your approach should of course be different from the approach to the customer who has ignored several previous contacts. Is the customer likely to be angry? Friendly? Cooperative? Hostile? The payment history is a good clue as to the way the customer will respond to your call.

3. Collect All Necessary Facts

    a. *Determine if your own company is at fault*. Were shipments and billings correct? Were all payments recorded? If you find errors, take time to have them corrected before calling the customer to bring the account up to date.

    b. *Check the past payment record*. How often have the customer's payments been delinquent in the past? How long past due is the account now? If the customer has been late only once in the last year, he or she will probably more readily accept a payment plan than the customer who has been delinquent most of the year.

4. Consider the Ideas to Cover

    a. *Prepare the questions* you'll ask the debtor to determine reasons for not paying bills on time. You'll want to make the customer feel that you are both on the same side. Plan open-end questions that allow the customer to do the talking rather than merely answering "yes" or "no." Good questions begin with the five W's—who, what, when, where, why—and the H—how.

    b. *Be ready to present a payment plan*. This is the heart of precall planning. The payment plan must account for all the overdue payments, not just one or two, and it must include a *specific* schedule that will bring the overdue account to current status. Prepare to sell the plan to the customer in a positive way, without insulting or harassing statements.

5. Plan and Organize

Prepare an opening statement and—at least in general—the order in which you'll present the material you want to cover.

Analysis of the Collection Call

Like the well-written collection letter, the collection call should be tactfully persuasive. The conversation contains the following parts:

1. Opening Statement

After identifying yourself and your firm, state the reason for calling. Then use a *strategic pause*—important in every call. If the customer is sincere in desiring to pay overdue bills, he or she will offer to pay or give a reason for not paying as soon as the reason for the phone call is given. Many collection calls are completed successfully immediately after this strategic pause.

2. Fact-Finding Questions

As you hear the customer's answers to your preplanned questions, try to determine whether the payment plan you designed is realistic. Be ready to adapt it to meet the customer's situation. When you think that using either your original payment plan or a newly devised one will get the account current, and it meets your company policy, proceed to the next step.

3. Presentation of Payment Plan

You might begin to focus the customer's attention on your plan by statements like these: "[Name], I've been thinking seriously about your account, and have come up with a plan of action that will get your account right back in good condition . . ."; or, "[Name], I'm glad you mentioned that you wish there were a way you could get your account paid up without having to do it today. I believe there is. How does this plan sound to you?" Now you have focused the customer's attention on the payment plan. If the final plan is a schedule of payments that will result in a paid-up account, it is a satisfactory arrangement regardless of who proposed the plan or how it is altered.

You have been successful if the customer agrees to a plan. You can then move directly to closing the call. However, if the customer does not agree to all or part of the payment plan, you will need to overcome objections.

4. Overcoming of Objections

Almost always, objections to a payment plan are based on a desire to postpone payments. You can take these three basic steps in overcoming objections:

a. Determine specifically what the customer is objecting to. You can't overcome an objection until you know what it is.

b. Get agreement on those parts to which the customer is not objecting. Maybe the customer's objection concerns only one of the payment dates in the plan. If so, get agreement on all the rest.

c. Work out the parts to which the customer objects. If the objections are minor, you can compromise so long as the plan is specific and it gets the account current. However, if the customer's objections are serious, you should be sure the reasons are valid. Then stress the benefits to the customer of paying and keeping the account current.

5. Closing Statement

Summarize the payment plan and thank the customer, as in the following example: "Fine, Mr. White. Now let me summarize to make sure that I have everything straight. You will mail me a payment of $45.30 on Monday, the 18th. I should have that by the following Thursday. Then you will send another payment of $45.30 on Monday, the 25th, which I should receive by the 28th. That will bring your account up to date. Thank you very much, Mr. White. Good-bye now."

After the call is finished, write down for future reference everything that was said. Note the pertinent information on a card, and file it with any other information on the account. (Of course, if the customer does not abide by the terms of the agreement, you or another collector must take further action.)

PROHIBITED COLLECTION PRACTICES

During the entire collection procedure—written and oral—creditors have, of course, the right to demand payment from debtors. However, they must be careful not to do anything illegal. The Federal Communications Commission released a public notice (70-609) reminding creditors that it is a violation of the telephone company's tariff to use the telephone to frighten, torment, or harass a person. The following practices are prohibited:

1. Calls to debtors at odd hours of the day or night

2. Repeated calls

3. Calls to friends, neighbors, relatives, and children, making threats

4. Calls asserting falsely that credit rating will be hurt

5. Calls stating that legal process is about to be served

6. Calls demanding payment for amounts not owed

7. Calls to place of employment

In addition, it is a crime under federal law when collecting private debts to use in any communication the words *national, federal,* or *United States (U.S.)* to convey a false impression that such communication is from a government-related department, agency, or bureau or in any manner represents the United States. Furthermore, various state laws condemn threats of violence to a debtor's person, property, or reputation; false accusation of fraud; threats of arrest; anonymous calls; deceptive or misleading representations regarding claims; and other unfair practices.[5]

SUMMARY

When a customer's account becomes past due, the creditor begins a collection series. Its goal is to collect the money and maintain goodwill. An effective collector must always treat the customer with consideration and courtesy. Though some customers do not always pay when they should, the collector should try in every way possible to help a defaulting customer arrange to pay an account. The creditor does not want to sue, because everyone but the collection agency or attorney loses.

The collection series is a preplanned but still flexible three-stage procedure—reminder, discussion, and urgency stages—to collect from the past-due customer. For the persuasive messages in the discussion and urgency stages, the collector may choose from five kinds of appeals. As the series progresses, each message places greater pressure on the customer to pay. The length of the series and insistence to pay depend on the credit record of the person.

Contacts with the customer can be by mail, telephone, wire, or personal visit. Written messages consist of statements, reminders, letters, Mailgrams, and wires. A collector who uses the telephone or makes a personal visit should plan carefully before each call and be tactfully persuasive during the call. In all collection procedures—both written and oral—creditors must be scrupulously careful that their practices are within both federal and state laws, and in keeping with company policies (if legal).

EXERCISES AND PROBLEMS

1. *Evaluations of early reminders:* Evaluate the effectiveness of the following early reminders that are sent after the statement(s). Which ones do you consider appropriate? Which ones do you consider inappropriate? Why?

   REMINDER 1   *Obvious form letter on letterhead stationery from an oil company (included are account number, personalized inside address, and salutation).*

   ```
   We know it is easy to lose a statement or forget to pay a
   bill, particularly if it is a small one.
   ```

In case one or the other happened in connection with your
account for $[amount], will you consider this as a reminder
to drop a check in the mail today?

REMINDER 2   *Personalized inside address and salutation with a typewritten body, on letterhead stationery from a bookstore.*

We want you to know that we appreciate your patronage, and
we hope therefore that we will not offend you when we mention that we haven't received anything on your account since
we sent you your statement. Evidently that was ignored. We
feel you will readily understand our anxiety.

We would appreciate it if you could send us something this
month.

REMINDER 3   *Obvious printed message on a 5½- by 7-inch paper from a weekly newsmagazine; no inside address or salutation.*

Just a brief note to repeat our thanks to you for your interest in [name of magazine] and for your order that will bring
you its quick, complete, and competent news briefing in the
many eventful weeks ahead. I feel sure you'll find both
pleasure and profit in its pages!

And may I add another thanks--in advance--to you for taking
care of the enclosed bill promptly. I've sent this copy in
case our previous invoice was mislaid or overlooked.

And from all of us at [name of magazine]--sincere wishes that
your [name of magazine] subscription will mean the best of good
news to you!

2. ***Evaluations of unusual collection messages:*** Which of the following
collection messages do you consider appropriate to send as reminders?
Which would you not send? Give reasons for your decision.

MESSAGE 1   *Obvious form letter—with the text (body) left blank.*

Dear Customer:

                                        Cordially yours,
                                        [signature, etc.]

P.S. I'm practically speechless, but could whisper a hearty
     "thank you" for your check for $131.32 to clean up
     that balance on your June purchases.

MESSAGE 2   *Obvious form letter with account number but no inside address. Attached is a real paper clip.*

No! That little paper clip in the upper-left-hand corner hasn't been left there by a careless stenographer. That's Elmer, our pet paper clip.

His sole purpose in life, as you know, is to hold two pieces of paper together. But our Elmer has enlarged his scope of usefulness and has accepted two very definite tasks that we have asked him to do:

1. Securely hold your check for $4,286.61 to this note when you mail both to us and thus clear up that little account we've talked about,
2. By doing so, bind the amicable relationship that exists between our two companies.

Let's get this little matter under the bridge. What do you say?

3. ***Evaluations of discussion-stage collection messages:*** What improvements can you suggest for each of the following collection messages in the discussion stage?

MESSAGE 1 *Personalized letter throughout; account number above inside addresses.*

Dear Mrs. Tomson:

This is not a dunning letter. Neither is it an attempt to gloss over a serious situation with fancy language concealing a strong-arm attempt to pry money out of you.

Distance and time make it impossible for me to come to you for a friendly chat, so I must ask you to accept this letter as the next best thing. You owe us $99.50, long past due. You have always paid your commitments promptly. Therefore, there must be some special reason for your delay in this case.

I am not so much interested in the cause of this delay as I am in how we can help you over the rough spot. If one can't look to friends for help in times of stress, who on earth can one look to--and I trust our past relationship entitles us to be classed among your friends.

We want our money, of course. But we also want to keep your friendship. I am sure we can accomplish both ends by being entirely frank with each other. What is wrong? What can we do to help you?

Please write me in full, in confidence. Perhaps between us we can work out some plan whereby you can take care of the past-due balance without crowding yourself too much, and, at the same time, we can continue to make shipments to take care of your immediate needs.

MESSAGE 2   *Obvious form letter with inside address, account number, and salutation typed in.*

You must have a good reason for not having paid anything on your account after our recent letter. But we do not know the reason.

If only you would tell us what the situation is, no doubt some arrangement could be made that would relieve your mind of the worry of an overdue debt, and satisfy us, too.

If you can, send in a part payment with your answer. Whether you can do that or not, at least tell us just what is wrong. Give us a chance to help. What do you say?

MESSAGE 3   *Personalized inside address and salutation, typewritten body. Dated May 31.*

Over a hundred and sixty years ago Sir Walter Scott said, "Credit is like a looking glass which, when once sullied by a breath, may be wiped clear again, but if once cracked can never be repaired." The importance of a good credit rating has not changed today.

The barbecue you bought at Wardman's in January will continue to give many hours of enjoyment as you use it in your backyard this summer. We, however, have become concerned about your account listing that purchase. It is past due almost four months. Because of our satisfactory past dealings with you, we feel there must be something wrong, but you have not indicated this by a response to the other letters sent to you.

Because of your very active participation in community affairs, you can realize the importance of having a high credit rating in order to keep in good standing with the other merchants about town. Your good rating was given to us originally by the Lakeview Merchants' Credit Association, of which we are a member. Our agreement with these people requires that we report all those accounts that are seriously past due. Because this is such a serious action, we

always wait with our better customers like you, hoping for
an explanation or, preferably, payment of the past-due account. In keeping with the credit association's requirements, we, however, will have to refer your name to them by
June 5.

To keep your credit "glass" from being broken, just mail
your check for $85.60 to us in the enclosed prepaid enve-
lope. Then come to the store and see the new attachments
and utensils for outdoor cooking, which you will continue to
enjoy this summer.

4. *Evaluations of urgency-stage collection messages:* Is the wording of
   the following messages too strong or not strong enough? Is the writer still
   trying to help the customer? Does the message accomplish the twofold job
   of collecting the money and retaining the customer's goodwill?

   MESSAGE 1   *Personalized inside address, account number, and salutation;
   typewritten body; dated March 8.*

   It seldom becomes necessary for us to turn an account over
   to an attorney for collection. And on those few occasions
   when circumstances leave us no other alternative, we consider it only fair to tell the customer exactly what we
   intend to do.

   Certainly, you must realize that we have made every effort
   to be fair and patient in requesting that you settle your
   January account of $205.40. We have written to you several
   times, asking that you let us know how we could cooperate
   with you in getting this indebtedness straightened out.

   Your continued silence leaves us no alternative but to refer
   your account to our attorney for collection--a step that we
   sincerely regret. So won't you respond to this final appeal
   for your cooperation and thereby avoid a procedure that can
   only mean embarrassment, inconvenience, and additional expense to you?

   Unless we hear from you by March 22, we shall be compelled
   to transfer your account to the office of our attorney.
   Please use the enclosed reply envelope to let us hear from
   you.

   MESSAGE 2   *Personalized inside address, account number, and salutation; typewritten body; dated October 16.*

   A short time ago you and Ed Taylor registered in our hotel
   on September 18 and stayed two days, checking out the 20th.
   The rate on this room is $80 per day. Our clerk, Mr. New-
   comer, was on duty (his first day) when you checked out and

```
he made an error and collected for only one day.  You still
owe us for that, and while Mr. Newcomer wrote you he would
have to stand good for the $80 we thought you would send it
to us.  However you probably didn't give it much thought and
perhaps have forgotten it.  So we will appreciate your send-
ing this to us at once.

For we are sure you would not intentionally dismiss the sub-
ject and refuse to pay.

However, if this is not paid by November 1st, we are forced
to turn the account over to the American Hotel Association
and they would print your name in all the hotel magazines as
one not paying hotel bill which would go to every hotel in
the U.S.

I know you are a fine fellow and will take care of this.
For we do appreciate the visit you made us and we want you
to come back next time you are in [city].  American [name] Show
is now on.  It's a wonderful show.  Why don't you come see
it.
```

5. ***Reminder letter for first-time overdue payment:*** Travelle Tire and Battery Company was established in your town (or city) to provide service stations and small garages with resale merchandise at low prices. You stock top-quality merchandise at reduced prices so that your customers can more effectively compete with the large chain stores and discount houses. At the low prices you charge the service stations and garages, all understand that any purchases from you must be paid within 10 days of the delivery date. (Otherwise, you could not afford to keep the prices so low, because of the high cost of doing credit business.)

   The RKM service station at 901 Parkway, in a town 20 miles from you, ordered $510.90 worth of tires, batteries, and fan belts on July 12. Your truck delivered them on July 14, and you expected payment no later than July 24. It is now August 3, and the bill has not yet been paid.

   Write to RKM service station and remind the owners of the overdue account. Be strict, but remember this is the first time that RKM has been late in payments; perhaps a mere oversight is involved. Ask for payment by return mail; enclose a stamped, addressed return envelope; and try to keep the goodwill of the station management.

6. ***Letter to collect balance of late and short payment:*** As controller for Toy Corporation, manufacturers of plastic toys and specialties, you need today to write a personalized collection letter. You have just received today (March 25), from QXY Distributors, a check dated March 22 for $265.37 in payment of your January 5 invoice of $313.15. You note they have deducted a $12.53 cash discount, which you can't allow, because of late payment. With terms of 2/10, e.o.m., this invoice should have been paid by February 10, but this customer's check was dated and mailed more than

a month later. Also you need to know why they deducted the $35.25; so far as your records show, there is no such amount anywhere. Write them an appropriate inquiry and request for their payment in full.

7. *Discussion-stage letter regarding broken promise:* You are a "collector" in a department store. The delinquent account of Mr. Jofah A. Lurns (228 High St., Topeka, KS 66622-3425) was turned over to you two months ago. At that time, Mr. Lurns's account (no. 264-555-3601) was four months overdue, and he owed the store $490.20 for purchases made five to six months ago.

Your first step was to call Mr. Lurns for an explanation of why he had not made payment. Mr. Lurns was apologetic and sounded somewhat embarrassed, as his account had never been delinquent before. He explained that his family had some unexpected medical bills and that he had been laid off his job in a manufacturing firm for two months because of a labor strike against a supplier. As a result, he had gotten behind in his payments to all his creditors.

As skillfully as you could, you tried to reassure Mr. Lurns that your store wanted to be fair and could appreciate his problem. You offered to work out a repayment plan that would stop the collection messages and help him recover slowly. Mr. Lurns agreed to pay $85 per month on the account until it was paid off. You confirmed the agreement in a letter, and the following week, you received a check from Mr. Lurns for $85. However, you did not receive his check this month, and your efforts to talk to him by phone have failed. (Either no one answers the phone, or when someone does answer, you are told that Mr. Lurns is not available.)

Now you must write a letter to Mr. Lurns to ask why he has broken his promise. Because you believe that he sincerely wants to take care of his account, you will offer to keep the agreed-upon repayment plan in effect if he sends you a check for $85 or more within a week and if he continues to send monthly checks until the account has been cleared. Write the letter, using the appropriate appeals.

8. *Discussion form letter to collect 90-day overdue payment:* You are credit and collection manager of the Loeso TV and Electronics Sales Company. Yours is one of the three major such stores in the city. Mr. Byron Tackson, a resident of your city, has been a credit customer of yours for six years, and his record is "good."

On February 8 this year, Mr. Tackson bought a portable video tape recorder for $250.50 and charged it to his account (#099002). March 1 you sent him a bill for this amount, due March 10. April 1, since you had not heard from him, you sent a second bill. May 1 you sent a third bill, with a sticker at the bottom saying, "Did you forget? Please mail us a check now—while you have it in mind." On June 10 the account is considered 90 days overdue. Address a discussion letter to Mr. Tackson, offering to help any way you can. Make the basic purpose of your letter a reply from him—a remittance, a letter, a phone call, or a personal visit. Prepare the letter as a form message with a personal inside address and salutation. Make it sound personal, but write it so that the body is applicable to any "good" customer with an account 90 days overdue.

9. *Second urgency-stage collection letter:* Your job today is to prepare the last urgency-stage collection letter for Mrs. James Beachton, 432 Columbia Avenue, Alexandria, VA 22344-3568. (You are assistant credit and collection manager for Calstrom Contemporary Furniture Showcase of Alexandria, Virginia.) Calstrom's policy is to repossess furniture after the fifth payment is missed unless the customer and you can agree on and implement a reasonable alternative payment plan.

   Four weeks ago, you notified Mrs. Beachton that repossession of her dining room suite, according to the terms of her conditional sales agreement, would be the logical action to take if she did not bring her account up to date or make some other payment arrangements. She had missed four monthly payments of $160 each and since then has made repeated promises to make payments, but so far she has paid nothing. Now she is five months behind in her payments.

   Your letter will be the last letter in the collection series. State clearly (but with an air of reluctance) that her dining room suite will be repossessed two weeks from today unless full payment of $800 is made, or another course of action is mutually agreed upon. For greater impact, this letter will be sent by certified mail and signed by one of the partners in the business. Although you must use the strong fear appeal and develop the unpleasant consequences of your drastic action, you still want to maintain Mrs. Beachton's goodwill as a potential cash customer. Therefore, incorporate one positive appeal.

10. *Urgency-stage collection letter to airline customer:* Assume that you are the credit collection manager for the Topway Airlines, whose air routes extend throughout the United States and overseas. The extensive routes that your planes travel make your airline very popular. In addition to the popularity that your airline already enjoys, your company has attempted to increase its passengers even further by offering a variety of credit plans to encourage travel.

    One plan that your company offers is a credit card that will allow a passenger to charge up to a limit of $900 for trips. The terms of the air travel credit card account are payable in full upon receipt of the bill.

    During the month of September, Ms. Marie Public, one of your credit card customers, charged several trips to her air travel credit card. The total amount of charges was $660. When Ms. Public mailed in her payment for September, she sent only $260 with a note that she would pay the remaining $400 in $100 installments.

    As credit collection manager, write Ms. Public a personal letter and request the full balance to be paid within 10 days. She has paid promptly in the past, but you must reluctantly tell her that credit privileges will be withdrawn until full payment is made. After full payment has been received by your office, full credit privileges will be restored. In your letter, reexplain the terms of the credit card account, but try to keep her as a customer. Prepare this letter for the signature of the president of Topway Airlines.

Chapter 15

Goodwill Messages

The messages discussed in Chapters 7 through 14 are necessary during the usual course of business. Their chief purpose is to take care of day-to-day problems through requests, replies, and announcements. In contrast, the *goodwill communications* covered in this chapter are not absolutely essential or required for the operation of a business. *Their main purpose is to convey a friendly, usually unexpected, message that builds goodwill.*

Besides being friendly, unexpected, and outside the usual course of business, goodwill messages have several other characteristics in common. Their *organizational plan resembles a good-news or neutral message—most important idea first, then brief comments and details (if any), and a final cordial ending (if needed). Like all others, goodwill messages should be honest and sincere and avoid gushiness or wordiness.* They can be sent to the recipient's home or office. Depending on their content, destination, and quantity, goodwill messages may be prepared on a typewriter or computer, or handwritten (for an extra, personal touch), or printed, perhaps on special paper appropriate for the occasion or season.

Unlike many business letters, however, *genuine goodwill messages should not contain statements that try to sell the recipients on buying additional products or service.* Most people dislike messages which pose as "goodwill only" but which actually mainly have sales motives.

A genuine goodwill message is almost always favorably received, for at least two reasons:

1. The sender presumably is not sending the message because of some business scheme.

2. The message comes as a pleasant surprise, for the recipient doesn't expect it. Bills will come if money is owed, but a thank-you from the seller for paying promptly or congratulations for winning an honor or celebrating a special anniversary aren't expected.

An unexpected benefit to firms that send goodwill messages is that they are remembered when the recipients want to buy products or services—sometimes months, even years, later.

Thoughtful persons often write messages designed to foster friendly relations in these ways:

Congratulating or giving deserved praise

Expressing appreciation

Conveying sympathy

Welcoming and offering favors

Showing continuing special concern

CONGRATULATING OR GIVING DESERVED PRAISE

A sincere, enthusiastic note of congratulations or deserved praise—sent promptly—can have an unforgettable impact on the recipient, especially because not many people take the initiative to send such messages.

Congratulatory Messages

The opportunities to congratulate are numerous, for congratulations may relate to any significant news about a person's business, family, or personal achievements. For instance, you might congratulate a business executive when her firm has opened a new branch, reached its twenty-fifth or fiftieth anniversary, moved to larger quarters, attained a publicized milestone in total volume of sales, received a well-known award for distinguished service to the industry or community, or achieved special favorable publicity. You might congratulate a person when he or someone in the family has made a significant achievement or won an honor. Among the events and activities that merit congratulations are election to an office, promotion, graduation, birth of a child; others include winning a competitive contest, scholarship, or prize; making an outstanding speech; writing a good magazine article or book; or performing well in a theater, debate, or other public gathering.

When you write a congratulation, "talk" informally and enthusiastically—without flattery—as you would in a personal contact with the recipient. Focus on your reader instead of on yourself. And write promptly—as soon as possible after you learn the good news. The letters below are examples of various congratulatory messages written by executives and other persons.

LETTER 1   *A congratulatory note with good tone and word choice.*

Main idea: promotion	Your promotion to vice president of General Construction Company was great news. I was happy to read about you in this week's Trade Press.
Compliments	If ever a person deserved company recognition, you do. Your courage and hard work in developing new ways to promote the services of your firm have won the admiration of many, including your competitors.
Congratulations	Congratulations to you--and best wishes for your continued success!

LETTER 2   *A banker congratulates a businessperson on an election. (A similar note brought the banker who wrote it millions of dollars of business in installment loans.)*

Congratulations, [*name*]

Main idea: congratulations, presidency	. . . upon being selected president of the Westside Lumber Dealers Association, as mentioned in yesterday's Times.
Compliments	Under your capable leadership, this organization will reach a new high in activity and service.

LETTER 3   *A manager congratulates a distant, out-of-state customer.*

Congratulations,
feature article

> Heartiest congratulations to you on the splendid
> progress you have made with your poultry plant!
> It was a real pleasure for me to see your pic-
> ture and read the feature article about your new
> cage house in the May issue of <u>American Poultry
> Journal</u>.

Compliments

> Verna Barns has spoken enthusiastically of your
> model operation and the excellent job you are
> doing. This article and its labor-saving sug-
> gestions have already been filed for future ref-
> erence in our "idea" folder.

Sincere
wishes

> On my next field trip to Minnesota I would like
> to meet you and visit your place. My very best
> wishes to you for your continued outstanding re-
> sults with Erving's Chicks.

Sometimes, in addition to congratulating a person, you may want to send along a clipping of a picture or article published concerning the event. Some firms have specially designed folders in which such clippings may be attached. Printed on the outside cover may be a message like "Congratulations" or "You're in the News," together with the company's trademark. For instance, the Carnation Company (dairy products) used a leaflet that pictured on the outside three carnations under the words "Carnations to You!" On the inside was an attractive design and this message:

> We Read With Interest . . . the attached clipping about you
>   and thought you would be inter-
>   ested in receiving our copy.
>
> At Carnation we are always pleased to read about those peo-
> ple who help make the Northwest such a wonderful place in
> which to live.

Sending an invitation or an inexpensive gift along with the congratulations, as in letter 4, can be an effective way to build goodwill. However, many other letters that begin with congratulations are actually not true goodwill messages, but disguised or obvious sales messages (to buy the firms' products).

LETTER 4   *A retail store sends layettes with congratulations to parents of twins.*
[Letterhead states: "Headquarters for clothes from crib to college"; saluta-
tion is "Dear Mr. and Mrs. (name)."]

Main idea:
congratulations
for twins

> May Barons add their congratulations to the many
> you have already received. With pleasure we send
> to you two layettes for your twin arrivals on
> April 23, 199-.

Gifts, compliments	Your babies will no doubt model all garments beautifully. We are happy to send you these "double congratulations" for your doubly happy event--with compliments of Barons.
Wishes for happiness	You can expect the layettes by mail within a few days. May you have many happy days and years ahead.

Praise for Unannounced Service

In addition to congratulating people for various achievements that are in the news, you may also find reason to give deserved praise for good service that has not been publicized.

For instance, you might compliment your employees on exceptionally fine work—perhaps for achieving a new high record of sales, accuracy, attendance, or other performance. Recognizing their good work with a sincere letter of praise can sometimes be a more lasting reward and benefit than giving a small monetary bonus.

Also, as a customer, you might write to a company executive to tell about unusually good service you received from his or her employees. Such sincere praise, as in letter 5, is appreciated by both the executive and the employees; often the sincere compliments stimulate recipients to do even higher quality work.

LETTER 5 *A customer praises a clerk's service by writing to the personnel manager.*

Main idea: thoughtful employee	You may be interested in the exceptionally thoughtful service I received from one of your employees.
Details, praise for excellent service	Recently I inquired about getting instructions for using an electrolysis kit I bought from The Bon some time ago. Gloria Jones, in your downtown store, explained that The Bon has been phasing that product out and no longer had any in stock. But Gloria's help to a customer continued also after store hours. She said she had the same kit at home and would copy the instructions and send them to me.
Appreciation, happy customer	Yesterday I received original instructions, not just a copy, in the mail. Gloria must have sent me her personal copy. I want you to know how much I appreciate that special attention and excellent service. Gloria turned my potential frustration into genuine pleasure at being treated so well. You have a happy customer who is spreading the word.

Whenever possible, the persons you want to praise should be mentioned by their names or identifying numbers. Military personnel also appreciate words of praise, as shown in the following example. A retired Army sergeant, after being treated in an overseas Navy hospital, wrote to the commanding officer of the overseas U.S. Naval Regional Medical Center, expressing grateful praise for the "highly qualified and dedicated" medical personnel. He included names of two doctors and three assistants and then also praised the "unseen and unsung people in the laboratories and in the supply kitchen, and other departments who help make things run smoothly." A few days later he received from the commanding officer the following pleasant reply, typewritten on official stationery:

LETTER 6   *A Navy commanding officer's reply to a letter of praise.*

Main idea: usefulness of letter	Your letter in appreciation for the care you received has been forwarded to all personnel concerned. A copy will be available in the appropriate records of those whom you named for commendation.
Compliment, thanks	We are grateful to know that there are recipients of our health care delivery efforts who are not only appreciative of our endeavors but also willing to express that appreciation in a letter.
Benefit to staff	You can be assured that your expression of satisfaction will enhance the motivation of the involved staff members not only to continue their good work but also to strive for improvement.

From time to time you will encounter employees—salespeople, bus drivers, police officers, teachers, clerks, and many others—whose service to you is far beyond the call of duty. A sincere note of praise written to an employee's superior—as in letter 5—has sometimes brought unexpected benefits to an otherwise unnoticed employee.

One of many true stories with a happy ending began when an airline passenger wrote a letter to the company president praising an employee (Paula) who had traveled 26 miles in her own car and at her own expense to get medical care for a traveler sick in a Hawaiian town. The president showed the letter to the vice president, who wrote the employee a message of praise (letter 7), and less than four months later Paula received a long-hoped-for promotion. Though her advancement was no doubt earned through years of good work, Paula felt that a letter such as the one the passenger wrote first brought her to the attention of management.

LETTER 7   *Praise from an airline executive vice president to an employee.*

Main idea:
compliment,
fine job

> Attached is a copy of a letter President Jack Doe
> has just received that is indicative of the unusu-
> ally fine job you are doing for us in [*name of town*].
> You surely made a lifelong friend for Hawaiian Air-
> lines.

Congratula-
tions

> Congratulations, Paula, on a job well done!

Benefit

> I am asking Bob Cann to make this letter a part of
> your permanent personnel file.

EXPRESSING APPRECIATION

Everyone likes to know that his or her efforts are appreciated. As a business executive, you can express appreciation to customers, suppliers, employees, stockholders, and many others whose activities relate to your business. Also, no matter what your occupation or rank may be, you will have opportunities to send personal goodwill messages. Some of these messages will pertain to favors extended repeatedly over a period of time; others will be for one-time kindnesses.

Appreciation for a Good Record or Favors Extended over a Period of Time

When you write to established customers, you can express appreciation for their patronage, for prompt payment of bills, for recommendation of your firm to friends, or for other courtesies. Some of these messages may be processed forms. Some contain both appreciation and praise; some also include a small gift or a special privilege, as in letter 8.

LETTER 8   *A computerized, personalized form letter sending appreciation and a privilege to a preferred credit customer.*

> Dear Ms. Sampson:

Main idea: thanks
for record of
prompt payment

> Many thanks for your promptness in paying your
> [*company name*] account each month and every
> year. Certainly you can be proud of the ex-
> cellent record you have established.

You-attitude,
special privileges

> In appreciation of you, one of our valued cus-
> tomers, we are pleased to enclose your new
> gold credit card. With it you will receive
> three special privileges, as explained on the
> enclosed sheet.

Assurance of continued good service

You may be sure we will continue to do the best we can to merit your continued patronage. Please call on us whenever we can be of assistance to you.

Though messages such as letter 8 are usually personalized form letters—with appropriate insertion of the customer's name and address—some large companies have found it desirable to send printed thanks, as in letter 9. Customers usually appreciate even a printed message—unless the same message arrives every month for six months, tucked in with the monthly statement (as it did for customers of one firm).

LETTER 9   *A manufacturer's thanks for patronage—printed on special letterhead showing two hands clasped and "THANKS" at the top in red.*

Main idea: thanks for patronage; desire to please

Too often in the rush of business life, we forget to say "THANK YOU" so that you can hear it, but you can be sure we always appreciate your patronage. It is our constant aim to please and satisfy you more each time.

Gratitude, easy action for services

Serving you is a real privilege, and we are grateful for your confidence in us. Anytime we can be of service to you in any way, just pick up the phone and call us collect at (209) 555-6499.

Some firms send their expressions of appreciation along with seasonal greetings. If appropriate, you can send a seasonal message near a special holiday—New Year's, Valentine's Day, Memorial Day, Independence Day, Thanksgiving, Christmas—or any other anniversary that may be meaningful to your recipients. Sometimes a small gift—calendar, ornament, picture—accompanies the greetings. In any case, the message should preferably be unique for the type of business as well as the season, and appropriately different from others the reader may receive during that season.

LESSON 10   *A company's greeting surrounded by 1-inch facial pictures and names of its 30 employees.*

Main idea: holiday greetings from employees

One of the real joys of the Holiday Season is the opportunity for the expression of goodwill and the exchange of friendly greetings.

Appreciation, sincere good wishes

In this spirit of friendship and with sincere appreciation for the pleasant business relations we have enjoyed with you, we extend Season's Greetings and wish you Health and Happiness every day of the New Year. . . .

The preceding examples of appreciation messages were sent by business firms. Also, it is good for every thoughtful person to express gratitude to the individuals—perhaps a relative, coach, scout leader, teacher, or former employer—who have contributed something memorable to his or her life—especially if (as in letter 11) years have passed since they met. A successful graduate student may write sincere thanks to a former "tough taskmaster" professor for the difficult required assignments, because the information learned is now essential in that person's job.

LETTER 11   *A professional person's thanks to a former Army officer.*

**Main idea:
thanks for
good deeds**

Eight years ago, a young 1st lieutenant at Fort
Ord, California, went out of his way to arrange
transportation for a young staff sergeant who
worked in his section. The transportation was
for a unique purpose--not for a pleasure trip
or for official duty, but for an education.

**Details, benefits,
appreciation**

Mr. Watters, I want you to know that the favors
you did for me have had a great influence on my
life. At the time you arranged for a jeep for
my use in attending high school classes at Palo
Alto, I thought it just another ordinary event
in my life. Never did I dream that those twice
weekly rides would become my first route on the
road to higher education.

**More details,
encouragement,
helpfulness**

The diploma I received was the ticket I needed
for admission to college. However, I needed
more than that. I needed someone to encourage
me and show me the benefits that a college education would give to me. You were persistently
trying to convince me of this value during my
last days of duty. And though your work was
filled with pressure and tension, you always
managed to remain calm and ready to cheer me
on.

**Gratitude, favor-
able results,
inspiration**

You helped me in so many ways; I'm deeply
grateful to you. You'll be glad to know that
your wise words didn't go unheeded. I graduated from the University of [*state*] last June and
am now in my first year of medical school.
Thank you for starting me on the road to a better education. I plan someday to help other
youngsters the way you helped me.

Such thank-you messages are an appreciated surprise to their recipients. Often they respond with sincere sentimental notes thanking the persons who wrote to them expressing appreciation for their favor.

Letters of appreciation are also due to people who have spent many hours on a worthy cause—such as serving on committees, soliciting funds, or helping with an election campaign. Each salutation may be personalized, or—to save expenses—addressed to "Dear (committee name) member."

Thanks for One-Time Favors and Kindnesses

Thanking people promptly for any significant one-time courtesy is desirable for a successful business- or professional person, as well as for everyone else with good manners. Whenever possible, a thank-you message should go to the person who gives a speech without honorarium; writes a letter of recommendation for you; helps you win an honor or award; grants an informative, lengthy interview; sends you a letter of praise or criticism about you, your business, your employees, or others in whom you are interested; donates money, gifts, or awards. Some firms even thank new customers for a first purchase or first use of a new charge account.

Of course, circumstances will govern the length and content of these thank-you notes, which may range from a few sentences to several paragraphs. Letters 12 through 15 are thank-you messages that thoughtful, courteous businesspersons have written on various occasions.

LETTER 12   *A program chairperson thanks a popular speaker—in an unusual, but gracious and sincere, letter.*

Main idea: thanks for outstanding speech	Sincere thanks to you for your delightful speech to the Uptown Business members yesterday. At the risk of contradicting the general theme of your message, "The Freedom of Movement," may I say that you made captives of us all.
Sincere compliment	Believe me, I did not--after noting what was a record attendance for our meeting--speak lightly when I told you that your reputation as a speaker, scholar, and, above all, a charming guest of honor had preceded you.
Compliments from members too	May I also state that, with all due apologies to Shaw--"What really flatters a man is that you think him worth flattering." On this point, certainly--and I speak with confidence for the club members and our guests--there is not the shadow of a doubt.
Courteous ending	We hope that your future will provide some respite from hard work and that you will be free to join us again. Thank you so very much!

When a customer compliments your firm or employees by letter, you should acknowledge the praise by writing a note similar to letter 13. [See also the Navy officer's reply (letter 6, page 418).]

LETTER 13   *A company president thanks a customer for her complimentary letter about the firm's employees.*

Main idea:
thanks for
cordial letter

Thank you very much for your warm and cordial letter of August 29. It is really a pleasure, upon opening the morning mail, to find a letter like yours.

Details,
gratitude

Nothing gratifies me more than to learn that the efforts of our employees are so thoroughly appreciated. Many people are quick to write criticisms, but seldom does anyone take the time to say something nice. So I am always pleased to hear from one of the many, many people who are satisfied.

Courtesy, promised
service

We will do our best to continue to provide you with the service you like.

Criticisms should also be acknowledged courteously. A large, nationally known firm sends a card labeled "Post-o-gram" with this message: "We appreciate your comments on (name of product) and the interest which prompted you to write. If we may serve you any time in the future, please let us know." Some acknowledgements of criticisms should include—in addition to thanks—an apology or explanation and perhaps brief resale on the firm's products or services.

For thank-you messages that acknowledge money donations, the explanation section usually should include a few details telling the success of the campaign or how the funds are being used, so that the donors will feel good about having contributed. If you are an officer in an organization that must solicit donations year after year, appreciative messages similar to letters 14 and 15 may well serve as incentives for future donations.

LETTER 14   *In a memo, a manager thanks employees for generous contributions.*

TO: All employees
FROM: John Mains, Manager, Plant 2
SUBJECT: Plant 2 UGN Contributions 199-

Main idea:
thanks for
contributions

On behalf of the United Good Neighbor Fund I thank all of you who so generously contributed to our UGN campaign.

Praise, details,
figures, results

This year, our plant had approximately the same number of contributors as last year, but a 21% increase in contributions! Our company goal was a 9% increase. Obviously we have substantially exceeded that amount.

Thanks for
strong, needed
support

Again, thanks for your strong support at a time
when it is needed more than ever!

LETTER 15   *The president of a civic charity club thanks donors.*

THANK YOU! THANK YOU! Your caring has made a
difference.

Main idea:
appreciation
for help

With deep appreciation we thank you for the
gifts and employment you have given this year
to help the poor. Because of kind-hearted
friends like you, this year the [*name*] Club
has:

Details: specific
ways large num-
bers of people
were helped

> Provided over 29,000 jobs in a wide
>   variety of work
> Assisted more than 7,000 families with
>   clothing and household items you helped
>   donate
> Served over 6,500,000 meals to hungry
>   men, women, and children
> Placed more than 300 people in full-time
>   jobs through Seminar and Job Search
> Sponsored a free walk-in Medical Center
>   Clinic for hundreds of people needing
>   health care

Thanks for
bringing happiness
to so many people

They are all grateful there are "people who
care." Thank you for your thoughtfulness and
generosity. You can be happy in knowing that
your contributions have helped bring happiness
to these deserving people.

CONVEYING SYMPATHY

When people suffer a serious misfortune, they may be encouraged by messages of sympathy from business associates as well as from personal friends. Because they pertain to sad or unpleasant circumstances, goodwill letters of this type are much harder to write than those already discussed. However, in times of distress, the recipient may value these messages even more highly than expressions of congratulation or thanks.

You can express condolence to a customer, competitor, colleague, business friend, or employee. The occasion may involve a death, accident, loss of material possessions (such as a business wiped out by fire or flood), sickness, major operation, or other misfortunes that can happen to an individual. Expressions of sympathy can be shown by cards, flowers, attendance at a funeral, offers of tangible help, visits, written messages, or a combination of several actions. This section concentrates on the individual messages you can write expressing sympathy.

If you are writing for your company and the relationship is purely a business one, your secretary can type the message on letterhead stationery. Otherwise, use your own stationery, and write in longhand what you want to convey.

Although you *cannot mechanically follow a set outline* for expression of sympathy, here are suggestions to consider:

1. Begin with the main idea—sympathy and tactful identification of the problem (such as accident, death, or loss of business).

2. Add only those details, if any, that are desirable for the circumstances. (For example, when writing to a survivor, you might express how much the survivor meant to the deceased.) Make all statements restrained and sincere.

3. Stress the positive—the good characteristics and best contributions of the deceased or ill person (if the person is known to you)—rather than the negative (pain, suffering, distress).

4. Offer assistance, if appropriate, but don't dwell on details. Perhaps you will offer to lighten a customer's monthly payments, move a due date forward, or make your warehouse available to a friend whose factory burned down. Omit such business matters as the amount the customer owes you, how long a debt is past due, or similar subjects that can and should be taken care of in another letter.

5. End on a pleasant, positive, reassuring idea, perhaps looking to the future. The following are acceptable messages of condolence.

MESSAGE 1   *Memo telling employees about the sudden death of a co-worker.*

TO ALL EMPLOYEES

Main idea: announcement, death, funeral services

We are saddened by the death of Thor Bjornsen. Thor was killed in a private-plane accident yesterday en route to a conference. Funeral services will be held [date] in [name] funeral home, 1111 Broadway Avenue, at 1:00 p.m.

Details, compliments

Thor was one of the finest chaps in the company--always helping others, especially newcomers. He was tops in his field and was generous and kind. We will all miss him.

Suggested memorial fund, easy action

Thor's family does not want flowers for him, so arrangements have been made with the Children's Orthopedic Hospital to receive sums for a memorial fund. Checks are to be made payable to that hospital. Address contributions to Thor

> Bjornsen Memorial, 333 Ridgeway Road, [*city, state, ZIP*], attention of Mrs. Jackson.

MESSAGE 2 *A personnel director's condolence to a widower customer (whose wife he had never met personally).*

Main idea: sympathy	With profound sorrow we have just learned of the death of your wife.
Sympathy from Boardson friends	Though there is little one can say or do to lessen the grief that must be yours, we want you to know that the heartfelt sympathy of all your friends at Boardson's is with you.
Focus on pleasant memories	We hope that the cherished memories you have of your many years together will comfort you in the months ahead.

MESSAGE 3 *Sympathy letter to a business friend whose store was destroyed.*

Dear Joan:

Main idea: sympathy, fire	The announcement on television yesterday about the widespread fire in your buildings distressed us greatly. I want to convey our sympathy to you and your employees.
Offer of tangible help; easy action	If there's anything that I as an individual can do to help you at this time, please call me (here at the office: 555-6666, ext. 562, or at home: 555-2323 evenings). Also you're welcome to use (at no charge, of course) our company's Lander Street warehouse (about 500 square feet) to store any materials during your reconstruction period, and our conference rooms for offices and meeting places as long as you need them.
Sincere wishes for recovery	All the employees at the [*name*] Company join me in wishing you a fast recovery.

If Joan were an out-of-town customer with an outstanding balance on her account, the sympathy message might have included an offer like the following to replace part of the second paragraph:

Further offer to help	If we can help you by extending your credit terms and the payment date on your account, just let me know. I'll consider it a privilege to come to your aid to show--even in a small way--how much we have appreciated your friendship and business through the years.

WELCOMING AND OFFERING FAVORS

Some of the good-news messages discussed in Chapter 8—for instance, those granting credit or acknowledging first orders—include a welcome to the customer, and some grant favors that the customer asked for. Also, many sales letters offer a favor or gift. All those messages are necessary in the daily course of business operations.

In contrast, the welcome and favor-offering letters discussed in this chapter are those "extra" messages that are not absolutely essential but are written mainly to build goodwill. The favors are freely offered, not written in answer to a request or in order to sell something.

Sometimes these welcome messages go to persons who have not yet dealt directly with your firm or perhaps not with your department. Among them are messages you may send to newcomers in a city or state, to new employees in your firm, or to new members of an organization whose work is related to that of your firm.

A letter from an officer of any business firm, welcoming a distinguished newcomer to the area and offering assistance, is usually a low-pressure *sales* message. Besides the welcome, it may include a city map, real estate guides, and a pamphlet or paragraph about the institution's services or products. Though such letters are useful for business, they are *not strictly goodwill* messages.

However, a welcoming message like letter 1 to a new customer can be considered mainly goodwill; it does not try to sell the reader on additional services but merely contains *resale* material (as in paragraph 2). Letter 2 is also a goodwill message—to let a once "lost" customer know that renewed patronage is appreciated.

LETTER 1   *A savings and loan officer welcomes a new account customer.*

Main idea: welcome, thanks	Welcome to membership in our organization. Many thanks for opening a savings account with First Federal.
Brief details on savings safeguards	Here your savings are safeguarded by careful management, investment in sound home loans, and insurance of accounts by the Federal Savings and Loan Insurance Corporation, an agency of the United States government. At the same time, we maintain ample reserves for the purpose of meeting withdrawals, should you need all or any part of your savings; in addition you earn an above-average dividend on your savings, compounded monthly at the regular rate.
Services in two areas	You receive the same personalized services at either of our offices--the Mountview Savings in the Southside Shopping Center or the downtown office.

Easy action

Please call on me or any member of our staff when we can be of service to you. Our telephone number is 555-4444.

LETTER 2   *A credit manager welcomes back a long-absent customer.*

Main idea:
appreciation
for customer's
return

The return of a good friend is as happy an occasion in the business world as it is in one's private life. Your recent purchase here at Baylor's was the first to be charged to your account for a considerable time . . .

Welcome and
thanks

and we take this opportunity to welcome you again to the Baylor Store. Thank you for your patronage.

Desire to
serve well

You can be sure that it is our sincere wish to serve you to your complete satisfaction.

The last example, letter 3, is an offer of a favor at "no charge or obligation" to noncustomers and customers. This message contains no direct sales plug for the writer's organization and does not ask the reader to buy or sell stock through the writer's firm. Thus, although the reason for the letter is probably to promote sales eventually, here it is mainly a goodwill message.

LETTER 3   *A stock brokerage firm's vice president offers a free current report. (A small, printed fill-in form is at the top of the letter; salutation is personalized.)*

Main idea:
offer of re-
port on stock;
easy action

I'd like to offer you a Bronson Fynch service that many of the investors in [city] have come to value highly: our research department's opinion about any stock listed on the New York Stock Exchange. If you'll just write the name of the stock on the form above and mail it to our Central Information Bureau, I'll get an up-to-date report from our research department back to you just as promptly as I can.

Invitation
to phone

Then, if you have any questions about the report, please call me at (206) 555-2222. I'll be glad to make an appointment at your convenience.

No charge
or obligation
for service

We are pleased to do this, [name], whether you have an account with us or not. There is no charge or obligation for this service. In fact, the only charge you ever pay at Bronson Fynch is the minimum commission when you buy or sell securities.

SHOWING CONTINUING SPECIAL CONCERN

A business firm may indicate goodwill and special concern in various ways. Among them is the goodwill message that shows you are sincerely interested in maintaining confidence in your firm's goods and services. To demonstrate your concern, you can write follow-up requests and announcements to customers, stockholders, suppliers, or employees. The purpose of these goodwill messages is to get feedback on products or services used, to maintain the firm's good image, or to help the customer get the best use from your products that she or he has already bought.

For example, some firms systematically send messages similar to letters 1 and 2 to solicit comments from their customers and maintain quality control.

LETTER 1   *The manager of a video and television repair shop shows sincere concern for customer satisfaction.*

Dear Mr. Donnelly:

Main idea: concern for customer satisfaction

Your video recorder was repaired two months ago by our service department, and I'd like to make sure that everything is still O.K., to your complete satisfaction.

Promise to please

We firmly believe that our most valued possession is the confidence and goodwill of our customers. My promise is to do everything possible to be certain you are pleased that you've chosen us to care for your home electronic equipment.

Appreciation and resale

Your confidence in our service department is sincerely appreciated. All of us at Bancroft's pledge to provide our customers with the finest service available in today's technology. Also, here you receive the kind of old-fashioned courtesy and personal attention that are hard to find in some industries.

Easy action, sincere desire to help

If we can be of benefit to you, please call me today--at [number]. I really do care, and want to help so that you'll continue to be pleased with our service in years to come.

LETTER 2   *A department store manager shows concern for customer desires by inviting comments and reasons for return of merchandise.*

Dear Mrs. Lighten:

Main idea: concern for customer opinions

Recently you returned, for a $235.40 refund, an item purchased from [store name]. Your opinions regarding that item and our service are valued highly.

Store's goal of quality and courteous service	We desire to provide a selection of quality merchandise and to see that our sales personnel are courteous at all times. In this instance we are sorry the product did not fulfill your desires, and we want to be sure that in returning the item you received the same courtesy as when it was purchased.
Easy action; appreciation for requested comments	Will you please jot your comments and suggestions for improvement on the enclosed sheet and mail it to us in the enclosed stamped envelope? We will very much appreciate your assistance, for it will enable us to provide the kind of service you like.

Still other ways that business firms show special concern and build goodwill are by contributing their time and money to various worthy causes. For example, some encourage their employees and managers to help on tutoring programs, or in child and family resource centers, or on community development events—sometimes even during company time if necessary.

Other firms make significant charitable contributions to mental health clinics or hospitals, city parks, museums, university or college or high school departments, or goodwill industries. Others participate in helping to rebuild disaster areas, or establishing foundation grants, or funding various needy public projects to show their continuing concern. All these services and contributions are, basically, prompted by a spirit of goodwill.

SUMMARY

Goodwill messages are ones that you don't *have* to send and that don't include a sales pitch or have strings attached. These messages congratulate, praise, thank, greet, sympathize, welcome, offer favors, or show special concern for the recipients—without including any obvious sales material. The message plan is direct—main idea, appropriate details, courteous close.

EXERCISES AND PROBLEMS

1. *Evaluations:* Below are two messages about gifts two companies offer. Is each one truly a goodwill message? If not, why not? What do you like or dislike about each one? Suggest needed improvements.

   a. We know you will enjoy having this special edition of your 199- color calendar, compliments of [*name*] Travel Service. We hope that it proves to be both useful and convenient in your office.

This affords us the opportunity to let you know that we appreciate the privilege of serving as your travel agent. We thank you for your past business, and we look forward to hearing from you whenever we can assist you with future travel plans in connection with business or pleasure.

We handle all forms of transportation--air, rail, steamship, bus, as well as reservations for hotels, motels and U-drive service. Our daily delivery system to any downtown business office is a time-saver for you and your staff, and we want you to feel free to make use of it.

ONE CALL DOES IT ALL! --555-0020

b. The Next Issue of [*name of free booklet*]

will be mailed on Monday, October 25. The [*name of booklet*] is sent free each month to business firms employing three or more department heads.

Before we address the envelopes for this issue, we want to make sure that our mailing list is complete and accurate. On the sheet that comes with this letter, you will find a list of all the names we have for members of your staff who are department heads or managers.

Please take just a minute to go over the list. Note any needed corrections. Cross out names of people who are no longer there. Add the names of members of your staff who are department heads or managers or supervisors and who are not on this list.

The [*name of booklet*] is "different." Each issue is of direct interest to supervisors and managers working with people daily.

Please correct and mail the sheet today--in the enclosed envelope. No stamp is needed. You and your associates will then be sure of getting [*booklet*] free throughout the year.

2. *Letter returning a lost sorority pin:* As assistant customer service manager of a national airline, you need to write a letter to accompany a lost sorority pin that you are returning to its owner. The pin had fallen under one of the coach seats on flight 742 to Chicago, June 29. No one wrote to report this lost pin; thus there has been considerable delay in establishing ownership. You first had to identify the sorority and then the chapter and

where it was located, all of which was time-consuming. However, you were eventually successful in learning this traveler's identity through Joanne Jones, president, Alpha chapter at Texas State College.

Ask the recipient of your letter to sign an attached lost property card and return it to you. Will your reply be a goodwill letter with no strings attached? Or will you include some sales talk and a look forward to future business?

3. *Evaluation of a hotel manager's letter:* The following message was sent by the general manager of a hotel to each business executive who had attended a national convention there seven months earlier. Is this letter a goodwill builder? Why or why not? What improvements can you suggest?

> May I take this opportunity to thank you for your patronage to [name] Hotel, and all of us here sincerely hope that you enjoyed your visit to [city].
>
> Have you any friends or business associates that might be coming to [city]? I would appreciate it very much if you would give me their names and addresses on the enclosed card so that I may send them a brochure of our hotel and invite them to stay with us while they are in [city].
>
> The staff of the [hotel name] joins me in looking forward to your future visits with us.

4. *Letter showing appreciation for a friend's lasting help:* This assignment can be a message you will actually mail. (If your instructor approves, you can hand in your carbon copy and mail the original.) Write a sincere letter of appreciation to one person who has had a profound and lasting good effect on your life. Perhaps he or she encouraged you to stick with a job when you almost quit, helped pay your college expenses, or contributed in any other special way to your well-being and achievements.

5. *Letter of appreciation and congratulations:* As manager of a wholesale hardware firm with customers in three states, you have just heard that Mr. Archie Oltimer will retire next month, after being in business for 45 years and your customer for 15. Mr. Oltimer's store is over 500 miles from your office—in a town not served by an airline—and you have never met him personally. However, his orders have come regularly through the years, and his payments have been prompt. Now he has sold his store to a younger man. Write him a sincere message of appreciation and congratulations.

6. *Letter congratulating a former college classmate:* Assume that one day six years from now you happen to read, in a professional or business journal, about a former college classmate of yours. She has been chosen to deliver the main address at the next regional convention of a national organization

you belong to. You're pleased that she has gained a distinguished reputation as a technical expert in the field—all in the few years since her graduation. Write her an appropriate note of congratulations.

7. ***Letter congratulating new Pan Xenia president:*** As manager of the foreign department of Your City Bank, write a congratulatory letter to Mr. Paul Mifford, recently elected president of Pan Xenia, international business honorary. Make up any other pertinent facts.

8. ***Rewrite of congratulatory letter:*** Improve the tone and you-attitude in the following message.

   ```
   I have just read that you have been promoted to vice presi-
   dent of your company.

   I am sure your attainment unequivocally substantiates the
   exemplary service you are giving your employer.  I believe
   you can be justifiably proud of your outstanding performance
   in the industry.

   I forward my heartiest congratulations and wishes for your
   continued success in your endeavors.
   ```

9. ***Letter congratulating each Quarter Century Club member:*** You are business manager of the Nelson Jewelry firm, registered jewelers in the American Gem Society. The largest bank in your city has just bought from you 35 of your $160 watches, which the bank will present to its employees who become members of the Quarter Century Club (25-year employees of the bank). The watches will be presented at a banquet two weeks from today. Your jewelry store has agreed to take care of all the service on these watches for one year free of charge. Write a letter of congratulations to be addressed individually to each new Quarter Century Club member, and include whatever goodwill-building material about your store is desirable. Make these people feel welcome to use your services.

10. ***Letter thanking instructor for help on fund-raising:*** Assume you graduated from college six years ago and have been successfully employed in work you like. You have also been active in a volunteer organization that helps a clinic for handicapped people in your community. Recently you were appointed chairperson of a fund-raising committee that decided to send persuasive letters to three groups of people, asking for donations. Because you felt you needed some (free) expert advice on your three rough drafts, you phoned your former business communication instructor. Though that particular week happened to be a time when this professor was heavily involved with responsibilities and deadlines on previous professional commitments, she (or he) willingly devoted an entire evening to your drafts and rewrote one of them almost completely.

   During the past three weeks since these letters were mailed, they have

already raised $3,450 in donations, and the committee plans to use them
again and again for future fund-raising compaigns. Write a letter of appreciation to your former professor for time and help given. Perhaps you can
make up some definite equipment or services that the $3,450 has already
purchased, and invite this professor to come visit the facilities at the clinic.
Be sincere in your thanks and comments.

11. *Five choices for a goodwill letter:* Write (or revise) a goodwill message
    that relates to one of the following situations.
    a. Condolence to the wife or husband of a long-time employee who died.
    b. Message to someone in the hospital because of an automobile accident.
    c. Thanks to a customer for being prompt in making loan payments the
    last three years. (Assume a bank or savings and loan association.)
    d. A message to accompany a clipping you're sending to a business friend.
    e. Thanks to a former teacher or professor for an exceptionally helpful
    course.

12. *Letter showing concern for machine performance:* As customer rela-
    tions manager of the Yurway Products Company, write a checkup letter to
    all business executives who have bought one of your machines to be used
    in their offices. (Assume any machine with which you are familiar.) Your
    letter is to be mailed one month after a machine is sold—to check on
    performance and to catch minor annoyances before they become major
    grievances. You want to make sure the machine is doing a good job for the
    reader, or you might want to know if the operators have any questions you
    can help answer. Will you enclose something for easy answering? Make
    sure your readers understand that your purpose is to help maintain the
    high standards for which your products have been famous, not to sell more
    machines.

13. *Evaluation:* The following letter from an auditor to the office manager of
    a business firm he visited uses play on words. Do you think the tone is
    appropriate and the message pleasingly unique? What do you like or dislike
    about the letter? It is dated December 18 and addressed individually,
    "Dear Mr. (name)."

```
I enjoyed the friendly atmosphere of your office during the
brief time I was with you this year.  Then your financial
statements were done, and I was on my way--to another office
and another short story.

With 199- almost gone, it's time again for a statement--this
time a personal one in which friendship and goodwill rank
high.

As I look back over my own accounts, I know that many things
have been left undone.  With the end of the calendar period
```

coming near, it's time to stop and credit them to your
account.

I wish to enter my appreciation for the courtesies you and
your staff showed me, the pleasure I felt in working with
all of you, and the "thank you" I thought of but might
have left unsaid.

Let me record all these, so my thoughts will be clear, while
I send you BEST WISHES for a HAPPY NEW YEAR.

14. ***Letter congratulating a customer:*** You are public relations manager of
a firm that manufactures lighting fixtures. Yesterday you read in *Illuminating News,* a trade journal, that one of your good customers—Janet Hilter—
has just opened her fifth lighting goods store in Florida this month. The
article states that the store is considered the largest and most modern store
of its kind in the Southeast, in keeping with the tremendous growth of the
area. You recall that eight years ago, when you were credit manager, you
first opened Ms. Hilter's charge account with your factory; she then had
only one store. Through the years she has placed increasingly larger orders
with your firm and has paid them all promptly. Though your lighting fixtures
have had a part in her success, resist the temptation to claim credit yourself
or to dwell on the merits of your products. Write Ms. Hilter a letter of
congratulations.

Reports

Chapter 16

Business Reports: Types, Preparation, Organization, Presentation

To carry on efficient operations, businesses need various reports. In almost any kind of responsible business job—whether you are a management trainee, a salesperson, an accountant, a scientist, a junior executive, or a vice president, you may have to write reports. Your communication effectiveness and, often, your promotion and salary increases are affected by the quality of reports you write.

Four chapters in this text are devoted exclusively to written reports. This chapter provides a *general overview* of business reports. It includes their meaning, classifications, and three main parts. It discusses how to prepare, organize, and outline reports; illustrates visual aids; and summarizes how to achieve the C qualities in written business reports. This information is essential for all business reports. In addition, Chapters 17 through 19 present details, suggestions, and examples for specific types of reports.

MEANING AND CLASSIFICATION OF BUSINESS REPORTS

Because of the wide variety of reports, they can be and have been defined and classified in a variety of ways.

What Is a Business Report?

Although the following statement is only one of many good ways to define a report, it covers adequately the types of reports presented in this book: A business report is an impartial, objective, planned presentation of facts to one or more persons for a specific, significant business purpose. The report facts may pertain to events, conditions, qualities, progress, results, products, problems, or suggested solutions. They may help the receivers understand a complex business situation; carry out operational or technical assignments; or plan procedures, solve problems, and make policy decisions about strategic planning.

Usually a report presents more detail than is covered by the typical one-page factual business letter or memorandum. It requires more attention to organization, visual aids, and other techniques for improving readability. Also, to be impartial and objective a report presents accurate, reliable information logically, without emotional appeals.

Reports travel upward to supervisors and management policymakers; downward and horizontally to those who carry out the work and policies; and outward (outside the firm) to stockholders, customers, the general public, specific firms or individuals, and perhaps government officials. A report may be both written and oral, the written usually preceding an oral presentation based on the written document.

How Are Business Reports Classified?

You can classify business reports in at least six different ways—according to:

1. *Function:* whether to inform or to analyze. The informational report presents the facts and a summary—without stating analyses, conclusions, or recom-

mendations. Among the special names for informational reports are "progress reports," "interim reports," and "quarterly reports." Each company has its own titles.

The analytical report presents facts, analyzes and interprets them, and then draws conclusions. It may also make recommendations to change or remain with the status quo. Analytical reports, for example, may be labeled "recommendation reports," "proposals," or "justification reports."

2. *Subject matter:* usually in keeping with the department from which the report originates. Examples include accounting, advertising, collection, credit, engineering, finance, insurance, marketing, operations, personnel, production, statistical, and technical reports.

3. *Formality:* whether formal or informal. Formal reports are generally long— more than 10 pages—and encompass complex problems. Informal reports are generally short. However, meanings of the terms "long" and "short" vary depending on circumstances as illustrated in Chapters 17 and 18. *General differences* in the main parts of formal and informal reports are noteworthy here.

Formal reports always include—in addition to the body (introduction, text, terminal section)—some of or all these prefatory and supplemental parts:

Prefatory parts—cover; title fly; title page; letters of authorization, acceptance, approval, transmittal; acknowledgments: synopsis, abstract, executive summary; table of contents; table of tables

Supplemental parts—appendix, bibliography or endnotes, glossary, index

Informal reports usually include only the body. Some informal reports, however, may have a title page, transmittal, endnotes, and appendix.

4. *Origin:* whether authorized or voluntary; also whether private or public. Authorized reports are requested or authorized by another person or committee; voluntary reports are written on your own initiative. The private report originates in a private business firm; public reports originate in a government, school, or other publicly financed office.

5. *Frequency of issue:* whether periodic or special. The periodic report comes out at regular intervals—daily, weekly, monthly, or yearly. The special report involves a single occasion or unique situation.

6. *Type or appearance:* mainly influenced by report length and formality. Entries **a, b,** and **c,** below, mention popular types of informal, short reports; **d** refers to the formal, long report.

   a. The *memorandum report* uses memo format with TO, FROM, SUBJECT, DATE; it is usually single-spaced and sent within the organization.
   b. The *letter report* uses letter format with letterhead, inside address, sal-

utation, complimentary close, signature area, and reference section; it is usually single-spaced and may go outside or stay inside the organization.

c. The *report on a printed form* has printed headings, instructions, blank lines, and spaces for the writer to fill in pertinent, specific facts and figures. It is used both inside and outside the firm, is a time-saver, and is adaptable to a variety of uses. Among well-known examples are salespersons' expense vouchers, job application forms, Internal Revenue Form 1040, automobile accident reports, insurance claim reports, employee appraisal reports.

d. The *formal report* is usually longer than the above reports and includes parts other reports don't have. It is used both inside and outside the organization.

You have probably noticed that the various classifications do not place reports into mutually exclusive categories. In fact, one report may have elements of all the categories—as, for example, an authorized, monthly, analytical memo report from the marketing department, written in a standardized form.

PREPARATION BEFORE WRITING REPORTS

As with letters and memos, you want to consider the planning steps before you begin to write a report. This planning process is, of course, much more detailed for long, formal reports than for shorter presentations. Nevertheless, for all reports adequate preparaton *before* writing involves the following *six important planning steps regarding purpose, reader, ideas to include, facts to collect, interpretation, and organization.*

1. Define the Problem, Purpose, and Scope

The first planning step is to analyze the problem involved and know the purpose of your report. Ask questions like *"What* is wanted?" *"How much?" "Why?" "When?"* Answers to those questions will help you determine your problem, purpose, scope, limitations (in time and perhaps funds), and title of the report. Then try to write your purpose in one concise, clear sentence.

A central purpose of many business reports often is to help the receiver solve a problem and make a decision. For example, if your firm is experiencing too great a turnover of employees, that's a problem. The purpose of the report may be to find out what causes the high turnover and how to keep the employees after they have been hired. Your scope might include surveying all employees or a random sample; you might also need to find out how other firms have solved similar problems. Or, in other reports, your problem may be concerned with an investment and a choice between two or more methods, machines, or policies. Your purpose might be to determine "Which proposal is better?" "Should we buy, rent, or lease?" "Should we choose *x, y,* or *z* machines?" and so on. Your scope states boundaries of the problem your report covers.

2. Consider Who Will Receive the Report

Visualizing your reader or listener and his or her needs is an extremely important step in business report preparation. Who wants (or needs) this report? Who will read (or hear) it? How much detail do they prefer? What is the reader's (or listener's) point of view? Experience? Knowledge? Prejudice? Responsibility? Is the recipient an officer of your firm? Stockholder? Customer? Government official? Will the report be sent to several—or perhaps hundreds of—persons at the same time?

In Chapter 25 you will learn that writing to a foreign location also demands awareness of another culture. In those cases, your report may be translated into another language. If your report is primarily for internal use, say, for your supervisor, you can use technical terms used in your area. If it is going overseas, those technical terms may be unfamiliar or be translated with a different meaning. Your language in some instances—particularly when going outside your firm—should be nontechnical.

3. Determine Ideas to Include

In short reports this third step usually involves writing down—in no particular order—any general idea you'll need to develop in order to meet the report's purpose. If the report is long, a detailed working plan follows. For some reports, formulating hypotheses is desirable (even essential) as a basis for determining what information you'll need, and then you will jot down the tentative topic headings in a preliminary, tentative outline.

For instance, if your purpose is to find out what causes the high turnover within the company, you might first jot down ideas concerning working conditions, supervision, salaries, promotion policies, fringe benefits. Then you might consider subdivisions of these topics. Working conditions might involve ideas about physical environment (location of offices or factory; conveniences such as desks, chairs; temperatures; lighting; employee lounge; cafeteria) and intangible factors (such as noise, odors, and transportation). This step helps guide you to kinds of facts you'll need to gather as the basis for a tentative outline.

4. Collect Needed Material

The fourth step in report preparation is to gather needed facts thoughtfully from reliable sources. For some reports you may have all the data in your head or nearby records. For others you may have to do extensive secondary and primary research involving "legwork" in addition to brain work. Databases provide excellent sources of research information.

Secondary Research

Research through published material is *secondary research*. Publications already in print—books, magazines, newspapers, pamphlets, government documents, atlases, reports, encyclopedias—are known as *secondary data*. A good start for your research may be in company, city, or college libraries, to find relevant materials that have been gathered and reported by other persons.

Experienced researchers and report writers advise collecting all possible data that might be needed and recording—in addition to your electronic search materials—your notes on cards or sheets of paper, usually with only one fact or idea on each.

a. At the top of the sheet (or card) place the heading under which the information will be filed. (See your preliminary plan, made in step 3.)

b. Next, write the data source—author, book name or title of article and magazine name, edition, publisher, city, state, date, page numbers. If you already have this biographical information on a master list of sources, you need to write on your note cards only the source number and page. For example, "5:82" means "source 5, page 82."

Some students put all their notes on floppy disks or diskettes, then later call up information via key words or phrases relating to the issues before them. Thus they electronically transfer previously collected notes from their own database directly to their final reports.

c. Record the facts you need, or keep a hard copy of a computer-generated printout of needed information. To avoid plagiarism, indicate whether you are quoting verbatim, paraphrasing, or merely recording the gist in your own summary necessary, as shown in Chapter 18.

Primary Research

To collect *primary data* (that which you "dig up" firsthand from unpublished information), you may use—with permission:

a. Records from your organization's files

b. Original letters, diaries, minutes, reports

c. Questionnaires—mailed, telephoned, or taken in person

d. Handwritten notes and tape recordings made during interviews

e. Personal observations—such as counting cars in a parking lot at different hours of the day, observing mannerisms of individuals as they approach a cashier to pay their bills, or witnessing a car accident

f. Experiments—such as comparing two groups in which all factors, except for one independent factor with which you are "experimenting," are the same

For suggestions on wording and arrangement of questions in direct-request survey inquiries (by questionnaires, letters, or interviews), see pages 141–142 and References and Notes footnote 1, Chapter 7.

In primary research the unpublished sources and recording methods you choose will of course vary with the purpose and problem your report covers. You will need to prepare desirable forms on which to record and tabulate interview replies, observations, and experiments. For additional information on specifics, consult books devoted exclusively to business report writing; these are available in your city and school libraries.

Electronic Databases

While hard copy print material is abundant for your secondary research, the newer electronic databases offer thousands of sources for reports and information about companies and topics. Instead of reading an article in the actual journal, you can obtain an abstract or complete copy of that article on a computer screen. For instance, two prominent on-line, up-to-the-minute databases are Dow Jones News Retrieval and LEXIS; additionally there are over 4,000 other electronic databases. A check with your computer center or library will indicate which databases are available.

The following is one example of the wide range of electronic sources available, and the large amount of information contained in each. Chapter 18 has a more complete example and its Exercise 3 requests a detailed listing of online data bases.

```
ABI/INFORM, 1971-present.
Abstracts over 500 publications; covers all phases of busi-
ness management and administration.
```

Keystroking a key word or words on the computer will call up the articles that have that word or those words in them. You can first review the titles of the articles, then view an abstract, and then in many instances view the entire article. It is a simple step from there to have either the abstract or the entire article printed as hard copy. Libraries and computing centers generally charge for this service; some computers accept cards from which magnetic "credits" (previously purchased by the user) are automatically deducted during printing of the information.

Electronic searching is instantaneous. Your problem often will not be locating material, but deciding what material to omit from your report. As cooperation between libraries around the country increases, even wider electronic data searching will be possible.

5. Sort, Analyze, and Interpret Data

In this fifth step the amount of brain work depends of course on the complexity of your research as determined by *purpose and reader needs.* In a short, informational report this step may take only a few minutes. In a long, analytical report based on masses of detailed data from many sources, this step may require weeks of study, arranging, and analysis between the first sorting and the final interpreting of data. Your analysis and interpretations should of course be objective, free from your own personal bias (if you have any). To be honest, never omit or manipulate relevant facts, though they may be contrary to your own preferences or may require a decision different from what you had expected.

Now is also the time to reconsider the logic of your hypotheses and whether any main ideas in your original, tentative outline (in step 3) should be revised. Occasionally, after investigating your primary and secondary sources, you may find that some points in your tentative outline are not logical or possible to complete. Conversely, some areas that should have been included in the outline may have been omitted. And so you now revise, add, and delete topics where necessary.

6. Organize Data and Prepare Final Outline

After careful analysis and interpretation, you will organize the findings and make the final outline. But before preparing such an outline, you need to know what constitutes a report body and to consider various methods of organizing and outlining. These areas are discussed in the next two sections of this chapter.

MAIN PARTS OF THE REPORT

After you have completed the six preparation steps, you turn to the main parts of the report. These usually contain three sections: introduction, text or body, and terminal section.

Introduction: Eleven Elements to Consider

The introduction should orient the reader toward better understanding of the report. For a short report the introduction requires considerably fewer elements than for long reports. You can include in the introduction any of the following elements if they are helpful to the reader and apply to your report:

Authorization	Scope	Definition of terms
Plan of presentation	Methodology	Limitations
or layout	Sources	Brief statement of the
Problem	Background	results
Purpose		

1. *Authorization* names the person or committee (if any) requesting the report. If it is a voluntary report, this introductory element is omitted. When you include the authorization, use conversational language—such as "as you requested" or "as (name and title) authorized"—rather than stilted words like "pursuant to your request."

2. *Plan of presentation or layout* (also called *structural organizer*) tells the reader in what broad areas (major divisions) the text is developed

and in what order the topics will be presented. For instance, the following statement was included in a long report:

```
Thus background will include a history of the situation,
followed by a discussion of the problem, criteria which a
solution must meet, solution alternatives, and then our
final recommendation.
```

The *layout* is a stated agenda that the report will follow. In a one-page report the layout may be omitted, because the reader can see at a glance what the report will cover. (Note that this book uses layouts: most major sections are introduced with a statement of what topics will follow in the section.)

3. *Problem* is usually defined early in the introduction. In fact, many introductions begin with stating the problem and then proceeding to the purpose—which is often determined by the problem.

4. *Purpose* must appear in every introduction. It is the most important single element because it should determine what the writer includes in the report. Among other names for purpose are "objective," "aim," "goal," "mission," "object," "strategy."

5. *Scope* relates to the extent and boundary of the investigation and of the report. For instance, if you are inquiring by questionnaire what married women customers between 25 and 35 years of age living in your city think about something—that's your scope. You don't include anyone else. (See also suggestions about scope on page 442.)

6. *Methodology* refers to the methods of collecting information. You might get data by reading library materials or reviewing databases or by conducting interviews, surveys, or experiments or simply by observing. In production reports, you may need to describe apparatus and materials used for experiments.

7. *Sources*—primary and secondary—are those that furnished the main information for your report. You may include publications, databases, company records, letters, minutes, documents, interviewees, employees, homeowners, and so forth.

   If you are writing a report of your own experience, you are your own source for the statements made in the report. But if you consulted other sources, you mention them—usually in a general summary statement. (Specifics come later, in the text section and bibliography.)

8. *Background* (or history) of the situation being investigated is sometimes included if the reader needs background information to grasp the overall picture and clearly understand the present discussion.

9. *Definition of terms* is necessary if you use any terms that have several possible interpretations. You need to tell the reader the exact meaning you have in mind. You can define terms in three different places—in

the introduction, in a glossary at the end of the report, or within the text of the report. The introduction is the best place when you have only a few (one to five) terms to define and the terms occur with this meaning throughout the report. If you have many definitions, a glossary is the best. Defining each word as you develop the text is also quite acceptable—especially when the word being defined doesn't occur throughout the report. Abbreviations should always be defined—usually in parentheses—when they are first used.

10. *Limitations* refer to restrictions such as time, money, research assistance, or available data. Without sounding negative, the writer should mention those factors that precluded further investigation.

11. *Brief statement of the results or recommendation* tells the decision—whether or not to buy, which machine is the best, who is your choice of applicant, or what is your recommendation. Then as the reader reads the details in the text, he or she knows how the facts affect the decision. This element is appropriate only when the terminal section comes at the end of the report body and when revealing the decision before the discussion is psychologically sound.

In short reports the few needed elements may be combined into one or two paragraphs with or without the title "Introduction." In some short, periodic reports (especially those covering the same topics every period) you might even omit the introduction if its contents are the same each period and your reader knows them.

For long, formal reports the introduction may occupy several pages, but usually less than one-tenth of the entire report. In these long reports the introductory section always has a title—"Introduction" or a meaningful substitute. Also, subheadings (for example: "Problem and Purpose," "Scope," "Background," "Methodology," "Plan of Organization") should be used whenever such guides would be helpful to the reader. If one or more lengthy elements tend to make the introduction disproportionately long, you can take them out of the introduction and place them separately under specific headings in the text or as part of the appendix.

Text: All Necessary Explanation and Support

The longest portion of any report body is the text. In fact, sometimes (in short, routine, periodic reports) the text may be the whole report—if introduction and terminal section are omitted. In this section you discuss and develop the necessary details that help you fulfill the report's purpose. As with all good business writing, include pertinent facts and trim away nonessentials.

The text is never labeled "Text." Its title may be "Discussion," "Findings," "Data," or other meaningful words. Or, instead of one main title for this section, you may use a series of headings throughout the text, corresponding to the main topics discussed in it. (Chapters 17 and 18 illustrate various headings for the text portion.)

Terminal Section: Summary, Conclusions, Recommendations

Whether the terminal section appears before or after the text, it should definitely add to its value. Its functions are to summarize clearly the highlights of the whole report, or to conclude, recommend, or both. This terminal section should be based on the text discussion and should include no new material.

The terminal section for an *informational* report is usually called "Summary." For an *analytical* report, it is usually called "Conclusions" or "Recommendations" (or a combination—such as "Conclusions and Recommendations"). Sometimes it is named "A Plan of Action," or "Propositions." The terminal section is never labeled merely "Terminal Section."

1. A *summary* condenses the text discussion, but not necessarily the entire text. Sometimes only the main points, strong and weak points, or benefits and disadvantages are summarized.

2. The *conclusions* evaluate facts discussed, without including the writer's personal opinion. Actually it is difficult to filter out personal opinion completely, but you should be careful to make your evaluation only from data in your text.

3. *Recommendations* suggest a program of action based on the conclusions. If you make recommendations throughout the report, you will probably summarize them here. (The same is true for conclusions.)

4. A *plan of action*, as a last statement, may include a time line as to when implementation will occur, attribution of responsibility for sections of the recommendation, and often budget concerns relating to implementation.

5. *Propositions*, recently being used in academic or scholarly journals, are a series of assertions based on the article or report. The intent is to state conclusions in a more assertive manner.

In some reports an unusual title, such as "Benefits," or "Recommended Solutions," or "Suggested Action," is appropriate for the terminal section. Among other possible titles are "Probable Developments," "Pertinent Suggestions," "Merits of the Plan," "Final Decision," "Forecast" (as an economist might make), "Important Precautions," and "Future Directions."

ORGANIZATION AND OUTLINE OF REPORT BODY

How a report is organized has a distinct bearing on the manner in which it will be received and acted upon. The report's readers, purpose, and subject matter must be considered when you choose the organizational plan for the entire report body and the text section. Then you will need to outline the topics correctly.

Plans for Organizing Report Body

The two usual ways to organize a report body are by the deductive (direct) and inductive (indirect) plans. Most business reports are organized deductively because readers wish to know early the recommendation or conclusions.

Deductive Arrangement

The word *deductive,* or *direct,* means describing up front in your report *the main ideas or main recommendations before presenting detailed evidence and explanation.*[1] It is comparable to the direct plan used for direct requests and good-news messages (see Chapter 6, pages 120 and 121). For reports following the deductive pattern, the three sections may be arranged in one of these two ways:

Terminal section	Introduction
Introduction	Terminal section
Text (discussion and	Text (discussion and
explanation)	explanation)

or

In a lengthy report, readers usually prefer the deductive arrangement because it gives them an immediate picture before they delve into the mass of supporting details. If the terminal section is *not* at the beginning, some readers skip to the end of the report, read the terminal section, and then return to the beginning. Even in the one- or two-page memo report, many business executives prefer the deductive to the inductive order. In general, you may (or should) use the deductive plan if your reader:

1. Is a busy executive who wishes to know first what the conclusions are or what action is to be taken, where, and who has the responsibility

2. Prefers to determine quickly whether to scan the text for confirmation of conclusions or recommendations and whether the rest of the report is worth reading

3. Will consider your conclusions good news or neutral information

4. Can better analyze data if conclusions or recommendations are given first

5. Wants the writer's point of view promptly

6. Dislikes suspense and prefers to see the recommended action first so that the discussion then substantiates it

7. Prefers that the report (or all reports) be organized in this order

8. Is basically friendly and receptive to the report's conclusions and recommendations

Inductive Arrangement

The words *indirect* and *known to unknown* highlight the inductive organizational plan. It is basically the same indirect plan you have used for bad-news and persuasive-request messages (as outlined in Chapter 6, pages 122 and 123). You present the *explanation before the main ideas or recommendation.*

You present much evidence and supporting materials before arriving at the main recommendation or conclusion. What the inductive approach does is hold the reader in suspense, with an end toward making him or her more receptive to what is a potentially unfavorable conclusion. For reports, the three sections are organized in this order:

Introduction

Text (discussion and explanation)

Terminal section

When should you choose the inductive arrangement for a report? In general, you may use this plan if you estimate that your reader:

1. Must have a detailed explanation first in order to understand the conclusions and/or recommendations; for example, in scientific and technical reports

2. Is the type who will fight your decision unless he or she is first given complete details and becomes convinced by logical development of evidence

3. Will consider your conclusions bad news, because they are contrary to the expected outcome of the study

4. Might feel less bias toward conclusions and be more likely to accept them if first given an analysis of important factors

5. Needs to be encouraged to read the entire report, not just the terminal section

6. Prefers that this report (or all reports) be organized in this order

7. Is potentially hostile to the report, to you, or to the committee asked to present the material

Ways to Organize Report Text Section

One of the most challenging tasks in report writing is to decide on the best way to organize the mass of details in the text section. You must make this decision before you prepare the final outline and, of course, before you begin writing the report. You can develop the text in one (or more) of the following ways:

1. *By criteria or topics*. This is the most common. Your main headings may be the standards, factors, solution options, benefits, or characteristics—criteria—on which a decision rests. For example, if your report's purpose is to determine whether the firm should buy, rent, or lease trucks, or whether it should open a new branch in City X or Y, or which applicant it should hire for a management job, and so on, you first decide which criteria are important for the decision. You use them as headings; also, you try to determine subtopics (subheadings) that relate to them.

2. *By order of occurrence*. Agendas, minutes of meetings, convention programs, progress reports, and write-ups of events or procedures may follow this chronological arrangement. The time periods may be by the hour, day, season, year, or whatever best fits the subject matter.

3. *By order of location or space*. This organization is useful for any orderly description focusing on space location of units—whether they are in a house, factory, office building, shopping center, or international firm with branches widely distributed geographically. For instance, the main divisions in a report on a national firm's operations could be by regions—Northeast, Southeast, Central, and so on. To illustrate the political implications of a policy change, you can write about its influence in Europe, the Middle East, the Far East, and the Western Hemisphere. Or, only the southern, eastern, and central states could be compared on an issue.

4. *By procedure or process*. While close to the chronological pattern, this method traces the steps of, say, a policy, or the operations of a machine, or the step-by-step procedure a bank teller might use in handling a deposit or withdrawal.

5. *By order of importance or by alphabetization*. First present the most important ideas, events, or topics, and proceed to the less important points. If all items are of almost equal importance, arrange them by some other reasonable plan, perhaps alphabetically. Also, when you organize your text by criteria, you can arrange them by order of importance, if desirable.

6. *By order of familiarity*. Always proceed from the simple or familiar to the complex or unfamiliar, because the reader can comprehend better what is known than what is not known. Likewise, begin with present circumstances and then proceed to the proposed situation.

7. *By sources*. This method is less desirable unless you are sure your reader is most interested in what each source revealed rather than in the criteria or other important ideas. You can use this way if, for example, you are reporting on prominent experts who spoke at the convention your firm asked you to attend.

8. *By problem solution.* This popular structure is just that: an initial discussion of the problem followed by a solution. It is also a common way to organize an oral persuasive presentation.

Methods of Outlining

After you have decided how to organize the body and the text, you will arrange the headings and subheadings in an outline. A good outline, especially for reports two or more pages long, is an essential tool and a real time-saver. It will become your guide for writing the report. In a long, formal report, it also becomes your table of contents.

The outline helps you—before you write the report—to see the relationship between topics, compare proportions and headings, check for loopholes in logical order, and eliminate overlapping. Before you word and set up the headings and subheads in your outline, you need to consider types of headings, formats of outlines, and parallelism in headings.

Types of Headings

For the wording of headings, you can choose from four heading types: *topic, complete sentence, imperative sentence, or variant.* Topic headings are the most common. They consist of single words (nouns), a few words, or short phrases. Complete sentence headings always include a subject and a verb. Imperative sentence headings (like commands) begin with a verb and omit the subject, which is an understood "you." Variant headings usually begin with a participle. Compare these examples of different ways to write one heading:

Topic headings
Preparation   *or*   Preparation before Writing

Complete sentence headings
Preparation Is   A Writer Should
   Essential before *or*   Prepare before   *or*   Preparing Is
   Writing Reports   Writing Reports   Essential

Imperative sentence headings
Prepare Efficiently   *or*   Prepare before Writing Reports

Variant headings
Preparing   *or*   Preparing before Writing Reports

A good heading should clearly indicate the subject matter below it, preferably using no more than eight words. If you choose a one-word topic heading, be sure it doesn't indicate broader discussion than actually is included under it.

For instance, the heading "Students" would be far too broad and vague for a report on the living expenses of college seniors at a particular college.

Formats of Outlines

Having chosen your organizational plan and the wording of your main headings, you next choose a way to show levels (degrees) for the various items in your outline. For short outlines (or only three or four headings and subheadings), you may prefer a format of simple indentions or bullets. Longer outlines will be clearer if you use one of the three ways to number heading degrees shown in Figure 16-1.

The traditional *numeral-letter combination* is popular in businesses and schools. The *decimal system* is favored in scientific and technical reports. The *letter-numeral combination* is used by those who prefer letters before main headings and do not need in their reports the additional degree that is possible with Roman numerals.

When arranging your headings and subheadings in the outline of the report's text, remember these five important cautions:

1. Place the most important ideas (for instance, your criteria) in the highest degrees of headings, considering report length, subject matter, and reader.

2. Try to balance the sections as well as possible. For example, if section II.A, in Figure 16-1, had 12 subheadings and section II.B had no subheadings, the proportion would be lopsided. You might then try to narrow the scope of heading II.A (by rewarding it and by rearranging facts) and broaden II.B.

3. Have at least two subheadings if you divide any topic; for example, A.1 and A.2, *never* merely A.1.

4. Use good judgment in the number of section headings for readability—neither too many (which could be annoying) nor too few. (Usually three to seven main sections are considered desirable.)

5. Never use the report title as a section heading. Also do not begin the first sentence with exactly the same words as the heading.

Parallelism in Headings

For parallel—and consistent—construction, all headings of the same degree within any part of an outline should be parallel to each other. This means they should have the same grammatical form—all nouns, all phrases, or all clauses or sentences. For example, in the Figure 16-1 numeral-letter outline the following headings should be parallel to each other: I, II, III, IV, V; A, B, C, D under I; 1, 2, 3 under II.A; 1 and 2 under II.B; a and b under II.B.2, and so on. However, subheadings 1, 2, 3 under II.A need not be parallel with subheadings 1 and 2 under II.B, nor with other third-degree subheadings in other sections. Compare the following headings for parallelism:

	Degree of Heading	Numeral-Letter Combination	Decimal System	Letter-Numeral Combination
Introduction	1st 2d 2d 2d 2d	I. A. B. C. D.	1.0 1.1 1.2 1.3 1.4	A. 1. 2. 3. 4.
Text/ Discussion	1st 2d 3d 3d 3d 2d 3d 3d 4th 4th 5th 5th	II. A. 1. 2. 3 B. 1. 2. a. b. (1) (2)	2.0 2.1 2.11 2.12 2.13 2.2 2.21 2.22 2.221 2.222 2.2221 2.2222	B. 1. a. b. c 2. a. b. (1) (2) (a) (b)
	1st 2d 3d 3d 2d 3d 3d 3d	III. A. 1. 2. B. 1. 2. 3.	3.0 3.1 3.11 3.12 3.2 3.21 3.22 3.23	C. 1. a. b. 2. a. b. c.
	1st 2d 3d 3d 2d 3d 3d	IV. A. 1. 2. B. 1. 2.	4.0 4.1 4.11 4.12 4.2 4.21 4.22	D. 1. a. b. 2. a. b.
Summary/ Conclusions/ Recommendations	1st 2d 2d 2d	V. A. B. C.	5.0 5.1 5.2 5.3	E. 1. 2. 3.

Figure 16–1   Three ways to indicate heading degrees in report outlines. This sample is arranged for an inductively organized report. (For deductive organization the introduction and terminal section will be I and II; the text will be III, IV, V, etc.)

Parallel (all topic headings—phrases)	Parallel (all imperative sentence headings)	Not parallel (topic, variant, and sentence headings)
Types of Headings	Select Heading Types	Types of Headings
Formats of Outlines	Choose Outline Formats	Choosing Outline Format
Parallelism, in Headings	Make Headings Parallel	Make Headings Parallel
Purposes of Calendars	Keep Calendars Current	Calendars Must Be Current

VISUAL AIDS

To help improve both readability and appearance of a report, good writers use headings and—when desirable—also graphic materials. Modern graphic packages for use on personal computers or word processors make creating a visual relatively simple and easily amendable. Because of their importance, these visual aids deserve special attention both before and during the actual writing of the report.

Headings and Subheadings as Directional Signs

The headings you have selected for your final outline will be directional signs for the reader of the finished report. Headings help direct the reader through the entire presentation.

When a heading has subheadings, usually first tell your reader what the subheadings are *before* you discuss them. See, for example, the various transitional introductory sentences and paragraphs in this chapter (and throughout the text) after most headings that have subheadings. However, sometimes transitional sentences are unnecessary and may be omitted. If the material under each subhead has only a few lines, these subheads will follow each other so closely that the reader needs no sentence to introduce them.

Figure 16-2 shows one popular system of styling the headings you may need for reports of various lengths. The paragraph or paragraphs under each heading include detailed suggestions regarding use, placement, type style, underlining, and capitalization. The following example briefly summarizes (in brackets) noteworthy points about headings like those in Figure 16-2.

FIRST-DEGREE HEADINGS [Centered and in all capitals-caps]

Second-Degree Headings [Centered, caps and lowercase, underlined]

Third-Degree Headings [Left margin, caps and lowercase, underlined]

FIRST-DEGREE HEADINGS

In a report that requires four or five degrees of main headings
you can type the first-degree headings in all capitals for the
introduction, text main divisions, and terminal section. They
are centered and are usually placed with three blank lines above
them and two blank lines below them. (The title of such a
report may be all capitals and underlined or typed with
S P A C E D   C A P I T A L S.)

Second-Degree Headings

If in a long report you use first-degree headings for the main
sections, then the highest-level subheadings within those sections will have second-degree headings. They are centered
and typed with or without underscoring. You capitalize the
first word and all others except prepositions (such as through,
to, of, with, on), conjunctions (for example, and, but, as,
when), and articles (the, a, an). Some authorities prefer
capitalizing prepositions with more than five letters. Leaving
at least two blank lines above these headings and one blank line
below is desirable.

If your report's title is the all-capitals, first-degree heading, you may use second-degree headings for main sections--
introduction, text main divisions, and terminal section. In a
short report that has only two or three degrees of headings, you
may if you wish use a second-degree heading for its title. Then
the subheadings will be third-degree and lower.

Third-Degree Headings

Placed flush with the left margin, third-degree headings are
underscored (in typing). Leave a blank line before them and (usually) a blank line after them. Capitalization can be the same
as for the second degree (as in this example), or only the first
word need be capitalized. (Then "D" in "Degree" and "H" in
"Headings" would be in lowercase.)

    Fourth-degree headings.--When you need a fourth level for
subheadings, you can type them just like the third-degree headings except that they are indented, usually five spaces, from
the left margin and followed by a period. Adding a dash is
optional. These headings are usually underscored if regular type
is used. The paragraph begins on the same line as the heading,
which is typed with one blank line above it.

    Fifth-degree headings consist of merely the underscored (or
italicized) first key word or words of the first sentence in the
paragraph. Use this degree of heading when the report requires
all five degrees or when you started with third-degree and are
using third-, fourth-, and fifth-degree headings.

Figure 16–2 *Levels of headings.*

Fourth-degree headings. [Indented, underlined, lowercase; paragraph begins on same
line]
Fifth-degree headings [Indented, underlined; sentence
begins with the heading]

Other type styles and placement of headings may be acceptable too. For instance, using boldface type is popular in first-degree and second-degree headings. Whatever is your chosen style, it should be used *consistently throughout the report*. Margin width may easily be set with software packages, along with type styles, underlining, bold letters, italics, and a host of other variations. Standard typewriters do not have as many options, but will permit different type sizes, styles, italics, and underlinings.

Microcomputer Graphics for Quantitative and Other Data

Whenever you must present numerous figures (quantitative data) or describe a technical process or a procedure, well-planned graphic materials will help give the picture more quickly—and interestingly—for your reader or listeners. Some graphic aids (also called *visual aids* or *illustrations*) are still constructed by hand. Today, microcomputers and readily available graphic packages make that task easier.

Equipment

What you need with microcomputer equipment depends on the software package you choose. For instance, *Harvard Graphics* demands a DOS-compatible system with at least 512K of memory; Microsoft *Chart* requires an IBM PC or compatible machine, with at least 256K of memory; while Claris *MacPaint 2.0* works on the Macintosh 512 enhanced, Macintosh enhanced, Macintosh SE, and Macintosh II. Each system has its own variables for graphic display. Your budget and equipment are the only hindrance to obtaining a wide-ranging, though similar, microcomputer graphics package. A periodical, *The Office*, can keep you up to date on office equipment capable of the latest microcomputer graphics.

Graphics Packages for Visual Aids

The jargon of each graphics package is different. In *MacPaint* you will use such tools as *rectangle* (selects a rectangular portion of a picture), *lasso* (selects irregular shapes in a picture), *grabber* (permits scrolling within a picture), *paint bucket* (fills in patterns), *spray can* (applies spots of paint or continuously paints a pattern), *paintbrush* (determines the paint strokes within a current paint pattern), and numerous other variations.

A representative sample of what software packages can do to enhance your presentations is seen in the following list of *MacPaint's* options:[2]

- Draw straight lines and round circles and create precise shapes and intricate patterns
- Add patterns to your pictures by "painting" with several sizes and shapes of brushes
- Select any part of a picture and move, duplicate, rotate, flip, stretch, shrink, or invert it
- Add text to a picture in a variety of fonts, font sizes, and font styles
- Move in for close-up views of a picture—as if you had a magnifying glass—so you can do detail work
- Enjoy the freedom to experiment, try new effects, undo what you don't like, create several versions of an idea, combine images from several different sources, and finally, put your work on paper
- Create or edit pictures that you can "paste" into documents created with word processing or page-layout programs
- Open up to nine documents at a time
- Zoom in to magnify a picture 200, 400, or 800 percent
- Draw ovals, circles, rectangles, and rounded rectangles from the center outward or from corner to corner
- Take a snapshot of a picture, permitting later changes to that snapshot.

Sample Graphics for Quantitative and Other Data

Following are illustrations and brief explanations of the more popular graphics that can enhance your written and oral presentations; all can be created using a graphics package. Each, clearly, has its own strengths and weaknesses.

Tables

Perhaps the easiest table to prepare is the numbered list, in which quantitative information, or words, or a combination of the two are presented in rows and columns. The titles of the rows (horizontal lines) are usually called *stubs*, and the titles of the columns (vertical lines, sometimes called *variables*) are *captions*. Tables have the following strengths and weaknesses:

Strengths	**Weaknesses**
Permit precise figures to be used	Do not visually show differences in data
Make complete decimal detail possible	May be too detailed; with too many items, values may distract reader
Allow numeric data to be combined with nonnumeric information	Are more useful in written than in oral presentations
Allow reader to return for in-depth review	May be visually dull

A table is illustrated in Figure 16–3.

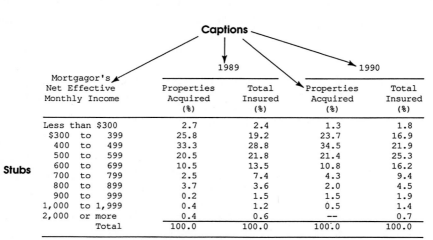

Table 3 Percentages of Properties Acquired and Insured,
1989 and 1990

Figure 16–3   *Illustration of a numbered table.*

Bar Graphs

Easy to construct and understand, column and bar graphs and bar charts—
often in color—are among the most common and adaptable types of graphic
presentation. Each has its own strengths and weaknesses:

Strengths	Weaknesses
Comparisons or trends easily shown	Inclusion of too much detail may require lettering too small to read
Main titles and subtitles for data easily added	Precise distinctions between variables harder to see
Oral presentations possible, if simple in form	Not all headings consistent between graphs on x and y axes
Color and cross-hatching add to visual appeal	Visual impact may overwhelm content

Vertical Bar Graphs.   When a time factor is considered, vertical bars are
especially useful (see Figure 16–4).

Stacked Vertical Bar Graphs.   When two or more items or parts of a subject
are being compared for the same year, a stacked vertical bar graph is helpful.
Each item on a bar has different color or cross-hatching (Figure 16–5).

Notice that in Figure 16-4 the dates are placed across the bottom scale. Millions of dollars beginning with zero at the bottom are listed upward at the left, to help determine the height of each bar. A figure above each bar shows its total.

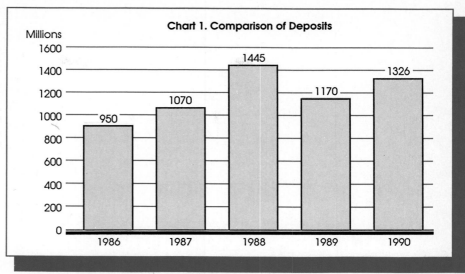

Figure 16—4 A vertical bar graph.

In Figure 16-5 one can see easily how a firm's two branch stores-A and B-compared in total number of cars sold each year.

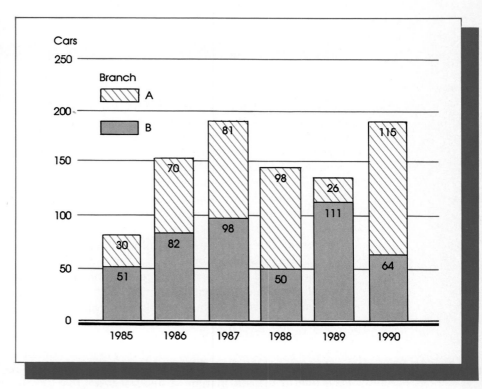

Figure 16—5 A stacked vertical bar graph.

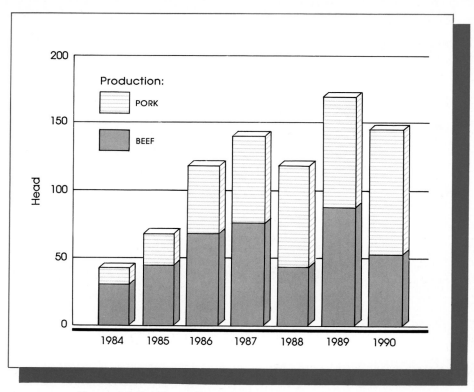

Figure 16–6   Three-dimensional stacked vertical bar graph.

Three-Dimensional, Stacked, Vertical Bar Graphs.   With a software package for a microcomputer, labeling of variables and alteration of legends can be easily done. In fact, *Cricket Graph, MacDraw II, MacPaint*, and others[3] permit numerous variations to be added to the basic bar or column graph, including changing text, font, size, style, and orientation. Additionally, a graph can be redrawn in a three-dimensional stacked appearance, illustrated in Figure 16–6. Adding depth further enhances the visual appearance of the bar graph and, for that matter, many other visuals.

Horizontal Bar Graphs.   The information presented in a vertical bar graph may also be presented horizontally. Visual variations—to hold the attention of the reader—add interest to the presentation. Figure 16–7 is an example of a three-dimensional horizontal bar graph that adds a "stacked" value.

Many uses and variations are possible with horizontal bar graphs. They may include single bars or multiple bars, with or without stacks. Suppose, for example, a report focuses on comparing beef and pork production in seven regions (or states or countries) during one year. Then the horizontal, three-dimensional, stacked bar graph would have the names of those seven regions placed one on each line in the left margin (instead of years that are in Figure 16–7). At the bottom, the *x*-axis would show number of head, as in Figure 16–7.

This graph illustrates beef and pork production in one country during each of seven years. The x-axis (on the bottom) indicates the numbers of cattle heads, while the y-axis (vertical, at left) lists the years.

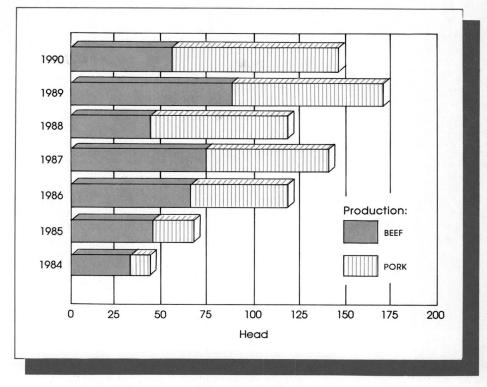

Figure 16–7 *Three-dimensional stacked horizontal bar graph.*

For a different business, Figure 16–8 illustrates a simple horizontal multiple bar graph comparing percent of associations that issued plastic cards for six different uses during two years. Notice that the categories (uses) are at the left, percents are across the bottom of the bars, and the years are identified in the key.

Pie Charts

When you wish to show relative sizes of various categories and the percent that each category adds to the whole, pie charts are the most popular and helpful. To make a comparison of facts easier, the pie segments (pieces) may be shown with percentages—all placed *consistently* either within a slice or outside but near it, as in Figure 16–9.

Strengths and weaknesses of pie charts are as follows:

Strengths	**Weaknesses**
Segment of pie may be lifted out for visual emphasis	Precise distinctions are not as visible when decimal distinctions are needed
Parts of a whole may be shown	

To distinguish the years in each double bar, cross-hatching, shading, or colors may be used. The key to the years (or whatever the variables are) is placed wherever space is available.

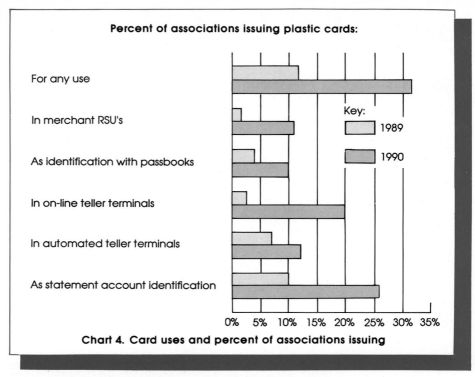

Figure 16–8   *A horizontal multiple-bar graph.*

Strengths

Values, headings, legends may be placed below, inside, or aside data

Both oral and written presentations can use pie charts

Weaknesses

Use of too many parts and values may blur distinctions

Distortions may occur if similar patterns are next to each other

As with bar graphs, you can "explode" or "drag out" a piece of the pie, thereby emphasizing that category. You can also add a three-dimensional variation, as seen in Figure 16–9.

Typically, the legend contains the major category names for the pieces in the pie; preferably there should not be more than six. The names may be listed in a key, or inside each slice if space allows, or outside the pie near the percentages. The third method is shown in Figure 16–9.

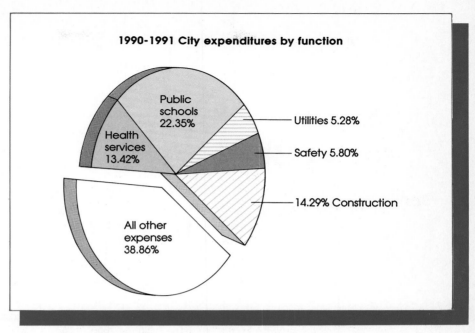

Figure 16–9 *Three-dimensional pie chart with exploded section.*

Line Graphs

Indicating trends over time is a central purpose for the line graph. So too is the wish to compare the distribution of one variable with another, over time. As in our preceding discussions, the line graph may be constructed using a computer software package or drawn with the aid of a drawing board. Several types of graphs involving lines, to indicate changes over time, are available in various software packages: line and area graphs are some of the most common. Linegraphs have the following strengths and weaknesses:

Strengths	Weaknesses
Trends over time, for several variables, permit comparisons	Too many variables and too many dates clutter information
Tick marks indicate increments between values	Fine, precise distinctions are difficult to determine
Symbols on lines aid clarity	Inconsistency for heading on x and y axes may confuse the reader, viewer

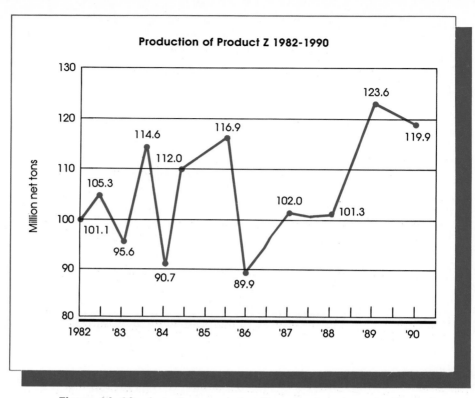

Figure 16–10   *A single-line graph with marked peaks and valleys.*

In a line graph the time increments are usually along the bottom, or *x* axis, and the magnitudes are along the side, or *y* axis. Some software packages, for instance, *Cricket Graph*, accept only figures along the *y* axis.

One feature of a line graph is that the various data points along the lines may each be marked with a small circle or square, and with figures that show totals, as in Figure 16-10.

In Figure 16-11 the line graph compares two categories. To distinguish them from each other, one has small squares; the other, circles. Some graphs may use a different color for each line.

Area Graph

You will see that there is a high similarity between a line graph and an area graph. The major difference in an area graph is that the space or area under the line is filled in. When additional categories are entered, the graph shows, through colors, hues, and other variations, the differences between the cate-

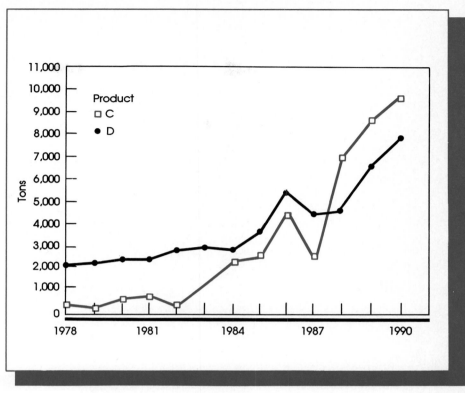

Figure 16–11   *Line graph with two variables.*

gories. Figure 16–12 illustrates how such a graph might look with two variables. It is easily constructed with a graphic software package. Area graphs have the following strengths and weaknesses:

Strengths	Weaknesses
Simple, one-variable changes in volume emphasis aid clarity	Small changes in data may be concealed
Multiple sets of data, in different configurations, can be instantly visible	Dramatic shifts in data are not handled well

Pictograms

Data may also be presented in the form of small pictures (pictograms). They may be arranged in various ways. When used on vertical or horizontal bar graphs, the small pictures—instead of lines—can form the bar rectangles. Depending on your subject matter, these miniature pictures may be created from scratch on a drafting table, taken from a bank of software designs, or formed freehand on a computer. While formal business reports may not make extensive

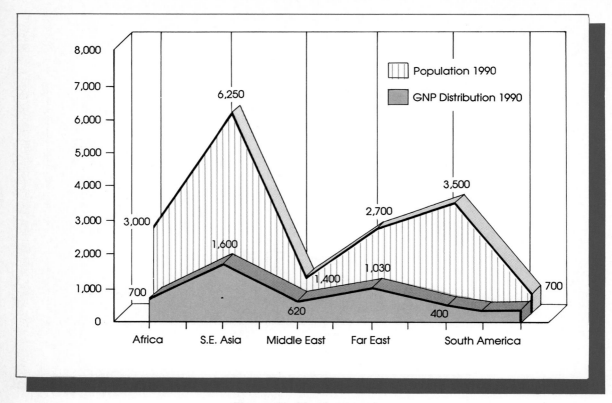

Figure 16–12 Area graph.

use of pictograms, reports to the general public in annual reports to stockholders, company advertising booklets, and desktop publishing may include numerous inventive pictograms such as people, houses, and cars:

All the preceding visual aids may be created on software programs on microcomputers, or if you have the patience, by using drafting materials. Slides and overhead transparencies of any of the preceding visuals can also be rapidly produced.

Other Visual Aids

A wide variety of additional visual aids can be used to help enliven the appearance of a report. Among them are maps, cutaway drawings (like those showing parts of a machine), organizational charts, flowcharts, polar graphs,[4] scatter-

Figure 16-13 uses ▲ ,
■ , and ● symbols
plus three colors to
indicate a firm's
overseas
exploration and
operations

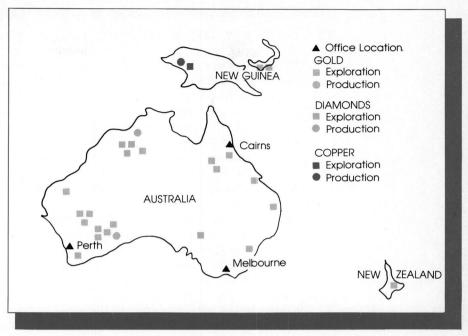

Figure 16–13   A map showing locations of gold, diamond, and copper resources.

grams, photographs, and various design sketches as seen in some labeled figures in Chapters 2, 17, 21, 22, 23, and 25.

Maps help reveal geographic facts and comparisons. They can show locations of natural resources—as in Figure 16-13—or company offices, transportation routes, environmental or weather patterns, quantities of products sold in certain areas, and various other data. To mark locations of pertinent data, you can use small squares, triangles, crosses, circles, cross-hatching, colors, designs, numbers, sketches, or small pictures.

Drawings of maps can be easily made into transparencies or pages in reports. If you work in a highly technical industry, software packages permit drawings of machines and processes, thus helping to clarify an idea or process. Today there are almost limitless possibilities in linking words with visual aids.

Checklist for Effective Visual Presentations

The following suggestions give a general overview of the essentials for effective presentation of graphic materials in your reports.[5]

■ Checklist for Effective Visual Presentations

1. *Placement*. Place your visual as close as possible to the paragraphs wherein the subject is discussed. You may also include graphs in appendices and, if small, in footnotes.
2. *Introduction and interpretation*. Introduce the reader to the visual *before* you show it. One to three sentences may be sufficient. If the graphic is simple, avoid obvious interpretations.
3. *Lead-in sentence*. The sentence before the visual aid may end with words like "as the following table (chart, picture, graph) shows (or illustrates)." If the visual aid is in the appendix, refer to it in the introduction, the text, or both.
4. *Simplicity*. Limit the number of categories in the visual. Six slices in a pie are clear; so are six sets of data in a stacked bar graph, or three to four lines in a line graph. Avoid crowding of labels.
5. *Emphasis*. Add arrows, underlining, vivid color, cross-hatching, "exploding" pie charts for important data.
6. *Scale, patterns, and color*. We read from left to right; colors should be lighter on the left and darker to the right. Avoid placing similar patterns next to one another. In graphs, a height-to-width ratio of 3:4 is pleasing to the eye.
7. *Number and labels*. Most often use the left margin for the vertical axis labels. Normally, do not assign numbers to small tables, charts, graphs when they are placed within a paragraph and occupy only a few lines (perhaps under 10). When there are many illustrations, number them consecutively (as in this chapter). For easy reference, you can have a separate list of tables or figures after the table of contents.
8. *Consistency*. Be consistent in size, style, fonts, patterns, and other variations within a document. Thus axis labels should be consistent from figure to figure within a report or a long memorandum.
9. *Expression of figures*. Round off figures, for instance, "$8,200" instead of "$8,213.41." (Do not round off before multiplying, for the results may be distorted.) Percentages and values are common ways to indicate differences between variations.

SUMMARY—QUALITIES OF WELL-WRITTEN REPORTS

After you have completed your outline and any needed visual aids (in rough draft), you are ready to write the report. and then—before you transmit it—you'll revise wherever necessary. The way you present the report often determines whether it will be accepted by the management people involved.

The following checklist summarizes ways to achieve the seven C qualities for good report writing. Chapters 17 and 18 provide additional details and examples about various parts, procedures, and requirements referred to in this checklist.

■ Checklist of C Qualities in Well-Written Reports

A.   Completeness and Conciseness

1. *Include in the report all facts needed to answer both primary and secondary readers' questions relevant to the report's purpose.* Use an appendix for relevant facts too detailed to be in the body.
2. *Cover the what, why, when, where, who, and how* whenever appropriate for purpose and reader(s).
3. *Give the person who requested the report what he or she wants*— detailed descriptions and figures or mainly highlights with minimum supporting data.
4. *Trim the report to essentials that fit the purpose and reader requirements.* Omit all irrelevant material even if you devoted many hours, days, or weeks to gathering and preparing it.
5. *Avoid wordy, trite expressions, unnecessary repetitions, and overuse of articles and prepositional phrases.* Instead of "Analysis of the data shows," write "Data analysis shows." Good business writing averages only 1 prepositional phrase to every 11 words.
6. *Present both favorable and unfavorable factors* that affect the situation your report covers.
7. *Include whatever prefatory and supplemental parts are desirable,* depending on the report's complexity, length, and "formality." Avoid unnecessary overlapping with the report body (for instance, in the transmittal letter and the introduction).

B.   Concreteness, Conviction, Objectivity

1. *Use specific words and figures* ("52 percent" or "8,100 employees" instead of "many" employees), because they are essential for fair and convincing reports.
2. *Identify information sources* within the introduction, text, or supplemental list. Include appropriate documentation.
3. *Substantiate a source's reliability (if necessary for reader conviction),* by stating truthfully (briefly) whether the source is a recognized authority; where, when, how, and under what conditions the person made the quoted statements; and whether they are likely to be biased.
4. *Be sure you yourself are objective in your quotations, paraphrasing, and abstracting.* Do not quote a source out of context or slant

(continued)

statements with your own intentional bias or opinion. Try to make the abstracted material a fair representation of the whole situation or area from which you abstracted.

5. *Consider carefully the bases for your inferences.* Inform your readers as to what portions of your statements are mere assumptions. Distinguish between verifiable facts, inferences based on facts, and your own assumptions, throughout the report.

6. *Avoid emotional writing*, with glowing adjectives and abverbs based on your opinions.

7. *Present facts impartially*, showing both sides whenever necessary. Don't discolor facts with your personal feelings and prejudices.

8. *Use concrete nouns as subjects of sentences.* Whenever possible, avoid beginning sentences with abstract, intangible nouns or with expletives (*it* is, *there* are, etc.).

9. *Place action in verbs, not in nouns.* Instead of "The function of this department is the *collection* of payments and *notification* of. . . ." say "This department *collects* payments and *notifies*. . . ."

10. *Use mostly active—not passive—verbs.* Instead of the passive verbs in "An observer *was sent* around the plant to . . . , and it *was found* that . . . ," use active verbs: "Management *dispatched* an impartial observer to officially record incidents of. . . . He (or she) *discovered* that. . . ."

11. *Avoid the subjunctive whenever possible*, because it conveys contrary-to-fact ideas in the reader's mind. Instead of *would, could,* and *might* (all subjunctive), use *will* (future) or *can* and *may* (present tense). For example, instead of "For better product distribution your firm *would need* three branch stores; each *would have* a manager who *would* . . . ," write "For better . . . , your firm *needs* three branch stores; each *will* (or *can*) *have* a manager who *can.* . . ."

12. *Write in present tense whenever possible.* Besides using present tense when you refer to the present, use it also when stating a fact that was true in the past and is still true: "The manager informed the employees that promptness *is* (not *was*) expected." Furthermore, use present—not future—tense when referring to something that seems to be happening in the future but actually exists now:

    a. In the introduction write, "This report *shows.* . . ." (not *will show*), because the reader has the completed report before him or her and whatever you're referring to is present now.

    b. Instead of future tense, "Two years of challenging work *will be* ahead for those who *will enter* this program. They *will spend* six months in each area . . . ," write in the present tense: "Two years of challenging work *are* ahead for those who *enter* the program. They *spend* six months in. . . ."

13. *Base your conclusions (if any) or your summary statements on adequate facts, and be sure your written presentation is logical.* Avoid unwarranted, hasty generalizations.

C. Consideration and Courtesy
  1. *Be honest in your research, analysis, interpretation, organization, and presentation of all facts, figures, comments.*
  2. *Choose your organizational plan (inductive or deductive) for the most effective reader reaction.*
  3. *Organize text topics after considering what will be most meaningful for the reader.* If possible, place favorable aspects before the unfavorable and the simpler ideas before the complex.
  4. *Adapt writing style and formality to the reader* by using one of these choices:
      a. In all *memo* and *letter reports* and in other *informal reports* use the same informal style as in letters and memos—personal pronouns (I, we, you, us, our).
      b. In *longer, formal reports*—for instance to top company, public, **or government officials or to the general public (and sometimes** also in reports with controversial subject matter)—you can use an impersonal style in which you never refer to yourself at all. But try to avoid overuse of passive verbs and expletives with this style.
      c. In a more *formal report style*—seldom necessary or desirable in business reports—you might refer to yourself as "the author" and your assistants as "the research staff," "committee," or a similar title.
  5. *Handle disagreeable material tactfully and courteously.* If you know your findings are contrary to the reader's opinions or expectations, you might precede your unfavorable statements by a tactful statement like, "Although one might have expected a different outcome, nevertheless . . . ," or, "Considering your previous experience, a study of these data leads to an unexpected conclusion and. . . ."
  6. *Watch your tone and logic,* to establish or reinforce the reader's confidence in you, the writer.
  7. *Base your recommendations, if any, on logical conclusions resulting from objective presentation of facts—and not on emotional appeals.*
  8. *Omit your own opinions unless the reader asked for them and you clearly label them.*
  9. *Make your report interesting as well as readable* by using topic sentences; headings; and tables, graphs, charts, pictures, or other graphic aids if they will be helpful. Also, occasional questions, pertinent stories, and examples spark interest—if appropriately related to the report's purpose.
  10. *When a decision is close, present in the terminal section both the pros and the cons;* list favorable aspects (advantages) before the unfavorable ones (disadvantages), usually in the same order as in the text discussion. Some reports also include brief opposition or disagreement statements, described in *Robert's Rules of Order*[6] as *minority recommendations*. These statements permit the reader to determine the validity of counterarguments.

(continued)

D. Clarity

1. *Phrase all statements so the reader can easily understand them.* Keep average sentence length within 16 to 20 words, paragraphs an average of 7 to 9 typewritten lines. Include a topic sentence for each paragraph whenever desirable.

2. *Include definitions of any technical terms or abbreviations*—in the introduction, text, or appendix.

3. *In comparing figures, use percentages, ranks, ratios, or rounded-off figures for easier reader comprehension.* But show exact figures somewhere in the report, perhaps in a table right in the text or the appendix.

4. *Use graphic aids*—charts, graphs, pictures, etc.—whenever they help clarify your presentation of quantitative data.

5. *Discuss a graphic aid briefly (the highlights) before you present it.*

6. *Use headings to guide the reader, but be sure your writing is clear and coherent without them.* In the sentence immediately following a heading, do *not* refer to the heading by the word *this* or another pronoun.

7. *Use transitional words and phrases* (such as *also, on the other hand, similarly, for example) to link sentences and tie ideas together.* (For a list of transitional words and phrases see page 779 in Appendix A.)

8. *Use transitional sentences with forward or backward references to link paragraphs or sections.*

   a. A *forward* reference is placed at the end of a paragraph. For example, the last sentence in a paragraph about education might lead to the next paragraph this way: "Thus education of the recent college graduate is important, but so is attitude toward employment."

   b. A *backward* reference sentence can effectively begin a paragraph and serve as both a transition and a topic sentence of that paragraph. In the previous situation, the attitude-toward-employment paragraph could begin with a topic sentence that ties the two paragraphs together, like this: "Education is an important job qualification for a recent college graduate, but so is attitude. . . ." (Do not use both **a** and **b** in consecutive paragraphs.)

9. *Use introductory, summary or concluding, and transitional paragraphs to tie together sections of a report.*

   a. The *introductory* paragraph of a section serves a section the same way a topic sentence serves a paragraph. If a section has two or more subdivisions, always introduce them; provide a brief layout to the reader before you discuss them.

   b. A *summary* or *concluding* paragraph can be effective if a section is quite long—say, three or more typewritten pages—but this final paragraph must definitely be helpful to the reader.

   c. A *transitional* paragraph is especially helpful in a very long report—perhaps with 30 or more typewritten pages. You add this paragraph somewhere in the middle of the report body to tell the reader where she or he is; it tells what has been covered and what is yet to come.

   d. An *internal summary* is sometimes used at the conclusion of a long section of a report; it is an interim statement before the reader gets to the end of the entire document.

10. *List and number conclusions or recommendations* if you have more than one.

E. Correctness

1. *Double-check accuracy of facts, grammar, nondiscriminatory expressions, spelling, parallel structure; relationship of prefatory and supplemental parts (if any) to the text; typing; and mechanics.* (Appendix A includes suggestions you may find helpful regarding abbreviations, numbers, punctuation, syllabication, transitional words, and other elements of mechanics.)

2. *Observe the five important cautions* (page 454) regarding arrangement of headings and subheadings.

3. *Word your conclusions accurately*, with conservative, unexaggerated statements. If they are based on an estimate, state the basis.

4. *Edit to see that your report has all the other good qualities* of report language, readability, and objectivity already mentioned in this checklist, and that important ideas are correctly emphasized (by adequate details, placement, headings, and other visual aids).

5. *Revise your draft(s), and correct errors.*

6. *See that report layout is attractive and uncrowded*, with pleasing margins and white space.

7. *In a long report, check for accuracy of all prefatory and supplemental parts* (Chapter 18) as well as of the body, and see that all parts are placed in correct order.

8. *Include no new material in the terminal section*. It must be based on facts in the discussion section.

EXERCISES AND PROBLEMS

1. ***Report after interviews with two frequent report writers:*** Understanding the process of how others put together a report is helpful in one's own report writing. This chapter suggests the methods to consider when writing a report. However, organizations have their own procedures, their own corporate cultures, and their own suggestions on putting a report together.

   This exercise asks you to interview two persons who write frequently on the job; your task is to report on the process they go through in completing a report. The conclusion of the assignment should give an overview of their personal writing process and the potential influence of the organization on that process. Questions to consider in framing the brief interview follow:

Organizational Process

- What is the organization and what position does the writer hold in that organization?
- To whom are reports most often directed? Do the readers rank above or below the writer?
- Are the reports primarily informative or persuasive?
- Are there any company or organizational constraints on writing reports?
- Is the report recurring, or is it entirely new?

Individual Process

- What kinds of information-gathering steps are followed?
- What are the specific problems the writer faces in the writing process?
- What is the most important element in writing a report?
- What background for writing does the writer bring to the project?
- What length of time is spent writing the report?

After the data are assembled, write a two- to three-page report summarizing your findings and ending with some conclusions or recommendations. Be prepared for a class discussion.

2. *Paragraph revision with inserted transitional words and phrases:* Assume the paragraph just before the one below discusses a firm's tax difficulties. In place of the bracketed words insert a transitional word or phrase from the list on page 779 (or any other source). The words in brackets guide you toward the intended meanings.

```
Wages.   Labor relations present an even more pressing prob-
lem. The cost-of-living index is rising; [result], the company's
wage policy may have to be reexamined.  It is true that the
ABC Amendment permits wage raises to be passed on to the con-
sumer [contrast], many branches of the company will not recover
the increased costs.  The appliance division [instances], would
encounter heavy sales resistance.  [Addition], management will
have to consider the effects of price increases or labor dif-
ficulties in an election year.  [Summary], negotiations with
labor will have to be taken with caution.
```

3. *Evaluations and suggestions for improving this two-page report:*
   a. What improvement can you make in the subject line?
   b. Does the introduction orient the reader to the material that follows? Why or why not? What elements do you find in the introduction? Should it have a heading?
   c. What is the purpose of the introductory paragraph immediately following the "Discussion" heading? Can you suggest a way to improve it?
   d. If the writer had chosen to omit the heading "Discussion" and instead

had placed the titles of the three reports as second-degree headings, what change would this choice have required in the introduction? Which setup do you prefer?

e. What degrees of headings does this report have? What degrees would it have if the change suggested in **d** were made?

f. Is the text organized inductively or deductively?

g. Underline all passive verbs. How many do you find?

h. Circle the active verbs. Does the report have more active than passive verbs?

i. Does each paragraph have a topic sentence?

j. Is the terminal section correctly labeled? Does it satisfactorily carry out its function? Why or why not?

k. Can you suggest any other corrections or improvements?

```
TO:        Layton Browne                    November 10, 199-
FROM:      Thomas Jones   J.J.
SUBJECT:   Installment Credit Department Reports
```

As you requested, I have compared reports written by one commercial bank here in [*city*]. I interviewed Diana Whitelon, assistant cashier at State National Bank, concerning business reports used in her organization. As you are especially interested in installment credit, I have limited my discussion to reports prepared and used by the Installment Credit Department.

Discussion

The three types of reports used in this department and discussed in this report are the Interoffice Memorandum Report, Statistical Report, and Memorandum Report for the Credit File.

Statistical Report

Employees of the installment credit department compile the statistical report monthly under Miss Whitelon's supervision. The report is a statistical presentation of the total loan balance of each of the department's individual accounts. These individual accounts are then divided between punctual and delinquent accounts.

The purpose of a statistical report is to inform the department manager and the branch manager of the quantitative and qualitative aspects of the department's operations. The branch manager consolidates this report into a branch report, which she or he then sends to the divisional manager and ultimately the executive vice president in charge of operations.

To provide quick evaluation of the department's performance, the report is presented in table form. It shows delinquent accounts, but these are given closer examination in the interoffice type discussed next. Little or no discussion is included, because only statistic are emphasized.

Interoffice Memorandum Report

The interoffice memorandum report is written by Miss Whitelon or employees in her department to supply credit information to upper management and any other bank officers, concerning any of their installment credit accounts. The most important are the upper-management reports concerned with delinquent accounts.

All bank officers receive report-writing training that provides standard guidelines for credit appraising. Delinquent-account credit reports are evaluated by upper management by thorough application of these guidelines and the validity of corrective action taken. The reports are usually one page or less in length.

Credit File Memorandum Report

Any bank officer may write the credit file memorandum report. Whenever a bank officer contacts an installment credit account, he or she makes a report of any new information that has been acquired. This report is then included in the credit file account and provides the bank with a more detailed picture of the account. This procedure guards against the possibility of one officer's being the sole contact with an account and also enables any other officer to become familiar with that account quickly and easily by reading the credit file.

Copies of these reports are sometimes sent to other interested bank officers, although the credit file memorandum becomes part of an account's files. For example, sometimes there is a person who mentions over lunch that she or he wishes to organize an employee trust fund. The officer, upon learning this information, then makes a comment on a memorandum-for-credit-file form. A subject line is provided for the account name, and a colume is provided for the date and origin of the report. In the column the bank officer places the date and his or her name, and any persons to recieve copies, in this case the Trust Department. The comment is entered opposite the date and is usually no longer than two lines.

Summary

The Installment Credit Department of State National Bank uses three types of reports: statistical report, inter-office memorandum report, and memorandum report for the credit file.

The statistical report is an operating report to upper management for the department with little or no discussion,
while the other two are written reports concerned with individual accounts. The inter-office memorandum is used mostly
for delinquent-account evaluation for upper management, while
the credit file memorandum contains any pertinent information
about an account. A copy of the credit file memorandum is
retained in the account credit file to build a more complete
file, but all three reports go outside the department.

4. *Evaluations and suggestions for improving the following report:*
   a. Does the subject line clearly identify the subject of this memo report:
   b. Why should a wrtier initial the report?
   c. What improvements can you suggest for the format and spacing of the
   TO-FROM-SUBJECT lines?
   d. Does the introduction orient the reader to the material that follows? Why
   or why not? What element do you find in this introduction? What improvements can you suggest?
   e. What degrees of headings does this report have? Are they appropriate?
   f. Do you like the three major divisions of the text, or would you prefer
   only two? If two, and they were "Skills Needed" and "Training Needed,"
   what would be the two subdivisions under "Skills Needed?" How would
   these changes affect the degrees of headings in this report?
   g. How can you improve the format and spacing of the numbered items?
   h. How can you improve the third sentence under "Training is Needed"?
   i. Is the terminal section correctly labeled? Why or why not?
   j. Circle active verbs and underline passive verbs. How many of each do
   you find? What derivatives of "to be" and "to have" do you find?

                                                    Date: April 21, 199-

TO: Superintendent Robin James
FROM: Roberta Cutting, High School Placement Counselor
SUBJECT: Communication Skills Audio-Visual Center Needs

On April 12, as you requested, I asked Mr. Eric Mott, management representative of the Audio-Visual center in [city], what
communication skills high school people need to work for his
company. This report will give the results.

Students need training in both oral and written communication, according to Mr. Mott. Even though new workers may not
be responsible immediately for writing, there writing skills
are considered at this time of employment and during their
early days on the job. This is because the Audio-Visual Center generally advances personnel from within the company.

Oral Skills Needed

Because the Audio-Visual Center hires most beginning workers
in clerical positions, they must be able to communicate or-

ally in the following ways. (1) Talking and listening on the telephone, (2) Receiving and introducing callers, (3) Working well with many other people.

Although these are beginning jobs, the employee is responsible for the image of the company and must be able to communicate clearly and tactfully with customers and other employees.

Written Skills Needed

The beginning worker needs to write more and more as he or she advances. However, even a beginner's duties could include the following. (1) Taking telephone messages. (2) Filling in office forms. (3) Writing routine letters. (4) Addressing envelopes. If an employee advances to a supervisory position, he or she needs to write periodic evaluation reports on the people in the unit.

Training Is Needed

The Audio-Visual Center does not have any in-service training or company manual. Therefore, applicants must get their training in school. There are several specific areas that Mr. Mott thinks the schools should be teaching.

1. Students should learn correct telephone techniques
2. Everyone, including young men, should learn to type
3. Students must learn to write legibly
4. All future employees should learn to spell correctly and use a dictionary
5. Learning desirable business attitudes.

The last item is perhaps most important. Students must be aware that regular attendance, punctuality, appropriate dress, and getting along with others are every bit as necessary as their skills.

Conclusions

Teachers cannot assume that students can communicate well: they must teach them to speak, listen, and write. The Audio-Visual Center feels that these are qualifications for even the most basic job.

5. **Collection of various published or report examples using deductive or inductive organization:** In order to better understand the differences between deductive (direct) and inductive (indirect) organization of reports, come to class with examples of either form taken from (1) newspaper stories, (2) books, (3) actual reports, and/or (4) advertisements. Can you estimate why the writer's chosen organizational plan for each example you have is deductive or inductive?

Chapter 17

Short Reports

What business executives look for in either short or long reports is concise, accurate, unbiased material with appropriate supporting evidence to help them make needed decisions. Chapter 16 can serve as your general guide for good work in planning, organizing, and writing the body of any report, regardless of its length. However, short, informal reports require fewer elements in their introductions, fewer transitional devices for continuity, fewer headings, and usually a more personal writing style than do long, formal reports.

This chapter begins with suggestions for writing short business reports, then presents examples of informational and analytical business memorandum reports and letter reports.

SUGGESTIONS FOR SHORT REPORTS

When writing short reports one should observe important guidelines regarding the main sections and desirable additional parts.

Writing the Main Sections

The body of short reports usually includes introduction, text (or body), and terminal section. Suggestions for their content are in the following checklist:

■ Writing the Main Sections of Short Reports—A Checklist

1. **Introduction**
   a. Some of these elements (defined in Chapter 16) may be included if desirable: purpose (always), authorization, sources, scope, definitions, background, limits, brief mention of results, list of topics (layout) to be discussed.
   b. If a report's introductory elements are stated in one or two short paragraphs at the beginning, the title "Introduction" is usually omitted.
2. **Text (discussion, body)**
   a. *Present all relevant facts accurately and impartially.* Do not allow your personal feelings and prejudices to affect the facts.
   b. *Organize* your report by the inductive plan or the deductive plan; usually business people prefer the deductive method.
   c. *Emphasize important ideas* by showing details, placing them in prominent positions (with the highest degrees of headings that are appropriate) and using mechanical means such as capitalization, underscoring, boldface, more space, and repetition.
   d. *Include visual aids*—graphs, tables, pictures—whenever they will help clarify information for your readers (or listeners).

    e. *Use headings* to guide the reader through the report, but write your sentences and paragraphs so they can stand alone—as if the headings didn't exist. Usually headings range from second- or third- to fifth-degree, with not more than two or three degrees of headings in any one short report.

    f. *Use topic sentences* for most paragraphs, and *use an introductory paragraph at the beginning of a major section* that contains two or more subdivisions.

    g. *Apply the seven C writing principles.* Throughout, make your writing easy to read. Use understandable words, sentences averaging 16 to 20 words, concrete nouns, few adverbs, few adjectives, and paragraphs whose average length is about seven typewritten lines.

3. Terminal section (summary, conclusions, recommendations)

    a. Be sure that your *terminal section is an integral part of the report and follows logically from the facts already presented* in the text.

    b. Remember that *a summary condenses the text, conclusions evaluate the text, and recommendations offer specific courses of action.*

    c. *Don't include any new material* in the terminal section of the report.

    d. Usually *list summary points in the same order as topics are discussed* in the text.

    e. *If* you have *more than one conclusion or recommendation, list and number them.* You might do the same in a summary, if desirable.

    f. *Support your conclusions or recommendations* with ample appropriate facts that are up to date and accurate.

Including Other Desirable Parts

The format of a short report may be like a memorandum, a letter, or a shortened formal report. Memorandum reports and letter reports may have a subject line before their body. The shortened formal report may have prefatory and supplemental parts.

Subject Line

For directional clarity consider adding a verb in the subject line. In so doing, you give the reader an immediate up-front sense of direction for the deductive, direct report. Some companies have a preprinted form for memorandums where little space is left for a subject line; they may therefore prefer a brief subject line, permitting the idea to be developed in the document. Contrast the following examples:

Brief Subject Line	More Complete Subject Line
`Expatriate Concerns`	`First-Month Problems of Expatriate Workers`

Brief Subject Line	More Complete Subject Line
Weekly Reports	Recommend Weekly Marketing Reports to All Staff
Automation	Resolving Interoffice Communication Problems through Computer Nets
Attrition	Report on High Employee Turnover
Data between ME and IE	Recommend Improving Data Transmission between Manufacturing and Industrial Engineering

Prefatory and Supplemental Parts

In some situations a short, comprehensive, important memo report or letter report would be more impressive if it had some of the prominent features of a long report. If your report is, for example, five or six single-spaced typewritten pages long and has several attachments, you might consider using a title page, a transmittal letter or memo, the report body (typed in single or double space), plus an appendix for the attachments. In the appendix put material that belongs in the report but would clutter the text and isn't vital to its development or presentation. (For discussion and illustrations of these prefatory and supplemental parts, see Chapter 18.)

INFORMATIONAL MEMORANDUM REPORTS

The central purpose of informational reports is to inform and to summarize facts, similarly to the speech that is intended to inform. Obviously, these reports vary widely in content, depending on type of business, purpose, topics discussed, and readers' needs. While there are many kinds of informational reports, the following examples illustrate three general kinds often used in organizations: conference reports, progress reports, and periodic reports.

Conference Reports

The subject matter of conference reports ranges from summaries of personal sales call conferences to write-ups of meetings attended by hundreds of persons.

For example, an advertising account executive may write a conference report (contact report) after every meeting or phone call between the agent and a client. Its purpose is to record all decisions and discussions. A credit or collection manager or account executive may make similar reports after conferences with clients. Likewise, many other employees as well as executives may be responsible for writing reports after any significant conferences with individuals or committees. *The text of such reports is usually organized by topics discussed or simply in a chronological progression.* Some firms have standardized headings for the often-written reports to assure that the same information or main topics are recorded in all of them.

In a different situation, a company's delegate to an important convention may be asked to present a report to superiors. Its purpose is to inform other management personnel of significant happenings, decisions, or topics discussed. How would you organize the text of such a report? You might choose to organize by order of time, topics (criteria), importance, or sources. In report 1, which follows, an assistant sales manager (who attended the firm's regional conference of sales managers) used a combination of the first two choices. The two main topics and their subtopics serve as guides (or *criteria*) for planning this particular sales campaign. Under the "Open Houses" heading, the subheads are *arranged by order of time*. This report—to the sales manager—uses second-, third-, and fourth-degree headings (as shown on page 455 and in Figure 16–2).

MEMO REPORT 1   *Assistant sales manager's report on regional conference.*

```
TO:    Matt Deaning          DATE:  June 8, 199-
FROM:  Martha Gerbman        SUBJECT:  Report on Open Houses and
                                       XL Promotion Programs

The following is a report on the items we discussed during
our June 6 meeting in [city] regarding our XL product.  Topics
pertain to the scheduled open houses and our promotional
programs.  The names of those who were asked and agreed to
be responsible for the various parts of these plans are
listed in the right-hand column below.

                        Events and Programs


Open Houses

Here is the tentative schedule that was established for
three events, subject primarily to availability of digni-
taries at the ribbon-cutting ceremony.

        Employees' Meeting - Thursday, July 30.  Fam-
ilies will be invited and sandwiches and refresh-                Terry
ments provided.  This will provide an opportunity               Moran
to dry-run the tours being conducted later.


        Ribbon-Cutting Ceremony - Friday, July 31.
Dignitaries to be invited need to be agreed upon.
We generally agreed that this occasion presents an             Jack
exceptional opportunity to publicize the growth of          Donalson
new and nonpolluting industry in our state.


        Distributor Event - Saturday, August 1.  The
tour will begin at 10 a.m., followed by lunch at
Ritz Plaza Hotel.  The program will impress upon           Martha
the distributors our program for XL Product Divi-          Gerbman
sion.
```

Promotional Programs

The discussion regarding our Promotional Programs focused on
two brochures, an advertising and direct-mail campaign, and
identification signs.

The XL Product Brochure. After we reviewed this product brochure, relatively minor changes were agreed upon. Another draft will be sent to Bill Campbell for approval before setting type. He will prepare and forward guarantee copy to the agency.	Bill Campbell
Introduction Brochure. We agreed that a brochure to familiarize our customers with the operation of the XL will be desirable. We agreed that the procedure used formerly in materials, showing photographs of the various personnel, will be a good approach.	Erick Brown

Those to be included in this brochure will be
Matt Deaning, Terry Moran, Jack Donalson, Martha
Gerbman, Bill Campbell, Erick Brown, Frieda
Dinson, Pete Mallon, Tyna Green, and John Raney,
the sales secretary.

Advertising and Direct Mail. We agreed that advertising promotion should be expanded to cover the entire region. This project will be further. . . .	Frieda Dinson, Pete Mallon
Identification Signs. White cardboard unit signs that will fold over the top edges of displayed XL. . . .	Tyna Green

Summary

The following open houses have been tentatively scheduled
for these dates: July 30--Employees' Meeting; July 31--Rib-
bon-Cutting Ceremony; and August 1--Distributor Event.

The promotional program is to include: a slightly changed
XL product brochure, an introduction brochure, expanded advertising and direct mail, and special signs for XL products
plus buildings and property. The introduction brochure will
include your picture and those of our nine staff members who
are in charge of these various activities.

c: Brown, Campbell, Dinson, Donalson, Green, Malon, Moran,
Raney

In report 2 the assistant manager organized his conference report by *sources*. It has only second-degree headings.

MEMO REPORT 2   *A conference report organized by sources.*

TO: Thomas Glook   DATE: October 2, 199-
FROM: Vernon Bennett *V. B.*
SUBJECT: Summary of St. Louis Regional Conference

Here is a brief summary of the St. Louis meeting that I
attended September 30 on coin service at military installations. Because you are mainly interested in the presentations of John Klinest, Wardman Jones, and Kathy Cummings, I
am focusing this report on their contributions to this
conference.

John Klinest's Presentation

John Klinest conducted our meeting and introduced the subject. Because of the current situation at military posts,
coin service at these posts will be a problem for years to
come. It's important to improve our service because:

1. The need is there. The present military situation
   requires more coin service.
2. Many of the young men and women on these posts are making
   their first real acquaintance with public telephone
   service. Their opinions of our service now are likely to
   be lasting.

A series of slides shown by Klinest pointed out that coin
conditions around the country vary from very bad (standing
in mud puddles to use coin kiosks) to very good. The coin
center at [*name*] is so plush it is used as a reception center
for guests.

Wardman Jones's Presentation

Wardman Jones talked about some of the revenue characteristics of military coin service. . . .

> [*Three paragraphs follow, including itemized facts and figures.*]

Kathy Cummings's Presentation

Regarding the traffic considerations, these were enumerated
by Kathy Cummings. She emphasized that. . . .

> [*Three paragraphs follow, highlighting her suggestions.*]

<u>Plan of Action</u>

These speakers recommend formation of an interdepartmental
district team to evaluate our coin service at [names] and report its findings to higher management. The team will use
the attached checklist for guidelines in its evaluations of
our services.

Progress Reports

As the name implies, progress reports show "progress," accomplishments, or
activity over time or at a given stage of a major assignment. The organizational
plan is usually inductive, including topics similar to these:

- Introduction (purpose, nature of project)
- Description of accomplishments during the reporting period
- Unanticipated problems (if any)
- Plans for the next reporting period
- Summary (overall appraisal of progress to date)

The example below is a general chairperson's progress report to the vice
president of a company, which is hosting the first purchasing managers' regional
convention in its city. The report uses the inductive organization plan, with
third- and fourth-degree headings.

MEMO REPORT 3   *A chairperson's report on convention plans.*

TO: Bruce Boyne, Vice President DATE: November 9, 199-
FROM: Vivian Porte, Convention Chairperson   *V. Porte*
SUBJECT: Progress Report on Purchasing Managers' Convention,
          January 26, 199-

To keep you informed about the activities of our planning
committee for the first regional purchasing managers' convention to be held in our city, here is a brief report of
our progress so far.

<u>Date, Time, and Place</u>

The Tower Oaks Hotel offices are holding these reservations
for us:

Date: Tuesday, January 26, 199-
Informal luncheon: 12:15 - 1:30
                      Regency Room--for up to 150 persons
Conference rooms: 9:00 - 4:30 Mezzanine rooms 202, 203,
                      204--each accommodating up
                      to 60 persons plus exhibit
                      tables

Tentative Program

So that the convention will have an appropriate official
opening, the committee members are delighted that you have
agreed to express the opening welcome.

    Keynote Speaker.--You will probably be glad to hear
that for keynoter we can count on having Jonathan Harrison,
vice president and general manager of National Products Company. The topic he has chosen is "The Challenge Ahead for
Purchasing Shortage Items."

    Other Participants.--As the attached tentative program
(Exhibit A) shows, we will have 10 outstanding business
leaders on panel discussions in the morning and afternoon
sessions. . . .

Publicity

Our first announcement in newspapers (local and in three
states) will be early in December. One or two other news
stories should appear during January.

If funds allow, we would like to mail two letters to all
purchasing managers in this region, along with a colorful
brochure of the conference program, exhibits, film specials,
and evening entertainment for those staying in the city
overnight. Exhibit B shows the planned layout. The ABC
Printer has quoted a price of $[amount] for 200 copies and
$[amount] for 150 copies.

Estimated Financial Requirements

Exhibit C, attached, is a tentative suggested budget. The
estimated total of $[amount] excludes the cost of stationery,
typing of master copies, and mailing services. Norma Henry
has assured me that these expenses can be taken care of
through our company's usual supplies and postage budget and
need not be itemized here.

We will appreciate any suggestions you may have about our
estimated expenses and your approval of the needed funds.

Summary

To date, many persons have already assisted our committee
with their expressions of preferences and suggestions. We
have hotel reservations; firm acceptances from our official
welcomer, keynote speaker, and panelists; price quotations
on a brochure for mailing; and tentative publicity plans.

```
You will receive from us a definite program, soon after
plans are completed, and another progress report on December
10.

In the meantime, your preferences regarding the publicity
brochure and estimated financial needs and any other sugges-
tions you may have will be sincerely appreciated.  Just jot
your comments on the enclosed sheet and return it to me.  If
you prefer, I'll gladly come to your office at your conveni-
ence to answer any questions you may have.

VP:wh
Attachments:  Exhibits A, B, C
Enclosure:  Comment sheet
```

Periodic Reports

Some periodic reports are written to correspond with the company's fiscal year. Others may be written weekly, monthly, quarterly, or annually, or in other regular recurring periods.

When a memorandum report is written each month about the same department and to the same readers, an introduction and terminal section are unnecessary. Many business firms use printed forms and standardized headings for the text section of such reports. These all save time—for those who must present the needed information in the reports and for those who receive them. They assure uniformity and completeness of coverage and permit the reader to know what to expect so he or she can compare the data by periods. Also, the suggested format makes it easy for the report writer to include the data the receiver wants. The writer merely adds the needed information under each heading, without worrying about what headings should be used.

Most organizations—business, government, religious, athletic, and so forth—write annual reports to summarize activities and financial affairs. For some small concerns the report is exceptionally short—consisting of perhaps a brief transmittal letter with one or two pages of financial statements. For other organizations—especially corporations that must report to their stockholders—the annual report may begin with a top official's letter report. Sometimes the letter is the entire report (perhaps eight or more pages). If not, then the report body discusses operations and activities; and of course every annual report should have a balance sheet and statement of earnings and expenses. Some also include pictures of officers, employees, products, machines, operations—plus charts or graphs.[1]

ANALYTICAL MEMORANDUM REPORTS

In contrast to the informational memorandum report, the analytical memorandum report seeks to analyze a situation or problem; it may end with or without a specific recommendation. The following discussion first suggests a step-by-step analysis of a personnel situation, leading to a conclusion without a recommendation. Thereafter are illustrated three ways to organize justification-recommendation reports.

Steps in Preparing an Analytical Personnel Report

Assume that Gene Mohr, manager of your bank's head office savings department has asked you (assistant manager of the personnel department) to help find a replacement for a teller who is quitting work and moving to another city. You advertised, and 15 people applied for the job. After carefully checking their application forms, test scores, and your own interview notes, you narrowed your list to the five best applicants. Then you wrote to their references for recommendations. After receiving the replies, you have chosen the three best-qualified candidates. Your task now is to evaluate each of the three in a memo report to Mr. Mohr. He likes you to analyze the facts for him—and rank the applicants—but he wants to make his own recommendations and decision.

Here are the facts about the three applicants:

Helen True: One year business college; high school graduate with a 3.0 (out of a possible 4.0) grade-point average; completed in high school an office machines course with a grade of B; typing, 60 words per minute; arithmetic aptitude, excellent; neatly groomed for business appearance; excellent references—"highly dependable, courteous, and honest"; excellent health; 11 years of business experience—all with one company.

James Mace: High school graduate with a 2.6 GPA; completed in high school an office machines course with a grade of C; typing, 50 wpm; arithmetic aptitude, good; fairly neat and well groomed; good references—"dependable, tactful"; good health, six years of business experience with two different firms; two years' military service.

Beth Astor: One year at the local four-year university, with a 3.1 GPA; high school graduate with a 3.2 GPA; completed in high school an office machines course with grade of A; typing, 65 wpm; arithmetic aptitude, excellent; very neat, well-groomed; references—"good worker but has difficulty getting along with others"; fair health; three years' business experience with three different firms; attendance irregular in two.

With all these figures facing you, where do you begin? One way is to group these facts under headings representing the *criteria* (see item 1, page 452) you will be using to measure the three people's qualifications. Notice that if you merely group them by their names as in the above list, comparisons are difficult. After some juggling, you decide that all the data fall under the headings of "Education and Skills," "Personal Qualifications," or "Probable Permanency with Bank." (Many times, when organizing, you have material that could fit under more than one heading: health is an example. So you organize such material the best way you can; in this report it can fit under "Personal Qualifications" or "Probable Permanency with Firm.") You can now arrange the backgrounds of the three applicants in a working table like the following, in rough-draft form:

	True	Mace	Astor
	Education and Skills		
Education	High school graduate 1 year business college	High school graduate	High school graduate 1 year at university
Grade point	3.0	2.6	3.2 in high school 3.1 at university
Arithmetic aptitude	Excellent	Good	Excellent
Typing	60 wpm	50 wpm	65 wpm
High school grade in machines	Grade B	Grade C	Grade A
	Personal Qualifications		
Appearance	Neat and well-groomed	Fairly neat; well-groomed	Very neat and well-groomed
Dependability	Excellent	Good	Fair; but good worker
Compatibility	Excellent	Good	Fair; difficulty working with others
	Probable Permanency with Bank		
Number of jobs	1	2	3
Years of work	11	6 plus 2 military	3
Health	Excellent	Good	Fair
Attendance record	Excellent	Good	Fair (irregular in two firms)

Now you can begin to analyze and interpret the material. Suppose your interpretation results in the following ranks and points for these candidates (assuming you decide to assign 6 points for first place, 4 points for second place, and 2 points for third place):

	True		Mace		Astor	
Criterion	Rank	Points	Rank	Points	Rank	Points
Education and skills	2d	4	3d	2	1st	6
Personal qualifications	1st	6	2d	4	3d	2
Probable permanency	1st	6	2d	4	3d	2
Total score		16		10		10

From this analysis Helen True wins first place, and although Mace and Astor are tied for second place in scores, it is obvious that Mace is ahead of Astor in two of three criteria. Thus he wins second place, and Astor third.

Your next step is to write the report, in rough draft. Then you'll edit it and revise wherever desirable. You'll use the inductive organizational plan because Mr. Mohr told you once he preferred that plan for all memo reports.

The following discussion assumes you have already studied and interpreted the data in the tables shown above. In the first table, you decide to leave the contents of the section "Education and Skills" as they are and to place "Appearance" as the third item in the second section ("Personal Qualifications"). In the "Probable Permanancy" section you decide on these new titles and arrangements: "Experience" (instead of "Years of work"); "Previous jobs" (instead of "number of jobs"). You have omitted such items as marital status and ages because the hiring decision is based on other criteria.[2]

With that groundwork completed, you begin to write—first the *subject line*, which should contain no more than five to seven words, preferably. You decide on "Evaluation of Three Teller Applicants." Then you write the introduction, next the major divisions of the text, and finally the terminal section.

Introduction

The following list shows which of the 11 introductory elements (pages 446 to 448) you should include in this particular report. (The others are irrelevant.)

Element	Comment
Authorization	Mr. Mohr asked you to assume the assignment.
Purpose	To evaluate the three applicants' qualifications for one opening as teller.
Background	From 15 applicants you selected 3.
Methodology sources	You used application blanks, test scores, your own interview notes, and recommendations from references.
Plan of presentation	You will develop the text according to the three criteria for a teller.
Brief statement of your decision	Optional. You may tell Mr. Mohr that Mrs. True ranks highest of the three candidates, or wait to tell this in the terminal section. Your choice will depend on what you think Mr. Mohr prefers.

When you put these five or six elements into words and sentences, you might have an introductory paragraph like one of the following:[3]

```
As you requested, here is the report concerning evaluation
of candidates for a suitable replacement for your retiring
teller.  On the basis of company test scores, screening of
initial applications, my personal interview with each appli-
cant, and recommendations from references, 3 final candi-
dates have been chosen from 15 who applied.  In evaluating
```

```
the candidates, I have placed primary importance on (1) edu-
cation and skills, (2) personal qualifications, (3) probable
permanency.  On the basis of these considerations, Mrs. True
rates the highest of the 3 candidates.
```

or (for the reader who fights your decision before reading the text):

```
Here is the report you requested concerning the evaluation
of candidates for a teller as a replacement for the employee
who is resigning.  Through careful screening of application
forms, test scores, my own interview notes, and recommenda-
tions from references, I have selected 3 out of 15 appli-
cants for your final consideration.  Mrs. Helen True, Mr.
James Mace, and Miss Beth Astor were chosen on the basis of
their education and skills, personal qualifications, and
probable permanency of their employment with our bank.
```

Main Divisions of the Text

You will use three main sections for your text—one for each criterion. You will study the working table and analyze the facts. If your reader wants all the details, you will include each table section or a variation of it within the text. Assume that you now decide to change the sequence of the sections within the table. "Probable Permanency" will be placed first; "Education and Skills," second; "Personal Qualifications," third.

The following discussion concentrates on the section labeled "Probable Permanency." Your procedure for the other two sections will, of course, be similar. What are the most important facts you can pull from the table? Avoid saying in sentence form before or after a table everything that's in the table; that wastes time and is monotonous. After careful thought you might write a paragraph like this to place before the table:

```
Ms. Helen True's experience and her previous job responsi-
bilities show a background and future potential for a
greater degree of permanence with our organization than
either Mr. Mace or Ms. Astor.  The following table shows
that both Mr. Mace and Ms. Astor might have a greater ten-
dency to leave, since they have less stable past employment
records and they do not possess the excellent health that is
preferable for the teller work.
```

After the table you might include comments like these:

```
Mr. Mace rates as a second choice.  His two jobs in 6 years
and good health are a better record than that for Ms.
Astor.  Also in his favor is the fact that he plans to make
a career of working with people.
```

Terminal Section

Will you choose a summary (condensation) or conclusions (evaluation)? The decision depends on what Mr. Mohr prefers. Because he asked you to analyze the facts and present your evaluation and he wants to make his own recommendations, your terminal section should include conclusions, not merely a summary, and you'll omit recommendations.

The following illustration (memo report 4) shows one of several ways this completed report may be worded. It is presented on your bank's memo stationery, addressed to Mr. Gene Mohr, without his title as manager of the head office savings department. This title could, however, be included if company policy so dictates or when the organization is large enough to justify a title for clarification. (Usually memos and memo reports don't include the title, because the people involved know one another and don't need any identification other than the name itself.) When you're writing to a superior, it may be wise to include the courtesy title ("Mr." here).

Notice that the introduction for this memo report doesn't require a heading, but the main sections within the text and the terminal section have headings—second-degree, parallel grammatically. Also, the headings and subject line should be underlined for emphasis.

MEMO REPORT 4 *A personnel department officer's analytical report (with conclusions only) to a savings department director.*

```
                    MEMORANDUM                 [bank name]
TO:       Mr. Gene Mohr              DATE: March 15, 199-
FROM:     [your name]
SUBJECT:  Evaluation of Three Teller Applicants

Here is the report you requested concerning the choice of a
replacement for your teller who is resigning.  On the basis
of information obtained from applications, test scores, per-
sonal interviews, and recommendations from references, I
have selected 3 out of 15 applicants for your final consid-
eration.  Of these 3, I feel that Ms. Helen True best meets
the job requirements of permanency, education and skills,
and basic personal qualifications, as discussed below.


                    Probable Permanency

Ms. Helen True's background of experience and previous job
responsibilities indicates potential for a greater degree of
permanence with our organization than either Mr. Mace or Ms.
Astor.  The following table shows that both Mr. Mace and Ms.
Astor have less stable past employment records and that they
do not possess the excellent health that is preferabe for
the teller work.
```

Criterion	Helen True	James Mace	Beth Astor
Experience	11 years	6 years	3 years
Previous jobs	1 firm	2 firms	3 firms
Health	Excellent	Good	Fair
Attendance record	Excellent	Good	Fair (irregular in 2 firms)

Mr. Mace rates as second choice. His 2 jobs in 6 years and
good health are a much better record than that for Ms.
Astor. Also in his favor is the fact that he plans to make
a career of working with people.

Education and Skills

On the basis of education and skills, Ms. Astor is an outstanding applicant. The table below provides facts in which
Ms. Astor ranks consistently higher than the other 2 in education, grades, and skills.

Criterion	Helen True	James Mace	Beth Astor
Education	H.S. graduate; 1 year business college	H.S. graduate	H.S. graduate; 1 year at university
Grade point	3.0 in H.S.	2.6	3.2 in H.S.; 3.1 at university
Arithmetic aptitude	Excellent	Good	Excellent
Typing	60 wpm	50 wpm	65 wpm
H.S. grade in machines	Grade B	Grade C	Grade A

Although Ms. True's results are not as high as those of Ms.
Astor, she shows a more than adequate proficiency in her
skills. She should prove just as efficient and capable as
Ms. Astor in a teller's position.

Personal Qualifications

Mainly on the basis of references from past employers, Ms.
True has the personality that best fits the performance and
image of the position. As the following table shows, she is
the only applicant of the 3 who has excellent references
with no additional qualifying statements by those references.

Criterion	Helen True	James Mace	Beth Astor
Dependability	Excellent	Good	Fair, but good worker
Compatibility	Excellent	Good	Fair; difficulty working with others
Appearance	Neat and well-groomed	Fairly neat; well-groomed	Very neat; well-groomed

The references of Ms. Astor are somewhat disturbing because of former employers' comments about her ability to get along with her co-workers.

<u>Conclusions</u>

1. Ms. Helen True is the best-qualified to fill your teller vacancy. She rates highest in degree of expected permanence and in personal qualifications for the job. Although her professional ability does not rate highest of the 3 applicants, she ranks second and indicates a more than adequate proficiency.
2. Mr. James Mace rates as a good second choice, mainly on the basis of his expected permanence and his compatibility. Although he does not rank as high on skills and grades as either of the other 2 applicants, his education and scores indicate he can perform the job adequately.
3. Because of the questions raised in her references, I feel Ms. Beth Astor is definitely in third place among these 3 candidates for this position. Other less desirable factors are her "fair" health and the uncertainty of her permanency with our organization. Her outstanding professional ability is too greatly outweighed by these 2 factors.

While the above memorandum report does not specifically recommend that Ms. True be hired, Mr. Mohr could infer that recommendation. It is now his decision—in light of the presented analysis—to take final action.

This report could become a good example of a "shortened formal report"—with some prefatory and supplemental parts as mentioned on page 484. Suppose you were also required to attach to this report confidential copies of recommendation letters and test sheets for each of the three tellers. Your report would then have 12 pages of attachments plus 3 single-spaced or 5 double-spaced pages of body (tables would remain single-spaced). If you decide to add a title page, it will include the TO, FROM, SUBJECT, DATE information, attractively set up in these four parts: (1) "Evaluation of Three Teller Applicants," (2)

"Prepared for Mr. Gene Mohr, Manager, Savings Department," (3) "By (your name), Assistant Manager, Personnel Department," and (4) "March 15, 199–." You will then omit this information from the first page of the report. If you use a transmittal memo, you'll also make a few changes in the first paragraph of the report introduction (as discussed on pages 536 and 537, in Chapter 18). Your 12 pages of attachments can become the appendix; pages will be numbered consecutively after the last page of your report. For example, if your report body (double-spaced) ends on page 5, the appendix first page will be page 6, and so on through page 17.

Justification-Recommendation Reports

Many analytical memorandum reports have a special purpose: to recommend a change—often in policy—or recommend no change, to justify an expenditure, or to suggest a different interpretation of what is considered a fact or value. Often these reports are in answer to a specific request, or they may be voluntary.

The following are items to consider including in the main sections of a problem-solution or recommendation report.

Introduction

You may restate the subject line, give brief authorization and purpose statements, include some background or history, and end with a brief statement on the report's organization (layout) of included material.

Text (discussion, body)

Before offering a recommendation to solve a problem, you must first analyze the situation or problem. Some readers may have to be convinced that a problem actually exists. Thus the text may include evidence on the current situation, along with undesirable effects. After proving the existence of a problem, you recommend how the problem may be solved. Some text sections include these headings: "Current State of Problem," "Effects of Problem," "Recommended Solution."

Terminal Section

Here you will include a summary of the major points and the recommendations. It is usually brief, with each recommendation numbered consecutively.

Organizational Plans

Justification-recommendation reports may be organized in one of the following three ways. Plans 1 (deductive) and 2 (a variation of deductive) are used most often, but plan 3 (inductive) will be used if the reader is someone who may react negatively toward a recommendation unless convincing facts are presented first.

1. *Deductive plan* (report 5): Conclusions or recommendations are stated before or after the introduction but always before the discussion.

2. *Variation of deductive plan* (report 6): This justification report includes criteria for judging the recommendation and organizes the information in a visually stimulating pattern. In other reports the facts may be presented with different variations. For example, in some the arrangement might be purpose, cost and savings (sometimes, criteria for installing an intricate system), conclusions, recommendations, discussion.

3. *Inductive plan* (reports 7 and 8): Introduction (background) and discussion (problem and/or possible savings) are presented before conclusions and recommendations. When the introduction has only one or two short paragraphs and is stated first, the heading "Introduction" may be omitted, as in memo reports 7 and 8.

The discussion section in any of these reports usually is 50 to 75 percent of the entire body.

MEMO REPORT 5   *An assistant manager's justification for purchasing a machine (deductive plan, with second- and third-degree headings).*

<pre>
                                             DATE: May 3, 199-
TO: David Willys, Director, Purchasing
FROM: Joan Swanson, Assistant Manager, Electrical
SUBJECT: Justifying Purchase of Wire-Measuring Machine
</pre>

Conclusions

<pre>
1. A capital outlay of $335 for a wire-measuring machine
   will save us $940 gross or $605 net the first year and
   $4,365 net for the 5-year guarantee period.
2. The machine will save the clerk the cumbersome job of
   coiling up the wire and also free the customer's time and
   our clerk's time by 10 minutes for each wire purchase.
</pre>

Introduction

<pre>
Recently I became aware of a costly procedure in the elec-
trical department--a procedure of hand-measuring wire, which
we should change, because it is costing us about $940 of un-
necessary expense each year. In addition to possible dollar
savings, this report shows a convenience to both the clerks
and the customers with the purchase of a wire-measuring
machine manufactured by the Ace Tool Company.
</pre>

Possible Savings

In our downtown hardware store we can expect savings in
wages and in elimination of losses due to measurement errors
after we change from the present hand measurement system to
machine measurement of wire. (Similar benefits may be expected for our branch stores, but this report covers only
the downtown store.)

Possible Savings on Wages

Currently we are hand-measuring the electrical (copper) wire
on a yardstick that is permanently affixed to the counter.
I made a random check of 100 purchases and found it takes an
average of 15 minutes for one clerk to measure, coil, and
price 50 yards of wire. The measuring machine can perform
the same job in 5 minutes--a savings of 10 minutes, or 1/6
of an hour for every 50 yards of wire.

Since our business volume requires that we always have to
hire extra help throughout the year, time saved in measuring
means money saved in wages. We sell an average of 2,000
yards of wire a month, or 24,000 yards yearly, and clerks'
rate of pay is $8 an hour. With a measuring machine there
is a possible annual savings of $640 in wages, as shown
below.

Estimated time saved: 24,000 ÷ 50 × 1/6 = 80 hours

Estimated savings in wages: 80 × $8 = $640 yearly

Possible Savings on Measurements

During the past 6 months, in my quarterly inventory checkups, I have found that an average of 50 yards had left the
store but was not accounted for over each 3-month period.
This 50-yard loss was attributed to errors in measurement,
although we have had no complaints of short measurement nor
reports of excessive measurements.

At 50 cents a foot (or $1.50 a yard) for the wire, we can
save annually an additional $300, as the following figures
show:

50 × 4 (quarters) × 1.50 = $300 savings realized

if we eliminate shortage loss caused by hand measuring.

We can realize a total gross savings of $940 ($640 and $300)
yearly with the measuring machine. And because the machine

sells for $335 and carries a 5-year guarantee, we can save
$605 net the first year, or $4,365 within 5 years--$605 +
($940 × 4).

Convenience Factor

In addition to the dollar savings, both the clerks and the
customers will appreciate the convenience factor of the machine. Because the wire comes in spools of 1,000 yards, the
clerks now have difficulty in hand-measuring less than a
whole spool--but a large quantity, say, 150 yards--of wire.
They must measure off 150 yards and then coil it in some
fashion so that it won't tangle and will be easy to carry.

As a contrast, the machine measures wire of all diameters,
meters up to 1,000 yards, and includes 3 parts:

    1. A spindle to hold the spool of wire to be measured
    2. A meter that measures and prices the wire
    3. A spindle to receive and coil the wire that has been
       measured.

Thus, this machine (manufactured by Ace Tool Company) not
only will eliminate mistakes in measurement and pricing, but
also will save the clerk the cumbersome job of coiling up
the wire and free the customer's time by 10 minutes for each
wire purchase.

MEMO REPORT 6 *Variation of deductive plan; note format and highlighted
recommendation.*

```
TO:       Board of Directors, [company name]
FROM:     Dave Allen, Senior Vice President--Tobacco Products
SUBJECT:  Recommended expansion of [name] into Western Samoa
DATE:     June 5, 199-
```

+--+
| RECOMMENDATION |
| |
| PURCHASE THE EXISTING CIGARETTE FACTORY ON WESTERN SAMOA |
| AS PART OF OUR PACIFIC RIM EXPANSION PLAN |
+--+

INTRODUCTION

The Company produces and internationally markets
tobacco products, packaged food, and distilled and brewed
beverages. Last year [name] made $1.209 billion on $15.766
billion in sales. Worldwide tobacco sales in 199- were
$6.35 billion, an 8% increase over the previous year.

Today's proposal is part of our overall plan to domi-
nate Pacific Rim tobacco markets within 5 years.

PROPOSAL

Fact: Negotiations are currently in progress which will
allow U.S. tobacco companies limited access to the
Chinese market within one to two years.

Fact: 50% of Chinese males smoke--a market of 439 million
customers, or almost twice the population of the
United States.

Strategy: Develop a tobacco industry in the Pacific Islands
which will foster indigenous consumption while developing sufficient capacity to supply the Chinese
market.

Criteria: 1. Find a stable political and ecological climate.
2. Ensure a consistent supply of quality leaf.
3. Locate near major trade routes.
4. Develop a model easily adaptable to other
   islands.

THE ISLAND OF WESTERN SAMOA MEETS THE ABOVE CRITERIA.

BACKGROUND

Land area: 3,900 sq km   Population: 161,000
Climate: Tropical (24-28 C)   Language: English spoken
               Distance from China: 5,400 miles

History: Separated from New Zealand in 1962. All land
owned tribally. Traditional tribal culture.

Politics: Executive and parliament (the Fono) elected by
chiefs of the tribes. Human Rights Protection
Party has held a majority since 1982. Stable,
with no violence or uprisings.

Economy: Subsistence agriculture based on coconuts (40%),
cocoa (30%), and taro (30%). Economy ebbs and
flows with international coconut prices. Growth
in the small-manufacturing sector slight.

Tobacco: Government owns only cigarette plant, with production currently 4% below 1982 levels. No information available on indigenous consumption.

SATISFYING THE CRITERIA

1. Politically and ecologically stable. Tropical climate is not ideal for tobacco cultivation, but a satisfactory leaf is produced in the region. (See attached Exhibit A for location.)
2. Some leaf is already grown on Western Samoa. Company-sponsored education in modern agricultural techniques will increase yield and quality.
3. Western Samoa is near several major shipping lanes.
4. Our model is simple: purchase or construct tobacco facilities which will process locally grown tobacco. The Company will, at first, subsidize and educate tobacco farmers to encourage the conversion of more acreage from coconuts to tobacco. Initially producing to support endemic consumption, these factories will eventually increase production to supply the Chinese market. (We do not recommend building in China or buying Chinese leaf because of the country's still unpredictable politics.) Within 5 years, tobacco will become the primary cash crop of the Pacific Islands, replacing the less lucrative coconut crop.

RATIONALE FOR PURCHASE OF FACTORY

1. An existing factory and work force are already in place.
2. Small scale will allow for experimentation in the model.

   Selling points to the government of Western Samoa:
1. Greater tobacco plantings will stabilize economy.
2. Greater value of tobacco will provide more taxes.

   The Company should enter into negotiations with the government of Western Samoa to purchase its cigarette factory. Using the Samoan model that we will build, [company] can island-hop to develop a strong tobacco trade in the Pacific Islands. Eventually, our system of growers and factories will produce enough cigarettes to supply the local as well as the Chinese markets.

MEMO REPORT 7 *Organized by plan 3—inductive; same facts as report 5: justification for purchasing a machine.*

TO: [*Same as report 5*]   May 3, 199-
FROM: [*Same as report 5*]
SUBJECT: [*Same as report 5, or change to noncommital*]: <u>Cost Comparison of Hand and Machine Wire-Measuring Methods</u>

[Noncommittal introduction] Recently I became aware of a costly procedure in the electrical department--a procedure of hand-measuring wire. This report compares cost and convenience factors of two alternatives--continuing with the present and hand method or buying a wire-measuring machine manufactured by the Ace Tool Company.

[The title "Introduction" is omitted because this short paragraph is the first part of this report body.]

Possible Savings

[Same as that section in deductive plan, report 5.]

Convenience Factor

[Same as that section in deductive plan, report 5.]

Conclusions

[Same as those shown in deductive plan, report 5.]

MEMO REPORT 8   *Recommendation for change in communication procedure (inductive plan).*

November 10, 199-

TO: David Bank, Unit Manager
FROM: Marianne Clauw
SUBJECT: Inefficient Communication between Data Processing
          and Consulting Departments

As you requested on October 1, I have investigated the state of communication between the Consulting Department and the Data Processing (D.P.) Department. Six months ago our company formed an internal consulting department to interface between the D.P. Department and the departments that use data processing services. The reason for this organizational change was to facilitate communication between the users and the D.P. Department.

Current Situation

Since the formation of the Consulting Department, the consultants have complained that their communication with D.P. personnel is inadequate. The recent relocation of the D.P. Department to Flint aggravated the problem, since the consultants remain in our Detroit office. The following are some problems that resulted.

<u>Problems</u>

1. The interoffice mail turnaround is approximately 3 days, which makes it inappropriate for urgent messages.
2. D.P. personnel are difficult to reach by phone because they are frequently away from their desks.
3. There is no message-taking procedure in the D.P. Department.
4. D.P. personnel state that they are unable to service user needs efficiently because the needs are not communicated in a timely fashion.

<u>Conclusion and Recommendations</u>

To provide efficient service to the user departments, timely communications between the consultants and the D.P. personnel are necessary. Implementing the following recommendations will facilitate quick and efficient communication between the departments.

1. Assign a receptionist to the D.P. Department to answer the phone, sort interoffice mail, and page persons who are called.
2. Strongly encourage all personnel to acknowledge phone messages and return phone calls the same day.
3. Institute special daily facsimile services to handle written communications between the D.P. Department and the Consulting Department. Also use facsimile machines daily to transmit documents between the Detroit consultants and the Flint D.P. personnel.

REPORTS WITH GRAPHS

When many figures are in the text of informational or analytical memo or letter reports, they demand special attention for clarity. Various graphic materials, as emphasized in Chapter 16, can help your reader or listener to understand and visualize quantitative data more quickly.

Notice how the three graphs illustrated in report 9 help clarify analyses regarding prices. (This report is addressed to the manager of a city commission, on which the accountant is a staff member.) Because of the technical nature of the utility industry, the introduction includes a few terms that have specific meaning in the report. It is organized by the deductive plan, and uses second-, third-, and fourth-degree headings.

MEMO REPORT 9   *An accountant's analytical report* with graphs regarding a utility's practicing policies.

MEMORANDUM

January 30, 199-

TO: Thomas L. Hummer
FROM: Don Cascade
SUBJECT: Some Pricing Policies of XYZ Natural Gas Company

Introduction

This report, which you requested on January 16, 199-, explores some pricing policies of XYZ Natural Gas Company during the past year. The study was initiated in response to public criticisms of the prices charged by that utility. The report answers the following questions:

1. How did prices vary during 199- for XYZ's general classes of customers--residential, commercial, and industrial?
2. Were prices related to heating degree-days?
3. How did prices compare with percentages of gas used by the three classes of customers?

Sources

Information in this report is based on data in Schedules X and XI of the Uniform Statistical Report for the year ending December 31, 199-. The Uniform Statistical Report is submitted annually by public utilities to our State Utilities Commission. Attached to my report are copies of the two statistical schedules that detail the data I used in deriving the figures for this report. Our analysis is not intended to be a final statement on XYZ's pricing; rather, it is an initial exploration into the situation, to answer first the above three questions.

Definitions of Terms

   Residential-Class Customers: Those in single-family dwellings, condominiums, and apartments. Their primary use of gas is heating, but they also use gas for cooking, water heating, and appliances.

   Commercial-Class Customers: These are retailers and wholesalers. Their primary use of gas is central and space heating.

   Industrial-Class Customers: These are in manufacturing. They use gas as an energy source in the manufacturing process and also use it for central and space heat.

   Therm: A unit of heat equal to 100,000 British thermal units. (A Btu is a unit of heat required to raise the temperature of 1 pound of water 1°F.)

2

Heating Degree-Day: A unit of measure used to estimate fuel requirements. One degree-day represents a 1° declination from a standard temperature in the average temperature of one day. XYZ uses a standard temperature
of 65°F. For example, if the average temperature for a day were 62°F, this
would represent 3 degree-days (65 - 62).

Conclusions

1. Pricing policies for non-residential-service customers appear much more
   stable than pricing policies for residential customers. Prices were
   higher for residential customers, and they varied significantly during
   the months--from a low of $0.41/therm to a high of $0.58/therm. Commercial customer prices ranged from $0.381/therm to $0.459/therm, and
   industrial prices from $0.35/therm to $0.43/therm.

2. Prices were not related to heating degree-days last year. Exact correla-
   tion of price to heating cannot be made based on the data from one year.
   Additional years would need to be compared to complete the analysis.

3. The prices paid by the three classes of customers were inconsistent with
   their percentages and the percentages of gas they used. Though 91.9% of
   the customers were residential, they used only 36.5% of the therms but
   paid 40.7% of the revenues. In contrast, commercial customers--7.3% of the
   total--used 23.2% of the therms and paid 22.8% of the revenues. Industrial
   customers--only 0.8% of the total customers--used 40.3% of the therms and
   paid only 36.5% of the revenues.

Discussion

This part of the report discusses the findings related to each of the three
questions about last year's pricing policies of XYZ. They pertain to price
variations for the three general classes and their relation to heating
degree-days and to percentages of gas used.

How Did Prices Vary during 199-
among XYZ's General Classes of Customers?

The line graph in Figure 1 depicts the prices charged to each class of
customer for each month in 199-.

Residential Customers: Residential customers were charged a wide range
of prices in 199-. Prices varied from a low of $0.41/therm in January to a
high of $0.58/therm in September. Prices fluctuated from month to month.
For example, the price in July was $0.53/therm, which was followed in
August by a price of $0.43/therm. This was a decrease of $0.10/therm. In
September the price was $.58/therm--an increase of $.15/therm over August's
price.

From the data available to me I was not able to discern the reasons for
these wide fluctuations in price. Overall, prices were lowest in the first
three months of the year, then increased through the summer months (except
for August), followed by a slight decrease in the final three months.

3

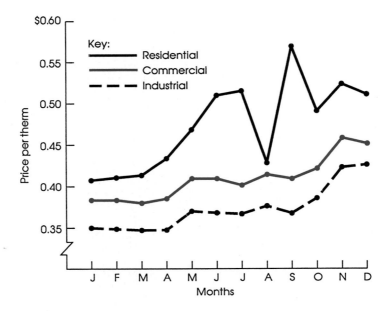

FIGURE 1. Price per therm for residential, commercial, and industrial customers during 199-.

Commercial Customers: Prices for commercial customers increased in May, August, October, and again November. Prices ranged from $0.381/therm in January to $0.459 in November.

Industrial Customers: Price increases to industrial customers came in the same months as those for commercial customers: May, August, October, and November. The lowest price paid was $0.35/therm; the highest was $0.43/therm.

Comparison of Residential, Commercial, and Industrial Prices: Residential customers paid higher prices than commercial customers, and commercial

4

customers paid more than industrial customers. The disparity between costs to residential customers and costs to commercial and industrial customers increased throughout most of the year, then decreased slightly in October and December.

Residential customers' costs exceeded those of commercial customers by $0.03/therm in January to $0.17/therm in September. Industrial customers paid $0.03 to $0.04 less than did the commercial customers throughout the year. This relationship can be seen in Figure 1 in the distance between the lines of the graph for each type of customer. Please note that the distance between the data for commercial and industrial customers is fairly constant throughout the year. If you contrast that constancy with distance between the data for residential and commercial customers, you can see that there was a disproportionate increase in residential rates.

<u>Were Prices Related to Heating Degree-Days?</u>

The answer to this question is a definite "No." Prices and heating degree-days were not related. This conclusion is supported by Figure 2, which

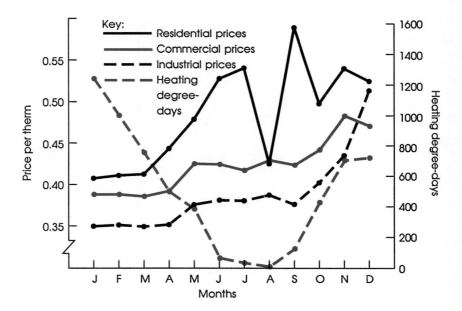

Figure 2. Comparison of prices with heating degree-days.

5

compares heating degrees and prices for the three classes of customers. If there were a positive relationship between heating degree-days and prices, the lines would be similar in shape. If there were a negative relationship, the lines would be opposite in shape. Instead, Figure 2 illustrates the noncorrelation of these two factors. For some months of the year prices remained the same or increased as heating degree-days decreased. Although prices and heating degree-days did increase simultaneously from October to November, this pattern is not sufficient to come to a conclusion of a significant relationship between the two for the year.

How Did Prices Compare with Percentages of Gas Used by the Three Classes of Customers?

An interesting relationship can be seen in Figure 3. The percentage of customers who were residential is 91.9; they used 36.5% of the therms and paid 40.7% of the revenues. Commercial customers comprised 7.3% of the customers, 23.2% of the sales, and 22.8% of the revenues. The remaining 0.8% of the customers were industrial. They used 40.3% of the gas sold and contributed 36.5% of the revenues.

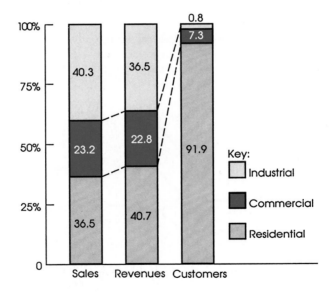

FIGURE 3. Percentage breakdown of sales, revenues, and customers by type of customer

6

The implications of these figures are that residential customers use a
comparatively small amount of gas and pay for a larger portion of it than
they actually use. Commercial customers break about even between what they
use and what they end up paying for. However, they tend to use an amount of
gas disproportionate to their numbers. And industrial customers represent
an extremely small number of customers, yet they use more of the gas than any
other class and pay much less for it.

Such differential pricing, though, might well be logical and reasonable.
For example, the costs of supplying equipment and materials to many
different residences are likely to be much greater than the costs of
providing equipment and materials to fewer commercial businesses in a
relatively confined geographic area, and to even fewer industries, which
are usually even more physically concentrated.

Attachments: 2

Thus informational memorandum reports seek to inform; analytical memorandum reports seek either to recommend or to analyze. Evidence is needed in both forms of reports, but especially in the analytical one, when persuasion of the reader is desired.

LETTER REPORTS—INFORMATIONAL AND ANALYTICAL

A letter report is most often used when sending information to a reader outside your organization. As the title indicates, a letter report uses the format of a letter—with date, inside address, salutation, body (different from a letter), complimentary close, signature, reference section. It is typed on the firm's letterhead. Often it has a subject line, usually placed a line or two below the salutation. Its length may range from two to five (seldom more) pages. The heading for pages beyond the first is the same as for a letter—reader's name, page number, date.

Letter reports may be informational in purpose, simply informing the reader about facts relating to a topic. Thus informational letter reports may summarize conferences, present progress reports or periodic reports, or have a variety of other purposes. An analytical letter report has some of the same characteristics as the analytical memo, seeking to analyze a situation or problem, ending possibly with a recommendation.

Though the general format of the letter report is like that of a letter, its body requires some of the special qualities of short reports, as discussed below.

1. *The first paragraph* usually includes the following elements found in an introduction:

> Authorization (if any, mention date of and person making request)
> Purpose (always)
> Problem (if one exists)
> Importance of issue (optional)
> Statement of the results (optional)
> Plan of presentation (depends on length of report)

Examples:

a. As requested in your January 7 letter, I have investigated the delivery service department with regard to reducing its operating cost.

b. While auditing your books last month, I noticed your firm does not have a centralized receiving department. The purpose of this report is to explain the present setup and then show how a receiving department will benefit your organization.

c. With pleasure we report to you our progress in the year just completed and look ahead with you for this year just started.

d. In response to your committee's request of October 199-, we have investigated the problem of high employee turn- over. Four options were considered, with one of those four recommended for implementation.

2. *The middle paragraphs* of the text should present objectively, without emotional appeals, all pertinent facts—both favorable and unfavorable. Sources and methods should be mentioned along with emphasis on findings or results. Headings, visual aids, and transitional sentences are also included wherever desirable.

3. *The last paragraph* brings the letter report to a pleasant, friendly close, as for letters. If you need to conclude or recommend, do so just before the last paragraph. If appropriate, offer to discuss further or to come to the reader's office.

Informational Letter Reports

One use of letter reports is to answer inquiries. For example, in letter report 1 Mr. Mains, graphic services manager of a corporation with 23 branches, informs Ms. Golden, vice president of a corporation in another state, about the firm's one-year experience with the Compugraphic composition system. Ms. Golden wrote that the manufacturer had given her Mr. Mains's name as an example of a new (one-year) customer. She said she is especially interested in Mr. Mains's comments on performance and dependability of this system.

LETTER REPORT 1   *A manager's informational letter report on his firm's use of a graphic system.*

Dear Ms. Golden:

Regarding your inquiry of July 15, I am glad to tell you of our experience with the Compugraphic system. We have been pleased with its performance, advantages, and dependability. It has given us better technology and also new types for copy and headlines.

Performance

By using the keyboards with video display terminals our operator can see the copy as it will come out and can easily plug in any changes. When the type is set in these Editwriters, it is run out on a related machine that does fast, high-quality typesetting. It has produced our bulletins, charts, forms, illustrations, and other nonstandard graphics in a much more efficient manner than was possible with our previous equipment.

Advantages

An important feature of this equipment is its storage capability. Everything can be stored on disks and can be called up later when needed. This new system has saved us considerable time, because it allows us to typeset documents without rekeystroking. Now, although work volume in the department is up significantly, the projects are getting done, more of the corporate need can be met in house, and we are producing more professional-looking products efficiently. Graphics users throughout our corporation are seeing new capabilities and results.

Dependability

This new system has served exceptionally well the needs of several departments this year. It has required only one minor repair, which the factory service representative took care of promptly. The scheduled six-month checkups also were thorough and dependable. . . .

[Two paragraphs include more compliments about uses, results, and satisfied major users in the firm's communications and publication departments.]

```
Ms. Golden, please write again or phone me--(999)555-6266--
if you have any other questions regarding our use of the
Compugraphic system.  It is a pleasure to help you.
```

Perhaps you have already noticed that a letter report like the one above about a system or machine is organized the same way as a letter of recommendation you might write about a person—his or her work for you or credit record with your firm. In fact, basically a recommendation is a confidential report. If the inquirer asks you several (five or more) questions about broad areas and doesn't furnish a printed report form for your answers, you will need to write a long, factual, objective message that is really a letter report. If your answers require more than one paragraph under each question, you should of course number the questions or use headings or do both to help improve readability.

Another popular use of letter reports is the annual message the company president sends to stockholders. In many firms—especially the larger ones—this letter report is usually in the initial section of the printed annual report.

Though letter reports usually go outside the company, some are used inside. For example, in some firms traveling salespersons write letter reports back to their firm from the field.

In addition to the various kinds of letter reports already mentioned, one more deserves mention here. It is the *progress report*. If you are a management consultant, an independent researcher, or a representative of a firm doing work under contract on a long-term (perhaps yearly) project for another company, you should report your progress periodically—in letter-report form. Under some agreements such reports must be made monthly, quarterly, semiannually, or annually. Basically, the general topics discussed in a progress report in letter form are similar to those outlined for a progress report in memorandum format on pages 488 and 489.

Analytical Letter Reports

Often used in letter reports is the problem-solution format. For example, an outside consultant to a company is asked to investigate an issue or a perceived problem. That final report may be submitted in letter-report form. You may also represent your company on an outside board and would write that group an analytical letter report in response to a specific request. One example of an analytical letter report (deductive in format) from an American overseas follows.

LETTER REPORT 2   *An American expatriate's analytical letter on problems faced in the Far East; the salutation is "Dear Ted."*

```
You asked us in your fax of April 10 to tell you what
problems the eight of us faced in adapting to work in Hong
Kong and give you suggested changes in preparing Americans
```

for an overseas assignment. Your request was most timely,
because we consider the issue to be highly important.

Recommendations

Our company should subscribe to English periodicals and
newspapers published in Hong Kong, place in your office the
periodic and annual reports of our Far East subsidiaries,
and begin planning a two-week seminar on cultural differences between the West and the Far East.

Problems

We recommend the above three suggestions on how our concerns
here might be met. Let me summarize some problems we Americans faced when working in the Far East, particularly in
Hong Kong.

1. Our undergraduate training in international business was
   founded primarily on readings and the expertise of instructors. Such learning is useful, but "reality" is
   considerably different from simply reading about a situation. We feel our training in the classroom was insufficient preparation.

2. Business is transacted differently over here. That
   statement is not a criticism; rather, it suggests that
   not all businesses--accounting firms, legal offices,
   banking systems, for example--operate the same way we do
   in the States. It took me, and my colleagues had the
   same experience, almost six months to learn my way
   around. And we have a long way to go.

3. While English is a common language over here, we all wish
   we knew more basic Cantonese phrases and terms relating
   to business. Our Chinese counterparts know English well:
   they have no problem conversing with us on business matters. We Americans have a problem of communication when
   sitting in a meeting where some of the discussion is in
   their language. . . .

These problems are of immediate concern. Surely there are
others, but these are major. Our three recommendations are
briefly mentioned above; here they are discussed in more
detail.

Solutions-Recommendations

1. Before coming to the Far East, employees should be exposed to publications of the host country. That suggestion seems relatively simple. It is recommended because

none of us even knew about the <u>South China Morning Post</u>, or the <u>Executive</u>, or the many other publications that summarize what's going on.

We know you are aware of the many publications in English, that daily are sold over here. Literally hundreds of English magazines and papers report on both local and international affairs. We recommend that our company subscribe to at least five publications and make them available to others who will join us in the future.

2. If one accepts the proposal that we should have current reading material, it is equally important that the company collect the annual reports of our subsidiary. Those reports are well written. They are as informative as ours in the States. They are an excellent summary of past business happenings and would be useful for us to read before arriving here. . . .

3. [*This paragraph suggests that a seminar in the States could include cultural, business, political, social, and even religious discussions on the Far East. Writer offers to recommend instructors.*]

<u>Benefits</u>

All of us feel that our productivity would improve if the preceding recommendations are accepted. Our families would more quickly become involved. We would know issues early. We would not be as surprised. And certainly most important of all, there would be fewer persons packing up and moving home, to the dismay of the company and to the discomfort of the families.

Ted, you asked for our brief statement on better preparing us as Americans to work in the Far East. Although I wrote the letter, the ideas represent the thinking of the eight of us, and our spouses. We look forward to your reaction and response.

SUMMARY

The preceding illustrations and discussions have indicated the wide variety of subject matter, uses, and formats for informational and analytical memorandum and letter reports. One of the distinguishing features of reports is their three parts: introduction, text or body, and terminal section. Yet the headings, placement, and contents of these parts vary widely—depending on purpose, audience, problems, complexity of subject matter, and other significant concerns. In addition, some short reports may have a few prefatory and supplemental parts similar to those in a formal report. Also, in printed form reports and some recurring periodic reports the introduction or terminal section or both may be unnecessary and therefore omitted.

Basically, however, all short reports have various characteristics in common. When you understand the basic plans, think logically and objectively, consider your purpose and your readers, use good judgment with facts, plan and organize carefully for direct or indirect plan, and achieve the qualities of well-written reports as suggested in both Chapters 16 and 17, you will turn out commendable short reports on the job.

EXERCISES AND PROBLEMS

1. ***Rewrite of savings association letter report:*** The following letter report (answering an inquiry) is quite good. Your job is to make it even better. Assume the customer asked about all the topics mentioned; thus, keep all the ideas but improve the report in these ways:

    a. Insert headings—second- and third-degree or third- and fourth-degree headings.

    b. Show more you-attitude.

    c. Change at least five passive verbs to active voice (and of course make whatever subject changes are necessary).

    d. Tabulate some listed details—for easier reading.

    e. Make any other minor changes desirable for good business writing.

    Thank you for your request for information relating to INSURED savings accounts in this association. This reply includes facts concerning types of savings plans, security of savings, withdrawal of funds, and necessary forms for opening an account. I am also enclosing a copy of our latest financial statement and several pamphlets of general information that give you essential facts you desire about us and the savings accounts we issue.

    We have two types of savings plans available--a passbook savings account and a 6-month savings certificate.

    Briefly, an insured passbook savings account may be opened for any amount at any time. Upon receipt of your remittance, we issue to you our savings passbook with the amount credited inside. Additional sums may be added in any amount and at any time you desire. Interest earnings are credited to passbook savings accounts on March 31, June 30, September 30, and December 31 of each year. This is done automatically on these dates whether you send in your passbook or not. Gold Bond stamps are given as a bonus to passbook savers, as outlined on the enclosed card. The current rate of dividend on passbook savings is $5\frac{1}{2}$% per year, compounded daily.

In addition to our savings passbooks, we also issue insured
6-month savings certificates. Designed to offer larger,
longer-term investors the maximum rate for insured savings,
these certificates are issued for a minimum of $1,000, with
larger amounts in multiples of $100. They differ from pass-
book accounts in several respects. Earnings on certificates
begin on the day of purchase and are paid at the end of each
6 months on maturity dates. The certificates are in certificate form, and checks are mailed to the certificate holders
every 6 months from the date of issue, instead of being automatically credited to the account as is done on passbook
accounts. Of course, if you have a passbook savings account
with State Federal, the dividends on your savings certificate
may be automatically credited to your passbook account upon
your request. For your convenience, savings certificates are
automatically renewed on the maturity dates for an additional
6 months unless you are notified at least 30 days prior to a
maturity date. The current interest rate on 6-month savings
certificates is $8\frac{1}{4}\%$ per year.

Savings in this association are INSURED up to $100,000 by the
Federal Savings and Loan Insurance Corporation, Washington,
D.C. We are also members of the Federal Home Loan Bank
System, a reserve credit system for associations. We lend
our funds upon the security of selected monthly reducing
first mortgages on homes. So, you will see, there is really
exceptional security for savings placed with us.

You will probably wish some information concerning withdrawal
of your funds. It has always been the policy of this association to pay withdrawals IN PART OR IN FULL without notice.
We have followed this policy ever since organization in 1926.
However, a savings and loan association may require notice of
withdrawal if necessary. If the country should again experience an economic emergency such as prevailed in 1932-1933, it
is possible that we would require notice. Under such circumstances it is quite likely that every financial institution
would necessarily restrict withdrawals. This provision in
the savings and loan laws is a wise one for the protection of
the customers.

For your convenience I am enclosing a signature card that may
be used for either an individual or a joint account. If you
desire to open an account in your own name alone, you should
use Form 100. If, however, you wish to open an account in
your name jointly with some other person, probably another
member of your family, you should use Form 200, on the
reverse side of the card. If you desire a 6-month savings
certificate, the same signature card may be used.

We also have trust accounts, frequently used by parents in
carrying savings accounts for children, or by persons who
desire to hold funds in trusts for another. Signature card
forms for this type of account will be mailed to you upon
request.

I thank you kindly for your inquiry and extend to you a cordial invitation to use the facilities of this association.

2. ***Rewrite of annual letter report, with tables and other improvements:***
   Given below is a report to shareholders. Assume this message appears on
   one side of an 8½- by 11-inch sheet and the annual statement of condition
   appears on the opposite side. Rewrite it so that the information is easier
   to read. For example, can you put in table form some of or all the figures
   given in the first three paragraphs? And can you list the names and titles
   in the last two paragraphs? Also, add an appropriate rounding-out last
   paragraph.

   Report to the Shareholders
   We ended our 61st year May 3, 199-, which proved to be a
   very good year. Our assets totaled almost $12,000,000 being
   $11,997,728.90, representing an increase of $430,315.75,
   which was due princially to the increase in home loans of
   $538,622.30.

   Savings accounts reflected a total of $11,013,074.26, rep-
   resenting a gain for the year of $385,321.70, which was
   substantially greater than the gain in the previous year.
   During the year the association repaid $265,000 to the Fed-
   eral Home Loan Bank and had no notes payable May 3, 199-.
   Net operating income, after expenses, amounted to
   $558,293.40, reflecting an increase of $32,423.01 over the
   previous year. The operating ratio of the association for
   the fiscal year was 17.87% of gross operating income, which
   was substantially lower than the national average, which is
   in excess of 27%.

   During the year, $42,000 was added to reserves, $495,810.52
   was distributed as earning on savings accounts, and
   $20,482.88 was added to undivided profit. Total reserves
   were $514,000 and undivided profit $87,505.03, making a
   total of $601,505.03, representing over 5% of total liabili-
   ties. Our reserves and undivided profit place us in a
   rather enviable position and leave no question, in my opinion, of our ability to continue at our present rate of return to our savings accounts.

   At our shareholders' meeting held Monday, April 5, the following were elected to serve as directors for the ensuing

year: William E. Brady, Robert E. Becker, Stephen G. Mills,
Mary A. Aitken, Daniel A. Roberts, Lisa L. Gifford, and
Louise G. Hulett.

At the directors' reorganization meeting, immediately fol-
lowing the shareholders' meeting, the following officers
were elected: Chairperson of the Board of Directors and
President, William E. Brady; Vice Chairperson, Robert E.
Becker; Executive Vice President, Secretary and Treasurer,
Stephen G. Mills; Vice President and Assistant Secretary and
Treasurer, Louise G. Hulett, and Assistant Secretary,
William A. Dugger. Sylvia Reddie was reappointed Savings
Officer, and Bonnie Whittemore was appointed Head Book-
keeper. Fred L. Sharp was reappointed attorney.

3. *Informational letter report to Dr. Inquire:* Assume you have received
   a letter from the assistant dean of students, Dr. Jean Inquire, Administration Building, your college or university, stating that you have been selected
   in a random sample to take part in a survey. The information gathered will
   be included—without student names—in an orientation booklet for entering students. She asks you to answer these questions regarding your course
   costs for this quarter (or semester):

   a. What is your year in college and major?

   b. How much did your textbooks cost you? Please mention
      course names and book titles, too.

   c. What other required course materials did you have to pay
      for, and how much did they cost? (Include lab fees, if
      any, but exclude tuition fees.) Figure only prices of
      new texts and materials (but you may mention any savings
      you gained if you bought used items).

   d. What relation, if any, do you find between these total
      course costs and the number of credit hours your courses
      carry?

   e. What relation, if any, do you find between these total
      course costs and the college (Arts & Sciences, Engineer-
      ing, etc.) or department (Business, Education, Art) in
      which they are offered? (Answer this question if you are
      taking courses in more than one department or college of
      this institution.)

   The only data you need are the prices of *new* (*or used*) books and
   materials plus lab fees, if any, for each course you are carrying *and* the
   credit hours of each course.

   In case you feel that this quarter or semester is atypical for you
   (perhaps because you are taking only one or two courses), you may, if you

wish, include information for both last quarter and this one. Indicate clearly the costs and credits in each.

Suggestions: Write your report in good business letter-report form—with heading, inside address, subject line, salutation, and closing. Use well-chosen headings to mark the main divisions of your report. Construct a table that includes your courses, credit hours, book titles, and costs of required books. Keep your report factual, objective, and well organized.[4]

4. ***Analytical memorandum report on a litter problem:*** Assume that the public relations manager of your city or town (or a nearby city) has been receiving numerous complaints from local people about the excessive amounts of litter lying on sidewalks and under cars parked in the downtown area. He has hired you as a consultant to help identify and solve the problem.

The manager would like you to think of as many problems as possible and offer several solutions to each problem. Your memo report will serve (1) as a discussion tool for the manager in an upcoming meeting of the city council and (2) as a resource to be used in developing a grant proposal (later) to a federal agency that funds studies of environmental problems.

Assume that you and an assistant took random samples of litter on three blocks in the central downtown area every day during the previous two weeks. You now have some facts and percentages regarding the kinds (or sources) of litter there. Also you can estimate probable causes for the litter and suggest possible desirable solutions.

Write the memo report in three or four pages (single-spaced). Remember that all sorts of problems could be occurring—some much less obvious than others. For example, one problem could be inadequate litter pickup.

5. ***Analytical memo report or letter report—justification-recommendation:*** The following are requirements in this assignment for you and your classmates:

Subject:	Presenting an individual research memorandum or letter report on a foreign country investment
Goal of assignment:	1. To recommend whether a company (of your choice) should expand, establish a subsidiary, permit franchising, locate an overseas office in a foreign country.
	2. To bring together (*a*) original work and (*b*) secondary information in a memorandum or letter report which includes a clear recommendation on whether a company (selected by you) should or should not invest resources in that country.
	3. To present the results of your research to the class.

Procedure: 1. Each class member will select a foreign country for analysis, selecting his or her own criteria as to whether investing resources in that country is desirable or undesirable.

2. The instructor will receive two copies of your memorandum or letter (maximum of two pages) on the day of your presentation. All class members will on the day of your presentation also receive a copy of your material.

3. Each member will orally present to the class (*time limits to be set by your instructor*) the specific recommendations contained in the written document.

Possible macro sources for background research:

■ *The Economist Intelligence Unit* (EIU), Country Profile (country reports on 92 countries).

■ *Area Handbook Series*, Foreign Area Studies, The American University (country reports on 107 countries).

■ United States Department of State, *Background Notes*, Washington, D.C. (country reports on about 180 countries).

On which country will you base your report? You and each of your classmates are asked to choose *one* of the following countries. Every student will have a different country. (Your instructor, your class, or both may decide on a fair method of choosing.)

1. Argentina	12. India	23. Pakistan
2. Australia	13. Indonesia	24. Panama
3. Austria	14. Israel	25. Philippines
4. Belgium	15. Italy	26. Singapore
5. Brazil	16. Japan	27. South Korea
6. Burma	17. Laos	28. Spain
7. China (PRC)	18. Macau	29. Thailand
8. China (ROC)	19. Malaysia	30. Turkey
9. Egypt	20. Mexico	31. United Kingdom
10. Greece	21. Netherlands	32. West Germany
11. Hong Kong	22. New Zealand	33. Western Samoa

6. *Analytical memo report—justification-recommendation of hot-air hand dryers:* One of your duties as assistant manager of Raney's Manufacturing is to check the plant's suggestion box. Recently a number of complaints have appeared about the unsightly, unsanitary mess in the

washroom. Some employees have been careless about using and disposing of paper towels. Each dispenser has a built-in trash basket and even a sticker to remind employees to place used towels in the basket. However, the problem still persists.

As a solution, you have decided to replace paper towels with a hot-air hand dryer. At your request, Haworth Inc., makers of the Jetaire Hand Dryer, sent a salesperson to evaluate your needs. The salesperson made a cost analysis of your situation and also presented an estimate of the cost for changing to the Jetaire Hand Dryer. Raney's has 240 employees, and each employee visits the washroom an average of 4 times a day. An average of 2½ paper towels is used each visit, at a cost of $0.003 a towel. Assuming 22 working days a month, a 3-year cost figure for towels alone was derived. Haworth's salesperson also pointed out that there are "intangible" costs involved with paper towels. These include time spent in filling out purchase orders and the cost of mailing the order, cost per square foot of storage of the paper towels, and plumbing expenses for toilets and sinks clogged with paper towels. These intangible costs usually amount to 50 percent of the three-year total cost of paper towels for any business.

According to the salesperson, each of the four washrooms in your plant should have three Jetaire units. The units cost $150 apiece and together use about $4.50 in electricity per month. There is also an installation fee of $120 (for 12 machines).

Because the estimated acquisition cost of the Jetaire Hand Dryers is over $1,000, it is necessary to receive authorization from Mr. Steve Batter, the plant superintendent. He is a very busy person and often does not have the time to sort through a lengthy cost analysis report. He likes to know immediately what the cost and savings are to the company. Write a memo report bringing to Mr. Batter's attention these points as well as other facts such as employee benefits. Include in your discussion section two concise, easy-to-read columns of labeled figures showing calculations that lead to your important totals. For your organizational plan will you use plan 1, 2, or 3 on pages 498 and 499?

7. *Informational memo report about C.A.A. account executives' reports:* You are a management trainee for Central Advertising Agency, in which the ability to write good reports is an important qualification. Two days ago Mr. Larry Morgens, training director, asked you to find out what types of reports are written by account executives in this firm. He suggested you interview Ms. Jane Mersen, vice president and account executive at Central and then write him the best report you can about your findings. Yesterday during your interview with Ms. Mersen you jotted down the following notes (with her permission). Ms. Mersen also gave you a sample of each of the four reports most often written in the company, and she added general comments on agency reports. Your notes are as follows:

```
Account (a/c) executive writes reports when directly in-
volved in the situation.  Otherwise, person involved and
```

a/c exec decide together who writes report. In all
cases concerning client, however, a/c exec is ultimately
responsible for reports concerning client's campaign.

Bulk of reports written by a/c exec: job memo, memo report, conference (or meeting) report, and recommendation
report.

Job memo report--most important in the office. An in-
traoffice report written to all depts. of the agency.
Written by a/c exec as often as necessary whenever any
action on client's campaign is called for. Gives authorization and instruction concerning client's campaign. Generally, a/c exec writes such reports daily.

Memo report written as often as necessary--usually
daily. Short (usually one page)--to communicate information to a specific person within agency. This report
concerns information dealing with many facets of
client's advertising campaign needed by the a/c exec in
performing his or her job.

Recommendation reports--most extensive and comprehensive
report by a/c exec. Written perhaps once or twice a
year; gives client the agency's recommendations, marketing plan, budget analysis, and advertising approach for
campaign. Agency and client both have copy of this report; many are 20-30 pages long. Not only does a/c exec
receive a copy, but so does head of agency and heads of
all depts. involved with a/c.

Important that a/c exec and client understand always
where ad campaign stands and how it is progressing. So
that each one has a record of all the decisions made
concerning the campaign, the conference report is used.
Written immediately after a conference or meeting between agency and client. Purpose: clarify discussion
and the decisions made at the meeting.

General comments:

General purpose of reports--no matter what type--is to
ensure and expedite communication between agency and
client or between depts. of agency. Mersen pointed out
several items she thought this agency's reports could be
improved upon. Also those items she thought made for
good reports. Also provided information on format this
agency uses for reports and what they have done to improve quality of their reports.

Too many reports not concise. Tend to be wordy and too
long; lack clarity; negative. Ms. M. thought that if

```
reports were more objective and emphasized position
rather than neg., they wd. help communication more.
Also desirable factors:  brevity and conciseness.  In
general, reports should communicate entire message in
fewest words possible without sounding abrupt.

Format--no particular order or format is strictly ad-
hered to.  Whether text or terminal section comes first
is not a written policy, but main points of discussion
should ideally precede the discussion to expedite read-
ing of report.

Company does not use any printed forms for reports, ex-
cept for the job memo report.  Nature of a/c in question
dictates form used for recommendation or conference re-
ports.  Headings are used to assist reader of report.
Because of volatile nature of advertising business, no
formal school in better report-writing techniques is
conducted.  However, the American Assoc. of Advertising
Agencies does provide some bulletins on better writing
techniques.  These help improve agency reports.  Also,
the a/c exec attempts to stress qualities of concise-
ness, clarity, and other desirable points of report
writing in informal discussions with other execs and
their subordinates.
```

Organize these rough-draft notes into a complete, well-written, concise memorandum report. Use the inductive plan and two degrees of headings. Assume you are attaching the four exhibits; be sure to refer to them appropriately within your report text. Remember to use topic sentences for paragraphs and to introduce subheadings properly.

8. ***Analytical memo report about three managerial candidates:*** One month ago Jim South, manager (since 1985) of the appliance department, Gaton's Department Store, announced his upcoming retirement. As the supervisor of all departments, you were asked by Lars Gaton (vice president in charge of personnel) to recommend a suitable replacement. For three weeks you have been interviewing applicants and compiling profiles on currently employed personnel who are qualified to handle the position. Gaton's has no seniority policy for hiring departmental managers. Emphasis is placed on individual qualities of leadership, ability to work with others, and a general knowledge of business operations. Previous management experience is not necessary, since most of the daily management routine can be quickly learned on the job.

Having carefully considered 12 qualified employees and applicants, you have narrowed the field down to 3 main candidates, one of whom you must recommend—in an analytical memo report—to Mr. Gaton. On the basis of your recommendation, he will make the final decision.

In your report consider the following three candidates' qualifications:

Thomas Tenon: Tom, a high school graduate, received an honorable discharge after serving 5 years in the Army (2 years as a master sergeant), worked 4 years in construction and then 7 years selling magazines on the road, and has worked in Gaton's appliance department the last 12 years. Now 48, he has the most seniority among the clerks. Often when Mr. South was absent because of illness or business reasons, Tom was asked to act as manager. Company policy requires that each departmental manager keep a personality and efficiency inventory on all employees in her or his department. In the inventory Mr. South praised Tom's ability to handle the managerial duties in his absence, but he also noted that Tom had trouble in getting along with some of the employees. At times Tom was "bossy" toward new employees, even when he was not acting as manager.

Carol Latson: Carol has a B.A. degree in history and English, taught high school English eight years, and worked in Gaton's home furnishings department for two years and in the appliance department the last four years. She is now 36. The principal of the high school where Carol taught told Mr. South by letter that he has no unfavorable criticism of her work at any time, but that Carol quit teaching because she had disciplinary problems. However, both faculty and students in high school liked her. In the personality and efficiency inventory, Mr. South wrote that Carol is one of the best workers he has ever managed. She never questions any request given her by Mr. South or by any of the other employees. Carol also gets along with all employees and seems to be the most popular among them. She has never been in a managerial position, but she does have a sound knowledge of the operations of the appliance department.

Don Korr: Next month Don will receive his master's degree in marketing. From Don's resume and an interview with him, you know he is a capable leader and has the type of personality that will allow him to get along well with employees in the department. In college he was captain of the track team. Most of Don's working experience has been part-time or full-time summer employment. For the last six years he has worked in an appliance store in the university district. A reference from the store manager was complimentary and noted especially Don's ability to keep himself busy when there were no customers to wait on. He is now 28.

9. ***Informational letter report about tutoring program:*** Assume your employer's public relations department sponsored a volunteer program one year ago to show the firm's concern for helping with certain needs of people in the community. You have become active in one phase of that program—as chairperson of a special tutoring committee that works with foreign students at a nearby college.

Yesterday you received a letter from Mr. Lawrence Gentro, public relations manager of a business firm in a nearby city. Having heard about your program, he asks you for information about it because he is interested in setting up a similar project.

The aim of your committee is to give foreign students the individual help they need in their conversational English. One volunteer employee is assigned to each foreign student seeking help. These two agree to meet at least once a week for a 10-week period. Some volunteer–foreign student pairs have sessions that last longer than one hour a week. No sessions are scheduled during company working hours.

Publicity is important to keep the program going. Notices in the firm's employee news bulletin and in the college newspaper are instrumental in recruiting volunteers and informing the foreign students. (Occasional write-ups by city newspapers have brought unsolicited, favorable publicity to your firm.)

Because of the intrinsic appeal of this program, many people volunteer. So far you have kept up with the foreign student demand. Some tutors are poor. Some say they will help and don't; others contribute a lot of time and effort.

In addition to meeting with the foreign student one hour a week, each tutor is required to meet with the other tutors and your company's public relations director one Saturday morning each month (in the company lounge). They discuss problems and ways to add variety in their sessions with the foreign students. As a result, you made a list of activities—including sports, recreation, studies, trips, shopping, and games that require practicing English.

You give both the tutors and the students a way to end the relationship if they don't get along. The students are free to terminate the meeting arrangements at any time and ask for a new tutor. Also the tutor can ask for a new student. Strict confidence is maintained in this matter; a lot of juggling does occur. Volunteers have paid their own expenses for the sessions. However, recently the company has established a small fund to cover some general costs—including a semiannual reception or luncheon for the participants.

On the whole, the program has been a great success. Many new and lasting friendships have resulted. The tutors also have learned a tremendous amount from the foreign students. The cultural exchange has helped both the students and the tutors.

Reply to Mr. Gentro's request and report your experience. Under appropriate headings, mention both the good and the difficult areas in organizing and operating the program.

10. *Informational memo report with table or other comparisons:* Your employer, Bryson Novak, wants to expand the business and asks you· to present some information about the following cities: New Orleans, Louisiana; Kansas City, Missouri; Omaha, Nebraska; and Portland, Oregon.

Though he is interested in many geographic and special-event topics, he asks you to begin your study on only these four topics:

a. Population

b. Area size

c. Educational institutions and facilities

d. Major businesses similar to your company

Make brief but specific comparisons on the topics for each of the cities. Your employer is in a retail business, specializing in one area. For this assignment, assume it is in an area you prefer. Choose one of these, if possible: books, clothing, videos, software, electronic equipment.

Usually good places to find information on topics **a**, **b**, and **c** are the most recent almanacs, atlases, and encyclopedias. For topic **d** various industrial and business directories list helpful details about cities, state by state. You can also get general business information from on-line data bases or optical disk sources in your library or computer center.

Try to collect the most up-to-date facts available. Whatever sources you use, mention their names and dates in footnotes, or perhaps in your introduction or the discussion section.

In this informational report use whatever organizational plan, headings, tables, graphs, and content are desirable for a complete answer. Keep the report to no more than three typewritten (single-spaced) pages.

Mr. Kovak, your employer, is owner and general manager of the business firm. Remember that if you write a complete, useful report for him, you will probably be chosen to do additional research on this project. With that in mind, you might mention tactfully your willingness to do future research.

Chapter 18

Formal (Long) Reports

Though formal (also called "long") report is an expansion of the shorter one. As discussed in Chapter 16, the body of a short report and a formal report consists of an introduction, a text or body, and a terminal section, more often organized deductively than inductively. Headings and other visual guideposts—easily done with word processing systems—are often used.

The formal report includes prefatory and supplemental parts. Its length may range from a few to hundreds of pages. *Formal* does not mean the level of language is formal. You should continue to use easily understood words and apply the C qualities found in well-written reports (summarized on pages 470) to 475). The formal report usually covers a more complex problem than the short report. Consequently, the needed preliminary investigation and gathering, sorting, and interpretation of data, as well as the writing and editing, are often far more time-consuming and costly than for short reports.

This chapter presents additional information you will need regarding the following aspects of formal-report writing: working plans; prefatory parts; documentation and explanatory notations; supplemental parts; writing, editing, revising, and typing.

WORKING PLANS

When someone—inside or outside your company—requests that you investigate a problem and write a report, you must know clearly what is expected of you.[1] You should know the problem, purpose, scope, procedure to follow in collecting data, and deadline for completion. If your employer (or whoever requested the report) doesn't give you complete information, you need to ask questions until you understand the assignment thoroughly.

After you receive the assignment, you may use the given facts for informal talks with authorities on the subject and people associated with the problem, preliminary review of materials existing in libraries, study of company records, and so on. Use whatever sources will give you the necessary background and understanding to proceed further with the investigation—through the first three planning steps (discussed on pages 442 to 443). Given here are a suggested working plan outline and a sample plan.

Outline

The culmination of preliminary investigation is a working plan that you'll present to the person who asked you to make the report. If no one authorized you to take the assignment, you still should make a working plan for your own benefit. In this working plan—perhaps a memo to the employer in your own organization or a letter to someone outside the firm—you'll include:

1. Problem
2. Purpose
3. Scope

4. Limitations

5. Use of the report

6. Type of reader(s)

7. Tentative outline (your main text and terminal section headings)

8. Method(s) of collecting data

9. Work progress schedule

The whole idea of the working plan is to tell the one who authorized the report (or yourself) the way you understand the problem, purpose, use of the report, and so on, and to make sure you see eye to eye. Be sure you understand who your readers will be. Do you have both primary and secondary readers? Are they familiar with the subject, or will they need background material? Are they biased, antagonistic, or favorably inclined toward the subject?

In the outline you show the areas you'll investigate and discuss in the report—and, if possible, subdivisions for each major area. Also indicate the type of terminal section you'll have—summary, conclusions, recommendations, or all three—and the arrangement of the parts, that is, by either the direct or the indirect plan.

Example

The following working plan is from a researcher in a management consulting firm to a department head. It is typewritten on the firm's memo stationery. (Though a blank line is usually left after each third-degree heading, it may be omitted in an internal memo report such as this when only one or two short paragraphs follow most headings.)

```
TO:      Nine Vandeline          DATE: April 12, 199-
FROM:    Tom Browne
SUBJECT: Working Plan for Study on Treelane Homeowners Asso-
         ciation
```

Confirming our conversation of April 8, here is my working plan for the study you requested concerning Treelane Home-owners Association, a development in south XY County.

Problems
The association's programs are not meeting the needs of its members. The benefits the association affords are rarely taken advantage of by homeowners. They share assets con-sisting of a clubhouse, park, swimming pool, and fishing pond. In addition, the association has a charter that out-lines rules and guidelines all homeowners are supposed to follow for (1) changes in their property, (2) general regu-lation of pets, and (3) use of the common area.

However, rules are often ignored. Social activities are
rarely attended by many homeowners. Business meetings have
a very poor attendance record. Communication is poor. Some
owners are hostile.

Purpose and Objective
I will determine the causes for the problems and make recommendations to help Treelane become a more effective organization.

My plan is to find the attitudes and interests of individual
homeowners and apply my findings to aid officers in modifying the organization. My findings and proposals will hopefully lead to an organization that involves homeowners and
helps them to receive benefits they are paying for.

Limitations
My evaluations must be limited to programs that are useful
and stimulate interest and modifications of property within
the budget. The study is limited in time in that the recommendations are needed one month from today.

Scope
I will evaluate only those changes which are practical and
feasible and which have apparent potential for bettering
Treelane.

Procedures for Gathering Data
A questionnaire will be sent to all homeowners. In addition
to studying replies received from homeowners, I plan to interview all officers and to examine--with your permission--
records of the association.

Division of Problem and Tentative General Outline
The problem will be divided into three parts: (1) social
activities, (2) physical property, and (3) rules.

First, a questionnaire must be prepared to find out what
preferences, dislikes, and ideas property owners have. The
data will be analyzed, and selected recommendations will be
evaluated by talking with officers and looking at the
budget.

Tentative Conclusion
The homeowners' association needs social activities that
will involve more property owners. This change will stimulate interest in the organization and decrease the hostili-
ties now present.

Work Progress Schedules
Data will be collected by Friday, April 22; organized and

```
interpreted by Monday, May 2.  The report outline will be
ready by May 9.  The final report will be submitted by
May 12.
```

After completing the preliminary investigation, the authorizer and report writer might have further consultations. Some authorizers wish close involvement and frequent progress reports. If there are few progress reports, additional contacts might occur (1) at the completion of the investigation, (2) after the writer has made the final report outline, and (3) after the writer has completed the report along with specific recommendations but before he or she officially submits the finished report to the receiver.

PREFATORY PARTS

One of the distinguishing features of a formal (or long) report is that it has some of or all the following prefatory parts that are placed before the report's body: cover, title fly, title page, letter or memo of authorization, letter or memo of transmittal, table of contents, table of tables, abstract.

Cover Design and Wording of Title

Many reports combine the cover and title page for the top page. Indeed, one can purchase professionally produced covers that have space for a title. In large companies or in some government offices specially printed covers have the title of the report printed on them.

More traditional reports simply have a hard cover with the title typed on a gummed label attached to the cover. Depending on the culture of a company, one can use varying degrees of imagination in designing covers to call attention to the material enclosed, as seen in the following:

Cover of Report	Title
Side from breakfast cereal box	`How Should Our Industry React to the Alleged Shared Monopoly?`
Movie advertisement	`Drawing the Line on Pornographic Films`
Airline ticket folder	`Travel Costs: A Problem in our Company`
Record cover	`Recommendations on Handling Home Entertainment Piracy`

Choosing a report title should indicate briefly and clearly what the report covers. Here are a few suggestions:

1. Include whichever of the five W's—*who, what, when, where, why*—are pertinent. For instance, suppose your report discusses detailed market-

ing procedures that the ABC Company should adopt to increase its sales in Canada during a certain year. To select the title, you might begin with this analysis:

Who:	ABC Company	*Where:*	Canada
What:	Marketing procedures	*Why:*	To increase sales
When:	1995		

Possible titles could be:

```
-Steps for Increasing ABC's 1995 Canadian Sales
-Increasing ABC's 1995 Canadian Sales
-A New Marketing Emphasis for 1995 Canadian Sales
```

2. Keep title length within a maximum of about 8 to 10 words. Try to omit articles such as *the, a,* and *an* whenever possible. Try also to omit *a report,* or *study of,* or *survey of.*

3. Add a subtitle—often indicated with a colon—for additional clarity if it is truly necessary. For example:

```
Child Care: Options for Full-Time Employees

Contending with Literacy: Two Recommendations for All
Employees

Industrial Water Pollution: What Strategy Should Be
Adopted?
```

4. Avoid vague, extremely short, too broad titles.

Unclear	Better
Ed Costs	Company Contributions to Higher Education Costs
Marijuana	Drugs and Organizational Abuse
International Trade	Improving International Trade with China
Company History	Strategic Marketing Plans: 1980–199–

5. Avoid evaluation terms in titles, as in the following:

```
Why Accounting Is Poor

Personnel Department's Selection Errors

Unnecessary Interventions from Finance Department
```

Title Fly and Title Page

Only when you have both a cover and a title page can you use the *title fly*— usually a blank sheet of paper located between the two parts. As in books, it acts as a buffer before the reader opens the book or as a protection of the title page.

The *title page*—usually symmetrically arranged—most often contains the title, the names of the recipient and sender, and the completion date. Each component may constitute a separate focal point on the page, as seen in Figure 18-4 (page 560) and in the following:

EXAMPLE 1

Title	Meeting the Challenge of Drugs in the Workplace
Recipient	Prepared for ABC's Board of Directors
Sender	Prepared by the Task Force on Organizational Drug Abuse
Date	October 9, 199–

EXAMPLE 2

Title	Product Liability in the Pharmaceutical Industry
Recipient	For the Legal Department, Company RLM
Sender	Nina Fitzgerald Pamela Kunick Scott Morris Bill Potter, Chairman
Date	November 5, 199–

If you arrange the title page in three sections, you combine the date with the author's identification. If appropriate, you may add pertinent facts about the people involved, such as title, department, and organization. The date of completion must agree with the date on the letter of transmittal.

When used with a separate cover, the title page is the same weight paper as the text sheets. As a combination cover and title page, this part might have a heavier-weight paper.

Letter or Memorandum of Authorization

The person or secretary of the group authorizing or commissioning the formal report notifies the report writer in a letter or memorandum of authorization. The letter format is used always when the report writer is outside the authorizer's organization. In a formal report of a public nature, the authorization message becomes one of the bound prefatory pages. Although it is often omitted from the business formal report, it may of course be included. If the authorizer is within the same firm as the report writer, the authorization may be in memorandum format.

When you are in the position of authorizing a report, organize your message by the direct-request or good-news plan. And be sure to make clear just what you are authorizing, as in the following memorandum of authorization.

To:	John Paul, Chairman, Task Force on Retirement Options
From:	Nadine Hunt, Secretary Board of Directors
Subject:	Request for Recommendations on Retirement Options
Date:	December 15, 199-

Request

As you know, the Board of Directors at their December 6 meeting requested that you chair a task force to investigate possible changes in our current retirement program.

Details

Specifically, the Board requests that you provide retirement recommendations for these categories: employees with the company 1-10 years, 11-20 years, 21-25 years, and over 25 years.

Furthermore they would like comparative data for other companies in our industry.

Date when needed

The Board hopes that your committee's recommendations can be presented at the May 10, 199-, meeting, or before, if that is possible.

Courtesy

If you have any questions, I will be pleased to respond and review further details.

Letter or Memorandum of Transmittal

The message that conveys the report from the writer to the reader in another organization is the letter of transmittal. In some formal, long reports—especially those written to a large group of readers—the author's message is labeled "Preface" (as in books) or "Foreword." If the reader (addressee) is in the report writer's organization, the transmittal may be in memorandum or letter format within the report.

The transmittal message is usually worded in conversational language (with first- and second-person pronouns—I, we, you) as you would talk if you were handing the report to the recipient in person. Only if you are writing to a formal, distinguished group—for instance, top government officials—might you use impersonal language and "the writer." Even prefaces may use the first-person pronoun.

Organization of the transmittal message may follow the direct, good-news plan: main idea, explanation, courteous ending. The following are topics that may be included—arranged in any appropriate, desirable order.

Main idea

Transmittal

Authorization

Purpose

Need or use of report

Explanation and/or highlights

Perhaps a brief indication of outcome—in general only. Indicate conclusions and/or recommendations *if* you think the reader will consider them good (or neutral) news and *if* an abstract or terminal section with the same information doesn't appear at the beginning of the report—just a few pages after the transmittal.

Maybe a comment or two to help the reader use and appreciate the report.

Background, methodology, limitations sometimes—stated briefly.

Courteous ending

Acknowledgments to people who assisted. (In some formal reports acknowledgments are in a separate section instead of in the transmittal or preface.)

Indication that later reports may be necessary or forthcoming.

Expression of appreciation for the assignment.

Willingness to discuss, do additional research, or assist with future projects.

You need to be careful not to include the same elements in both the transmittal and the introduction, or in the transmittal and the abstract or executive summary, for the needless repetition would be annoying.

The example which follows is a transmittal letter for a 67-page report and includes the final recommendation. The company letterhead and inside address have been omitted here.

Dear Mr. McShea:

Transmittal

Purpose

Enclosed is the report which you requested on January 5, 199-, on the issue of what policy our firm should follow regarding the rights of those judged mentally ill.

Highlights

The nature of XYZ's problem, its history, causes and effects are explained in the report. Four recommended solutions to the problem are judged in light of the three criteria of fairness, workability, and cost-effectiveness.

Recommendation

As a committee we propose this recommendation: those persons judged mentally ill by a medical practitioner be given the same rights as those with other illnesses.

Courtesy

```
We hope the report is acceptable.  Preparing
it has been a rewarding and enlightening expe-
rience.  If you or other members of the execu-
tive team have further questions, we will be
happy to discuss them with you.

Sincerely,

[Signature
[Typed name, title]
```

Table of Contents

You should include a table of contents as a prefatory part of your long report whenever such a table would be a helpful guide for your reader. The table of contents lists the main headings of the report outline plus page numbers showing where the sections begin in the finished report. This table is especially useful for the reader who wants to see a concise overview of the report's contents and needs to read only a few scattered, selected sections or parts.

Figure 18-6, page 562, illustrates a table of contents with two degrees of headings. These are preceded by the Roman numerals (I–V) and alphabetic letters (A–E). Including the numerals and letters is optional. (Notice that the Roman numerals are typed so that their last digits are aligned.) For reports that also have third-degree headings, these too may be included in the table of contents, but doing so is optional.

Though the table of contents is placed before the report body, you must, of course, prepare the table after the entire report is typed—so you will know the correct page numbers. Use leaders (spaced dots) to lead the eye from the name of each entry to the page column on the right. Every entry shown in the table of contents should appear exactly as it does in the body. But not every heading in the body has to appear in the contents. Usually you show no more than three degrees (first, second, and third) of headings.

If the appendix includes several different entries (questionnaire, reprint of a statute or regulation, various tables, or other visual aids), you can show them in one of two locations: (1) as subdivisions of the appendix on the contents page if you have only a few entries or (2) as subdivisions of the appendix on a separate appendix title page if you have a rather extensive appendix.

Table of Tables

The label for this prefatory part depends on the type of formal visual aids shown throughout the text. If the illustrations are all tables, you can label the page "Table of Tables" or "List of Tables." Follow the same procedure for charts, pictures, and so forth. If you have a mixture of tables, charts, and other visual aids, consider a title that encompasses them all; perhaps "Table of Illustrations" will suffice.

This prefatory page serves the same function for the visual aids as the contents page does for the sections covered in the report. Whether the table of tables is placed on the same page with the table of contents or by itself on a page, the layout is similar to the following:

Table of Tables

Table		Page
1	(Title)	6
2	(Title)	9
3	(Title)	11
4	(Title)	23

Abstract, Synopsis, Executive Summary

The informative abstract (also labeled "synopsis," "executive summary," "epitome," "precis," "digest") performs a vital timesaving service for the reader. It is a condensed, concise, accurate statement of what is important in the report. Usually its length is between 5 and 10 percent—or less—of the whole report. The busy manager and even those tangentially interested, after scanning it, can determine whether they want to read further.

This prefatory part may be organized inductively (introduction, text, terminal section) or deductively (terminal section before the text). Either way, it *may include purpose, scope, methods, data sources, sometimes committee members (if significant for the reader), major facts and figures, statement of results, conclusions, and recommendations.* Generally it is placed on a separate page between the table of contents and the report body.

Besides being a useful prefatory part of a long, formal report, informative abstracts also serve other important functions. Some firms circulate to all their management personnel the abstract *without* the report. (The person who originally authorized the report of course gets the complete, original report.) Those who receive only the abstract can decide whether they need the original report, which is then sent to them upon their request.

Another important use of abstracts is for reports, articles, documents, and such that are published. A well-written abstract can communicate essential contents to hundreds, even thousands, of business associates. In a brief reading time, colleagues can scan abstracts in their professional and business journals, thus keeping up to date on literature in their special field. The quality of an abstract may determine which people and how many wish to see the full document.

Good examples of abstracted articles are found in electronic databases. Each database uses a similar method, as seen in the **ABI/INFORM** on-line system:

86-31193

Title   Transferring American Management Know-How to the People's Republic of China

Author   Wang, Ruth L.

Journal	Advanced Mgmt Jrnl Vol: 51 Iss: 3 Date: Summer 1986 pp. 4-8 Jrnl Code: AMJ ISSN: Ex 0036-0805
Terms	Peoples Republic of China; Management Style; Japan; Management; Comparative Analysis; Managers
Codes	9180 (International); 2500 (Organizational behavior)
Abstract	The People's Republic of China seems determined to modernize its economy despite fears that modernization may lead to capitalism. Both Japanese and US management styles have factors that the Chinese, whose state enterprises are known for their slow and ineffective decision making, might well emulate. The American style is known for its effective decision making and entrepreneurship, while the Japanese style emphasizes human resources management. . . . Tables. References.

Though the abstract length varies somewhat in proportion to the report length, it should be confined to fewer than 500 words (preferably on one page). To show you how abstracts vary, here are three examples:

EXAMPLE 1   *An abstract of an energy conservation report (parts of that report are shown on pages 560–565).*

Purpose, scope, method	This report analyzes the energy conservation effort at Central Diesel, Inc., in three dimensions. They are based mainly on interviews, and include usage before the shortage, usage currently, and projected usage after proposed changes within separate areas of special concentration.
Major facts, figures, results	Before last winter's energy shortage, the firm, like many others, had no conservation policy. After realizing an energy crisis existed, all departments cooperated. Savings totaling about 14% energy usage were made by reducing temperatures, removing unnecessary lighting tubes, and reducing heat-loss sources plus excessive waste in convenience electricity and company vehicles.
Recommendations	Five recommendations for future improvements to achieve an estimated 35% total savings include installing certain access doors, repairing an air compressor, replacing one inefficient heating system, changing the diesel generator testing procedures to cut fuel consumption, and replacing older vehicles with smaller economy models.

EXAMPLE 2   *A short abstract on a 75-page published report.*

**Purpose,
scope,
method,
sources,
major
facts and
figures**

To determine the basic vocabulary of written
business communications, a computer count was made
of 2,504 letters, memorandums, and business
reports, submitted by 1,411 companies representative of the population of industries
nationwide. A total of 606,496 running words and
15,522 different words were identified, with the
100 most frequently occurring words accounting for
half of all word occurrences. Major differences
between this list and previous lists were noted. A
separate analysis of 500 letters, 300 memorandums,
and 200 reports was made to identify the physical
format, sentence structure, and readability levels
of the documents.[2]

EXAMPLE 3   *Executive summary of consultant recommendations.*

Purpose

International Substance Abuse Consultants was asked
to analyze this specific question: What should be
done within the company regarding alleged substance
abuse?

Consultants

Before making a specific recommendation, our staff
consultants investigated these five major background issues:

Scope

Definition and history
Measurable loss
Hidden losses
Causes of the problem
The current situation

**Methods,
sources**

Preparation work was done over a period of five
weeks, with each member contributing information to
other members. Data came from books, periodicals,
newspapers, and interviews with 323 employees of
your company. Additionally, numerous contacts were
made with substance abuse organizations.

**Criteria,
options**

The consultant group felt that regardless of the
kind of substance abuse, each recommendation should
be measured against a consistent set of criteria:
(1) cost-effectiveness, (2) feasibility, (3) sen-

```
                    sitivity, and (4) legality.  On the basis of these
                    criteria, members reviewed each of the following
                    five options:

                         Detection and termination
                         Health maintenance programs
                         Employee education programs
                         Employee assistance programs--in-placement
                         Employee assistance programs--out-placement
```

Result   Education came closest to meeting all the criteria.

Recommen-   Our <u>final recommendation</u> is that your company begin
dation   an employee education program to inform employees
                    on these topics.

```
                         Kinds of substance abuse
                         Effects of substance abuse on the employee
                         Effects of substance abuse on the company
```

DOCUMENTATION AND OTHER NOTES

When your report contains paraphrases, specific facts, or quotations from various sources, you must document your sources. In addition to notes citing sources, some reports (also articles, chapters, or books) may have other notes too. This section first discusses briefly the kinds and purposes of footnotes, plus superscripts that precede the footnotes. Then it focuses in detail on the content of *source* footnotes, and, finally, on placement of footnotes.

Footnotes—Kinds, Purposes, and Superscripts

Kinds and Purposes

The three kinds of footnotes are source, cross-reference, and explanatory. They meet the following purposes:

1. *Source footnotes give credit to sources you used.* Any quotations and important factual statements that are not common knowledge or based on your experience must be supported by references to your sources. If you quote someone else's statement verbatim or you paraphrase it in other words and you don't credit that source, you are plagiarizing—

committing "literary theft." By citing sources, you give credit where credit is due. Additionally, you (1) improve your own credibility as a writer, (2) help convince your readers that your data are trustworthy, and (3) provide an opportunity for readers to examine your sources.

2. *Cross-reference footnotes direct the reader to another place within the report.* For instance, they may mention a detailed discussion, examples of important principles, or perhaps a page in the appendix. These footnotes help to emphasize significant points without unnecessary repetition.

3. *Explanatory footnotes discuss, explain, and/or give additional information.* This material relates to an idea in your report text that is incidental; or is too long, complicated, or technical to include in the text discussion; or shouldn't interrupt the flow of thought.

Superscripts

To refer your reader to footnotes and to number them, you may use superscript numerals, easily inserted with today's word processing systems. These are usually small Arabic numbers placed slightly above the line. You can number these superscripts consecutively throughout the report or begin a new series with each chapter (as in this book).

Superscripts are usually placed at the end of a sentence or a title, and always at the beginning of the footnote. (See, for instance, superscript 3 on this page. The actual footnote is in the References and Notes list, page 826. *Superscripts in tables and figures should be symbols* (asterisks, daggers—the ° and †) or *lowercase alphabetic letters*, not Arabic numbers. (For examples see Capsule Checklists, chapters 7–11.) The same sequence of symbols is repeated in *each* table or figure in a report (or article or book), unlike numbered superscripts, which would continue consecutively throughout the report, article, chapter, or book.

Content of Source Footnotes

The choice of content in source footnotes varies somewhat depending on the following:

1. Whether or not the report has a bibliography or other reference list

2. Whether the source footnote is being used for the first time or is being repeated

3. Which style handbook you are following

To avoid confusing you with several alternatives, this section summarizes briefly the main items included in a popular method. Remember that others may be equally desirable for different situations.[3] Use whatever is preferred by your instructor, employer, industry, business, editor (or by you), and be consistent.

1. Source Footnotes *without* Bibliography or Other Reference Lists

Footnotes citing sources the first time should always contain complete information if the report or chapter has no bibliography or other list of reference sources at its end. When the same source is repeated in later references, these footnotes may be shortened. Source footnotes may refer to published or unpublished materials.

Published Sources.   You get most of the information about a book source from title and copyright pages. For a periodical—published quarterly, monthly, weekly, or daily—you'll find needed information on the cover page and in the article itself. Though your reference materials will vary in content, try to include whatever facts about the composition and publication are available and helpful to identify specifically each source for your readers. Then arrange them in the sequence shown in the following checklist and examples.

The checklist guidelines on page 545 outline briefly the items that may be included in first-time, full-footnote references when the sources are books, periodicals, or newspapers. You can use these guidelines also for sources in other publications—encyclopedias, almanacs, annual reports, government documents. Of course, not all these items are available or essential for every footnote.

Unpublished Sources.   *For minutes of meetings, speeches, letters, theses, interviews*—you will find a variety of different citations used. However, as a general guide, the minimum items to include are:

Superscript

Name of author or sponsoring organization

Title or kind of material

Date

Page numbers, if these would be helpful to the reader

Examples.   The following illustrate first-time, full-source footnotes about published and unpublished materials. (In the first example, the italicized numbers in parentheses after each item are inserted to indicate the corresponding sections in column A of the checklist on page 545.

BOOKS   *With one, two, and four authors.*

[1]Oiva Laaksonen *(2.a)*, <u>Management in China during and after Mao in Enterprises, Government, and Party,</u> *(4.a)*,

■ CHECKLIST GUIDELINES FOR FIRST-TIME FOOTNOTES ABOUT PUBLISHED SOURCES

A. Books	B. Periodicals	C. Newspapers
1. Superscript	1. Superscript	1. Superscript

Facts about the Composition

A. Books	B. Periodicals	C. Newspapers

2. Author name(s)
  a. 1 to 3 ⎫ normal
    (or 1 to 5) ⎭ order
  b. Over 3 (or 5): 1st author plus "and others" or "et al."
3. Author capacity (used only if not really the author):
  a. Editor—typed "ed."
  b. Translator—"trans."
  c. Compiler—"comp."
4. Book title
  a. Typed: all capitals or underlined
  b. Printed: italics
5. Edition number or name (if not the first)
	2. Author name(s)
	  a. 1 to 3 ⎫ normal
	    (or 1 to 5) ⎭ order
	  b. Over 3 (or 5): 1st author plus "and others" or "et al."
	  c. Sometimes no person's name given
	  d. A bureau may be author
	
	3. Article title
	  a. Typed ⎫ in quota-
	  b. Printed ⎭ tion marks
		2. Author name(s)
		  a. 1 to 3 ⎫ normal
		    (or 1 to 5) ⎭ order
		  b. Over 3 (or 5): 1st author plus "and others" or "et al."
		  c. If no name, maybe give section (Editorial, Business), if any
		
		3. Article title
		  a. Typed ⎫ in quota-
		  b. Printed ⎭ tion marks

Facts about the Publication

A. Books	B. Periodicals	C. Newspapers

6. Publisher name
7. Publisher location (usually headquarters' city; add state if not well-known city; add country if foreign). *Note:* Items 6 and 7 may be reversed—"City: Publisher."
8. Date of publication—year of latest edition
9. Volume number, if more than one volume
10. Page(s) of the citation
	4. Periodical name
	  a. Typed: underlined
	  b. Printed: italics
	5. Publisher location—if desirable to include, same as A.7
	
	6. Date of issue (month and year) ⎫
	7. Volume number, if any ⎬ use either or both
	8. Page(s) of article ⎭
		4. Newspaper name
		  a. Typed: underlined
		  b. Printed: italics
		5. City and state may be inserted if not in name
		
		6. Date of newspaper—month, day, year
		7. Page(s) of article

Walter de Gruyter (6), Berlin (7), New York (7), 1988 (8), pp. 22–24 *(10)*.

[2]Young Yun Kim and William B. Gudykunst, <u>Theories in Intercultural Communication</u>, Sage, Newbury Park, 1988, p. 11.

[3]Richard W. Brislin, Kenneth Cushner, Craig Cherrie, Mahealani Yong, <u>Intercultural Interactions, A Practical Guide</u>, Sage, Beverly Hills, 1986, pp. 18–20.

PERIODICALS   *With author identified and no author identified.*

>   [4]Doug Rose, "An Update on Desktop Software," <u>Communication World</u>, November 1988, vol. 5, no. 11, p. 14.

>   [5]"Stock Market Picks Up in China," <u>Beijing Review</u>, December 19–25, 1988, vol. 31, no. 51, p. 40.

NEWSPAPERS   *With author identified and no author identified.*

>   [6]Dennis Kneale, "TV Networks Suffer Lasting Ill Effects of the Writers' Strike," <u>Wall Street Journal</u>, Jan. 5, 1989, p. A1.

>   [7]"Fundamental Fairness," <u>Wall Street Journal</u>, Jan. 5, 1989, p. A10.

GOVERNMENT AND FINANCIAL DATA PUBLICATIONS

>   [8]<u>Statistical Abstract of the United States, 1987</u>, U.S. Government Printing Office, U.S. Department of Commerce, Washington D.C., 1988.

>   [9]Chemical Bank, <u>Flexibility in Global Swaps</u>, 1988, p. 7.

UNPUBLISHED INFORMATION

>   [10]Thomas L. Brewer, "Country Creditworthiness and Political Instability," paper for presentation at the annual meeting of the Academy of International Business, San Diego, Oct. 20–23, 1988.

>   [11]Regional District Attorneys Association Symposium on White Collar Crime Enforcement, conducted at Battelle Research Center, Seattle, Wash., May 12, 1990.

>   [12]Randy Aprill, chief chef, Intercontinental Hotel, Washington, D.C., letter, Feb. 5, 1990.

>   [13]Steve Sarns, product manager, SI Corporation, Ann Arbor, Mich., personal interview, Mar. 6, 1990.

2. Source Footnotes *with* Bibliography or Other Reference Lists

When the report includes a bibliography or other list of references, the footnotes may (but not *must*) be shortened to these items:

Superscript

Surname(s) of author(s)

Title of book, article, report, or manuscript (possibly, shortened)

Page number(s) on which the information appears

For example, source footnotes 1 and 3 shown in the preceding list of footnotes could be shortened as follows:

¹Laaksonen, <u>Management in China</u>, pp. 22-24.

³Brislin et al. [*or* and others], <u>Intercultural Interac-</u><u>tions</u>, pp. 18-20.

Because the bibliography or reference list gives the complete citations, readers can refer to it if they wish more details about any source. Discussion and examples of these supplemental parts are on pages 551 to 554 and in Figures 18-2 and 18-3.

3. Repeated Source Footnote References

When you need to cite the same source more than once in a paper, the citations after the first time are usually shortened. Three methods are acceptable:

Method a.   Superscript, author surname(s), page number(s).

Method b.   Same as Source Footnotes *with* Bibliography (see preceding section).

Method c.   Standard Latin abbreviations (which many readers do not understand, but which may be required for some academic papers):

Ibid. (meaning "in the same place")—refers to the immediately preceding footnote, but a different page. Content: superscript, ibid., page(s)—as for footnote 2 in the examples at the top of page 548.

Op cit. ("in the work cited")—refers to a previously cited footnote that. is followed by at least one intervening footnote about another source. Content: superscript, author surname(s), op. cit., page(s). See footnote 4, in the following examples.

Loc. cit. ("in the place cited")—refers to same page in a previously cited footnote. (1) When one or more other source footnotes intervene, use superscript, author surname(s), loc. cit. See footnote 5 in the following examples. (2) When no other source footnote intervenes, use superscript, loc. cit. See footnote 6.

The following examples show how to shorten source footnotes by using methods **a** or **c** whenever source references are repeated:

[1]Donald Murray, <u>Write to Learn</u>, Holt, New York, 1984, pp. 185-187.

Method a	Method c
[2]Murray, p. 198.	[2]Ibid., p. 198.

[3]Thomas E. Harris and Jennings Bryant, "The Corporate Communication," <u>The Journal of Business Communication</u>, vol. 23, no. 3, Summer 1986, p. 25.

Method a	Method c
[4]Murray, p. 201.	[4]Murray, op cit., p. 201.
[5]Harris and Bryant, p. 25.	[5]Harris and Bryant, loc. cit., p. 25.
[6]Harris and Bryant, p. 25.	[6]Loc. cit.

Placement of Footnotes

If you use footnotes, they can be placed either at the bottom of the page or in a list (bibliography or endnotes) at the end of the report, or they may be placed in both places; sometimes they are situated parenthetically within a sentence or paragraph.

Bottom-of-Page Footnotes

The traditional placement of footnotes—source, cross-reference, or explanatory—is at the bottom ("foot") of the same page on which they are cited by superscripts. When typewritten, they are separated from the text by a typed solid line 1½ or 2 inches long—a double space below the last line of the text and beginning at the left margin. Each footnote is typed single-spaced, usually indented three to five spaces on its first line and even with the left margin on all succeeding lines. Double-space between footnotes, as shown in Figure 18-1.

Bibliography or Endnotes

A second way to place footnotes is the terminal method, in which all notations are in a list after the body of the report. This placement is discussed in the next section, Supplemental Parts.

Parenthetical Documentation

A method of documentation gaining favor in both the academic and the non-academic world is termed *parenthetical documentation*, in which a source citation is included within a sentence or paragraph. Such citations may be made in three ways: author-date method, number method, or full-citation method.

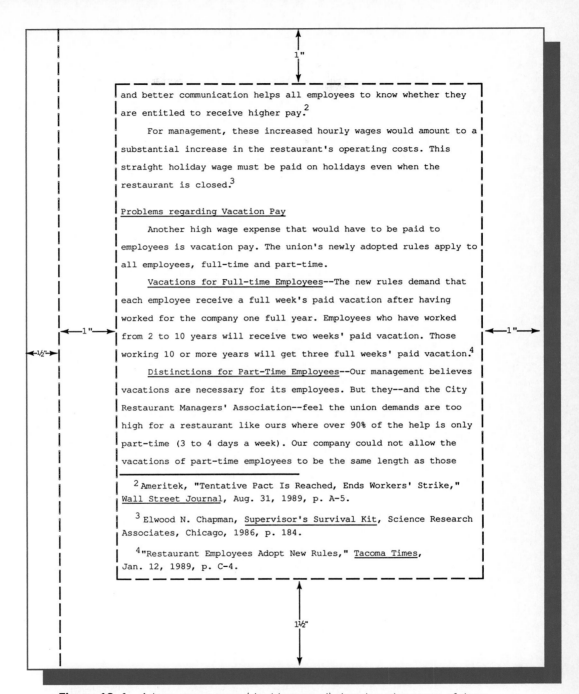

and better communication helps all employees to know whether they are entitled to receive higher pay.[2]

For management, these increased hourly wages would amount to a substantial increase in the restaurant's operating costs. This straight holiday wage must be paid on holidays even when the restaurant is closed.[3]

Problems regarding Vacation Pay

Another high wage expense that would have to be paid to employees is vacation pay. The union's newly adopted rules apply to all employees, full-time and part-time.

Vacations for Full-time Employees--The new rules demand that each employee receive a full week's paid vacation after having worked for the company one full year. Employees who have worked from 2 to 10 years will receive two weeks' paid vacation. Those working 10 or more years will get three full weeks' paid vacation.[4]

Distinctions for Part-Time Employees--Our management believes vacations are necessary for its employees. But they--and the City Restaurant Managers' Association--feel the union demands are too high for a restaurant like ours where over 90% of the help is only part-time (3 to 4 days a week). Our company could not allow the vacations of part-time employees to be the same length as those

[2] Ameritek, "Tentative Pact Is Reached, Ends Workers' Strike," Wall Street Journal, Aug. 31, 1989, p. A-5.

[3] Elwood N. Chapman, Supervisor's Survival Kit, Science Research Associates, Chicago, 1986, p. 184.

[4] "Restaurant Employees Adopt New Rules," Tacoma Times, Jan. 12, 1989, p. C-4.

Figure 18–1 *A long-report page (double-spaced) showing placement of three superscripts and three complete footnotes.*

Author-Date Method.   This placement requires that the surname of the author or authors, the year of publication, and a page number [for example (Stewart, Cash, 1988, 102)] be inserted parenthetically in the text sentence whenever you wish to give credit to the author. No footnote appears. Instead, the reader would look to the rear of the report for the alphabetically arranged bibliography where Stewart and Cash would be included along with their work published in 1988. The American Psychological Association (APA) would have the bibliography citation in this order:

> Stewart, C. J., & Cash, W. B., Jr. (1988). <u>Interviewing:</u>
> <u>Principles and Practices</u> (5th ed.). Dubuque, IA: Wm. C.
> Brown

The Modern Language Association (MLA) would have this order:

> Stewart, C. J., and W. B. Cash, Jr. <u>Interviewing: Princi-</u>
> <u>ples and Practices</u>. 5th ed. Dubuque, IA: Wm. C. Brown.
> 1988.

Other kinds of bibliographies and manuals may arrange some citations a little differently. For details on numerous variations, you might refer to publications listed in footnote 3, page 543.

Number Method.   This approach uses Arabic numerals—usually underlined—within parentheses [for example (2, 1988, 46-54)] to indicate the number of the citation in the reference list, the date of the citation, and the pages. Or, simply the number alone [for example (2)] is used. Sometimes the bibliographic reference list is numbered in the order in which the citations occur in the text.

When either the authors or the text title is mentioned in a sentence, only the citation number need be included, as in this example:

> <u>U.S.-China Trade, Problems and Prospects</u> (<u>17</u>) has as its
> main theme potentials for opening trade with China.

Full-Citation Method.   If a report has few (perhaps only two or three) citations, you may wish to include the complete notation in a sentence within the discussion. Then you would have no end bibliography or reference list.

> In the edited work by Eugene Lawson, <u>U.S.-China Trade, Prob-</u>
> <u>lems and Prospects</u>, (1988, New York, Praeger), the majority
> of the authors have worked in the area of China trade.

This form is particularly acceptable for brief memorandums.

The above information is not at odds with regular footnote procedures. Rather, parenthetical documentation is a method which may be requested by your company, particularly if it has a high-technology interest. You should, therefore, determine early the citation style preferred.[4]

SUPPLEMENTAL PARTS

The special parts that are added after the body of a report are called *supplemental* or *appended parts,* or *addenda.* They may include a bibliography or other list of references, an appendix, a glossary, and an index.

Bibliography or Other Appropriate List

List of Sources in Bibliography

The bibliography is a list of all sources you cited in the footnotes as documentation and also other relevant references you consulted for the content of your report. Among the published sources included in a bibliography are those from books, government publications, yearbooks, public documents, encyclopedias, pamphlets, bulletins, magazines, newspapers, and databases. It is possible that a report, article, or other paper may have full-citation footnotes but no bibliography; also, a bibliography may be included without any footnote source citations.

You can present bibliographic entries in a single alphabetic list or under various headings. One could, for example, arrange sources within broad groups such as books, periodicals, newspapers, and other major categories of your choosing, as in Figure 18-2.

If you also consulted unpublished sources such as manuscripts, interviews, responses to surveys, and organization letters or documents, the title of your list of sources may be Sources Consulted, Reference Sources, or whatever adequately covers its contents. For example, see Figure 18-9.

Bibliographies (also called *sources, references, works cited, selected bibliography, annotated bibliography, works consulted*) are often arranged alphabetically by author surnames or titles. Such sources usually differ from the footnote setup in the following three ways, as in Figure 18-2:

1. The first word of each entry begins at the left margin and all other lines are indented—usually three to five spaces. For footnotes, as previously shown in Figure 18-1, the opposite setup is used: each first line is indented, and all succeeding lines start at the left margin.

2. The author's surname is listed first, for alphabetizing. If a source includes two or more authors, only the first author's name is reversed. (An alternative arrangement by some writers is to reverse all authors' names, not just the first name.)

3. For books and other bound volumes, the total pages may be stated, but not the specific pages consulted.

Some bibliographies are annotated. They contain, just after the composition and publication information about each entry, a brief statement about its content and value. For example:

BIBLIOGRAPHY

Books

Huseman, Richard C., James M. Lahiff, John M. Penrose, Jr., and John D. Hatfield, Business Communication Strategies and Skills, Dryden Press, Chicago, 1984.

Murray, Donald, Write to Learn, Holt, New York, 1984.

Peters, Tom, and Nancy Austin, A Passion for Excellence, The Leadership Difference, Random House and Warner Books, New York, 1985.

Timm, P. R., Managerial Communication, Prentice-Hall, Englewood Cliffs, N.J., 1986.

Willingham, John R., and Donald F. Warders, A Handbook for Student Writers, 2d Edition, Harcourt Brace Jovanovich, New York, 1978.

Periodicals and Newspapers

Bekassy, Virginia, "Boosting Productivity with the Four-Day Week," Management World, June 1987. p. 12.

Carroll, Paul B., "New Systems Tackle Problem of Tapping In to Data Bases," Wall Street Journal, Oct. 31, 1986, sec. 2, p. 1.

"Discretionary Justice," Business Week, May 6, 1986, p. 9.

Editorial, Los Angeles Times, May 1, 1990, B-7.

Weatherly, Richard, Michael Lipsky, and Thomas Jones, "Street-Level Bureaucrats and Institutional Reform," Harvard Educational Review, May 1987, p. 172.

Weinrauch, J. E., and J. R. Swandra, Jr., "Examining the Significance of Listening: An Exploratory Study of Contemporary Managers, Journal of Business Communication, 13:1, 1975, p. 54.

Government and Financial Data Publications

Freeport McMoRan, Inc., Quarterly Report, June 30, 1990.

U.S. Postal Service, International Postal Rates and Fees, U.S. Government Printing Office, Washington, D.C., 1990.

Figure 18–2 *A bibliography. This one shows how 13 source footnotes are arranged alphabetically under three subheads.*

```
Concentrates on basic principles and techniques of writing
technical reports.  Focuses on data gathering, data analy-
sis, and the scientific method.  Contains good examples.
```

List of References and Notes

If a report includes cross-references and incidental explanatory notations in addition to sources, and the writer chooses the terminal method of listing notations, the list after the report is usually quite different from the bibliography. Entries appear on the list in the same numerical order that the citations and superscripts occur in the report; author names are not arranged alphabetically. The list may be titled References and Notes, or List of References, or, sometimes, merely Endnotes. This method is used by many professional journals and academic writers.

Figure 18-3 is an example of an endnotes list in the terminal section. It includes 12 entries—8 sources, a cross-reference, and 3 explanatory notes. All are ordered by superscript number.

A similar method is used in this textbook. For every chapter that has superscripts, the designated notations are listed in the same order—under References and Notes, near end of the book, on pages 818 to 830.

Appendix

You put materials into the appendix when you need to include them somewhere in the report but they aren't essential in developing any part of the text. The appendix permits you to avoid cluttering the discussion (text) with exhibits, copies of questionnaires, or pamphlets which are unnecessary to read for the right understanding of the report but which may be useful for reference or as supporting information.

With short reports, you merely add the appendix sheets directly to the report. But for a formal report, you place a sheet of paper (the appendix title page) between the last page of the body and the first page of the appendix. If you have enough material in the appendix to justify a separate table of contents, show the contents below the title on the appendix dividing sheet.

Each separate entry (sample forms, detailed data for reference, tables, pictures, questionnaires, charts, maps, graphic representations, blueprints) in the appendix naturally requires an identifying title. As a rule you should refer the reader to every entry in the appendix in the report body (within the discussion itself or in a footnote).

The last page of the appendix is the ideal place for any table or illustration the reader will need to refer to throughout the report. You can set up this table on a pull-out sheet and tell the reader about the sheet in the letter of transmittal or introduction. Such an arrangement permits the reader to keep this master table—or whatever is on the sheet—in full view at all times.

Endnotes

1. Oiva Laaksonen, Management in China during and after Mao in Enterprises, Government, and Party, Walter de Gruyter, Berlin 1988.

2. Young Yun Kim and William B. Gudykunst, Theories in Intercultural Communication, Sage, Newbury Park, 1988.

3. Richard W. Brislin, Kenneth Cushner, Craig Cherrie, Mahealani Yong, Intercultural Interactions, A Practical Guide, Sage, Beverly Hills, 1986.

4. Doug Rose, "An Update on Desktop Software," Communication World, vol. 5, no. 11, November 1988, p. 14.

5. For details and illustrations of these documents see pages 32-36.

6. "Stock Market Picks Up in China," Beijing Review, vol. 31, no. 51, December 19-25, 1988, p. 40.

7. Dennis Kneale, "TV Networks Suffer Lasting Ill Effects of the Writers' Strike, Wall Street Journal, Jan. 5, 1989, p. A-1.

8. The citation "Abstracts of Working Papers in Economics, 1982-present," includes abstracts of key economic papers issued by over 50 of the world's major research organizations, including graduate schools of business.

9. "Fundamental Fairness," Wall Street Journal, Jan. 5, 1989, p. A-10.

10. The statement about discretion applies only to social service agencies. Laborers in an industrial assembly line exercise little discretion.

11. This work was used in translation; the original article appeared in German as "Der Vorstand."

12. Statistical Abstract of the United States, 1988, U.S. Government Printing Office, U.S. Department of Commerce, Washington D.C., 1989

Figure 18–3 List of references, sources, and notes. Numbers are in the same order as in text discussion. *No* footnotes appear on text pages. List of 12 includes 8 different sources, 1 cross-reference (5), and 3 explanatory notes (8, 10, and 11).

Glossary

When your report includes any terms that have several possible interpretations, definitions should be inserted—in one of three places. If you have many definitions (for instance, in a technical report), a glossary at the end is preferable. Mention in your introduction that the report includes a glossary. It will be useful to readers who wish to check on some meanings even though the terms are not essential for understanding the report.

As shown in Chapters 16 and 17, when you have a few terms whose exact meaning is essential for understanding your report, a desirable place for definitions is the introduction. Other choices are to include a brief definition parenthetically after the unclear referent or as a footnote.

Index

The index lists topics alphabetically and guides the reader to various places that discuss certain subject matter in the report. Only in very long reports will you need an index.

PRESENTATION OF THE FORMAL REPORT

Before you begin to write your formal-report body and other parts, you should, of course, have completed all preliminary work. You have defined the problem and purpose, collected all needed material, sorted and interpreted data, organized the final outline, and prepared visual aids. If it is required or desirable, you also have presented a working plan for approval by whoever assigned the report. The next steps are writing, editing, revising, and typing the report.

Writing the First Draft

With your research materials close at hand—sorted in piles or in folders under your outline headings—you can now begin writing. Perhaps you'll start with a section you consider easiest for you: that's a good way to become comfortable with the job. Writing a long report will seem easier if you think of it as a series of short reports (your main report sections), linked coherently by your well-planned outline and appropriate transitional devices.

In the first draft just get your ideas down on paper or into your word processing system without stopping to correct spelling, punctuation, or grammar. Also, make your first draft as complete as possible. Later, when revising, you'll find it is easier to delete material if necessary than to insert new material.

Introduction

You can begin with the introduction, or finish the text first. Either way is acceptable. Be sure to include those elements in the introduction that will best orient the reader to the rest of the report. For a 15- to 25-page, double-spaced, typewritten report the introduction should be no more than 1½ or 2 pages. If, for example, it is four pages long because the problem or background material has required three of the pages, take the problem or background material out of the introduction and make it the first main section of the text.

Text

For a 15- to 25-page report, the text probably shouldn't have more than three or four major divisions. If you have more than that, look critically at your outline to see whether you can and should regroup or combine sections. Although the divisions don't all have to be the same length, every main division should include enough substance and length to justify its position of importance. Of course, a report with a hundred or several hundred pages will have proportionately more main divisions; in fact, it may have "chapters," each with its own main divisions and subdivisions. Remember to insert documentation where necessary, too.

Terminal Section

As you know, you may label the terminal section "Summary," "Conclusions," or "Conclusions and Recommendations." Or you may want to consider one of the other possible titles, such as those listed on page 449.

Besides completing a first draft of the report body, you should also write a draft of the abstract, letter of transmittal, and bibliography or endnotes list, if you'll have one. You can also set up the table of contents and the table of tables (if any) in rough draft; but only after the final typing is finished can you know correct page numbers for these tables.

Editing and Revising the Rough Drafts

After you have finished the first draft, lay it aside for at least one day. Doing this will help you look objectively at the material and see more clearly the weaknesses in the draft. Editing requires objective self-criticism. What seemed right in the first writing may seem seriously out of place upon second reading. Remember too that the best writers revise and rewrite several times, when necessary!

A few handy supplies are useful when you revise a long report. You'll need a pencil, a stapler, cellophane tape, extra paper, and a pair of scissors or a razor blade. As you read your draft critically, you can use your pencils for small corrections in the margins and between lines, or for deletion of unneeded sentences. However, if you find a section that needs major reorganizing use your scissors (or razor). A paragraph out of place on one page may be cut out and stapled or taped in the correct position. (Use a backing sheet underneath each cut page if necessary.) Likewise you may need to write an entirely new paragraph; you can insert it, too, into a section after you have cut the sheet at the right place.

If you use a word processing system, text editing and revising functions can be accomplished quickly and easily. After your material has been entered in the machine's memory, you will be able to revise with only a few keystrokes—condensing, changing or adding words, rearranging paragraphs, adjusting margins, detecting spelling errors, and, with the correct programs, constructing graphic aids and tables.

Nevertheless, *you* still need to think. You should:

1. Check critically the title, abstract (or synopsis or executive summary), introduction, and terminal section. The title should tell concisely what the subject of the entire report is. In the abstract, if any, you should reveal the problem, purpose, sources used, results (usually), and whatever else is pertinent. The introduction should include all needed elements. Finally, the terminal section should contain no new material and should stem logically from the information in the text.

2. Compare the letter of transmittal, introduction, and terminal section (if it precedes the introduction and text); avoid repetition. The reader who has to read the same information two or three times in close sequence will react unfavorably.

3. Check the table of contents to make sure that all major and minor sections match the headings in the text. Not all headings in the text (such as fourth- or fifth-degree headings) need to appear in the table of contents. Check also to see that you have indicated correctly the relation of major and minor parts and that headings of the same degree are parallel.

4. Check footnotes, if any, for consecutive numbering and correct placement in the bibliography, or whatever endnotes list you have.

5. Now edit the entire report for the C qualities. If your report violates any, try again to improve it wherever possible.

Typing the Formal Report

After you have revised the draft or drafts to your satisfaction, the report is ready to be typed. Although various authorities have different rules for typing this material, the suggestions here are for one of the acceptable methods. Whatever method you use, be consistent. Consistency is easy with today's software packages. The report should make a favorable impression in its overall appearance, spacing, margins, and pagination, in addition to its well-written content.

Overall Appearance

Regardless of how well written your report is, if its appearance is untidy or inaccurate, it will create an unfavorable impression in the mind of the reader. See that the cover is appropriately attractive, that typing is neat and on quality bond paper, that visual aids and footnotes are correctly placed. Avoid smudges, streaks, curled ends, wrinkled paper, and any other nonverbal distractions that might divert your reader's attention from the message. Noteworthy also are any errors in mechanics, discussed in Appendix A.

Double Spacing versus Single Spacing

Reports may be typewritten with double or single spacing. Those who prefer double spacing feel it is easily read; it is also preferred by printers. Single-spaced reports have become popular in recent years not only because they save paper, but also—with fewer pages for the same amount of report data—because they save in several other ways: (1) typing time, (2) filing space, (3) expense of both duplicating time and materials when multiple copies of a report are needed, and (4) reading time when turning fewer pages.

If you double-space the report, the first word of each paragraph should be indented (usually five spaces). In a single-spaced report, paragraphs may be indented or begin at the left margin. However, always double-space between paragraphs and both before and after long quotations, visual aids, and footnotes.

Regardless of whether the report is typed in double or single spacing, the following parts should be single-spaced:

1. Transmittal letter—typed on company letterhead if you are writing it as an employee of the firm. And, of course, the letter should be centered attractively on the page.

2. Quotations and examples, of three or more typewritten lines. If this material consists of two or more paragraphs, double-space (leave a blank line) between them. Also, indent margins of the quote five spaces to the right and left of the double- or single-spaced text material. Use ellipses (. . .) to indicate omissions if you are quoting only parts of an author's paragraph. In long quotations you can show lengthy omissions by either a full line of periods or by four periods at the end of the paragraph before the omission.

3. A list of items you want to set off or emphasize.

4. Footnotes (but double-space between them).

5. Some tables and other visuals aids.

Margins

In addition to the following suggested margins, you need to add ½ inch for binding on each page. Although the report is usually bound on the left-hand side—like a book—you can bind it at the top. Acceptable margins are as follows:

First page of each prefatory part (preface or letter of transmittal, table of contents, table of tables, abstract), *body,* and *supplemental parts* (appendix, bibliography or endnotes, index): top margin of 1½ or 2 inches.

All other pages: Top, bottom, and side margins are 1 or 1½ inches (plus the ½-inch allowance for binding at either left side or top).

Pagination

Every page in the report—except the cover and title fly—should have a number, but not all numbers are actually typed on each page. For the prefatory sheets use small Roman numerals; for the body and supplemental sheets use Arabic numbers, according to these guidelines:

1. *Prefatory parts page numbers* are centered and placed ½ inch below the imaginary line that frames the bottom of the typewritten material. Count and number the prefatory pages as shown below:

Cover and title fly	Don't count or number.
Title page	Count (i) but don't insert number.
Letter of transmittal	Count, but usually don't insert number. A one-page letter is page ii at the bottom; a second page of the transmittal is page iii.
Table of contents	Count and number each page.
Table of tables	Count and number.
Abstract	Count and number.

2. *Body and supplemental parts page numbers:*
   a. If your report is bound at the left, page numbers are usually placed near the upper-right corner of the page, aligned with the right margin and ½ inch (or a double space) above the top imaginary line that frames the typewritten material. The exception is that the numbers for first pages of parts are either omitted (though counted) or placed ½ inch (or double space) below the imaginary line that frames the bottom of the typed material. They are centered with the typing on the page (as for prefatory parts pages).
   b. If your report is bound at the top, page numbers are usually placed in the center at the bottom of the page, ½ inch, or a double space, below the imaginary line that frames the bottom of the typewritten text.

EXAMPLE OF PAGES FROM A FORMAL ANALYTICAL REPORT

The following pages from a 27-page energy conservation report within a company apply many of the suggestions in this chapter and Chapter 16 for writing a formal report. They are illustrated not as models of perfection but as one way to present parts about which students most often have questions:

Title page (Figure 18-4)

Letter of transmittal (Figure 18-5)

Table of contents—deductive organization (Figure 18-6)

First and second pages of text—single-spaced (Figures 18-7 and 18-8)

List of sources consulted (Figure 18-9)

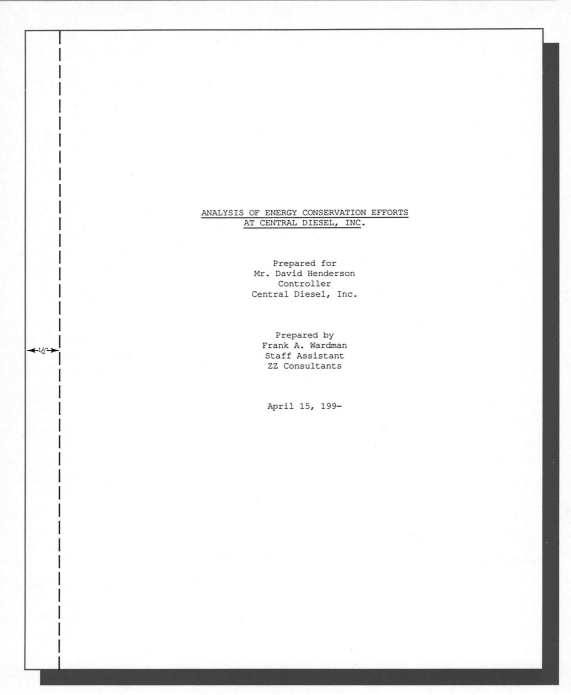

ANALYSIS OF ENERGY CONSERVATION EFFORTS
AT CENTRAL DIESEL, INC.

Prepared for
Mr. David Henderson
Controller
Central Diesel, Inc.

Prepared by
Frank A. Wardman
Staff Assistant
ZZ Consultants

April 15, 199-

←½"→

Figure 18–4 Title page.

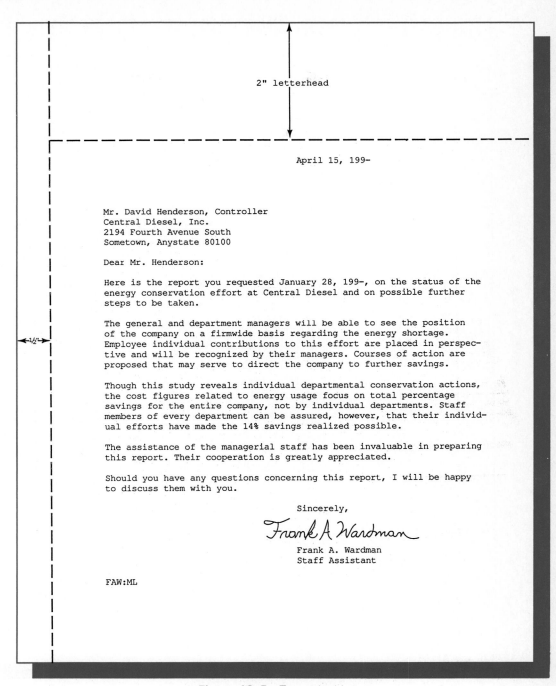

2" letterhead

April 15, 199-

Mr. David Henderson, Controller
Central Diesel, Inc.
2194 Fourth Avenue South
Sometown, Anystate 80100

Dear Mr. Henderson:

Here is the report you requested January 28, 199-, on the status of the
energy conservation effort at Central Diesel and on possible further
steps to be taken.

The general and department managers will be able to see the position
of the company on a firmwide basis regarding the energy shortage.
Employee individual contributions to this effort are placed in perspective and will be recognized by their managers. Courses of action are
proposed that may serve to direct the company to further savings.

Though this study reveals individual departmental conservation actions,
the cost figures related to energy usage focus on total percentage
savings for the entire company, not by individual departments. Staff
members of every department can be assured, however, that their individual efforts have made the 14% savings realized possible.

The assistance of the managerial staff has been invaluable in preparing
this report. Their cooperation is greatly appreciated.

Should you have any questions concerning this report, I will be happy
to discuss them with you.

                                        Sincerely,

                                        Frank A. Wardman

                                        Frank A. Wardman
                                        Staff Assistant

FAW:ML

Figure 18–5 Transmittal letter.

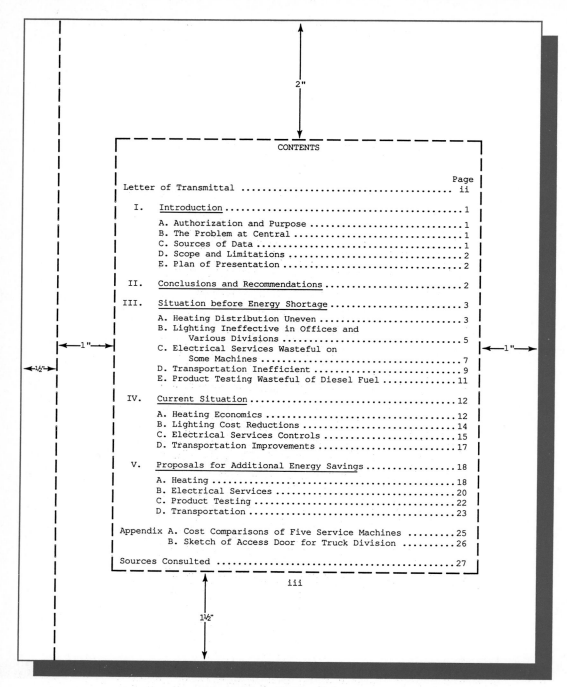

2"

CONTENTS

1"   1"

½"

iii

1½"

Figure 18–6 Table of contents.

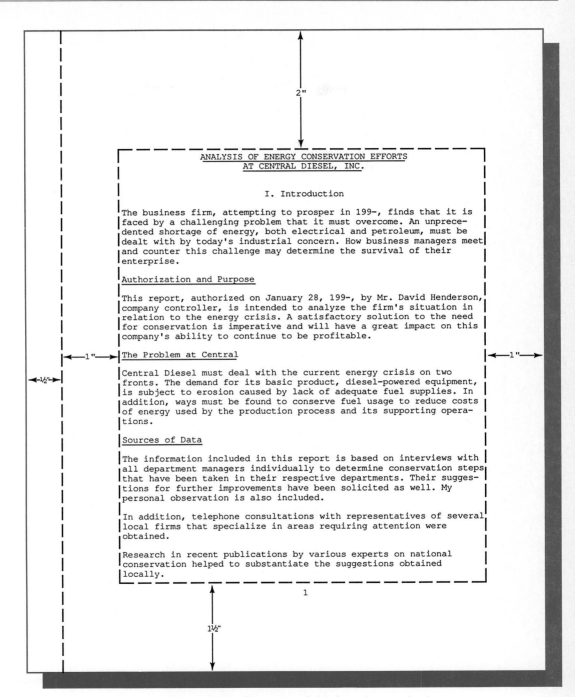

2"

ANALYSIS OF ENERGY CONSERVATION EFFORTS
AT CENTRAL DIESEL, INC.

I. Introduction

The business firm, attempting to prosper in 199-, finds that it is
faced by a challenging problem that it must overcome. An unprece-
dented shortage of energy, both electrical and petroleum, must be
dealt with by today's industrial concern. How business managers meet
and counter this challenge may determine the survival of their
enterprise.

Authorization and Purpose

This report, authorized on January 28, 199-, by Mr. David Henderson,
company controller, is intended to analyze the firm's situation in
relation to the energy crisis. A satisfactory solution to the need
for conservation is imperative and will have a great impact on this
company's ability to continue to be profitable.

The Problem at Central

Central Diesel must deal with the current energy crisis on two
fronts. The demand for its basic product, diesel-powered equipment,
is subject to erosion caused by lack of adequate fuel supplies. In
addition, ways must be found to conserve fuel usage to reduce costs
of energy used by the production process and its supporting operations.

Sources of Data

The information included in this report is based on interviews with
all department managers individually to determine conservation steps
that have been taken in their respective departments. Their suggestions for further improvements have been solicited as well. My
personal observation is also included.

In addition, telephone consultations with representatives of several
local firms that specialize in areas requiring attention were
obtained.

Research in recent publications by various experts on national
conservation helped to substantiate the suggestions obtained
locally.

1

1"   1"   ½"   1½"

Figure 18–7   *First page of this formal report body.*
(Either single or double spacing is acceptable).

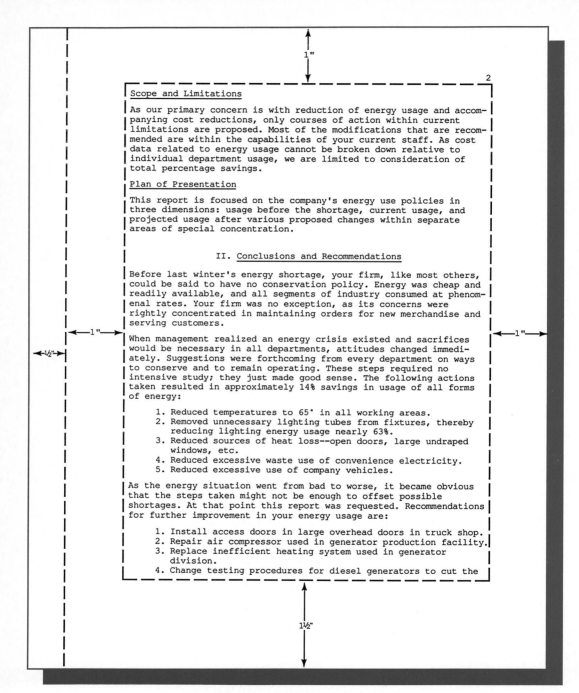

2

Scope and Limitations

As our primary concern is with reduction of energy usage and accompanying cost reductions, only courses of action within current limitations are proposed. Most of the modifications that are recommended are within the capabilities of your current staff. As cost data related to energy usage cannot be broken down relative to individual department usage, we are limited to consideration of total percentage savings.

Plan of Presentation

This report is focused on the company's energy use policies in three dimensions: usage before the shortage, current usage, and projected usage after various proposed changes within separate areas of special concentration.

II. Conclusions and Recommendations

Before last winter's energy shortage, your firm, like most others, could be said to have no conservation policy. Energy was cheap and readily available, and all segments of industry consumed at phenomenal rates. Your firm was no exception, as its concerns were rightly concentrated in maintaining orders for new merchandise and serving customers.

When management realized an energy crisis existed and sacrifices would be necessary in all departments, attitudes changed immediately. Suggestions were forthcoming from every department on ways to conserve and to remain operating. These steps required no intensive study; they just made good sense. The following actions taken resulted in approximately 14% savings in usage of all forms of energy:

1. Reduced temperatures to 65° in all working areas.
2. Removed unnecessary lighting tubes from fixtures, thereby reducing lighting energy usage nearly 63%.
3. Reduced sources of heat loss--open doors, large undraped windows, etc.
4. Reduced excessive waste use of convenience electricity.
5. Reduced excessive use of company vehicles.

As the energy situation went from bad to worse, it became obvious that the steps taken might not be enough to offset possible shortages. At that point this report was requested. Recommendations for further improvement in your energy usage are:

1. Install access doors in large overhead doors in truck shop.
2. Repair air compressor used in generator production facility.
3. Replace inefficient heating system used in generator division.
4. Change testing procedures for diesel generators to cut the

Figure 18–8   *Page 2 of this formal report.*

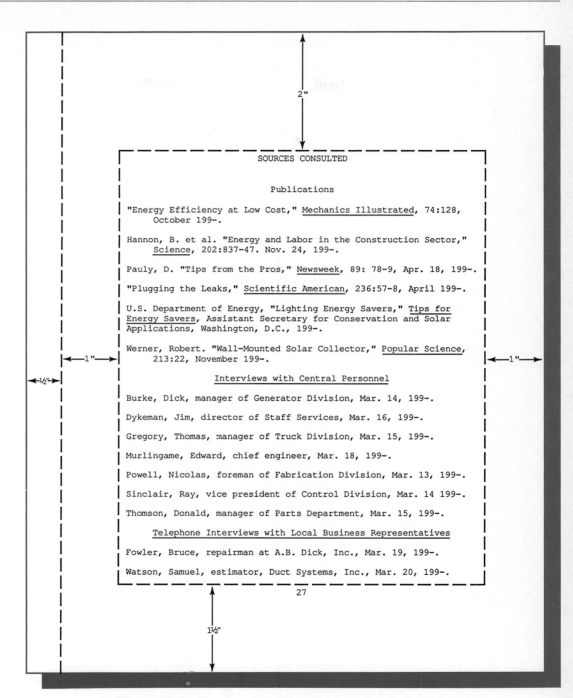

2"

SOURCES CONSULTED

Publications

"Energy Efficiency at Low Cost," <u>Mechanics Illustrated</u>, 74:128,
      October 199-.

Hannon, B. et al. "Energy and Labor in the Construction Sector,"
      <u>Science</u>, 202:837-47. Nov. 24, 199-.

Pauly, D. "Tips from the Pros," <u>Newsweek</u>, 89: 78-9, Apr. 18, 199-.

"Plugging the Leaks," <u>Scientific American</u>, 236:57-8, April 199-.

U.S. Department of Energy, "Lighting Energy Savers," <u>Tips for
Energy Savers</u>, Assistant Secretary for Conservation and Solar
Applications, Washington, D.C., 199-.

Werner, Robert. "Wall-Mounted Solar Collector," <u>Popular Science</u>,
      213:22, November 199-.

Interviews with Central Personnel

Burke, Dick, manager of Generator Division, Mar. 14, 199-.

Dykeman, Jim, director of Staff Services, Mar. 16, 199-.

Gregory, Thomas, manager of Truck Division, Mar. 15, 199-.

Murlingame, Edward, chief engineer, Mar. 18, 199-.

Powell, Nicolas, foreman of Fabrication Division, Mar. 13, 199-.

Sinclair, Ray, vice president of Control Division, Mar. 14 199-.

Thomson, Donald, manager of Parts Department, Mar. 15, 199-.

Telephone Interviews with Local Business Representatives

Fowler, Bruce, repairman at A.B. Dick, Inc., Mar. 19, 199-.

Watson, Samuel, estimator, Duct Systems, Inc., Mar. 20, 199-.

27

1"   1"   ½"   1½"

Figure 18–9   List of sources consulted, including both published
materials and interviews.

Other pages in the text section of this report are arranged and numbered as shown on its page 2. The main headings—III, IV, and V—are centered horizontally (on pages 3, 12, and 18, as indicated in the table of contents). They do not begin new pages, but merely follow the preceding text paragraphs. Subheadings for them are third-degree headings placed at the left margin like those on the report's page 1—Authorization and Purpose, The Problem at Central, and Sources of Data. (To protect anonymity, in the six illustrated report pages here the names of persons and of the company as well as some numbers in the pages have been changed.)

Though the report is a long, formal report with prefatory and supplemental parts, the wording throughout is appropriately informal. (Typed single-spaced, this report occupies about half as many pages as if it were typed double-spaced. The broken lines and arrows are inserted in these illustrations to show you the widths of the imaginary margins.) The bibliography is titled Sources Consulted because most of the information came from interviews rather than publications. If you are wondering how footnotes are typed on single-spaced pages, the answer is that they are placed at the bottom of pages with the same spacing as shown in Figure 18-1—though it is a double-spaced report. (See also Placement of Footnotes, on pages 548 to 550.)

SUMMARY

The formal business report is "formal" because of its parts—not because it uses formal language. These reports generally cover more complex problems and are longer than short reports. In addition to the body (with introduction, text, and terminal sections) they include prefatory and supplemental parts. Each part should serve a useful purpose for the reader; if it doesn't, it should not appear in the report. Accurate documentation is important. So determine early the desired citation format, as used in this text, or as in the MLA, APA, or other stylistic handbooks. Effective preparation of long reports requires careful, thorough planning, organizing, draft writing, editing, revising, typing, and proofreading. The writer should continue to apply the C qualities for well-written reports (summarized in Chapter 16).

EXERCISES AND PROBLEMS

1. *Topic outline:* If you need practice in organizing topics under meaningful headings, try this assignment. Assume the sales manager of ABC New Car Agency in your city has asked you, a management consultant, to review and evaluate the agency's sales system. The internal control seems to be weak, and something is causing problems.

    The main purpose of your study is to determine the strength of the internal control and its effect on the financial papers for new-car sales.

    You have just finished both secondary and primary research. Two new accounting books (make up names) substantiate your concept for internal control. In your primary research you interviewed 4 middle managers and 15 or 20 employees. You studied the personality of the sales staff and the viewpoints of other personnel. You observed the personnel performing their duties and their interactions. Up to now you have information under the following topics, jumbled and in no useful order:

```
File clerk's job

Keypunch operator's responsibility

Dealership's environment

Title clerk's functions

Salesperson's personality

Internal control by buyers' orders

Personnel system's internal control

Dealership's history

Sequence of signatures in sale of a car

Accounting clerks' duties

Control system's procedure

Title clerk's work

Sales staff's functions

Flowchart of new-vehicle sales system [you have drawn this on
seven pages]

Dealership's new-vehicle sales system

Introduction

Conclusions

Sales manager's part

Bibliography
```

Choose main headings for the text of this report (three or four should be sufficient). Then organize; place these 19 topics under the headings wherever they belong, in a complete outline of the well-planned formal report.

2. ***Long formal report:*** Your assignment is to write a formal informational or analytical report whose body is approximately 15 to 25 double-spaced pages. Choose a topic that is broad enough to justify the length. Yet beware of a topic so broad that it would require volumes. If possible, consider a subject that you know something about or one that especially interests you.

   Try to find a topic that involves a business problem. (For example, you might know there's too great a turnover of employees in a certain department.) From the problem, and with some thought on your part, you can determine the purpose of your report. Other ideas that you can use as a springboard for a topic are listed below, pertaining to problems involved in:

Accounting, credits, collections

The accountant's role in cost reduction and analysis

Computer programming and errors in monthly statements

Problems and progress of accounting in X Company

Accounting contributions to the effective management of X Company

Problems involved in a bank's converting to a computerized operation

Policy or procedure and degree of communications used by X Company in collecting retail accounts

General management and/or labor

The functioning and problems of your campus student-body governing organization; accomplishments and recommendations for greater effectiveness

A profit-sharing plan for X Company

Hiring handicapped workers: whether it would be charity or good business for X Company

A program for achieving optimum discipline in X Company

Business outlook for Y industry or X Company

Proposed plan for hiring and training minority groups in X Company

Development of a profitable ski area on a certain mountain

Suggestions for X Company's response to Z Union's attempt to organize workers

Recommendations for a formal salary scale for X Company

Personnel administration

Development of a personnel testing program for X Company

Analysis of the merit rating system of X Company

A safety program for X Company

The performance of women in top executive positions

Survey, interpretation, and recommendation—after a study on attitudes toward certain recent troublesome problems:

a Opinion of X Company's employees regarding wages, working hours, parking, food services, promotion plan

b Opinion of students in your school regarding grading, credit hours for certain courses, student parking, housing

c Opinion of X organization's members regarding membership dues, requirements, privileges, new clubhouse

Marketing

A promotional program for introduction of X product

A new plan for X Company to offer incentives to sales personnel

Where X Company should locate its next supermarket

How X Company can measure effectiveness in its advertising

How downtown merchants can cope with suburban shopping centers

After you have clearly determined the purpose of your report, state it in one sentence. Continue your preliminary preparation (steps 1, 2, and 3 on pages 442–443). At this point in your research submit to your professor (or anyone he or she suggests) a memo report of your working plan. Be sure to include in this memo at least the following: problem, purpose, methodology, readers (both primary and secondary), and suggested outline. In this outline show the order for the introduction, major divisions of the text, subheadings for each major division, and the type of terminal section.

After you have approval of your working plan, you can begin to collect your data; then organize this material and interpret it. With the completion of this last stage—interpretation—you can draw conclusions and make recommendations. Naturally, if you're writing an informational report, you'll skip interpretation of material and merely summarize. Also at this time you should prepare (at least in rough-draft form) your tables and any other necessary visual aids. If your professor requests it, submit the final outline that you'll follow in writing your report—the one that will become your table of contents.

Now you should be ready to write. Choose the right time and place and follow the rules outlined in the chapter—for both the first draft and the revisions. After your final revision, you can type (or have typed) the body of the report in final draft, or you can first write the necessary prefatory and supplemental parts. In this report assignment include at least the following: cover, title page, letter of transmittal (or preface), and table of contents. Also, you'll need to include other parts—especially appendix and bibliography—if your report requires them. If the transmittal may affect part of what's included in the body, you should at least plan the transmittal before the final typing of the body.

Although the content and presentation of the material are most important, also remember the role that mechanics play. Be sure you have nothing that distracts your reader from concentrating on what you want to tell. Thus, be sure the spelling, grammar, punctuation, and appearance are acceptable.

3. *Information available on on-line or optical disks:* Go either to your library or to your computer center where on-line databases or disks are located. Report to the class—with actual printouts—the various kinds of data available under common headings such as the following:

   a. General business information
   b. Company financial information
   c. Statistical data
   d. Industry-specific information, or
   e. Other categories noted in on-line or business disks

Your goal is to offer information as to the many kinds of electronic business data that are available. Sample printouts will permit your classmates to examine your collected information.

4. ***Bibliography styles by MLA and APA:*** Obtain from your library or local bookstore the *MLA Handbook for Writers of Research Papers* or *Publication Manual of the American Psychological Association* and give the class examples of the citation style in a bibliography from either of the two works for each of the following references:

   a. A one-author source; a two-author source
   b. A computer software source
   c. A doctoral dissertation
   d. Two books by the same person in a bibliography

Proposals

A special type of report that is important in business, industry, government, and academia is the *proposal*. Like other reports, proposals range in length from short (fewer than 10 pages) to long, "formal" documents of 50 or more pages. Some proposals can be measured in volumes. For instance, one report for a major project contained 12 volumes of exposition and graphics, weighing over 25 pounds. Of course that proposal was for a project for hundreds of millions of dollars.

In a survey of chief executives for nearly 50 randomly selected manufacturing firms with $1 million minimum annual sales volume, 65 percent report that proposals play an important role in the operations of their firms. Of these, over 50 percent said the part is "great" or "crucial."[1] In a survey of 837 university business graduates working in 35 states and the District of Columbia, 59 percent stated they write proposals to customers and clients at least "sometimes"; and within this group 22 percent write proposals "often."[2]

This chapter discusses proposal purposes, kinds, parts; short and long proposals; and writing style and appearance. Illustrations and examples are included.

PURPOSES OF PROPOSALS

A business, a university, a private group, or an individual that seeks the award of a contract from a firm—even one's own firm—a government agency, or a private foundation must submit a proposal (bid) before being considered. Often, individuals or firms skilled in a special area are asked to submit a proposal that could help in solving a problem. On the other hand, proposal writers may indirectly learn of an opportunity to solve a problem or investigate a topic and on their own submit a proposal. Examples of publicly announced requests for proposals might include the following topics:[3]

- Business contributions on solving urban poverty
- Plans for solving rural poverty and needed resources
- Human rights and social justice
- Governance and public policy
- Education and culture
- International affairs

Some organizations have more narrowly defined purposes, as seen in the following shortened list of business research objectives noted by the American Production and Inventory Control Society Education and Research Foundation:[4]

- The migration from job shop to repetitive manufacturing
- The application of just-in-time (JIT) in the job shop
- Performance measurements in the just-in-time (JIT) environment
- Engineering and just-in-time (JIT)
- Preventive maintenance related to downtime and quality

- Changes in skill requirements for direct labor employees in a computer-integrated manufacturing job shop
- Skill diversification requirement and how to satisfy it

The purpose of proposals is—in one way—similar to that for memorandum justification-recommendation reports, discussed in Chapter 17. Both aim to solve a problem, alter a procedure, find answers to questions, or conduct research on a topic of mutual interest.

However, important differences are that the proposal is most often sent to readers or a review committee outside the writer's organization. Then outside experts evaluate and make a recommendation concerning the benefits of the proposed services, products, or topic. Also evaluated is the worth of the project, based on a proposed budget. Money is the common medium of exchange, but some firms also barter (offer their services or product for another's services or product).

A university researcher who needs a grant, most often on a research topic, undertakes a similar procedure: he or she also completes a formal research proposal to either the government, private industry, or private foundations.

KINDS OF PROPOSALS

Basically, proposals are persuasive (sales) presentations. The thousands of proposals that organizations and individuals send are concerned with a wide variety of topics and problems to be solved.

In general, however, we may refer to proposals in three ways—according to their purpose, length, and origin. As mentioned in the preceding paragraphs under Purposes of Proposals, there are *business proposals* and *research proposals*. In length, proposals may be similar to other reports—*short* or *long and formal*. Also, like reports, proposals may be *solicited* or *unsolicited*. An organization or government office that solicits proposals may invite qualified firms or persons to bid on performing an extensive job and solving a problem. Its request for proposals may be by mail (as shown in an example later within this chapter), or it may be published widely in business journals or government announcements.[5]

When you write a solicited business proposal, remember you most likely will have many competitors also bidding for that contract (and the remuneration). Follow meticulously the proposal requirements of the solicitor, regarding problem, needed solution, specific work to be done or equipment to be installed, even the format of the proposal, number of copies desired, deadlines, and so forth. Whenever possible, use the outline and same words the agency has in its literature or guidelines. Don't use jargon that only you and your assistants can understand.

Likewise, when you write an *unsolicited* proposal, you need to convince the reader or review committee that you understand the organization's problem and that your firm or you are qualified to solve it successfully.

PARTS OF A PROPOSAL

The parts of a proposal are listed below. They may be used in major business proposals on sales of your company's services, expertise, equipment, or extensive installation facilities. Or they may be adapted for a research study within your own firm or for another company outside your firm. Of course, only long, comprehensive proposals require most of or all these parts. Smaller projects may use only a few. Information required for a $5 million grant or sales contract will surely be longer and more profound than for a $200 research allowance. Therefore, *consider carefully which parts are desirable for your specific proposal outline.*

Title Page

Most organizations specify the information to be included in the title page, some even providing special forms which summarize basic administrative and fiscal data. As a minimum, the title page should include the title, the name of the person or company to whom the proposal is submitted, the person submitting the proposal, and the date. When in doubt, follow the suggestions in Chapter 18 concerning the title page for a report.

Some titles are one line long, occasionally two. Some even include a colon—followed by words to clarify the thought. Clarity and comprehensiveness are dual criteria for a good proposal title.

Abstract, Executive Summary, Synopsis

Even brief proposals should have an abstract. Because you will be competing with others for the same opportunity, some evaluators will initially read only the abstract, seeking to gain a quick overview. In fact, the abstract should speak for the complete proposal, it should be able to stand alone, and it should summarize how objectives will be met and what procedures will be followed. Budget figures are frequently omitted because proposal abstracts may receive wide distribution.

Some proposal readers feel that the abstract is one of the most important parts of a proposal; give it careful time and effort.

Table of Contents

Brief proposals usually do not require a table of contents. Long proposals do require one, as well as a list of tables, figures, and illustrations.

Introduction

Purpose

A somewhat safe assumption is that your reader may have a general knowledge of the purpose, and that he or she will send the proposal to others for a more rigorous evaluation of its technical competence. Therefore, write the introduction as if approaching an informed nonspecialist. Purposes are often stated in infinitive form:

- To propose options for evaluating forward pricing strategies
- To prepare an environmental impact statement for the North Bend Generating Plant Site
- To construct three cooling towers to go with the North Bend Generating Project
- To rewrite the Defense Contract Audit Manuals

Problem

In a business proposal show clearly that you understand the problem or problems. Does your reader need a complex remodeling and construction job or extensive equipment replacement? If pertinent, mention difficulties that may be encountered and consider how you propose to overcome them. If your proposal concerns a research study, is it a community problem, for the local area or a general area? If it's about a company problem—such as shipping delays, shoplifting, inventory control, poor customer relations, excessive purchase returns, inadequate communication—does it concern a certain branch or area?

Scope

If your proposal is for service or equipment you are selling, in what areas will it serve the prospective buyer? Define the boundaries of your project. If you're proposing a research study, will you study one area of a community, company, department, or severe problem? What boundaries are you setting to accomplish your objectives?

Background

If your proposal is short, the background may be omitted; in a longer proposal, information such as the following is usually included:

- Previous work completed on identical or related projects
- Possibly, literature reviews on the subject, particularly your evaluation of them
- Statements showing how your proposal will build on the already completed projects and research

Procedures

Of course, the procedures section is the heart of your proposal; it addresses how you will meet the requirements of your reader. There is no hard and fast rule as to what is to be included in this section, for each proposal will be different. A few suggestions may be helpful:

1. Be realistic as to what can be accomplished. Don't overextend your company's or your capabilities.

2. Be specific on how your methods will meet the goal and purpose you stated earlier.

3. Be precise on time schedule, perhaps breaking down the project into phases.

4. Be clear on how you will evaluate the quality of your work, or production, or product.

5. Be exact as to the limits: what you will do and what you will not do.

6. Be sure the method of solving the problem connects with the objectives and goals for the project.

Equipment and Facilities

Show you have thought deeply enough to realize what facilities will be needed. If your proposal is for your company's bid on an enormous construction job, probably several departments will cooperate with you in presenting needed facts and figures.

For a research project, state what equipment and facilities you aready have for use, and assure that you can get the rest. Depending on the type of project, you might, for example, need everything from an electronic blackboard to a small airplane.

Personnel

Two sections make up this topic: (1) the personnel arrangements and their involved company areas, and (2) their qualifications, often expressed in complete biographic data. Included here are also the percentages of time that personnel will devote to the project.

Especially important is information on the project director, project associates, and other assistants. It is they who will direct the project and with whom the reader (contractor) will establish an ongoing relationship if the project is approved. If you will be the project director, state your own experience and past successes with similar projects. Include dates and references (with permission) so that the prospective funder can verify your statements.

Budget

Sponsors or organizations requesting proposals frequently specify how the budget should be presented. Read such specifications carefully. Not all groups allow the same costs.

While some budget sections may be in tabular form, it is customary to include a "budget justification" section, stating in paragraph form a further rationale for your financial figures.

A sample tabular 12-month budget is shown in Figure 19-1. "Sponsor" is the government office or organization for which the work will be done; "Company" is the firm that requests the funding.

Appendixes

Some reviewers of proposals leave reading of appendixes to the last, if they read them at all. Additional bulk may to the reader represent additional padding, and could produce a negative reaction. Certainly, visuals (maps or graphs) and some pertinent letters of support and endorsement can be added. But when in doubt, leave out.

A SHORT PROPOSAL

The following proposal is a short sales presentation a firm made to a prospective buyer. (Do not consider it a model of perfection; it is, however, an example of a fairly typical informal proposal to sell an installation product.) Before sending the proposal, the writer visited the company's place of business, studied its setup, and discussed its needs. The proposal objectively and persuasively presents evidence that the seller's filing system will solve a problem of the reader's firm and offer it six specific advantages. This proposal consists of:

> One prefatory part—transmittal letter (Figure 19-2)
> Attached proposal body (Figures 19-3 and 19-4) with concise details on:
> > Efficiency factors of Spacefinder Filing System
> > Advantages of Spacefinder system
> > Present system
> > Proposed system
> > Conversion
> > Summary
> > Cost of proposed equipment
> A supplemental part—vault sketch plus overlay

Notice that the letter follows the AIDA formula for sales letters. The first paragraph catches the reader's attention; the second and third paragraphs create desire by referring to facts and figures in the attached pages (about the present system and benefits of the Spacefinder system); the last paragraph asks for action.

As with any good sales pitch, the "attached proposal" body leads the reader through an explanation and a discussion of the Spacefinder advantages and details of the present and proposed systems before it mentions cost. The letter and the report together constitute the proposal that is to convince the reader to convert to the new system.

TWELVE-MONTH BUDGET

	Sponsor	Company	Total
PERSONNEL			
Project director, quarter-time	$ --	$ --	$ --
Project associate, 10%	--	--	--
Research assistant, half-time	--	--	--
Clerk-typist, half-time	--	--	--
Subtotal	$ --	$ --	$ --
Staff benefits (21% of			
salaries and wages)	$ --	$ --	$ --
Subtotal	$ --	$ --	$ --
CONSULTANTS	$ --	$ --	$ --
MATERIALS AND SUPPLIES			
Miscellaneous office supplies	$ --	$ --	$ --
Glassware	--	--	--
Chemicals	--	--	--
Subtotal	$ --	$ --	$ --
TRAVEL			
Project director consultation with sponsor, Washington, D.C., and return. 1 person, 2 days:			
Air fare	$ --	$ --	$ --
Per diem @ $100/day	--	--	--
Local transportation	--	--	--
Subtotal	$ --	$ --	$ --
TOTAL DIRECT COSTS	$ --	$ --	$ --
INDIRECT COSTS (60% of modified total direct costs)	$ --	$ --	$ --
GRAND TOTAL	$41,064	$5,808	$46,872

Figure 19–1   Sample budget.

TAB PRODUCTS, INC.
928 Hampston Street
[*City, State, ZIP*]

September 20, 199-

Mr. R L. Foster
[*Company name*]
1220 Empire Building
[*City, state, ZIP*]

Dear Mr. Foster:

Attention:
reader
benefits

The attached proposal is for a conversion by your firm from
drawer files to the TAB PRODUCTS Spacefinder Filing System.
This conversion will result in significantly increased filing
efficiency and a saving of floor space. It is a proven fact
that the Unit Spacefinder Filing System does increase filing
efficiency up to 50%.

Interest,
desire:
enclosures,
product
advantages

The system you now use in the vault on the third floor is
sketched on the enclosed quarter-inch grid paper. The vault is
drawn to exact scale, and the drawer files now being used are
placed in their present position. Using the overlay, you will
notice how much space you can save in this vault when you have
the TAB PRODUCTS Unit Spacefinder Filing System. It also increases efficiency in locating records and returning them to the
file. Furthermore, you can use this floor plan in the future to
expand storage in the same area.

Conviction:
attachments,
figures,
advantages

The attached pages explain the Spacefinder system and quote figures showing advantages to your firm in floor space savings and
efficiency. You are welcome also to see time studies made by
other firms that achieved 50% increased efficiency.

Action and
courtesy

Please call upon me for assistance and further information. My
telephone number is 555-2222. Thank you for this opportunity to
quote on the TAB PRODUCTS Unit Spacefinder Filing System.

Sincerely,

MIG:jm   Mark X. Greene
Enclosures and   Customer Service Department
attachment

Figure 19–2 *Transmittal letter for a short proposal.*

PROPOSAL
to [*name of receiver's firm*]
for conversion to the TAB PRODUCTS Unit Spacefinder
Filing System

Efficiency Factors of Spacefinder Filing System

The Unit Spacefinder Filing System differs from shelf and drawer filing in many respects. Listed below are the efficiency factors of Unit Spacefinder:

1. You file in a container, not a drawer, on a shelf, or in a cabinet. The unit box is 4" wide. This means that the documents have support every 4". This need is one of the most important required in lateral filing. The more support, the easier it is to "in-file" and pull records. (See sketches attached.)

2. The unique "stair-step" effect, caused by the angle in which unit boxes are hung, gives you accessibility never before possible. This accessibility is an exclusive feature of Unit Spacefinder. Every folder is easy to reach and easy to see.

3. You get flexibility. You can rearrange and expand without a lot of time-consuming bother, such as in the case of drawer files or shelf files. You create space where you need it simply by sliding boxes easily along rails. There is no need to transfer records handful by handful.

Advantages of Unit Spacefinder Lateral Filing System

1. The stair-step effect allows folders to be readily identified, removed, and replaced with the least effort.

2. The unit boxes can be removed from the racks, a feature that allows:
   a. Work with the records at a desk for purging or for checking, etc.
   b. Fast fleeting of records by rearrangement of the unit boxes.

3. Visibility is a definite advantage. All folders are exposed to the file clerks and with proper indexing can be located at least 50% faster than when the folders are used in drawer files.

4. A 50% increased efficiency by record staffs handling their workload has been proved in many filing areas, both large and small. Efficiency means saved person-hours, which in turn mean saved dollars.

5. Flexibility of the unit enables us to assure you we can tailor the Unit Spacefinder framework to fit your needs. It is freestanding and does not have to be anchored to the walls or floor; therefore, if you need a different configuration to fit a particular location, we can easily meet your desires.

6. You get more filing space in less than half the floor space.

Figure 19–3   *Body of the short proposal, page 1.*

Present System Now in Operation

12 ea. 5-drawer legal-size files
 8 ea. 4-drawer legal size files
Total filing inches: 2,300"
Total floor space: 122.11 sq. ft. (including drawer pull)

Folders used are 3d cut, top position right-hand side, legal. Filed in
numerical sequence.

1. Conversion factor--use same folders.
2. Use Colorvue Guide Cards, which reveal inserted number on both sides.

Proposed System

Use combination of 42" and 30" single-face sections of Unit Spacefinder
against wall and double-face Unit Spacefinder spaced 42" to provide
ample aisle space.
Total filing inches: 2.380"
Total floor space: 47.02 sq. ft.

Conversion

Present folders can be used. Right-hand tab allows easy identification
of numbers.
Guide Cards should be inserted in file every 2 to 3 feet.

Summary

1. Increase in filing inches--80"
2. Floor space released for expansion or other purposes--75.09 square feet
3. Efficiency increase--minimum 35%

Cost of Proposed Equipment

1 ea. 5422	Initial 45" legal-size single		$_____	$_____
2 ea. 5334	Additional 42" legal-size with worktshelf, single			
3 ea. 5404	Additional 30" legal-size single		___.__	___.__
1 ea. 5430	Initial 45" legal-size double with two workshelves		___.__	___.__
1 ea. 5408	Additional 30" legal-size double		___.__	___.__
				$_,___.__

Figure 19–4   *Page 2 of the short proposal.*

LONG FORMAL PROPOSALS

Many projects require proposals with comprehensive, detailed, elaborate presentations about various intricate problems. The following section includes an example of a solicitation letter for a proposal; a sample chronology of procedures for solicited major proposals; a discussion of where to send proposals invited by the U.S. government; and examples of sections in long proposals of a general nature, a major construction project, and a research proposal.

Solicitation for Proposals

Frequently a firm or agency requests a proposal letter from outside vendors who they feel are qualified, telling them what kind of preliminary information concerning a proposal should be returned. That information, submitted in similar form from several outside groups, makes it easier for the soliciting company to compare data, aiding it in determining who will be asked to submit a more detailed proposal. In large contracts—for instance those in excess of $25 million—a two-step process may occur. The soliciting company (1) sends a preliminary request to possible interested parties and (2), through this initial screening, eliminates some companies, then asks for more detailed information from the finalists still in the running for the contract.

For instance, a soliciting group interested in constructing a large automotive facility sent the following cover letter to a small group of companies competent to accomplish the task. This preliminary statement sought to determine which companies had some interest in the project—before requesting more detailed information as a second step. (The message was typewritten on company letterhead and dated November 8, 199-.)

Gentlemen:

Main idea; implied request, reasons

The X Company is engaged in designing, engineering, and constructing a unique automotive manufacturing facility in [*city, state*]. We would like to discuss your firm's capability, resources, experience, philosophy, and innovative approaches to assist in our team approach to the design and engineering of our facility.

Explanation: desirable details

X Company expects to provide a complete conceptual package containing master specifications, building sections and elevations, a construction budget, scope of services, etc. Your organization, if ultimately selected, will perform complete engineering services to generate construction bid documents to be defined by the construction assistance firm. These services will be rendered on a lump sum basis.

Invited
easy action;
attached
information

If your firm is interested in being a partner in
this endeavor, we would like to hear from you and
arrange for discussions in your facilities within
the next few weeks. In line with the X Company
team approach, we have attached certain preliminary information and would present further details
related to the project upon our visit. To make
arrangements, please call, . . .

                                    Sincerely,

Attached to the preceding cover letter were four pages requesting preliminary information, divided into four major categories and related subpoints.

X Company's philosophy and mission
Corporate philosophy
People philosophy
Mission

General description of possible facilities
Administration and support facilities
Ancillary facilities
General assembly facility
Body shop facility
Manufacturing facility
Paint shop facility
Powerhouse-cogeneration facility
Powertrain facility
Site work
Stamping facility
Water-wastewater facility

Tentative X Company engineering schedule

General X Company technical requirements

Chronology of Procedure for Solicited Major Proposals

A complete chronology of the entire process for a major proposal could go
through eight steps.

1. The soliciting company publicly announces a project in professional
    publications, newspapers, and newsletters or writes to certain companies
    asking if they are interested in bidding on the project. (See the preceding
    cover letter as an example of such an initial request.)

2. Contacted companies, and others reacting to the public announcement, submit preliminary proposals based on initial request information.

3. The soliciting company reviews all submitted documents, eliminates some companies on the basis of this preliminary review, and establishes a "short list" of finalists.

4. The soliciting company (1) asks each of the finalists bidding for the contract to submit a highly detailed proposal and (2) sets deadlines for receiving the proposal.

5. Finalist companies select their written and oral presentation teams; writing of their proposal proceeds through several editions; oral rehearsals of statements based on the proposal occur.

6. Finalist companies submit proposals to the soliciting group; dates are established for the oral presentation to the soliciting group.

7. Finalist companies make their presentations.

8. Finalist companies wait for response—from one month to as long as half a year, or longer.

U.S. Government Proposals

The preceding eight-step process is common in business proposals, and the federal government—one of the largest receivers of proposals—has a similar review process. There, however, the soliciting agency will hold its own internal review, but may also involve outside experts, frequently including representatives, for instance, from the Defense Contract Audit Agency.

When one is writing a proposal for the government, it is necessary to meet strictly each agency's proposal requirements, learned through contacting a contracting officer or requesting proposal specifications as announced in the *Commerce Business Daily*. Such a request for a proposal follows:[6]

Expert and Consultant Services

Office, city, contact person, phone	Louisiana Dept. of Environmental Quality. POB 94381, Baton Rouge, LA 70804, attn Phyllis Baxter, 504/3429034
Basic information as to proposal requirements found in solicitation for proposal document	H-Records Management System. BOD 27 Jan 89. SOL for Proposals (SFPs) 22100-89-01. Proposals will be evaluated according to criteria defined in the SPF, and all proposers will be notified by mail of any contract awarded after such evaluation within thirty days of the closing date.

After reading the above proposal solicitation, you would contact the person named in the first paragraph. She would give you additional information and send appropriate forms and a more detailed request for a proposal statement. Large contractors with the government also have their own offices in Washington, D.C., and elsewhere. They would make personal contacts before submitting the proposal. These same large contractors would have on file numerous examples of previously submitted proposals.

Sample Sections of Long Proposals

So important are proposals for some firms that they have spent thousands of dollars to equip their own company libraries with individual study rooms and up-to-date research facilities plus a staff of typists, designers, photographers, editors, and computer experts. Their main purpose is to help their marketing representatives turn out top-quality, winning proposals—solicited and unsolicited.

Nor is visual persuasion on the written proposal neglected. Company logos often appear on each page and name card. Color is used extensively. All visual aids may be bound in a separate booklet or appear on various pages of the proposal.

For example, one marketing executive's successful unsolicited major proposal has on its colorful cover an accurate sketch of the prospective customer's buildings. The proposal—32 pages, single-spaced—is attractively bound and protected by a plastic cover. Inside are also five appropriate full-page pictures. Here is that proposal's considerate transmittal letter (with changed names); it was typed on the company's letterhead and bound in the proposal:

Dear Mr. Johnson:

Purpose:
review of
RASC needs

Thank you for the opportunity to review the communication needs of the Region Administrative Services Center.

Problem
areas and
solutions
to be
discussed

In the past few years this administrative center has grown rapidly in both staff and services to the community. Because your communications system has not kept pace with your growth, a number of communication-related problems have developed.

Your department heads, receptionists, and employees have been most cooperative during our discussions to determine major communication problem areas. The problems uncovered, and the solutions to them, are discussed in the following pages.

Metrodynamic Communications looks forward to providing a telecommunications system that will grow and expand as your Center expands. To meet that

RACS benefits from 2 proposed systems

goal, we recommend a Direction PBX. The Direction PBX features stored program control combined with time division switching, which provides exceptional versatility for today's needs and is easily adaptable to future requirements.

As an alternative, Centrex II will also respond to your needs, with capabilities somewhat different from the Direction system.

Benefits now and in future

Either system will provide the Regional Administrative Services Center with an efficient, flexible, versatile system for today and tomorrow. I am looking forward to working with you on a continuing basis.

$$\text{Sincerely,}$$

This proposal's table of contents includes six major parts. Each part is preceded by a title listing its topics, some with subheads and pertinent pictures. The body of the proposal is neatly typed with helpful headings (second-, third-, and fourth-degree). Colorful illustrations and pictures help emphasize that the proposed system is "efficient, economical, flexible." Important figures, rates, charges, and other details are shown in tables both within the text and in the appendix.

The following are sample headings found in longer formal proposals for (1) a general proposal, (2) a construction management proposal for several million dollars, and (3) a research proposal.

PROPOSAL 1   *A general formal proposal.*

1. *Prefatory parts*
Title page
Letter of transmittal
Table of contents
List of tables and/or figures (if any)
Executive summary or abstract

2. *Body of proposal*
Introduction
   Problem
   Need
   Background
   Objectives or purpose
Procedures (discussion section)
   Methods and sources
   Plan of attack
   Sequence of activities
   Equipment, facilities, products
   Personnel qualifications

Evaluation and benefits of project
Budget or costs, prices, total bid

3. *Supplementary parts*
Agency forms
Budget justification
References
Tables, maps, or graphs (if any)

PROPOSAL 2 *A construction management proposal.*

1. *Prefatory parts*
Cover, with title
Inside title page
Table of contents
Request for proposal letter (owner's solicitation letter)
Response to proposal letter (company's cover letter)
Description of owner's requirements
Scope of services
Description of facilities
Working relationship
Contracts
Schedule for selecting architect or engineer
Phase 1, qualifying firms
Phase 2, interviews
Phase 3, negotiations of fees and notice to proceed

2. *Body of proposal*
General format
Approach to delivery of services
Capabilities of firm
Demonstration of management system
Personnel in delivery of services
Contract terms and conditions
Firm information
Fee

3. *Supplementary parts*
Master project schedule
Vendor surveillance
Projected fuel analysis
Table defining direct costs, overhead fees

PROPOSAL 3 *A research proposal.*

1. *Prefatory parts*
Title

Abstract
Table of contents
Introduction (including statement of problem, purpose of research, and
   significance of research)

2. *Body of proposal*
Background (including literature survey)
Description of proposed research (including method or approach)
Description of relevant institutional resources
List of references
Personnel
Budget

WRITING STYLE AND APPEARANCE

You will be wise to apply all business communication principles and report-writing techniques when writing the proposal—whether it is for a research grant or for a million-dollar sales contract by your company. Remember also that appearance throughout your proposal makes important nonverbal impressions.

In its digest on proposal writing, the Washington State Office of Economic Opportunity includes the following excellent advice:

First impressions are very critical. None is more so than that first impression your proposal gives to the reader when submitted to an agency or foundation for consideration. Many proposals are lost at the first look by the reader. He [or she] appraises the proposal immediately in terms of:

1. General appearance
2. Neatness
3. Specific appearance of:
   a. Table of contents
   b. List of figures
   c. Title page
   d. Maps
   e. Graphs
   f. Charts

4. Consistency of style
5. Title—is it grandiose or does it properly describe the project?
6. Completeness
7. Professionalism

Therefore, you cannot afford to skimp on the time you spend in "polishing" your proposal. Each item must be checked and re-checked. Since you have spent many hours developing the proposal idea, and further hours researching and writing before your first draft, why risk your investment over poor typing, proofing, graphics, etc.? Some of the most important time spent working on the proposal will be that spent on the final draft.

If you are not an artist, it might be advisable to employ one to prepare the cover, charts, graphs, etc. The cost is minimal when you consider the potential return.

Be sure you and your typist are familiar with an appropriate typing style. Learn it well and be sure to follow it consistently. . . . Select one which best fits your needs and adopt it for all your proposals.

Don't accept or be satisfied with sloppy typing or artwork. Make sure it is reworked until satisfactory. You want all the final copy to be neat and clean prior to submission.[7]

The preceding suggestions on proposal outline, format, writing style and appearance can be adapted to all kinds of proposals. If, instead of seeking funds for a comprehensive research study, you are writing a proposal that is your company's bid on a $5 million sales or construction contract, the basic characteristics of the formal proposal are similar.

SUMMARY

A proposal is a report offering to solve a perceived problem in exchange for remuneration to the writer or the writer's organization. Proposals are significantly important in business, industry, government, and academia.

Basically, proposals—like other reports—should be factual, objective, logical, well written. They should also be persuasive. All proposals should present facts honestly to justify the requested expenditure to be paid by the reader's organization to the writer's firm or to an individual for solving a problem or altering a procedure.

Proposals may be short or long and formal, solicited or unsolicited. They may aim to solve business problems or research projects. The writer should consider carefully certain parts that may be desirable for each proposal outline. Among the common parts of a proposal are title page; abstract; table of contents; introduction with purpose, problem, and scope; background; procedures; equipment and facilities; personnel; budget; and appendixes.

Both solicited and unsolicited proposals should scrupulously follow all requirements to meet the reader's need. The federal government, one of the largest solicitors of proposals, demands very specific requirements.

The body of both short and long proposals consists of introduction, discussion, and terminal section. Many proposals also include one or more prefatory and supplemental parts. Writing style and appearance make first impressions that may be critical for acceptance of the proposal. In all, proposals should follow the suggestions for well-written reports and also for persuasive messages, adapted to the reader's requirements.

EXERCISES AND PROBLEMS

1. ***Proposal to Development Foundation regarding research project:*** Your instructor may on occasions submit a proposal either to begin or to finish a research project. Assume that he or she has asked you to join in applying to a foundation to begin a research project on the general topic of the formal preparation needed for today's executives.

Assume further that you have investigated the various private foundations in the United States and located one which has in the past funded educational research. In writing to the Development Foundation, you discover that it has specific requirements.

a. An initial summary page should be limited to the following information:
Institution
Principal investigators
Brief title
Descriptive title
Time period for the investigation
Budget

b. The contents of the proposal should use the following headings:
Request
Purpose of research
Procedure
Intended results
Time schedule
Budget (first, second year)
Investigators

Your responsibility is to (1) create a title page for the proposal and (2) develop an outline of the ideas to be included under the Development Foundation's major headings.

2. ***Proposal to another firm to distribute your firm's products:*** Assume you are marketing manager in a manufacturing firm whose products are now successfully marketed by distributors in 15 states. Assume products with which you are somewhat familiar or on which you can get specific information. They may be furniture items, building construction materials, electronic office equipment, or others. After careful research by your staff members, you have found that a certain five-state region in the United States is expanding rapidly for various reasons (make up the reasons).

You have never before marketed your products in that region, and in the past two months you—with your assistant manager—have visited the area in person. Also, you have conversed with the vice president and purchasing manager of a large firm that distributes other products related in general to those your firm manufactures. However, neither that distributor nor any dealer in the area has products similar to yours. You feel sure that dealers, business firms, builders, and individual customers need and should have your products. Being without them could cause problems.

In this assignment you are to write a convincing proposal to the distributing firm's purchasing manager. Your purpose is to persuade him that the area needs the products you are selling. State the problem, purpose and benefits, scope (area in which your products will help the distributor's business), your marketing procedure, quality and prices of your products, and any other pertinent information.

3. ***Report on a proposal's process from initial request to winning bid:*** Some local companies (engineering firms, ad agencies, and others) attempt to win contracts through submitting proposals. Your task in this exercise is to interview someone who is or was involved in preparing a proposal in one of those firms. Your goal is to trace the proposal's process: from initial request for a proposal to final selection of the winning bidder. Not all firms use identical procedures or formats; thus, you and your classmates will each learn different formats for the respective firms in your area. (1) Present a brief written report on the results of your investigation, and (2) on the option of your instructor offer a brief oral report based on the written statement.

   Some interview questions helpful for your report might include the following:

   a. How were you or your firm contacted? How did you find out about the opportunity for submitting a proposal?

   b. Who determined the team to work on the proposal? What were the central goals of the proposal?

   c. Was a project leader or chairperson of the project appointed? What were his or her responsibilities?

   d. What were the major headings or parts of the proposal?

   e. Which modern technological approaches were used to supplement the oral presentation?

   f. If the company was denied the proposal, were any reasons given for denial?

4. ***Proposal to a chosen organization or agency:*** Choose a problem that you can solve by experimentation, survey, observation, or any combination of these, and write your proposal to the organization that is concerned with the problem. Or (if more appropriate) assume your proposal goes to a funding agency whose philosophy is in keeping with the problem you propose to research. Here are suggestions for topics—but feel free to choose your own.

   a. Try to solve a problem related to a firm's product development; plant expansion; improvement of a sales, accounting, or purchasing system; or curtailment of shoplifting.

   b. Analyze a problem in your community—crime in a certain area, a traffic snarl situation, poor citizen involvement in local issues, need for attracting new industry or keeping young, educated persons in the community.

   c. Undertake a project in one of your college classes—or survey a sample of the student body regarding an important campus problem.

   Follow thoughtfully the suggestions in this chapter regarding proposal writing. Organize your topics under appropriate headings, and write a proposal that meets all requirements as to content, format, and writing style. Then submit your complete proposal to (a) your instructor and/or (b) your class in an oral presentation. Be prepared to defend your proposal and to have the class critique it.

5. ***Proposals for sponsored research to the government, foundations, or inside school groups:*** Some schools and universities follow a basic format when submitting proposals for sponsored research, either to the government, to private foundations, or even to inside school groups. If your school has an office that helps with preparing such proposals, speak with a member of that office and determine (1) the recommended inclusions in an academic research proposal and (2) some reasons for acceptance or rejection of a proposal. Present to the class, in an oral report complete with some visual aids, the results of your findings.

6. ***Report on a sample instructor proposal:*** If your school does not have an office assisting in developing proposals for either internal or external sponsored research, speak with a professor or teacher who has submitted a proposal. Determine (1) what the purpose of the proposal was, (2) what major points were covered in the proposal, and (3) what he or she felt helped the proposal to be accepted or rejected. Here too you could orally present to the class the results of your investigation, along with a visual aid that summarizes your main points.

7. ***Report on annotated bibliography regarding proposal writing:*** In your library or a school office devoted to helping write proposals, compile an annotated bibliography on works that discuss proposal writing. When reporting on your investigation, give (1) the bibliographic citation for your source and (2) a brief statement on the contents of the work.

PART FIVE

Oral Communications

Chapter 20

Successful Oral Presentations and Successful Listening

The ability to communicate effectively through speaking as well as in writing is highly valued, and demanded, in business. Knowing the content of the functional areas of business is important, but to give life to those ideas—in meetings or in solo presentations—demands an effective oral presentation.

Throughout each working day you as a business or professional person communicate orally with customers, colleagues, associates, supervisors, employees, inquirers, and others. Besides speaking with individuals face to face or by telephone, you will at times also be asked to address various groups of people; in other words—to make a speech. You will also need to listen to the ideas of many persons.

This chapter introduces you to improving your oral presentations within and to groups, as well as developing your listening skills within those groups. Chapters after this focus on informative and persuasive speaking, followed by a chapter on communication within business meetings, and then a section on interpersonal communication

IMPROVING YOUR ORAL PRESENTATIONS

Whether the group to which you speak consists of 10 colleagues around a conference table, 30 students in a class, a thousand in an auditorium, or a wider television audience, the ability to speak effectively is important (sometimes crucial) for your success.

The objectives of this section are to give you an overview of:

- Various kinds of oral presentations
- Essential steps for preparing effectively
- Methods of delivering the message
- Suggestions and requirements for speaker

Types of Oral Presentations

The types of talks and speeches given daily throughout the United States are of course so numerous that only a few highlights can be included here.

Short talks may range from 1 to 10 minutes in length. Many are periodic, brief progress or committee reports. Some talks introduce new managers or employees (usually during special events), or they may introduce distinguished guests or speakers and panel members at conferences. Other short talks are presentations of awards to people who have earned recognition and thanks for outstanding work on the job, in the community, in sports, or whatever. Still others may be words of welcome to visitors touring your plant or attending the organization's anniversary reception. Or you might be asked to give a short, cordial welcome to the audience gathering to hear how your company's products protect the environment; and so on and on.

Long, or formal, presentations may vary from 10 minutes to 1 hour. Some organizations observe 20- or 30-minute time limits for speeches. Often, long oral reports or proposals are presented within the organization at important management or staff meetings. They often restate or summarize significant main points on complex problems that are detailed in long written reports.

Also, long speeches are frequently scheduled at regional, national, or international conferences of business, professional, religious, social, political, and other associations. Their subject matter varies widely, ranging from information on research studies and projects to discussion of controversial issues.

Essential Steps for Preparing Talks Effectively

Careful planning is essential for successful speeches, short or long. The better you prepare in advance, the more confidence you will have on stage. Preparation usually requires the following seven steps. Most of them include important concepts similar to those for writing letters, memos, and reports (as discussed in previous chapters, especially 2, 3, 4, 5, 6, and 16).

1. Determine the purpose.

2. Analyze the audience and the situation.

3. Choose the main ideas for your message.

4. Research your topic thoroughly.

5. Organize the data and write your draft.

6. Plan visual aids if desirable.

7. Rehearse the talk and revise where necessary.

1. Determine the Purpose

Each speech can have a general and a specific purpose. The most common general purpose—or "mega purpose"—of business talks is one of these: to inform or instruct, to persuade, to entertain. The specific purpose—more narrow, or micro—is to achieve a definite, specific result.

To Inform or Instruct.   You will on occasions be asked to make an idea clear, explain the results of an investigation, demonstrate a process, give instructions to new employees, or report on surveys. Your purpose is to promote understanding.

In short committee reports the specific purpose is generally to inform executives and employees (or other group members) about significant activities during a particular period. Sometimes the aim is to teach a new procedure. Chapter 21 discusses in detail the speech to inform or instruct.

To Persuade.   The goal of persuasive speaking is to get your listeners willingly to act or accept your beliefs. In business you do this through logically proving your contention, policy, resolution, or claim. Chapter 22 discusses in detail the speech to persuade.

Some other forms of persuasion are to stimulate, motivate, inspire, and get a group more enthused. These kinds of talks, while complete with evidence and reasoning, will also include emotional persuasion, such as one hears at sales meetings. As a leadoff speaker to your firm's salespeople—who already agree with you and support a product—your goal may be to intensify the listeners' desire to make more contacts and increase sales.

To Entertain.   As businesspersons, you will sometimes be asked to give speeches to entertain (though less often than for other forms of speaking). Occasions may be social and connected with colleagues' promotions or retirements, or with anniversaries of the organization, committees, or persons. Humor is a likely ingredient of your talk, but one may also include stories and illustrations. Some people are good at using puns, wild exaggerations, irony, or even poking fun at authority. Yet humor without some serious thought is just as uninteresting as total seriousness without some humor.[1]

You will also make special-occasion speeches to *introduce, welcome,* and *present.* Each seeks to create a pleasant atmosphere.

Introducing a speaker may require as much preparation as a major speech. All facts must be correct. Your goal is to present the qualifications of the speaker, mention the occasion, suggest how the topic is important, and then present the speaker to the group. This talk, often brief, demands several rehearsals.

Speeches of welcome should make the individual or group pleased that they have come to your company, to a meeting, or to some other event. Your goal is to create goodwill. Keep in mind that you are welcoming on behalf of your organization, ending with the idea that you pledge cooperation and look forward to a successful association.

Depending on the culture of an organization, you may have to present someone with a recognition award: for services performed or, at a retirement ceremony, for years of service. Your goal is to honor the person and increase the morale of the group attending. If a formal written citation accompanies an award, that may be read; the other parts should be delivered extemporaneously.

2. Analyze the Audience and Situation

As emphasized in previous chapters, the message—whether oral or written—should be adapted to the audience. If your talk is within your organization, you will have some idea about who and how many will be in the audience.

When your talk or speech is outside your organization—to a business, public, government, or social group—less information is available. You need to find out the size of the group, age range, interests, goals, occupations (at least in general). Usually you can get this information from the person who asked you to speak and from other members of the group. If all in your audience have the same occupation, for instance, computer specialists or purchasing agents, you can use appropriate technical expressions and illustrations.

Specific analysis of the audience and the situation for information and persuasive speaking is in Chapters 21 and 22.

3. Choose the Main Ideas for Your Message

Arising out of the general and specific purpose should come the main ideas you intend to cover. Clearly, presenting a speech of introduction demands knowing about the speaker. That preparation may be more intensive than preparing for an informative statement. Regardless of speech type, jot down many main ideas, then edit until you have a workable number of main headings.

4. Research Your Topic Thoroughly

When you know your purpose, your audience, and have some idea of the main ideas to be covered, you proceed to collect the needed facts. Don't feel you must stay with your first main ideas; these may change as you research your topic. Your research approach may follow the same procedure the writer uses when preparing a written report.

5. Organize the Data and Write Your Draft

After you have gathered all needed information, you should organize your speech and write the draft, as either a complete outline or a complete manuscript. A good speech has three parts—*introduction, body (usually called* text *or* discussion *section in reports),* and *summary or conclusions.* The choice of whether to organize in either the direct (deductive) or the indirect (inductive) order depends on your listeners' knowledge and attitudes toward the subject matter. If you are planning an oral report, you may find helpful suggestions on pages 449 to 456, because steps in organizing oral and written reports are similar.

Introduction.   Your opening statements should capture your listeners' attention and help create confidence in you. An introduction is of special importance, for it assists in getting your listeners into the right frame of mind, gives some background to the topic, and sets the direction for the rest of your talk.

Gaining audience interest and attention may be accomplished using some of the following:

Purpose statement	Personal story
Quotation	Reference to the occasion
Question	Humorous story
Startling statement	

Body (Text, or Discussion).   The main part of your speech must present whatever material is necessary to achieve your specific purpose. If you are giving a short talk to introduce a speaker or to present an award for an outstanding achievement, you can use that person's resume as a basis of your text. Sincerely highlight the attributes: *don't* just read everything on the resume! Try also to add some interesting incident that the audience will enjoy hearing.

Developing an oral report is similar to developing the text of a written report—organized under appropriate headings, followed by facts to support your main points. However, because of a specified time limit for the speech, you usually must omit much of the detailed data of a long written report and concentrate on perhaps one to three topics.

Summary or Conclusions.   The last part of your speech presents briefly the key points or perhaps repeats a quotation that best emphasizes what you wanted to convey. Words like "in closing" or "one last point is" are appropriate signals for the ending. The last one or two sentences might produce special applause.

6. Plan Visual Aids if Desirable

To help get your message across to the audience, you may also need to plan meaningful visual aids for display at appropriate times. First decide whether you will distribute handouts for each person in the audience or whether you will display all visual aids from one spot. The latter procedure is usually better because your audience will focus attention on what you are displaying instead of shuffling papers and reading when you would rather have them listen. (However, if you think they would benefit from taking copies home, you can distribute them after your talk.)

The most common devices for "one spot" displays are chalkboards or whiteboards, flip sheets or charts, projectors, and high-technology visuals. Each has some advantages, depending on subject matter and audience size.

Chalkboards or Whiteboards.   When you wish to write brief, significant points or figures either before your talk begins or while you are talking, a chalkboard or whiteboard is useful. If you will have much material for the board, plan, if possible, to place it there before your talk begins. The board can be covered until you wish to reveal your display, especially if the drawing is complex. Before large audiences, avoid speaking as you draw because your back will be toward the audience and your body will cover your drawing. Boards are usable only if the audience can see from all corners of the room.

Flip Sheets or Charts.   A variety of material on large separate pages can be on flip sheets, fastened at the top and attached to an easel or stand. The size of sheets as well as the words, charts, tables, or drawings on them can be modified somewhat, in keeping with expected audience and room size. Even so, of course, their use has limits, for they may be hard to read in large auditoriums seating hundreds of people.

One advantage of using flip sheets or charts instead of a chalkboard or whiteboard is that you can prepare them before you come to the room where you'll be speaking. Another is that the material written or printed on them can be larger and of better quality when prepared with colored markers than when material is written with chalk or marking pencils. Also, you can skip pages or add facts on sheets whenever desirable. You can even insert small handwritten notes—not for the audience, but as cues for yourself to guide you to the next topic. And if you are speaking to a small group around a conference table, you can use smaller "table flipsheets" easily read by your audience. Furthermore, during your talk you need merely flip pages in any order you wish and more quickly focus your eyes again on your audience.

Projectors.   Adaptable for displaying business materials are the slide projector, the overhead, and the opaque projector.

With *slide projectors* or *carousels* the illustrations should be shown in a darkened or semidarkened room. The material must be prepared in advance on slides. These are especially useful when you have a series of photographs taken by a camera and developed directly on slides. However, you can also begin with designs or written materials on paper; from them, computer-generated, 35-millimeter, full-color slides may be made in your office or by professional studios.

The *overhead projector* has the advantage of being usable in daylight or a lighted room. To use the overhead you must first convert your display materials into transparencies. These can be prepared quite inexpensively, in a few seconds, on your company's spirit duplicating or photocopying machine, on one of the various other modern transparency makers, or by professional photographic methods. While projecting the transparencies to your audience you can write on them (with marking pens or pencils). You can add overlays or more drawings when necessary, as when explaining the development of a certain manufacturing or marketing process. Also (as with the opaque) you can cover up and reveal your display material point by point so your audience can't read ahead or jump to a conclusion.

With the *opaque projector* (now falling into disuse) you can use any typewritten, handwritten, or printed materials or various specimens just as they come from your files. The risk is that some of the material will be too small to be seen by all the audience. Therefore, use large lettering and examples. The opaque projector should be used preferably in a semidarkened room.

High-Technology Visuals.   With the advent of the computer it is possible to project on a large screen the words and drawings appearing on a small computer screen. The results of each of your keystrokes is immediately projected to the larger screen.

Electronic blackboards are useful when a coparticipant in your presentation is in another location, his or her printed words appearing on the board before your audience. Videotapes are also used, their images appearing on large screens before the audience. Some companies also use satellite transmission for voice hookups, by which audience members may question the speaker or the coparticipant in another country. (The prologue in this book describes briefly how visuals and oral statements are presented in a video conference.)

In summary, adapt your visuals to the size of your audience; realize that visuals should add to, but not distract from, the presentation.

■ Checklist for Visual Aids in Oral Presentations

- ■ Avoid too many lines; eight large lines are generally easily read by all the audience.
- ■ Be sure all can see your visual; stand to one side after referring to the aid.
- ■ Use a pointer; one saying is "T + T," that is, touch and turn—touch where the audience should look; turn back to them as you add your oral comments.
- ■ Be creative; simply projecting a visual with 52 lines does not hold attention, whereas a creative visual with color and drawings and interesting headings can hold the audience.
- ■ Relate the visual aid to your talk; use and refer to visual aids as supplements to what you say.
- ■ Speak to the audience, not the visual; turning your back on the audience suggests the aid is more important than what you are saying.

7. Rehearse the Talk and Revise Where Necessary

After you have considered the preceding six steps, you are ready to apply them through rehearsals. And you will revise wherever improvements are needed. Some executives go through numerous drafts before presenting an important speech. To develop confidence, you should know the subject better than anyone else in the audience.

When rehearsing, stand and deliver your speech out loud—maybe in front of a mirror. To get the feel of the volume level you will use for the presentation (in case the lectern has no microphone) talk so that a friend (real or imaginary) in the back row can easily hear you.

- ■ Always imagine the audience in front of you.
- ■ Use transitional phrases and sentences to show your listeners the relationships between sections of your report. Avoid long sentences and unusual words.
- ■ Take each of the main points one at a time and learn to present each with its supporting material as a unit.
- ■ Include the visual aids you'll use—and in the margin, note where each aid should be used.
- ■ Anticipate questions from the audience. Jot them on paper and consider thoughtful answers.

■ Stop at the allotted time. Then cut and revise the speech accordingly until you can deliver it within the time limit—allowing also for a question-and-answer period.

A frequently asked question is "How many times should I rehearse?" At least two or three times is recommended, or until you feel comfortable. That comfort level will vary with the speaker and the occasion: how often you have given the presentation, what your position is in the company, which group you are speaking to, and how knowledgeable you are on the topic.

A company president delivering a Christmas greeting rehearsed four times; a vice president making a presentation to a congressional committee went through his talk three times; a vice president at a new car announcement rehearsed five times; a president of a foreign subsidiary visiting the home company rehearsed eight times; some speakers go through still more rehearsals and revisions. The final decision is up to you.

Four Methods of Delivering the Message

To make your oral presentations, you have four choices of kinds of speaking: extemporaneous, manuscript-reading, memorization, and impromptu.

1. Extemporaneous Method

With the extemporaneous method—which is usually preferred—you speak from a previously prepared outline or notes. Your outline may be detailed with some comments, quotations, and statistics—all typed on 8½- by 11-inch paper, with pages numbered. For short talks, your notes may be on numbered 3- by 5-inch cards, but some speakers prefer the larger 5- by 8-inch cards or sheets, especially for longer speeches.

Use this extemporaneous method of speaking whenever possible, because it permits more eye contact with the group and you can more easily establish rapport with your audience. After you have given numerous oral presentations, you will be able to use fewer notes and feel more at ease and more confident than a beginning speaker does. Also, you will likely prefer to deliver your talks extemporaneously.

2. Manuscript-Reading Method

For some long speeches it may be necessary to read parts of your manuscript. Technical or complex data and, certainly, quotations from authorities will be read verbatim. Be sure to look at the audience often. Avoid reading the entire speech word for word.

Some top-level executives and government officials find it necessary to read their speeches. If they will be filmed on television or quoted in news media, ad-libbing could sometimes lead to problems. Also, of course, laws and rules must be read verbatim. In these cases reading is safest and acceptable, but the reader must still maintain eye contact with the audience.

Large type, wide margins, and double or triple spacing of lines are helpful aids when you must read from the manuscript. Some speakers use a page style similar to a TV script, leaving a left margin of about one-third of the page. In that wide margin you can write comments to yourself, such as "slide 2" or "move to screen," or you can insert last-minute changes to your talk. Try, as do some radio and TV announcers, to underline important words or phrases.

3. Memorization Method

The beginning speaker might memorize a short talk, but the delivery should be made to sound spontaneous. Rarely ever should a long speech be memorized.

Some of the best speakers memorize—but *not* word for word—the purpose statement and main points of their speech. Try to memorize not the exact words you will use but the *ideas*. Also it may be helpful to memorize your first sentence—especially if you are inclined to feel stage fright at the beginning.

4. Impromptu Method

When you are called upon for comments—on the spur of the moment—you speak impromptu. In discussions and conferences, or in your classroom, a request for a response is frequent. How can you prepare? Winston Churchill, the consummate British prime minister during the Second World War, rehearsed his "impromptu" comments first at home, though later, in the House of Commons, his remarks appeared to be entirely on the spur of the moment. Another example is a university vice president who seemed to be doodling throughout a discussion; in reality he was also jotting down notes for use in his later impromptu remarks. In short, good listening (discussed later in this chapter), plus a few jotted notes, can help an impromptu statement.

Oral and Nonverbal Requirements in Delivery

Communicating successfully before an audience demands actions and qualities not found in writing. In addition to completing the seven steps for preparing your speech, and choosing the method of delivering it, you need also to focus on your oral delivery, control of stage fright, and nonverbal behavior.

Oral Delivery

Your voice during your communication adds to a verbal impression of you. You can use voice more effectively in business speaking by following a few suggestions regarding pitch, rate, volume, quality, and pronunciation.

1. Pitch. A simplistic definition of *pitch* is the highness or lowness of your voice. The following are some problems in pitch:

Monotone. A sameness in pitch level. An oscilloscope of your voice in a monotone range would show a rather flat line: little variation, little rising or falling of the voice.

Voice too high or low. An excited speaker would be in the upper range (during a heated conversation between people), while the dull, monotonous speaker would rest at the lower pitch level.

Lack of word value. Each word, regardless of its importance in a thought group, receives the same pitch emphasis, the speaker not distinguishing with vocal stress between important and unimportant words in a sentence.

These problems are corrected by pitch changes, accomplished through steps and glides—from a higher to a lower level, abruptly. Say this sentence out loud: "Bill, don't do that!" On which word did you raise your pitch? For emphasis each word can receive a higher pitch depending on the precise word you wish to stress.

Bill, don't do that!	Bill, don't *do* that!
Bill, *don't* do that!	Bill, don't do *that*!

When we wish to emphasize an entire sentence, usually the strong declarative thoughts end with downward pitch changes, giving the feeling of finality, determination. A rising inflection is more appropriate to asking questions or suggesting indecision.

Variety in pitch is necessary. Not to use variation is risking being called a monotonous or uninteresting speaker.

2. Rate.   The speed, or rate, at which people speak varies. Sameness in rate also enhances monotony. A speaker may be considered dull when the rate is slow and unvarying, even though that speaker's content may be superior. Conversely, the fast speaker also causes discomfort: we wish the rapid-fire speaker to slow down so that we can digest the thoughts.

Communication experts suggest that the range for public speakers lies between 80 and 160 words per minute. For some people conversing informally, the rate may range from 80 to 250.

A key word related to rate is *pause*. Let oral "white space" occur in your speech, just as you use white space in a written document. As in writing, a pause in speaking lets your receiver reflect on the message and helps break the flow of thought. A pause also lets you collect your thoughts, take time to move a visual, or rest your voice. Silence, through a pause, is an excellent way to regain audience attention.

A pause is also a good way to indicate that you are ending a point and will move on to another. Just as paragraphs are indented to indicate a new subject, so the pause can also alert listeners that a new topic is coming.

3. Volume.   To utter the admonition "Speak up, please" from the rear of the room demands listener courage. But to sit passively while unintelligible words flow by is a disservice to the audience and to the speaker. *Volume* is the loudness or softness of your voice. How do you improve it?

By contrast in emphasis, louder or softer volume. How would you express the following thought at the end of an oral proposal presentation?

```
And with that we conclude our remarks.  Personally, I look
forward to working with you and the other members of your
project team.  I can't forget that at one time I was asked
to join your firm.  Now I'm on the other side, offering a
proposal that I hope you'll accept.  Regardless of your fi-
nal decision, we wish you to know that we enjoyed this morn-
ing with you.
```

The man who gave that statement lowered his voice—made it a moving personal appeal at the end of a rigorous three-hour team presentation. His soft volume matched the intimacy of his thoughts.

You can also accent syllables, as well as important words, you feel should orally stand out.

By controlled breathing. Unless you breathe deeply, from the diaphragm, you cannot generate a strong volume. Your lungs must be filled with air to produce a pressure level high enough to propel the air forcefully past your vocal cords. Incidentally, slow, deep breathing before beginning to speak also relaxes you, decreasing some stage fright symptoms.

Certainly you must adapt your volume level to the size of the audience and room. Speaking to 50 people in a room without an amplification aid would surely demand more volume than when you speak to 5 people in a small room.

4. Vocal Quality.   Here are words to describe voice: *husky, throaty, loud, vibrant, dynamic, moving, weak, strong, harsh, shrill, effeminate, masculine, gentle, squeaky, muffled, falsetto, silvery, ravishing, clean, ringing, effortless, secure, flexible, serene, pliable, vibrant, colorful.* We perceive people in great measure by their voice quality, that indefinable something that distinguishes their voices from others.

The size and shape of the following parts of our body affect voice quality: mouth, tongue, lips, teeth, vocal cords, sinuses, hard and soft palate, and nose. In fact, the voices of great singers, and speakers, each have their own elusive, individual quality because of some anatomical difference, for which the performers are personally and financially grateful.

If you're unhappy with your voice, see a competent speech therapist for professional help. Improved voice quality is helped by deep breathing and a conscientious attempt at relaxing the throat. That way, some suggest, a full, unrestricted voice can enter the resonating chambers such as the mouth, throat, and nasal cavities.

5. Pronunciation.   We are displeased when people mispronounce our name. In fact, we subconsciously register a reaction when any word is mispronounced— relative to our concept of how it should be pronounced. (We may be wrong; the speaker, right.)

Additional pronunciation problems need to be mentioned.

Jargon. Within your organization you will learn jargon pronunciations, often for abbreviations. Thus "cam" used within one group will mean "contract audit manual," but to outsiders could mean a part that forces a roller to move. A danger, clearly, lies in using these in-group pronunciations outside your group, with inevitable quizzical nonverbal reactions from your listeners.

Varied regional accents. For many words, southern pronunciation and accents, for example, differ from those in Chicago or Boston. For most of these words, however, there is a common standard throughout the states, as there must be for us to understand quickly.

Added or omitted sounds. Speakers should, of course, be careful not to add such sounds as *uh, hm, y'know, er, OK* between words or sentences. If one has many of these interjections (one speaker had 24, another 42, another 147), they break up the flow of words for the listener. The result is similar to the negative impression writing errors leave with a reader. Some speakers literally don't hear their interjections until they hear them played back on a videotape.

Other bad habits of adding and omitting may also affect pronunciation. In the following examples, the preferred pronunciation is second:

Adding		Omitting	
idear	idea	gonna	going to
athalete	athlete	watcha say	what did you say
arthuritis	arthritis	meetn	meeting
hunerd	hundred	dija	did you

Suggestions for improving pronunciation are:

Listen to the educated and cultured people of your community. You can usually assume that their standard is correct and acceptable for their region of the country. A public speech by a respected businessperson is also a good guide.

Consult a recent dictionary. More options on pronunciations of words are included in recent editions. When in doubt, get a consensus from your class members or your instructors.

Control of Stage Fright

Few people can approach an audience without some feeling of discomfort. Many good speakers and actors experience symptoms of stage fright—wobbly knees, rapid heartbeat, trembling hands, "butterflies" in the stomach. Actually, the uneasy feelings are the body's way of providing extra emotional and physical energy to help a person rise to the occasion.

Luciano Pavarotti, the great contemporary singer, said of stage fright, "I would not want even an enemy to suffer those terrible moments." The former, eminent radio newscaster of World War II, Edward R. Murrow, called it the "sweat of perfection." A former head of General Motors, on the front page of the *Wall Street Journal*, on his retirement indicated he bordered on becoming physically ill from nervousness. The list goes on: for singers, dancers, musicians, speakers. What can be done for this universal fear, this common malady of nervousness when speaking?

In a real sense it's mind over matter, it's confidence above all, it's feeling that you know the subject better than anyone else, it's the internal feeling that you're in charge. If it makes you feel any better, football players have similar feelings of fear before a game; the coach then tells them they're the best, they're good, they're in control, they're ready!

Here are suggestions used by successful speakers and performers to help control stage fright:

■ Checklist for Decreasing Stage Fright

- ■ Know your subject well. Prepare with the attitude that on that subject on that day you know more than anyone else.
- ■ Rehearse your talk several times (as suggested on pages 602 and 603. If possible, rehearse in the same room where you'll speak. This can easily be done within your company. But if your speech will be outside your company, try to arrive at the place early and take a look around. (Actors frequently have a short rehearsal in the hall where they will later appear.)
- ■ Request—in advance—a lectern. It helps to hold not only your notes but also, occasionally, a trembling hand. But avoid leaning on the lectern excessively.
- ■ Precheck any equipment you'll need—projector, screen, extension cord— and know which electric outlet is nearest the podium or lectern.
- ■ Take an object with you—a pen, your notes, a marking pencil. Of course one should not play with the object, but using it as a pointer and as something to touch has helped calm some speakers.
- ■ Breathe deeply and slowly before speaking. Try moving a little in your chair: cross and uncross your legs. Even that slight movement decreases some muscle tenseness.
- ■ Move during the speech. (See the comments on pages 610 and 611.) Some movement holds audience attention and releases nervous energy. Even behind a lectern one can move slightly or use a lavaliere mike and, thereby, increase the possible range of movement. If you're seated, shift positions in your chair or gesture a bit more with your arms.
- ■ Approach the lectern with assurance and enthusiasm.

Nonverbal Behavior

The speaker's posture, movement, gestures, facial expressions, and appearance all convey external nonverbal cues. Some of the negative impressions to avoid are sketched in Figure 20-1.[2]

1. Posture.   When you're depressed, your shoulders sag and your head drops forward. On the other hand, when you have good news to tell, you stand upright, possibly square your shoulders, and hold your head high. Your outward appearance mirrors your inner mood. Thus good posture suggests poise and confidence; stand neither at rigid attention nor with sloppy casualness draped over the podium, but erect with your weight about equally distributed on each foot.

Posture may also be adapted to the audience. When speaking to a small business conference of, say, 12 people, you might sit on the edge of the table, or in some groups even in a high swivel chair. An informative talk to 200 people would demand more formality, and more postural variety, particularly during transitions to suggest a change in topic.

Some women prefer shorter heels when speaking. Too high a heel causes

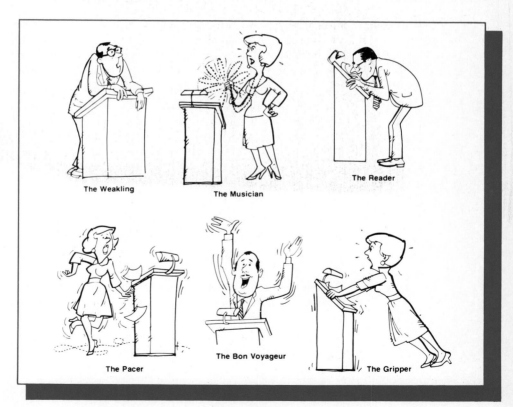

The Weakling

The Musician

The Reader

The Pacer

The Bon Voyageur

The Gripper

Figure 20–1   *Undesirable attitudes and postures for speakers and meeting leaders.*

some female speakers to rock from side to side. Choose a comfortable set of shoes to avoid conveying a negative, ill-at-ease impression because your shoes are bothering you.

2. Movement.   Taking a few steps during a presentation can hold attention, as does any moving object. There are times, however, when a lectern precludes extensive movement other than short steps to its side. Yet, move if possible, for the following reasons:

> *Move to hold attention.* At large sessions, lecterns restrict your movement. In business meetings the audience may be smaller, thus permitting you to stand behind a desk or table. Move more often from side to side rather than back and forth. But don't move continuously, like a caged lion!
>
> *Move to get rid of nervousness.* A way of decreasing stage fright is to move about, especially in the beginning of your talk. Even the manner in which you approach the lectern tells something about you nonverbally. Are you slow and plodding, or do you move with assurance, determination, enthusiasm? The latter approach gives a confident feeling while decreasing some of your initial nervousness.
>
> *Move to suggest transitions.* Cues for transitions in writing include headings, words, and numerical hints such as (1), (2), (3) or (a), (b), (c). In your talk, you visually supplement the oral words of transition by physically moving when making a direction shift. The audience follows you more easily.
>
> *Move to increase emphasis.* In writing we use exclamation points following emphatic statements. In speaking, a movement toward the audience, accompanied by a gesture, can imply you are stressing a point. Emphasis through movement suggests idea importance and holds group attention.

3. Gestures.   Briefly, gestures are movements of the hands, arms, head, shoulders. Hand and arm gestures are used for several reasons:

> *To emphasize.* For example, the clenched fist emphasizes a point by either hitting the palm of the hand or shaking it upright before an audience.
>
> *To point.* The index finger calls attention, indicating either locations or directions.
>
> *To reject.* A sample phrase accompanying this gesture would be "I can't believe the actions of our competitors." Here the hand may go to the side in an act of rejection.
>
> *To describe.* Clearly, though your hands cannot give the precise picture of the idea or thing you are speaking about, even an approximation of size is worthwhile.

Head and shoulders drooped or turned to one side indicate different nonverbal messages than if these physical parts are erect and the speaker faces the audience—the desired stance.

A few suggestions regarding gestures are noteworthy:

Vary gestures. Using the same action repetitiously is boring to the audience and suggests lack of creativity on your part.

Avoid continuous gestures. Visually the audience needs a rest from the speaker's frequent gestures. Overuse can weaken the emphasis.

Watch timing. The gesture should accompany the oral thought, not precede or follow it.

Adapt gestures. Seated at a table is not the time for broad, all-inclusive gestures. On the other hand, a large audience would not see a small gesture. Adapt to the size of the group.

The key to good gestures is enthusiasm; you must feel excited about the topic, have a strong sense of involvement.

4. Facial expressions.   When you smile or laugh, your face suggests that your topic interests you. A frowning or glaring facial expression may convey nonverbal impressions that you are worried, angry, or perhaps ill at ease. Show enthusiasm and vitality. You must not only *feel* but *show* your interest in your ideas. Sincerity is important. Your enthusiasm must reflect your sincere belief in your ideas and a sincere desire to share them with your listeners.

Facial expression includes eye contact. Speakers who bury their head in their notes or who speak to the board lose a sense of directness with the audience. Eye contact with your listeners suggests respect and goodwill, adding to a favorable impression of you as a speaker.

5. Appearance.   How you look, what you wear affect listeners. One may smile at the stereotype of the blue suit, white shirt for men or the dark suit, white blouse for women, yet, this "uniform" is appropriate and quietly demanded— or sometimes overtly required—within some companies. When you are speaking, it is necessary to know these unwritten and written rules of dress.

By contrast, in some companies casualness is the norm. Pants and any shirts for men, slacks and any blouses for women are appropriate. It is up to you, as a speaker inside the company or coming from the outside, to know the norms for clothing. Appropriate dress, along with good grooming, can give you a feeling of confidence, and the audience a sense of respect for you.

IMPROVING YOUR LISTENING

"Nobody listens to me" is a common complaint. It is so common that businesses spend large sums of money teaching their employees how to listen. All of us spend much of our lives speaking, writing, *and* listening—the last, far in excess of the other acts of communication. The subject is important.[3]

Most of your listening, as a learner, is comprehensive listening: that is, you're seeking to understand and, sometimes, to evaluate information given you orally. You, and many others, also engage in enjoyable, relaxed listening, as when watching movies, plays, or television or when playing records or tapes.

So you're already engaged in the kind of listening you will do in business, namely, trying to absorb as much information as possible through your ears. Thus, even now, it pays to improve your listening ability. It is important in business, whether you are an executive or a subordinate employee, as the following statement from a company's management brochure indicates:

> Poor listening habits can keep an organization from functioning properly. Verbal information can be misunderstood. Those with public contact may misinterpret what a customer wants. A manager who doesn't listen efficiently cannot pass along instructions, and subordinates who don't listen well often have difficulty carrying out instructions.
>
> The benefits of applied listening skills are impressive. Good listeners make a company a more effective organization. They have better rapport with others, they get more out of meetings and are more effective in conferences, and they are better at understanding the needs of others.[4]

Common Faults of Listening

Studies agree that our listening efficiency is no better than 25 to 30 percent. That means, foremost, that considerable information given us orally is lost. Why? Some reasons follow.

1. *Prejudice against the speaker.* Perhaps you have heard this quotation: "Who is saying it shouts so loudly that what is said is easily forgotten." We are distracted because who the speaker is conflicts with our attitudes. For example, can you maintain attention when the speaker's position, attitude, or belief is entirely contrary to your own?

2. *External distractions.* The preceding fault was more of an internal distraction. Some nonverbal cues are strong external distractions. Does the speaker stammer? Wear loud clothing? Dress sloppily? Walk or gesture excessively? Reek of perfume or cologne? All of these and more cause persons to tune out on speakers.

   Actually, the entire physical environment affects listening. Among the negative factors are noisy fans, poor or glaring lights, distracting background music, overheated or cold or oddly shaped or gaudily decorated rooms, excessive draft from a window or register, and so on. Also, sitting near disturbing individuals in the audience might distract a listener's attention from the speaker's message.

3. *Thinking speed.* Most of us speak between 80 and 160 words per minute. Yet people have the capacity to think at the phenomenal rate of up to 800 words per minute. That leaves time on the listener's hands (or in his or her head). What do you do during all that time when you're not actually processing the speaker's words? Do you go off on tangents, focus your attention elsewhere, begin to daydream, shift your attention?

Soon you can be off, far away from the words of the speaker—missing some important points.

4. *Premature evaluation.* How many times have you interrupted persons before they completed their thought? Finished their sentence? Stated *their* conclusions? Directly as a result of our rapid thinking speed, we race ahead to what we feel is the conclusion. We anticipate. We arrive at the concluding thought quickly—although often one that is quite different from what the speaker intended.

5. *Semantic stereotypes.* As certain kinds of people bother us, so too do their words. An interesting class interchange occurs when discussing this question: What is your favorite word, and why? Opposite that question is, What words bother you, and why?

    Internal reaction words vary from person to person, each list influenced by feelings, attitudes, prejudices, and biases we carry inside ourselves. (See the communication model in Chapter 2.) Hence, some words cause negative reactions. We tune out the speaker because the word annoys us; it shouts so loudly in our brain that effective listening is impaired.

6. *Delivery.* A monotone can readily put listeners to sleep—or cause them to lose interest. Sadly, some teachers speak in monotones. So do significant people in government or business. How a speaker delivers his or her message does annoy some people—and they become bored, uninterested, and critical of the message. "He's a bore" is more a critique of delivery than an assessment of a speaker's mental abilities.

Good listening is hard work—and important. It is easier to listen to what we enjoy, and to those we enjoy—more quickly following arguments and ideas that link with our own way of thinking.

Listening with a Purpose

Up to this point you may feel that getting an audience to listen is entirely up to the speaker. Wrong. All of us have had the experience of reading to the bottom of a page and being unable to tell what we have read. Similarly, it's possible to hear someone and be unable to summarize or repeat a word of what we heard. The fault is not entirely that of the sender. The audience (or you as a member of that audience) must answer this question: Why listen?

To Gain New Information and Ideas

Throughout our lifetimes there are kernels of information that become a part of us through the spoken word. Lectures in class, for example, can supplement and clarify a textbook; informative indoctrinations give new employees background to a company; persuasive statements to clients give both information and reasons for buying. New ideas are received daily, via the oral medium, if one listens.

To Question and Test Evidence and Assumptions

When a speaker presents a message, much of what is said is based on either verifiable facts or his or her opinions. A good listener tests those facts and opinions against his or her assumptions, then questions the speaker. The goal is to arrive at what is true, workable, and acceptable to most people.

To Be Inspired

Sales meeting audiences know the value of a stimulating keynote speaker. He or she sets the tone, direction, mood for the entire meeting. A well-delivered poem or a moving speech can be motivational, provided that the listeners focus on the inspiring statements.

To Improve Your Own Communication

Role models and mentors are valuable to young people entering the business world. If your role model is also an effective communicator, you are lucky. However, if your mentor lacks some communication skills, and thus cannot serve as a resource, other excellent ways exist to study communicators: attending meetings, hearing speeches, or even observing famous officials speaking on television. Choose the best techniques; listen for and adopt those that are done well. Add them to your list of desirable speaking attributes. Omit undesirable habits that you see and hear.

The preceding discussion suggests reasons why you should listen. You, as a listener, can help ensure achieving those listening goals by doing the following:

■ Checklist for Improved Listening

1. *Be prepared.* For a class, this means completing your reading and assignment responsibilities. For an outside speaker, you can learn something about the speaker, the topic, the audience, the situation even before attending. In a sense you are preparing yourself to listen.
2. *Accent the positive.* "If you have to do it, do it with a positive attitude" is a centerpiece of many modern self-help books—and a good model for life. In listening, too, we ought to leave our negative baggage at home, taking along only a constructive attitude. Find something interesting or useful in the message.
3. *Listen to understand, not refute.* Respect the viewpoint of those you disagree with. Try to understand the points they emphasize and why they have such feelings (training, background, etc.). Don't allow your personal biases and attitudes regarding the speakers or their views to influence your listening to their message. To deny hearing a view with which you disagree is to possess a closed mind and ear.
4. *Focus your attention.* Tune out internal and external distractions by facing and maintaining contact with the speaker. If you experience some neg-

ative environment factors, you can sometimes move to another location in the room. Blot out your meandering thoughts and focus on what is being said.

5. *Concentrate on context*. Search out the main ideas. Construct a mental outline of where the speaker is going. Listen for transitions and the progression of ideas. Look for supports that develop the thesis.

6. *Take notes*. If you focus on content, the physical act of writing main points reinforces the mental outline you are constructing. Jot down ideas. Even incomplete sentences or single words will later be a memory jogger of what was said. But avoid trying to record entire sentences verbatim, for while you are writing them, you may miss the next significant points the speaker is presenting. Note the general principles, and record the supporting facts for them whenever possible.

7. *Curb the impulse to interrupt*. This suggestion applies to interviews, conferences, job instructions, and meetings. Listen attentively until the speaker invites questions. Don't assume conclusions (perhaps wrongly) before the speaker has stated them.

8. *Summarize and evaluate*. Restate—in your own words—just what you think was said. You should also question evidence used and mentally test the validity of evidence in support of a proposition. Furthermore, during the speech, you can also note nonverbal cues (gestures, eye contact, tone) that help indicate whether the speaker appears to be sincere in his or her statements. At the conclusion of the talk, during a question period, it is your right to ask questions about material presented.

Results of Good Listening

Positive, purposive listening—to speakers in discussions, in interviews, in speeches, or in one-on-one situations—yields valuable benefits:

1. Leads to helpful, positive attitudes—by understanding the hindrances that lie in the way of good listening.

2. Permits the speaker and listeners to improve communication, because each side is more aware of and receptive to the other's viewpoint.

3. Indicates by feedback to the speaker that listeners are interested; in turn, the speaker tries harder to give his or her best presentation.

4. Helps listeners obtain useful information on which they can make accurate decisions.

5. Creates better understanding of others and thus helps listeners work with others.

6. Assists the speaker (especially in an interview) in talking out a problem. A person needs to receive, as well as give, help.

SUMMARY

When you can communicate effectively orally, you have an important skill to help you advance in business and in the professions. For short talks you may be asked to present periodic, brief progress reports, introduce various persons, present awards, and occasionally welcome visitors or meeting attendees. Longer speeches may be presentations of proposals or highlights of research reports or complex problems—to audiences within or outside your organization.

Careful planning is essential for successful speeches, short or long. Steps for preparing effectively require thoughtful consideration of purpose, audience and situation, ideas, research, organization, visual aids, and revisions. An important extra step is rehearsals—to build confidence and reduce or eliminate possible stage fright.

The general purposes of speeches business people give are to inform, to persuade, (less often) to entertain, or to create goodwill. The specific purpose of each speech is best stated in an infinitive phrase that ties in with your speech title and focuses on your precise goal to meet the audience and occasion. Organization and evidence are logical parts of good business speaking. To neglect either is to wander aimlessly and to employ unsupported generalizations.

The extemporaneous method of presentation is preferable to reading from a manuscript and to memorization. The extemporaneous method allows more visual and nonverbal contact with an audience. *Variety* and *enthusiasm* greatly influence pitch, rate, volume and quality of voice. Posture, movement, gestures, facial expressions, and appearance convey nonverbal cues that give vitality and sincere meaning to any presentation.

Good listening is demanding, requiring omission of personal biases as well as external distractions. With a positive attitude and active involvement through personal summaries and evaluation, you can have fruitful listening experiences.

EXERCISES AND PROBLEMS

1. *Informative talk to Business and Professional Club members:* Assume the Business and Professional Club in your city has invited you and six other students to a dinner meeting. Each of you is to present an informative five- or six-minute talk on how the current curriculum in your chosen major field prepares students for successfully filling jobs in business or a profession. Choose at least three main topics for your talk, and back them up with specific facts. Adapt your carefully organized talk to your listeners' interests. Talk with sincerity and enthusiasm, mindful of your physical and vocal behavior.

2. *Informative four-minute talk to instruct or entertain:* For a four-minute talk, select any topic you are familiar with—a sport, a favorite food, an event, a place, a gadget. Introduce yourself to the class, tell what your topic is, develop it in any instructive or entertaining way you wish, and summarize your talk. After you have finished, your class members will make constructive suggestions.

3. ***Short informative talk to introduce speaker or award winner:*** For this assignment each student will give a short (three- to five-minute) talk to introduce a member of the class as either a speaker or an award winner. First, choose a classmate (by any method your instructor suggests). Then exchange resumes with that person. Confer with each other to get acquainted. (Your classmate needs information to introduce you, too.)

   You may each assume that your classmate is a speaker about a certain topic at a meeting of a business, professional, campus, or other club of which you are both members. You have been chosen to introduce him or her. If you prefer, instead of introducing your classmate as a speaker, you may assume you were asked to present him or her with an award.

   Whichever specific purpose you choose for your talk, select from your classmate's resume at least four pertinent facts—with his or her approval. All statements in your talk should be true—except of course the assumption that this classmate is a speaker or award winner. To support either of these assumptions you may need to add a few made-up incidents. For instance, if you will present an award, be sure to mention clearly a (made-up) noteworthy achievement—on the job or in scholarship or in community activities, sports, music, or whatever. Organize your talk well, and present it enthusiastically to your audience.

4. ***Nonverbal communication log:*** The purpose of this assignment is to make you more aware of cues that one receives nonverbally. Each day for seven days keep a log, noting nonverbal cues you feel communicate something to you. Note any situations you wish, but you should have at least three examples per day for seven days. In addition to the discussion on nonverbal cues in this chapter, you may also find useful suggestions in the section Nonverbal Communication in Chapter 2.

   a. Keep a nonverbal communication log, which you will hand in to your instructor on a prearranged date. Divide your paper into two columns: on the left put the heading "Situation," and on the right "Conclusions." Under "Situation" describe the incident observed and under "Conclusions" draw some inferences as to what you felt was communicated.

   b. Be prepared to discuss the assignment orally in class.

5. ***Oral presentation based on resume:*** One way to break down some nervousness is to speak on a well-known topic—yourself. Therefore, prepare an assignment that (1) presents a brief oral statement in support of your future goals, backed up by (2) your resume prepared as a transparency. You may simply use the resume form your school uses or create a new one, including the usual information such as opening section, education, work experience, activities, personal data, and references. (See Chapter 12 for additional comments on resume construction.)

   Suggestion: Begin by stating your personal goals (either short- or long-term), and then refer to your resume (lying on an overhead projector) as evidence that you possess the qualifications to meet your goals.

Successful Informative Speaking

I n a business environment you will give informative and persuasive speeches. Both are mentioned in Figure 21-1. This chapter focuses on the first kind, presentations that make ideas clear and promote understanding for listeners either inside or outside your company. The persuasive end of the continuum is discussed in the next chapter.

How to achieve clarity in informative speaking is explained through examining purposes and kinds of informative speaking, the importance of audience analysis, ways to organize informative data, and supports for informative data.

PURPOSES OF INFORMATIVE SPEAKING

In the preceding chapter you learned about general and specific purposes, the former being the overall, more "mega" purpose of your talk. The specific purpose is more narrowly defined. It is the precise, exact result you hope to achieve with your listeners.

Specific Purpose

Take time to decide on the specific purpose of your speech. Naturally, that purpose will vary with the kind of speech and audience, but begin by writing out what you wish your listeners to remember and take with them. One way to do this is through stating your specific purpose in a precise infinitive phrase.

Vague Specific Purpose	Better Specific Purpose
Computers	To inform the group about using the UNISYS <u>Write One</u> system of word processing
Health Care	To inform employees on differences between Blue Cross/Blue Shield and local HMOs
Investing	To explain the advantages of joining an investment club
Vacation Periods	To discuss company vacation policies for new employees
Changes in Retirement	To note the process employees should follow for retirement benefits

Once you define your specific purpose, you can begin to link three preparation steps together: title, general purpose, specific purpose, as in the following examples:

Title:	Where Do All the Workers Go?
General purpose:	To inform
Specific purpose:	To discuss the human-resource dilemmas occurring after a merger and acquisition

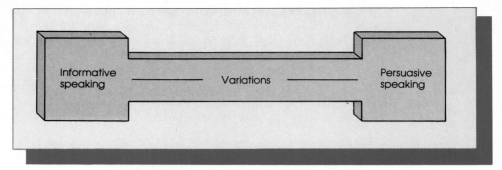

Figure 21–1   *Informative-persuasive continuum.*

```
Title:              What Happens after 55?
Purpose:            To inform
Specific purpose:   To review changes in our organization's re-
                    tirement policy for employees over age 55

Title:              Women Managers--Paths to Follow on the Way
                    Up
Purpose:            To inform
Specific purpose:   To report on survey results of 700 women
                    managers and their recommendations for suc-
                    cess in business
```

Note that to this point you have given little effort toward constructing the speech; you're still laying the foundation. You should consider one more thing before locating detailed supporting materials—whether you'll speak about a process or a policy.

Process as Purpose

This book focuses heavily on process. Your authors inform you about the steps you can take to be better communicators in written and oral communication. A study of process is knowing the systematic steps needed to bring about a desired result. In a company you could speak about how a machine works, how a product is made, how to construct a good auditing report, how to prepare for retirement, how to merge two benefit packages, or how to use a word processing program.

Most often your speech's organization will be chronological, starting at the beginning and tracing that process to the end. Therefore you must know the major steps before communicating them to your listeners. For instance, the following example takes listeners through the process of preparing for an overseas assignment:

```
Title:              Our Employees Overseas
General purpose:    To inform
Specific purpose:   To suggest the procedures in preparing for
                    overseas work
```

```
Main points:    I.      Contact with personnel office
               II.      Visit to overseas location
              III.      Debriefing with previous personnel in over-
                        seas location
```

If a process is complex and is not really organized chronologically, you may wish to select headings that give only the main points of that process. A good example is the self-learning exercises of software programs, which often begin with general headings of the entire process, then are divided into smaller segments. Microsoft *Word*[1] has such an approach.

```
Title:                  Learning Microsoft Word
General purpose:        To inform
Specific purpose:       To introduce users to the basic process of
                        learning Microsoft Word
Main points:    I.      Word disks
               II.      Microsoft Word manual
              III.      Word Pocket Guide
               IV.      Fast Results:  A Sampler
                V.      Quick Help
```

You should think of the kinds of visuals to supplement your process presentation. These may be self-created or taken—with proper citation, of course—from materials already available on your topic.

For instance, a Human Resources Manager might wish to use his or her "Main Points" headings on the visual aids, as taken from the following example:

```
Title:                  How to Develop an Employee Attitude Survey
General purpose:        To inform
Specific purpose:       To discuss phases of an employee survey
Main points:    I.      Decisions on survey and questions
               II.      Distribution and collection of question-
                        naires
              III.      Tabulation and analysis of data
               IV.      Implementation and follow-up
```

A detailed outline for development of an employee attitude survey might be similar to Figure 21-2, adapted from suggested plans by Leland G. Verheyen.[2]

Policy as Purpose

New employees often have a series of get-acquainted sessions wherein company policies are clarified. The topics can be on a process but can also clarify company policies or concepts. You therefore may inform groups on a new policy, a current policy, or changes to existing company policy.

In some ways policy speeches are more difficult to give than ones explaining the steps in a process or the functioning of a machine. With policies or directives

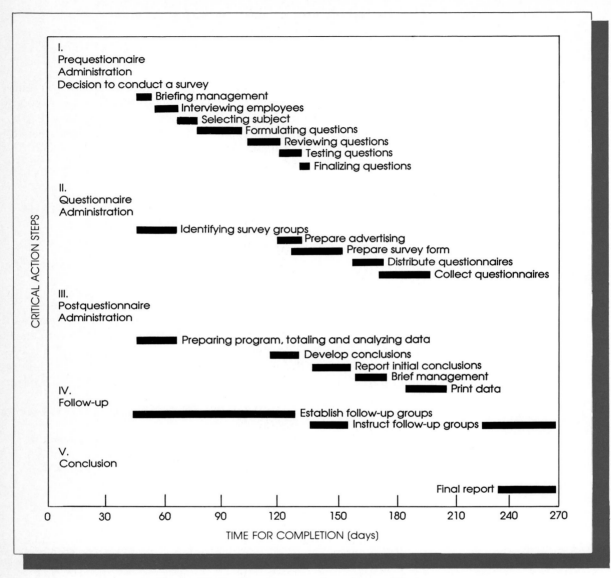

Figure 21–2 *Development of employee attitude survey.*

you deal with ideas more than with things that you can touch and feel or see. Visual aids, then, become valuable additions to your speeches on policy matters.

```
Title:              Drugs in the Workplace
General purpose:    To inform
Specific purpose:   To clarify company policy on use of drugs
                    in the workplace
```

```
Main points:    I.      Company definitions of what drugs are
                II.     Company policy on administered drug tests
                III.    Company evaluation of results and employee
                        rights
                IV.     Company rehabilitation policy

Title:                  Your Child in Day Care
General purpose:        To inform
Specific purpose:       To introduce employees to the new company
                        policy on day care
Main points:    I.      On-site day care facilities
                II.     Off-site day care facilities
                III.    Employee financial arrangements
```

KINDS OF INFORMATIVE SPEAKING

When you have done the preliminary analysis on purposes of your speech, you will present your information in one of these four types of informative situations: reports, community goodwill, briefings, instruction.

Reports

Ask some business people what they dislike most about weekly or monthly meetings. Frequently their response is "I don't like the reports; they're too long, too detailed—they don't hold my interest." Sadly, many oral reports fall into that category. Why? Because the speaker did little to make them interesting or to organize clearly.

Oral informative business reports include many kinds; among them are:

- Periodic department reports
- Progress reports on sales or ongoing committee activities
- Statements on area, division responsibilities
- Reports on manufacturing problems in the plant
- Reports on competitive operations
- Reports on problems with vendors
- Monthly personnel reports
- Abstract of contact reports for month

A weekly staff meeting, a monthly board of directors' meeting, a yearly stockholders' meeting, or even a yearly visit overseas to hear reports from functional units of a large multinational corporation can be the setting for making something clear to listeners.

A common characteristic of oral informative reports is that written material accompanies or precedes them. It is your decision whether to hand out in advance a brief abstract or executive summary, or to hand it out at the meeting. Longer progress or periodic reports—on which your oral report is based—are sent in advance, and at the meeting you add highlights and answer questions. The examples on pages 621 to 623 were first written, then speeches given as supplements.

Community Goodwill

Large organizations realize the value of remaining in contact with the community. To promote goodwill, companies devote considerable money supporting their public relations offices, seeking to offer and leave a positive company image in the community. While written communication often dominates in release of information to the public, the oral speech is often used.

Thus many companies have speakers' bureaus. Company employees—top-level executives—speak in a variety of public settings, often on topics about which the speakers have considerable knowledge. Announcements in local papers occasionally name topics on which employees will speak to local civic, church, or other community groups. Even agencies of the federal or state government present informative statements to the public. A phone call to a company's speaker's bureau or to a government public relations office or consumer affairs office could bring a speaker on topics as varied as the following:

- Preparing for a career with the public utility industry
- A history of solar energy
- Old power plants as early generators of electricity
- Protecting our environment
- Changes in the 199- income tax form
- Proposed DNR changes for refuse disposal

Frequently the speaker brings along a company-produced film as a supplement to the remarks. Needless to say, only the better speakers are selected to represent the company.

Less frequent, but also important, are the various other short goodwill-building talks. Long before you are a top-level executive, you may be asked to welcome visitors, introduce speakers, or confer awards within your company or in the community. Such talks have been discussed in Chapter 20.

Briefings

Some organizations define "short" problem-solving sessions as *briefings*—in which are offered information, background, options, alternatives, pro and con sides of arguments, which management must have before making a decision. Often you as a staff person will make concise presentations to a group of executives, giving them facts and opinions, then letting them make the final decision, based on your analysis.

For instance, a utility preparing for an increase in utility rates (a rate case) had numerous brief staff meetings to decide on which strategies to follow. A chronology of topics in preparation for its rate case followed this pattern:

1. Selection of rate case manager

2. Selection of potential witnesses

3. Meeting of all team members to select initial strategy

4. Writing and redrafting of case

5. Assembly of final case of direct testimony

6. Rehearsal of witnesses; work with manager

7. Filing of case

8. Rehearsal in preparation for cross-examination before public service commissioners.

Hence, there are many meetings, occasionally several a week, to hear oral informative statements and to make decisions. Much informative speaking precedes any final decision in the world of business.

Instruction

A common belief is that the longer you are with a firm the more instruction you will give: to younger employees, to others who can benefit from your experience. Your responsibility may be to instruct either several people or on some occasions an entire class of recruits new to the firm. The central goal, again, is to make clear a process, policy, or even the philosophy of the company.

Your goal as an instructor is to have listeners follow your explanations, learn from your instruction, and then apply it within the organization. Examples of topics offered in an organization are these:

- Using our word processor—an introduction
- Completing the sickness and accident forms
- Setting up a retirement plan
- Using recent tax law changes in auditing
- Conserving energy

Speaking in such situations as reporting, community goodwill, and briefings gives you less freedom than when instructing. Here you have more room for individual creativity: choice of subtopics, arrangement of material, structure of the classroom.

That there is a need to teach employees to instruct more effectively has not gone unnoticed. Some universities offer in their management or education programs, for example, seminars on training the trainer, training in the organization, and instructional development workshops.[3] All of these seminars focus on one core idea: preparing employees to do a better job of managing, and then preparing them to instruct others.

ANALYSIS OF AUDIENCE

If possible, learn several things about your audience: their attitudes and some general characteristics. Consider also the occasion and the location for your speech.

Some things you will not know in advance, nor find out about until you arrive. An entirely new audience, for instance, will be harder to assess than one you have appeared before many times. For example, a large firm bought out a smaller 44-member firm, and an executive wished to explain—in a formal talk to all employees and in small group meetings—a new health policy. Only after the speaker arrived did the president of the small firm state this admonition: "Down here we're used to speaking straight. Let me do all the talking and explaining. You just answer questions, and we'll do all right."

Attitudes

Helpful here is noting the familiar five-part continuum used in forced-choice questionnaires. Figure 21-3 places degrees of familiarity on a five point scale, from 1 "Very Familiar" to 5 "Very Unfamiliar."

Allied to familiarity is another factor, an audience's degree of interest. Figure 21-4 is also constructed according to values, from "Very Interested" to "Very Uninterested."

If your assessment shows that an audience is very familiar with the topic, you omit the elementary, the obvious, the simple, and go on to a more advanced explanation. Conversely, an audience totally unfamiliar with the topic would require a more basic explanation. You could ask:

- How much do my listeners know about the topic?
- What is their level of comprehension?
- What percentage of the group is well informed? Uninformed?

Knowing where most people lie on the familiar-unfamiliar, interested-uninterested continuum permits more precise adaptation to the audience's characteristics. For instance, assemblers on a production line would probably be less aware of management principles such as organizing, directing, and controlling than would top-level executives. Speaking about management principles to production personnel would therefore require more examples, more definitions, and more background.

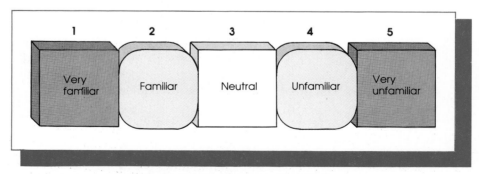

Figure 21–3 *Degrees of familiarity.*

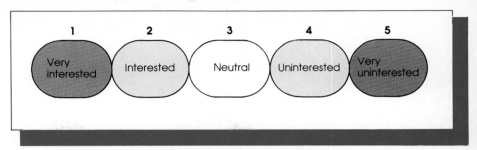

Figure 21–4   *Degrees of interest.*

An uninterested audience requires that you get its attention: through show-ing the value of the material, bringing in examples of the topic's importance to others in the company, using a videotape or film, asking for a senior officer of the company to introduce you, or involving the audience through questions and answers. Anything you can do when using attention getters such as suspense, conflict, familiarity, novelty, or humor will help your cause.

Occasion

Within organizations most of your speaking will occur during meetings, either to members of your own work group or to other functional areas. Daily, weekly, or monthly staff meetings are a way to review the progress of the company. Thus your analysis of the occasion is not as difficult as when speaking to persons outside an organization. Your own work group is relatively constant, many of the same people being present from session to session.

When speaking to outside groups, you must devote more thought to the occasion. Are you the main speaker? Are you first or last on a program? Is the meeting a regular meeting or one specially called to hear you? How much time has been allowed for your talk? Is the occasion formal or informal? Other questions can readily be supplied, but your task is to consider the occasion and your place in the proceedings, and then to adapt your material.

Location

Each location has its own peculiar environment. Members of company speakers' bureaus have spoken in church basements, large auditoriums, small conference rooms, even in the lounge of a local bar.

Determine the physical arrangements. Will you speak from behind a table or a podium on a stage? How far will you be from the audience—near the first row or some distance away? And perhaps most important of all, will you have a public address system that functions well?

In informative speaking, you will likely use visual aids to supplement your remarks. You must be heard. Your overheads and slides must be seen. You must know whether you have room to move about. Not knowing anything about the location has caused speakers to communicate poorly.

General Characteristics

When regularly speaking to the same group members, you may know them well; you probably have been friends for some time. You know their approximate ages, their functions in the company, their sex, the size of the group, something about their education and special interests, and the clubs to which they belong. This knowledge permits you to omit or include familiar information, for better understanding of the topic.

Speaking to outside groups is more of a challenge. To adapt examples to their interests you should find out whether the group is young, middle-aged, or older and something about its education, and perhaps also its occupations or interests in general.

To summarize, audience attitudes on a subject affect the level of adaptation you will use in informing. Knowing the occasion will give you some idea as to your precise involvement in the session. Understanding the location will affect your choice of visuals and degree of formality. And knowing some general characteristics will permit specific references to the interests and backgrounds of the audience.

ORGANIZATION AND OUTLINE OF THE INFORMATIVE SPEECH

Your preparatory work is over. You have determined the kind of informative talk you will give, stated your specific purpose, analyzed your audience. You have begun collecting data and, if desirable, planned visual aids as discussed in Chapter 20. Now you must organize your information into a clear pattern. Since ancient times (Chapter 1), speeches have been constructed in three parts: introduction, body (text, or discussion), summary or conclusion. These are now discussed, along with how to organize the entire speech.

Main Parts of the Speech

Introduction

Here are six ways that introductions for informative speeches may begin:

1. *State your purpose.*

    "I'm here to discuss three major costs connected with product liability."

    "Today I'll concentrate on the cultural problem abroad regarding different concepts of keeping time."

"Management has approved two changes in health care benefits for employees; the memo sent you earlier explained them. I'd like to review them with you and then answer questions."

2. **Tell an anecdote, appropriate joke, or good-natured story relating to your subject.**

"Funny things happen to people between 40 and 60; here's one incident that's common to that group."

"An interesting communication story is of a speaker mistaking a restroom in a London airport. I'll begin there."

"Merit pay increases may have two definitions: the company's and mine. You'll like mine better."

3. **Use a quotation that gives some background or inspiration to your speech.**

"As Oliver Wendell Holmes wrote, 'A great thing in this world is not so much where we stand as in what direction we are moving.' That's my theme: In which direction are we headed?"

" 'No man is an island,' John Donne said. That's the basic idea we promote in this company."

" 'The shadows are lengthening for me. The twilight is here.' The words of General MacArthur in 1962 are not a drumroll for ending; they were the beginning of a new resolve for the rest of us."

4. **Greet your audience sincerely.**

"Two places I especially enjoy coming to are home and your community. It's good to be with you."

"The sound of your applause is indeed a warm greeting; I thank you. It's good to be here."

5. **Make a startling statement.**

"By the end of my talk, over 2,000 new babies will have been born: over 1,800 people will have died."

"Last year we had the lowest turnover rate in the industry, 6 percent."

"One of you has just won dinner for two. A look on page 27 of the workbook, with my signature, indicates the lucky winner."

6. **Ask questions that make audiences start to think.**

"Let me begin by asking some general questions: What's the average age of a company president? Which area of study do managers say is the most important in reaching the top?"

"Three questions are foremost: What are the architectural plans for the company condominiums?—Who gets first claim on applying for entrance?—How much will they cost?"

After your appropriate, pleasant beginning, you can continue the introduction by supplying whatever definitions, background information, or topics will help orient your listeners. State the limits, if any, you will impose on your discussion. The end result of your introduction is that you have clarified your specific purpose and gotten their attention. You may do two more things in the introduction: set the direction and offer a layout of where you will go.

"Now I'll discuss the values of three different advertising campaigns: first, print media; second, television; and third, door hangers."

"Our goal is to focus on regulations affecting employment of the handicapped. We are concerned with that topic in three ways."

"Four amendments are important in the food and drug laws; let's look at each of them."

Body (Text, or Discussion)

Known variously as the *body*, the *discussion*, the *text*, or the *main section*, this part of your speech supports your specific purpose. Here, major themes are developed, leading to understanding.

In organizing this main section of your informative speech you can choose from several ways to make ideas clear.

1. By Topical Organization. This means you organize topics into natural divisions or into some kind of general classification. No two people organize a topic in an identical manner; each would be correct according to his or her own purpose. A speech on "The Automobile as a People Mover" could be variously organized:

```
    I. The electrical system        I. Rubber and its use in an
   II. The lubrication system or       automobile
  III. The cooling system          II. Plastics as a major por-
                                        tion of the automobile
                                   III. Steel's contribution to
                                        an automobile.
```

You decide on the major sections in the body of your speech. Then—to make those sections clear—determine the supports (as discussed later in this chapter).

2. By Chronological Organization. Listeners like to follow material according to the order in which events or happenings take place: past, present, and future. That's chronological. The previous discussion in this chapter on process as a purpose in informative speaking, page 620, suggested that chronological organization was common in matters having a sequence of events. If that sequence is obvious, has a beginning and ending, has a definite sequential motion, has a prescribed order of events, use the chronological order.

An informational speech on "Steps in Preparing a Utility Rate Case" could have the following major headings:

```
  I. Background material needed [earliest]
 II. Staff to work on project [later]
III. Major final arguments [latest]
```

Instructing a group of middle managers on "Preparing for Meetings" could include:

```
  I. Decisions before the meeting
 II. Notification of members
III. Arrangements for the meeting
 IV. The leader's role
  V. The participants' role
 VI. Evaluating the meeting
```

While the headings in the above example are chronological—from before the meeting to after the meeting—you may use your own subheadings within the chronological pattern.

3. By Cause to Effect.   We know that certain pressures and stimuli cause other things to happen: pressing down on the accelerator makes a car go faster; opening a refrigerator door lets cool air escape; investing money in a bond results in dividend payments; advertising a sale should bring in more customers.

In the preceding examples there is a high chance that the causes produced the stated effects. If the cause were not there, no effect would have occurred. But three caveats are noteworthy in considering causal reasoning.

a. Avoid assuming that a single cause produces a precise result.

Effect	**Questionable Cause**
Low earnings per share	are not solely the result of decreased sales.
Spelling errors	may or may not be due to a faulty spell-checker.
Takeovers and mergers	are not entirely due to the actions of greedy people.
Your low raise	is not wholly due to your boss's not liking you.
A low grade on an assignment	does not necessarily mean the instructor dislikes you.

b. Avoid assuming a false connection, that is, presuming that because one event occurred after another the two are linked. In the following examples, ask yourself if there is a precise, infallible connection between the cause and the effect.

Effect	False Linking Causes
Sales were up in 199-	after new management took over.
The consulting area of the Big Eight has grown	since deregulation.
She's been a problem	since she's been here.
Unemployment is up,	stocks are down.
I got an A;	I changed instructors.

   c. Realize there may be multiple causes, some major, some minor. Not all causes are of equal value. A speaker who states that a minor cause is major is open to challenge. Such is often the basis of argument—discussed in the next chapter—as two different teams or individuals try to determine causes for a problem and try to correct it.

You frequently may use cause-to-effect organization. Select carefully what you presume to be the main causes, but be prepared to defend that selection.

An informative talk on "Rumors in the Organization" could have these headings in the body of the speech:

```
    I. Causes of company rumors
       A. Wishful thinking
       B. Dislike for certain procedures
       C. Attitudes of individuals

   II. Effects of rumors
       A. Lower morale in company
       B. Distortion of facts
```

Most often the preceding three organizational patterns are used in informative speaking. One could also organize by the familiar to the unfamiliar (easiest to hardest), location (east to west, top to bottom, left to right), or question (how, what, when, where, why). Regardless of the method, clear organization of ideas is essential so that listeners understand the presentation.

Summary

A well-organized informative speech should have a well-organized summary. This is where you briefly pull together the two or three main points of your speech, telling the audience—as is done at the end of each chapter in this book—what are the major points to remember. It helps the audience to recall what was presented.

If your informative talk has true symmetry, the summary will closely mirror the purpose and layout as expressed in your introduction.

INTRODUCTION

> In January 199-, MCA announced that it had agreed with Nip-
> pon Steel Corporation of Japan to explore various types of
> joint opportunities in the entertainment and leisure field.
> You asked that I investigate some of those possibilities and
> provide both positive and negative views on various options
> and then come in with a recommendation.

SUMMARY:

> In summary, current successes of theme parks in Japan offer
> great opportunities for our company. My review of several
> options, both pluses and minuses, leads to one recommenda-
> tion: MCA and Nippon Steel should establish a joint venture
> tour and entertainment facility in Tokyo.

While the summary may closely mirror the introduction, using a visual aid—perhaps the same one used in the beginning of the speech—is a good way to add visual emphasis and provide a frame for the entire speech.

Outline of the Speech

Before delivering your oral informative talk, outline it. This task is as essential as for a written report. The structure most often used is a complete sentence outline, alone or in combination with a key-word outline. Beginning speakers tend to use more detail; then, as they gain confidence, they turn to a more skeletal form.

The following example suggests how a short topical outline might look for the introduction, body (discussion), and summary of an informative talk to a group of consultants in a Big Eight accounting firm. Note that the specific purpose occurs first in the introduction. It is there because not all members may know the purpose or some may have forgotten. Then, too, there may be guests, with less preparation. Take a moment to explain your purpose, particularly when the audience may be uninformed or when the topic is noncontroversial.

EXAMPLE 1   *Outline of informative talk.*

> Title: Those Who Lead: Top-Level Executives in U.S. Busi-
>   ness
> Purpose: To inform
>
>   Introduction
>
>   I. Specific purpose: To inform you about three character-
>   istics of chairmen and chairwomen, presidents, and
>   vice presidents in U.S. business.

```
 II. Three Trivial Pursuit questions set the direction of
     my talk:
     --In which functional area in business do most execu-
       tives begin their careers?
     --What percentage of executives received just a high
       school education?
     --What percentage of executives' spouses hold a full-
       time job?

III. Background to those questions will include career pat-
     terns, education, and personal background.

                              Body

 IV. Career patterns of executives
     A. First, second, and third job area
     B. Size of company for which they work
     C. Average salary of male and female executives
  V. Education of executives
     A. Levels of education
     B. Kinds of undergraduate degrees
     C. Recommendations to students regarding their under-
        graduate work

 VI. Personal background of executives
     A. Income level of their parental home
     B. Parents' dominant occupation
     C. Occupation of spouse

                            Summary

VII. Most executive careers began in finance in companies
     with a gross operating revenue in excess of $200 mil-
     lion a year.  They have average salaries of $129,000
     for males and $87,000 for females.

VIII. They are highly educated, less than 0.02% having only
      a high school education.  As undergraduates, most ma-
      jored in engineering and business; they recommend that
      same kind of preparation for students today.

 IX. Most come from middle-income homes, and their parents
     worked in professional areas.  Less than 10% of execu-
     tives' spouses work full time.

  X. The foregoing information should have added to your
     understanding about people who head U.S. companies.
     You may wish to do further research to better prepare
     yourself for responsible executive work in the busi-
     ness world.
```

It's your decision on how detailed an outline you wish to construct. Some speakers first create a more fully developed outline, even a script; then rehearse it; then edit again, ending with a shorter version for use as their presentation notes. The preceding informative outline was quite detailed, including some complete sentences. If you were confidently familiar with the topic, you could shorten it to a version similar to this second example.

EXAMPLE 2   *Outline of informative talk (example 1 condensed).*

```
Title:    Those Who Lead: Top-Level Executives in U.S. Busi-
          ness
Purpose:  To inform

                           Introduction
    I. Chairmen and chairwomen, presidents, VPs in U.S. busi-
       ness

   II. Three Trivial Pursuit questions:
       --Where executives begin careers?
       --How many received HS education?
       --Spouses in full-time jobs?

  III. Career patterns, education, and personal

                              Body

   IV. Careers:  jobs, company size, average salary

    V. Education:  levels, undergrad, recommendations on un-
       dergrad degree

   VI. Personal:  income-home; parents' occupation; spouse's
       occupation

                            Summary

Career patterns; highly educated; middle-income home
```

SUPPORT FOR INFORMATIVE SPEECHES

Clarity and understanding are the core purposes of informative speaking. To accomplish these tasks requires, in addition to clear organization, evidence. Facts and opinions are two categories of evidence that provide support for your ideas.

Facts and Opinions

Information presented for evidence may include demonstrable or historical facts and, sometimes, opinions.

Demonstrable Facts

Facts include information that is verifiable. *Demonstrable facts* are ones we personally experience when collecting data for our talk: through conducting interviews or our own survey or through reading what others have said on a topic. If co-workers have data about a subsidiary in London, and they are reliable observers, there is no need for you to visit London to get the same facts. Demonstrable facts are secured firsthand through personal observation and examination, but lacking that we depend on other verifiable sources.

Historical Facts

Historical facts are true information from the past. We accept last year's earnings per share because there are records to verify them. If we have not seen past information, we depend on those reliable persons, writers, authors, executives who have seen or worked with the data. You can see that the validity of historical facts is only as good as the sources—people, publications, citations—on which you depend.

Opinions

The preceding two categories are realities that are verifiable and observable by several people, in whom you have confidence. *Opinions*, for the most part, draw a conclusion, infer from data, and conclude. You can see that a fact is highly reliable. An opinion is less so, because it expresses a judgment; it is only as valid as the person expressing that judgment. Thus if you make a statement on a subject of which you know little, your opinion has little weight. On the other hand, if you speak about your area of expertise, your opinion is more accepted.

What makes your opinion or that of others more qualified? Your education is a main criterion. So is your work experience, your background, your position in the company. A B.B.A. or M.B.A. degree is a visual cue that you have gained some expertise in understanding business. Your remarks on the economy would have more reliability than a nonbusinessperson's remarks.

We will now turn to how facts and opinions are used in various forms of support in informative speaking, and other forms of speaking as well.

Seven Forms of Support

Facts and opinions are used in either written or oral form. Here we focus only on the oral clarification and supports for your ideas. Seven common support and clarification methods using facts and opinions are *examples, illustrations, statistics, quotations, analogies, definitions, and repetition and restatement.*[4]

Examples

Of all ways to make ideas clear, the example is used most often. It is a brief, specific instance, holding attention and clarifying at the same time.

"For instance, out of 5,299 companies included in our response, less than 500 executives worked in industries with a gross operating revenue of less than $100 million yearly."

"For example, when executives were asked where they would like to begin their careers if starting over again, at least 25 percent replied they would recommend the area of marketing and sales."

While the above examples present clear ideas about the topic of top executives, based on facts and generally valid findings, you may also turn to hypothetical examples, those not founded on fact. You could make up a situation, put the listener into a hypothetical example, perhaps beginning with "Suppose you were an executive. What changes would you make in your career path . . . ?" But when in doubt, try to remain with verifiable (and, therefore, credible) information.

Illustrations

An easy way to remember what an illustration is, is to think of it as an elongated example; it amplifies a point in detail. Some call this method "explanation" or, even, "story," but regardless of its name an illustration holds the attention of an audience.

"One illustration will make my point clear: Our executive is male, is married in over 80 percent of the instances to his first wife, and considers his home life more important than his job. He is also devoted to his spouse, considers her of utmost importance in offering emotional support and maintaining a satisfying and well-run home. In this regard, his wife is perceived as ministering to his personal needs, as well as being involved in other aspects of his life not directly related to work. Top executives illustrate concern for the home, more so than most of us think."

Statistics

In business, "number crunching" provides the raw material of many written and oral reports. But remember that while numbers clarify, too many of them, too much detail, or too many abstract figures can cloud instead of clarify. Do not rattle off a long series of figures without relating them to the audience's level of understanding. Preferably, round off figures, and for clarity use precise numbers in place of such general terms as *many, some, few,* or *most.*

Figures can be made even more vivid when you can refer or point to them on a visual aid; then listeners can both hear and see the statistics you're using to clarify.

"Taken as a whole, newly promoted executives come from middle-income homes (57.5 percent), followed by lower-income (29.9 percent) and upper-income homes (12.6 percent). Interestingly, more chairmen (70 percent) come from homes of lower- and upper-income families than do presidents and vice presidents. As a generalization, nearly a third of newly promoted executives come from relatively humble beginnings."

Quotations or Testimony

Frequently an audience desires to hear what others have to say on your topic. You may have done your research well, but your credibility improves through occasionally turning to the words of others. A *literal* quotation or testimony states the words of a true expert, a genuinely informed person on a topic. It is the kind of quotation most often used in business speaking.

A *literary* quotation uses the words of a source more for their emotional, philosophical support. Thus a quotation from Shakespeare or Abraham Lincoln or a poem could be used at an award ceremony or retirement party, or as a way to get an audience's attention in the introduction to a speech. In a business meeting you clearly would use the *literal* quotation.

Analogies (Comparisons)

Analogies help to make the unknown clear by comparing it to the known. Thus in speaking of an auto fuel pump (relatively unknown) we compare its pumping action to that of the human heart (generally known), or in speaking of departments in an organization (sometimes unknown) we may compare them to slices of a pie (quite well known). These are *figurative* analogies, comparing something relatively unknown to something more familiar.

Literal analogies—most often used in business—are comparisons between things in the same class, same category, same overall group. You could, for example, compare a classroom (known) with another classroom (probably unknown); the earnings per share in the current year (known) with a previous year (probably unknown or forgotten).

At best only a degree of similarity exists between any two comparisons, yet the analogy is a common way to clarify and make a topic vivid.

Definitions

Definitions are not exactly forms of support, yet they clarify and define the meaning the speaker will employ in informative speaking. Defining terms puts everyone, speaker and audience, on common ground.

> "Here is my understanding of who is included in the term 'top-level executive': CEOs (chairmen of the board), presidents, and vice presidents. 'Middle managers' are those people I shall position below the level of the vice president."

The preceding definition is the speaker's definition. He did not depend on the dictionary, but defined "top-level executive" as he wished the term defined. Such a definition oriented listeners to his subject, put them in his frame of reference, and removed from their minds other definitions they may have heard previously.

Dictionaries are adequate sources for how words are used *in general*. As a speaker you have the responsibility to convey to your listeners the *specific* meaning you intend. If you intend a meaning not in the dictionary, you must make that meaning clear to your audience.

Repetition and Restatement

How many times do you have to repeat an idea before it is remembered? "Three times" is often mentioned: at the beginning, the middle, and the end of a talk. Regardless of where you present ideas again, you have two ways of doing so: repetition and restatement.

Repetition is the repeated statement of an idea in basically the same words.

Restatement is rephrasing an idea through other words.

Not everyone may draw a distinction between the two terms, but remember that learning relies on repetition and restatement, a principle particularly relevant to informative speaking.

Try all the preceding seven forms of support in your informative speaking; use them to clarify and to hold attention. If you use them well, your audience will say, "Well, that's the clearest explanation I've ever heard on that topic."

SUMMARY

The general purpose of informative speaking is to make ideas clear and to secure understanding. The specific purpose relates to effecting a precise result. To accomplish this may require specific explanations and visual aids regarding steps in a process or details in policy matters.

Business speaking is often informative and may be in the form of (1) giving an oral report, often based on your written report, (2) presenting useful information orally in briefings before important decisions are made, (3) instructing or teaching within an organization, or (4) speaking for the organization in a goodwill capacity, frequently to outside groups. Clearly, you are a teacher in all these situations.

Audience analysis must occur early in planning for informative speaking, so that you can adapt your material to the level of your audience. Such preparation demands that you have knowledge about your listeners. How much do they know about your topic? What are their attitudes, the occasion, the location, and general factors such as sex, age, and size of the audience?

Informative speaking is organized in the traditional pattern of introduction, body, and summary. You first get the attention of the audience in your introduction through such ways as (1) stating your purpose, (2) telling an anecdote, (3) using a quotation, (4) greeting the group, (5) making a startling statement, or (6) asking thoughtful questions. You may also include brief background material, if desirable, and usually include a forecast of major sections your speech will cover.

The body—the main discussion section—of the talk, including detailed support for your specific purpose, usually is organized by topics, by chronological order, or by cause to effect. Throughout, interest is held through clear transitions, vivid examples, and clear organization.

A summary is a common way to end an informative talk. In it you state concisely the main points, perhaps adding why the information was important and where one could go for additional detail.

Preparing a well-organized outline is essential before delivering a successful speech. It may be a detailed sentence outline, useful especially for beginning speakers, or a brief topical outline, for experienced speakers.

To make informative talks clear you should use facts and opinions. Various forms of support for them include (1) examples, (2) illustrations, (3) statistics, (4) quotations, (5) analogies, (6) definitions, and (7) repetition and restatement. Not using supports will leave the talks abstract and unclear.

Our focus has been on the oral; audio-visual aids can also be used to assist clarification.

EXERCISES AND PROBLEMS

1. *Information speech to peers:* Prepare an informative speech on any topic of your choice. Your goal is to make clear an idea to an audience of peers. As you prepare the talk, be sure to do the following: use clear organization, support your specific purpose with a variety of support forms, and deliver with desirable pitch, rate, and volume. For a three- to five-minute talk, use the following format:

```
Title: _____
General purpose: to inform

                         Introduction

   I. Specific purpose _____
  II.

                            Body

 III.
  IV.
   V.

                          Summary

  VI.
 VII.
```

2. ***Informative speech to clarify an idea or explain a purpose:*** Prepare an informative presentation that makes an idea clear or explains a process. This speech should be about four to six minutes in length. Criteria are organizational clarity, a good delivery, and content that supports your ideas. Try also to use visual aids. You may choose from these topics or others:

> The steps involved in buying stock
>
> What is meant by the "invisible hand" in business
>
> Characteristics of rejection letters
>
> How a word processor works
>
> What is meant by "first-in–last-out" in the accounting field

3. ***Oral report using information from corporate annual reports:*** The corporate annual report is perhaps the best known and most widely circulated business report. Virtually every public, college, and university library receives copies of annual reports from business and industrial firms. Some libraries catalog the printed reports and store them in filing cabinets; others store annual reports in some other form, such as on microfiche or microfilm.

   Your assignment here is to make an oral report, using information collected from corporate annual reports. You will concentrate on a comparison of certain key financial ratios for the company or companies chosen. Information on computing ratios (such as the current ratio, the acid-test ratio, the net-profit-to-net-sales ratio, and the inventory-turnover ratio) can be found in most financial management textbooks or in *Key Business Ratios*, a booklet available free from Dun & Bradstreet, Inc.

   You have your choice of two options in making the comparisons. The first option is to choose *one* company and make a comparison of at least three ratios computed for each of two recent years. Of course, you will compute the ratios yourself. Obviously, your comparisons must be between ratios that compare the same things. For example, you could choose to compare the current ratio, and acid-test ratio, and the inventory-turnover for Company X for the two most recent years.

   The second option is to compare the ratios computed for *two* companies, using annual reports for the *same* fiscal year. For example, you could compare the current ratio, the acid-test ratio, and the net-profit-to-net-sales ratio for Company A for the most recent year with the same ratios of Company B for the same year.

   To make your presentation complete, explain how the ratios were computed and what the ratios mean. For this purpose, you should prepare a visual aid (such as a poster or a transparency for use with an overhead projector). A visual aid should also be used to enhance your comparison of the ratios between years or companies.

   The time limits for your report will be assigned by your instructor. In most instances, the report called for here will fall in the four- to six-minute range.

4. **Evaluations of introductions:** The press appears to give much attention to business and government speakers. Their speeches are often printed in their entirety, in such places as *Vital Speeches*, The Economic Club of Detroit, the *New York Times,* and other publications. For this exercise read the introductions to five different speeches. (1) Indicate what kind of introduction the speaker used based on those discussed in this chapter, and (2) determine whether the speaker used that type of introduction effectively.

5. **Assessing periodicals for credibility:** After reading this chapter you should be more attuned to the credibility of sources used for your facts and opinions. Daily you are bombarded with visual and auditory stimuli. And it is from some of these stimuli that you collect forms of support for your speeches, or papers.

   Divide a paper into two parts, as follows:

   ```
   NAME OF
   PERIODICAL                ASSESSMENT

   1.                        1.
   2.                        2.
   ```

   On the left side name a periodical (daily paper, magazine), on the right side assess the credibility of that publication as a source for financial news. Number one could be your selection as the most credible source; your last number in that column—at least five—could be your lowest-ranking source. Give reasons—support why one periodical has higher credibility than another.

6. **Noting comparisons between an informative talk and a stockholder letter:** Go to your library and locate three different annual reports. These could be in similar product categories (all chemical or all automotive or all fast-food, for example). Read only the letter to the stockholders, usually signed by the president or CEO (chief executive officer). Your task will be to determine answers to the following questions:
   a. Is the structure similar to that of an informative speech? Does it have an introduction, body, and conclusion?
   b. What is the specific purpose of the letter?
   c. Is the letter informative or persuasive? Why?
   d. What forms of evidence are used in the letter?
   e. Was the letter effective?

Successful Persuasive Speaking

Advertisements bombard us daily with appeals: buy this object, try this product, go on this cruise, invest your money here, sign on the bottom line, send in a reply. Oral, visual, and written media carry persuasive messages.

While the above examples illustrate general persuasion directed to us through TV, newspapers, radio, and magazines, business organizations also use persuasion. In fact, the early chapters in this book have many examples on how to get readers to accept your idea.

Chapter 21 focused on the informative end of the communication continuum, making an idea clear. Now we will look at the other end of the continuum, persuading others to accept your point of view. Five major divisions of this chapter look at the purposes of persuasive speaking, the kinds of persuasive speaking, the importance of audience analysis, organization of your ideas to persuade, and use of supports for your persuasive position.

PURPOSES OF PERSUASIVE SPEAKING

The *general* purpose of persuasive speaking is to get listeners to accept willingly your idea or point of view. The key word is "willingly." Your goal is that after you have finished your presentation, listeners will accept your proposal, do as you ask them to do, follow where you suggest they go.

The *specific* purpose is the precise response you wish your audience to give. Phrasing your specific purpose in infinitive form will channel your thinking into a precise statement of purpose.

Vague Specific Purpose:	Better Specific Purpose
The United Fund	To convince listeners that the United Fund makes many positive contributions to the community
College Recruiting	To persuade the staff that company recruiters should interview at state colleges in addition to the large state universities
Teleconferencing	To convince the group that our own in-house teleconferencing equipment will be cost-effective compared with rental of such equipment
Japan as the Theme	To recommend that X company, in conjunction with Y company, develop a theme park in Japan

When you have determined your general purpose (to persuade) and selected an interesting title that gets attention, you turn to stating the precise response you wish to get from your audience.

Persuasion is difficult. The more thoughtful you are and the more time you take in preparing carefully—as in the informative speeches—the better chance for later success. It is a good idea to write out the specific purpose. The purpose becomes the central theme around which you build your speech to achieve the desired response. Note in the following examples how the titles get attention. The general purpose reminds you of the overall goal; and the specific purpose, in an infinitive phrase, is exact.

```
Title:              Effective Employee Training Techniques
General purpose:    To persuade
Specific purpose:   To recommend that all instructors in the
                    company training program enroll in the
                    course "Effective Training"

Title:              Enchanting Summer Interns
General purpose:    To persuade
Specific purpose:   To recommend using guidelines, orientation
                    booklets, and a feedback mechanism for im-
                    proving work with summer interns

Title:              Seven Days of Reporting
General purpose:    To persuade
Specific purpose:   To convince listeners that four changes have
                    to be made in the weekly sales reports
```

KINDS OF PERSUASIVE SPEAKING

Each of the advertisements (stimuli) directed at you has a precise purpose (response) in mind. Ad agencies, for example, hired by corporations exist for several purposes: to create a favorable image of the client, to sell the product to consumers, and to devise strategic plans involving all media. Large companies have their own departments or depend on outside companies to help implement company persuasion goals. Some examples include:

- PR (public relations)[1] firms—in the thousands—seek to enhance the image of a company or even an individual in society.
- Internal company PR departments write speeches for executives, oversee internal communication, and handle news releases for the public.
- Advertising agencies—also in the thousands—write advertising copy (persuasion) directed at the public.
- Private consultants work with smaller firms on their public persuasion.
- Lobbyists for organizations, companies, universities, government agencies, all seek to "sell"—persuade for various reasons.

At first glance you might presume that the written medium is a major part of the above-mentioned groups. It is important, but oral persuasion plays just as significant a role. So you, as a member of a PR company or an ad agency, as a staff member in your company's own PR department, or as an employee, will use oral persuasion to get your ideas accepted.

Opportunities to persuade are endless; however, persuasion can be classified into four major categories: policy, procedure, value, or fact.

Policy

Policy refers to a course of action that should or should not be taken. Policy is formulated in response to questions such as the following:

- Should our company divest its holdings in companies doing business in South Africa?
- What should our policy be concerning adding Martin Luther King's birthday to the list of elective vacation days?
- Should the committee's two recommended options concerning health care providers be given to employees?
- Which procedure should the company follow in accepting outside bids on a new warehouse?
- How should we react to the government's request that we collect for savings bonds?
- What should company policy be for using company computers at home?
- How many follow-up collection letters should be sent before we engage an outside collection agency?

Try answering the above questions. Some of you will immediately seize upon a single solution, while others will let several choices or answers run through their minds. Your goal in answering a policy question is to arrive at a decision and then recommend that decision to another person or group. To do that requires persuasion, supplying reasons for accepting your recommendation.

Be prepared to answer this audience question after you have made a policy proposal: Have you considered alternatives? None of the preceding questions can be answered with a simple "yes" or "no." Therefore, you must show that your solution—adopted after you have reviewed and then dropped other alternatives—is the one the group or individual should accept.

Also be prepared for changes to your proposal. In public groups parliamentary procedure permits formal first- and second-level amendments to proposals.[2] Corporate meetings move more informally, using fewer votes. Regardless, your persuasion may not be entirely over after making the presentation; questions and changes to your original proposal may occur. Thus, be prepared to defend your original position and be prepared to respond to proposed changes.

Procedure

Closely allied to policy questions and statements are those of procedure, that is, how should a policy be implemented? What steps should be carried out? Who should carry out the decision? Questions and statements of procedure parallel those seen in the discussion of process relating to informative speeches

(Chapter 21, pp. 620 to 621). There, speakers attempt to make a process clear; in persuasive speaking the speaker persuades that one procedure or process is better than another.

- What's the best way to assemble a bicycle?
- In formulating a PR strategy for the next year, which steps should we follow with our ad agency?
- In rewriting the company bylaws, where should items on the foreign subsidiaries be placed?
- Crises may hit our company. Which persons and offices should handle crisis communication?
- The agenda for the directors' meeting should have six major categories.
- Ranking of retirement benefits should be reordered according to this pattern. . . .
- Let's add the electrical harness for the automobile at step 12.

One has only to speak to employees in a manufacturing facility to learn that there are other ways of doing things. Company manuals, standard operating procedures (SOPs), and traditions play forceful roles in how things are carried out. When you propose changes to established procedures, you really have two tasks: you must first show why the previous system is inadequate, and you must persuade that your new proposal is better, and perhaps more cost-efficient and effective. An initial outline for a speech about a change in procedure may look like the following (taken from an actual study by a review committee):

```
Title:              Proposals: A Needed Change
General purpose:    To persuade
Specific purpose:   To recommend a change in proposal prepara-
                    tion for contracts over $1 million
Main points:  I.    Current preparation procedure
             II.    Problems with current method
                    A. To us as the proposers
                    B. To proposal requesters
            III.    Recommended changes to procedure
             IV.    Anticipated positive results of accepting
                    proposed changes
```

Visual aids often accompany requests for change from the current position. The proposal review committee in the above example used visual supports such as (1) cost figures, based on hours worked, for the several departments compiling the internal data; (2) memorandums which showed that several departments were working on the identical background information; (3) pages from the proposal—showing errors of fact and costing, poor grammar and spelling.

Additionally, the committee interviewed persons at the company soliciting the proposal and in so doing received overlapping data, some of which were inconsistent. They read written summaries of telephone contacts, again showing inconsistencies, and they even listened to a recorded telephone conversation in which obvious inaccuracies existed between the oral statements and printed material.

The end of the story is that all proposed procedural changes were accepted. Evidence in support of the changes by the proposal review committee was so varied and well presented that today—four years later—the procedures are still in place.

Presenting a new, first-time proposal is a bit easier. There, your persuasion is based on a process you may have worked out alone or in conjunction with a committee. In any event, recommending your procedural choice demands that the audience understand the process (informing) and reasons (persuasion) for the procedure.

Value

A question or statement of value involves a judgment, most often expressed in words.[3] Using many adjectives and adverbs to express our attitude and judgment may fail to convey our intent to the listener because of the many different connotations such modifiers have for people. In Chapter 21, pp. 635 to 639, we noted that facts are verifiable. Value judgments are harder, if not impossible, to quantify. How do you measure a precise emotional or attitudinal reaction to a word, an idea, or a person?

The following questions and statements imply a value judgment. Try to select the words that suggest how they differ from questions and statements of policy and procedure.

- What is it worth to our company to contribute funds to the Olympics?
- Would our publishing a newsletter for overseas personnel have any value?
- Will we benefit by appearing before the Investment Club of New York?
- Who are the better speakers in our organization?
- Which employee made the most significant contribution to the community this past year?
- It's unwise to compete in three areas at once.
- The personnel office is more trouble than it's worth.
- The X agency does a superior job.
- That's the poorest memorandum I've seen today.

A value judgment is needed to answer the questions above and react to the assertions. While you can still turn to facts to support your view, it is quite difficult, for instance, to find many facts in support of the term *better*. All of us carry around in our heads a concept of "better," but therein lies the problem: We must persuade others that our interpretation of the term *better* is the one to accept.

Words and their opposites, as in the following list, imply some kind of value judgment:

Fair/unfair	Honest/dishonest
Good/bad	Valuable/valueless
Interesting/uninteresting	Brave/cowardly
Beautiful/ugly	Advantageous/disadvantageous
Sincere/insincere	Modern/outdated
Leader/follower	Progressive/nonprogressive
Creative/noncreative	Traditional/modern

You may ask how does one handle value terms? In informative speaking (Chapter 21) one suggestion for clarity was *definition*. Define, early, what you mean by a *modifier*. For instance, the following is an adaptation of a statement made in an actual persuasive speech.

"I know that we will consider the matter closely, for that's the policy of this company. But I have one favor to ask. Keep in mind what I mean by 'acceptable.' For me it means that no worker will be displaced because of the changes; no parachute will be opened for employees here less than 15 years; no retirement benefits will be impacted in any way."

What the speaker did was laudatory: she defined and made public her criteria for her use of the term *acceptable*. This definition, in part, clarified her judgment term and permitted at least a crude form of measurement. It would be ludicrous to try to define each evaluative term we use. To define the statement "It's a nice day" or "That's a good memo" each time it's used goes beyond common sense, a quality needed in handling value situations.

Accordingly, define and clarify—but accept the idea that you may not be able to define and clarify every term, and that even when you do, there may still be disagreement on your interpretation. Your task when persuading on value judgments is to persuade the audience that your interpretation is correct.

Fact (Present or Past)

One would think that matters of fact should raise few questions as to what happened, when something occurred, or who did what? You are seeking answers to what is true and verifiable. But if you are alone in believing something is true, you may have to convince others of that position.

Business questions and statements of fact are represented in the following:

- What were our earnings per share in 199-?
- What did our letter of August 4, 199-, promise those who responded within two weeks?
- How many miles did the sales staff travel in November?

- What is the economic history of Hong Kong in its relationship to foreign banks?
- What is the cost per operation in our local hospital?
- Your department had the highest absenteeism in 199-.
- Our 10-K report was misquoted by the financial news services here and abroad.
- The dollar percentage quoted in the article was off by 5 percent.

On the surface, answers to questions of fact may appear clear—perhaps to only one person. Under close examination, some supposed facts may be totally in error, owing to a misreading of data, a misunderstanding of data entered into the computer, or a host of other reasons. Witness a court of law where 12 jurors try to decide the "facts" of a case; there is rarely 100 percent agreement, and in some cases so divergent are interpretations of facts that no decision is reached.

Or, note how many clarifying statements companies and the government send out if an apparent fact is taken out of context by writers, listeners, and readers. The situation of one executive, for example, and his joining and then leaving the board of directors of General Motors, is an example of clarification piled on clarification. Internal conflicts on what is true, what are the facts, can and do take considerable communication time.

Some facts may be wrong, for in a large company unintentional misrepresentation of facts may occur. We say "unintentional," yet unethical persons may deliberately alter figures to suit their own ends. Entrance to computer files, resulting in falsification of data, has been too common an occurrence.

Your goal, then, is to persuade listeners that your data are correct, verifiable, and acceptable.

Fact (Future)

A relatively new area for business is called *strategic planning*, laying out long-term goals for an entire company or for departments within that company. In stating these goals, many internal and external impediments must be considered. Since future planning is based on projections from the past, there is much guesswork involved. The speaker recommending future company directions will therefore face inaccuracies in data; he or she will have to predict future facts.

This book makes no attempt at analyzing the various statistical methods and probabilities regarding future data. Predicting the future, inevitably, is risky. Yet, few people can avoid offering interpretations of data, of facts that may impact a company's future. Some companies lay out their sales projections for an entire year, and adjust them every several months in view of changes affecting the original projections. All you can do is try to be as correct as possible, building on past facts as the foundation for future projections.

AUDIENCE ANALYSIS

The preceding chapter discussed audience attributes a speaker must know before informing. Here we review similar topics, but focus on persuasion: listener attitudes, the occasion, the location, and some general characteristics.

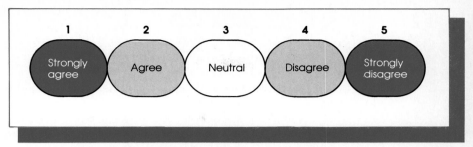

Figure 22–1   *Degrees of agreement.*

Attitudes

The discussion of attitudes in informative speaking (Chapter 21) focused on the characteristics of the familiar versus the unfamiliar and interested versus uninterested in an audience. Those same points pertain to persuasive speaking. Yet one factor more relevant for persuasion is the attitude of being for (pro) or against (con) your position.

Here too the five-point scale is relevant, knowing where your audience is on the agree-disagree continuum (Figure 22-1). Certainly you will not know precisely where an audience lies, but early soundings can give you a general sense of an audience's position.

Your assessment focuses on what you think the attitude of your audience is toward accepting your proposal. If they strongly agree with you, your task is easier; if they strongly disagree, your task is more difficult. We should *also differentiate two kinds of disagreement*.

1. An audience may disagree with your facts. That problem must be removed before you proceed toward the second point of opposition.

2. Unhappiness with your suggested action is the second negative attitude. It is more difficult to resolve. Here one faces the ingrained prejudices that deny listeners flexibility. They may be outright hostile toward your position, for any number of hidden reasons.

How can you face the hostile, prejudiced audience? Among various ways, you may possibly choose these two: search for commonality and compare agreements with disagreements.

Search for Commonality

A favorite technique of speakers facing a hostile audience is to begin with familiar, commonly accepted topics—before moving to the areas of disagreement. You begin inductively, using examples, illustrations, and goodwill comments that produce little disagreement. The following are a few desirable topics:

- Praise for the organization and its members
- Names of colleagues with whom you have worked for long periods of time
- Patriotism, group support, cooperation

A further listing of introductory comments is included in this chapter's section titled "Introduction," page 654.

Not all the above commonalities will work for all United States and foreign companies. Anytime one speaks in a foreign country or attempts to effect change, a new set of cultural adaptations to that country must be made. Chapter 25 discusses cultural concerns in more detail.[4]

Compare Agreements with Disagreements

A second approach to breaking down attitudinal hindrances to your position is to list prospective areas of agreement and disagreement before you give your speech. Such a listing depends heavily on facts but may also include value judgments. Your goal is to force yourself to see the areas of differences before you offer your main position. Labor negotiators when preparing their review of a controversy between two groups often use the parallel-column, agree-disagree approach.

A controversial day care issue in the workplace could have parallel agree-disagree columns, as in this example:

Agreements	Disagreements
1. On-site day care permits the mother to work.	1. A mother's place is in the home.
2. Five percent of industry today offers day care.	2. Costs will outweigh the advantages, and influence my earnings.
3. Children deserve the best care during their early, formative years.	3. Those with no children feel they are discriminated against and will not receive equal benefits.
4. Most people desire some kind of day care as part of their benefit package.	4. Rules and regulations will make the task difficult.
5. Child and parent share a closeness.	

The point is to collect facts that are accurate, for both sides of the issue. Then, as would a good debater, collect additional counterarguments on the points of disagreement, review what objections might be, and hope that your information produces a change in attitude.

Surely you are interested in the knowledge that audiences possess on your topic, but a series of questions can make more specific their depth of understanding on your proposal.

Does the audience know both the pro and con arguments surrounding my thesis?

To what extent has the audience collected information from a wide variety of sources?

Are some staff members already set in their attitudes against me and my topic? Is this the first time members will be exposed to my point of view on the issue?

How open-minded is the group to a different position, one radically different from their own?

Most of the above questions relate to audience attitude toward a topic, trying to assess their knowledge and perceptions. A group strongly opposed to your idea will force a change in your approach, while a more neutral group offers fewer problems.

Occasion

Corporate grapevines are often so accurate that you should sense the type of opposition to expect toward your position. A good secretary, a member of your staff, or an "assistant to" should know in advance the kinds of counterarguments to expect at a staff session, a discussion, or even a board of directors meeting. In your favor at regular staff meetings is the chair's predictable consistency in group leadership; thus, the procedure and occasion are well known and permit careful advance preparation. Knowing potential opposition arguments will permit you more extensive evidence gathering to counter those arguments.

Earlier we suggested that corporate meetings usually do not entangle themselves in formal voting; consensus (general agreement) is more common. However, some managers ask for votes on proposals. Again, a good corporate underground will tell you the opposition to expect at the occasion. It is well to know potential positional differences before you go to a meeting, and whether a decision will be made or delayed until later.

In meetings outside the corporation it is more difficult to summarize group attitudes. Indeed, there may not be a group attitude unless you are, for example, a supporter of nuclear power speaking to an antinuclear group. You may be asked to participate in a public debate, supporting your company's position in contrast to an outside opposing group; there you would know the format in advance and could bring in material strongly founded on logical supports. Here too you must know—particularly when addressing government groups on behalf of the company—whether your proposal is being given a first reading, or whether a decision will be made later. Knowledge of political parties and their position to your company's proposal is a must before attending a city government meeting.

Location

"Good luck on entering the lion's den" carries a meaning quite clear to business speakers: they're giving a speech on the home ground of the opposition. Presidential candidates must feel that way when addressing members of the opposition; as do public utility executives when addressing a state rate hearing; auto executives, when speaking to a congressional committee considering emission standards; CIA interviewers, when debating with certain student groups; or an advertising agency, when speaking to homeowners on expanding the agency offices into a residential area. These are examples of psychological and attitudinal problems, caused in part by the physical location of the meeting.

Surely size of the room, ventilation, heat, and light are important, but underlying all of these is the attitudinal influence of the room on you, the speaker. You cannot help but be affected, reacting to both the physical and the psychological pressures of the situation.

General Characteristics

Much of our discussion on audience analysis necessary for persuasive speaking has focused on attitudes, perceptions, biases, prejudices of groups. Often these attitudes get in the way of accepting a speaker's point of view; in addition, are the usual characteristics such as age, sex, size of the group, and even time of the presentation.

In sum, audience analysis for the persuasive speaker demands more research than does informative speaking, particularly for learning audience attitudes. Knowing those attitudes, the framework of the occasion, the influence of the location, and other aspects will help you to persuade with more assurance.

ORGANIZATION OF THE PERSUASIVE SPEECH

Assume you have analyzed your audience and the occasion, collected your material, and are now ready to arrange your data into a persuasive statement.

As in written sales messages, the AIDA organization works with persuasive speaking as well: attention, interest, desire, and action. The persuasive speech has an introduction, body (text, or discussion), and conclusion—as shown in the following discussion and outline.

Introduction

Chapter 6 states that when the reader is likely to consider a message favorably or at least neutrally, you can use the deductive or direct approach. Likewise, in speeches when you have good news and the chances of the audience's accepting your position are good, you can use deductive organization. Via this method you will in the beginning offer your specific purpose, request, proposition, solution, claim, resolution, or assertion. You can use the same kinds of openings for these persuasive statements as for informative speeches: giving a specific purpose, telling an anecdote, using a quotation, offering a greeting, making a startling statement, or asking a series of questions. Then you can follow with reasons and supports for that position.

In contrast, an audience that may react unfavorably to your persuasion or that has hostile attitudes toward the subject should be approached inductively, or indirectly. Announcing your position in the first sentence could turn off a hostile group. Listeners might sit there politely, but inwardly their bias or prejudice would deny giving you a fair hearing.

Approaching a hostile audience is similar to meeting a stranger. We begin with a semantic ritual, searching through words for areas of possible agreement and disagreement. Initially, our physical behavior is more formal, our words are not inflammatory, we avoid excessive value judgments, the topics under discussion are quite narrow. Only with an expanding intimacy do we expose more of ourselves and our positions, and only after knowing what our stranger's attitude is on a position. That semantic and nonverbal sparring is quite like approaching an audience, especially during the introduction.

If the audience is hostile, begin your talk on topics about which you both agree. You might start by noting that fairness is common to all people and that you know you will receive such treatment before the group. Others have used humor, telling a joke on themselves or commenting on the goodwill shown to them in other groups.

To get the attention of the hostile audience, you might use some of the following approaches:

■ Checklist for Approaching a Hostile Group

1. Offer a greeting to gain goodwill.

"We have differences in philosophy, yet I bring you greetings from many friends of yours whom I have met during this past year."

"I've spoken to many groups over the years; each has given me a hearing. I bring you greetings from your colleagues in. . . ."

2. Make use of the fairness concept.

"All of us in this room have a degree of freedom not experienced anywhere else in the world; I'm using that freedom to bring a different point of view."

"This group is known for its many representatives of fairness; I trust you'll consider my remarks fair."

(Continued)

3. Appeal to a sense of human weakness.

"Well, I've made mistakes in my days; may I tell you about one I made in my first appearance before this group."

4. Quote from a supporter of the audience's views.

"One of the directors of your association strongly supported the concept of brotherhood. I'll begin with a quotation he uttered last year."

"Your newsletter has this heading: 'Unity as based on truth.' I like that, and believe I can pass that test."

With a well-stated introduction you will have gotten the attention of the group whether receptive or unfavorable to you, obtained their goodwill, and introduced the general direction for your talk.

You may do one final thing: set out the precise direction or offer a preview, a layout of what will be covered in the body.

"So first I'll offer a brief history of the problem and then make three recommendations."

"The key to implementing programs successfully involves approving four measures as expressed in four verbs: *identify, define, resolve,* and *maintain.*"

"May I begin with suggestions where we agree, then move to where we disagree."

"Word processing software programs lie on my desk; I'll make a final recommendation after discussing the pros and cons of two others."

Body (Text, or Discussion)

Major arguments supporting your position are put in the body—the text, or discussion—of the speech. Now your responsibility is to get the audience to accept your position, often expressed as a claim, assertion, generalization, proposition, resolution, or even formal legal statement.

Position:	That utility executives attend at least one management improvement seminar a year.
Claim:	I claim that most women executives read the *Wall Street Journal*.
Assertion:	The assertion is frequently made that a high correlation exists between drinking and one's appraised age.
Generalization:	Businessmen smoke more than do businesswomen.
Position:	Our sales are adequate, and therefore we can remain with our current advertising agency.

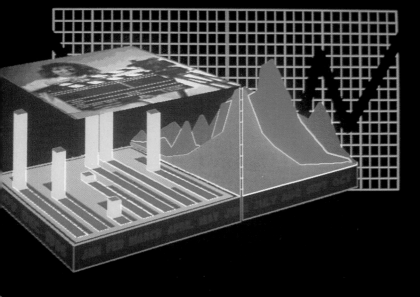

Courtesy Chyron

❏ Colorful and informative graphs, charts, maps, and other visual aids can easily be created with the use of a microcomputer and one of many available graphics software packages. High-resolution color images that make use of various styles and sizes of typography and highlighting devices help bring to life quantitative data and technical processes. When included with business reports, letters, and presentations, computer-generated graphic aids not only reinforce the message being conveyed, but also allow audiences to perceive at a glance various trends, patterns, changes, and relationships that might not otherwise be immediately apparent.

Performance data presented in a vertical bar graph, a pie chart, and a line graph

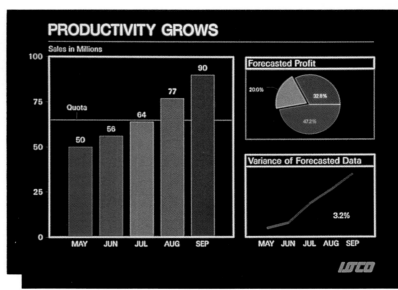

Courtesy ISSCO

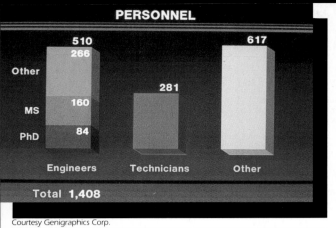

Courtesy Genigraphics Corp.

Three-dimensional stacked vertical bar graph

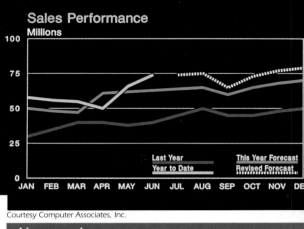

Courtesy Computer Associates, Inc.

Line graph

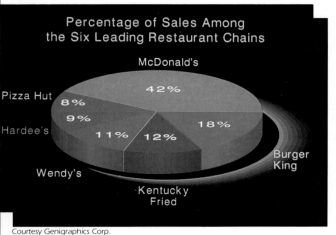

Courtesy Genigraphics Corp.

Three-dimensional pie chart

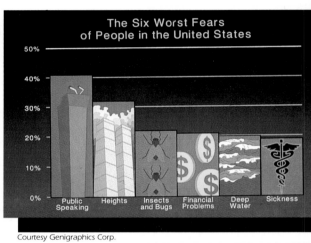

Courtesy Genigraphics Corp.

Vertical bar graph with computer-generated pictograms

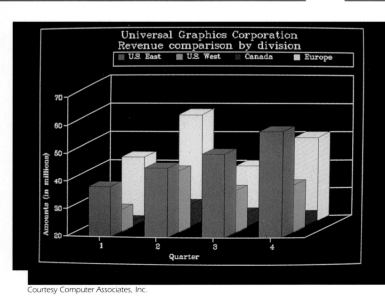

Courtesy Computer Associates, Inc.

Three-dimensional bar graph

Resolution:	Whereas, lack of exercise in utility executives is a concern of health officials, and
	Whereas, high correlations exist between exercise and decreases in stress, now therefore
	Be it resolved: that our corporation support the construction of a physical fitness and wellness center, and that it be available to all employees.
Legal proposition:	Article XII, Section 1C, of the code suggests that four members of the financial staff be endorsed by the chief financial officer. Therefore, an amendment through addition should be inserted into Article XII, Section 1C, as follows, "That all. . . ."

What all the above terms in the left-hand column have in common is that each asserts that something should be done, accepted, or believed. Each demands proof before listeners will willingly go along with you.

In persuasive speaking one can use the same kinds of organization discussed under informative speaking (topical, chronological, and cause-to-effect). But most persuasive business speaking uses the problem-solution format, proposing either that a change occur or that things remain as they are.

Problem-Solution—For Change

Frequently your intent will be to argue that something is wrong and that a change is in order; you are unhappy with the status quo. For this reason you must convince listeners that a problem exists and that you have a solution to remedy the problem. You begin with proving the existence of a problem.

The Problem.   Central to your thinking is the idea that something is wrong; there is dissatisfaction; flaws exist in the way things are going; failures far outnumber successes; costs are outrunning profits; negatives exceed the positives; the situation is so bad that something must be done; difficulties are many; there is a need for change; things are a mess. Remember, not all your listeners may feel there is a problem, so your first step is proving that one exists. Three brief examples of the problem section in the body follow:

Problem: Industrial distributors intentionally misrepresent delivery dates.
1. Casual "week or 10-day" responses are frequent.
2. Distributors join competitors who also misrepresent delivery dates.
3. Deceitful practices are common.

Problem: Our company communicates poorly between upper and lower management.
1. Lower management feels they are being talked down to.

```
        2. Downward communication is often without explana-
           tion.
        3. Little personal contact occurs between the two lev-
           els.

Problem:  Hindrances to Sino-U.S. business cooperation
          1. Policy issue 1: Foreign exchange balance
          2. Policy issue 2: Import substitution
          3. Policy issue 3: Local content requirements
          4. Policy issue 4: Policy fluctuation
          5. Policy issue 5: Development of a national market
```

This last example, taken from a section of a report on the Chinese auto-mobile industry,[5] further developed each of the problems with third-degree headings, such as "Current Situation" followed by "Effects of Current Practice." The reader was then supplied with facts—as well as they were known—followed by interpretation of those facts. It is a good example of proving the existence of issues which have to be addressed in order to propose a solution.

A good speaker, basing the problem section on verifiable facts, has met half the persuasive responsibility. The second half now demands recommending a solution for solving the problem.

The Solution, or Recommendation.   You will politely state your solution and then give your reasons. Keep in mind that several questions may run through your listeners' minds:

- Do we really need to change from what we're now doing?
- Will the proposal really solve the problem?
- Can one be sure that the solution will work? Be practical? Be effective? Be cost-effective?
- Will the benefits of the solution outweigh the negatives?
- Will the proposal create a host of entirely new problems?

Having answered what debaters call these "stock issues," you are ready to amplify your solution. Three examples of organizing solutions or recommendations follow:

```
Improving customer relations through accurate delivery
dates.
1. Give realistic delivery dates to customers.
2. Submit daily interoffice inventory memos between sales-
   persons and purchasing agents.
3. Monitor key accounts.

Recommendations for opening lines of communication between
upper and lower management.
1. Publish monthly newsletters; inform all levels of the or-
   ganization.
```

```
2. Institute a "Good Idea Program" to encourage employee
   involvement at all levels.
3. Promote visits between levels of management.

Overview of forms of cooperation.
1. Restricted investment.
2. Technology licenses.
3. Customer and supplier.
4. Joint venture.
```

Your solution is a mixture of laying out your recommendation and at the same time showing how it will remove the problems you cited earlier. One more thing remains to be done in the body of the speech advocating change: show the benefits of adopting your solution and the disadvantages of not accepting the solution.

The Benefits from the Solution. Briefly, you can insert in your talk positive results if your solution is adopted. You're trying to heighten desire for acceptance, summarizing future desirable effects. Your answers would be "yes" to the questions raised on page 658. Yes, we really do need to change; yes, my proposal would solve the problem, along with producing the following benefits; yes, my proposal would work, would be practical, would be effective, would be cost-effective; yes, by accepting my proposal the benefits would outweigh the negatives; yes, my solution implies that a change is needed and would not create a series of new problems.

The Disadvantages of Not Accepting the Solution. Conversely, you may also use a negative approach. A typical method is to suggest that if your recommendation or solution is not accepted, undesirable consequences will occur. You project into the future, suggesting that the current situation will continue (the status quo will be maintained); current problems, as you have defined them, will continue; undesirable consequences, such as costs, work force issues, or examples relevant to your topic, will not be removed. An example of two negatives and one positive is seen in the following:

Negative:
```
Relations with customers will not improve if mis-
representation of delivery dates continues.
1. Company's service image will continue to deterio-
   rate.
2. Customers will seek other sources if promised
   dates are not met.
3. Salespersons will be defensive in meeting custom-
   ers.
```

Negative:
```
Not adopting an open line communication system will
permit the current problem to continue.
1. Team spirit will not increase.
2. Vested interests will continue in strength.
```

```
Positive:     Advantages of restricted investment
              1. Maintains operational autonomy
              2. Provides immediate source of capital
              3. Ensures some projects will grow substantially
```

Thus the problem-solution-benefit form of organizing the body of the persuasive speech first proves the existence of a problem, supplies a remedy to that problem, and then projects positive benefits if the solution is adopted or negative consequences if the recommendation is not accepted.

Problem-Solution—For No Change

Any hint at changing a procedure or accepting a different idea within an organization is to some people a red flag. Indeed, most people like things to remain as they are. We all have heard statements such as "What's wrong with the way we're now doing it?" "Why should we tamper with success?" "There's no problem; why can't we leave things alone?" "That recommendation is worse than what we've got now." "Over my dead body will that solution be adopted," and so forth through a series of statements reflecting resistance to change.

The Problem.   If you feel the current situation is acceptable as is, you're in favor of the status quo. Such an attitude may be as legitimate as that of those who wish a change, except that you must prove that no problem or need to change exists. All your subheads in support of the proposition must leave one impression: There is no problem; things are fine.

If you are in favor, for example, of keeping your training program in your company as now structured, you might formulate the following generic main headings, which may be adapted to other topics as well:

```
Problem:     Current situation for training managers
             1. In-house programs
             2. Use of outside consultants and trainers
             3. Release time for on-site programs
```

The Solution.   Debaters on the negative side of an issue—those opposed to change and in favor of the status quo—would argue that no new solution is needed, things are currently acceptable. By analogy, a political party out of power contends that so many problems exist that a change in the administration should be made; the group in power argues that to continue success, the current party must remain.

```
             Recommendation that we remain with the current system
             1. Continue in-house programs along with release time
             2. Continue use of outside expert consultants and trainers
```

The Benefits from No Change.   Two alternatives are present: (1) arguing that staying with the current situation will produce positive results, continue benefits, promote efficiencies, strengthen morale, or even increase profits, or (2) arguing that trying a new solution produces more negatives, creates new, troublesome issues, decreases benefits, increases costs, accepts a drastic proposal for a minor concern, or enlarges a problem that for the moment is minor.

```
Benefits continue to result from the present system.
1. Travel time is negligible.
2. Costs are less:  rooms, travel, per diem.
3. Consultants and trainers continue up to date on issues.
```

Conclusion, Final Recommendation

As with informative speeches, persuasive speeches should end quickly. A summary can be used, but more important is making one last call to action, one final appeal that your proposal be accepted. If you have done a good job, it will be quite clear, early, what you wish your audience to do.

"And so I recommend that our current procedure for training managers continue."

"To review, I ask for your support in trying different methods of opening lines of communication between upper and lower management: through newsletters, through a 'Good Idea Program,' and through visits between management levels."

Outline of the Speech to Persuade

Accepting the principle that most persuasive speeches in business follow the problem-solution form of organization, the following brief outline suggests how the AIDA method can apply to persuasion.

```
                    Outline of Persuasive Talk


        Title:          Coping with Problems in Interna-
                        tional Business
        General purpose: To persuade
        Specific purpose: To persuade the personnel office
                        that a precise training program
                        is necessary


                        Introduction

        I. An employee of our Korean office made this
           observation: "Effective communication in in-
           ternational business is a challenging task
           and one we need to improve upon."
Attention
        II. I'd like to suggest that we have several
            problems, recommend a course of action, and
```

end with some benefits if my proposal is
adopted.

Body

III. Discussion of the problems
   A. Language differences
   B. Translation errors
   C. Cultural barriers

IV. Discussion of the solution
   A. Language training as a requirement for em-
      ployees sent overseas
      1. For the overseas manager
      2. For the family of the expatriate
   B. Language training for the U.S. and Korean
      staff
      1. Emphasis on daily correspondence
      2. Creation of company in-house transla-
         tion office
   C. Temporary assignments in home and host
      country
      1. Cultural similarities and differences
         would increase understanding of fellow
         employees.
      2. Work in actual foreign environment
         would be helpful.
      3. Adaptability of employees for foreign
         assignments could be determined.

Interest

Desire

V. Discussion of benefits from accepting solu-
   tion.
   A. Precision in understanding language dif-
      ferences would be heightened.
   B. Decrease in errors on both sides would oc-
      cur.
   C. Awareness of others' point of view, or
      their cultural heritage, would improve un-
      derstanding.

Conclusion

VI. We need to act quickly to resolve the commu-
    nication and intercultural problems within
    our company, such as language, translation,
    and cultural concerns.

**Agreement:
acceptance;
action**

VII. My threefold solution of training will de-
     crease our concerns and result in positive
     results for our company.

VIII. I recommend that you accept my proposal.

Note that the preceding example is a detailed outline of your remarks. As with the informative talk, how detailed your notes are is up to you. They could be as brief as the following:

Title:	Coping with Problems in International Business
General purpose:	To persuade
Specific purpose:	To persuade the personnel office that a precise training program is necessary

Introduction

Attention

    I. Korean quotation

  II. Problems, action, benefits

Body

 III. Problems: language, translation, culture

Interest

  IV. Solution: language training--employee; language training--staff; temporary assignments in home and host country

Desire

   V. Benefits

Conclusion

Agreement; acceptance; action

 VI. Act quickly

VII. Threefold solution decreases concerns

SUPPORT FOR PERSUASIVE SPEECHES

Since the time of Aristotle and Cicero—writers on persuasion in the ancient world—speakers have been told that persuasion rests upon three bases: *ethos*, *pathos*, and *logos*. These Greek terms are not a part of a businessperson's vocabulary, yet you have already used what they mean in your writing and will do so in your persuasive speaking.

Ethos concerns the credibility of the speaker, what he or she does that suggests good sense or a high moral character. You give your listeners the impression that you are a believable person. You do that through knowing your subject, giving the feeling that you are fairly presenting your information via a delivery that is enthusiastic and believable. In other words, both you as a person and the contents of your speech must give an image of high credibility.

Pathos is the emotion to support your ideas. Few of us would admit—especially in the business world—that we are moved to action on the basis of our emotions. Our advertising and marketing friends have been using emotions for years. But few speeches in staff meetings or before company groups depend on the emotional impact left on listeners. Surely, we are influenced by appeals to fear, to self-preservation, to physical well-being, to self-esteem, and to a host of other needs, but they do not often find a prominent place in internal business communication.

It is *logos*, the third part of ancient rhetorical principles, that receives major emphasis in both written and oral persuasion. *Logos* involves using evidence and reasoning, organizing supports into logical patterns of argument. All of us hope that rational thinking governs our actions. And to a great extent speaking to your peers within a company is based on rational thinking.

We will focus on facts and opinions and then on the seven kinds of evidence that are used to support persuasive positions.

Facts and Opinions

The discussion on facts and opinions relating to informative speaking (pages 635 to 636) is applicable to persuasive speaking as well. All information used as supports, either facts or opinions that are verifiable, is the raw material for supporting your points. In persuasion, supports are used to back up assertions, to give your audience logical reasons for actions you wish them to take or beliefs you wish them to accept. After we have looked at how facts and opinions are used in seven different kinds of support, we will suggest ways to test their reliability.

Seven Forms of Support

Examples

In informative speaking you used the specific instance or example to make an idea clear. In persuasive speaking the same form of evidence supports a proposition in the body of the speech.

> "For instance, last month one translation error resulted in six telexes being sent between here and Korea. That's one problem."
>
> "Here is an example: It took my secretary three phone calls in addition to those telexes to sort out the problem."

The speaker then draws conclusions from those examples, offering judgments based on the presented evidence. Examples should be true, based on information about which two or more people agree.

Illustrations

Illustrations are elongated examples; they lay out in detail a specific situation, suggesting, for example, that your proposed solution has worked successfully elsewhere.

> "TV teaching is used in this manner by X company in successfully preparing employees for overseas work. They began with a film on intercultural problems, followed that with a written analysis of what participants felt was the problem, and ended with a discussion with people who had spent time in that country. The whole process took place over three weeks."

Statistics

Many of the statistics (numbers) you use in persuasion in the business world are self-generated. They are therefore dependent on your method of collection and the inferences you draw from them. You should know what statistical measures to use to prove the validity of your data.

You will also use statistics from sources other than yourself. If statistics come from members of your own staff, you are in a good position to gauge the reliability of the data. On the other hand, turning to secondary sources outside your immediate area demands knowing the credibility of that source and the secondary source in which the information may have been reported. The person who wrote the following extract sought out a reputable source, the *Institutional Investor*, in gathering data for her paper:

> Thailand's labor force is among the most skilled in Asia yet remains one of the most inexpensive. The literacy rate averaged 91 percent in 1984 while unemployment reached nearly 7 percent in 1986. Outside of Bangkok the minimum hourly wage reached approximately $2.00 in 1987.[6]

Quotations

Testimony is another term for using the words of a literal expert in support of your proposition. We tend to listen when respected and trustworthy authorities are quoted. For that matter, a quotation from a respected journal has just as much weight. What you are trying to do is use an expert to enhance your credibility, to establish more reliability for your thoughts. An expert's words must carry high reliability.

> "The head of our investment office, Mr. Rogers, states that 'our company's rate of return on outside investments surpassed by 1.2 percent that of the Dow Jones averages during the last year.' What I'm saying is that we should not turn to an outside firm; we need not change, because our own internal investment group is doing so well."

Analogies

Most often used in business speaking is the literal analogy, comparing things in the same class. Thus with personal computers, it is simple, for example, to call up comparative figures on similar companies, their earnings per share or percentages of increases over the past year. That same data can be used as support in an oral statement. Quarterly reports to stockholders make extensive use of comparisons; so do popular business magazines. At a glance, or via the spoken word, an audience can immediately see comparative advantages and disadvantages.

> "X is a large corporation; in fact, it has subsidiaries in 17 different countries. The communication network back to the home office is circuitous, tortuous, because of the size of the company. Some say we've got an elephant here: large, slow moving, and covered with many ripples in the skin. An elephant can't change direction quickly because of its size, much like company X."

Definitions

As in informative speeches, persuasive speeches have denotative (dictionary) definitions and definitions which you personally link to your ideas. Often your definitions build on those supplied in a written document, as in the following example, which are then consistently carried over into your oral presentation.

> "*Engineer* refers to the duly authorized representative of the Purchaser for expediting and administering the contract."

Note that the above definition is beyond the usual meaning of the term *engineer*. The firm wishes to emphasize that only one person—bearing that title—is to represent them.

> "*Amendment* shall mean a written supplemental agreement (Form 238) entered into by the Purchaser and Seller to modify the executed contract."

While sounding like legalese, the definition is specific: all changes will be in writing, and on a specific form.

Repetition and Restatement

An adage familiar to most of us goes like this: "Tell them what you're going to tell them, tell them, and then tell them what you've told them." Repeating arguments in the same way (repetition) impresses an idea on listeners' memory. Separating these repetitions within the speech decreases the chance for monotony. Restating an idea (the same idea but in different words) also reinforces an argument.

Those are the seven common forms of support in persuasive speaking, in fact in any kind of speaking where you try to influence the thinking of others. To restate an old classical axiom, first state your point and then prove it. Using evidence well is a way to get that done.

Questions on Forms of Support

Recall what was said earlier: All listeners and readers come with their own biases and prejudices on topics. So do we as speakers; we too select—edit out—opinions, even facts that do not conform to our way of thinking. In collecting evidence we must be careful about the accuracy and neutrality of our sources. One way an audience counters your arguments is to raise questions such as the following, all of which you should consider in selecting your evidence:

■ Checklist for Selecting Evidence

- ■ Is the source reliable? Is the material taken from data considered valid by common standards of honesty and integrity?
- ■ Does the person whom you are quoting have a reputation for credibility? For fairness? For careful research?
- ■ Is your information true? Valid? Is it accurate or taken out of context?
- ■ What is the recency of your data? How old is the information? Is it out of date? Are more recent statements available on the same topic?
- ■ Are your statistics valid? Have you used commonly accepted means of determining reliability?
- ■ Have you indicated how you obtained your evidence? Do you make it clear when you are moving from your opinion to what is considered fact?
- ■ How wide is your scope? How many others agree with your evidence?
- ■ Is your evidence ambiguous? Do you go through it with generalities, rather than specifics?

Do the facts agree with other facts? If there is conflict between two sets of facts, both may be wrong. If the facts you use are supported by others, the data are more valid.

Are the opinions you use or depend on reliable? Just because a person is a respected member of the community does not make him or her an expert on every subject. Search for expert, rather than lay, opinions.

Answering these and other questions better prepares you for responding to possible objections and at the same time gives you confidence that your choice of evidence is acceptable and valid.

SUMMARY

We daily are approached to buy something or to think in a certain way about a product. Persuasive business speaking also tries to get others to change: to change a policy, to accept a value judgment of a person or process, or to recognize the truth or falsity of information. You try to get listeners willingly to accept your point of view and then act according to your wishes.

Persuasion demands knowing your audience, its knowledge of your topic and its attitudes; the occasion, whether you are persuading members within the company or without; the location, its degree of formality and the environment of the room; and some general characteristics, such as size, sex, and age of the audience. Most important is being aware of an audience's attitudes: Are they in favor of your position, neutral, or opposed to your ideas?

Audiences that are neutral or favorable to your proposals are less traumatic to address than those that are hostile toward you; hence, your introduction will vary according to the makeup of that audience. More often than not, your major form of organization for the body will be problem-solution—first proving the existence or nonexistence of a problem, then supplying a solution or a recommendation to remain with the status quo. You may also add benefits, those effects occurring in the future when your solution is adopted and the problem removed. Your conclusion is a short call to action and expression of hope that your recommendations will be accepted.

Your evidence will be founded on facts and opinions, then used in the traditional forms of support: (1) examples, (2) illustrations, (3) statistics, (4) quotations, (5) analogies, (6) definitions, and (7) repetition and restatement. These can logically support your position if they are reliable, credible as to source, honest, recent and statistically valid, gathered in an unbiased manner, supported by others, and clearly stated.

EXERCISES AND PROBLEMS

1. *Persuasive speech on a controversial topic:* Prepare a five-minute oral statement on a controversial topic that you wish to defend before the class. You will make but one main point. Clearly, you will have to present evidence so the group will accept your proposition. Your support (evidence) should come from reliable outside sources and individual investigation. Prepare an outline similar to the following:

   ```
   Title of one-point proposition: _____
   General purpose:  To persuade
   Specific purpose: _____
   Specific main point: _____
    First support: _____
    Second support: _____
    Third support: _____
   ```

The following are some sample one-point assertions:

- Age should be left off resumes.
- Writing is more effective than oral communication for communicating reprimands.
- Some good-paying jobs do not require a college education.
- English is the language of business throughout the world.
- Nonverbal communication is as effective as oral communication.

2. ***Revision of general purposes into specific phrases:*** Rewrite into a specific infinitive phrase the following general purposes for speeches to persuade:

Unions in the United States

Social Security reforms

Retirement at 62

Government bonds

Advertising in the Yellow Pages

Telegrams versus letters

Lawyers make significant contributions to business

Communicating effectively in business

Surveys gather information

Dress affects the listener

3. ***Oral presentation of long formal report:*** Assume you have been asked to present your long, formal report orally at an informal conference attended by 10 managers in your company. (See Exercise 2, pages 567 to 569.) Their work is closely concerned with the subject matter of your report. Prepare your report presentation thoughtfully. Usually a mere "summary" of the report is not the best method, because it may be too general to be meaningful to your listeners. In addition, if appropriate, select specific highlights about the problem and its solution. Choose the ideas that are most likely to be of interest and importance to your audience. For example, you might introduce to them the three or four most important factors you considered in the report. Be well informed about the overall highlights of your report, and be prepared to defend your findings in a question-and-answer session (with your class members) immediately after you have presented your report. (In your presentation, you will of course *not* read many parts of the report to the audience.) Make your talk businesslike, with the right tone; it may be 20 or more minutes in length.

4. ***Persuasive talk to class members as salespersons in a sales meeting:*** Prepare a persuasive oral presentation for members of the class, who will assume the role of salespersons attending a sales meeting. They are present to gain helpful tips on how to be persuasive when giving sales presentations.

As the basis for your persuasive talk, use a sales letter you prepared in Chapter 11. Or you may sell any product on which you can gather sufficient information—using popular ads; sales letters you or friends have received; facts about the product's content, price, advantages; and your own firsthand knowledge or use of that product. Remember to attract favorable audience attention, and create interest, then desire. Emphasize specific benefits the customer will receive. Use visual aids to stress the importance of creating a desire in the customer to do what it is you want done. The visual aids you could use might include one or more of the following: transparencies, flip charts, posters, a chalkboard, a projector, slides.

The following is a sample persuasion problem for your talk: Make a presentation to a group of college students and extend to them an invitation to become a subscriber to a popular magazine. Place emphasis on items such as the savings of 50 percent off the regular newsstand rate, features in the magazine, how it will supplement their textbooks, and the ease in placing the order.

5. ***Persuasive speech to support keeping things as they are:*** You occasionally may make a speech opposing a change; instead, you suggest that things are fine just as they are. Prepare a five-minute statement wherein you are opposed to change. Some possible topics include the following:

- Keep the present political party in power.
- Retain the present set of core course requirements.
- Support candidate X for another term.
- Current tuition rates are just fine.
- Current rules on pornography are acceptable.
- Insider trading rules are adequate.

6. ***Analysis of a campus or community speech:*** Attend a speech on campus or in your local community. This speech may be either to inform or to persuade. Complete the following analysis form for this presentation.

Title of speech: _____

General purpose: _____ Speaker: _____

First major point: _____

Kinds of support (evidence) used to back up first major point:

    a. _____

    b. _____

    c. _____

Second major point: _____

Kinds of support used to back up second major point:

a. _____

b. _____

c. _____

What statements, if any, were merely the speaker's opinions, not true and verifiable facts? _____

_____

What were the speaker's conclusions? _____

_____

Your evaluation of speech: _____

_____

7. **_Critical analysis of a paragraph:_** The statement that follows is attributed to no particular speaker. However, it does illustrate some flaws in critical thinking. It could have been spoken at a sales meeting or in another persuasive situation.

   Analyze the statement at each of the numbered points in the statement. Each one is a location for potential critical thinking errors. You might think of content, reasoning, language, and sources for the information.

   "There is no doubt [1] that every [2] home in the United States needs [3] a microwave oven. Most [4] homes have it [5] already. In fact, statistics suggest [6] that microwave ovens are the fastest growing item added to every [7] new home. Years ago [8] the outdated [9] woodstove, the bane [10] of every farm woman [11], was the center of the family. While the microwave oven cannot match that emotional and desirable bond, it can add the same speed and efficiency enjoyed by others." [12]

Successful Business Meetings

E very week across the United States thousands of meetings are held—in educational, business, industrial, professional, government, athletic, religious, and other organizations. Well-planned, productive group communications are essential for conducting modern business. But too often we hear the remark "That meeting was a waste of time." Because time is valuable, meetings should be held only when absolutely necessary—to achieve objectives and results that cannot be accomplished effectively in any other way.

The cost of business meetings is, of course, influenced by many factors. If 10 supervisors meet two hours every week on company time and their salaries average $35 an hour, each meeting represents at least $700 weekly salary cost, or over $36,000 for 52 meetings a year. To this should be added the time devoted for planning and presentations; secretarial time for typing agendas, handouts, minutes; overhead expenses for meeting room facilities; and travel expenses if some representatives come from distant units. When you add these meeting costs to those of the numerous other time-consuming meetings business executives and employees attend, the figures are surprisingly high. Do the results justify the investment?

The purpose of this chapter is to suggest how your meetings can be more successful when leadership and participant skills are of high quality. Four topics are discussed:

- Meetings in business
- Leadership responsibilities
- Participant responsibilities
- Methods of solving problems

MEETINGS IN BUSINESS

This section considers briefly the definition, group process, purposes and kinds of meetings; the importance of oral and written communication in them; and authorization for a committee.

Definition

Numerous writers have wrestled with their definition for a meeting. Perhaps you have heard this negative comment from some attendants: "A meeting is an event at which minutes are kept and hours are lost." In contrast, let us use this positive definition: A *business meeting* is a gathering where purposive discourse occurs among three or more people who exchange information on a common topic or problem, for better understanding or for solving a problem. The key words are "purposive," "understanding," and "solving."

A meeting is useful when the group leader and participants know the reason—"specific purpose"—for the meeting. What is your evaluation of the following memorandum announcing a meeting?

```
TO:       Members of personnel staff

FROM:     J. Rankin

SUBJECT:  Meeting on the 5th


     Please join the heads of our three personnel departments
for a discussion on compensation.  Hope to see you August 5,
at 11:00.
```

You may say, "I don't know where the meeting will be held, who will be there, or what its purpose is." The brief meeting announcement is unclear. Sadly, too many meetings are called in such an imprecise manner.

The word "understanding" in our definition suggests that learning from the information presented at a meeting is a first purpose. You will gain something if there is an effort to understand, through asking questions or listening.

"Solving" a problem is a second and major reason for a business meeting. The action steps leading to this goal are discussed later.

Group Process

You should know that all groups go through cycles between their initial meeting and later meetings. Uncertainty as to purpose, type of organization, and interpersonal relationships typifies beginning meetings. After a time the goals of a group are sorted out, patterns of problem solving are resolved, personal and authority relationships are clarified. In short, each group—and you as a new member of a group—go through a period of feeling out both the purposes of the group and its members.

While numerous studies have attempted to categorize the development of groups, one author capably suggested that the group process goes through four phases.[1]

Forming	Here the emphasis is on getting the group started. It is an orientation phase for group members.
Storming	Members at this stage search out their position; conflicts and arguments arise.
Norming	Actual progress begins to occur. Members begin to resolve conflicts and recognize acceptable kinds of conduct.
Performing	Once the interpersonal and group structures are accepted, the group begins to achieve its goals.

Clearly, you most likely will join a group or attend meetings that have been held for some time. You, as the newcomer, will be under review. After a get-acquainted time, your contributions will most likely begin with the norming process; then you will begin to help solve problems or give information, and you will be performing.

Purposes and Kinds

As implied above, meetings are held for two basic purposes: to present information and to help solve problems. What often happens is that both these purposes may occur in one meeting, a part of the meeting devoted to giving information and the other devoted to problem solving. Three types of meetings usually help achieve these objectives.

Informational Meetings

In the environment of an informal group, informative meetings are held to disseminate information and check on the understanding of those who attend. For example, the following notice appeared in an employee bulletin:

> All department purchasing personnel should attend a meeting on Thursday, December 4, at 3 p.m. in the Personnel Conference Room. The topic will be a discussion of the new staff categories approved by the Personnel Office.

At that meeting the staff learned, asked questions, understood the new categories. No problems were solved, no recommendations for change in policy occurred; rather, each person gained an improved understanding of the issue. A usual format is to have an opening informative speech, by a person highly knowledgeable on the topic, followed by a discussion.

Other internal informational meetings may be held to brief employees on changes in procedure, on policy amendments regarding a specific topic (policy), on profit-and-loss data (present and past facts), and on a host of other topics. You can see that these kinds of informational meetings involve purposes and use of data similar to those of informative speaking (Chapter 21). In discussion, however, there is the opportunity to clarify understanding through give and take, not so easily achieved when simply listening to an informative talk.

One also holds discussions with outside clients, for example, in an advertising agency: informing the client on next quarter's advertising schedule, on promotion plans, on the use of print and TV media, on proposed income schedules. During those meetings questions are asked and clarifications occur—for both the client and the agency.

Suggested-Solution Meetings

Two kinds of discussions are concerned with problems and solutions. The simpler is when a manager wishes to hear about options for solving a company problem. The scenario proceeds like this:

1. There is a feeling that a problem exists.

2. A question is phrased that seeks to get to the heart of the issue, such as "What should be done to control training costs?"

3. A person or committee is assigned to investigate.

4. A meeting is called to discuss possible answers, solutions, or recommendations to the question.

Note that no decision is reached. The manager, and the review committee, listen to all points of view. Comments on the options and perhaps a potential final solution are discussed. But no decision is made. The meeting was informative and exploratory. A final decision may be made at a second, problem-solving meeting.

Problem-Solving Meetings

Meetings that result in decisions for action predominate in the business world. When the executive or even a committee has no adequate solution for a problem, he or she or the committee seeks suggested solutions in a problem-solving meeting. The problem is presented at the beginning by either the executive or someone previously appointed to prepare a written report on it. The meeting participants suggest solutions, discuss and evaluate them, and arrive at a decision on which action is to be taken.

Because the problem-solving meeting requires the most careful planning and presiding over by the leader, as well as challenging participation by those attending, the remainder of this chapter focuses on this type of meeting. You can use most of the suggestions, of course, for all types of meetings.

Importance of Oral and Written Communication

It makes no difference whether you are a leader or a participant in a discussion; you will use both written and oral means of communication. Frequently a position paper or a request for action will be written, then followed by an oral discussion of the proposal. Persuasion of either the reader or the listener is a central purpose in these media.

In numerous business meetings a written problem-solution organization is presented as background, then followed by oral discussion that may lead to a decision. That decision is then further supported and defended orally against opposition by others. Persuasion and debate occur; you defend your decision, you participate in the discussion, and you argue logically for the group-supported decision.

Authorization for a Committee

You as an individual or chairperson of a committee may receive a formal letter or memo of authorization to investigate an issue. Often such notification is sent by the corporate secretary or your immediate superior. In some instances you too will authorize others to proceed.

The letter or memo of authorization will be similar to the information sent in connection with a formal report (Chapter 18). Who, what, when, and where are good cornerstone questions to answer. Such a format is used by the Department of the Treasury along with a detailed "Statement of Work" plan that is a good model for laying out committee responsibilities and goals. It illustrates the basic kind of information needed by persons who were to investigate a problem and who came from all across the United States.

While your authorization for an internal group may not be so detailed, the core ideas in the following well-organized statement of work are generally applicable.

U.S. Department of the Treasury
Office of the Fiscal Assistant Secretary
Washington, D.C.

STATEMENT OF WORK

<u>Project</u>:	Treasury Investment Program (TIP) Design and Implementation Plan
<u>Objective</u>:	To provide advice and assistance on the design and implementation of a new Treasury Investment Program under the guidance of the Office of the Fiscal Assistant Secretary. The design will include the identification of Congressional and/or legislative actions that may be required, financial institution criteria for participation, and an implementation plan or schedule.
	Major decisions will be required concerning collateralization of Investment Account balances, rate of interest for Investment Account Funds, classification of depositaries, and various operational details.
<u>Benefits Expected</u>:	This system will be a requirement for the new Federal Tax Deposit (FTD) System (an electronically based program). Benefits will be derived through better cash management, increased collateral capacity, and increased predictability of Federal government cash flow transactions.
<u>Type of Expertise</u>:	Background in banking and finance and knowledge of the Treasury Tax and Loan Account System and the Federal Tax Deposit System.
<u>Product Desired</u>:	Design recommendations and an implementation schedule.
<u>Time Estimates</u>:	Panel members will be expected to work an estimated one day a month for a period of one year.
<u>Work Location</u>:	Washington, D.C.

<u>Background</u>:   In January 199-, Deputy Secretary [*name*] approved the conceptual design of a new FTD program, the Electronic Revenue Network (ERN).

The conceptual redesigned FTD System would cause immediate withdrawal of FTD funds from depositaries, placing these funds in the Treasury operating account at the Federal Reserve Banks.

While this action could physically be implemented, without consideration of the impact on the existing Treasury Tax and Loan Investment Program it could have serious impact on the management of monetary policy and other consequences.

To ensure the success of the new FTD System, a well-developed and -designed Investment Program must be made available for implementation either simultaneously with or before implementation of the new FTD System. Otherwise, the redesigned FTD System could be a step backwards to the mid-1970s instead of a step forward into the 1990s.

Treasury has a major responsibility to ensure that the movement of large government funds does not disrupt bank reserves or financial markets, and this was the driving factor behind development of the present Investment Program in 1978. Therefore, Treasury must provide for a smooth transition to the electronic era of the 1990s with the design of a new investment program to manage annual revenue flows in the range of $1 trillion.

What the above clearly does is to cover a wide range of requirements, from the kind of expertise required to the final decision, along with a time schedule for implementation. In brief, panel members had a good background as to what was expected of them at the meeting.

LEADERSHIP RESPONSIBILITIES

Thus far, the focus of this chapter has been on background information, for both leaders and participants, but essential to any successful meeting is the competence of the leader. He or she should know the different kinds of leadership and its functions—before, during, and after the meeting—to be effective.

Kinds of Leadership

Some persons find it hard to accept that leadership functions during a meeting shift back and forth between the leader and group members. That is usual, unless the leader loses complete control of the meeting. What follows focuses only on the person formally designated as the leader. Traditionally leadership kinds lie on a continuum from authoritarian through democratic to leaderless (Figure 23-1).

Authoritarian

The behavior of the autocratic leader could range from firm suggestions which must be accepted to commands which must be carried out. A leader in this position has quiet contempt for participants, dominates the thinking of a group, manipulates others to his or her advantage, praises those who agree with his or her position, resents questions, issues orders and commands, puts self above all. Clearly, this type of leadership should be avoided.

Leaderless

On the other end of the continuum is the leader who gives up all his or her leadership functions to the group. This person believes that shared leadership is appropriate to problem solving, and thus the meeting has no leader. Certainly you have chance meetings where quick discussions occur without a leader. Sometimes such leaderless groups are successful with high-ability people who need little direction and control. Yet even they depend on someone finally offering guidance and a summary of what they achieved, though the leader exerts little control.

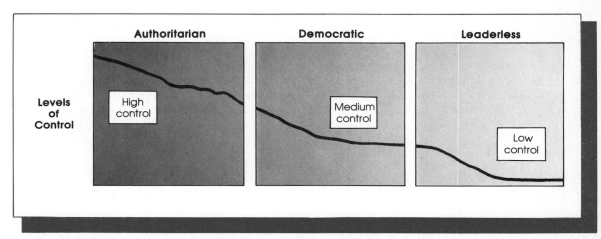

Figure 23–1   Leadership styles.

Democratic, Participative

The ideal leadership role for your business meeting is the democratic one. This role lies between the two extremes and seeks to win cooperation of the group as it moves toward a solution. It works on the principle of participation. The democratic leader realizes that the group has final authority, knows that groups vary in their ability to make decisions, helps the group make the decision rather than forcing the decision on it, facilitates productive group discussion, promotes minority opinions, evaluates unsupported generalizations, clarifies vague statements.

Democratic leadership takes time; that is, democratic discussion is slow. It takes patience to listen to the opinions and views of others. Authoritarian leadership is faster, the leader making many decisions with or without approval of the group. In the end, however, it is you as a democratic and participatory leader who best guides the group through the following functions.

Planning Steps before the Meeting

It is incorrect to assume that one person will always call a group together. Sometimes a committee is authorized by another group, as high as the board of directors. The secretary of the authorizing group is then empowered to implement the board's decision, he or she working with the chairperson to appoint the committee and set out the responsibilities. Such initial planning involves five factors: purpose; members; meeting date, time, place; announcements and agenda; physical arrangements.

1. Consider the Problem and Determine the Purpose

First, the leader must decide whether the meeting should be called at all. In one sentence he or she should write the problem and specific purpose. If the purpose can be better attained by telephone, memos, letters, video teleconferencing, or electronic mail, the participants should not be called together for a meeting.

A good meeting topic must be timely, genuine, really important, and meaningful for the conferees. It must present a difficulty that is within the experience of the meeting attendees. Also, the problem should be limited adequately so that conferees are able to solve it—at least partially—within the conference time. It should be about a matter that can immediately be decided by the group or about which recommendations can be made to a higher administrative body.

2. Decide Who Should Participate

Many business committees have a consistent group of attendees. For instance, executive committees may comprise vice presidents, other committees may be made up of account executives (persons working on a given account), or finance committees may consist of staff members from purchasing to disbursements.

Additional members are also invited to supplement the regular members' contributions or to appear to make a specific report.

Regardless of whether or not the meeting is to solve a difficult, top-level problem, the invitees should be those who can make special contributions.

Usually, the more difficult the problem, the smaller the group—sometimes five or fewer. But if an executive needs mainly a list of possible solutions from a "solution discovery" meeting, perhaps 10 to 20 participants would be desirable for a brainstorming session. To review and discuss regular department activities, 30 might be invited. And for some informational meetings, hundreds may be interested and gain useful explanations.

3. Arrange for Meeting Date, Time, Place

Date and Time.   Generally the better days for meetings are Tuesdays through Thursdays. However, some executive groups consistently meet early on Monday or Friday. Considered a poor time is Friday afternoon, and immediately after lunch. Good times are 9 to 11 a.m. and 2 to 4 p.m., but some leaders have found that to keep a one-hour meeting "on the beam," 11 a.m. is psychologically a desirable starting time. Participants then work more alertly to help accomplish the goals of the meeting so that it will end on time for their lunches.[2]

Place.   Depending on audience size and makeup (and purpose of the meeting), the chosen place may be in the executive suite, a company conference room, an auditorium, a hotel, or a convention center.

4. Announce Agenda

Most often it is the meeting leader who words the question, with precision, and prepares the agenda so the participants know in advance the direction of the meeting. The announcement should be sent early enough to give them adequate time to prepare their thoughts on the matter.

Wording the Question Properly.   There are three types of problems underlying discussion: questions of fact, value, and policy.[3]

Fact questions are concerned with what is true and what are the facts, as in these examples:

> What is the strategic plan our PR agency proposes for the next year?
>
> What are the media constraints we will face in Germany?
>
> Which fast-food chains are expanding to the Far East?
>
> What is the project path followed in our advertising agency?

Value questions depend on words implying appraisal and judgment of the goodness or badness, rightness or wrongness, merits or demerits of a person, place, or thing. Value words, such as "fair," "justify," "worth," "merits," and "value," in the following questions steer discussants to a judgment based on a mixture of factual content and feelings about an issue:

> Is the current system of bonuses *fair* for salespersons whose gross sales are in excess of $50,000 a month?
>
> Can you *justify* our current mileage allowance in contrast to other firms of a similar size?
>
> What is the *worth* of continuing our in-house programs on team building?
>
> What are the *merits* of sending a common rejection letter to all interviewed students who don't fit into our plans?
>
> What is the *value* to us in terms of new personnel and cost-effectiveness over the next year?

Policy or *procedure* questions occupy most business meetings: What should be done? What action should we take? Who should carry out the actions? Implicit in these questions is the idea of options.

> What should be our policy on building our own motors for our heart-lung machines?
>
> What should be the decision path in dealing with our major client?
>
> Which marketing media should we follow during this next year?
>
> To what extent should we do three things: invest money and time in the Far East; align ourselves with a foreign investment firm; send representatives to the trade show in Beijing?

You as a leader, manager, caller of the meeting, will get off on the right foot when your worded questions are short, clear, unbiased. Poor questions like the following should never be used:

> What's the problem in personnel? [*Unclear referent.*]
>
> Why are our salespeople so poor in comparison with others in the firm? [*Prejudgment.*]
>
> Our company letters stink; what can we do about it? [*Prejudgment, bias.*]
>
> How do we get out of the problem of trade barriers? [*Broad, vague topic.*]

Preparing the Announcement.   Five ingredients make up a good announcement: topic, date, time, place, responsibilities of participants. For some meetings it is also desirable to stimulate participants' interest in the problem by stating its importance before they come to the meeting. The following memo begins with mention of a related news item.

October 7, 199–

Title of topic

```
To:       Warehouse salespeople
From:     Chris
Subject:  Potential computer market for home use
```

Importance	<u>Electronic Topics</u> suggests in its October issue that a potential market exists for increased sales of computers in the home.
Topic question Responsibilities	Will each of you please give thought to this question: How can we increase sales of our personal computer hardware and software in our immediate area? This will be the first meeting on the issue; we'll assign more responsibilities at the meeting.
Date, time, place	We'll meet two weeks from now, Tuesday, October 21, 199-, in my office, at 9:00 a.m.

In addition to the five ingredients listed above and "importance" of the topic, you may also—when desirable—include suggested reference materials, as sent with this announcement:

May 22, 199-

Date, time, place	To: Product Planning Committee From: RNS, President Subject: Monthly meeting, Wednesday, June 6, 10:00 a.m., Rm. 816
Responsibility	Two questions are to be discussed in our monthly meeting:
Specific topic questions	1. What other uses can you suggest for our disposable tubing? 2. What policy should we follow about producing intravenous suckers that use internal wiring for support?
Individual Responsibilities Responsibilities of group	Beyond these two questions we will have a review of progress on our redesigned modules--by Mike S. and Tom G.--and the usual monthly review of our ongoing new-product items, by all of you.
Responsibilities of group	My staff has prepared the background and history of the two questions above. I ask you to come prepared to recommend options. Suggested reference material is enclosed with this announcement for the meeting.

If the agenda is not announced in the call to the meeting, a good chairperson comes prepared with a handout to be distributed—as a first item of business. In essence the agenda is a simple listing of topics to be covered. One such sample is illustrated below:

```
        Agenda for Executive Officers' Strategic
                  Planning Session

                 October 21, 199-

     Agenda

        1. Approval of minutes of October 14.

        2. First report on concepts involved in a
           Full-Service Agency                        Ernie P.

        3. Decision to be made on enclosed document:
           Which criteria should be used in considering new
           business?                                  Jan M.

        4. Report/listing of clients to be considered
           for potential new business contacts        Glen M.

        5. Reactions to proposal on restructuring
           Account Services                           Ernie P.
```

As you probably noticed, of the above five items, a decision was required for (1), the minutes, and (3), which criteria to use. Agenda items (2) and (4) appear mainly informative, while (5) is informative and could lead to a decision.

5. Take Care of Physical Arrangements

As the last step before any meeting, the leader should consider such physical arrangements as seating, materials, equipment, atmosphere.

Seating.   Most likely the chairperson will arrange seating, perhaps in a circle, or around a conference table, or in a diamond or U shape, so all conferees can easily see one another and the chairperson.

Materials, Equipment, Atmosphere.   Items to consider are chalkboards, whiteboards, marking pencils, chalk, erasers, pencils, paper, flip sheets, microphones, lectern, projectors, visual aids (charts, tables, graphs). Drinking water, glasses, and ashtrays (if smoking is allowed) should be handy. Name cards may be desirable if participants come from different firms or widely separated departments and are not personally acquainted. A secretary—or someone else—should be asked in advance to take minutes at the meeting.

Procedures during the Meeting

For success of the problem-solving meeting the leader's attitude and efficiency—from the beginning statement through the entire discussion—are critically important. The leader should be well prepared, be able to think and act quickly, get along with others, respect their opinions, know objectives of discussion and the reasoning process, be patient, and have a sincere interest in the values of cooperative group action. This section lists procedures the leader should follow in conducting the meeting.

1. Begin with Appropriate Opening Statement

Obviously, you should prepare your introductory statement before the meeting, but neither memorize nor read it. Present it informally and naturally—in one or more of these suggested ways:

■ Checklist for Beginning Problem-Solving Meeting

State the Problem

> "We're here today for an analysis of this question: 'Which divisions are not meeting the financial goals set last January?' "

Indicate Importance of Problem

> "At no time in the history of this company have we faced more serious problems. Without exaggeration, I suggest that we must come up with a firm answer to the question I put on the agenda: 'What should be our position on expanding our overseas data processing operations?' "

Suggest Issues

> "It appears three issues relate to our question of overseas expansion: (1) What is the political base of those countries in which we wish to expand, (2) what is the economic base, and (3) under what conditions should we consider moving more production to foreign countries?"

Use a Quotation

> "*Jobber News*'s editorial has this comment: 'Revising a ruling last year by an administrative judge, the Federal Trade Commission has ordered Tenleso, Inc., to sell off its Martoe Equipment Co. unit.' That opening comment is a good springboard to our meeting today: Which units in our organization are possible targets for court action?"

State Cause for Discussion

> "The Citizens' Lobby in the House is prepared to offer two bills on the issue of regulating content and sale of dread-disease insurance policies. They were kind to send us copies of those two possible options, and wish our suggestions for change. Before we begin our discussion, I suggest we examine both versions, then move into our discussion."

Other possibilities are open to you as chairperson, but the above are some of the most common. Some chairpersons have also used visual aids, case analysis of a situation, or videotaped statements by superiors.

2. Stimulate Discussion for Solution Discovery

In general, try to encourage all conferees to participate, and do keep the discussion moving forward. To help spark discussion on each topic, write on the board or on the overhead projector the criteria a solution should meet. List on another board the possible solutions of the problem as conferees suggest them. Ask questions and keep participants from wandering onto irrelevant paths. Get conferees to analyze their own thinking as much as possible. Sometimes if the original contributor of an idea cannot add to it, another conferee may be able to carry it further. If a participant's statement is vague, rephrase it clearly before you write it on the board.

Maintain an atmosphere of goodwill and cooperation throughout the meeting. If a situation becomes tense or some members are reluctant to speak or are annoying or antagonistic, apply the techniques you have learned for handling bad-news situations. Even taking a recess diffuses tensions. Try to be tactful, considerate, and understanding and show a sense of humor.

3. Understand Roles of Participants

A widely used classification—though completed some time ago—of member roles within meetings was developed by Benne and Sheats[4] at the National Training Laboratory in Group Development. It helps a leader to know these roles in order to understand group process better.

Group Task Roles.   Any individual may play these roles, including the chairperson.

Initiator-contributor	Coordinator
Information seeker	Orienter
Opinion seeker	Evaluator-critic
Information giver	Energizer
Opinion giver	Procedural technician
Elaborator	Recorder

Group Building and Maintenance Roles.   Keeping the goals of the group in mind through group-centered attitudes characterizes these roles.

Encourager	Group observer
Harmonizer	Compromiser
Standard setter	Follower
Gatekeeper (opens channels of communication)	

"Individual" Roles.   The emphasis here is self-oriented roles, often at odds with group building and maintenance roles.

Aggressor	Recognition seeker
Blocker	Self-confessor
Playboy	Dominator
Help seeker	Special interest pleader

Knowing the various roles being played by group members assists the leader in knowing how to react, how to handle role statements made during a meeting.

Particularly important, however, is handling the problem participant. Here are some suggestions for leaders on handling difficult conferees:

The Reticent, Nonparticipating Member.   First ask this person a question he or she can answer by a simple "yes" or "no." Then whenever possible, ask this member to give the conferees some information that he or she is sure to know because of job, training, or experience. Thank and praise the person as much as you can; he or she may then be more likely to enter the discussion confidently.

The "Know-It-All."   This person may be asked to justify every statement he or she makes. Whenever possible, ask other conferees for their opinions of these statements. Sometimes, if necessary and you feel the majority are annoyed by this person's arrogance, you may tactfully quiet the person by asking for a show of hands from the group, which strongly outvotes the know-it-all's suggestions.

If the negative member still insists on knowing all the answers, a private, outside-the-meeting session can bring the group's concern to the person. This one-on-one meeting in a nonthreatening atmosphere may produce more positive results.

The Long-Winded Speaker.   You may thank this excessive talker when he or she is at the end of a sentence, and then recognize someone else. Or you might move the discussion to another highly important point, perhaps with a statement like "Well, we have two more points to consider before we wind up this meeting, so let's move along to the next topic."

The Erroneous Member.   If the other members—out of respect—are reluctant to correct this person, an especially tactful comment by you, the leader, may be required. As with any bad-news message, avoid direct criticism, sarcasm, or ridicule. Shield the person's pride. "When praising people, single them out; when criticizing them, put them in a group." Perhaps analyze a similar case, without referring to the speaker personally.

The Conferee Who Shows Personal Animosity.   Though rare, sometimes an angry member shouts hateful, tactless comments toward another member or members. You can show an attitude of calm understanding and turn him or her off by directing a question to another conferee.

4. Sort, Select, Interpret Data for Solution Evaluation

After you have listed conferees' suggestions on the board, encourage participants to consider advantages and disadvantages of each suggested course of action. List them separately. As leader, be careful not to impose your own opinions on the group, or if you wish to participate, ask another member to chair the meeting. Encourage each group member to feel a sense of responsibility for the success of the analysis. Good listening by everyone to what others offer is extremely important.

5. State the Conclusion and Plan of Action

As with a written analytical report, the terminal section is of major importance. Before you dismiss the meeting, review what the group has accomplished. Summarize what parts of the problem members have solved or partially solved. State the decision (conclusion) clearly and definitely. You might begin your statement of the conclusion by saying "You have agreed. . . . " or "You have suggested. . . ." or "It's my interpretation that we have approved. . . ." rather than, "I think this is what should be done." If the group arrived at several conclusions, list them, preferably in order of importance.

Make some statement about how the solution the group decided on will be carried out. Appointments may be made then or announced later in a memo regarding the action. (The following example of meeting minutes suggests accountability by a person and a precise date.)

Follow-Up after the Meeting

Two functions after the meeting are distribution of the minutes and—most important—seeing that responsible committees, departments, or individuals are appointed to carry out the chosen action. In some situations the meeting leader may have to confer with other executives of higher authority before appointments are made regarding policy decisions.

Copies of the minutes your secretary or assistant prepared should be sent to the meeting participants soon after the meeting. They usually should include:

Name of the organization, department, or group

Date, time, place of the meeting

Names of members present

Names of any others present as invited visitors

Name of chairperson and (at the end) recording secretary

Brief summary of reports, if any, by those listed on the agenda

Highlights of solutions presented and decisions made

Time of adjournment and (if announced) date for next meeting

Example of Meeting Minutes

Two people's minutes of the same meeting will rarely be identical. Yet, if you follow the pattern above, your minutes of a meeting might look similar to the following (except that agenda items 4 through 7 are omitted in this example).

```
Minutes of ET (Executive Team) meeting      September 16, 199-
Executive Conference Room

Present:  Jan M. (chairperson), Eric M., Julie D., Diane M.,
          Marsha K., Jim D., Pam M., Jon D., Ernie P., and
          Carey F.  Also Present:  Kay G., David J., and
          Richard S.
```

Review of Actions Taken at September 9 Meeting

```
   1. Kay G. to prepare a job flow chart of a work order and
      report to ET group.                    Due: September 30

   2. Diane M. to present a report on salary compensation
      currently offered by the company.     Due: September 30

   3. Eric M. to prepare a report comparing the bank require-
      ments with the current budget projections.
                                               Due: October 28
```

Minutes of September 16 Meeting

```
   1. The minutes of September 9 were approved as presented.

   2. Job Costing and Time Reporting
      Kay G. presented a brief report on how the new Adware
      system for agency-client profitability will work.  An
      internal methods team headed by Kay has been estab-
      lished with the intent of standardizing communication
      with clients.

   3. Training Program--Tuition Reimbursement
      David J. outlined a proposed tuition-reimbursement pro-
      gram to be offered to all full-time employees after six
      months of employment.  He proposed that a limit of
      $1,000 be instituted.

      Action to be taken: The ET group suggested that the
      proposal wait until the question of agency compensation
```

was solved. The chairperson suggested that a detailed report of all perquisites and salary compensation be presented before a final decision was made, that report to be completed by October 30.

Agenda items 4 through 7.

8. New Business Development
   Julie D. reported that our company now has a one-year agreement with [*company*] to provide graphics, packaging, and marketing for a total of $120,000. She asked whether the ET group would encourage her to pursue other clients similar in purpose.

   Action to be taken: The ET group, after discussion, recommended that she proceed in contacting and offering proposals to new clients, offering similar services as noted in the $120,000 project.

The chairperson adjourned the meeting at 3:50 p.m. and reminded the group that the next meeting would be held on September 30.

Respectifully submitted,
Vicki R.
Recording Secretary

PARTICIPANT RESPONSIBILITIES

Implicit in the preceding section was the idea that some leadership functions may be assumed by participants. If it were not so, the leader could be accused of being autocratic. But more often you will be a discussant in a meeting.

Preparation for Meetings

You will surely bring to any meeting some general knowledge and innate understanding. The more specific preparation, however, will occur in terms of a precise problem and the expressed purpose of the meeting.

As part of your preparation you will gather evidence, the raw material on which to base generalizations and logical comments. Examples, statistics, quotations, definitions, and analogies will make up much of your data, ready to be injected into the discussion.

You cannot be overprepared for a meeting. The phrase "I don't know" in response to your supervisor's question will communicate more than the fact that you are not prepared. That negative answer can be avoided if before a meeting you observe, interview experts on the issue, listen well, and spend time on background reading about the topic. In brief, some kind of preparation is needed for you to make a significant contribution.

Effective Participant Roles in Meetings

Having collected information beforehand, you can express your ideas objectively in meetings and listen open-mindedly to ideas others present. With a positive attitude you can have the following nine participant roles, suggested by the late William M. Sattler and N. Edd Miller in a classic text on discussion and meeting process.[5]

1. Organizer

Business meetings, with little difficulty, get away from their central topic. When you assume the role of organizer, you make comments that steer the group back to main issues. You suggest procedure, note points that have not been discussed, or summarize where the group has been. Typical of procedural comments are these:

> "I'm sure we're interested in your personal reminiscences, but we seem to be losing sight of our major purpose. I suggest we get back to the main question of the meeting: What are the criteria for selecting a new agency?"

> "Could I pause a moment and see if I know where we are. I understand two issues face us: What will be the reaction of our stockholders, and what will be the response of the stock market?"

> "Madam chairperson, we seem to have resolved item one on the agenda; in the interest of time, perhaps we could go to item two which demands a decision within one month."

Such procedural suggestions—by you if the leader does not do so—are of inestimable value in keeping a group on the right path.

2. Clarifier

In the role of clarifier you point out misunderstandings and clarify complex or foggy ideas. Your statements could be similar to these two examples:

> "Well, it seems we've gotten lost in understanding the meaning of the term 'strategic'. Some of you are speaking of it as those plans under one year, while others are out at least three years. I suggest we first agree on a common definition."

> "Let me add one comment: Some of you are talking about the foreign rate of exchange on the German mark two months ago, while the rest of you are speaking in terms of today, when the rate is 15 cents higher on each dollar. That 15 cents will make a lot of difference in our overseas budget of 8 million. Let's agree on a common time frame so that we're all talking about the same thing."

3. Questioner

Most questions ask for further information. You wish to fill in the knowledge gaps for yourself and for the group, some of whom also do not know but are too hesitant to ask.

One danger in asking questions is that they may be too broad. The result is answers that come back with such diversity that time is wasted before zeroing in occurs. Knowing the difference between the vital and the inconsequential will help you to be a productive participant.

4. Factual Contributor

Preparing thoroughly permits you to make substantive contributions. A caution is not to monopolize or suggest in an overbearing manner that you have *the* information. The tone of your oral statement will say as much as the content. A few desirable comments follow.

"Your point is interesting. I wonder if I may add some data from a study appearing in the December issue of the *Journal of Business Communication.*"

"Concerning the length of memorandums, Mr. Paul Blank, president and chief executive of [*name*] Chemical Company, made this statement: 'Memorandums crossing my desk should be limited to one page.' My inference is that here is a busy man who demands brevity in written communication."

"I like what you say, but my information based on the October 4 *Wall Street Journal* gives different data."

5. Energizer

Sometimes you can keep the discussion moving, stimulating the members to reach their goals when gloom or frustration has set in. You suggest there is light at the end of the tunnel when some feel the problem is incapable of being solved.

"We're almost there. If we give it another half hour, I'm sure we can arrive at a consensus on the issue."

"I suggest a brief recess, say, 10 minutes. Then let's come back and show the exec committee we can come in with a proposal on time."

6. Idea Creator

When you play this role, your comments may be offered in this manner:

"After listening to the discussion I feel we have at least four options to consider today."

"Before coming to the meeting I made several phone calls for others' ideas; here are their comments on the issue before us."

"My guess is we're working so hard on a single solution that we're blind to the possibility of combining all our options."

"*Fortune Magazine* had a superb article on technological innovations in the workplace. I suggest we look at their list as a start for our discussion."

And so on. Creativity in problem solving means you are capable of thinking through hypotheses amidst a potpourri of seemingly disorganized data. But out of this disorganization you are able to synthesize, arriving at a solution you were seeking, one you discovered accidentally, or one you were bright enough to see arising out of the discussion. With the ability to suggest creative responses you will be looked upon as an invaluable member of any group.

7. Critical Tester

Every meeting needs a person willing to challenge, tactfully, the validity and reasonableness of contributions. Note that the stress is on what is said rather than who is saying it. Focus on the idea, the content, the evidence, the reasoning, leaving out all references to the person. All persons have the right to do so whenever a misleading or inaccurate statement is made. The following are questions to keep in mind, similar to the questions on forms of support in Chapter 22.

- Were a sufficient number of facts given on which to build a conclusion?
- Is the information consistent, or do some contradictions get in the way of accepting the information?
- Are the facts—and the language—clear?
- Are the sources of information and the statistics reliable?
- Is the information recent; can one see the source and verify the evidence given?
- Was the cause sufficiently powerful to produce the alleged effect?
- Have some data been omitted in leading to the conclusion?

You should not hesitate to challenge an unsupported conclusion, an out-of-date source, a biased piece of information, an incomplete recital of facts, an unclear cause producing even more unclear effects, an unclear referent or source—and other illogical matters that potentially can negatively influence the discussion. Not to do so is to omit good participant responsibility when reading a report or participating in a discussion.

8. Conciliator

Mutual interaction can turn into violent disagreements as opponents debate an issue. Deadlocks may result. Positions can become so polarized that losing face in addition to losing the argument is at stake. You as a conciliator seek to find a middle ground, seek to restructure positions that are acceptable to the opposing parties. Some examples are these:

"Here's my suggestion: Instead of a four-year term of office, the tenure, as a compromise, might be a two-year term, with an evaluation for a longer term to occur at the end of that time."

"Let me suggest a way out of this impasse: We've heard arguments from the two main groups. I suggest a drafting group, two from each of the opposing groups and three from the rest of the body, to come in with a merger of the positions. Let's look at that, then make a final decision at our next meeting."

"I've heard what you've both said. Your positions are now on the table. I suggest you both take a day to put them in writing and send them to the committee, then all of us will meet in a week to bring closure to the issue."

9. Helper of Others

A final suggestion is that you can help other participants as well as the leader. Sensitivity to others through tact and cooperativeness characterizes this role. You do not seek to embarrass but rather to help those who feel inadequate or frustrated, giving them the feeling of being accepted and wanted. You might do that in several ways:

"We've heard from most of us around this table. I'm eager to hear what Paul has to suggest on this topic [*invitation to participate*]."

"Mr. Chairman, you may have misunderstood, What I think Kathy was saying was this . . . [*clarification and further support for her idea*]."

"That's a superior suggestion, Donna. Let's take a couple of minutes and see what others think [*praise of member*]."

"Eric was a little harsh on you. Can you take a few moments to develop your second point [*support of a member*]."

You rarely will use all the preceding nine roles in a single meeting, nor should you be expected to. But to be proficient in perhaps four of them would be making a significant participant contribution to a group meeting.

METHODS OF SOLVING PROBLEMS IN MEETINGS

How do you think through a problem? Some of you may use intuition (rapid insight into a problem), rationalization (justification attempts over time), or scientific, reflective thinking (logical progression) to come to an answer. The last method is the method discussed in this section, and the one most used in business.

To aid you as a meeting chairperson or participant, moving from a felt awareness of a problem to its eventual solution, some of John Dewey's seminal ideas on problem solving (in his classic book *How We Think*, Heath, Boston,

1909) are adapted here. Four stages are involved in problem-solving meetings: background analysis, solution discovery, solution evaluation, and choice of action.

Background Analysis

You feel a problem exists; you sense something is wrong; you hear contradictory information; you are confused, frustrated that something is not going well in your organization. This stage has three steps, similar to the planning steps discussed in Chapters 6 and 20 for written and oral communication.

1. State the Problem in the Form of an Affirmative Question

An important first step at solving any problem is phrasing the central issue in a neutral question form. Affirmative wording is preferable because a negatively worded question—"How do we not handle personnel dismissal?"—is a bit more confusing. If the question clearly states what is assumed to be the problem, it follows that the answer or answers will help solve the problem. Rules for writing the question should meet the criteria discussed earlier in this text—conciseness, concreteness, and clarity.

> What should be the policy of our company regarding alternative sources of energy?
> Which criteria should be used in selecting new clients for our firm?
> Which accounting firm should we hire for the next five years?
> In which related businesses should we consider expansion?

2. Define and Limit the Problem

The preceding questions are concise, but they demand some clarification. For example:

> By "alternative sources" we mean coal, atomic energy, water, sunlight, oil, and gas.
> By "criteria" we mean those limited to ROI (rate of return on our investment).
> By "accounting firm" we mean one of our outside consultants.
> By "related" we mean those firms only in the fast-food area.

3. Collect Facts on the History of the Problem

What you consider in this step can be suggested by possible questions:

> What is the history of the problem?
> What are some symptoms of the problem?

What is the extent and seriousness of the problem?

What is the size of the problem?

What are some possible causes and effects of the problem (for example, management, labor unions, government)?

How do other companies handle the problem?

What do other countries do in facing the problem?

What previous things have been done to solve the problem?

Your thoughtful examination of background material will have helped to prepare you for the role of either leader or discussant. And, if you have prepared written background material for the group, it will serve as backup material to prepare for the next stage—solution discovery.

Solution Discovery

Two steps occur in identifying solutions to a problem.

1. Establish Criteria

Basically, this step involves stating criteria by which all group members and others can judge solutions in order to weed out alternatives that do not fit the criteria or goals set. Frequent criteria for assessing solutions include workability, feasibility, acceptability, positive or negative consequences, costs, number of people impacted, and return on investment.

In response to the question "What should be the policy of our company regarding alternative sources of energy?" a discussion group might set up the following criteria for judging alternatives:

The solution must be *equitable*—from the environmental perspective and from the company's position.

The solution must be *easily implemented*. Societal and structural modifications should be minimal; legislation required, if any, must receive majority support.

The supply of the source must be *consistently adequate* for the company's production program in three plants.

The solution must provide *economic advantages*. Manufacturers' incentives to comply with the proposed solution, industrial incentives to innovate and improve efficiency must not be inhibited.

A company report on the question of "What should be the company policy on drugs in the workplace?" included criteria for evaluating options in this manner.

Criteria

1. Practicality: Will the proposed procedures and tests create
                         more personnel problems than we have now in
                         this case?

2. Feasibility: Even if practical, will the recommended solution be
                         implementable, especially considering cost factors?

3. Rights: Are the employees' personal rights as well as the
                         less well defined employer rights protected? (One
                         might consider employer rights to include expec-
                         tancy of average performance levels and produc-
                         tivity.)

Thus all proposed solutions are measured against consistent criteria. Interestingly, some criteria may change during a meeting, new criteria may be added
or different weights may be attached. You, as chairperson, must adapt to those
group-proposed changes.

2. List Possible Solutions

You as a new graduate may often offer in a meeting a solution that you feel has
been logically thought out, based on time and research, and then firmly insist
that the problem can be solved in only one way. It is a rude introduction to the
business world when others suggest that your solution has little merit. Hence,
the thoughtful chairperson and participants should consider several alternative
solutions, perhaps ranging from the practical to the highly innovative.

A good technique at this point in the problem-solving process is simply to
list alternatives. *Brainstorming*—the process of listing as many ideas as possible
without judgment from any group member—is a favored method. Here persons,
interested in solving a problem, offer ideas in a freewheeling atmosphere. No
criticisms are allowed, even for off-the-wall solutions.

After everyone has had a chance to voice suggestions, the list is shortened,
usually in light of stated criteria. Several good ideas may thus arise, and later
serve as a list from which may come the final solution.

What list of solutions, for example, would you propose to the question
stated above, "What should be the company policy on drugs in the workplace?"
A shortened list of possibile solutions from one company looked like this:

```
--During recruitment let candidates sign release forms for
  drug testing.

--Managers should orally and in writing communicate this
  message:  Employees will be fired if caught using drugs on
  the job.

--External drug rehabilitation programs will be used for
  those using drugs.
```

--"No Drugs in the Workplace" should be posted throughout
  the company.

--An employee assistance program (EAP) is the central goal
  in the war against drugs.

--Drug testing must be used in conjunction with other means
  of employee assistance.

Solution Evaluation

The preceding step was simply formulating a list of *tentative* suggestions on solving a problem. Now you must evaluate all suggestions in light of your stated criteria. In other words, you begin testing, locating pro and con reasons about a solution, answering whether a preferred solution truly will solve a problem or create new ones. As you work through the process in a discussion, you may end with selecting one of your tentative proposals, create an entirely new solution, or combine parts of several solutions. Your responsibility is this: You should arrive at a solution during this evaluation phase.

A series of questions can serve as hints to what you could be asking, for example, on this problem: "What health programs will best meet the needs of our workers?"

What will be the consequences of adopting one of the tentative solutions?

Will any of the solutions introduce new dangers or new problems?

Will all the causes of the problem be removed?

How does each of the solutions meet the criteria established for judgment of the solutions?

What are the advantages and disadvantages of each solution?

What effect will the solution have on the future?

Has the solution proved workable at another company or in a similar situation?

Is there a professional organization or a person held in high regard in support of one of the options?

In each of us are hidden reasons why we support or do not support a proposed solution. Our reasons may be based on personal attitudes, opinions, bias, or prejudice, as discussed in Chapters 2 and 21. But the rational person will try to apply a reasoned approach to problem-solving meetings. Consensus, or formal vote, then determines the solution to be accepted.

With the solution accepted, you still have one more thing to decide.

Choice of Action

Unless your group is the final decision maker, your recommendation to a higher administrative unit should include specifics on implementing the solution. A precise person or office within the firm may be asked to implement the proposal and be assigned a budget. Central to the action step is setting a time for completing the solution; that step places accountability on either the individual or the department asked to oversee implementation.

A company submitted the following action steps to accompany a proposed recommendation on new and continuing building projects:

```
                        OUTLAY REQUESTS

In accordance with the procedures established by the Board
of Directors, the Building Services Office will implement
the newly approved building program and continue ongoing
projects.

New Projects

1. Site development                              $   400,000
   [Details on plans for new projects,
   contractors, etc.]

2. Utilities                                     $   900,000
   [Similar detail as above.]

Continuing Projects

1. Laboratory building                           $1,960,000
   [Update on progress, who's in charge,
   how time line fits in with agreed-upon
   completion time. . . .]

Summary
```

[*Brief summary statement on the 16 projects included in the report.*]

The document was signed by the vice president in charge of the Building Services office.

Example of Complete Outline Using Scientific, Reflective Process

Assume for this example that you are an employee of an automotive organization and that your superior asked you to do two things: (1) prepare a written report and (2) lead a discussion on the general topic of productivity improvement in the auto industry. Your complete outline—a mix of the written and oral—could progress in the following manner:

```
I. Background Analysis
   A. Problem in form of question
      "What can be done to increase productivity in the
      American automotive industry?"
```

   B. <u>Defining, limiting problem</u>
      1. Productivity may be defined as the "percentage change in output divided by a percentage change in input."
      2. A limiting factor is that productivity is rarely constant in the automotive industry, because of variances in models, schedules, and the like.
      3. <u>Input</u> is defined as labor, invested capital, materials, or the effort or ingenuity of management.
   C. <u>Background, history of problem</u>
      1. Importance of the problem in the declining productivity effects on the American household
      2. Automotive production history
         a. 1950–1960   c. 1970–1980
         b. 1960–1970   d. 1980–1990
      3. Possible causes of productivity decline
         a. Management is confronted with unpredictable long-run costs, financial markets, foreign competition, stockholders.
         b. Work force problems include boredom and frustration, job movement, absenteeism, high turnover rate.
         c. Labor unions are affected by rates higher than in Japanese auto plants, restriction on output, cost-of-living allowances.
         d. Government excessive regulation in the seventies, tax structure for business, devalued asset allowance are noteworthy.
      4. The Japanese approach to productivity
         a. Culture and philosophy of Japanese people
         b. Work force of Japan's auto companies
         c. Organizational structure of Japanese auto industry
         d. Use of automation in Japanese auto industry
      5. Effects of productivity decline
         a. Poor quality of product
         b. GNP affected; one-fifth of GNP auto-related
         c. Competitive edge lost
         d. American dollar decrease in value

II. <u>Solution Discovery</u>
   A. <u>Establishing criteria</u>
      1. Low cost: Costs may be dollar costs or social costs.
      2. Time: Notice time before solution implementation and time before measurable results are obtainable.
      3. Effectiveness: Must produce measurable, positive results for consumer, worker, manager.

```
                    4. Feasibility:   affordability and practicality of
                                      solution must be considered
             B. Possible solution
                    1. Motivation of the worker
                    2. Use of improved technology
                    3. Management changes
                    4. Labor and their unions
                    5. Government:  law and regulations

       III. Solution Evaluation
             A. Advantages of solutions 1, 2, 3, 4, 5
             B. Disadvantages of solutions 1, 2, 3, 4, 5
             C. Acceptance of solution:  combination of all five
                solutions

        IV. Choice of Action
             A. A committee of five persons, selected by the chair-
                person, will contact (1) legislators, (2) American
                Association of Manufacturers, (3) labor leaders.
             B. The committee will submit a cover letter and full
                report, with final recommendation, to the groups
                named above by August 31, 199-.
```

The preceding example is the ideal; it is included as a preeminent example of what one could do to prepare for a meeting. Surely a shorter version is possible, but how condensed is dependent on your familiarity with the issue.

SUMMARY

Two basic purposes of business meetings are (1) to present information and (2) to solve problems. Many business meetings are based on written reports or papers submitted in advance. Such information includes background material leading to the solving of a problem; oral discussion follows.

In a meeting the democratic and participative leader is most desired. The authoritarian leader is concerned with self and is dogmatic, while a leaderless group has little guidance and shares leadership functions.

Effective leadership requires careful planning before the meeting—to consider the problem and purpose; participants; meeting date, time, place; wording of the question for the meeting; preparation of agenda announcement; and physical arrangements within the meeting.

During the meeting the leader has responsibilities of beginning with an appropriate opening statement and stimulating discussion for solution discovery, evaluation, and choice of action. The chairperson also encourages minority opinions, tests unsupported generalizations, clarifies vague statements, and maintains an atmosphere of goodwill and cooperation.

After the meeting, the leader's functions include distributing the minutes and seeing that responsible appointments are made and that a date is set to carry out the necessary action.

Desirable responsibilities as a participant include thorough preparation for a meeting followed by effective role participation in that meeting. The participant may be an organizer, clarifier, questioner, factual contributor, energizer, idea creator, critical tester, conciliator, and helper of others. All these roles may be used in a meeting, or you may perhaps use only four or five; regardless, you will be making a positive contribution to the group.

The rational, logical, reflective pattern of solving problems is most effective in business meetings. You begin with background material on a problem, arrive at a tentative list of solutions, evaluate those solutions on the basis of stated criteria, and ultimately decide on a plan of action.

EXERCISES AND PROBLEMS

1. Supply definitions for the following terms that have a relationship to meetings and group discussion:

Conference	Colloquy
Symposium	Committee
Panel forum	Parliamentary procedure
Debate	

2. ***Report on a meeting, chairperson, and participants:*** Attend a meeting on your campus or in your community; report back on the following questions:

    a. Was the purpose of the meeting clear?

    b. What were some actions by the chairperson:

    - How was the meeting begun?
    - Was the chairperson democratic, or were other kinds of leadership exhibited?
    - What was done to move the group along toward a decision?
    - How was the decision regarding a problem announced?

    c. What roles were played by participants?

    - Were negative characteristics exhibited by some members? If so, what were those characteristics?
    - What kinds of support did members bring to the discussion? How did they support their ideas?
    - Describe the most useful member in the group; what made that person effective?

3. ***Evaluations of questions for problem-solving discussion:*** The following questions have been posed by other students as they considered topics for a discussion. Their goal was to have a problem-solving discussion before the class. Evaluate these questions: which are satisfactory and which are not?

    a. New products for next year?

    b. What's the problem with our new administration and education building?

    c. Is our economy getting better or worse?

     d. What should be the policy of the government on allowing banks to sell securities?

     e. Oral communication in business—what makes it effective?

     f. What steps can business take to improve business relations with Third World countries?

     g. Should the B.B.A. students go on in school and obtain their M.B.A. degree?

     h. Which of the Big Eight accounting firms is the most respected in our state?

4. *Fact, value, policy questions for meetings:* Wording the question for a meeting is important. Write at least three questions each on fact, value, and policy. Bring these to class and defend them as being of fact, value, and policy.

5. *Evaluations of participants' contributions during a public meeting:* Attend a public meeting of a local school board, a city council, or a student organization. Use the following evaluation form for determining the number and kinds of contributions made by the participants. Bring the form to class for a report on the roles participants played in the meeting.

PARTICIPATION FORM

Discussion group: _____

Date: _____

Check in the appropriate category the type of contribution made by each of the participants. (See the discussion of participant roles in this chapter.)

Type of contribution   *Participant*

	#1	#2	#3	#4	#5	#6	#7
Organizer							
Clarifier							
Questioner							
Factual contributor							
Energizer							
Idea creator							
Critical tester							
Conciliator							
Helper of others							

Which type of contribution was made most often? Why? _____

_____

_____

_____

_____

6. ***Oral-written group work using scientific, reflective method:*** The information below summarizes the basic requirements of this oral written assignment involving extensive group work on employing the scientific, reflective method.

 a. Each member of the class will be assigned to a group.

 b. Each group will select its own chairperson, set its own meetings outside of class, meet the deadlines imposed, select its own problem for the assignment.

 c. Each group will present to the class and instructor the following information:

   (1) On the day before the background-analysis presentation, distribute to the class—or announce—the topic to be discussed in the following class period.

   (2) On the day of the informative, background-analysis presentation about the group problem:

     (a) The group distributes the agenda for the meeting.

     (b) The chairperson introduces group members, sets out the direction for the meeting.

     (c) Each member in the group orally presents one part of the background, location, recognition, description of the problem chosen by the group.

      - Definitions needed to understand discussion
      - History of problem
      - Effects of problem
      - Causes of problem
      - Importance of problem
      - Evolution of problem (early period; late period)
      - Comparison of problem

     (d) The chairperson concludes the presentation and allows questions and discussion with members of the class.

     (e) A secretary can take minutes on the presentations of group members.

     (f) The meeting is adjourned.

   (3) On the day of the persuasive solution presentations about the group problem:

     (a) The minutes of the preceding meeting may be presented to the class for approval.

(b) The chairperson of the group summarizes the preceding background presentation of the group.

(c) Each member in the group orally offers his or her own solution to the group problem.

- Criteria for evaluating alternatives to solving the problem
- Overview or range or listing of solutions available to solve the problem
- Solution A
- Solution B
- Solution C
- Solution A/B
- Solution C/D

(d) The chairperson concludes the presentation by summarizing the alternative solutions presented and allows questions and discussion with group members.

(e) A secretary may record the presentations of the group members.

(f) The class or group may or may not decide on a single solution.

7. ***Review of the decision process on a published issue:*** Review in a local newspaper, a campus paper, or a national business journal an issue that ultimately was solved, by vote of a governing body. Such an issue may have consumed several months of deliberations and be a business issue, a school issue, or a governmental issue. Your task is to review the process of arriving at the final decision, through doing the following:

   a. State the problem as you perceive it as a question of fact, value, or policy.
   b. List the various options that were considered.
   c. State whether criteria were announced before or during any discussion.
   d. Summarize, briefly, the final solution or recommendation voted on or approved by the approval body.

Having presented that outline, offer an analysis as to where you think the major problems lay in arriving at the final decision.

Chapter 24

Successful Interpersonal and Other Oral Communications

Within business, professional, and governmental organizations you have many opportunities for one-to-one communication. Much of that will be casual, but a considerable amount of time will focus on purposeful two-person (dyadic) communication. Your work will likely include interviewing, telephoning, and dictating. This chapter begins with a background statement on one-to-one communication and then offers suggestions for handling the three above common forms of interpersonal communication.

DYADIC COMMUNICATION

A *dyad* is defined as two persons who seek to exchange information. In fact numerous writers center their entire discussion of interpersonal communication on that term. Communication which is unidirectional is one-way communication.

What is lacking in Figure 24-1 is a feedback loop. In the top example listener B simply receives information and does not communicate back to sender A. The second example suggests that listener B is a sender (speaker) and in turn does not receive feedback from listener C. Is such communication true interpersonal communication? No. Some might argue that it is impossible *not* to communicate. Even averting one's eyes or not responding orally is a form of response. However, a more purposeful exchange between two people must occur for good interpersonal communication to exist (Figure 24-2).

How would you respond to this question: What are the kinds of two-person interaction occurring during your business day? Your response might be that telephone conversations and discussions with your boss or subordinates are the ost frequent. That may be true, but casual conversations with one other person also dyadic, yet less structured, less formal. We can classify two-person versations two ways—by function and by type.

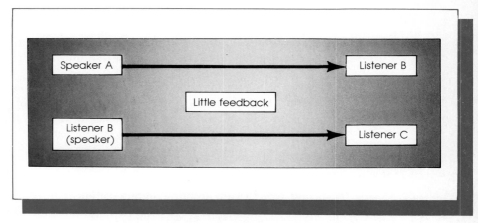

Figure 24–1   Little speaker-listener feedback.

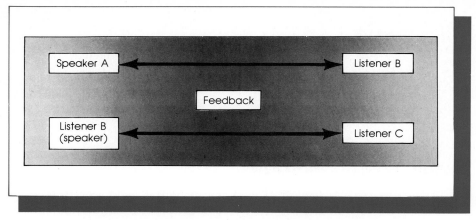

Figure 24–2   *Considerable speaker-listener feedback.*

Functional Relationships

In the business world a purposeful meeting between two people may fall into several major categories, based on why the meeting is held. The key word here is "purposeful," which excludes the numerous casual, impromptu meetings which occur.

> Employment interview (evaluating qualifications for a position)
>
> Training and instructional interview (informing each new employee about specific duties in the position)
>
> Counseling interview (understanding work-related personal problems or questions—financial, health, family)
>
> Work evaluation interview (reviewing job performance)
>
> Disciplining interview (discussing potential reprimands)
>
> Complaint interview (expressing complaint on an annoying situation)
>
> Job termination (exit) interview (getting the departing employee's reasons or feelings about company policies that may need changes)

Note that each of these categories has a purpose, a distinct function. Underlying each of these functions is an exchange of information to assist, guide, or inform both employee and manager. Most of, if not all, the interviews would be between two people, a dyadic relationship.

Types of Relationships

A second way to view dyadic communication is to think of the level at which you relate to other people. A possible continuum of communication relationships—out of an endless list of possibilities—could include those shown in Figure 24-3.

The words exchanged between persons in an intimate relationship (spouses, significant others, dates, partners) are clearly at a different level of exposure and intimacy than the other relationship categories. While some intimate relationships do exist in a work setting, your communication will more likely avoid the kinds of topics and intimacy reserved for your family and those close to you.

Most of your interpersonal communication at work will be at the "friend" and "acquaintances" levels. It will be more formal, with the topics heavily business-related. At meetings you may see people you do not know; they are strangers and completely nonintimate.

Review for a moment. What sort of oral or nonverbal greeting did you receive from complete strangers today? Were you greeted orally or given some form of recognition as a stranger passed you? Maybe even eye contact was avoided.

As your intimacy with another person increases, the kinds of communication you exchange and kinds of things you talk about also change. Thus speaking about the weather is a safe, nonthreatening oral greeting; or a slight nod, or a hesitant wave to a stranger is usually acceptable. Rare is the person who launches into controversy immediately on meeting a stranger. Only after some sharing of pleasantries do both persons begin to open up and make public their views on issues. Time generally raises the level of intimacy. Some forms of address may become more familiar; first names replace last names.

To dissect minutely how one classifies one's relationships with others serves little purpose. What is important, however, is that communication with one other person in a work relationship is different from speaking to your spouse, a family member, a friend, or a total stranger. How to communicate effectively

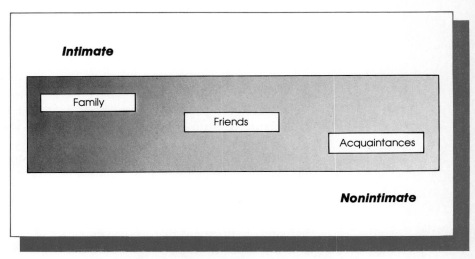

Figure 24–3 *Interpersonal relationships.*

on a functional level with an employee or a superior in an interview situation is the focus of the following section.

INTERVIEWING

The interview is the most often used form of dyadic communication in business. Though specific functions may vary, the steps in planning for interviews have basic similarities. This section summarizes seven common interview objectives, notes the essentials common to both parties for successful interviews, discusses the responsibilities of the interviewer, and ends with a checklist for the interviewer. (Chapter 13 includes a checklist for interviewees who are job applicants, and provides suggestions for answering interviewers' questions.)

Uses of the Interview

The following list summarizes the various ways interviews are used:

Use	Procedure	Example
Seeking position	Candidates speak with company representative.	Recruiter meets with graduating students or job seekers.
Informing on job	Job requirements are stated as based on job description or job experience.	Senior member or boss meets with new employee early in job experience.
Solving problem	Facts are collected, options reviewed, decision is made.	Employer talks with successful employee who is abrasive.
Supporting solution	Information is collected and arguments are planned to persuade.	Manager persuades employee who is opposed to recommendation.
Counseling employee	Facts are used to support contention that employee needs help.	Employee, accused of drug abuse on the job, is presented with treatment options.
Evaluating employee	Job performance review form is discussed.	Supervisor makes yearly review of employee.
Gathering information	Data are gathered on why employees leave; emphasis is on events and not personalities.	Manager conducts exit interview.

Undoubtedly there are many other examples of the one-to-one interview, but the above examples suggest that you as an employee or as a manager will be involved in interviews. How to make them more effective is the topic of the next section.

Essentials for Successful Interviews

To be effective, interviews require preparation beforehand; efficient, thoughtful procedures during the discussion; and follow-up afterward.

Preparation before the Interview

As emphasized often in this text regarding written and oral presentations, careful preparation is essential. Whether you are interviewer (the one who conducts the interview) or interviewee, you should usually go through the following planning steps:

1. Know the specific purpose at the time the appointment is made.

2. Find out as much as will be useful about the other person—name, position, attitude, work, needs, biases, background.

3. Collect all facts and materials necessary for attaining the objective.

4. Plan questions you will ask and consider answers you may give to questions the other person asks you.

The place chosen for the interview should be appropriately quiet, comfortable, and free of distracting interruptions.

Procedures during the Interview

1. Begin with sincere, pleasant comments that establish harmony and goodwill; get "in step" with each other.

2. State the purpose of the interview. (This statement is usually given by the interviewer.)

3. Present facts and questions in language that follows the seven C principles. Be concise, complete, considerate, concrete, clear, courteous, correct. Allow time for the other person to speak before you proceed to the next point. This discussion is the main part of the interview—comparable to the body of a speech, and text section of a report.

4. Listen attentively to each other's views, be receptive to suggested solutions, and be courteous also when you disagree.

5. Notice meaningful nonverbal cues that sometimes are different from the spoken words (a forced smile on the outside, crying or anger inside?).

6. Work to achieve agreement on action to be taken—what, when, why, where, by whom, and how.

7. If you are the interviewer, before closing summarize the main points and make sure that you both understand the conclusions or actions to be taken.

Follow-Up after the Interview

The need and extent of follow-up activities depend on the specific purpose of the interview and the decisions reached in it. Whatever future actions are agreed upon should be carried out within the scheduled time. The interviewer (or a dependable assistant) should check on them. Other interviews may be necessary and should be scheduled.

Interviewer's Responsibilities in Employment Interviews

This section presents detailed suggestions for the interviewer—recruiter—who interviews job applicants. The following topics are included: objectives, preparation before the interview, procedures during the interview, evaluations afterward, and a checklist for the interviewer. In Chapter 13 you can reread suggestions for the interviewee—the job applicant. Chapter 5 mentions some legal aspects regarding interview questions.

Objectives of the Patterned Interview

A patterned interview is more often used in reviewing job candidates. Some companies use a consistent evaluation form—for all company interviewers—to be sure all of them collect similar information. Some schools have consistent resume forms that permit quick, standardized review of resumes before the interviewers meet the candidates. In a patterned interview the interviewer controls the direction of the conversation.

The interview's threefold objective for the patterned interview of a job applicant is to:

1. Help evaluate job qualifications that other sources cannot assess as well

2. Give the applicant essential facts about the job and the company

3. Create and promote goodwill toward the company

Interviewer's Preparation before Employment Interview

If you are an interviewer of job applicants, prepare in the following ways before the interview:

1. Read each applicant's resume before the interview.

2. Know your company's organizational structure; also know the requirements and work environment of the job about which you are interviewing applicants.

3. Decide what information you need from each applicant. Usually the areas pertain to character, personality, work experience, training, interests, and activities.

4. Know the current regulations—national and those in your state—regarding fair employment practices.

5. Plan your questions. Be sure they are within the laws concerning marital status, age, race, sex, religion, and other matters. Some schools have an interview review committee to be sure the questions and behavior of the interviewers are appropriate, and legal. (For a list of suggestions, see Chapter 5.)

6. Make your questions clear, free from personal bias, and essentially the same for all candidates you will interview for the same position. For a list of questions that might be asked during the interview, see pages 359–363).

7. Choose a quiet, distraction-free room for the interview. (If you are interviewing on a campus, you will of course adapt to whatever facilities are available.)

8. Arrange your schedule so that no one will have to wait long.

Warm-Up Period of the Interview

Earlier we considered how we communicate with strangers, trying to avoid controversial topics as both persons search for a common ground. Nonverbally, greet the candidate with a firm handshake and a warm smile. Orally, suggest a degree of enthusiasm in your greeting; be sincere and friendly. It is up to the interviewer to set the interviewee at ease, perhaps building on some current topic as suggested in the resume. A candidate's hobbies are a nice noncontroversial beginning to an interview.

Main Content of the Interview

After the brief warm-up, you make clear the purpose of the interview and the topics you plan to cover. You encourage the applicant to do most of the talking, but you control the interview and see that it does not wander aimlessly. You ask appropriate planned questions, use desirable methods throughout the interview, and avoid pitfalls.

Asking Appropriate Questions.   You might begin by letting the applicant describe his or her education, then move to the work history and off-the-job activities. Focus on relevant information that cannot be obtained as well from other sources.

Open-ended questions and statements are usually preferred because the applicant can give you more information—both verbal and nonverbal. Among useful open-ended questions you might ask are those that begin with "what," "which," "why," "how," or "tell me"—like some of the suggested questions on pages 359 to 361.

Which courses were the most useful in your degree program? Why?

Which courses did you like best? Least? Why?

Please describe yourself in comparison with other members of your class.

Outside of school what are your interests?

What experiences in your previous jobs have helped you prepare for the job you are now seeking?

Describe the kind of manager for whom you would like to work.

Why are you leaving your present job? [*If the applicant mentions "problems with my supervisor" or other vague reasons, you may tactfully probe for clarification.*]

Dead-end questions (also called *closed questions*) usually ask for only "yes" or "no" or other one-word answers.

How many people graduated in your class?

Can you give me the percentage of foreign graduates who majored in accounting? Marketing? Finance?

How many accounting courses did you have in college? Did you enjoy college? Which course was most difficult?

Questions similar to these elicit quick responses that are easy to tabulate. But the information is often less helpful than that from open-ended questions—unless you probe for an explanation or reasons for the answers.

Using Effective Methods.   A few cautions regarding wording of questions are noteworthy. To be fair, avoid leading questions that invite a given response or that show your own preferences. They may tempt a tense applicant to slant answers accordingly, especially if he or she is reluctant to admit having no knowledge of the matter at all.

I'm personally in favor of . . . ; what's your view?

What is your opinion of the unfair ruling our state legislature recently made regarding . . . ?

Questions should be neutral and not be about provocative, controversial issues or personal matters that will embarrass the applicant and are irrelevant to the job.

Additional suggestions for effective methods during the interview are in the checklist for interviewer, pages 715 and 716.

Evaluation after the Interview

Immediately after closing the interview, write notes on all important points. Using the information you have obtained from the candidate during the interview, and supplementing it with vital facts from other sources, you must form an overall opinion. In your evaluation of the interview, the following clues should prove useful in determining the applicant's state of mind and general makeup.[1]

Positive	Negative
1. Behavioral and psychological symptoms	
a. Early arrival	**a.** Late arrival
b. Alert, responsive attitude	**b.** Inattentive, dull attitude
c. Emphatic attitude	**c.** Condescending or withdrawn attitude
d. Relaxed manner	**d.** Tenseness, fidgetiness, body tremors
e. Smiling	**e.** Frowning
f. Clear voice	**f.** Choked voice, mumbling
2. Verbal symptoms	
a. Sticking to the main point	**a.** Changing the subject
b. Incisiveness	**b.** Overgeneralizing or providing of too much detail
c. Relevant responses	**c.** Irrelevant responses
d. Well-organized presentation	**d.** Disorganized presentation
e. Appropriate use of humor	**e.** Uncalled-for levity
f. Spontaneous replies	**f.** Long pauses before replying
g. Speaking well of people	**g.** Criticism of others
h. Candor	**h.** Rationalization, evasiveness

After the interview you may prepare an "interview write-up," consisting of a one- or two-page report with a paragraph on whatever areas are pertinent to the interview. It may cover such items as education and training, work experience, current off-the-job life, personal characteristics, and overall summary. The beginning of the report shows the interviewee's name, the date, topics considered, and the name of interviewer. At the end (you might call it "conclusion") is a scale where the interviewer checks his or her overall rating of the applicant in relation to others interviewed.

■ Checklist for Interviewer

Before Interview

■ Read resume.
■ Know structure, philosophy of company.
■ Plan questions.

(continued)

- Choose comfortable room.
- Know which questions may not be asked.

During Interview

- Warmup through familiar, comfortable topics.
- Use open-ended questions; ask for details when necessary.
- Listen, let candidate do most of the talking, but tactfully control direction of interview.
- Avoid biased, illegal questions.
- Omit personal bias as basis for likes and dislikes.
- Note oral and nonverbal skills, as a guide to degree of social skills. Keep your own opinions and nonverbal cues to yourself.
- Give interviewee chance to ask questions.
- Jot down a few notes, but do detailed notes later.
- End with courtesy, indicating what applicant should do next or when a decision may be expected.

After Interview

- If possible, immediately dictate or record major points to be remembered about person.
- Use consistent criteria on education, work experience, etc.
- Keep records straight; if possible, indicate applicant's overall rating in relation to others interviewed.

TELEPHONING

Throughout the world the telephone, along with face-to-face communication, is the most used mode of communication, but it is often ill used. Because most of its uses and values are familiar, we will look only at how to be more effective in using it.

Suggestions for Effective Telephoning (One to One)

As with all other successful written and oral communication, telephoning requires preplanning by the caller and desirable behavior during the conversation by both persons who are conversing. As some commercials advise, "Reach out and touch someone." Though you are not meeting face to face, your conversation will be voice to voice and you want it to be as favorable as possible.

Preplanning by the Caller

1. Know the specific purpose of your call.

2. Know the name and occupation (if pertinent) of the person you are calling.

3. Consider the best time to phone, from the standpoint of that person and of your company. Usually, avoid calling just before lunch or at closing time. If you are calling long-distance, be sure to consider time zones; consult your phone directory map. Choose discount times whenever possible and desirable.

4. Plan your opening statement.

5. Jot down the questions you want to ask. Try to limit your call to one main point. If you are calling to sell something, know your sales psychology and have factual suggestions for listener benefits. The suggestions for unsolicited sales letters—in Chapter 11—may be helpful for your phoning, too.

6. Have paper and pen handy for note-taking; also place near the phone any figures, files, former correspondence, or whatever may be necessary for reference during the conversation.

Behavior during the Telephone Conversation

When You Are the Caller.   Introduce yourself, and if you are calling long-distance, say so at the beginning. Secretaries are more willing to interrupt their bosses if they know you are calling from out of town. Person-to-person calls add importance and a feeling of urgency. If the person you are calling is not in, ask whoever answers the phone for the best time to reach that person. Or you can leave a message with your number and time to have your call returned.

When You Answer a Phone Call.   With a clear, pleasant voice answer promptly, usually with your name and department. If you are answering for your employer or a co-worker, you might say, "Mr. Brown's office. This is Martha. How may I help you?" If Mr. Brown happens to be in another office, you might transfer the call (with the caller's permission) or suggest when Mr. Brown can be reached in his office. The tone of your voice, your language, and courtesy to the caller can often create impressions that are critically important for personal and organizational success.

When You Record on a Recording Device.   Many business- and professional persons now use a recording device when they do not wish to answer the phone or when they are absent from their office. "I'm not available right now, but when you hear the tone, please leave your message, name, the date and time you called, and your phone number; I will get back to you" is a sample recording.

When you respond to this invitation, speak slowly, giving your message as naturally as possible. Then add your name, phone number, day and time when you called, and when you can be reached.

■ Checklist for Telephone Communication

1. At the beginning of your conversation with the desired person, smile. Though your listener cannot see you, the tone of your voice will sound more pleasant when you smile.
2. Establish rapport—preferably with some item of interest or benefit to your listener.
3. State the purpose of your call and proceed—with a clear, enthusiastic voice—to one of your questions or to your main point, unless it is bad news that should come only after other material has been tactfully presented.
4. Listen to the other person's views, ideas, and suggested solutions; don't interrupt.
5. Listen also for the tone of the other person's voice; if it sounds annoyed, negative, angry, try to be helpful without arguing immediately.
6. If you are trying to sell something, never read a sales pitch word for word. It will sound insincere and canned. Adjust your presentation to your listener as well as possible. Be sincere and truthful.
7. Before closing, restate the main decisions, if any, that were made, and check that your listener agrees with your statements.
8. Thank your listener, and let him or her hang up before you do.

Variety of Telephoning Equipment and Uses

During the past decade amazing new electronic technological advancements have widely expanded the ways telephones can be used. Still further significant inventions are progressing rapidly each year (see also the prologue). The following is just a brief sample of some popular kinds of special telephone equipment for efficient oral communication.[2]

■ *Automated attendant* is a computer-controlled answering machine that responds to incoming telephone calls and presents the caller with a series of options to reach individuals or departments within the system. It can also respond to calls made directly to specific stations by playing a prerecorded announcement from the person called. Through the use of touch tone codes, these announcements can be changed quickly from any telephone, inside or outside of the system.

- *Automatic call distributors* answer numerous incoming calls, play a prerecorded message to the callers, place them on "hold" (sometimes with music background and additional announcements played periodically as long as the callers remain on the line), and forward each call to the first available operator. These are especially useful in a telemarketing environment—for airline and hotel reservations, credit and adjustment inquiries, department stores, and any other offices having a high volume of incoming calls.
- *Cellular mobile phone service* enables people to make local and long-distance calls to and from cars, trucks, buses, boats, and ferries that have phones. Calls can be completed by dialing direct or calling the operator.
- *Data communications* can electronically route information from computer terminals or personal computers by using the existing telecommunications network with the help of modems. Many businesses have developed data communication networks that interconnect all their branch offices to a central computer in their headquarters location.
- *800 service* lets out-of-town customers dial businesses without charge; they can place orders, ask questions, or check on orders.
- *Facsimile telecommunication equipment* transmits drawings, graphs, pictures, and written messages using data impulses and signals by means of the telecommunication network.
- *Integrated Services Digital Network (ISDN)* is an evolutionary communication system that replaces analog transmission with digital. When in place, special ISDN equipment on a person's desk or in the home will be able to transmit voice, data, fax images, and a host of other communications devices over the same pair of wires at the same time.
- *Intercoms* enable persons within an organization to have direct telephone connections with each other simply by dialing one- to four-digit code numbers. There's no need to walk to see co-workers; participants can stay at their own desks with all information needed right at their fingertips.
- *International calls* can be placed to practically any country in the world either by direct dialing or by assistance from an operator.
- *Message waiting service* lights a "lamp" on the user's phone, indicating that a message was taken while the person was away. This system is especially useful for hotel guests as well as for executives and everyone else who needs to know who called during his or her absence.
- *Outdoor phones* protected in weather-resistant housing are for emergency calls on highways, construction sites, forestry stations, streets. The new "911" service in communities that have it will automatically route calls to the nearest speedy emergency service.
- *Paging equipment* broadcasts messages (by a loudspeaker voice or beeps) to various locations within the organization, to locate "missing" persons in the office, thus giving better service to callers.
- *Pocket pagers* alert their users to calls when they are in a meeting,

restaurant, or anywhere within a given number of miles from their offices. The pagers are 24-hour conveniences with an optional dual-tone feature that lets users distinguish between emergencies and routine calls; they also have built-in memory to collect messages and relay them when users turn them back on.

- *Private Branch Exchange (PBX)* switchboard and its extensions serve as a telephone exchange performed by operators within an organization, enabling speedy, direct internal dialing and forwarding of incoming calls.

- *Recording equipment* automatically answers incoming calls, states a prerecorded message to the caller, records the caller's message, and disconnects.

- *Remote Call Forwarding (RCF)* is a unique telephone service that gives out-of-town customers a local number to a firm's home office. For the business firm it's like having a branch office in all or any of 350 markets nationwide—at a mere fraction of the cost. Listings can be in local directories wherever the service is available, and customers call as easily as a local call.

- *Special attachments for handicapped* listeners convert telephone sounds into comprehensible signals for those who have impaired or lost hearing, sight, or speech.

- *Speed calling* abbreviates a 7- or 10-digit telephone number to 1 or 2 digits for faster, easier, more accurate dialing of frequently called telephone numbers. Speed calling is available from your local telephone company in most computerized central offices, and can also be obtained through certain types of telephone equipment.

- *Teleconferences* among three or more people in two or more locations widely separated geographically can be valuable savers of travel time, fuel, and money when used in place of face-to-face meetings.

- *Videoconferencing* among three or more people in two or more locations has the added advantage that participants *see and hear* those who are in the meeting—on their respective home premises or on telephone company property or leased premises that have the needed equipment.

- *Voice mail* is a system that provides a quick, easy way to leave messages for individuals or groups within a business telephone system. When used with a computer-controlled attendant, the voice mail system allows callers to leave a message for the person dialed. Through the use of a touch-tone telephone, these messages are easily retrieved, saved, transferred to others' mailboxes, or erased.

- *WATS (Wide Area Telecommunication Service)* enables persons to call from a WATS line to order telephone numbers within a designated service area or zone. WATS customers pay for long-distance calls based on the monthly usage of network time; details of each call are not included in the service. WATS is used for outgoing calls only.

DICTATING

Up to now the discussion in this chapter has focused on direct oral conversations between two persons (dyadic communication) speaking either face to face in an interview or voice to voice in a telephone conversation. Dictation is also oral communication—to an intermediary who transcribes the spoken words into a written message that is to be sent to an addressee. Because a frequent complaint of secretaries pertains to the poor dictating habits of executives, this section focuses on both the importance of good dictation and suggestions for better dictation.

Importance of Dictation

The person who can dictate messages clearly and quickly (instead of writing them all out in longhand) saves time and money for the employer and also, indirectly, helps build goodwill with customers.

The importance of good, clear dictation is especially noteworthy when one considers the enormous costs of errors resulting from poor dictation. Transcription errors because of dictators' lack of care have ranged from embarrassing or comical to costly and disastrous. Five examples are mentioned here.

1. A department supervisor, intending to write to the Dungeness Crab Company, began his dictation (to a new secretary) with this statement: "Send the following letter to Dungeness Crab Co." (He pronounced the last word as "ko.") The result? His letter—which he unfortunately signed and mailed without reading the inside address—was addressed to "Mr. Dunjen S. Crabco."

2. An insurance agent with a southern accent found that a secretary had transcribed what he dictated as "Mr. Robert's heart murmur" as "Mr. Robert's hot mama."

3. Another dictator's poor enunciation and omission of spelling on an unusual name resulted in a $4,000 damage suit. Her firm's wrecking crew—instead of razing an empty house at 560 McDonough Street—had begun to tear down an empty house at 516 McDonald Street!

4. A chief engineer had a habit of uttering "huh" and "er" between phrases while dictating into a microphone, and of dropping off word endings—saying, for instance, "hund" instead of "hundred." On one important material requisition for this international construction company a new typist misinterpreted this engineer's "uh" for "hundred," and thus she typed 111,000 feet of a certain dimension of lumber instead of the intended 11,000 feet. The requisition with the unnoticed error was duplicated and mailed to the company's 50 construction engineering branch offices. Can you estimate the cost of that error causing all those offices to buy 100,000 extra feet of unneeded lumber?

5. A new skilled and intelligent foreign worker joined an engineering firm. Face-to-face oral communication went well because listeners could ask questions of clarification if words were misunderstood. When he dictated his first tape, three secretaries in the "pool" refused to work on it; it was unintelligible to them. (The engineer later took a class in improving English for the nonnative speaker.)

Suggestions for Better Dictation

Before you dictate, prepare! Know your purpose. Visualize your reader, and consider also your secretary who will listen to your oral message and transcribe it. Collect all material and facts you will need for the content of your message. Organize your thoughts. Prepare an outline—with key words or phrases. If you are answering a letter, you might jot main points in its margin. Set aside sufficient time so you are not pressured and are free from interruptions—especially if your dictation is directly to a stenographer instead of to a machine.

Here are good oral practices to follow while dictating:

1. Dictate from your outline, using language that follows the C principles and good organization as discussed in previous chapters of this book.

2. Enunciate clearly. Very few people can speak clearly with candy, gum, or cigarettes in their mouths. Be especially careful with plurals, and figures that sound similar, such as fifty and sixty ("five o" and "six o" are much more definite). Distinguish clearly between similar sounds like p and b, m and n, f and v, t and d. Sometimes you need to say "T as in tape" or the like.

3. Spell unusual words and names when using them for the first time. Also be especially careful with the many English words that are similar in sound but different in meaning and spelling. Here are a few examples:

accept, except	ordinance, ordnance
addition, edition	practical, practicable
affect, effect	principal, principle
assistance, assistants	residence, residents
brake, break	right, rite, write
cease, seize	sight, site, cite
coarse, course	stationary, stationery
compliment, complement	straight, strait
council, consul, counsel	their, there, they're
formally, formerly	to, too, two
its, it's	waive, wave
latter, ladder	weather, whether
	who's, whose

4. Dictate—at the beginning of the message—any special instructions such as extra copies for certain persons, unusual tabulation of figures, or your desire for a rough draft only. For a complicated message—report, letter, memo, speech, etc.—you will surely want to edit and revise before it is mailed. Thus be sure to ask for a rough draft, double-spaced. Your correct instruction can save time as well as paper and supplies.

   Most dictators desire to edit their transcribed work, much as members of Congress edit their words before they become a part of the *Congressional Record*. It is a humbling experience to see your oral words put into print, without amendment. Much changing and rearranging often occur on the draft statement. Word processing equipment and magnetic tapes make the task for the secretary relatively easy; changes can quickly be made and new drafts prepared before you accept the final version.

5. The length of time you have worked with a secretary will determine the degree of oral punctuation signs you will include in your dictation. Some dictators include only "paragraph" to suggest a change in direction. Others, especially when dictating to a pool of secretaries, include "quote" and "unquote" or "parenthesis" and "close parenthesis." If the same paragraph will be used in several letters, this too is indicated—the secretary can through a few keystrokes insert the stored paragraph or data.

6. Dictate at a normal rate, as you talk. Avoid long pauses followed by rapid dictation.

7. Let your secretary use his or her initiative as to grammar corrections, additional punctuation, and arrangement of your letters, memos, and reports.

8. When dictating a reply to a letter received, you can save both your time and your stenographer's time if you dictate only the name of the addressee. Your stenographer can later copy the full address from the letter you returned after you have dictated your reply.

9. Especially when dictating by telephone or on a machine (not face to face to a secretary), be sure to omit any side comments that are neither for the operator's instructions nor for your addressee. For instance, some careless dictators have found statements like "That guy is really nuts" or "I don't believe what this darn customer wrote" within the transcribed letter. Naturally, it had to be revised.

10. If you have many important figures to be tabulated, write them on paper from which the stenographer can copy them.

11. Keep the mail you are answering in an orderly pile by turning each letter (or memo) upside down when you have finished answering it.

After all your dictation is completed, your entire pile of answered incoming correspondence will be in order for your stenographer to obtain needed information, attach file copies, and so forth.

12. Set aside definite dictation periods (for instance, a set time for each morning or afternoon) with no interruptions by telephone or callers. Of course the preceding suggestion applies only when you are at work. Numerous managers and executives do much dictating on the return flight from a meeting, using the now familiar hand-held microcassette recorder.

13. Standardize basic instructions, and put them in writing for your transcribers—to eliminate needless repetition. Develop simple code words to indicate frequently used instructions—such as "CEPO" for "Send a copy with enclosure to our Portland office."

14. Dictate less and delegate more—if you have an experienced secretary. For repetitive situations, develop effective interchangeable form paragraphs she or he can use easily. Dictate only the basic ideas, and let your secretary compose the routine letters.

Example of Dictation

The following opening and closing sections from a good-news reply to a phoned request for product information simulate how an orally dictated letter might "sound" to the transcriber. If you dictate to the secretary face to face, most of the words below in italics will be omitted. If, however, you use a voice-recording instrument, your instructions to the transcriber may be similar to those in italics below. Of course, voice inflection conveys additional (unspoken) instructions—for instance at the end of each sentence.

"Good morning, operator. This is Robert Bridges in the consumer service department. Extension 507. Please transcribe this letter addressed to Mr. Phillip *P-h-i-double l-i-p* Jones, Department four two, Harrington *H-a-double r-i-n-g-t-o-n* Corporation, one six zero zero Avenue of the Americas *plural*. New York, New York, one zero zero three eight. Dear Mr. Jones.

"Thank you for your inquiry about our, *operator, next two words all caps* ELECTRO *hyphen* SPEED, *operator, cap M as in Mary* Model 28, *operator, cap T* Typewriter. Yes, *comma* indeed *comma* this model has proved very popular in such applications as yours in which, *operator, one word* downtime must be minimized. *Paragraph."*

[*Middle paragraphs dictated in similar fashion*]

"Our sales representative in the *cap E* Eastern *cap T* Territory *comma* Tanya *T-a-n-y-a* Brickler *B-r-i-c-k-l-e-r comma* will call you next week to set up a meeting to discuss your needs more specifically *semicolon* she will then be able to inventory your needs and give you a price quotation. To help you investigate our product line more thoroughly *comma* I have enclosed six colorful brochures *period, parenthesis*. Note the blue leaflet that describes the automatic *quote, initial cap N* Never *hyphen, initial cap F* Forget *end quote* one zero zero *hyphen* character memory system *period, close parenthesis, paragraph*.

Please call me at six two one *hyphen* double nine eight seven if we can answer additional inquiries about our typewriters. Cordially yours, Robert Bridges, Customer Service Representative. Enclosures, six.

A shortened version of the same material—providing your secretary knows your style—might proceed in this manner.

"Joanne, I'll give you the business cards for all the next couple of letters when I return. Just omit the inside address. This is letter one.

"Dear Mr. Jones. Thanks for your inquiry about our ELECTRO-SPEED Model 28 Typewriter. Yes, this model has proved very popular in such applications as yours in which downtime must be minimized. Next Paragraph. . . ."

Joanne would know, from previous letters dictated by her boss, which words to capitalize, where the dictator wishes abbreviations, and even what the preferred ending should be.

SUMMARY

A dyad includes two persons seeking to exchange information. In such a relationship communication is two-way, both speaker and listener offering feedback during the exchange of ideas. Whereas intimate communication is usually reserved for family and friends, business communication is less so and may be categorized on the basis of function or types.

The most common form of dyadic communication is the interview, which has the general purposes to inform, persuade, or solve a problem. These general purposes can be found in such situations as seeking a position, informing about job requirements, solving a company problem, counseling an employee, and evaluating an employee.

The job interviewer's preparation should include knowing pertinent facts about the company, job requirements, applicant's resume (if available), and fair employment laws; also preplanning appropriate job-related questions. During the interview—after a brief, friendly warm-up period—the interviewer should courteously ask preferably more open-ended than yes-no questions, and should listen impartially for both verbal and nonverbal messages before evaluating the applicant.

A telephone conversation can often (but not always) take the place of two written messages or a face-to-face interview between two persons. Along with face-to-face communication, it is the most common form of communication used in the business world. A variety of new electronic equipment is available.

For effective telephoning the caller must preplan regarding purpose, listener, best time to phone, opening statement, questions, and supplies to have nearby. During the telephone conversation both caller and called should observe the C principles in their behavior and language while expressing ideas.

Dictation is oral communication to an intermediary who transcribes the spoken words into a written message that is to be sent to an addressee. Careful preparation includes many of the essential planning steps recommended also for interviews and telephoning. In addition, the dictator must consider the intermediary (secretary). Dictation should preferably be from an outline of key words or phrases. Desirable dictation practices include clear enunciation, spelling of unusual words (when appropriate), and adequate instructions to the transcriber—especially in machine dictation. With today's word processing systems, a secretary can quite easily prepare several drafts before the final version of the transcribed document is completed.

EXERCISES AND PROBLEMS

1. ***Oral report after an interview:*** This project involves an interview (for information-gathering purposes) and an oral presentation (for information-dissemination purposes). Your first task is to identify and interview a person who has a type of job or career that you hope to enter upon graduation. The purpose of the interview is to determine what kinds of communication activities that person must engage in during a typical week. You should not only cover the types of written messages sent and received but also determine the volume or frequency, the job title for the originator of the incoming messages, and the disposition of the messages (what your interviewee does when he or she receives each type of message). Don't forget to cover oral communication messages (verbal orders or directives, telephone requests, etc.). For outgoing written or oral messages, find out to whom (title of person) the messages are directed. Unless the interviewee keeps a log of such activities, you will have to depend on the interviewee's estimates for some of the information.

   The second part of this assignment requires you to make a formal oral report of your findings in class. A three- to five-minute time limit should be sufficient; however, your instructor may wish to establish other limits.

2. ***Exit interview planned to gather useful information:*** For efficiently handling a situation in which your oral communication skills are important to a company, you must do some preliminary planning and practice.

   Assume that you work for a firm with high employee turnover. Your responsibility is to gather information that will be useful to management in determining why so many employees leave. This information will be gathered in an exit interview procedure used by your company and conducted with every employee who leaves. You are to establish specific objectives to be followed during the interview, set up strategies that can be followed, and develop a specific list of questions that you will ask during the interview.

Try these questions out in an interview setting in class, using another member of the class as the employee who is leaving the company. In your interview, you should first express appreciation to the employee for his or her service. (This should be done in order to set the tone for a positive and relaxed interview.) You should then emphasize to the employee that in no way will the information gathered be used against the employee when seeking employment elsewhere. Stress the fact that the information will be used to help management improve working conditions in the company and perhaps help cut down on employee turnover. Use any technique that you believe will assure a nonthreatening situation.

Your primary functions during the interview are to solicit the information your company needs and to provide information that will be helpful to the employee.

3. ***Oral presentation of answers to two job-interview questions:*** For this project choose two questions from the list of preemployment questions on pages 359–361, and assume your interviewer has asked you to answer them. Then prepare a three-minute presentation to your class (or to smaller groups). Your instructor, your class members, or both will "interview" you on what you said or on any other pertinent question. They will offer constructive criticism on your persuasiveness in answering the two questions that you assumed they asked you, and will comment on both your verbal and your nonverbal expressions. An alternative to this assignment is to divide the class into groups of two to five persons. Each student will then be interviewed by the group or by one student interviewer instead of by the whole class. The other members of each group will take turns being the interviewee—to present their three-minute talks answering their two chosen preemployment questions.

4. ***Dictation of a letter, using a tape recorder:*** You are correspondent for a company with a centralized word processing department. By dialing a special number, you dictate correspondence from your desk telephone. This dictation is recorded in the word processing department on tape for later transcription. The typed document is routed to you for signature and mailing— or editing and retyping if necessary.

Dictate a solution for a letter-writing exercise in Chapter 7 or 8. To simulate dictating to a word processing department, use a tape recorder. Experienced dictators can dictate routine correspondence from nothing more than a mental outline; however, you probably will need to consider the best organizational pattern to use, jot down a brief outline with major points for development, and then dictate. Be sure to indicate your name and department. Then, using the dictation suggestions on pages 722–725, dictate your letter from inside address to your name and title.

5. ***Oral instructive explanation about a particular job:*** Present to the class a five-minute instructive explanation on how to perform the duties of a particular job you are familiar with. After you finish, call on a class member to tell as well as possible what she or he learned. (This procedure tests not only your instructional clarity but also the listener's attentiveness.)

6. ***Oral improvements on three telephone responses to customers:*** The following replies are similar to some that employees have given to customers when answering telephone calls. What impressions do you think they make? Write your suggestions for improving each. Then be prepared to share your ideas orally in class.
   a. "Hello. Yeah, it's Jake. Huh? What kinda TV do ya have? I dunno if we have a part to fit it. I can't tell ya; I have ta know the model number of your TV. Wait a sec. I'll look. Woops. Got a customer here just now. Call again. Bye." [*Click*]
   b. "Hi, nope. This is not Mr. Brown. Wow! I'm not sure if he's out or just not taking calls. Maybe he's still out to lunch. What was your name? Hang on."
   c. "Hello. XY repair service. Gosh, we're so far behind today. Have a stack of cars here. No way we could getcha in today. Well, maybe. Don't call until after tomorrow."

7. ***A difficult job interview question for class discussion:*** As a class exercise you are asked to bring in one question that you consider difficult to answer in an interview. The question may be one actually asked in a job interview or a potential question about which you feel uncomfortable in answering. Because each of your classmates will also bring a question to read in class, you will all hear a variety of questions. Some class members may then try responding to them—tactfully, truthfully, as specifically as possible.

8. ***Discussion on a visual aid regarding Johari Window:*** The Johari window is also important to interpersonal communication. It is a model that suggests the communication interrelationships between you and others. Prepare a visual aid of that model and discuss its implications for interpersonal communication. See Joseph Luft, *Of Human Interaction*, Mayfield, Palo Alto, Calif., 1989.

PART SIX

Significant Concerns for Effective Business Communicators

Chapter 25

International and Intercultural Communication

For some time the American Assembly of Collegiate Schools of Business (AACSB), the accrediting agency for business schools in the United States, has supported internationalizing the business school curriculum. That concern is built in part on the "globalizing" of business and your potential for working in and understanding the intercultural environment that goes with that.[1]

Both large and small companies, manufacturing and nonmanufacturing, are exporting and importing goods and services. A report from the President's Commission on Foreign Language and International Studies suggests that over 6,000 American companies have foreign operations, and more than 20,000 American firms export products or services abroad.[2] Another study indicates that numerous top-level executives have worked out of the country—6.7 percent of the CEOs, 18.8 percent of the presidents, and 17.2 percent of the vice presidents. They spend an average of about three years in a foreign country.[3]

If one can judge by the numerous books and articles that discuss intercultural communication and adaptation,[4] there is a heightened concern about the issues discussed in this chapter. The task of communicating and working overseas is not easy, as suggested in the following statements:

> A few American companies have attempted to take their uniquely American approach to management and transplant it in Japan. Without exception, every attempt has been a complete and total disaster.[5]

> Ethnocentrism . . . the emotional attitude that one's own ethnic group, nation, or culture is superior. An excessive or inappropriate concern for racial matters.[6]

> You've got a choice: either you're on the plane with me this evening or I return home alone. [Actual statement of a spouse after one day visiting a foreign country.]

As an introduction to basic information you need for working and communicating effectively with people in or from other countries, this chapter includes four topics:

Background to intercultural adaptation

National environmental variables

Individual environmental variables

Preparation for overseas work

BACKGROUND TO INTERCULTURAL ADAPTATION

One of the major concerns of executives is global competition. Statistically, over 50 percent of chairpersons, presidents, and vice presidents feel a "global village" will lead to more competition from abroad and also give the United States more opportunity to export goods.[7] In other words, both executives and employees can no longer ignore the influences of the Far East or Europe, culturally or economically.

Culture

As the term *communication* is difficult to define, so too is the term *culture*. Two authors' research suggests that at least 164 definitions exist, with at least 6 categories predominating.[8] For our purposes, *culture* is the behavioral characteristics typical of a group. What this definition implies is that communications, oral and nonverbal, within a group also are typical of that group and often are unique. Thus, to assume that all the suggestions for improving your written and oral communication as noted in this book are true throughout the world is incorrect.

Another term you should know is *ethnocentrism*, that is, judging other groups or countries by the cultural standards of your group. While the focus in this chapter is primarily on communication, you must understand the many other factors that make up a culture, discussed later in this chapter. A series of questions may help you to consider how you react to communication differences.

1. What do you think of a culture in which people sign their last names first?

2. What is your reaction when two signatures appear at the bottom of a business letter?

3. Why don't people put the month first, then the day, rather than day first, then the month?

4. What is your impression of a foreign letter that is intentionally not concise?

5. Some salutations are overly formal; so are endings. Is that a concern when your letters have been more casual?

6. How do you react to long sentences in letters when you were taught to have shorter sentences?

7. What's your reaction when a letter ends without a clear statement of purpose or action?

8. What is your feeling toward a meeting in which there is little discussion, little comment until the senior, and usually older, person speaks and recommends an answer?

All the above are, respectively, the actual characteristics of communication for the following nationalities: (1) Chinese, (2) German, (3) Europeans and others, (4) French and German, (5) French and German, (6) French and German, (7) Chinese, and (8) Chinese. If you reacted negatively toward any of the different communication styles in the above questions, you tended to judge them in light of your own cultural standards.

Each time you hold up your standards of what is good when judging written or oral communication from another culture, you must be careful. To say, as did an American manager, "German reports begin with Adam and Eve" misses the point: Germans are more thorough in submitting reports than we are. Withhold evaluative statements on foreign communication styles until you recognize that different cultures use different communication methods.

An Intergroup Model

The underlying assertion in the previous discussion is that you are more comfortable with familiar surroundings and people. That makes sense. As a basis for developing that thought further we will use Figures 25-1 and 25-2 as the basis for our discussion.

Figure 25-1 suggests that at the core of the four daisy wheel petals is a hub: a commonality that all humans possess. Thus a doctor in Germany understands the workings of the body of an American, a Chinese, a Malaysian, a Briton. In other words, certain physical, anatomical traits are common to mankind, regardless of country, race, or origin.

Note that in the figure, cultures I and II have a significant overlap; an additional commonality exists between them—beyond the core. Both cultures, for example, might speak English, use knives and forks, drive on the right side of the road, address a letter with last names last. Cultures III and IV have fewer things in common with I and II, but have some commonality between them-

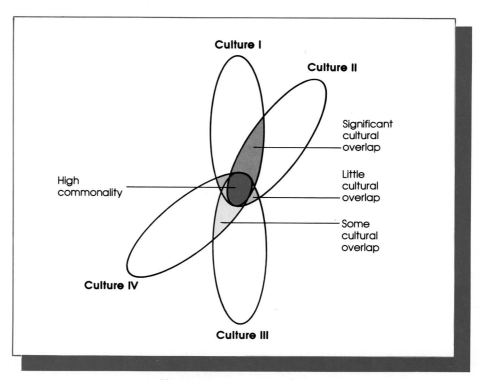

Figure 25–1 Cultural overlap.

selves. They speak a similar language, drive on the left side of the road, and write in a similar script.

Despite such areas of overlap, it is still easier for you, as a member of culture I, to communicate with someone else in that culture; so, too, a doctor, businessperson, brother, sister, mother, or father also from culture I would be more comfortable with others from that same group.

Toward the end of each petal—in all four of the cultures—there is little commonality with other groups. Religions are different, as are values, beliefs, attitudes, verbal and nonverbal means of communication. Such differences can lead to a nationalism that makes it difficult even to imagine changing the national anthem, or the pledge of allegiance, or the motto on our coinage.

Each country represented by the petals is different. You can see what happens if petals are added for each country in the world. Some would have much overlapping, while others would have little. To complicate the issue just a bit more, within each country are individuals. You, within culture I, may not have the same intensity of belief or acceptance of an idea as someone else within that same group. Thus while we accept certain underlying principles, attitudes, ideals, and values, there are still differences between each of us. Witness the differences in our political parties, which although subscribing to the principles of democracy, still have many other differences.

Figure 25-2 suggests a slightly different arrangement and size of the petals and cultural patterns. Here three of the cultures are highly similar; each to a

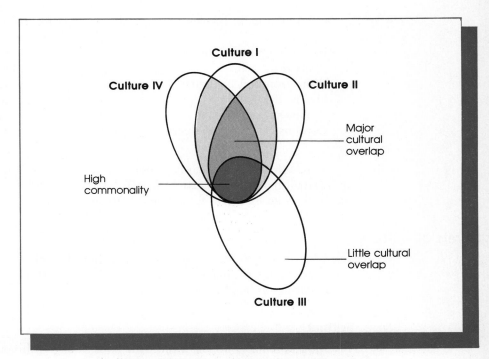

Figure 25–2 *Cultural similarity and dissimilarity.*

high degree overlaps the others. Thus all may accept Christianity as the dominant religion, the language is the same, dress is similar, letter size is identical, formality in address dominates, telephones look alike.

What does the configuration of culture III suggest? A quick inference is that petal III has little in common with the other three. As one moves outward from a core sameness, each of the cultures represented by the petals begins to change, some more than others. Why? Tradition plays a part, so does teaching, so does habit, so do attitudes, so do any number of reasons for which few have logical answers. However, note that at one point several of the petals overlap, suggesting that some things (for example, eating with chopsticks rather than forks or spoons) are common while most of the other things are not.

Assume for a moment that you're in culture III. Although you possess the core attributes of the other cultures, it is difficult for you to accept their differences. You have lived and learned and accepted certain values and ways of doing things. The following list gives some typical attitudes and attributes of U.S. culture and compares them with possible alternatives you might find abroad:[9]

U.S. Culture	Possible Alternatives
Individuals can influence the future.	Life's path is preordained.
First names should come first.	Last names are used first.
Punctuality is important.	There is much time available; we'll get there.
Get to the point quickly.	Get to know the individual first; then conduct business.
Remove a person when he or she does poorly.	Rarely remove a person; he or she will lose face.
Write from left to right.	Write from right to left.
Day is divided into two 12-hour segments.	Day is continuous; hours numbered from 1–24.
Consensus makes the decision.	The senior member makes the decision.

Although the preceding has been an overview of culture, a seminal writer on intercultural communication, Edward T. Hall, suggests that culture can be analyzed on an informal, formal, and technical level.[10]

Levels of Culture

The triad of the formal, informal, and technical levels of culture as noted in *The Silent Language* suggests that we react to life on three levels. Each of these has a bearing on how we view others.

Formal

Tradition dominates at this level. This book, along with your instructor, is an example of formal learning structured more or less on a pattern followed for centuries. You are presented a way to proceed, you try it, and you are corrected. You proceed again, hopefully correctly. Your parents' approach was even more prescriptive: "Don't do it that way; do it this way." Grammar is formal; all languages have rules of structure. Driving on the right side of the road, for Americans, is the "right" way to proceed. Tradition dominates; reasons are few.

Interestingly, ask yourself why Americans drive on the right side. Why shouldn't sentences end with a preposition? Why does a letter begin with "*Dear*"? Why does *b* follow *a*? Absolute logical answers are difficult to find. We do some things because we were taught that "that's the way we do things here."

Prescribed limits for verbal and nonverbal behavior are also formal. We don't shout fire in a theater or undress in class. Some tend to wear black at funerals; brides often wear white; time is measured in centuries, years, months, days, hours, minutes, seconds, milliseconds. On viewing people who disturb formal norms you may become agitated, emotionally aroused, angry.

Informal

At this level it is equally hard to answer the question "Why do we do it this way?" We act certain ways because that's the way our parents (role models) acted; we write "Dear [*name*]" because that's the way other letters were addressed. Hundreds of things, details, ideals, customs are passed along from generation to generation without our knowing why. We learn much from watching others, hearing how they speak, how loudly they speak, what they wear when they speak. We depend on models, and act accordingly. If our parents say they'll be somewhere at 7:30 and consistently arrive between 7:45 to 8:00, they have an informal concept of time.

The informal level also affects the degree of acceptance accorded the formal level. Hence we can go 2 or 3 miles over the formal speed limit and not be arrested; we can split an infinitive and not get a C grade; we can call some professors "Prof," and they are unperturbed. On the other hand, some people really mean precisely 8:15 when they state they'll be someplace then; they feel the speed limit should be obeyed precisely; they believe a letter must always have two signatures. The problem arises when we confuse the formal limits with the informal.

Technical

At the technical level evidence and rules are foremost. There is a logical explanation of why certain things are done. Emotion is low. Whereas the formal level of learning in a culture includes learning patterns of behavior, at the technical level the attempt is to convey precise logical rules. Mathematics is highly logical; so is NASA's keeping track of time. We have little emotional reaction to a formula or measurements in milliseconds.

In summary, Hall wrote that to understand differences in culture better you should analyze culture on three levels. For him formal learning was a two-way process: the learner tried, made a mistake, was corrected, and went on. Formal learning depended heavily on tradition and an emotional attachment for doing things in a certain way—without knowing the logical reason. Technical learning is highly dependent on a teacher, or someone who gives logical, impersonal reasons for actions.

Cultural Adaptation

Knowing some of the general background issues should help you understand why differences between peoples and nations exist. Yet, even tourists experience *cultural shock*, that is, surprise that so many things can be so different. You may experience similar reactions. Four stages make up a typical adaptation to an unfamiliar culture: anticipation, disillusionment, adaptation, and final acceptance.

Anticipation

Some call this first period *expectation*, looking forward to the foreign experience. Your family is excited. You begin reading and looking at pictures of your assigned country. You are enthusiastic. If your company does much overseas work, it might have you and your family attend cross-cultural training programs in the United States, similar to those given Peace Corps volunteers.

Your first contact on foreign soil is often the airport, usually crowded, often with police in evidence. The language may sound strange to your ear. You have arrived.

Often you will be met by representatives of your company already stationed there, who take you to your living quarters.

During the first several days abroad much is new and exciting. You discover that many of the people you deal with know English, and you feel comfortable. Other expatriates—persons working and living abroad—are usually helpful as both you and your family begin to adapt to the culture.

How long such a positive attitude continues varies. For some people the "honeymoon" period lasts from one day to a week or a month.

Toward the end of this initial period things that were similar to home are now overlooked; differences between your own culture and the foreign one become more obvious. And you may begin to have doubts.

Disillusionment

It is hard to distinguish a precise time when anticipation may turn to disillusionment. Little things begin to bother you: there's a smog in the air most of the time; few drivers speak English; television is on only during certain hours, and not in English; fewer people speak English than you thought; the food is totally different; typewriters are manual; and a host of other things.

Some human-resource persons suggest that certain behavioral patterns tend to emerge that reflect a turning inward rather than a facing of the culture. Following are a few of the many behavioral changes that may occur:

■ Speaking and going out only with friends who speak English; establishing friends on the basis of language.

- Reading books and magazines from home, in English.
- Writing and calling home extensively.
- Avoiding parties and contacts that demand eating native foods and joining in native customs. Shielding your children from neighbors; riding rather than walking.
- Criticizing the government, the city, the local officials; finding fault with any public service.
- Joining gossip sessions with other Americans who feel the same as you; waiting to greet new arrivals with the latest negative experiences.

It is not too strong to suggest that all the above are unhealthy and affect the working and living experience. The end result is that all suffer: you as the employee who does a poor job, your family who also reacts negatively, and your company, which because of your negative behavior does not receive a fair effort.

Adaptation

A positive sign that you are beginning to adapt to a culture is when a sense of humor returns. You laugh at obvious errors—as when a homemaker who wanted chicken bought a can with a picture of a chicken on the outside, only to discover on returning home that it was a can of oil in which to fry the chicken. Or, one can laugh at discovering that "WC" does not mean "Westminster Cathedral," but rather "water closet," or bathroom.

Some people adapt quickly. They begin adapting immediately on arrival, tasting, testing their new foreign environment. Some new employees overseas within one week feel little discomfort, and toward the end of their tour request another stay.

It is a positive step that, more and more, human-resource officers are testing more carefully, screening both employees and their families for potential for cultural adaptation. The earlier that employees reach the adaptation period, the more successful they will be.

Final Acceptance

Often it is said that when you dream in the language of your host country, you have reached the stage of final acceptance. That's a subjective view. What is not subjective is when you accept the differences and easily move between the two cultures. Of course there will be moments of discomfort—these occur in your own country—but they are momentary as you continue with the task of work and daily living.

Not specifically noted in the above discussion is the effect of communication, written and oral, on a foreign employee. Not all letters will be in the same form as in the United States: many other parts of the world are more formal; many reports, letters, and memorandums incorporate the formality of the British, even their spelling. Even mainland China, closed for many years to the outside world, still adheres to British formality. British spelling is in the communication texts. An American student while living abroad was the shining star in an English class, but had numerous spelling errors because she followed American rather than British spelling. It took some discussion to permit her American English spelling to be accepted.

Orally there will also be differences. Europeans are more formal in speech. First names are avoided. Mr. and Mrs. or Miss are the norm. Students of a foreign language know that the word *you* can be both formal and informal in speaking. In German, for example, the informal *du* is used with close friends, and *Sie* with strangers or those on the edge of friendship. A bow in Japan, even the depth of the bow and distance from you, communicates your degree of acceptance by the sender.

What follows in this chapter now are the variables that must be understood in order to adapt quickly to a culture. This means understanding the national and individual environmental factors.

NATIONAL ENVIRONMENTAL VARIABLES

As the communication model (Figure 2-1) in Chapter 2 shows, the message sender and the receiver are both affected by external and internal stimuli. When communicating with business people in a foreign country, you must realize that overall national and individual environmental differences within the cultures further affect those stimuli. Figure 25-3 suggests the macro, or global, constraints and variables that communicators must face when working with foreign receivers of their messages. The items in the left-hand column are mainly national environmental variables. You should understand them, know they exist. They could influence your perceptions of the country and the people with whom you may work and communicate.

Education

In many countries throughout the world, the employees, including factory managers, are not as well educated as their United States counterparts. For instance, if your future work takes you to the Far East, Chinese and other Asian managers have less formal education than you do.[11]

■ EDUCATION LEVELS OF CHINESE, ASIAN, AND U.S. MANAGERS

Highest Level of Education	Chinese, %	Asian, %	U.S., %
Less than high school	5.4	2.5	0.1
High school graduate	31.8	12.4	3.2
Some college	34.6	19.4	16.9
Undergraduate degree	27.6	65.4	79.8
Postgraduate degree	0.7	25.0	30.0

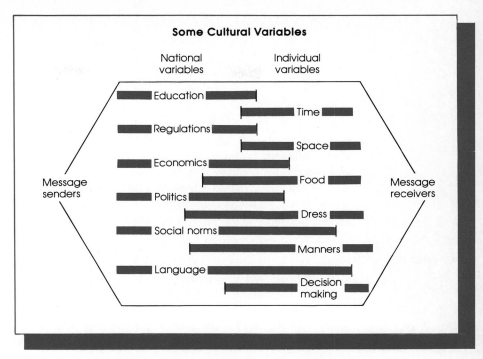

Figure 25–3 *Overlapping cultural variables.*

A quick conclusion may be that the Asians, particularly the Chinese, are less interested in education, that the nation is ill equipped to hold its own with other parts of the world. You would be wrong. You must go beyond your initial inference and assess the reasons why Chinese managers lack extensive education. You must go beyond surface conclusions.

1. In relation to its size, China does not have many institutions of higher education—in contrast to the United States. In 1980 there were only 675 institutions of higher education, increasing to 902 in 1984, and by 1985—the latest figures—the number had reached 1,016.

2. China is an agrarian economy. Over 800 million people still live in the countryside; 69 percent of the labor force is agricultural. Education, some early Chinese leaders felt, was unneeded in such an environment.

3. Most universities were closed during the Cultural Revolution (1966–1976).

4. Self-study and private tutoring occurred during the Cultural Revolution, but for most young, college-aged people education was not available.

5. A less educated Chinese manager—except between 1977–1980—faced an age maximum (age 25) for taking a college entrance examination.

In short, there are reasons for lower levels of education in Chinese managers. It's not that they did not wish an education; they were not in a position to receive one.

In the United States, education is available to all persons from kindergarten through high school. College and graduate studies are then further options.

Other countries have different systems. German students must decide early as to whether they wish to follow a college track or pursue a trade. Hong Kong parents early begin teaching their children at home in hopes of getting them into a good church school. Some Indian parents search out private schools for their children. In Japan over 90 percent graduate from high school, and 35 percent attend college.

Whatever a nation's people have learned becomes part of their culture. Thus, in international communication people from different cultures may interpret and react differently to a situation or message.

Law and Regulations

In developed and developing nations various regulations affect business communications and salable products. For example, advertising to children is restricted in the United States, Canada, and Scandinavia. Even the type of product to be advertised—for instance, cigarettes—is restricted in Europe. Also there is a stricture on the amount of money that can be spent on advertising. Other countries, such as France, Mexico, and the Province of Quebec, also have a restriction on the use of foreign languages in advertisements.

In Iran, western publications showing unveiled women are forbidden. No fashion magazines are allowed into the country, and cosmetic makeup—including perfume—is prohibited. Women must wear either a *chador* (a head-to-toe veil) or a manteau (a loose smock worn over pants) with a scarf on the head. Men cannot wear short sleeves or T-shirts. (Some of these rules may change in the 1990s.)

Economics

Availability of capital and transportation and the standard of living per capita vary from nation to nation. The opportunity to borrow money, the rate of inflation, the exchange rates influence business and a country's ability to communicate concerning that business.

With our free-enterprise system in the United States, competitors usually set their own prices. In contrast, OPEC (Organization of Petroleum Exporting Countries), as a cartel, sets oil prices. Israeli agricultural competitors mutually agree on a price. Some Japanese businesses check with the government before initiating major production and trading changes.

Politics

Even concepts of democracy will vary as interpreted in Korea, the Philippines, or Great Britain. Indeed, the sweeping political changes in Eastern Europe and its altered concepts of government will affect future business relations. Or, the events in Tiananmen Square, where thousands of Chinese advocated a more democratic form of government, will affect future contacts with mainland China.

All those events affect communication, understanding of a country, and a company's willingness to do business in an unclear political environment.

For the measurement of potential political instability, there are classic indices and research studies[12] that consider events—such as antigovernment demonstrations, arrests, assassinations, elections, exile, general strikes, guerrilla warfare, government crises, purges, revolutions, and riots—in determining the stability of a country.

Religion

Religious beliefs can affect business communication and influence an entire nation: toward the present, the future, and the hereafter. Iran, for instance, is a nation profoundly influencing others because of its beliefs.

You could, with some class discussion, arrive at the similarities among Protestant, Catholic, and Jewish faiths. All three religions are found abroad— sometimes in the minority. Also Buddhism, Hinduism, and the Moslem religion are found in many parts of the world, affecting values (and attire) of the people who profess these faiths. These three religions forbid consumption of alcohol; thus no liquor is served at business affairs.

Even religious holidays can affect international communication, interrupting work schedules or delaying responses to requests. Often the role of women is influenced by religion, affecting their consumption patterns and positions within an economy. Know the religion of your host country.

Social Norms

In various ways any national environmental constraints—education, law and regulations, economics, politics, religion—affect a nation's social norms.

In many countries a male line of the family profoundly influences some business decisions. Then the family and how its members relate to one another— decisions, buying patterns, pooling of resources, special interests—affect behavior and business communication.

Beyond the immediate family a bond may exist between persons, based on caste, class, age, or even special interests. Be aware of a nation's social norms.

Language

An important constraint that undergirds all the preceding constraints is language. Obviously, unless both sender and receiver know a common language, the opportunities for successful business communication are significantly limited.

English is a world language—and to some extent the language of business. *But*, you will do a better job overseas if at a minimum you know some basic vocabulary of your host country. Your informal contacts and your off-the-road visits and travels will take you to places where "no speak the English" will be heard. Younger people overseas know English; fewer older people do. Yet interpersonal bonds are forged between you and your hosts by your trying to learn the language—with all your errors. Each language has its own sentence patterns and vocabulary.

INDIVIDUAL ENVIRONMENTAL VARIABLES

The preceding discussion noted the mega national characteristics affecting communication with and within a country. They are all parts of the cultural petals discussed earlier. Living within that overall culture is the individual, exhibiting his or her own personal habits and lifestyles. Also each culture, on the micro and more personal level, has differences in verbal and nonverbal cues expressed through varying concepts of time, individual space, food, acceptable dress, manners at home and at work, decision-making patterns, and other verbal and nonverbal variations.

Time (Chronemics)

Persons in Latin America and the Middle East treat time more casually than do Americans, who usually prefer promptness. Germans are time-precise; rarely do you wait for an appointment in Germany. In Latin America—and in Buddhist cultures—you may wait an hour; your host is not showing disrespect thereby, just reflecting a different concept of time; arriving late is a socially accepted custom.

In some cultures business people take afternoon naps, close shops, and postpone times for business meetings and dinner. Germans have, by law, definite opening and closing hours for business.

Even when referring to seasons of a year, countries differ. Some speak of the rainy and the dry season; Americans and Europeans think of spring, summer, fall, and winter.

The following opposing statements give you some feeling of time-opposite concepts.

Culture I	**Culture II**
"Let's get on with it."	"Mañana" (tomorrow)
"Time-saving devices"	"Efficient devices"
"In how many minutes can you get here?"	"What will be will be."
"Let's set a phone appointment for 8:15."	"We'll give you a call."
"The future is now."	"The old way is a good way."
"Live for today."	"Traditions should be honored."
"8:15"	"Some time tomorrow"
"You're late."	"Oh?"
"Dinner at eight"	"See if we can make it."

It should not take you long to recognize which is the time-conscious culture opposed to one more concerned with the past and less with precision in time. Knowing cultural differences in time will help you understand why some responses are slow—by your standards.

Space (Proxemics)

How close may people approach before you feel uncomfortable? A foot, 2 feet, 5 feet? Most Americans feel uncomfortable if a stranger comes closer than 18 inches, comfortable at 5 feet. How will you react in Saudi Arabia when someone's breath brushes you in conversation? How will you feel, crowded into a train in Japan or India where you are so close you cannot fall down? How do you account for the cold stare of a German whose yard or home you have invaded with your eyes?

Americans demand more room, buffer space, between themselves and others when speaking. To some cultures (Arabs, Latin Americans) Americans thus appear cold and aloof; the interpersonal space is too great. You, on the other hand, may consider speakers who stand close to you as being intrusive, rude, pushy.

Even concepts of office space differ across cultures. In China many people occupy the same office, or have none. In Germany you knock before entering an office—even the secretary who frequently must enter the private space of his or her superior. In other words, you cannot assume that your Western concept of space will be understood throughout the world.

Food

It used to be that tourists visiting Hong Kong or Tokyo, for example, would rush off to the ubiquitous McDonald's, or order a Domino's pizza or a meal at Kentucky Fried Chicken in Beijing. Natives in those countries now also frequent such places. When we get off the beaten path, however, food, its preparation, its cleanliness will vary. Pork is forbidden in middle eastern countries but is a part of the Chinese diet and that of many other countries; beef is hard to find in India; veal is plentiful in Europe; rice is ever present in Hong Kong and China.

In the Far East dark and light tea are national drinks—they also have good beer—while in Europe French workers enjoy a glass of wine with lunch, often a stated codicil in a labor contract. Alcohol, as stated in the preceding section under Religion, is forbidden for Buddhists, Moslems, and Hindus. You can get into trouble by carrying liquor into some countries.

Cheese may be dessert in France, part of a sandwich in Denmark, or an hors d'oeuvre in Germany. Your palate must adapt as well as your view of time and space.

Acceptable Dress

The western business suit for males and dresses or suits for women are the common western uniform for doing business. The British businessman may wear a bowler along with a dark suit and an umbrella; an Indian, a Nehru jacket.

Ask foreign students what is the dress of American students and they respond "jeans." But with the worldwide market for jeans, the youth culture has taken hold of this attire overseas as well.

In the Middle East, long cotton coats are acceptable. In some situations you may see the Hawaiian muumuu, the Polynesian sarong, the Japanese kimono, the Iranian chador, or the Mao dark-blue jacket and pants.

Manners

Some cultural anthropologists suggest you should observe children in foreign cultures, for by watching them you learn the behavioral habits of elders. Children shake your hand in Germany, hug you in Italy, often stay in the background in India. In fact, the ritual of the greeting and the farewell is more formal overseas with adults and children. You bring a gift when visiting most homes in Europe or in Japan. If you bring flowers, you avoid gifts of red roses in Germany or white chrysanthemums in France, Belgium, and Japan. Adopting the manners of a country may mean a two- to three-hour lunch in Europe is acceptable, if you can call up your patience.

In Saudi Arabia you will learn that sons defer to their fathers, that age is paramount, that a junior prince is silent when a senior enters. At the heart of their system is the family, the House of Saud. To know even these few cultural manners is to begin understanding this country in the Middle East.

Decision Making

Americans are accused of being brusk; we wish to get to the point—fast. "Getting down to business" is a trait of our western culture. The Germans, Swiss, Dutch, and Scandinavians are similar, quickly getting to the issue. The Italians, French, and British prefer more leisurely social amenities.

When one reaches Japan, decision time is held back as group consensus moves you toward a decision. Participation, by many people, is the touchstone. You can imagine that much time, therefore, is spent in reaching an answer. That is what frustrates Americans; that is where we throw up our hands. Unhappily, we do not try to understand that for the Japanese the system of participative decision making works, that the *ringi* process (stamps of approval by many people on a proposal) means underlying agreement is obtained in advance of beginning an action.

An interesting study of Japanese management style—as preparation to understanding both the decision-making process and the culture—is provided in the article "Maverick Managers," in the *Wall Street Journal*.[13]

Thus patience, and understanding of the decision process, add to your understanding of a foreign environment.

Verbal and Nonverbal Communication

Although verbal and nonverbal forms of communication have appeared in the preceding discussions, a separate section is required to point up additional specific differences.

Verbal

A kind of verbal sparring occurs when strangers meet, each seeking to determine which topics are acceptable and noncontroversial. Additionally, *how* in tone of voice these initial words are spoken can influence your initial perception of whether the meeting is positive or negative.

Even the oral phrase "how would you like to" can have either a direct or an indirect meaning; it could be a command or a question. In Australia it is taken as a request and not a question; in the United States it is a question. "See you later" can mean the same day to some Asian workers or some indefinite time in the future to Americans. "Yes" for an Asian may mean "yes" or "no." "Anytime" to a Greek means he or she would welcome you with no time limit. In China you may utter the Chinese expression *"She she"* ("thank you") for your tea, or drum your fingers on the tablecloth, nonverbally indicating gratitude.

If you have traveled abroad or flown on foreign airlines, you may be surprised at the volume level of some persons. What to us is a loud volume and carries the inference of a fight is normal and accepted by Arabs. Some Japanese use little volume, again accepted and part of a cultural heritage.

Nonverbal

A handshake is a traditional form of greeting in the West. In Polynesia, the traditional greeting is embracing and rubbing each other's back. Eskimos rub noses as a form of greeting; a kiss on the cheek or lips signifies the same thing in many western cultures. In China and Japan public kissing is frowned on, an action reserved for one's private life. Touch as a form of behavior varies and is limited to certain persons.

Facial expressions vary across cultures. You could get the wrong impression when some Filipinos smile and laugh, when underneath this behavior they are angry. Or, the inscrutable facial expression of the Japanese does not suggest disinterest, rather an unwillingness to make public one's inner thoughts.

The meaning of gestures varies. What we think is an innocent gesture (the "O.K." sign with thumb and forefinger together) may be obscene in parts of Italy; a thumbs up is a positive sign in the United States; in Greece it is negative, suggesting "sit on this." This is not the place to review the hundreds of gestures and body motions used in different cultures; several good books devoted solely to this topic exist.[14]

You can see that it is not safe to assume that gestures used in all innocence in the United States are accepted in the same manner throughout the world. Be aware; be cautious; know the variations that could cause failures in communication, or complete distrust of you as a communicator.

PREPARATION FOR OVERSEAS WORK

A list of variables representing the world's cultures is endless. On the other hand, it is possible to overgeneralize, for no two people within any culture are identical. Each of us is even different from day to day. Thus it is possible for our individual personalities to interact with the individual and national environmental variables. Over time there may be many dramatic changes, or none. You may have problems coping with changes in your own culture; add the foreign element, and the problems are compounded.

No magic formula is available for your foreign work. The Peace Corps quickly found this out. Yet, to prepare for overseas work and to improve your intercultural communication you should try to learn some of the language; to be aware of specific communication differences, including differences in writing; and to do some specific research.

Learn the Language

The most often heard request by foreign businesspersons is that American students should know a foreign language. The rapport between you and your foreign colleagues increases when you attempt to speak their language. Your foreign friends will forgive your grammatical errors—perhaps one of the few times in your life—when you make attempts at communicating in their tongue.

If you are like most students, you may have had one year, perhaps two, of a foreign language. Which language should you learn? Germans advise German; French suggest French; Chinese propose Cantonese or Mandarin; Japanese hint Japanese; and South Americans counsel Spanish. When you know in which country you will work, begin language training—not only for yourself but for other members of your family as well. Numerous private companies offer language training via cassettes or through total immersion, from 60 to 80 hours; or your company may hire a tutor to prepare you in basic language familiarity.

Obtain copies of documents and types of correspondence you will work with overseas. Take these documents to your language class, and learn the form, style, and basic rudiments of what to expect. Emphasize the oral as well. The written will take more time, often demanding assistance from a bilingual secretary or assistant.

Know Communication Differences

While the letter has similarities the world over, in short and long reports differences occur. Germans have much background information, while some Chinese reports are general and vague, lacking specificity. Foreign reports are often consistent from month to month, simply having spaces for figures, giving little chance for interpretative comments. You may actually do less writing of formal reports overseas than in your home country.

Learn the rules for handling written material. For example, in the United States one signature is sufficient on letters, while in Germany some letters require two signatures, often with completely illegible names. Learn due dates for major reports. Foreign countries have more holidays than we do. You may be completing a report for your United States office on a day when everyone in the foreign country is celebrating a national event—unfamiliar, uninteresting, or unknown to you.

Of course the hardest problem will be merging your native language with that of your host country. In some research done between a German subsidiary and its U.S. home office, one U.S. manager of the German headquarters offered this scenario of communicating between a home office and its subsidiary.[15]

1. Written request for a proposal is written in the United States. (English language.)

2. Proposal arrives at regional office to keep them informed. (English.)

3. Regional office may or may not attach cover letter. Proposal request arrives at German subsidiary, where manager has request translated into German for distribution to staff. (English-German.)

4. Staff meeting called. Request discussed and responsibilities laid out. (German.)

5. Staff person or vice president has staff meeting with colleagues. (German.)

6. Initial report written by staff person and his or her staff. (German.)

7. Response to proposal request reviewed by vice president at staff meeting. (German.)

8. Discussions with U.S. managers. (English.)

9. Redrafting of report by members of staff and vice president. (German.)

10. Report translated into English for U.S. vice presidents and others. (German-English.)

11. Managing director receives report. (German-English.)

12. Report sent to regional director and on to parent company in the United States. (English.)

That rather tortuous path suggests many opportunities for communication breakdowns. Fortunately in the above scenario an able secretary who knew both German and English made it easier for the U.S. managers.

Understand Some Differences in Writing

British politeness and spelling; the absence of some definite and indefinite articles; the order of the month, day, and year; obvious spelling and grammatical errors; and a mixture of letter and memorandum forms characterize some foreign correspondence. The following is an untouched sample of a letter sent in the Far East.

```
                                                        23 may 199-

        Safe Deposit Department
        The Hong Kong and Shanghai Banking Corporation
        Kowloon, Hong Kong

        Subject: Approval of shipment

        Dear Yavonne:

        It is with extreme pleasure that I notify you of GOP level
        of model xxx is being processed by the local buying location
        and the state of formal sign-off is being reached.

        Once this formal approval is granted, there will almost cer-
        tainly be a running chyange from old level to new level
        within a short lapse of time.

        Further to our discussion we favour your bank presenting
        your confirmation to us that we may proceed on our end.  I
        hope to hear from you by week of 1 June this year.

        We have pleasure to work with your office.

        Yours sincerely,

        Jonathan Wong
```

The grammar and spelling are not perfect, yet the sense is clear. By strict classroom standards the letter needs work, but remember that the writer's native language is Cantonese.

Do not be surprised if some other cultures omit the period after *Mr.* or *Mrs.* when addressing you in a letter. The British—amply illustrated in one of their premier periodicals *The Economist*—frequently omit the period in forms of address.

In the following letter from the Far East, the punctuation and spelling are not correct; the writer's native language is Mandarin. The sense is correct, the structure is not.

```
                                                Beijing, 23, Jan. 199-.
        Dear Professor [name of addressee]:

        Thanks for your signed agreements, I am glad to sign it and
        back one of them to you, and enclosed two agreements in
        chinese, Please sign it, one of them will be returned.  I
        believe our cooperation will be very successful.
```

> Now, We start in new questionnaire to 20 chinese managers
> for experiment, then, We will revise it and prepare the last
> questionnaire table for our joint research. The parameters
> of chinese managers will be collected in data base of
> chinese managers by computer code in [*name of school*] Univer-
> sity. I think of that some of parameters are very interest-
> ing for make-decision of leaders of government in making
> policy in china. We must design a best computer program for
> it. . . .

Does the letter deserve a low grade? Would you refuse to have any further communication with the writer? Of course not. We are more tolerant than with native speakers and writers (which is the way *we* expect to be treated when writing or speaking in a second language). You must understand that not all letters and reports will be as faultless as those you write.

Do Some Research

Your company may have in place a program for handling your overseas assignment. If such a program is in place, your company recognizes the need to prepare you for foreign service work. If little help is given you, you may find some of the following information useful. Prepare by knowing about helpful organizations, reviewing published material, and speaking with returnees.

Contact Helpful Organizations

While your company may have on hand general information on various countries in which they do business, the following representative agencies are sources of additional help:

AFS International
313 East 43d St.
New York, NY 10017

Business Council for International Understanding
The American University
Washington, DC 20016

Center for International Business
Suite 184
World Trade Center
Dallas, TX 75258

Society for Intercultural Education, Training and Research, International
1414 22d St., NW
Washington, DC 20037

Asian Productivity Organization
4-14 Akasaka 8-Chome
Minato-ku, Tokyo 107, Japan

East-West Center Publications
1777 East-West Center Road
Honolulu, HI 96848

Consult Published Material

Some books have been referred to in the course of this chapter; you may find them and others helpful:

Adler, Nancy, *International Dimensions of Organizational Behavior*, Kent, Boston, 1986.

Brislin, Richard W., et al., *Intercultural Interactions, A Practical Guide*, Sage, Beverly Hills, Calif., 1986.

Furnham, Adrian, and Stephen Bochner, *Culture Shock*, Methuen, London, 1986.

Hall, Edward T., *The Silent Language*, Doubleday, Garden City, N.Y., 1959.

Harris, Philip R., and Robert T. Moran, *Managing Cultural Differences*, Gulf, Houston, 1987.

Kim, Young Yun, and William B. Gudykunst, *Theories in Intercultural Communication*, Sage, Newbury Park, Calif., 1988.

Lonner, Walter J., and John W. Berry (eds.), *Field Methods in Cross Cultural Research*, Sage, Beverly Hills, Calif., 1986.

Post Reports (for major countries), U.S. Department of State, Government Printing Office, Washington D.C.

Seelye, H. Ned, *Teaching Culture*, National Textbook, Lincolnwood, Ill., 1988.

Singer, Marshall R., *Intercultural Communication, A Perceptual Approach*, Prentice-Hall, Englewood Cliffs, N.J., 1987.

Terpstra, Vern, *International Dimensions of Marketing*, Kent, Boston, 1988.

The periodicals listed below are representative. Your library or the foreign embassy (therein an office variously called *office of commerce* or *trade office*) of your host country may be able to recommend additional English publications. Even foreign tourist offices in this country are willing to recommend helpful publications.

A search of the databases will indicate literally hundreds of articles in a variety of journals on national and individual environmental variables. The following emphasize business issues:

Asia
P.O. Box 379
Fort Lee, NJ 07024

China Business Review
1818 N. Street, NW
Suite 500
Washington, DC 20036

International Business Magazine
14842 1st Avenue S
Seattle, WA 98169

Business Abroad
P.O. Box 3088
Grand Central Station
New York, NY 10017

Business Edition/Department Forum
U.N. Headquarters
Geneva, Switzerland

Overseas Living
International Orientation Service
P.O. Box 3567
Chapel Hill, NC 27515

Speak with Returnees

Occasionally companies permit an initial visit to your host country before your permanent placement. During that visit, ask questions of persons living there. More importantly, on the return of those persons to the United States, learn more of the positive and negative aspects of their stay. The following questions may help focus your direction. By identifying specific cultural elements in your own country, you can then consider their acceptability or unacceptability in your host country.

■ Checklist for Intercultural Communication

Your Country	**Your Host Country**
Communication Styles	
Verbal	What is acceptable and unaccept-able?
Nonverbal	Are any gestures offensive? Are there any issues relating to time, space, dress, manners to be avoided in order to avoid mis-communication?
Business Communication	
Informal and formal	What examples are there for a pre-ferred style in oral and written communication?
Common formats	Are memorandums, letters, reports produced in a similar format, similar organization?
Structure	Are organization of ideas, solving of problems approached similarly?
Language	Who will assist in translating both written and oral material?
Education	
Levels	What is the education of the per-sons with whom you will work? To what degree does the country support education?
Law and Regulations	
Formal and informal	Is there a degree of freedom or do either legal or governmental reg-ulations intrude?

(continued)

Your Country	Your Host Country

Economics

Past history and projections for future	To what extent are foreign companies licensed to engage in foreign trade? May funds, profits be removed, and under what conditions?

Politics

Past and future trends	Are there conventions, protocols that individuals are expected to observe? What influence do interest groups play in the company and have on the individual?

Religion

Homogeneity and diversity of belief structure	What are the significant religious or national holidays that impact both company and individual? What behavior is expected? What are the differences between the religion of your home country and of your host country?

Social Norms

Family, influence of past colonial history	Are there categories, a hierarchy in the social structure? To what extent does a possible former colonial power still exert an influence?

Languages

Single or several; extent of English usage	Is there one language or are several used? Which basic phrases should one know? What are the polite forms of address?

The above list could be extended indefinitely; the intent is to suggest a start at the kinds of questions you could ask relating to a potential foreign assignment.

Omitted entirely are the more personal questions on health, food, and other more private concerns. Those kinds of questions are captured in a useful list from Joan Wilson of the Foreign Service Institute, U.S. Department of State, as possible additional probes for thinking about overseas work:

- Who are the country's national heroes and heroines?
- What is the attitude toward gambling, drinking, dope, religion, education?
- What things are taboo in this society?
- Which colors are positive in tone? Which are negative?
- What are the special privileges of age and/or sex?
- What are the important holidays? How is each observed?
- What sports are popular?
- What is the normal work schedule? How does it accommodate to environmental or other conditions?
- How will your financial position and living conditions compare with those of the majority of people living in this country?
- What is the history of the relationship between this country and the United States?
- Where are the important universities of the country? If university education is sought abroad, to what countries and universities do students go?

Consider Maxims on Intercultural Communication

Following is a series of propositions regarding preparation for intercultural communication:

- It is impossible to generalize the cultural traits of an entire nation using only a few persons as a sample.
- Communication breakdowns are more the result of misunderstandings in culture than grammatical or stylistic issues.
- One's culture is a mixture of many inputs, some obvious and straightforward, others based purely on tradition and habit.
- The statement "When in Rome, do as the Romans do" carries a symbolic and useful truth.
- Preparation such as asking questions about your host country lessens the chance for personal and communication errors.
- Recognize that over time some national and personal environmental variables do change.
- Each culture has a strong allegiance to its way of doing things; the U.S. has no monopoly on national, personal, and communication procedures.

SUMMARY

Each country has a culture that results in a generally recognizable behavior. As part of that culture we are comfortable, but often are unable to explain why we act or communicate as we do. Some of our actions are based on tradition, emotion, or simply acceptance that "that's the way we've always done it"; others are based on what we have been taught. Consequently, it takes time to adapt to another culture, a person often going through stages such as anticipation, disillusionment, adaptation, and final acceptance.

Each country has variables on a national level—those that more indirectly affect its population. We learn something about a country's culture through knowing the educational levels of the population, the legal and regulatory restraints affecting business, the economic philosophies or national and foreign trade practices, the political attitudes, religion as practiced by the state or the individual, the social norms of the state, and the language, as it affects international communication.

Additionally, each person within a country has more personal behaviors. How they handle time, what a comfortable distance for interpersonal communication is, what foods are wholly acceptable, what is considered appropriate dress, what the unwritten personal manners within a home or office are, what procedures and speed are followed in arriving at personal and business decisions. Finally, cultures have both verbal and nonverbal communication characteristics; what is acceptable in one culture may be entirely unacceptable in another.

Your effectiveness in communicating well and succeeding overseas requires adapting to many factors. Knowing even the polite forms of a foreign language is helpful, as is knowing some differences in writing and speaking. Do some research into various organizations and journals interested in international business and communication. Last, ask questions, in both personal and business areas. Then you are on the way to successful intercultural communication.

EXERCISES AND PROBLEMS

1. *Significant and representative values of native country culture:* After reviewing the definition of *ethnocentrism*, list examples of those values you consider significant and representative of the culture in your native country. You could use these headings and others: politics, economy, manners, higher education.

2. *Oral team reports on a country's variables that may affect business and communication:* Appoint several teams within the class. Each team has the responsibility of selecting a single country and then orally reporting to the class some of that country's national environmental variables and individual environmental variables that may affect business and communication. A possible outline might include the following points:

The Country	The People of the Country
Land and climate	Population
History and government	Language
Economy	Religion
Education	Holidays
Transportation	Attitudes
Health	

Lifestyles of the Country	Cultural Customs
Position of the family	Methods of greeting one another
Social and economic levels	Nonverbal behavior
Business hours	
Food	**Words and Phrases**

3. ***Characteristics of people in another country:*** List what you consider to be characteristics of the people in a country you know or have read about. Clearly, no generalization will hold for an entire nation, but some surface qualities may appear with some consistency.

4. ***Comparison of U.S. and Chinese idioms:*** While numerous differences exist between cultures, there are also high degrees of commonality. One sees this commonness when comparing idioms or sayings between two cultures. We in the United States are familiar with the idioms in the left column. Match them with their Chinese counterparts in the right column.

Familiar to Americans	Familiar to Chinese
a. It's the bad apple that spoils the barrel.	— The head of the cow does not fit the mouth of the horse.
b. It takes two to tango.	— It's impossible to clap with only one hand.
c. Speak of the devil.	— Paper cannot wrap up fire.
d. It's like building castles in the air.	— One hair from nine oxen.
e. Don't bite off more than you can chew.	— The wood has already been used in making the boat.
f. A drop in the bucket.	— You ride a tiger and find it hard to get off.
g. As ye sow, so shall ye reap.	— To dig a well only after one is thirsty.
h. To lock the barn door after the horse is gone.	— Like ants on top of a hot cooking pot.
i. It's water over the dam.	— If one plants melons, one gets melons.
j. Where there's smoke, there's fire.	— Like climbing a tree to catch a fish.
k. Like comparing apples and oranges.	— The horse that leads the herd astray.
l. On pins and needles.	— Blow on the hair and search for tiny sores.
m. Picky, picky, picky.	— When you speak of Ts'ao Ts'ao, Ts'ao Ts'ao arrives.
n. The truth will out.	— There are no waves if there is no wind.

5. ***List of sources available for learning about a foreign country:*** Assume you wish to export a product to a foreign country or learn something about

that foreign country before taking any kind of action. Where would you go for information in the library? To whom or what would you turn for information? List sources one could turn to to find out more about doing business abroad.

6. ***Written memo report and oral presentation on a foreign country investment:*** Combine both an oral and a written assignment according to the following structure:

Subject:	Present an Individual Research Memorandum and Oral Presentation on a Foreign Country Investment
Action requested:	Recommend whether a company—of your choice—should expand, establish a subsidiary, permit franchising, or locate an overseas office in a named foreign country.
Goal of assignment:	**a.** To bring together (1) original work and (2) secondary information in a memorandum that includes a clear recommendation on whether a company—selected by you—should or should not invest resources in that country.
	b. To present the results of your research in an oral briefing, attempting to persuade the class on a course of action.
Procedure:	**a.** Each class member may select from the list at the end of this exercise a foreign country for analysis, setting his or her own criteria as to whether investing resources in that country is desirable or undesirable.
	b. Your instructor should receive two copies of your memorandum on the day of your oral presentation. All class members will on the day of your presentation also receive copies of your memorandum. Example of headings you may wish to include:

To:	International Review Committee (your class)
From:	Your name and the group or division you represent.
Subject:	Include a clear, definite statement of purpose. Include a verb to give a sense of direction.
Date:	

<u>Introduction</u>: (1) Opening paragraph important. Here restate what is being recommended or will be discussed. Why is topic im-

		portant? What is previous to discussion? What are criteria?
	(2)	Supply definitions if needed.
	(3)	Layout of position you wish accepted or will discuss; *divisio* (agenda) of how material will be developed.
Body:	(1)	Entire body of memorandum includes (1) background discussion and (2) rationale for your recommended action.
	(2)	Evidence for your recommendation should include findings, examples, statistics, analogies, quotations, charts. (An appendix may be added for visual supports or other related material.)
	(3)	Usually use one paragraph for each major issue or conclusion.
	(4)	Transitions may be used to clearly move ideas along.
Conclusion:	(1)	Restate recommendation you wish accepted.
	(2)	Look into the future, visualize what will occur if proposal or conclusions are or are not accepted.

    c. Class procedure:

      (1) Proper grammatical form, proper footnote and bibliographic form should be used throughout.

      (2) Distribute your memorandum to each member of the class.

      (3) The class will challenge or question you ***during*** your oral presentation.

      (4) You will receive a written critique of your memo and presentation from your instructor.

Possible macro sources for background research include the following:

The Economist Intelligence Unit (EIU), Country Profile (country reports on 92 countries).

Area Handbook Series, Foreign Area Studies, The American University (country reports on 107 countries).

United States Department of State, *Background Notes*, Washington, D.C. (country reports on about 180 countries).

Countries for Analysis

1.	Argentina	18.	Macau
2.	Australia	19.	Malaysia
3.	Austria	20.	Mexico
4.	Belgium	21.	Netherlands
5.	Brazil	22.	New Zealand
6.	Burma	23.	Pakistan
7.	China (PRC)	24.	Panama
8.	China (ROC)	25.	Philippines
9.	Egypt	26.	Singapore
10.	Greece	27.	South Korea
11.	Hong Kong	28.	Spain
12.	India	29.	Thailand
13.	Indonesia	30.	Turkey
14.	Israel	31.	United Kingdom
15.	Italy	32.	Western Samoa
16.	Japan	33.	West Germany
17.	Laos		

Appendixes

Appendix A

Mechanics and Style

Several chapters in this book include suggestions for desirable style plus construction of effective sentences and paragraphs for various kinds of messages. Among them are Chapters 3 and 4 (principles); 7 through 15 (direct requests, good news, bad news, persuasive requests); 16, with C qualities for effective reports; and 20 through 24 (oral communications). In this appendix, suggestions focus on additional matters and mechanics that should be correct in business communications. Some exercises are included too.

Abbreviations

In business letters and reports, abbreviations are appropriate for the following titles: Mr., Mrs., Ms., Messrs. (as for a law firm of Messrs. White, Green, and Black). Other common abbreviations are Jr., Sr., Mt. (Mount), St. (Saint), Inc. (Incorporated), Ltd. (Limited), D.C. (District of Columbia); compound directions, NW or NW. or N.W. (Northwest), with similar variations for SW, NE, SE; and the professional degree symbols such as B.B.A., Ph.D., M.D., C.P.A. The title Dr. (Doctor) is usually abbreviated, especially when the first name or the initials are used with the surname. [Some authorities suggest abbreviating "Doctor" when the first name or initials precede the surname (Dr. John Brown) but spelling it out in a salutation (Dear Doctor Brown). Businesspersons, however, feel that applying two rules is impractical, and they abbreviate "Doctor" in both situations.]

The following words should be spelled out whenever possible: *president, superintendent, honorable, reverend, professor, building, association, department;* also, *street, boulevard, avenue, east, west, north, south.* City names should be spelled out. It is best to use abbreviations sparingly within messages. A good rule is: "When in doubt, spell it out." However, if you are using the U.S. Post Office Department two-letter state abbreviations on envelopes, you should preferably also abbreviate the state the same way in the inside address for consistency. The U.S. Postal Service recommends use of the following two-letter abbreviations—two capitals without periods or spaces.

Alabama	AL	Illinois	IL	Nebraska	NE
Alaska	AK	Indiana	IN	Nevada	NV
Arizona	AZ	Iowa	IA	New Hampshire	NH
Arkansas	AR	Kansas	KS	New Jersey	NJ
California	CA	Kentucky	KY	New Mexico	NM
Colorado	CO	Louisiana	LA	New York	NY
Connecticut	CT	Maine	ME	North Carolina	NC
Delaware	DE	Maryland	MD	North Dakota	ND
District of Columbia	DC	Massachusetts	MA	Ohio	OH
		Michigan	MI	Oklahoma	OK
Florida	FL	Minnesota	MN	Oregon	OR
Georgia	GA	Mississippi	MS	Pennsylvania	PA
Hawaii	HI	Missouri	MO	Puerto Rico	PR
Idaho	ID	Montana	MT	Rhode Island	RI

South Carolina . . .SC	Utah . . . . UT	West Virginia . . . WV
South Dakota . . . SD	Vermont . . . . . . .VT	Wisconsin . . . . . .WI
Tennessee . . . . . TN	Virginia . . . . . . .VA	Wyoming . . . . . WY
Texas . . . . .TX	Washington . . . . WA	

Dangling Participles

A *participle* is a word that ends in "ing" or "ed" and looks like a verb; yet it actually is an adjective that must modify a specific noun or pronoun. If it doesn't or if it is positioned so that its relationship to the word it modifies is not clear, it is called a *dangling participle.*

The three most common forms of dangling participles are caused by the writer's not observing the following rules:

1. The participle should be placed close to the word to which it refers, and there should be no intervening noun to which the participle might seem to refer.

Unclear: `A complete` *report* `is submitted by our branch office,` *giving* `details about this transaction.` [`Giving` *is the participle; it should modify* `report`, *but it seems to modify the intervening noun* `office.`]

Clear: `Our branch office submitted a complete` *report, giving* `details about this transaction.` [*Now the participle clearly modifies* `report.`]

2. A participle at the beginning of a sentence (or at the beginning of a second independent clause in a compound sentence) should refer to the subject of the sentence or independent clause.

Unclear: *Having* `been boiled for the proper length of time, the` *homemaker* `took the shrimp off the stove.` [`Having` *seems to modify the subject* `homemaker`, *when the participle should modify* `shrimp.`]

Clear: *Having* `been boiled for the proper length of time, the` *shrimp* `were taken off the stove by the homemaker.` [*Now* `having` *modifies the right word—* `shrimp` *—which is the subject of the sentence.*]

> *or*

`After the shrimp had boiled for the proper length of time, the homemaker took them off the stove.` [*This sentence discards the participle.*]

Here's a simple way to see if the participle beginning the sentence properly modifies the subject: State the subject "shrimp" and follow it with the participial phrase, "having been boiled for the proper length of time." If the two parts give you the meaning you want, "shrimp, having been boiled for the proper length of time," then the participle is modifying the right word. But if you are boiling the homemaker, something is wrong.

3. A participle following the main clause should refer to a definite noun, not to the general thought expressed by the clause.

Unclear:
```
These accounts disappeared from the vault, thus caus-
ing us serious worry.
```
[*Instead of modifying a particular word,* causing *modifies the entire clause that appears before the comma. Suggestion: Reword so that you don't have the participle in the sentence.*]

Clear:
```
Because the accounts disappeared from the vault, we
are seriously worried.
```

Clear:
```
These accounts disappeared from the vault, a fact that
caused us much worry.
```

Numbers as Figures or Words

In general—use the figure instead of the word, because the reader can more easily read the figure and grasp its meaning. In invoices, tabular materials, purchase orders, and the like, always use figures. In letters and reports—use the rule of 10 (spell out numbers 1 through 9; use figures for numbers 10 or higher) except for amounts of money and for isolated cases, as shown below.

1. If a sentence begins with a number, express the number in words. This rule is used when the sentence cannot be effectively revised.

```
Fifty applicants were interviewed for the position.
```

2. When a number standing first in the sentence is followed by another number to form an approximation, express both in words.

```
Fifty or sixty will be enough.
```

Note: Try not to begin a sentence with a number. Rewrite the sentence to place the number within or at the end of the sentence.

```
The confirmation request was answered by 559 businesses.
```

3. When a sentence contains one series of numbers, express all members of the series in figures, unless they are all below 10.

```
We had 25 applicants from Arkansas, 15 applicants from
Texas, and 6 applicants from Oklahoma.
```

4. When a sentence contains two series of numbers, express the members of one series in words and those of the other series in figures. If this rule is not followed, confusion results because of too many groups of numbers.

```
Five students scored 95 points, seventeen students scored 30
points, and eleven students scored 75 points.
```

```
Three senior accountants made $100 a day, twelve semiseniors
made $80 a day, and five junior accountants made $40 a day.
```

Note: For clarity, tabulate more than two series of numbers.

Name of Accountant	Daily Rate, $	Estimated Working Days	Total Estimated Earnings, $
Barlow, Helen	80	3	240
Dickinson, Al	70	2	140
Oman, Charles	80	1	80

5. When one number immediately precedes another number of different context, express one number in words, the other in figures.

```
The specifications call for twenty-five 2 × 4's.
```

```
The deposit slip listed four 5's as the only currency.
```

```
You ordered 275 three-inch bolts.
```

6. When an isolated number is below 10, express it in words. This rule does not apply to exact dimensions or amounts of money.

```
The new salesperson sold eight refrigerators last month.
```

```
She hit a 6-foot pole.
```

```
This paper is 8½ inches wide.
```

7. When numbers are expressed in words, as at the beginning of a sentence, use a hyphen to join the compound numbers, twenty-one through ninety-nine. A compound number usually acts as a compound adjective.

```
Fifty-six accounts; twenty-one women; ninety-three men.
```

8. When a numerical quantity contains more than three digits, each group of three digits should be set off by a comma (starting at the right). (Obviously, this rule does *not* apply to dates, street numbers, serial numbers, and page numbers.)

```
1,000; 1,021; 5,280,000; 60,000; 600,000
```

9. Express amounts of money in figures. The following practices are recommended:

    a. When an amount of money consists of dollars and cents, always express the amount in figures. The dollar sign should precede the amount (unless in a tabulated column).

```
The invoice total was $5.51.  The bonds were sold at
$999.50.
```

    b. When an amount of money consists only of dollars, omit the decimal point and the double zero. *Exceptions:* (1) When the amount is tabulated in a column that includes both dollars and cents, include the double zero.

```
The invoice is $150.  The check is for $5.   $   250.80
                                                 200.00
                                                 312.70
                                                 286.50
                                             $1,050.00
```

    (2) When a series of money amounts contains mixed figures, include the double zero for consistency on all even figures.

```
The committee raised amounts of $15.00, $33.75, and $75.00
in the three rummage sales.
```

    c. When an amount of money consists only of cents, write the amount in any of the following ways:

```
The piggy bank yielded $.57.  The piggy bank yielded 57¢.
The piggy bank yielded 57 cents.  The piggy bank yielded 9
cents.
```

    d. As a rule, do not write an amount in both figures and words. This procedure is necessary only in legal and financial documents.

```
The check is for $7.  The total assets are $23,000.50.
```

    In financial and legal papers write:

```
Ninety-five dollars ($95.00)
seven dollars ($7.00)
twenty-three and 42/100 dollars ($23.42)
twenty-three dollars and forty-two cents ($23.42)
```

10. Express the following numbers in figures, unless otherwise indicated:
    a. Dates.

```
October 3, 1988
3d of October
Your letter of October 3 was most welcome.
```

b. House or room numbers (except number one).

```
1503 Thomas Street
One Lenox Drive
```

c. Numerical names of streets.

Over 10:   `315  69th Street or 315 - 69th Street`   [*Note two*
              spaces or space-hyphen-space to separate house and street number.]
Under 10: `2930 Third Avenue or 2930 3d Avenue`

d. Numbered items such as page numbers, chapter numbers, figure numbers, table numbers, chart numbers, serial numbers, and telephone numbers.

```
Page 10      Table X             Policy #V9109815
Chapter 10   Table 10            Policy V9109815
Chapter X    Chart 10            Claim No. 13189756
Figure 8     Chart X             Telephone 555-1111
Fig. 8       Service Serial No. 018452  Phone (206) 555-1111
```

e. Decimals.

```
10.25   3.1414   0.3535
```

f. Dimensions and exact age.

```
8 1/2 × 11 inches    2 × 4 inches    He is 24 years, 5 months,
8 1/2 by 11 inches   2 by 4 inches   and 8 days old
```

g. Time.

```
7 A.M. [reserved for headings]   7:35 P.M. [reserved for headings]
7 a.m. [more commonly used]      7:35 p.m. [more commonly used]
seven o'clock                    seven in the morning
```

h. Percentages

```
35%                  6%
99.99%               6 percent
 0.09%
```

i. Fractions.

```
1/32      one-third        4³/₄ or 4.75
3/64      two-thirds       ¹/₂ or 1/2
25/64     one-fourth
25/100    three-fourths
```

Punctuation

Punctuation is important because it helps the reader understand what you are saying. That's the whole purpose of commas, periods, dashes, and all those other little marks—to make reading easier and clearer.

Comma Is Used:

1. When you address the reader directly.

```
Please let me know, Mr. Jons, when you will be in Tucson.

I'll certainly appreciate your taking care of this as-
signment, John.

Ms. Smith, that was a fine speech you gave to our group
last week.
```

2. When you mention a person's title after his or her name or the name after the title.

```
This person is Ms. Fay Janson, president of Acme Company.

Mr. Julius Roller, Jr., has done a splendid job.

Our representative, Ms. Hall, will see you next week.
```

Note: You omit commas in an expression like "my brother George" when a one-word name ("George") follows the title ("brother") and you have more than one brother. If you have only one brother: "my brother, George, . . ."

3. When the year follows the month and the day.

```
On October 4, 1985, I started working for this company.
```

   but

```
I was born in July 1968.
```

4. When the sentence contains a series or list of more than two things or persons.

He raises turkeys, chickens, and geese.

Mr. Smith, Mr. Snow, and Mrs. Hull appeared in court.

But in the names of business firms, follow the usage of the particular firm.

Merrill Lynch, Pierce, Fenner & Smith Inc.

5. When you can add "and" between two words that describe something.

   You are an efficient, hard-working fellow. [You are an efficient *and* hard-working fellow.]

   but

   A right mental attitude helps for happiness. [*It doesn't make sense to say* A right *and* mental attitude helps for happiness.]

6. When a sentence has two clauses separated by "but." (A *clause* is a group of words that includes a subject and verb; on the other hand, a *phrase* is a group of words that does not include a subject and verb.)

   I like this car, but it is too expensive for me.

7. When a sentence has two clauses separated by "and" and one clause or both clauses are long.

   You need a thorough knowledge of forestry, and you can get that knowledge from on-the-job training.

   His name is John, and he told me some of the most fascinating tales about the South Pacific.

   but

   I like you and you like me. [*No comma is necessary when both clauses are short—say, usually no more than five words each.*]

8. When a sentence begins with a long dependent clause (one that cannot stand alone and that starts with such words as *although, since, because, as soon as, after, when*).

   As soon as your letter reached me this morning, I called Mr. Doe.

   Although his plan was incomplete, he received general approval.

> *but*

```
His plan received general approval when the president
read favorable comments to all his department heads.
```
[*When the dependent clause comes after the main clause and is closely con-
nected with it, no comma is used.*]

9. When a word or clause that follows the name of a person or thing isn't
    necessary to distinguish that person or thing from another.

```
This man, who went without sleep for two days, fell
asleep at the wheel.
```

```
Boston, the capital, is the largest city in Massachu-
setts.
```

> *but*

```
A man who went without sleep for two days fell asleep at
the wheel.
```
[*Here the "who" clause is necessary to identify "man."*]

```
Buy the book Investments the next time you go to the
bookstore.
```

10. When a sentence includes a loosely connected word or phrase, called
    a *parenthetical* word or expression.

```
You will agree with me, however, that he is a great risk.
```

```
Yes, I agree with you.
```

```
You did a fine job, to be sure.
```

11. When two verbs come together.

```
Whatever is, is right.
```

12. When two figures come together in a sentence.

```
In 1979, 432 employees took their vacations in July.
```

13. When two sentence elements may be misunderstood or look strange
    if read together.

Wrong:	`Ever since we have enjoyed working with him.`
Right:	`Ever since, we have enjoyed working with him.`
Confusing:	`That that is is that that is not is not.`
Clear:	`That that is, is; that that is not, is not.`

14. When a sentence contains a quotation.

    ```
    "Tom," he said, "will receive the Leadership award."

    He said, "Tom will receive the Leadership award."
    ```

15. When the first word of a sentence ends in "ing" and modifies the subject.

    ```
    Looking into this man's record, we find he was arrested
    twice.
    ```

16. When a sentence omits a word (usually a verb).

    ```
    One of the persons involved in the accident is a mill op-
    erator; the other, a logger.
    ```

17. When the state follows the city.

    ```
    Denver, Colorado, is called the mile-high city.
    ```

Period Is Used:

1. To end a sentence that is complete with subject and verb.

    ```
    This firm has several branches throughout the state.
    ```

2. Also to end an imperative (command) sentence that begins with a verb but omits the subject (usually "you"), which is understood.

    ```
    Choose colorful and meaningful visual aids.

    Drive carefully on that slippery road.
    ```

3. For an ellipsis—to show omission of words from a quoted sentence. Use three periods (with intervening spaces) to indicate words omitted within the sentence; add a fourth period (or question mark) if the omission is at the end of the sentence.

    ```
    "Fourscore and seven years ago our fathers brought forth
    upon this continent a new nation, . . . dedicated to the
    proposition that all. . . ."
    ```

4. To indicate abbreviations. *But* omit the period after acronyms for organizations or government agencies.

    ```
    Mr., Dr., Inc., a.m., p.m., N.E., NE., J. E. Doe
    AFL, RCA, TVA, AT&T
    ```

5. For decimal sign.

`13.5%, 0.04, $374.22.`

6. In tabulation.

`1.`
`2.`   *[Only one space after the period.]*
`3.`

Semicolon Is Used:

1. Between clauses that can stand alone, with the second clause beginning with words such as *however, nevertheless, consequently, therefore, moreover, hence, likewise, furthermore,* and *namely.*

`He has an excellent background in education and work experience; however, I cannot find much information concerning his extracurricular activities on or off campus.`

2. Between closely related clauses that can stand alone and don't have any word between them.

`I prefer a person who has worked her or his way through school; he prefers a person who has devoted the entire time to schooling and has a high grade-point average.`

But, you may use a comma to separate very short main clauses not joined by words listed in number 1 above.

`I stopped, I aimed, I fired.`

3. Before expressions such as *for example, that is, namely, for instance,* and *in fact* when they fall in the middle of the sentence.

`Three of our offices have been redecorated; namely, Everett, Longview, and Bellville.`

Note: Some writers use a comma before such expressions when they introduce a phrase or dependent clause, but use a semicolon before an independent clause, as in the following example.

`She is highly qualified for the position; for example, she has several years' experience as a research assistant.`

4. When a comma is in at least one of two clauses, both of which can stand alone and a word such as *but, and,* or *or* lies between the clauses.

```
On January 16, 1987, you mailed your report to us; but it
didn't arrive until January 27.
```

5. When a sentence contains a series and at least one part of the series has a comma.

```
The speakers included Ms. Roberta Jule, vice president of
sales; Mr. Dennis Greiner, secretary; and Mr. Jack Blue,
comptroller.
```

Colon Is Used:

1. To introduce any lengthy quotation, list, or table after such words as *the following, as follows, as, these, this*—stated or implied.

```
This is what he said: "Choose a job you'll enjoy living
with for the rest of your life, and then. . . ."
```

```
That house has four rooms: front room, dining room,
kitchen, and bedroom.
```

Note: To show emotions or emphasis, use dashes instead of colons.

2. To separate hours and minutes.

```
4:50 a.m.    8:35 p.m.
```

3. After the salutation in a business letter.

```
Dear Mr. Jones:
```

Dash Is Used:

1. To emphasize.

```
The suggested exercises every day--every day--are bene-
ficial for your health.
```

2. To set off a series within the sentence.

```
These people--Mr. Smith, Mr. Jones, and Mrs. Peterson--
asked me about this type of account.
```

Hyphen Is Used:

1. To break a word at the end of a line.

```
sub-              knowl-
stantial          edge
```

2. To tie together words thought of as a unit, except when the words follow the noun.

```
well-written report but report is well written
letter-writing contest but contest for letter writing
up-to-date rule but rule is up to date
secretary-treasurer
his take-it-or-leave-it attitude
40-foot pole
short- and long-run objectives.
```

But, don't hyphenate when the first word is an adverb ending in "ly."

```
slowly moving object
```

3. In numbers 21 through 99 when spelled out.

```
fifty-five
ninety-nine
one hundred seventy-six
```

4. To separate "ex," "elect," and "self" from the next word.

```
ex-president; ex-President Ford
president-elect
self-control
re-cover [cover again]
```

5. To avoid an ambiguous or awkward combination of letters.

```
re-address, pre-election [Some authorities use "readdress," "preelec-
tion."]
```

Exclamation Mark Is Used:

To indicate strong emotion.

```
What a beautiful car!
```

```
What a mess!
```

Questions Marks Are Used:

1. For direct question.

```
What have you found out about this person?
```

But, use a period or a question mark after a request.

```
May we hear from you within the next 10 days.

May we hear from you within 10 days?
```

   2. To show doubt.

```
In 1983 (?) that country had two earthquakes.
```

Quotation Marks Are Used:

   1. Around a direct quotation

   2. Around unusual, substandard, or inexact terms

   3. Around titles of magazine articles and book chapters (but not titles of magazines, books, and pamphlets)

   4. Around words to be set off

```
The "please" in a request is. . . .
```

Here are three good suggestions to remember about punctuation before and after quotation marks:

   1. All periods and commas go within the quotes.

   2. Semicolons and colons always go outside the quotes.

   3. Question marks, exclamation marks, and dashes
      a. Go outside the quotes when they punctuate the entire sentence.
      b. Go inside the quotes when they punctuate only the quoted matter.

Apostrophe Is Used:

1. To show possession.

```
child's, women's, anybody's, Jones's, Moses', father-in-
law's, someone else's
```

2. For omission of a letter or number.

```
I'll, you'll, we've, don't, can't, hasn't, o'clock, isn't,
it's, the blizzard of '89
```

3. For plural of:
      numbers (optional)   `7's look like 9's or 7s look like 9s`
      letters   `p's and q's`
      words used as words   `You have five "hope's" in this`
                          `letter.`

Syllabication (Division of Words)

Syllabication is the division of words at the ends of lines to avoid a ragged right margin. In general, avoid this division of words, because the material isn't as easy and as clear to read. The following rules will help you to syllabicate words correctly:

1. Divide words between syllables only. Examples: *prod-uct, knowl-edge*.

2. Do not divide at the ends of more than two consecutive lines of typing.

3. Limit the number of syllabicated words to no more than four on a full page of typewritten material.

4. Divide hyphenated words at the hyphen only. Examples: *self-control, half-brother*.

5. Never divide words of one syllable or words pronounced as one syllable. The addition of past tense does not necessarily add an extra syllable. For example, *guessed, slammed, learned, backed, seemed,* and *glanced* cannot be divided, because they are all one syllable.

6. Do not divide a four-letter word. If possible, avoid dividing words of five or six letters. Examples: *upon, final, avoid*.

7. In words having three syllables or more, a one-letter syllable should be typed on the preceding, rather than the succeeding, line. Example: *sepa-rate*, not *sep-arate*.

8. Avoid separating a one- or two-letter syllable at the beginning of a word from the rest of the word. Examples: *apti-tude*, not *ap-titude; enough*, not *e-nough*. Exception, if necessary: two-letter prefixes—*ad, de, en, ex, im, in, re, un, up,* etc.

9. Never carry just two letters of a word to the next line. Example: *newly*, not *new-ly*.

10. When two vowels coming together are pronounced separately, divide between the two vowels. Examples: *cre-ated, gradu-ation*.

11. As a rule, divide between a prefix and the rest of the word. Examples: *trans-pose, con-sign*.

12. As a rule, divide between a suffix and the stem of the word. Examples: *lov-able, announce-ment*.

    a. Note that in such words as *ame-na-ble, fea-si-ble,* and *de-fen-si-ble* the termination is "ble"—and the vowel preceding it is considered a part of the preceding syllable.

    b. When a root word ends with a double consonant, separate the suffix from the root word. Examples: *guess-ing, tell-ing*.

    c. When a final consonant is doubled before a suffix, the additional consonant goes with the suffix. Examples: *trip-ping, strag-gling, stop-ping*.

    d. Note that the endings *-cian, -cion, -gion, -sion,* and *-tion* are kept as syllables, regardless of word derivation. Example: *expres-sion*.

13. When a consonant is doubled within a word, divide the word between the consonants. Examples: *fer-ret, tal-low, shut-ter*.

14. Do not divide the last word on a page.

15. Do not divide abbreviations, contractions, figures, or proper names.

Transitional Words and Phrases to Help Tie Sentences Together

Addition:

again	equally im-	in addition	next
also	portant	last	others
and	finally	lastly	secondly
and then	first	likewise	thirdly [etc.]
besides	further	moreover	too
	furthermore		

Cause and Result:

accordingly	because of	hence	thus
as a result	consequently	therefore	unless
assuming	for this rea-	thereupon	
	son		

Comparison:

better yet	in like man-	similarly	an even
here again	ner	still worse	greater sum
	likewise		even more
			important

Contrast:

although, even	however	on the contrary
though	in contrast	on the other hand
and yet	nevertheless	still
at the same time	notwithstanding	yet
but		

Instances, Lists, Explanations:

in particular	for example	for instance	to illustrate

Place:

adjacent to	here	on the opposite
beyond	nearby	side
		opposite to

Summary:

as has been stated	for instance	in short	to be sure
as I have said	in brief	in sum	to sum up
for example	in other words	on the whole	

Time Sequence:

afterward	during	in the meantime	soon
at the same time	following	meanwhile	then
before	immediately	previously	while

Trite Expressions to Avoid

advise [*when you mean "tell" or "inform"*]
assuring you of our prompt attention, we remain
attached please find
attached hereto
Dear Madam, Dear Sir, Dear Sirs
don't hesitate to
enclosed please find
in re
in reply wish to state

kindly [*when you mean "please"*]
party [*when you mean a person*]
please be advised that
please find enclosed
re your letter of recent date
said [*the said individual*]
thank you in advance
we are in receipt of
we transmit herewith

Exercises

A. *Dangling participles:* Identify all dangling participles in these sentences, tell whether each one violates rule 1, 2, or 3 (pages 765 and 766), and then correct all errors on a separate sheet of paper.

1. Enjoying 6% earnings, a savings account should be opened.
2. The check arrived six days late, causing me to write a collection letter.
3. Realizing our mistake, a new check was immediately sent to replace the first one.
4. Being larger and more attractive, these offices should make your work more pleasant, thus enabling you to work better.
5. Being a savings association, our customers do not have checking accounts here.
6. Please go down to the main office, and lying on the manager's desk you will find a copy of the latest report.

7. Having been run through the computer, the clerk used the figures for his report.
8. Changing your monthly loan payments, it will be necessary to get approval from the loan department.
9. Having been an outstanding keynote speaker, we can offer you this special award.
10. Being an old customer, we know that you are familiar with our special holiday sales.

B. *Numbers as figures or words:* Listed below are sentences that contain numbers in the form of figures and words. If any number is used incorrectly, cross out what's wrong and write the corrections on a separate sheet of paper. Don't mark any number that is used correctly.

1. 5 policies lie on my desk.
2. Two men and 8 women work in this office.
3. The insured's car hit a 10-foot pole.
4. 10 men scored 94 points, 17 men scored 110 points, and 3 men scored 143 points.
5. May I have 100 12-inch rulers?
6. This morning I answered 17 letters.
7. You'll find the answer on page 8.
8. Mary came home at 7 o'clock.
9. She works from 8 a.m. until 5 p.m.
10. Thanks for the $50.00 loan.
11. The car hit a ten-foot pole, rolled over, and then fell down a 20-foot embankment.
12. The gate is six feet three inches tall.
13. Your lot is 45 feet wide and one hundred thirty-two feet deep.
14. Please send the policy to 1 South Fifteenth Street.
15. Thank you for your check for twenty dollars.
16. Please buy 17 3-cent stamps.
17. The 3 items are on sale for $15, $16.95, and $20.

C. *Sentences to punctuate:*

1. The price is high but the quality is low
2. Washington Lincoln and Franklin Roosevelt were well known presidents
3. Youll find up to date information in that book
4. My sister Mary now attends college
5. The person who finds my watch gets a $20 reward
6. The boys are smiling the girls are laughing
7. As we agreed on the telephone this policy will run until May 6 1984
8. What system of bridge do you play

9. The price is high and the quality is poor
10. You did a fine job Mary in handling this situation
11. When you come to the meeting you should see Mr. John Narver our personel manager
12. It is wise therefore to trade with reputable merchants
13. A stitch in time saves nine says an old proverb
14. You can be certain Ms. Corbett that you'll have our answer within a week
15. In 1970 72 persons from our office enrolled
16. Among those at the conference were Mr. A B Moe superintendent Mr. Harris Lobe sales manager and Ms. Rollow Butts educational director
17. Having read the policy twice he was familiar with its contents
18. There was nobody there in fact when I arrived
19. His suggestion was this Think before you write
20. I always thought he was loony
21. David Brown who found my watch gets a $20 reward
22. When she talks she lisps her ss and rolls her rs
23. Enclosed is a copy of our letter of February 12 1987 regarding the endorsement date January 30 1987
24. Seattle Washington is the largest city in the Northwest
25. Please send the following Form A Form B and Form C
26. Be certain to read pages 4 15 17 22 and 30
27. This is your desk that one is mine
28. Nothing has been done according to Joe to change the picture
29. John said that he would do it
30. It takes guts to publish that report
31. As Pete ate John gave him an account of the accident
32. For the next two weeks send my mail to 441 South Estelle Wichita Kansas
33. I saw this man hit that pale blue four door automobile
34. Wait for me shouted a man running toward the bus.
35. People who live in glass houses shouldn't throw stones
36. They asked me whether I had taken any courses in finance
37. My sister you will be pleased to hear is now an accountant
38. A person who is honest will succeed
39. Three students Henry Pete and Mary invariably have their assignments well prepared every day
40. Its true that plenty of practice with proper guidance will improve your writing ability

Appendix B

Appearance of Business Messages

mong various media you can choose for written messages are letters and memorandums—plus special timesaving memo-letters, postcards, Mailgrams, telegrams, cablegrams, radiograms, telexes, and facsimiles (faxes). This appendix offers a brief overview on the appearance and use of these media and on form messages.

BUSINESS LETTERS

The medium used most often for written messages to persons outside the firm is the business letter. It is judged on content, organization, and physical appearance. Planning the content and organization is your responsibility; typing the message so that it is neat, accurate, and attractive is usually your secretary's job.

The letter's appearance conveys nonverbal impressions that affect a recipient's attitude even before that person reads the letter. Modern word processing systems and accompanying printers, with many type styles and formats, can remove much visual dullness and negative reaction.

Elements of appearance that help produce favorable impressions are appropriate stationery, correct letter parts and layout, and properly addressed envelopes.

Stationery

Keep the following guidelines in mind if you have an opportunity to suggest or change your organization's stationery.

Quality, Size, Color

To help build an image of quality, the paper for general business correspondence should have at least 25 percent cotton content; cotton does not turn yellowish in time as does wood pulp. The paper quality is usually 20-pound weight, based on the actual weight of four reams (2,000 sheets) of standard-sized paper. The standard size is 8½ by 11 inches for letters, but legal documents from some law firms are 8½ by 14 inches. White is the most popular color, particularly with printers connected to word processing systems. However, some firms achieve a distinctive professional touch using cream or light-gray stationery.

Letterhead

The modern letterhead (see Figure B-1) usually occupies no more than 2 inches at the top of the page. Printed, embossed, or engraved are the firm's name and address, ZIP code, and sometimes telephone number, cable address, fax number, nature of the business, and name of the department or branch office sending the correspondence. (Some of these may be at the bottom of the page.)

Optional details are names of officers and directors, trademark, slogan, and starting date of the firm. Many firms are including the extended ZIP code–ZIP

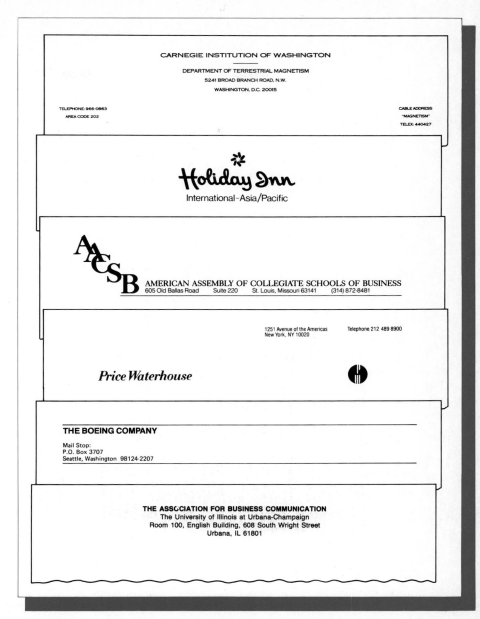

Figure B–1 Illustration of letterheads. (Holiday Inn's address, telephone number, telex and cable numbers are printed on two lines at the bottom of the page.)

+ four figures—assigned to buildings, residences, and floors within buildings. As stated in U.S. Postal Service Notice 221 (1985), "Addressing for Automation," the benefits of "ZIP + 4" are great. They include, among others, immediate postage discounts, high-speed sorting of your outgoing mail, and improved delivery services.

Standard Parts of the Letter

Most business letters have seven standard parts: (1) heading, (2) inside address, (3) salutation, (4) body, (5) complimentary close, (6) signature area, and (7) reference section, as shown in Figure B-2.

1. Heading—Letterhead and Date

The heading shows where the letter comes from and when it was written (or dictated). Usually the date is typewritten two to six lines below the last line of the letterhead—at the left margin, centered, begun at the center, or placed so it ends with the right margin. The preferred date sequence in American business is month, day, year—March 5, 1992, with the month spelled out. If you use the figures 3/5/92, the meaning in Europe, Latin America, and the Far East would be day, month, year—3 May, 1992. Thus, many multinational companies and organizations—the U.S. military has done so for years—write 5 March 1992 to avoid any confusion with subsidiaries around the world.

When you type a business letter on blank paper (for yourself, not an organization), your return address, but *not* your name, is typed directly above the date about 2 inches from the top, as in Figure B-3.

2. Inside Address

Always blocked at the left-hand margin, the inside address includes the name and address of the individual, group, or organization to whom you are writing. The person's name is preceded by a courtesy title and followed by a business or executive title, if any. All parts are typed single-spaced and arranged as in the examples on pages 788–789.

For guidelines on when it is appropriate to abbreviate titles, names of streets, states, and other items, see Abbreviations on the first page of Appendix A.

Courtesy Title and Name. If the addressee has no professional title—such as *Doctor, Reverend,* or *Professor*—the traditional courtesy titles are *Mr., Mrs., Miss,* or *Ms.* which stands for either *Miss* or *Mrs.* When you write to a married woman who prefers "Mrs." and her husband's name ("Mrs. John Jones"), address her that way. When in doubt about a woman's preference, use "Ms." plus her own first name and surname. The trend is to use *Ms.* as the courtesy title for all business and professional women, regardless of their marital status, unless of course they have a professional title that takes precedence.

After the courtesy title include your addressee's full first name, or two

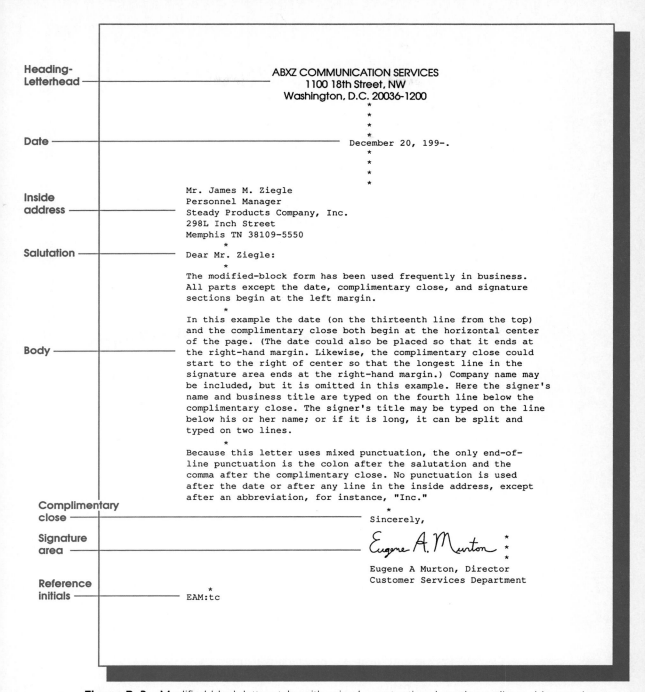

Heading-
Letterhead

Date

Inside
address

Salutation

Body

Complimentary
close

Signature
area

Reference
initials

ABXZ COMMUNICATION SERVICES
1100 18th Street, NW
Washington, D.C. 20036-1200
*
*
*
*
                                        December 20, 199-.
*
*
*
*
Mr. James M. Ziegle
Personnel Manager
Steady Products Company, Inc.
298L Inch Street
Memphis TN 38109-5550
*
Dear Mr. Ziegle:
*
The modified-block form has been used frequently in business.
All parts except the date, complimentary close, and signature
sections begin at the left margin.
*
In this example the date (on the thirteenth line from the top)
and the complimentary close both begin at the horizontal center
of the page. (The date could also be placed so that it ends at
the right-hand margin. Likewise, the complimentary close could
start to the right of center so that the longest line in the
signature area ends at the right-hand margin.) Company name may
be included, but it is omitted in this example. Here the signer's
name and business title are typed on the fourth line below the
complimentary close. The signer's title may be typed on the line
below his or her name; or if it is long, it can be split and
typed on two lines.
*
Because this letter uses mixed punctuation, the only end-of-
line punctuation is the colon after the salutation and the
comma after the complimentary close. No punctuation is used
after the date or after any line in the inside address, except
after an abbreviation, for instance, "Inc."
*
                                        Sincerely,

                                        Eugene A. Murton   *
                                                            *
                                                            *
                                        Eugene A Murton, Director
                                        Customer Services Department

*
EAM:tc

Figure B–2   *Modified-block letter style with mixed punctuation. Length, medium; side margins
1½ inches; line length, 5½ inches. Asterisk (*) indicates one blank line space. (The total
blank line spaces below the last line of a letterhead to the date, and to the inside address—also
from the reference initials to bottom of the page—vary depending on the length of each letter.)*

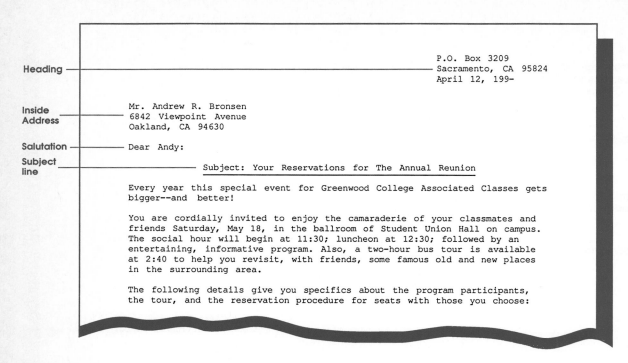

Heading

Inside
Address

Salutation

Subject
line

P.O. Box 3209
Sacramento, CA 95824
April 12, 199-

Mr. Andrew R. Bronsen
6842 Viewpoint Avenue
Oakland, CA 94630

Dear Andy:

Subject: Your Reservations for The Annual Reunion

Every year this special event for Greenwood College Associated Classes gets bigger--and better!

You are cordially invited to enjoy the camaraderie of your classmates and friends Saturday, May 18, in the ballroom of Student Union Hall on campus. The social hour will begin at 11:30; luncheon at 12:30; followed by an entertaining, informative program. Also, a two-hour bus tour is available at 2:40 to help you revisit, with friends, some famous old and new places in the surrounding area.

The following details give you specifics about the program participants, the tour, and the reservation procedure for seats with those you choose:

Figure B–3   *Illustration of heading with typed return address on plain stationery; also, inside address, nickname in salutation, and centered subject line. (This example is part of the first page of a two-page letter; the top margin is 1½ inches, the bottom and side margins are 1 inch; line length is 6½ inches.)*

initials, plus surname—for the first line of your inside address. When you do not know whether the initials are for a man or a woman, you can use *Mr. or Ms.* for the courtesy title—or omit it.

Business or Executive Title.   Depending on the relative length of lines, the business or executive title may be typed (1) on the same line as the addressee's name, as in example a below; (2) on the second line preceding the company's name, as in example b; or (3) on a line or two by itself, as in example c and in Figure B-2.

Order of Arrangement.   The various elements of the inside address are arranged like a pyramid. On the top line you place the smallest unit (an individual's name). The remaining items progress downward to the largest unit; lines usually range from three to six.

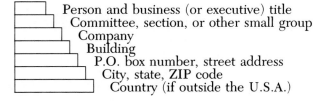

Person and business (or executive) title
Committee, section, or other small group
Company
Building
P.O. box number, street address
City, state, ZIP code
Country (if outside the U.S.A.)

a. Ms. Marietta K. Worthington
Treasurer, XXX Credit Company
P.O. Box 91467
Augusta, GA 30915-1234

c. Dr. Marlotte Lim, Sr.
Human Resources Officer
Esso Singapore Private Limited
1 Raffles Place
Singapore 0104

b. Mr. John Trimmer, President
General Construction Company
Larson Building
1380 Adams Street NW
Chicago, IL 60623-1122

3. Salutation

The salutation is the friendly greeting that precedes the body of the letter. It is typed on the second line below the inside address, two lines above the body and even with the left margin.

Acceptable Salutations.   The following list includes both traditional and comparatively recent salutations, all of which must be *appropriate for the first line of the inside address*. You have these choices:

a. `Dear Mr.` [*or* `Ms., Mrs., Miss`] `Doe:`—when the first line of an inside address is the name of an individual.

b. `Dear John` [*or* `Mary` *or* `nickname`]`:`—when you'd address the individual this way in person and when it is appropriate for you to do so in your letter on this occasion.

c. `Dear Manager` [*or* `Executive` *or* `Director`]`:` or `Dear Mr. or Ms. Doe:` or `Dear Sir or Madam:` or an appropriate variation—when the first line is a position within an organization and you have no person's name, or when it includes only initials before the surname.

`Manager, Service Department`

[Remainder of inside address.]

`Dear Manager:`
[*or* `Dear Mr. or Ms. Manager`]
[*or* `Dear Madam or Sir`]

`R. L. Macon`

[Remainder of inside address.]

`Dear R. L. Macon:` *or*
`Dear Mr. or Ms. Macon:`

d. `Ladies and Gentlemen` [*or* *reverse, or* `Gentlemen and Gentle-`
`women`]`:` or `Dear Members of . . .:` when the first line is a committee, company, or group of men and women; `Gentlemen` if all are men, and `Ladies` if all are women.

`ABC Toy Company`

[Remainder of inside address.]

`Public Relations Committee`

[Remainder of inside address.]

```
Ladies and Gentlemen:          Dear Committee members:
```
[*or others, as above*]   [*or others, as above*]

```
Professional Women's Club      XYZ Fraternity
```

[*Remainder of inside address.*]   [*Remainder of inside address.*]

```
Ladies:                        Gentlemen:
```
[*or* `Dear Professional`   [*or* `Dear Members of XYZ:`]
`Women:`]

e. `Dear Customer, Dear Homeowner, Dear Executive,` or `Dear Student` or `Occupant` or `Member of` [*name group*] or similar expressions—for messages that omit the inside address—as in sales letters, announcements, or other identical letters to more than one person.

Salutopenings.   Occasionally some business executives use "salutopenings" when they feel a salutation such as "Dear Mr. Brown" is not appropriate because he is a stranger, or "Dear" just seems unnatural. When you use a salutopening, type it on the salutation line, but omit "Dear" and begin with the first few words of your opening paragraph plus the reader's name. After the name, the sentence continues a double space down to the first line of the letter body, as below:

Salutation line   `What do you think, Mr. Brown,`

Body   `of the enclosed suggested arrangement for . . . ?`

Salutation line   `Good news, David,`

Body   `and thanks for your report on. . . .`

4. Body

Generally the body of all letters should be typed single-spaced, with double spacing (one blank line) between paragraphs, before and after the salutation, and before the complimentary close. Figure B-2 includes asterisks to indicate where all blank line spaces are in that letter.

A short letter of five or six lines in one paragraph could be entirely double spaced, except for additional blank line spaces before and after the date, and within the signature area.

When the body of a letter is two or more pages, each page beyond the first is headed by a combination of the addressee's name, page number, and date. This information is typed 1 to 2 inches from the top of the sheet, with the same margins as on the first page. In any of the accompanying examples shown here, leave a triple space between the last line in the header and the first line in the new paragraph.

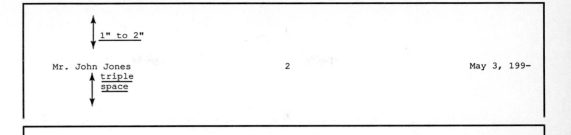

5. Complimentary Close

Most business letters use one of three key words in the complimentary close—*sincerely, cordially,* or *truly.* Only the first letter in the first word is capitalized, as shown in the following complimentary closes:

```
Sincerely,  [most popular]
Sincerely yours, Yours sincerely,
Very truly yours, Yours very truly,
Cordially,
```

When an informal salutation like "Dear Tom" ("Mary," or nickname) is used, the preferred complimentary closes are:

```
Sincerely, Cordially, Warm regards, Best regards, Best
wishes,
```

6. Signature Area

You can include in the signature area three or four identifications—name of your company, your signature, your typewritten name, and your business title.

Company Name.   If printed on the letterhead, your company name need not be typed after the complimentary close. However, if you wish to include the company name (some firms require it), type it in capital letters a double space under the complimentary close, as in the Bronson Company example below, and as in Figure B-4.

Signature, Typewritten Name, and Business Title.   Your signature is pen-written above your typed name, which appears three to five lines under either the company name (if included) or the complimentary close. The typed business title usually follows the typed name.

Very truly yours,	Sincerely,	Cordially,
Thomas L. Sutton	BRONSON COMPANY	*Roy Weber*
Thomas L. Sutton	*Mary P. Tracy*	Roy Weber,
Manager, Plant 2	Mary P. Tracy	President
	Personnel Manager	

Usually the signature is the same as the typed name. An exception is that if you have used your reader's first name for the salutation, you will usually sign only your first name above your typed name, as Roy Weber did in the example above.

For business and professional women, unnecessary reference to their marital status is avoided. In the signature area a married woman always signs *her* first name and not her husband's. Thus for "Mary P. Tracy, Personnel Manager" (example 2 above), though she is the wife of William R. Tracy, her professional messages are never signed (nor addressed to her as) "Mrs. William R. Tracy." If her name before marriage was Mary Pullman, she may sign either "Mary P. Tracy" or "Mary Pullman Tracy." (Of course, when she writes about a personal charge account, for instance, that is listed as "Mr. and Mrs. William R. Tracy," she should include the latter name in parentheses so as to correctly identify herself.)

It is also noteworthy that many married women, especially professionals, do not use their husbands' surname. Their signatures continue as before marriage, and they prefer the title "Ms."

Usually both men and women omit the courtesy title from their typewritten names and their signatures. However, if a man or a woman uses only initials before his or her surname, or the first name is not clearly male or female (for example, Chris, Robin), then it can be helpful to the recipient for the man to include "(Mr.)" and the woman to include "(Ms.)" in front of their typewritten names.

7. Reference Section

Your initials as dictator or drafter of the message, and those of your typist, usually appear at the left margin on the same line with the last line of the

REGENCY OFFICE EQUIPMENT COMPANY

312 Zero Street
Somecity, NY 10002-0000

June 22, 199-

REGISTERED MAIL

Ms. Jeanette Darlene, Consultant
Interoffice Appliance Company
456 Exchange Building
Sometown, Anystate 99988-4000

Dear Ms. Darlene

This full-block letter is typed single-spaced with a
blank line between paragraphs. Every line begins at
the left margin. "REGISTERED MAIL" is a double space
from the date.

Many firms prefer open punctuation with this form,
but mixed may also be used. The writer's company
name may be typed under the complimentary close, as
here, or omitted.

Other accepted forms of reference initials could, of
course, be used with this letter style. Also the
"REGISTERED MAIL" notation could be typed at the
bottom, a double space after the reference initials.
The postscript, handwritten or typewritten, would then
be placed a double space under "REGISTERED MAIL."

Sincerely yours,

REGENCY OFFICE EQUIPMENT COMPANY

James Briggs

James Briggs, Manager
Customer Service Department

JB/jd

P.S. *Best of success on your speech!*

Figure B–4   Full-block letter style, with open punctuation. Length, short;
side margins, 2 inches; line length, 4½ inches.

signature area (your name or title) or one or two lines below that. (If your name is typed at the left margin—as in Figure B-5—instead of in the signature area, the typist's initials follow it.) Among the common forms used are:

```
KLM:tr        KLM:TR        KLM/tsr        tr        KM/tr
```

Use of word processing systems adds another dimension. Then the initials of the dictator; the disk; sometimes abbreviations for the subject; and the typist are recorded.

```
HWH<3>:jr    [HWH is dictator; disk 3; jr is typist.]
LDM<6>F.E.:bn  [LDM is dictator; disk 6; F.E. is abbreviation for topic title;
               bn is typist.]
```

If someone other than the signer of the letter composes it, practice varies regarding reference initials. Many firms show at least on the file copy the initials of the signer, writer, and typist (KLM:JC:tr). The original, to the addressee, may omit all or the writer's initials, to avoid showing that the signer did not dictate the letter.

Optional Parts of the Letter

When appropriate, any of these optional parts can be included: (1) attention line, (2) subject line, (3) enclosure(s), (4) copy notation, (5) file or account number, (6) mailing notation, and (7) postscript.

Attention Line

The attention line directs a letter to a particular person or title or department when the letter is addressed to a company. It is useful when the writer (1) doesn't know an individual's name but wants the message to go to a particular title (sales or adjustment director) or department (personnel), (2) knows only the person's surname and thus cannot use that name on the first line of the inside address, or (3) expects that the addressee travels often, and the writer wants the letter to be attended to promptly by whoever takes care of the addressee's business.

The usual placement of the attention line has been between the inside address and salutation (a blank line before and after it). It may be flush with the left margin as in Figure B-5, or indented with the paragraphs, or centered. A salutation in the letter should be appropriate for whatever name is on the first line of the inside address. Notice that in Figure B-5 the salutation is plural because the first line is to a department. The intervening attention line has no effect on the salutation. A salutation in the letter should also be plural when a *company name* is on the first line of the inside address.

Some firms with large mailings tend to place an attention notation within the inside address—under the company name, which is on the first line. (Then

LETTERHEAD

_ _

December 1, 199-

Accounting Department
Eastern Register Company
1969 Fourth Avenue, NE
Sometown, Anystate 99999-2000

Attention: Mr. Johnson

Ladies and Gentlemen:

    This modified-block form is like that in Figure B-2 except that its par-
agraphs are indented five or more spaces. The date may be centered or placed to
the right of center, so long as it does not extend into the right margin. In this
example the date begins at the horizontal center of the page.

    The attention line here is at the left margin, two lines below the inside
address, and underlined. It could also have been centered and typed in all capital
letters without underscoring. If you wanted Mr. Johnson's name in the salutation,
you would type his first name (or two initials) and his surname above "Accounting
Department." Then you would omit the attention line and use "Dear Mr. Johnson"
(or "Dear Bill") in the salutation.

    In this example the complimentary close, like the date, begins at the center
of the page. The company name is omitted, but it could have been included. Also
the signer's name--instead of being at the left--could have been typed in the usual
place--or just "hw" above "General Manager," and reference initials (like"mm:hw"
could then have been used at the left margin.

    The term "Enclosures 3" in the reference section shows that three additional
items are being enclosed in the envelope. Each different item is counted as one,
regardless of the number of pages it may have. The notation "cc" indicates that
a carbon copy is being sent to Mr. Jami and Ms. Krown. Names are in alphabetical
order or by rank. The address of each may be included if needed for filing
information.

    The right-hand margins are "justified" in this example. Doing so is optional
for this and all other letter styles.

                        Very truly yours,

                        Millard M. Morrison

Millard M. Morrison/hw   General Manager

Enclosures 3
cc: Mr. Thomas Jami
     Ms. Helen Krown

Figure B–5   Modified-block letter style, with paragraph indentions and mixed
punctuation. Length, long; side margins, 1 inch; line length, 6½ inches;
right-hand margins justified (vertically straight).

in word processing, the section can be copied and used for both the inside address and the envelope.)

Subject Line

Considered part of the body of the letter, the subject line helps to tell your reader at a glance what your letter is about. It also helps in filing. The subject line may include or omit the word *subject*. It is usually placed on the second line below the salutation and centered (Figure B-3), or placed flush with left margin (Figure B-6). The typing may be capitals and lowercase and underlined (Figure B-3), or all capitals (Figure B-6).

Enclosure Notation

To remind whoever prepares your envelope for mailing that something is to be enclosed, the enclosure notation is usually typed a single or double space under the reference initials. This notation also alerts the addressee's incoming mail department to check for enclosures. An enclosure is anything in the envelope other than the message itself. One enclosure is a unit that can consist of one or more pages (for example, a two-page resume with an application letter is only one enclosure). When more than one item is enclosed, your secretary should indicate the number: "Enclosures 3" (see Figure B-5). For an attachment, that word may be typed in place of "Enclosure."

When the enclosures are especially important (checks, legal documents, or blueprints), it is desirable to list in the enclosure notation exactly what the enclosures are:

    Enclosures 2--Policy #95999 and #23805.

Copy Notation

When you want other persons to receive a copy of the letter that you have written to the addressee, the names of these persons—arranged in order of importance or in alphabetical order—should be typed in a copy notation. Place it just below the reference initials or the enclosure notation. Type "cc" before the recipients' names (as in Figure B-5) if you are sending them a carbon copy. Type "c" or "pc" or "copy" if it is a photocopy. Recipients' addresses may be included after their names if desirable.

Sometimes you may not want the addressee to know that other persons are getting a copy of the letter. Then you (or your secretary) can type "bc" (blind copy) or "bpc" (blind photo copy) and the recipients' names *on the copies only*.

File or Account Number, and Mailing Notation

To aid in filing and quick recognition for both the sender's and the reader's company, some firms require that file, loan, or account numbers be typed above the body of the letter in a conspicuous place.

LETTERHEAD

_____

July 26, 199-

Mrs. Carl Lane
P.O. Box 3754
Sometown, Anystate 00000-1234

FORMAT FOR SIMPLIFIED LETTER

This letter form, Mrs. Lane, has been recommended by the
Administrative Management Society as a time saver when typing
business letters. Here are its features:

1. It uses full-block form and open punctuation.

2. It omits the salutation and complimentary close but--to
    personalize--may, if possible, use the reader's name in the
    first and last sentences.

3. The subject line is in all capitals, omits "Subject," and
    is typed where the salutation is usually placed.

4. The signer's name and business title are typed in all capi-
    tals, starting at the left margin at least four lines below
    the last line of the letter body.

5. The typist's initials are at the left margin two lines below
    the signer's name. Enclosures and names of persons receiving
    copies are on separate lines below the initials.

Mrs. Lane, the simplified letter not only saves time but also
avoids the risk of selecting an inappropriate salutation--or
using "Dear (name)" when the reader is in no way "dear." It
is also helpful when you are writing to a department and don't
know anyone's name or whether its members include men, women,
or both.

For most business letters, correspondents prefer to use the
traditional forms with salutations and complimentary closes.

Paul A. Mullins

PAUL A. MULLINS--RESEARCH DIRECTOR

hm
Enclosure
Messrs. Erich Wittor, Mike Luberts, Ron Scharf

Figure B–6   _AMS simplified style; full-block; open punctuation. Length, medium;_
side margins, 1½ inches; line length, 5½ inches.

Mailing notation words such as *Special Delivery, Certified*, or *Registered Mail*, when applicable, may be typed a double space below the date line and at least a double space before the inside address, as in Figure B-4. An alternative placement is below the last notation. For instance, the "Registered Mail" notation could be placed a double space under the reference initials and a double space above the postscript.

Postscript

To emphasize a point already in your letter or to include a personal brief message unrelated to the letter, a postscript, typed or handwritten (with or without "P.S.," "PS.," or "PS:") may be added below everything else typed on the page. (See Figure B-4.)

However, if you forgot to include an important idea in the letter body, it can easily be reprinted in the right paragraph if one is using a word processing system. If using a typewriter, it is usually better to retype the letter than to add the information in a postscript. In sales messages the postscript is overused and sends a negative message that the writer did not plan well.

If you have occasion to use several notations after the signature area, the initials *RECMP* may help you and your secretary remember the proper order for arranging them vertically at the left margin: reference initials, enclosures, copy notation, mailing notation, postscript.

Letter Layout

Although layout or format of the letter is primarily the typist's responsibility, it is covered briefly here to give you a basis of choosing the styles you prefer. Some companies have adopted a common word processing software package (that includes even punctuation) so that all their letters are uniform regardless of dictator, department, or secretary.

Punctuation Styles

Open and *mixed* punctuation are the two forms most used in business letters. In open punctuation no line of any letter part (except the body) has any punctuation at the end unless an abbreviation requires a period. In mixed punctuation a colon follows the salutation; a comma follows the complimentary close.

Letter Styles

Business letters are usually arranged in one of the letter styles described briefly below and in Figures B-2 to B-6.

1. *Full-block* (Figure B-4). Every line begins at the left margin. This is the most common format, because it is quick and easy to set up.

2. *Modified-block* (Figures B-2 and B-3). The date, complimentary close, and signature sections begin at the horizontal center of the page or are placed so they end near the right-hand margin. Attention and subject lines may be indented, centered, or begin at the left margin, where all other parts begin. This letter style is still much used and is attractive on the page.

3. *Modified block with paragraphs indented* (Figure B-5). This style is used less, because the indented paragraphs are time-consuming to set up.

4. *AMS simplified style* (Figure B-6). AMS has been in use since the 1950s, but is not widely used.

Tips for Letter Placement

Software packages permit instant formatting (indents, spacing, margin width, type style, for example) of material according to the length of the letter or the size of the paper. The following suggestions are helpful for setting up your message on 8½ by 11-inch paper.

Letter Length	Words in Body	Side Margins, inches	Line Length, inches	Lines between Date and Inside Address	Examples
Short	Under 100	2	4½	4–10	Figure B-4
Medium	100–200	1½	5½	3–8	Figures B-2 and B-6
Long	200–300	1	6½	2–6	Figure B-5
2-page	Over 300	1	6½	2–6	Figure B-3

In summary, some software packages for word processing systems have taken out most of the guesswork in laying out or formatting a letter. Additional nonverbal cues of the letter's appearance are: its stationery, its placement of the standard parts on the page, and its envelope. When these are all desirable, the combination will help you to send a visually appealing letter.

Envelopes

The quality of envelope paper, pictures, slogans, and type style all contribute to your organization's image. Each envelope should—in the upper-left corner—show the sender's return address, usually printed like the letterhead or, if necessary, typewritten. The addressee's address (which is the inside address of the letter) should be placed on the envelope according to U.S. Postal Service published guidelines for location, legibility, abbreviations, and format.

It is costly to misaddress an envelope. During the fiscal year October 1, 1977, through September 30, 1988, 79.2 million pieces of mail ended up in the dead-letter office of the U.S. Postal Service. Found in those pieces of mail was a total of $849,235, of which only $61,514 could be returned. Over 323,000 employee hours were devoted to the dead-letter office, at an approximate cost of $4.5 million.[1]

Address Location and Legibility for Optical Character Recognition (OCR)

To quicken the process of sorting mail at the post office, correspondents should place the addressee's name and address on the envelope completely within the "OCR read area," because the electronic mail sorters—optical character readers (OCRs)—are programmed to scan this area automatically. The address should be clear, with dark print or typewriter type on a light background, and parallel to the envelope's bottom edge; slanted or crooked lines can confuse OCR recognition.

Address Format for OCR

The addressee's address should always be typed single-spaced in block form, with all lines beginning at a uniform left margin. Uppercase (capital) letters are preferred on all lines that must be within the OCR area. However, lowercase letters in various type styles are acceptable provided they meet the requirements of OCR readability. All punctuation is preferably omitted, except the hyphen in the ZIP + 4 code. Figure B-7 follows the most recently published preferences of the U.S. Postal Service.[2]

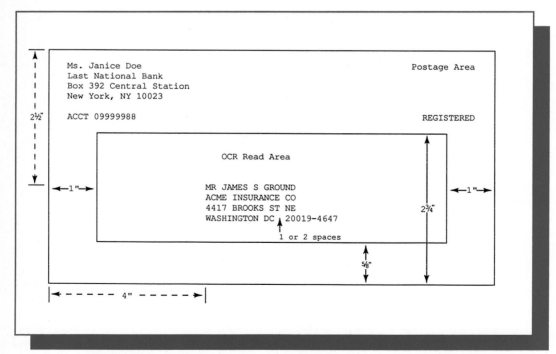

Figure B–7   *Large business envelope (no. 10 size—9½ by 4⅛ inches) properly addressed for optical character recognition.*

Mail notations such as "REGISTERED" or "SPECIAL DELIVERY" should be typed in all capitals below the postage area, outside the OCR area. Any on-arrival instructions, such as "CONFIDENTIAL," "HOLD FOR AR-RIVAL," "PLEASE FORWARD," or "ACCOUNT NUMBER," should be typed in all capitals below the return address near the left upper edge of the envelope, as shown in Figure B-7. All these must also be outside—and above—the OCR read area.

For the addressee's address to fall inside the OCR area of a no. 10–sized envelope, the first line should begin 2½ inches down from the top and 4 inches from the left edge. (See Figure B-7.) If the address contains five or six lines, the first line begins about 2¼ inches from the envelope top.

To speed machine sorting and processing while keeping postal operating costs and postage fees down, the Postal Service continues to make minor changes in published preferences wherever possible and desirable. They also have, in every large city, a joint Mailer/Postal Service organization that deals with mailer problems and suggestions. A free monthly pamphlet and various guides for successful envelope addressing are available from your local post office.

The following samples of OCR-referred formats for envelope addresses contain abbreviations, all uppercase letters, and no punctuation except for a hyphen in the ZIP codes.

```
ZYZ CORPORATION          MS KATHY STEVENS          MR EARL BROWN
ATTENTION H M JONES      CLIFTON TOWERS APT 952    342 HIGH DRIVE
PERSONNEL DEPT           3900 53D AVENUE W         LONDON W1P 6 HO
1096 S MILL DRIVE        SACRAMENTO CA 95816-1437  ENGLAND
ARLINGTON VA 22204-3152
```

Some firms use the "all-capitals, no-punctuation" layouts only for monthly billings and large-quantity mailings. When they prefer consistent appearance for the envelope and the inside addresses, the envelopes may be addressed the same as the letters' inside addresses. They have upper- and lowercase type-written characters (*not* all capitals), punctuation, and few or no abbreviations except states. Such envelopes can also be sorted and delivered by the Postal Service accurately and promptly—if the addresses meet requirements for OCR readability.

Folding of the Letter

Before a letter is inserted into the envelope it should be folded correctly. Doing this also affects the recipient's nonverbal impression of your organization.

When the 8½ by 11-inch standard-sized sheet is to be mailed in a no. 10 envelope, it should be folded in thirds. The bottom third is folded up first. Then the top third is folded down over it, preferably so its edge is about ¼ inch from the first fold. When inserted into the envelope, the open end of the folded message should be next to the back and top of the envelope.

MEMORANDUMS

In contrast to the letter, which is directed outside your organization, the memorandum (memo) goes within your organization. It is the most common form of written communication between people or departments. The stationery, parts, layout, and envelopes of the memo are somewhat different from those of the letters described in the preceding section.

Stationery

Memo stationery quality is changing with the increasing use of word processing systems. Managers using electronic mail (E-mail) send their message from their instrument to that of a colleague, and may simply have that message printed out on computer paper. For more permanency, though, a copy of the electronic memorandum is often reproduced on higher-quality stationery. Formal memorandum reports—composed on a word processing system and reproduced on a laser printer—may also use higher quality paper.

Preprinted memo stationery may include "MEMORANDUM" (or "INTERDEPARTMENTAL MEMORANDUM") and the company's name (but not address). Also, words naming various memo parts, as in Figure B-8, may be included.

MEMORANDUM   (Company name)

DATE: _____   FROM: _____

TO: _____   TELEPHONE: _____

DEPT: _____

SUBJECT: _____

                                For your

Message, Comment, or Reply   □ APPROVAL □ INFORMATION □ COMMENT

WRITE IT • DATE IT • SIGN IT   Oral messages waste time, cause annoying
                                  interruptions, and are likely to be misunder-
                                  stood or forgotten.

Figure B–8 Office interdepartmental memorandum.

Parts of the Memorandum

The standard memo parts of the memorandum are "to," "from," "subject," "date," and "message"; these can be programmed to appear automatically with just a keystroke in a word processing system. Optional are such items as reference initials, enclosures, file number, routing information, and the sender's department and telephone number. Some of these parts may be printed on the memo stationery. Unlike the letter, the memo requires no inside address, salutation, complimentary close, or full signature. The combination message-reply forms do, however, provide lines for both the writer's and the reader's signatures. (See Figures B-9 and B-10.)

The combination *message-and-reply memorandum* form is an especially good time and expense saver for both sender and recipient. A packet of three or more perforated sheets (white and colored), plus carbons (unless special "carbonless" paper is used), makes up a message-reply packet. Printed instruc-

Figure B–9   Interoffice memorandum packet containing either carbons under sheets of paper or carbon-treated paper (white, yellow, pink), with sections for both the message and the reply.

tions at the top or bottom tell the sender and the reader how to use the sheets. Printed lines may aid those who communicate in handwriting. Each sheet is divided into two sections—MESSAGE and REPLY. These two sections may be side by side or one above the other, as in Figure B-9.

What you write after the TO, FROM, and DATE will vary with the situation and your organization's practices. A courtesy title—Mr., Mrs., Miss, Ms.—before your reader's name (after TO) may be used or omitted, depending on your relationship with the reader (superior or subordinate) and the degree of informality within your organization. You omit the title before your name. Also, if the memo is a temporary message, not to be filed, and if you and the writer work together regularly, you may merely use initials, first name, or nickname after TO and FROM, and use all figures or abbreviations for the date. Place your handwritten initials above or to the right of your name.

```
TO:        J.E.H.              or    TO:        Jack
FROM:      T.R.M.                    FROM:      Ted
DATE:      10 Feb. [year]            DATE:      Feb. 10, 199-
SUBJECT:                             SUBJECT:
```

However, if the memo will be filed, the names of the sender and receiver should be spelled out:

```
TO:        Mr. [optional] James E. Hill, Personnel Manager
FROM:      Theodore R. Murdock, Accounting Department
DATE:      February 10, 199-
SUBJECT:
```

If you are sending the same message to several persons, their names, titles, or both should be typed after TO. If you write to the same persons often, you might have a form called a *routing slip* prepared with their names printed (or photocopied, or programmed into your word processing system) after the TO. When you have only one copy of a document, book, or other important papers that you want everyone in a certain group to read and comment on, circulate a covering memo—the single original, with no copies for readers to keep—among those on your list.

```
DATE:      May 2, 199-          Please read and initial the at-
TO:        Tom Brehm_____       tached: then send it to the next
           James Brown_____     reader. Last reader please re-
           Anita Jones_____     turn memo and attachment to
           Searl Lichen_____    sender.
FROM:      Kermit Hobson, Personnel
SUBJECT:   Request your Suggestions on Attached Procedures
           Manual
```

A subject line should include terms that instantly make the purpose of the memorandum clear. The length of the subject line may be up to seven words, sometimes longer if it has a verb.

Unclear Subject Lines	Clearer Subject Lines
Vacations	Vacation Policy for 199-
Expanded Operations	Recommend that EED Expand Operations into PRC
DPI's Problems	DPI Should Consider Expanding Its Recruiting Staff

The clearer subject line may include a verb to give an immediate sense of direction to a request or recommendation. The verb "recommend" suggests you are proposing that action should or should not be taken:

Recommend 8 Percent Increase in 199- Budget.

Recommend that Our Office Remain in City of New Delhi.

Layout of the Memorandum Body

The body of the memo, as for the letter, is its most important part because it contains your message. In general, you can use the same guidelines, principles, and organizational plans for the memo as for the letter.

The memo body, unlike that of a letter, is not centered on the page. The first line usually begins a triple space under the subject line regardless of message length. Left margins are usually lined up evenly below the TO. The body is typed single-spaced with double spacing between paragraphs. For memo pages beyond the first, headings are the same as those for the business letter: reader's name, page number, and date. Reference initials are typed a double space below the body, at the left margin. Copy notations may be placed after the reference initials (as in letters) or near the top of the memo between the TO and the FROM. If only your business title appears in the FROM line, or if the FROM line is omitted, you should sign your name a few spaces below the memo body.

Envelopes and Electronic Mail

How your memo is sent to the addressee depends on where you and the reader are located, and the degree of high technology in the office. Firms generally have messengers, preprinted company envelopes, or electronic mail. The envelope address contains your name and department in the upper-left corner and the reader's name, department, and address according to your organization's procedures.

SPECIAL TIMESAVING MESSAGE MEDIA

Included in this section are various message media that save time for both the sender and the recipient. The media that merit at least a brief discussion here

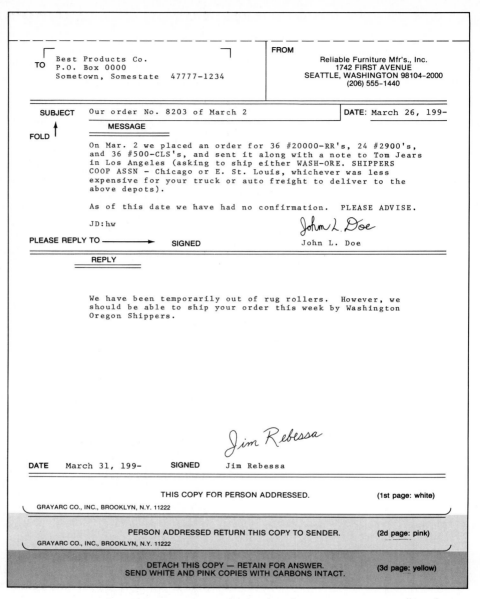

FROM

TO
Best Products Co.
P.O. Box 0000
Sometown, Somestate   47777-1234

Reliable Furniture Mfr's., Inc.
1742 FIRST AVENUE
SEATTLE, WASHINGTON 98104-2000
(206) 555-1440

SUBJECT   Our order No. 8203 of March 2   **DATE:** March 26, 199-

FOLD

MESSAGE

On Mar. 2 we placed an order for 36 #20000-RR's, 24 #2900's,
and 36 #500-CLS's, and sent it along with a note to Tom Jears
in Los Angeles (asking to ship either WASH-ORE. SHIPPERS
COOP ASSN – Chicago or E. St. Louis, whichever was less
expensive for your truck or auto freight to deliver to the
above depots).

As of this date we have had no confirmation. PLEASE ADVISE.

JD:hw

PLEASE REPLY TO ——————▶   **SIGNED**   *John L. Doe*
John L. Doe

REPLY

We have been temporarily out of rug rollers. However, we
should be able to ship your order this week by Washington
Oregon Shippers.

Jim Rebessa

DATE   March 31, 199-   **SIGNED**   Jim Rebessa

THIS COPY FOR PERSON ADDRESSED.   (1st page: white)
GRAYARC CO., INC., BROOKLYN, N.Y. 11222

PERSON ADDRESSED RETURN THIS COPY TO SENDER.   (2d page: pink)
GRAYARC CO., INC., BROOKLYN, N.Y. 11222

DETACH THIS COPY — RETAIN FOR ANSWER.   (3d page: yellow)
SEND WHITE AND PINK COPIES WITH CARBONS INTACT.

Figure B–10 *Memo-letter stationery for routine short messages—usually going outside your company.*

are memo-letters, postcards, Mailgrams, telegrams, cablegrams, radiograms, telexes, facsimiles (faxes), and form messages.

Memo-Letters

In the interest of speed and lower costs, many firms (especially wholesalers, publishers, and manufacturers) use a combination message-reply or memo-letter form for routine short messages directed *outside* their organization. In Figure B-10, after the FROM, the full name and address (perhaps also phone number) of the sender's company are printed and after the TO, a larger space is provided so that the typist can insert the full name and address of the recipient, because he or she is outside the sender's firm.

A further time-saver is the printed request-for-information form, illustrated in Figure B-11. Notice that besides the printed 28 requests this firm commonly uses, the form leaves spaces for 6 others to be inserted if desired. The bottom of this memo-letter form allows space for comments by both the sender and the receiver. This form also is a packet of three sheets with carbons preinserted. The memo-letter is mailed in the same kind of envelope as a regular business letter or in a window envelope (in which the address after the TO serves also as the envelope address).

Postcards

For short messages that are not confidential, companies may send postcards and reply cards for a wide variety of uses. The "blow in" postcards in magazines are an example of making replies easy in response to an advertising appeal. Order cards and colorful seller "miss you" cards to missing customers are additional ways to attract customers.

As a customer, you can use a postcard, for example, to inquire, to request a free advertised booklet, or to order a product that is to be charged to your account. You can often save time and expense by using postcards.

Mailgrams

When you need to reach any number of people simultaneously, in writing, with impact, and on the *next business day*—you can use Mailgrams. They are available for delivery overnight to any address in the United States and Canada.

Uses and Appearance

You can use Mailgrams in many ways—to announce important news speedily and simultaneously to sales representatives, distributors, stockholders, employees; quote special prices; acknowledge orders; congratulate; collect delinquent payments. Figure B-12 illustrates the Mailgram format and tells some advantages.

J. W. MICROELECTRONICS CORPORATION
REGIONAL TECHNOLOGY PARK - BLDG. C
4901 STENTON AVENUE • PHILADELPHIA, PENNSYLVANIA 19144-3040 • PHONE (215) 555-8681

REQUEST FOR INFORMATION

TO: _____   DATE _____   REQUEST NO. _____

_____   P.O. NO. _____   INV. NO. _____

_____   INV. DATE _____   INV. AMOUNT _____

PLEASE REPLY TODAY VIA   ☐ THIS FORM   ☐ WIRE   ☐ TELEPHONE   ☐ RETURN ENVELOPE ENCLOSED

☐ 1. PLEASE ACKNOWLEDGE OUR ORDER AND GIVE SHIPPING DATE.

☐ 2. PLEASE CHANGE ORDER AS NOTED BELOW AND ACKNOWLEDGE.

☐ 3. PLEASE ADVISE WHEN ORDER WILL BE SHIPPED.

☐ 4. MUST HAVE MORE SPECIFIC SHIPPING DATE.

☐ 5. CAN YOU MEET OUR SHIPPING DATE?

☐ 6. GOODS NOT RECEIVED; PLEASE TRACE SHIPMENT.

☐ 7. IF SHIPMENT HAS BEEN MADE, PLEASE MAIL INVOICE TODAY.

☐ 8. WHEN WILL BALANCE OF OUR ORDER BE SHIPPED?

☐ 9. PLEASE RUSH PRICES REQUESTED.

☐ 10. PLEASE SEND A SHIPPING NOTICE.

☐ 11. PLEASE SEND A RECEIPTED FREIGHT BILL.

☐ 12. PLEASE SEND A CERTIFIED WEIGHT SLIP.

☐ 13. PLEASE SEND ACCEPTANCE COPY OF OUR P.O.

☐ 14. RELEASE SHIPMENTS AS SHOWN UNDER "REMARKS" BELOW.

☐ 15. PUT OUR P.O. NUMBER ON ALL SHIPMENTS.

☐ 16. SHIP THIS ORDER TO ADDRESS BELOW.

☐ 17. WE HAVE NO RECORD OF TRANSACTION COVERED BY YOUR INVOICE. PLEASE GIVE US ORDER DATE, DATE SHIPPED, P. O. NUMBER, NAME OF PERSON PLACING THE ORDER, AND/OR SIGNED DELIVERY RECEIPT.

☐ 18. YOUR INVOICE IS RETURNED FOR REASON CHECKED:

☐ 19. WE REQUIRE_____COPIES OF EACH INVOICE.

☐ 20. PRICES DO NOT MATCH YOUR QUOTATION.

☐ 21. TERMS DO NOT MATCH OUR P.O.

☐ 22. QUANTITY DIFFERS FROM OUR P.O.

☐ 23. UNIT PRICE IS INCORRECT.

☐ 24. EXTENSION PRICE IS INCORRECT.

☐ 25. OUR P.O. NUMBER IS LACKING OR INCORRECT.

☐ 26. SALES TAX DOES/DOES NOT APPLY.

☐ 27. ORDER SHOULD BE BILLED F.O.B. DESTINATION.

☐ 28. ORDER MUST BE SHIPPED VIA _____

☐ 29. _____

☐ 30. _____

☐ 31. _____

☐ 32. _____

☐ 33. _____

☐ 34. _____

OUR REMARKS   **YOUR REPLY**

Form R-R113 The Drawing Board, Inc., Box 505, Dallas, Texas

Figure B–11   Printed request-for-information packet (three sheets) with numbered requests for easy checkoff; also, space for remarks and for recipient's reply.

WESTERN UNION TELEGRAPH CO
ONE LAKE STREET
UPPER SADDLE RIVER, NJ 07458

western union **Mailgram**

UNITED STATES POSTAL SERVICE
U.S. MAIL
★★★★★★

```
0-001012U056003 4/5/0- ICS NY 14233    MLTN
                                       *** BUSINESS REPLY***

L.B. JONES
32 SOUTH MAIN STREET
MAPLEWOOD, PA 15219-1001

HERE'S THE RESPONSE GETTER
YOU'VE BEEN WAITING FOR......

IT'S A BUSINESS REPLY MAILGRAM...DELIVERING YOUR MESSAGE WITH
THE IMPACT OF A TELEGRAM (AT A FRACTION OF THE COST)...ALL
WITH A BUILT-IN REPLY SLIP...A BUSINESS REPLY ENVELOPE FOR
IMMEDIATE TURNAROUND.

IT LETS YOU REACH HUNDREDS OR THOUSANDS OF PEOPLE IN THE NEXT
BUSINESS DAY'S MAIL...TO:

     ...GENERATE SALES LEADS
     ...COLLECT ON DELINQUENT ACCOUNTS
     ...OFFER SALES PROMOTION MATERIAL
     ...SOLICIT CONTRIBUTIONS OR PROXIES
     ...TAKE READER/CONSUMER AUDITS/SURVEYS
     ...RELEASE PRICE CHANGE INFORMATION

OR TO SEND ANY OTHER ANNOUNCEMENTS AND REQUESTS. YOU'LL GET
GREATER RESPONSE FASTER.

YOUR PROSPECTS AND CONSUMERS NEED MERELY FILL OUT THE REPLY
FORM AT THE BOTTOM OF YOUR MAILGRAM AND REFOLD IT SO THAT
YOUR RETURN ADDRESS AND PERMIT NUMBER SHOW THROUGH THE WINDOW
OF THE BUSINESS REPLY ENVELOPE. NO POSTAGE NEEDED.

WESTERN UNION WILL GLADLY ASSIST IN PREPARING YOUR MESSAGE
AND LIST FOR TRANSMISSION IN VOLUME ORDERS SO THAT YOU MAY
OBTAIN THE LOWEST COST POSSIBLE. FOR FURTHER INFORMATION CALL
WESTERN UNION TOLL-FREE.

MAILGRAM IS THE FASTEST WAY TO GET THE WORD AROUND...AND
BACK.

WESTERN UNION TELEGRAPH CO
ONE LAKE STREET
UPPER SADDLE RIVER, NJ 07458

06:14 EST

MGMCOMP MGM
```

Figure B–12   *Mailgram.*

Methods of Sending

Mailgrams may be sent by various means, including phoning a Western Union tollfree number. Direct input into the Western Union Mailgram system may be done by customers who have Telex I, Telex II, INFO-COM services, facsimile, or word processing terminals with capability of transmitting information telegraphically. Also, some direct computer transmission or magnetic and paper tape reels may be accepted at certain Western Union locations.

Each message is routed electronically by the Western Union network to a post office near your addressee and printed out individually. It is delivered in a Western Union blue and white Mailgram envelope with the next regular mail, usually the day after it's sent, sometimes the same day. The price structure and manner of counting words or characters differ for each type of Mailgram filing. Costs are also lower for quantity mailings ranging from 100 to over 25,000 messages.

Telegrams, Cablegrams, Radiograms, Telexes, Facsimiles

You can send a message by telegram within the continental United States and by cablegram or radiogram for overseas communication. The format of telegrams and cablegrams is similar to that of the Mailgram.

Telegrams

For domestic telegraphic service, you can choose full-rate telegrams or overnight telegrams. The fastest domestic service, for transmission within two hours, is the full-rate telegram with a minimum charge based on 10 words. The more economical overnight telegrams are messages accepted up to midnight for delivery not earlier than the following morning. If your firm sends numerous telegrams, a copy of *Domestic Telegraph Service Rules* is helpful. These sheets contain money-saving, specific details on how to count words, figures, forms of money, symbols, and punctuation.

Cablegrams and Radiograms

If you communicate frequently with representatives overseas, you might develop mutually understood code symbols to save costs. For example, notice how the following cable text from an insurance agent in Greece to her home office in the United States can be cut from a word count of 25 to only 10 words. (Words in the address count extra.)

CUSTOMER HAS TODAY ACCEPTED A NEW INSURANCE POLICY INCLUDING
FIRE EXTENDED COVERAGE AND VANDALISM ALSO PUBLIC LIABILITY
AND PROPERTY DAMAGE AS WELL AS WORKMEN'S COMPENSATION. [25 *words.*]

CUSTOMER TODAY ACCEPTED NEW POLICY INCLUDING FECVM PLPD AND
WC. [10 *words.*]

Telexes

All the preceding types of electronic mail may be sent directly from your secretary's computer or your company's computer. By definition, a *telex* is also an electronic message keyboarded on a word processing system, then sent over telegraph lines to compatible receivers of your own company or that of anyone who has a telex number.

Many companies, hotel chains, airlines, and a host of other groups communicate directly with their own offices. As with cablegrams, a common code of abbreviations saves costs and speeds messages, as in this excerpt from a telex:

```
IN YR TLX 4913 U AGREE TO HOLD PRICES FOR MDX TIL END YR.
OUR ODR XCI-530-MR IS FIRST OF 4.
```

Some common abbreviations used in international telexes are:

DER	Out of order	ENTER	Entertainment
JFE	Office closed, holiday	M.A.P.	Modified American Plan
*P	Stop your transmission	BANQ	Banquet
RAP	I shall call you back	F.A.P.	Full American Plan
SVP	Please	NGT	Night

In addition to the usual uses of telex, Western Union offers also its EasyLink and EasyLink Telex to give you access to a variety of other valuable services too.[3] Among them are the following:

InfoMaster—provides fast, economical information retrieval, easy access to the world's largest electronic library (over 800 databases) to research virtually anything on business, technology, current events, and published or public information.

FYI News—gives timely reports on world and national news events, money and stock updates, and more in just minutes.

Official Airline Guides—include, in the electronic edition, flight and hotel information; you can even make reservations.

Electronic mail network—enables you to reach 1.7 million domestic and worldwide telex terminals, facsimile machines worldwide, and over 170,000 EasyLink users—all with the same terminal.

Facsimiles (Faxes)

One of the fastest growing means of communication is the facsimile (fax) machine. It electronically transmits identical images from the sender's machine to the receiver's. Hence an entire memorandum or letter is inserted into the sender's machine and with the proper fax number will arrive quickly in the office of the receiver.

Noteworthy also is the Western Union Instant Mail Manager for the Macintosh computer. It is usable for message creation, transmission, and receipt.

"Fax for Macs" are delivered worldwide. From your Macintosh you can send messages to multiple fax machines as well as telex subscribers and EasyLink mailboxes simultaneously by using EasyLink's multiple address feature. You receive immediate information that your fax message has been delivered.

Form Messages

Whenever you want to send an identical message to at least two persons, you can write what is called a "form letter" or a "form memo," based on a master draft. The storage capabilities of computers permit storing complete sentences, paragraphs, or even entire letters. A simple keystroke allows immediate insertion of the stored material.

There are four kinds of form messages: complete form, fill-in form, guide form, and paragraph form.

Complete Form

Messages identical in every word are *complete forms*, especially useful for announcements, some collection reminders, and large-scale campaigns when being *impersonal* is acceptable. They may be reproduced on a printing press, computer, multigraph, photocopier, or laser printers.

In a complete-form *memo*, the word TO is followed by such terms as "All Employees" or "Management Personnel." In *letters*, a general salutation ("Dear Customer," "Homeowner," "Sports Buff," "Student") is chosen to fit the type of individuals getting the letter. Computers now easily store complete forms.

Sometimes the first few words of the opening sentence are placed where the inside address and salutation usually are:

"Faked" inside address	`The last time you had` `a chance like this` `to get ` <u>`World and Home News`</u>
"Faked" salutation	`at a big savings . . .`
Body	`. . . business was coasting along without any serious` `worries, the war in [country] seemed to be cooling off,` `the President had. . . .`

Fill-in Form

A message prepared in advance to meet a specific kind of situation may have spaces left for filling in variable information concerning the receiver. The date, customer's name and address, account number, payment due date, and so forth are machine-inserted in the right spaces on each individual letter. The fill-ins should match the type style and darkness intensity of the surrounding printed matter.

Some fill-in forms—for example, the one illustrated in Figure B-11—are obviously forms. They are useful in routine situations when both the writer and the reader consider forms acceptable.

However, when it is desirable to personalize each letter, fill-in forms can be reproduced by computer, automatic typewriter, or other high-speed automatic machines with magnetic tape capacity for inserting variable information at the time each form is reproduced. Thus, each person on your mailing list will receive a letter containing his or her name in one or more places and all the specific variables that apply to his or her case. The "fill-ins" are almost unnoticeable.

Guide Form

Sample letters prepared in advance for various situations can be kept on hand (usually in an office correspondence manual, or on a floppy disk) and referred to whenever a communicator writes similar messages. The communicator uses any sample as a guide only, inserting personal phrasing wherever desirable.

Paragraph Form

An office booklet or a magnetic disk for storing paragraphs to meet various situations is often an efficient way to save the letter writer's time. Several keystrokes can immediately make optional paragraphs available to the writer. The writer does, however, need to use good judgment in selecting appropriate paragraphs.

The booklet or disk usually contains various sections covering the frequently written messages. An airline, for example, may group its paragraphs under "Passenger Fares," "Flight Schedule Inquiries," "Air Cargo," "Adjustments," "Charter Flights," and "Goodwill." Each section contains numbered pages with various opening, closing, and intervening paragraphs that answer often-asked questions. Each paragraph may be marked by a number and a letter of the alphabet.

Thus, after choosing the appropriate paragraphs for your message, you need merely dictate the paragraph numbers, for instance, "2C, 5A, 9C, 15E." If you need a special paragraph that is not in the booklet (or on the disk), you dictate it. Your transcriber arranges the designated paragraphs and adds your specially dictated paragraph in the right order. (If a word processing system or automatic typewriter with magnetic tape or card is used, a letter can be completed in a few seconds.) Each customer gets an attractive, personalized letter composed of form paragraphs that exactly answer his or her questions and needs.

SUMMARY

Letters and memos are the most used written business message media. In addition, for special situations, memo-letters, postcards, Mailgrams, telexes, and facsimiles, plus other telegraphic and wireless media and forms, are also effective.

Attractive appearance of a business letter is an important aid to the reader's favorable first impression. Stationery, parts, layout (format), and envelope addressing should follow certain guidelines. For memorandums (sent within the organization) the stationery, parts, layout, and envelopes are different from those of letters. Memo-letters have a format more similar to a memo than to a letter. Postcards have certain timesaving features. Though the formats of Mailgrams, telegrams, and cablegrams are similar, these messages differ in methods of transmittal, word count, and costs. The facsimile machine electronically transmits the identical images from the sender's machine to the receiver's. All these media convey the impression that your message is important and urgent. To get the most economical rates, study the telegraph company's rules governing these services.

The four kinds of form messages—complete forms, fill-in forms, guide forms, and paragraph forms—offer advantages in time, cost, and quantity mailings. They must, however, be used with good judgment to avoid possible disadvantages.

This appendix is your guide for *formats* of business letters, memos, postcards, telegraphic media, and form letters and memos. In Chapters 7 to 15, which focus on *content*, most illustrations include only the message *body*—to save space. Therefore, when typing your complete messages, you may want to refer regularly to this appendix for correct layouts.

EXERCISES AND PROBLEMS

1. What are the standard and optional parts of a business letter?

2. How do the standard parts of the memo differ from those of the letter?

3. What are the advantages of using postcards, when desirable, for business messages? What disadvantages can you name?

4. Describe briefly five features of the AMS simplified letter.

5. Name three differences between a modified-block form and a full-block form of letter. Consider all standard and optional parts of these letters. Which of these two letter forms do you prefer and why?

6. What are the advantages—and possible disadvantages—of (a) form messages, (b) Mailgrams, (c) telegrams, (d) cablegrams, (e) telexes, (f) facsimiles?

7. Each of the following parts of a letter has one or more faults. Treat each part as an independent unit. Correct the errors, change all obsolete forms, and type each part correctly on a separate sheet of paper.

In the heading (stationery that doesn't have a letterhead):

a. 3 April 199-
   15,477 E. 5th St.,
   Spokane, Wn. 98155

b. Mr. Ray F. Byfield
   15 Mt. Vernon Ave.
   New Orleans, La. 70145
   Jan. 5th, 199-

In the inside address:

c. Mrs. John E. Henning,
   4317-18 Avenue N.E.
   Chicago,
   Illinois

d. Professor Lee Stephenson,
   School of Business Administration
   University of California
   BERKELEY 94700

e. Campbell and Morris Furniture Co.,
   1,496 Westlake Ave.
   City [*Sender is in same city as addressee.*]

In the signature and reference section:

f. [*open punctuation*]   Very Truly Yours,
                                 State Federal Savings Assn.,
   D.E.S./A.R.F.   Mr. Donald E. Smith
   INCLOSURE   President

g. [*mixed punctuation*]   Cordially yours
                                 MEURER & HOHANNES, INC.
   RAJ:AF   Raymond Jensen
   cc: Thomas Brown   Prod. Mgr.

In the inside address, salutation, and complimentary close (assume mixed punctuation):

h. Gladyne Lucchesini
   Des Moines, Ia. 50320
   Dear Miss Gladyne Luchesini
                          Yours truly

i. Dr. William Knapp, M.D.
   618 Wrigley Bldg.
   Chicago Ill. 60667
   Dear Carl,
                          Sincerely yours

j. B.K. Renshaw
   17,672 3rd St., N.E.,
   New York City 10011
   Dear Sir:-
                          Yours

k. Veterans Adm.
644a Liberty Bldg.
Detroit, Mich. 48256

Dear Dr. Chester Powers
                        Respectively yours,

l. Northwest Company, Inc.
Accounting Department
Phila, Penna. 19133

Dear Ms. Swanson

                        Your faithful friend
                        Pasco & Co.
Incl.   Clifford D. Bergerson
al: cdb: TR   Personnel Mgr.

m. Symon Manufacturing Company
Attention: Mr. David Burgess
13282 South Fifteenth St.
Kansas C'y, Mo. 64143

Dear Sirs: RE: February Sale

8. Which of the following three memorandums is best? Why? How does even this memo need improvement? In your evaluation, be sure to consider the probable purpose of the message and whether the memo is likely to be filed.

a. Jack to Bob, 4-23-[*year*]

BOOKLET SCHEDULE

Johnson now says Saturday sure.

b. TO: RJL
FROM: JS
April 23, 199-
HEALTH BOOKLET SCHEDULE

I checked with Johnson and now have a definite promise that the 6,000 Standard "Your Health" booklets will be delivered Saturday, April 26.

This rescheduling will not affect our production sched-ules.

c. TO: Dr. Robert Lawson, Vice President
FROM: John Spam, Managing Editor
April 23, 199-
RESCHEDULING OF STANDARD "YOUR HEALTH" BOOKLETS

```
I talked with Thomas Johnson this morning in an effort to
reschedule production of 6,000 Standard "Your Health"
booklets to permit delivery Saturday, April 26.

He indicated at first that such a rescheduling would delay
either the "Travel Plans" or the "Vacation Hints"
booklets, but after talking with his production manager,
he agreed to make the schedule change without delaying our
other production.

Thus we can definitely count on delivery of "Your
Health" Saturday.
```

9. Your corrected inside addresses for Exercises 7.c, d, and e may be typed in the same format on the envelopes, within the OCR read area. Assume, however, that your organization follows the Postal Service's preferred "all capitals, no punctuation" for envelope addresses. Thus, type these three envelope addresses in that format—next to the inside addresses on your answer sheet.

10. Changes in office technology occur frequently. Various periodicals may provide a quick resource for recent changes. Among them are these: ***Administrative Management, Boardroom Reports, Computers and People, Datamation, EDP Analyzer, Nation's Business, The Office,*** and ***Word Processing Directory.***

    For a fuller understanding of some terms used in the modern office, obtain a definition and a statement of how the following terms and phrases relate to the modern office:

Bits	Facsimile	Software
Bytes	Floppy disk	Stand-alone system
Boilerplate	Intelligent typewriter	Teleconferencing
CRT	Modem	Text editor
Dictation systems	Microfacsimile	Word processor
Electronic mail	Reprographics	Xerographic process

11. Review for the class an article on some aspect of modern technology in the office. Your subject may be similar to any mentioned in the Prologue: inputting systems; storage, and retrieval of information; reproduction of material; and dissemination of information.

References and Notes

*(**Note:** Numbers in parentheses indicate the page on which each superscript reference appears.)*

Chapter 1

(6)
1. Vernon M. Buehler and Y. K. Shetty, "Managerial Response to Social Responsibility Challenge," *Academy of Management Journal*, 19 (1): 66–78, March 1976; *Corporate Social Reporting in the United States and Western Europe*, U.S. Department of Commerce, Washington, D.C., 1979; Sandra L. Holmes, "Executives Should Be Seen and Heard," *Business Horizons*, April 1977, pp. 5–8; Rae Leaper, "CEO's of Nonprofit Organizations Agree: Communicate or Perish," *Journal of Organizational Communication*, **4**: 9, 1980; Gilda Parella, "Are Newsletters Read? Are They Remembered? Are They Needed?" *Journal of Organizational Communication*, **9**: 26, 1980; John F. Steiner, "The Business Response to Public Distrust," *Business Horizons*, April 1977, pp. 74–81; Albert Walker, "Anatomy of the Communication Audit," *Communication World*, **5**(9): 19–22, 1988.

(7)
2. The Association for Business Communication, with its national office at University of North Texas, Denton, has members in colleges and universities throughout the world.

(7)
(7)
3. Frances W. Weeks, "Communication Competencies Listed in Job Descriptions," *The ABCA Bulletin*, September 1971, pp. 18–37, and December 1974, pp. 22–34; Marie E. Flatley, "A Comparative Analysis of the Written Communication of Managers at Various Organizational Levels in the Private Business Sector," *The Journal of Business Communication*, Summer 1982, pp. 35–49; G. Gilbert Storms, "What Business School Graduates Say about the Writing They Do at Work. . . ," *The ABCA Bulletin*, December 1983, pp. 13–18; James C. Bennett and Robert J. Olney, "Executive Priorities for Effective Communication in an Information Society," *The Journal of Business Communication*, Spring 1986, pp. 13–22.

(7)
4. Betty Ann Stead, "Communication and the Accountant's Responsibility," *The Journal of Business Communication*, Spring 1977, p. 24, with citations from Editor's Notebook. "The CPA and the Second 'R'," *The Journal of Accountancy*, November 1969, pp. 39–40, and Robert H. Roy and James H. MacNeill, *Horizons for a Profession*, American Institute of Certified Public Accountants, New York, 1967, pp. 14–15.

(8)
5. *DCAA Contract Audit Manual*, Department of Defense Contract Audit Agency, Washington, D.C., July 1988 (published biannually).

(8)
6. John Fielden, "What Do You Mean I Can't Write?" *Harvard Business Review*, May–June 1964, pp. 144–145. Figure 1–1 adapted from original article.

(9)
7. Thomas W. Harrell and Bernard Alpert, "MBA's, Twenty Years After," Research Paper No. 75, Research Paper Series, Stanford University, pp. 1–14, 1984.

(9)
8. The following is a representative list of references: William Arthur Allee, "A Study of the Graduates of the College of Commerce, State University of Iowa, 1921–1951," Ph.D. dissertation, Iowa City, 1951; James C. Bennett, "The Communication Needs of Business Executives," *The ABCA Journal of Business Communication*, Spring 1971, pp. 5–11;

PAGE

Garda W. Bowman, "What Helps or Harms Promotability," *Harvard Business Review*, Jan.–Feb. 1964; William P. Carr, "An Evaluation of Accounting Curriculum Subjects" (Loyola University of the South, New Orleans), *Collegiate News and Views*, October 1952, pp. 5–10; Homer Cox, "The Voices of Experience: The Business Communication Alumnus Reports," *The Journal of Business Communication*, Summer 1976, pp. 35–46; Samuel D. Deep, *Human Relations in Management*, Glencoe, Encino, Calif., 1978, Chap. 1; H. C. Edgeworth, "Business Communication and Colleges of Business," *The ABCA Bulletin*, September 1978, pp. 34–36; William Grogg, "The Importance of Business Writing to the Student—A Businessman's Viewpoint," *The ABCA Bulletin*, June 1972, pp. 1–5; J. M. Hunter, Anthony Koo, and R. F. Voertman, "What Happens to Our Economics Majors" (Michigan State University, East Lansing), *Collegiate News and Views*, March 1954, pp. 11–13; R. R. Kay, "To Manage You Must Communicate," *Iron Age*, July 15, 1965, p. 55; Raymond V. Lesikar, *A Summary of Needs of Education for Small Business Based on a 1959 Survey of Louisiana Businessmen*, Louisiana State University Press, Baton Rouge, 1959; Charles E. Peck, "Survey of Curriculum Opinions of Business Administration," *University of Washington Business Review*, Seattle, 1958; Bill Rainey, "Professors and Executives Appraise Business Communication Education," *The ABCA Journal of Business Communication*, Summer 1972; C. Wilson Randle, "How to Identify Promotable Executives," *Harvard Business Review*, May–June 1956, pp. 122–124; Rollin H. Simonds, "Skills Businessmen Use the Most," *Nation's Business*, November 1960; J. B. Steinbruegee, T. J. Hailstones, and E. E. Roberts, "Personnel Managers Evaluate a College Business Program" (Xavier University, Cincinnati), *Collegiate News and Views*, May 1955, pp. 7–11; Stella Travaek, *An Opinion Report of the College of Business Administration, The University of Texas, 1917–1954*, Bureau of Business Research, University of Texas, Austin, 1954; Clarence E. Vincent, "Personnel Executives Examine the College Graduate" (Southern Illinois University, Carbondale), *Collegiate News and Views*, March 1966, pp. 12–16.

(9) **9.** H. W. Hildebrandt, F. A. Bond, E. L. Miller, and A. W. Swinyard, "An Executive Appraisal of Courses Which Best Prepare One for General Management," *The Journal of Business Communication*, Winter 1982, pp. 5–15. Additional publications also supporting the importance of communication, written and oral: Hildebrandt, Bond, Miller, and Dee Edington, *The Newly Promoted Executive: A Study in Corporate Leadership*, University of Michigan, Ann Arbor, 1985, 1986, 1987; *A Managerial Profile*, University of Michigan, 1984; and *A Managerial Profile: The Woman Manager*, University of Michigan, 1985.

(9) **10.** H. W. Hildebrandt, E. L. Miller, and D. W. Edington, *A Review of Managers in U.S. Industries*, University of Michigan, Ann Arbor, 1987.

(9) **11.** H. W. Hildebrandt and D. Edington, "In Singapore or New York, Executives Look Alike," *The Asian Wall Street Journal*, May 24–25, 1985, p. 6; "Comparative Profiles of Asian and U.S. Executives," Working Paper 399, Graduate School of Business Administration, University of Michigan, Ann Arbor, 1984, pp. 1–24; H. W. Hildebrandt, E. L. Miller, and D. W. Edington, *A Review of Managers in U.S. Industries*, University of Michigan, Ann Arbor, 1987.

(11) **12.** John D. deButts, "When We Tell Customers, 'We Hear You,' We'd Better Be Listening," *Bell Telephone Magazine*, September–October 1973. His suggestions are good advice for employees in any business organization or government office in the 1990s too.

Chapter 2

(16) **1.** William F. Eadie and Michael Sincoff, "Technical Communication in Written and Oral Modes," *Journal of Technical Writing and Communication*, **7**: 205–217, 1977; Dale A.

PAGE

Level, Jr, "Communication Effectiveness: Method and Situation," *Journal of Business Communication*, **10** (1): 19–25, Fall 1972; Sarah Ligett, "Speaking/Writing Relationships and Business Communication," *Journal of Business Communication*, **22** (2): 47–56, Spring 1985; Ingrid Pufahl Bax, "How to Assign Work in an Office: A Comparison of Spoken and Written Directives in American English," *Journal of Pragmatics* **10**: 673–692, 1986.

(21)

2. If you wish to read more details about communication and human relations, semantics, processes of speaking, listening, writing, reading, or group dynamics, you might begin with the following books (some of which are classics), plus any bibliographies they contain: Kurt Baldinger, *Semantic Theory*, St. Martin's, New York, 1980; Ernest Bormann, *Communication Theory*, Holt, New York, 1980; David K. Berlo, *The Process of Communication: An Introduction*, Holt, New York, 1960; Stuart Chase, *Power of Words*, Harcourt, Brace, New York, 1954; William V. Haney, *Communication and Interpersonal Relations*, Irwin, Homewood, Ill., 1986; A. Harris, *I'm OK—You're OK*, Avon, New York, 1982; S. I. Hayakawa, *Through the Communication Barrier*, Harper & Row, New York, 1979; Richard C. Huseman and Archie B. Carroll, *Readings in Organizational Behavior: Dimensions of Management Actions*, Allyn and Bacon, Newton, Mass., 1979; Alfred Korzybski, *Science and Sanity*, Institute of General Semantics, Lakeville, Conn., 1980; Irving J. Lee and Laura Lee, *Handling Barriers in Communication*, Harper, New York, 1978; Gail E. Myers and Michele T. Myers, *The Dynamics of Human Communication*, McGraw-Hill, New York, 1987; T. C. Pollock and J. G. Spaulding, *General Semantics: A Theory of Meaning Analyzed*, Institute of General Semantics, Lakeville, Conn.: 1942; Brent D. Ruben, *Communication and Human Behavior,* Macmillan, New York, 1988.

(28)

3. Nonverbal cues are mentioned also in Chaps. 12, 13, 18, 19, 20, 24, 26, and App. B. For more reading on nonverbal communication you might begin with these articles and books: D. Archer and M. Akert, "Words and Everything Else: Verbal and Nonverbal Cues in Social Interpretation," *Journal of Personality and Social Psychology*, **35**: 443–449, 1977; M. Argyle and J. Dean, "Eye Contact, Distance and Affiliation," *Sociometry*, **28**: 289–304, 1965; J. E. Baird, "Nonverbal Communication Can Be a Motivational Tool," *Personnel Journal*, September 1979, pp. 607–610; Ray L. Birdwhistell, *Kinesics and Context*, University of Pennsylvania Press, Philadelphia, 1970; Albert Mehrabian, *Nonverbal Communication*, Aldine-Atherton, Chicago, 1972; M. Bond and D. Sheraishi, "The Effect of Body Lean and Status of an Interviewer on Nonverbal Behavior," *International Journal of Psychology, 9* (2): 117–128, 1974; Julius Fast, *Body Language*, M. Evans, New York, 1984; Edward T. Hall, *The Silent Language*, Doubleday, Garden City, N.Y., 1959; Mark L. Knapp, *Essentials of Nonverbal Communication*, Holt, New York, 1980; Michael Korda, *Power! How to Get It: How to Use It*, Ballantine, Westminster, Md., 1976; Dale Leathers, *Successful Nonverbal Communication Principles and Applications*, Macmillan, New York, 1986; Robert W. Rasberry, "A Collection of Nonverbal Communication Research: An Annotated Bibliography," *ABCA Journal of Business Communication*, **16** (4): 21–29, Summer 1979; Pavel Machotka and John P. Spiegel, *Articulate Body*, Irvington, New York, 1982.

Chapter 3

(49)

1. Royal Bank of Canada, "Honest Communication," *Journal of Business Communication*, Winter 1973, pp. 19–27.

(50)

2. Steven N. Brenner and Earl A. Molander, "Is the Ethics of Business Changing?" *Harvard Business Review*, vol. 55, no. 1, January–February, 1977, pp. 59–64.

(50)

3. Phillip V. Lewis and N. L. Reinsch, Jr., "The Ethics of Business Communication," *ABCA National Convention Proceedings, 1981*, p. 9.

(50)

4. Lewis and Reinsch, "The Ethics of Business Communication," pp. 16–17.

(50)   **5.** Lewis and Reinsch, "The Ethics of Business Communication," pp. 16–17.

(51)   **6.** Phillip I. Blumberg, dean of the School of Law and professor of law and business at the University of Connecticut; excerpts from his *Invited Essay to Beta Gamma Sigma*, "Corporate Morality and the Crisis of Confidence in American Business," January 1977. Beta Gamma Sigma, national scholastic honorary for students pursuing degrees in business and management, has endeavored to foster integrity in business practice since its founding in 1913.

Chapter 4

(66)   **1.** Robert Gunning, *The Technique of Clear Writing*, rev. ed., McGraw-Hill, New York, 1968, p. 38. Used with permission of author, copyright owner.

(67)   **2.** See George Klare, *The Measurement of Readability*, Iowa State University Press, Ames, 1963, for a discussion of 31 different kinds of readability formulas.

(70)   **3.** From *Dear Sir*, vol. 3, no. 1, Correspondence Improvement Section, Public Relations Department, Prudential Insurance Company of America, Newark, N.J.

(76)   **4.** Any of the following contain helpful material on grammar and English for business communication: Greta Henderson and Price R. Voiles, *Business English Essentials*, 7th ed., McGraw-Hill, New York, 1987; Celia Millward, *Handbook for Writers: Grammar, Punctuation, Diction, Rhetoric, Research,* Holt, New York, 1983; Lois J. Bachman, Norman B. Sigband, and Theodore W. Hipple, *Successful Business English,* Scott, Foresman, Glenview, Ill., 1987.

(78)   **5.** The discussion in this section is adapted mainly from "Guidelines for Equal Treatment of the Sexes in McGraw-Hill Book Company Publications." For a bibliography of 16 publications about sexist and nondiscriminatory communication, see "Some Guidelines for Nondiscriminatory Communication," *The Journal of Business Communication*, Winter 1979, pp. 75–76. See, also, International Association of Business Communicators, *Without Bias: A Guidebook for Nondiscriminatory Communication*, Judy E. Pickens (ed.), Wiley, New York, 1982.

(82)   **6.** A good many organizations still prefer and consistently use *chairman* for both sexes. Among them are Toastmasters International and the National League of American Pen Women. As has been the accepted procedure for decades, a female presiding officer may be addressed "Madam Chairman." (Ardent nonsexist communicators have asked, humorously, how a male presiding officer would feel if he were addressed as "Sir Chairwoman.")

(85)   **7.** Jane Goodsell, Press Associates, Inc., prepared a syndicated column called "Soup to Nonsense." When she tried her skill at turning old proverbs into bureaucratic gobbledygook, these were some of her creations.

Chapter 5

(95)   **1.** Unless otherwise footnoted, this discussion on defamation is based on Arthur B. Hanson, *Libel and Related Torts*, vol. 1, American Newspaper Publishers Association Foundation, New York, 1969, pp. 21–195; Harold J. Grilliot, *Introduction to Law and the Legal System*, 3d ed., Houghton Mifflin, Boston, 1983, pp. 520–521; William L. Prosser and Robert E. Keeton, *Law of Torts*, Handbook Series, 5th ed., West, St. Paul, Minn., 1984. (This work may usefully be consulted in connection with most of the topics dealt with in this chapter.) We are particularly grateful to George C. Cameron and George Siedel, professors of business law, University of Michigan School of Business, and Lorraine R. Goldberg of the University of Washington for their assistance. Additionally, hundreds of cases cited in the LEXIS legal database system contributed to the content of this chapter.

PAGE

(96)
  2. Paul P. Ashley, *Say It Safely: Legal Limits in Publishing, Radio, and Television*, University of Washington Press, Seattle, 1966, pp. 43–47.

(97)
  3. Iris I. Varner and Carson H. Varner, Jr., "Business Communications and the Law," presented at the international convention of the American Business Communication Association, Atlanta, Dec. 28, 1978, pp. 7, 8; reviewed Dec. 1, 1982. Also, Varner and Varner, "Legal Issues in Business Communication," *ABCA Bulletin*, September 1983, p. 17.

(97)
  4. "Importance of Being Frank," *Newsweek*, Oct. 5, 1981, p. 87.

(98)
  5. S. G. Tenney, assistant attorney general, University of Washington, Seattle, interview, Nov. 29, 1982; and James B. Wilson, senior assistant attorney general, University of Washington, Seattle, interview, Mar. 18, 1986.

(98)
  6. Varner and Varner, *Business Communications and the Law*, pp. 7–10; also Carson Varner, examples in "Employee Evaluations, Letters of Recommendation and Legal Liability," presented at the international convention of the Association for Business Communication, Los Angeles, Nov. 14, 1986.

(100)
  7. Philip Wittenberg, *Dangerous Words: A Guide to the Law of Libel*, Columbia University Press, New York, 1947, pp. 282–308; and Bruce W. Sanford, *Libel and Privacy: The Prevention and Defense of Litigation*, Law & Business, Inc., New York/Prentice-Hall Law & Business, Washington, D.C., 1985, pp. 103–105.

(102)
  8. Hanson, *Libel and Related Torts*, pp. 197–206.

(102)
  9. Kenneth Donelson and Irene Donelson, *When You Need a Lawyer*, Doubleday, Garden City, N.Y., 1964, pp. 245–249.

(104)
  10. Robert Niel Corley, Robert L. Black, and O. Lee Reed, *The Legal Environment of Business*, 5th ed., McGraw-Hill, New York, 1981, pp. 535–542 and 240–247; and Robert N. Corley, O. Lee Reed, *Fundamentals of the Legal Environment of Business*, McGraw-Hill, New York, 1986, pp. 420–426.

(105)
  11. Jethro K. Lieberman and George J. Siedel, *Business Law and Legal Environment*, 2d ed., Harcourt Brace Jovanovich, New York, 1986.

(106)
  12. Adapted from *Mail Fraud Laws: Protecting Consumers, Investors, Businessmen, Medical Patients, Students*, U.S. Post Office Department, Washington, D.C., June 1969.

(107)
  13. Varner and Varner, *Business Communications and the Law*, pp. 9–11.

(107)
  14. Excerpts from *Pre-employment Inquiries and Screening*, Washington State Human Rights Commission, July 1977 and August 1988.

Chapter 7

(141)
  1. See also Stanley L. Payne, *The Art of Asking Questions* (especially Chap. 14, which lists 100 considerations), Princeton University Press, Princeton, N.J., 1980; and Donald R. Lehmann, *Market Research and Analysis*, Irwin, Homewood, Ill., 1985.

Chapter 8

(175)
  1. A "to-whom-it-may-concern" letter is sometimes given to a satisfactory employee before she or he leaves the company, but because it must necessarily be general and not confidential, it carries much less weight than the confidential, specific recommendation.

(187)
  2. Every city has a credit bureau—an association of credit grantors (stores, banks, car dealers, credit unions, and so forth). The function of the credit bureau is to collect the credit

PAGE

records of its customers and consolidate the information of each individual. Then, when a credit grantor receives a request for credit, it asks the credit bureau for the applicant's record and forms its own conclusions. The larger credit grantors are linked to the bureau by teletype, which enables them to get a printed record in seconds.

(188)   3. Some retailers mail all statements the same day each month. Others use *cycle billing* according to account numbers or names. This method helps to level out the billing department's load over a 30-day period. For example, customers whose names begin with A–C may be billed for 30-day purchases through the 5th of a month, and statements may be mailed on the 10th; those whose names begin with D–F may be billed through the 8th and statements mailed on the 14th; etc.

Chapter 9

(220)   1. See footnote 2 p. 187, about the functions of city credit bureaus. The Fair Credit Reporting Act gives rejected applicants certain rights to request from consumer reporting agencies disclosure of adverse information and correction of errors. Also, for a small fee, they may see their credit bureau report if they merely want to check its accuracy. If you are moving from one city to another, a good idea is to check your current report, then request that it be sent to the bureau nearest your new home.

Chapter 10

(268)   1. Adapted by courtesy of New York Life Insurance Company, *Effective Letters Bulletin*.

Chapter 11

(284)   1. Adapted by courtesy of Armstrong Cork Company, Lancaster, Pa.

(287)   2. In general, the term *direct mail* refers to any printed matter, other than periodicals, that attempts to sell or promote sales by mail. It includes—in addition to letters—postcards, manuals, brochures, order blanks, pamphlets, leaflets, gadgets, and reply forms. These items usually supplement the letter and help create a favorable seller-buyer relationship.

(290)   3. Many firms (except those with specially trained direct-mail staffs) ask outside specialists to write their sales letters and plan the enclosure.

(294)   4. Adapted by courtesy of Apple Computer, Inc., Los Angeles, Calif., July 1989.

(295)   5. Adapted by courtesy of Bell & Howell Document Management Products Co., Chicago, Ill. Their system won the Computerworld Smithsonian Award for Innovative Use of Information Technology; winner in the Business category, June 20, 1989.

(300)   6. Sweepstakes and other games of chance have been powerful action inducements. The prospect may be "eligible for winning any one of 5,000 prizes" if an enclosed card is mailed before midnight of a certain date. However, some states prohibit such methods. Furthermore, studies have shown gross inconsistencies between the prizes some companies advertise and the number they award.

(301)   7. Adapted by courtesy of Aeroil Products Company, West New York, N.J., and The Dartnell Corporation, *The Dartnell File of Tested Sales Letters*.

(302)   8. Letter and enclosure courtesy of The Bon Marche, Sales Promotion headquarters, Seattle, Wash., September 11, 1989; sent to customers in its 40 stores within six states.

(305)   9. Adapted by courtesy of S. Posner Sons, Brooklyn, N.Y., and The Dartnell Corporation, *The Dartnell File of Tested Sales Letters*.

PAGE

(307)   10. *The Reporter of Direct Mail Advertising*, September 1965, pp. 49–50. Though business conditions are different in the 1990s, persuasive sales letters can still bring back lost customers.

(307)   11. Adapted from an award-winning letter created by Spiro & Associates, Inc., Philadelphia, for the Mayflower Hotel in Washington, D.C.

(309)   12. Adapted by courtesy of Seth Thomas Clock Company, Thomaston, Conn.

Chapter 12

(321)   1. Bob Mascone, "Managing the Job Search," *Placement Handbook, First Year Students*, School of Business, University of Michigan, 1988–89, p. 16.

(330)   2. If a firm's name is now different from what it was when you were employed there, state the present name and "(formerly . . .)." If you are currently employed and do not wish to disclose your employer on your resume, you can merely identify the firm by industry; for example, you might say "a medium-sized manufacturer of electronic equipment."

(332)   3. To indicate industriousness previous to the earliest full job entry, "Other jobs before (year)" is acceptable for applicants in their early twenties but may be regarded as inappropriate for older applicants (over 30).

(334)   4. Some campus placement centers provide placement and credential file services on a fee basis for students and alumni seeking professional positions in K–12 public or private schools, colleges, or universities within five years of graduation. If you have such a credential file established, be sure your reference list (if any) includes the preparation date.

Chapter 13

(364)   1. A Cincinnati executive, reviewing 35 different jobs in his company for which hundreds of applications were received, gives this tip: "In each instance the job went to the thoughtful applicant who followed up the interview with a sincere thank-you note." Numerous other executives as well as applicants have confirmed the effectiveness of these follow-up messages.

(375)   2. For suggestions to employers regarding interviewing see Chapter 24, and for a list of fair and unfair preemployment inquiries see Chapter 5.

Chapter 14

(393)   1. Twice a year creditors must mail to all credit customers a printed form titled "In Case of Errors or Inquiries about Your Bill." (Creditors decide what months these will be sent; in large stores the mailing is automatically computerized along with two monthly statements a year.) This form explains rules about customers' rights and obligations if they question the accuracy of a bill. (See Chapter 5 under Credit and Collections.)

(398)   2. *How to Excel in the Art of Friendly Persuasion*, the Western Union Telegraph Company.

(399)   3. Courtesy of Tom Hardeman, sales representative, Western Union, Seattle, Wash., 1987. All employees handling telegrams and Mailgrams are (under the Communications Secrecy Act) bound to secrecy on the content of any message or even that a communication was made between any two people.

(400)   4. Theodore N. Beckman and Ronald S. Foster, *Credits and Collections*, 8th ed., McGraw-Hill, New York, 1969, p. 533. Though this comment was published years ago, it is still true in the decade of the 1990s.

PAGE
(404)

5. Adapted from "Legal Phases of Collections," *Credit Manual of Commercial Laws*, National Association of Credit Management, 1979, pp. 543–545; rev. ed., 1987, Chap. 23, pp. 3–4.

Chapter 16

(450)

1. This idea of presenting your conclusion or main point first is not new. It was a common method even during the time of Aristotle (384–322 B.C.). For those interested in historical background see Aristotle, *Rhetoric*, Lane Cooper (trans.), Appleton-Century Crofts, New York, 1932.

(458)

2. See Jim Raggerty and Rich Norling, *Cricket Graph, Presentation Graphics for Science and Business*, Cricket Software, Malvern, Pa., 1986. Other programs used in this text and which can be used to create visuals are *MacDraw II*, Claris Corp., Mountain View, Calif., 1988, and *MacPaint*, Claris Corp., Mountain View, Calif., 1987.

(462)

3. Raggerty and Norling, pp. 7–15.

(468)

4. *MacPaint*, 2.0, Claris Corp., Mountain View, Calif., 1987, pp. xiii, xv.

(469)

5. This book emphasizes presentation. If you need additional help in constructing tables, charts, and graphs, you can find complete chapters in texts devoted entirely to statistics or report writing. See also Michael C. Thomsett, *The Little Black Book of Business Report Writing*, Amacon, American Management Association, New York, N.Y., 1988. Furthermore, on the market are many graphic packages that may be compatible with your personal computer or your school's computer. If no computers are available, you can construct graphics yourself or engage an expert to assist you.

(473)

6. See Henry M. Robert, *Robert's Rules of Order*, rev., Scott, Foresman, Glenview, Ill., 1981.

Chapter 17

(490)

1. For some large national and international corporations annual reports are often elaborate, colorful brochures printed on glossy paper with 40 or more pages. As such, they are outside the scope of this chapter, for they are not "short." Actually, they are impressive advertising brochures for the public as well as stockholders. They also are informative for college graduates and others seeking jobs with reputable firms. Annual reports of some corporations are often prepared and printed by agencies that specialize in such publications.

(493)

2. Although Title VII of the Civil Rights Act does not specifically mention marital status, this topic is closely related to and often interpreted under sex discrimination. Also, many states have laws that employers may not discriminate against applicants on the basis of marital status, age, or sex.

(493)

3. Previous chapters in this book have adhered to the rule of 10 regarding numbers. As discussed in App. A, p. 766, you should write out (with exceptions) numbers one through nine, but beginning with 10 you use the figure. Departing from the rule of 10, this chapter uses—in some informal reports and messages—figures for all numbers, except the number one. Because of a trend in business toward writing figures for all numbers (unless the number begins the sentence), you can decide for yourself what you prefer and act accordingly—in informal reports and messages.

(521)

4. Actually, for a survey of this type the inquirer should send a questionnaire form on which each respondent merely fills in answers. However, for the purpose of this assignment, let's assume she sent merely a stamped envelope and that she is also interested in seeing how well college students express themselves in written reports. Make yours one of the best!

PAGE

(530)

Chapter 18

1. In a formal report of a public nature, the person or committee authorizing or commissioning the report notifies the report writer in a letter called a *letter of authorization*. The message will be bound with the formal report's prefatory pages, usually just before the transmittal letter. Some businesses also send a *memorandum of authorization*, particularly when the request comes from the top management level of an organization.

(541)

2. Adapted from Scot Ober, "The Basic Vocabulary of Written Business Communications," Alpha Sigma chapter, Delta Pi Epsilon, Arizona State University, Tempe, 1981.

(543)

3. Space in this book allows only highlights about bibliographies and footnotes. For additional details on numerous variations in content and setup, you may find these publications helpful: Walter S. Achtert and Joseph Gibaldi, *The MLA Style Manual*, Modern Language Association of America, New York, 1985; William Giles Campbell and Stephen V. Ballou, *Form and Style: Theses, Reports, Term Papers*, 7th ed., Houghton Mifflin, Boston, 1986; Joseph Gibaldi, and Walter S. Achtert, *MLA Handbook for Writers of Research Papers*, 3d ed., Modern Language Association of America, New York, 1988; *Publication Manual of American Psychological Association*, 3d ed., American Psychological Association, Washington, D.C., 1983; Kate L. Turabian, *A Manual for Writers of Term Papers, Theses, and Dissertations*, 5th ed., revised and extended by Bonnie Birtwistle Honigsblum, University of Chicago Press, Chicago, 1987; *United States Government Printing Office Style Manual*, U.S. Government Printing Office, Washington, D.C., 1984. If your report uses other sources and it is to be published, be sure you abide by copyright laws to avoid infringement. Information is available on "Publications of the Copyright Office," Register of Copyrights, Library of Congress, Washington, D.C. For other style manuals see John Bruce Howell, *Style Manuals of the English-Speaking World*, Oryx, Phoenix, 1982.

(550)

4. For a more detailed discussion, the reader is referred to two references that support the parenthetical documentation method: Gibaldi and Achtert, *MLA Handbook for Writers of Research Papers* and *Publication Manual of the American Psychological Association*.

Chapter 19

(572)

1. Bill G. Rainey, "Proposal Writing: A Neglected Area of Instruction," *The Journal of Business Communication*, vol. II, no. 4, Summer 1974.

(572)

2. C. Gilbert Storms, "What Business School Graduates Say about the Writing They Do at Work," *The ABCA Bulletin*, December 1983, pp. 15–16.

(572)

3. These topics were listed by the Ford Foundation as current research interests for 1988 and 1989.

(572)

4. Taken from database (SPIN) "Research Foundation of the State University of New York Sponsored Programs Information Network" for the American Products and Inventory Control Society, November 1988, ID: NR108.

(573)

5. The U.S. government daily solicits proposals (bids) on hundreds of subjects and projects, ranging from defense systems to seminars on communication topics. See *Commerce Business Daily*, subtitled a "daily list of U.S. government procurement invitations, contract awards, subcontracting leads, sales of surplus property, and foreign business opportunities." Issue PSA-9749, Jan. 3, 1989, included, for example, topics from "Expert and Consultant Services" to "Contracts Awarded," pp. 1–25.

(584)

6. *Business Commerce Daily*, U.S. Department of Commerce, Washington, D.C., Jan. 3, 1989, p. 1. For more details on contracts with the federal government, see Frank M. Alston, Margaret M. Worthington, and Louis P. Goldsman, *Contracting with the Federal*

PAGE

Government, 2d ed., Wiley, New York, 1988; *Doing Business with the Federal Government*, U.S. General Services Administration, Superintendent of Documents, Washington D.C., 1986.

(589)

7. Lon F. Backman, Program Development, *A Digest on the Elements of Proposal Writing*, Washington State Office of Economic Opportunity, Olympia, December 1971. This excellent advice is timeless, and still applies in the 1990s.

Chapter 20

(598)

1. See a particularly effective book on using humor in all kinds of business situations, Ed McManus and Bill Nichols, *We're Roasting Harry Tuesday Night*, Prentice-Hall, Englewood Cliffs, N.J., 1984.

(609)

2. B. Y. Auger, *How to Run Better Business Meetings: An Executive's Guide to Meetings That Get Things Done*, Minnesota Mining and Manufacturing Co. (3M), St. Paul, 1979, pp. 64–65.

(611)

3. A seminal study on listening was completed in 1948: Ralph Nichols, *Factors Accounting for Differences in Comprehension of Material Presented Orally in the Classroom*, unpubl. doctoral dissertation, State University of Iowa, 1948. At that time nearly 40 percent of Nichols's respondents spent the day listening. That high percentage has dropped somewhat, to 25.3 percent with Asian managers and to 30 percent with top-level U.S. executives. See H. W. Hildebrandt, "International/Intercultural Communication: A Comparative Study of Asian and U.S. Managers," *World Communication*, 17 (1): 49–68, Spring 1988; and H. W. Hildebrandt, *The Newly Promoted Executive, 1986–87*, School of Business, Division of Research, University of Michigan, Ann Arbor, 1987.

(612)

4. Pacific Northwest Bell, *Management Report*, issue 122, Oct. 4, 1974, pp. 2–3. This statement is still true in the 1990s. Excellent advice is timeless.

Chapter 21

(621)

1. *Using Microsoft Word*, Microsoft Corp., 1987. See also Peter Rinearson, *Word Processing Power with Microsoft Word*, Microsoft Press, 1987.

(621)

2. Leland G. Verheyen, "How to Develop an Employee Attitude Survey," *Training and Development Journal*, August 1988, pp. 72–76.

(625)

3. See also *Training and Development Journal*, American Society of Training Directors (ASTD), 1630 Duke St., Alexandria, VA 22313; also courses offered by the National Training Lab (NTL), 1240 N. Pitt St., Alexandria, VA 22314. One of the premier directories on executive programs is Christopher Billy and Ann Simmons (eds.), *Bricker's International Directory*, Peterson's Guides, Princeton, N.J. 1989.

(636)

4. All the following discussion on evidence and supports includes data from valid research studies. See especially Herbert W. Hildebrandt, "Learning from Top Women Executives—Their Perceptions on Business Communication, Careers, and Education," in William G. Neal, James C. Scott, and Carol Lundgren (eds.), *Business Communication—What's New*, Utah State University, 1984, pp. 149–161. Also, Floyd A. Bond et al., "The Newly Promoted Executive, A Study in Corporate Leadership," Division of Research, University of Michigan, Ann Arbor, 1980–1987; Herbert W. Hildebrandt and Jinyun Liu, "Chinese Women Managers: A Comparison with Their U.S. and Asian Counterparts," *Human Resource Management*, 27 (3): 291–314, Fall 1988.

PAGE

Chapter 22

(645)   **1.** One of the largest communication organizations, with over 12,000 members, including both PR specialists and business communicators, is the International Association of Business Communicators, One Hallidie Plaza, Suite 600, San Francisco, CA 94102.

(646)   **2.** See Henry M. Robert, *Robert's Rules of Order*, rev., Scott, Foresman, Glenview, Ill. 1981, pp. 108–140.

(648)   **3.** Editorial cartoons, however, may express value judgments nonverbally. The artist depicts, usually through gross exaggeration, a judgment in picture form. One need only look at the editorial cartoons during political campaigns to recognize the implied value judgment. Businesses are also not exempt from artistic and editorial cartoons; responding to them, if this is deemed desirable, takes skillful persuasion.

(652)   **4.** A recent book, devoted entirely to communication differences between selected U.S. and Japanese students, provides examples of attitudinal and communication differences for just one country. See Dean C. Barnlund, *Communication Styles of Japanese and Americans*, Wadsworth, Belmont, Calif., 1989. For an article on Chinese female managers, see Herbert W. Hildebrandt and Jinyun Liu, "Chinese Women Managers: A Comparison with Their U.S. and Asian Counterparts," *Human Resource Management*, **27** (3): 291–314, Fall 1988.

(658)   **5.** *U.S. China Automotive Industry Cooperation Project*, University of Michigan, Ann Arbor, 1988.

(665)   **6.** Molly Schmidt, *Asian Pacific Search Location for Trojan Facility in Thailand*, unpub. paper, University of Michigan, Ann Arbor, 1988. The source for the statement was "Thailand: A Golden Age of Economic Growth," *Institutional Investor*, international edition, 1987.

Chapter 23

(674)   **1.** B. W. Tuckman, "Development Sequences in Small Groups," *Psychological Bulletin*, vol. 63, 1965, pp. 384–399.

(681)   **2.** Virginia Johnson, market development supervisor, Visual Products Division, 3M, speaker on "More Effective Meetings" at the international convention of the American Business Communication Association, New Orleans, Oct. 22, 1982.

(681)   **3.** A fourth type of problem is procedure, but few discussions are concerned only with steps in a process. Procedure or action steps are part of the overall discussion on accepting and implementing a proposal.

(686)   **4.** Kenneth D. Benne and Paul Sheats, "Functional Roles of Group Members," *Journal of Social Issues*, vol. 4, Spring 1948, pp. 41–49.

(691)   **5.** William M. Sattler and N. Edd Miller, *Discussion and Conference*, Prentice-Hall, Englewood Cliffs, N.J., 1966, pp. 338–340.

Chapter 24

(715)   **1.** Theodore Hariton, *Interview: The Executive's Guide to Selecting the Right Personnel*, Hastings House, New York, 1970, p. 58; John D. Drake, *Interviewing for Managers: A Complete Guide to Employment Interviewing*, American Management Association, New York, 1982, pp. 160–161. See also useful topics in Arthur Bell, *A Complete Guide to Interviewing—How to Hire the Best*, Dow Jones-Irwin, Homewood, Ill., 1989; Auren Uris, *88 Mistakes Interviewers Make and How to Avoid Them*, Amacon, New York, N.Y.,

PAGE

1988; Martin Yate, *Hiring the Best: A Manager's Guide to Effective Interviewing*, B. Adams, Boston, 1988.

(718)

2. The overview of telephone equipment, techniques, and systems is courtesy of J. D. Murphy, account manager, U. S. WEST Communications Services, Inc., Seattle, Wash., January 1990.

Chapter 25

(732)

1. See the perceptive review of business education in the twenty-first century, Lyman W. Porter and Lawrence E. McKibbin, *Management Education and Development: Drift or Thrust into the 21st Century*, McGraw-Hill, New York, 1988. An additional resource for determining a school's degree of internationalizing its curriculum is in "Internationalizing? New Self-Audit Document Provides Progress Report," *Newsline AACSB*, **19** (2): 6, 1988.

(732)

2. *Strength through Wisdom: A Critique of Capability, A Report to the President,* from the President's Commission on Foreign Language and International Studies, Government Printing Office, Washington, D.C., 1979, p. 125.

(732)

3. See Herbert W. Hildebrandt, Edwin L. Miller, and Dee W. Edington, *The Newly Promoted Executive*, University of Michigan, Ann Arbor, 1987, p. 12.

(732)

4. See, for example, Walter J. Lonner and John W. Berry (eds.), *Field Methods in Cross Cultural Research*, Sage, Beverly Hills, Calif., 1986; Young Yun Kim and William B. Gudykunst (eds.), *Theories in Intercultural Communication*, Sage, Newbury Park, Calif., 1988; L. W. Sarbaugh, *Intercultural Communication*, rev. ed., Transaction, New Brunswick, N.J., 1987; and Marshall R. Singer, *Intercultural Communication: A Perceptual Approach*, Prentice-Hall, Englewood Cliffs, N.J., 1987.

(732)

5. Wilharn Ouchi, *Theory Z.*, Addison-Wesley, Reading, Mass., 1981, p. 14.

(732)

6. *Webster's New World Dictionary of American English*, Simon and Schuster, New York, 1988.

(732)

7. Hildebrandt, Miller, and Edington, *The Newly Promoted Executive*, 1987, p. 30.

(733)

8. A. L. Kroeber and Clyde Kluckhohn, *Culture—A Critical Review of Concepts and Definitions*, Random House, New York, n.d. (Originally published **47** (1), 1952, Papers of the Peabody Museum of American Archaeology and Ethnology, Harvard University.)

(736)

9. Over 20 other differences and alternatives are noted in Philip R. Harris and Robert T. Moran, *Managing Cultural Differences*, Gulf, Houston, 1987, pp. 76–77.

(736)

10. Edward T. Hall, *The Silent Language*, Doubleday, Garden City, N.Y., 1959, pp. 83–118.

(740)

11. Herbert W. Hildebrandt and Jinyun Liu, *A Managerial Profile: The Chinese Manager*, School of Business, University of Michigan, Ann Arbor, 1988, p. 36.

(743)

12. Ivo K. Feierabend and Rosalino L. Feierabend, "Cross National Data Bank of Political Instability Events" (code index), Public Affairs Research Institute, San Diego, Calif., 1965, pp. 2A–10A; Arthur S. Banks, *Cross-Polity Time-Series Data*, M.I.T. Press, Cambridge, Mass., 1971; Ivo K. Feierabend (compiler), *Anger, Violence, and Politics: Theories and Research* (collection by various authors, including a comparative analysis using new indices by T. R. Gurr), Prentice-Hall, Englewood Cliffs, N.J., 1972. An especially good bibliographic source is David A. Jodice, *Political Risk Assessment: An Annotated Bibliography*, Greenwood Press, Westport, Conn., 1985.

(746)

13. "Maverick Managers," *Wall Street Journal*, Nov. 14, 1988, p. R14.

PAGE
(747)

14. Desmond Morris et al., *Gestures: Their Origins and Distribution*, Stein and Day, New York, 1979. This book researches nonverbal gestures in foreign countries; it is useful for persons going abroad. See also Loretta A. Malandro et al., *Nonverbal Communication*, Random House, New York, 1989.

(749)

15. Herbert W. Hildebrandt, "Technical Written Reports from Germany," *Journal of Technical Writing and Communication*, **4** (4): 291–303, 1974.

Appendix B

(799)

1. Mr. Michael Powell, of Congressman Howard Berman's office, obtained information from Congressional Relations Office of the Postmaster General, December 1988.

(800)

2. United States Postal Service, *Postal Addressing Standards: Creative Solutions for Your Business Needs*, Publication 28, July 1989. For additional information on designing mail for OCR/BCS readability, the Postal Service suggests you obtain a current copy of Publication 25, *A Guide to Business Mail Preparation*, and Notice 221, *Addressing for Success*, from your local post office marketing and communications office.

(811)

3. Western Union, *EasyLink and EasyLink Telex—A Better Way to Send Your Telex Messages*, May 1989. Also *Western Union Instant Mail Manager for the Macintosh*. For more information call 1-800-247-1373, Dept. 320, or write to Western Union, 1 Lake Street, Upper Saddle River, NY 07458.

Index

Index